MOUS Essentials PowerPoint® 97 Expert

Jane Calabria

Dorothy Burke

Linda Bird

que E&T

An Imprint of Macmillan Computer Publishing

MOUS Essentials PowerPoint® 97 Expert

Copyright© 1999 by Que® Education and Training

Library of Congress Catalog No: 98-66775

ISBN: 1-58076-056-2

01   00   99   4   3   2   1

Interpretation of the printing code: the rightmost double-digit number is the year of the book's printing; the rightmost single-digit number, the number of the book's printing. For example, a printing code of 99-1 shows that the first printing of the book occurred in 1999.

Screens reproduced in this book were created using Collage Plus from Inner Media, Inc., Hollis, NH.

Composed in *Stone Serif* and *MCP Digital* by Que® Education and Training

Publisher:
Robert Linsky

Executive Editor:
Randy Haubner

Acquisitions Editor:
Jon Phillips

Director of Product Marketing:
Susan L. Kindel

Managing Editor:
Caroline Roop

Development Editor:
Nancy D. Warner

Project Editor:
Tim Tate

Copy Editor:
Susan Hobbs

Acquisitions Assistant:
Ken Schmidt

Technical Editor:
Asit Patel

Cover Designer:
Nathan Clement

Book Designer:
Louisa Klucznik

Production Team:
Steve Balle-Gifford
Megan Wade

About the Authors

Jane Calabria has authored 13 Macmillan Computer Publishing books. As a consultant, Jane works on a national level with large corporations and training organizations, developing user training programs and modeling help desk support structures. As a trainer, Jane teaches Microsoft desktop applications, operating systems, and Lotus Notes and Domino. She is a Certified Lotus Notes Professional (Principal level) and a Certified Microsoft User Specialist.

Jane and Dorothy Burke have teamed up successfully on several MCP books, including the *Certified Microsoft Office User Exam Guide for Microsoft Word 97, Microsoft Excel 97,* and *Microsoft Power Point 97.* They also co-authored *Microsoft Works 6-in-1, Microsoft Windows 95 6 in 1, Microsoft Windows 98 6 in 1, Using Microsoft Word 97,* and several Lotus Notes books.

Dorothy Burke has traveled a few career paths before becoming a computer instructor and consultant. She has worked as a magazine editor for an engineering trade magazine, in customer service and management in the home medical equipment industry, and in a management consulting firm as an office manager and editor of its newsletter and catalogs. Dorothy is a Certified Lotus Instructor and a Certified Lotus Professional in Lotus Notes. With a strong background in graphics and desktop publishing, Dorothy develops applications in Lotus Notes and for Domino Web sites. Writing with Jane Calabria, she has contributed to the *10 Minute Guide to Lotus Notes Mail 4.5* and *Lotus Notes 4.5 and the Internet 6-in-1* published by Que Corporation. She is also a contributing author to Que's *Special Edition Using PowerPoint 97* and is the co-author of the *10 Minute Guide to Lotus Notes Mail 4.6, 10 Minute Guide to Lotus Notes 4.6, Microsoft Works 4.5 6 in 1, Microsoft Windows 95 6 in 1, PowerPoint 97 Exam Guide, Word 97 Exam Guide, Excel 97 Exam Guide,* and *Using Microsoft Word 97.*

Linda Bird specializes in corporate training and support through Software Solutions, her own company. She has successfully trained users representing more than 75 businesses, including several Fortune 500 companies. Her clients include Appalachian Electric Power Co., Borg Warner Automotive, Goodyear, Pillsbury, Rockwell Automation, and Shell Chemical. Her background also includes teaching at Averett College and serving as computer trainer coordinator for Adult Services. She is currently associated with the University of Rio Grande.

Linda has written *PowerPoint 95 Essentials, PowerPoint 97 Essentials, Level I, PowerPoint 97 Essentials, Level II, Transition from PowerPoint 4.0 to PowerPoint 97, Transition from Word 6.0 to Word 95,* and *Power User's Guide to Windows 95.* Additionally, she has contributed to books and instructor's manuals on Word, WordPerfect, PowerPoint, Lotus 1-2-3, Access, and Windows 95. She writes customized training manuals for client businesses and monthly columns for *Smart Computing* magazine. A graduate of the University of Wisconsin, Linda lives in Gallipolis, Ohio, with her husband, Lonnie, and daughters, Rebecca and Sarah.

Trademark Acknowledgments

Preface

Que Education and Training is the educational publishing imprint of Macmillan Computer Publishing, the world's leading computer book publisher. Macmillan Computer Publishing books have taught more than 20 million people how to be productive with their computers.

This expertise in producing high-quality computer tutorial and reference books is evident in every Que Education and Training title we publish. The same tried-and-true writing and product-development process that makes Macmillan Computer Publishing books bestsellers is used to ensure that educational materials from Que Education and Training provide the most accurate and up-to-date information. Experienced and respected computer application instructors write and review every manuscript to provide class-tested pedagogy. Quality-assurance editors check every keystroke and command in Que Education and Training books to ensure that instructions are clear, accurate, and precise.

Above all, Macmillan Computer Publishing and, in turn, Que Education and Training have years of experience in meeting the learning demands of students across all disciplines.

The "MOUS Essentials" of Hands-On Learning

The *MOUS Essentials* are appropriate for use in both corporate training and college classroom settings. They can be used effectively as computer-lab applications modules to accompany any of Que Education and Training's computer concepts text or as stand-alone texts for an applications only course. The *MOUS Essentials* workbooks enable users to become self-sufficient quickly; encourage self-learning after instruction; maximize learning through clear, complete explanations; and serve as future references.

The *MOUS Essentials* series uses the following elements to get the most out of the material:

Objectives list what students do and learn from the project.

Required Activities are the objectives as they relate to the Microsoft Office User Specialist exams.

"Why Would I Do This?" shows students why the material is essential.

Step-by-Step Tutorials simplify the procedures with large screen shots, captions, and annotations.

If you have problems... anticipates common pitfalls and advises students accordingly.

Inside Stuff provides tips and shortcuts for more effective applications.

Key Terms are highlighted in the text and defined in the margin when they first appear, as well as in an end-of-book glossary.

Jargon Watch offers a layperson's view of "technobabble" in easily understandable terms.

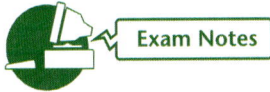

Exam Notes provide information and insight on topics that are covered on the MOUS exam and that should be reviewed carefully.

Checking Your Skills provides true/false, multiple choice, matching, and completion exercises.

Applying Your Skills contains directed, hands-on Practice exercises to check comprehension and reinforce learning, as well as self-directed Challenge exercises requiring students to use critical thinking skills.

CD-ROM contains files for the text's step-by-step tutorials and end of project exercises.

Annotated Instructor's Edition

If you have adopted this text for use in a college classroom, you will receive, upon request, an *Annotated Instructor's Edition* at no additional charge. The manual contains suggested curriculum guides for courses of varying lengths, teaching tips, answers to exercises in "Checking Your Skills" and "Applying Your Skills" sections, test questions and answers, and data files and solutions for each tutorial and exercise. Please contact your local representative or write to us on school or business letterhead at Macmillan Computer Publishing, 201 West 103rd Street, Indianapolis, IN 46290-1097, Attention: Education Channel Sales Support.

Microsoft Office User Specialist Exams

In order to validate your skills using Office, Microsoft has created the Microsoft Office User Specialist program. The Specialist Program is available for many Office 95 and Office 97 applications at both Proficient and Expert User levels.

The Specialist designation distinguishes you from your peers as knowledgeable in using Office products, which can also make you more competitive in the job market.

The *Microsoft Office User Specialist* exams are for anyone who:

- Wants to expand their skills.
- Is seeking certification in a particular software.
- Wants to learn or reference tasks in short, concise lessons.
- Is an instructor or trainer preparing groups of people for the Microsoft Exams.

Que Education & Training Certification Resource Center

To keep up to date on the Microsoft Office User Specialist program exams, check the following Web sites:

www.queet.com/certification

www.mous.net

www.microsoft.com/office/train_cert

MOUS PinPoint® Training and Testing CD-ROM

MOUS PinPoint training and testing software is designed to supplement the projects in this book. It aids you in your preparation for taking and passing the *Microsoft Office User Specialist* exams. The MOUS PinPoint software consists of:

- Trainers
- Evaluations

Each **trainer** asks you to perform specific tasks that were covered in a particular project of this book. If you don't know how to perform a particular task, you can watch a demonstration (**SHOW ME**) of the task. Immediate feedback (concerning the correctness of performance) is given after each task in each trainer. Each **evaluation** consists of the same questions that were given in the trainer. However, with an evaluation, you may not view demonstrations and you do not receive feedback after trying each task. After performing a **trainer** or **evaluation**, you can view a report of your overall performance.

Preparing to Install the MOUS PinPoint Training and Testing Software

To install the MOUS PinPoint training and testing software, we recommend following these steps:

1. Check to see if your computer meets the minimum requirements (see Table I.1).

2. Perform a full installation of Office 97 on your computer, if you have not already done so (see the section "Installing Office 97").

3. Install the MOUS PinPoint testing and training software (see the section "Installing the MOUS PinPoint Training and Testing Software").

Using the MOUS PinPoint Training and Testing Software

To use the MOUS PinPoint training and testing software, we recommend following these steps.

Study the projects in this book. After reading each project:

1. Run the **trainer** for the project (see the section "Running the MOUS PinPoint Software"). Then view a report on your performance (see the section "Viewing Reports").

2. Run the **evaluation** for the project (see the section "Running the MOUS PinPoint Software"). Then view a report on your performance (see the section "Viewing Reports"). Note: Some projects may not have a corresponding MOUS PinPoint trainer and evaluation.

After you have finished reading this book, take the MOUS PinPoint Final Exam:

1. Run the **evaluation** for the Final Exam Part 1. Final Exam Part 1 covers material included in the first half of this book.

2. Run the **trainer** for the Final Exam Part 1. Only the items missed in the trainer will be set to run.

3. Run the **evaluation** for the Final Exam Part 1 (again) as a final check.

4. Repeat steps 1–3 given for Final Exam Part 2. Final Exam Part 2 covers material from roughly the second half of this book.

5. When you are finished using the MOUS PinPoint software, you can remove it from your computer (see the section "Removing the MOUS PinPoint Training and Testing Software").

Running MOUS PinPoint Testing and Training Software Requirements

The system components in Table I.1 are required to run the MOUS PinPoint Testing and Training Software.

Table I.1 System Component Requirements		
Component	Minimum	Recommended
CPU	Pentium 90	Higher than Pentium 90
Operating System	Windows 95 or NT 4.0 Note: You must have an Administrator's or Power User's login if you are working on a Windows NT workstation.	N/A
Installed Apps (full installation)	Office 97	N/A
RAM	16 MB	32 MB or higher
Hard Drive	Adequate space for Office 97 and for MOUS PinPoint training and testing software	N/A
CD-ROM Drive	2X speed	4X speed or faster
Pointing Device	Windows-compatible mouse or pointing device	N/A
Video	Color VGA video display	N/A

Installing Office 97

Important: It is necessary to do a complete installation of Office 97. This means installing *all* components.

To perform a full installation of Office 97, complete the following steps:

1. Start Windows 95 or Windows NT 4.0 and close any applications that are running (other than Windows).

2. Insert the Office 97 CD and run **setup.exe**.

3. Click on the **Add/Remove** button, as shown in Figure I.1 (if a previous installation of Office 97 is already on your computer). If you do not have a previous installation of Office 97 on your computer, select **Custom** installation from a different screen.

Figure I.1
The Microsoft Office 97 Setup dialog box.

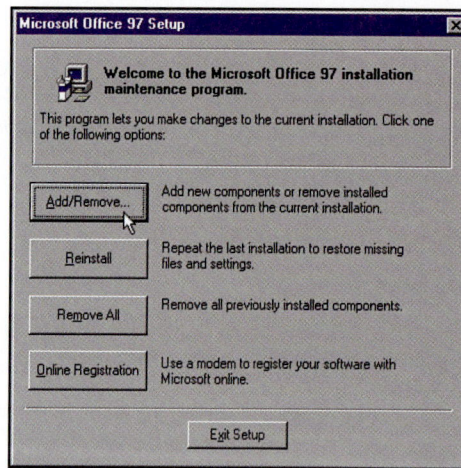

4. Click on the **Select All** button (see Figure I.2).

Figure I.2
Choosing the Select All button will install *all* Office 97 components to the system.

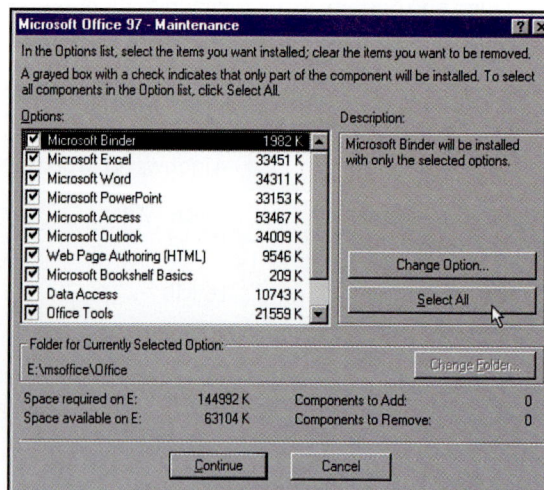

5. Click on the **Continue** button.

6. Continue with the installation until it is finished.

Installing the MOUS PinPoint Training and Testing Software

To install and run MOUS PinPoint trainers and evaluations on a single-user computer, you must first install the MOUS PinPoint **Launcher** by running a setup program from the MOUS PinPoint CD.

Installing the MOUS PinPoint Launcher

To run the setup program for the MOUS PinPoint Launcher:

1. Start Windows 95 or Windows NT 4.0 and insert the MOUS PinPoint CD into the CD-ROM drive.

2. Select **Start**/**Run** from the Windows desktop.

3. Enter (or browse to) **[Drive Letter]:\SETUP.EXE** (where **[Drive Letter]** is the assigned drive letter of the CD-ROM). See Figure I.3.

Figure I.3
Indicating the location of the setup.exe executable.

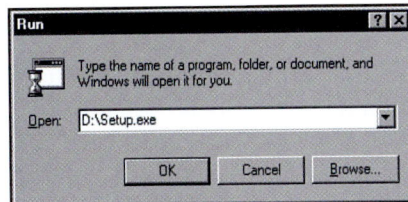

4. Click on **OK.** The setup program runs.

5. Answer the questions that appear during the installation.

6. When the dialog box in Figure I.4 displays, choose **Normal Single-User Installation**.

Figure I.4
The MOUS PinPoint Network Installation Setup dialog box.

7. Click **Yes** when you are asked if you want to install MOUS PinPoint modules to your hard disk. The dialog box in Figure I.5 appears. The installation program is getting ready to install the **Launcher** to your computer. It needs to know the directory where you would like it installed.

Figure I.5
The default location
Destination Folder is
shown.

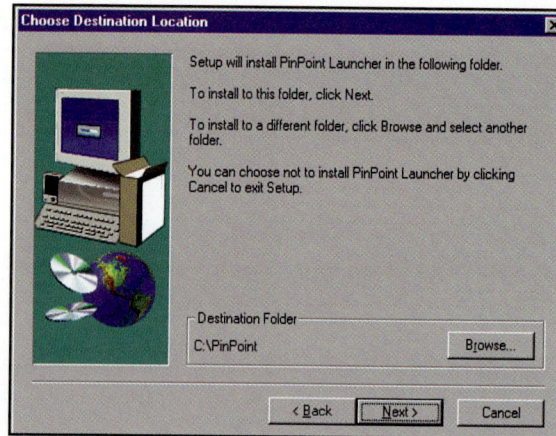

8. To install the **Launcher** to the default location, click on the **Next** button. Otherwise, enter a new path for the **Launcher** and then click on the **Next** button.

9. Confirm the installation location by clicking on **Yes** in the dialog box in Figure I.6.

Figure I.6
The destination folder
requires confirmation.

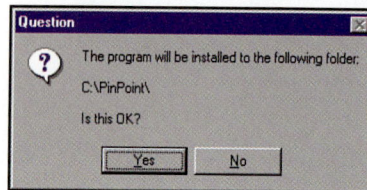

10. When Figure I.7 appears, click on Next.

Figure I.7
Creation of the Program
Folder.

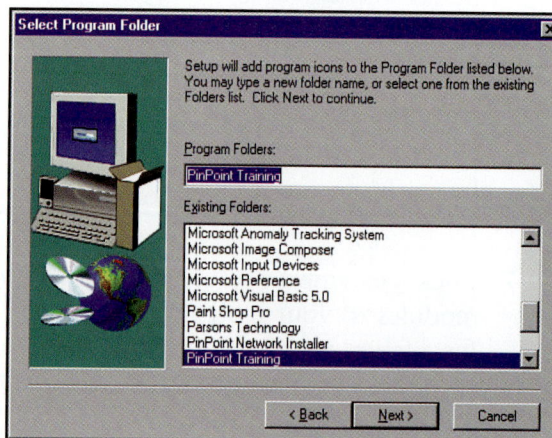

A **PinPoint Training** group window is created (see Figure I.8). You can close this window. It is not necessary to use this window to start the PinPoint Launcher in the future since you can always select Start/Programs/PinPoint Training/PinPoint Training from your desktop.

Figure I.8
The PinPoint Training group window that is created.

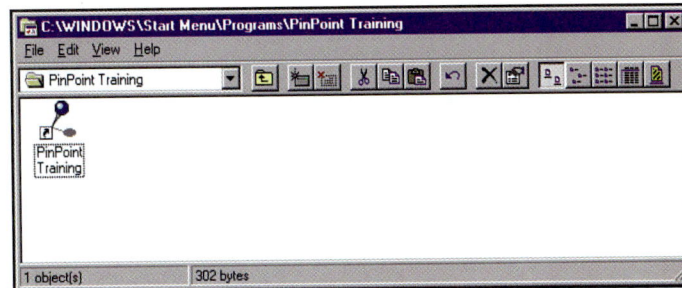

The PinPoint **Launcher** is used to:

- logon with your **UserID** and **Password**.
- install your MOUS PinPoint training and testing software for *an exam*.
- run your MOUS PinPoint training and testing software for *an exam*.
- view reports after you have run the MOUS PinPoint training and testing software.

To install the MOUS PinPoint training and testing software for *an exam*, continue with the next section.

Installing the MOUS PinPoint Software

To install the MOUS PinPoint training and testing software:

1. Start the Launcher by selecting Start/Programs/PinPoint Training/PinPoint Training (see Figure I.9).

Figure I.9
The Home screen of the Launcher.

2. Click on the **Installer** button (see Figure I.10).

Figure I.10
The **Installer** screen.

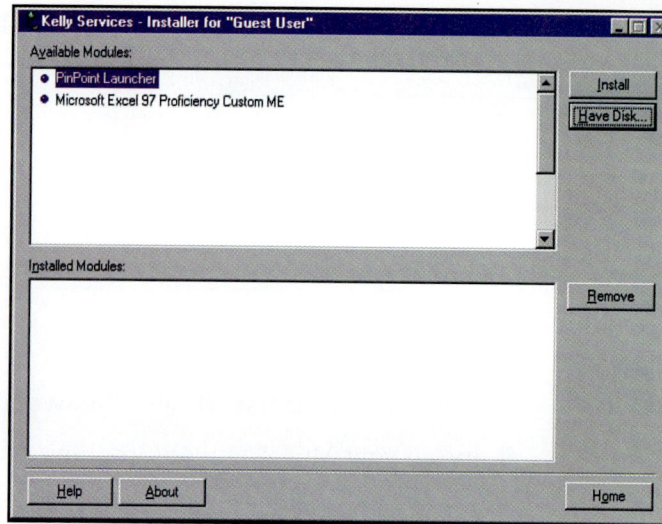

3. Install your MOUS PinPoint software by selecting the specific module (for example, **Microsoft Excel 97 Proficiency Custom ME**) from the **Available Modules** list box and clicking on the **Install** button. (Do not install the **Launcher**. It's already installed!)

4. Answer the questions that appear during installation. You are asked to verify the location where the MOUS PinPoint software will install to your hard drive (see Figure I.11).

Figure I.11
The default location Destination Folder is shown.

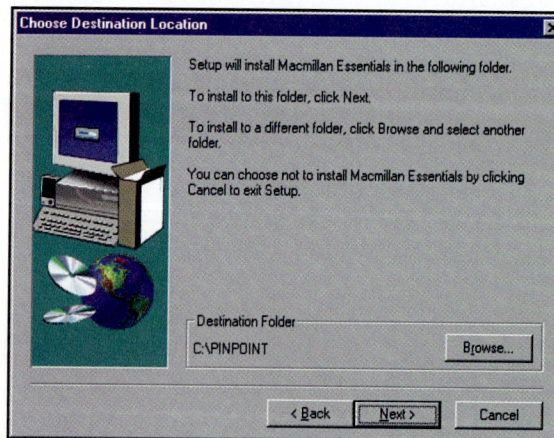

5. Make changes as necessary by clicking on **Browse** and selecting a different destination folder. Important: The MOUS PinPoint software for *the specific exam* and the PinPoint **Launcher** must be installed under the same main directory (for example, **C:\PinPoint**) in order to work properly.

6. Click on **Next**.

7. Accept the subdirectory (for example, **xl8prome**) where the MOUS PinPoint software will be placed. You do not have a choice concerning the name of this subdirectory.

Figure I.12
The destination folder requires confirmation.

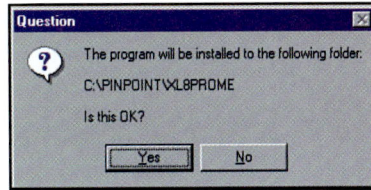

8. Click on **Yes**.

9. If you would like to view a README file concerning MOUS PinPoint software, click on **Yes** in the dialog box in Figure I.13. Otherwise, click on **No**.

Figure I.13
Specify whether you want to review the README.txt file.

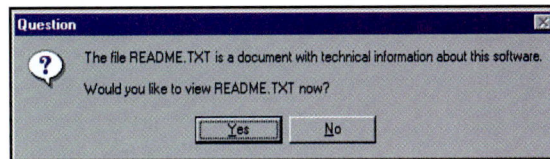

A PinPoint Training group window is created (see Figure I.14).

Figure I.14
The PinPoint Training group window that is created.

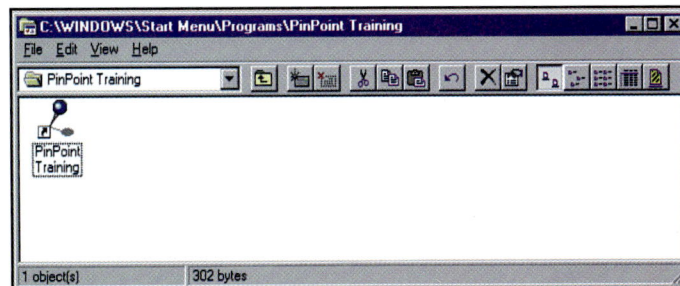

Close this window. It is not necessary to use this window to start the PinPoint **Launcher** in the future since you can always select **Start/Programs/PinPoint Training/PinPoint Training** from your desktop.

If you want to run the MOUS PinPoint software that you just installed, don't exit from the **Launcher**. Continue on with step 3 in the next section.

To exit from the **Launcher** to Windows, click on the **Exit** button.

Running the MOUS PinPoint Software

To run the MOUS PinPoint software, it is necessary to start the PinPoint **Launcher**. Important: Shut down all applications.

To run the MOUS PinPoint software:

1. Shut down all applications (except Windows and the Launcher) that are running, including any shortcut bars (such as Microsoft Office shortcut bar). If the Office 97 exam application is running, shut it down.

2. Start the Launcher by selecting Start/Programs/PinPoint Training/PinPoint Training from the Windows desktop.

3. Click on the User Logon button (see Figure I.15). Logging on under your name allows the **Launcher** to keep track of your personal progress. This enables the **Launcher** to reconfigure a module the next time you take it. It also enables the **Launcher** to create a report containing information about your training or evaluation sessions.

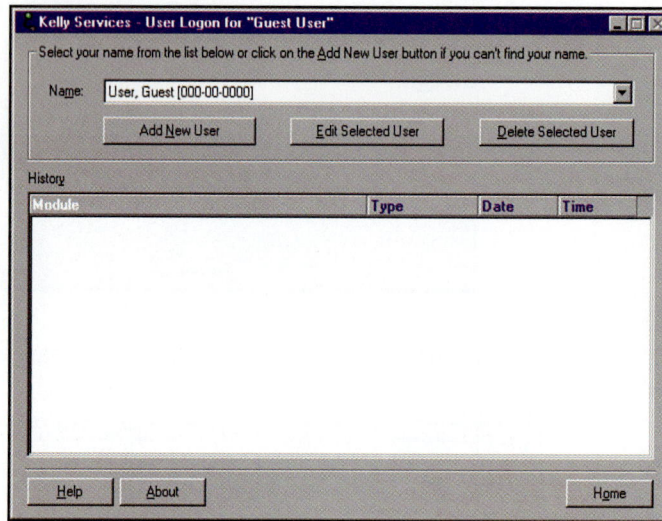

4. Select your name from the drop-down list in the **Name** combo box in Figure I.16:

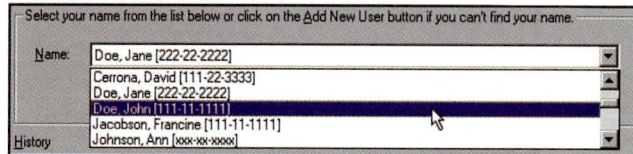

■ You may need to use the scroll bar to find your name.

■ If your name is not in the list, go to step 5.

■ If you found your name, skip to step 8.

5. If this is your first time running MOUS PinPoint software, your name will not be in the list. If that is the case, create a user account for yourself by clicking on the **Add New User** button.

6. Enter your personal data, tabbing between fields in Figure I.17:

■ Enter all five data items. If one or more of the data items are missing, the **OK** button will remain grayed out (disabled).

■ Your **User ID** and **Password** may both consist of up to fourteen characters and are both case sensitive.

■ After entering your **Password** in the **Password** field, you must confirm this **Password** by entering the identical **Password** again in the **Confirm Password** field.

Figure I.17
The Add New User dialog
box.

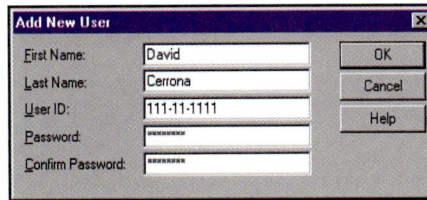

7. Click on **OK**. Your account is created and you are logged on. You are ready to move to the **Training & Testing** screen.

8. Click on the **Home** button to move to the **Home** screen.

9. Click on the **Training & Testing** button (see Figure I.18).

Figure I.18
The **Training & Testing**
screen.

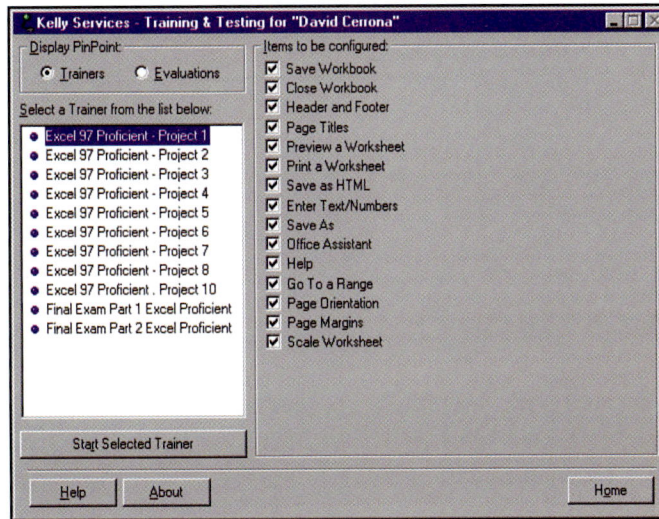

10. Select **Trainers** (or **Evaluations**), depending on which you would like to run (see Figure I.19). A list of trainers (or evaluations) displays.

Figure I.19
Selecting trainers or evaluations.

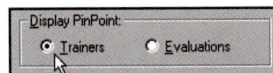

11. Select the particular trainer or evaluation that you would like to run. Each trainer and evaluation is named by the project that it covers. Trainers may be configured. That means you can select the tasks that you would like to run. The first time you run a trainer, all tasks will automatically be selected. (Note: Evaluations may not be configured.)

12. If you are running a trainer, configure it by selecting or deselecting tasks in the **Items to be configured** section:

    ■ A check indicates that the task will run.

    ■ No check indicates that the task will not run.

    You are now ready to start (launch) the trainer or evaluation for the project.

Figure I.20
Select the tasks you want
to configure.

Figure I.20
Select the tasks you want
to configure.

13. Click on the **Start Selected Trainer** button if you are starting a
trainer or the **Start Selected Evaluation** button if you are starting
an evaluation. Before the trainer or evaluation runs, you are asked to
confirm (see Figure I.21).

Figure I.21
Confirm the running of the
trainer or evaluation.

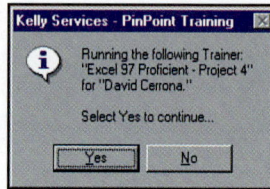

14. Click on **Yes** to confirm. While running the trainer or evaluation, you
may use the controls in Figure I.22.

**Show Me gives a step-by-step
demonstration using a similar example**

Done checks a finished task

Figure I.22
Controls available while
running the trainer or
evaluation.

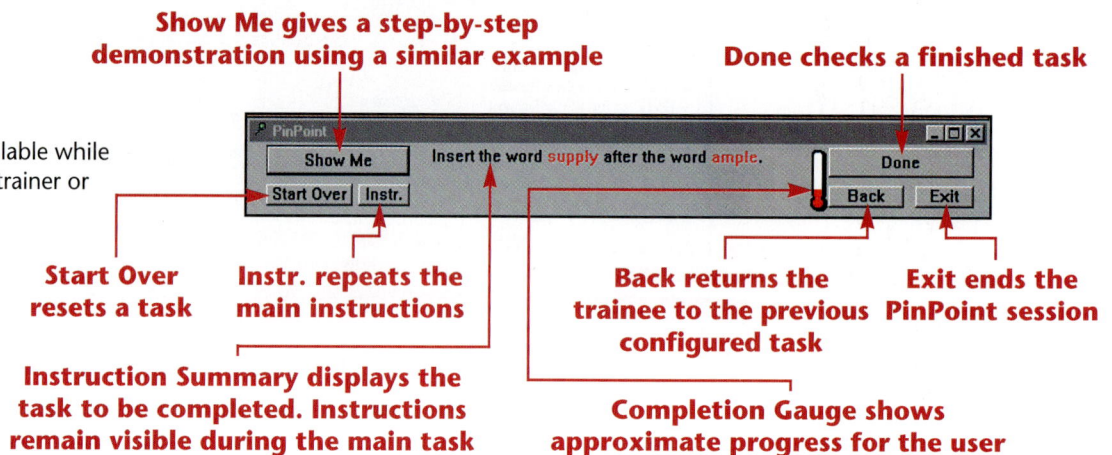

**Start Over
resets a task**

**Instr. repeats the
main instructions**

**Back returns the
trainee to the previous
configured task**

**Exit ends the
PinPoint session**

**Instruction Summary displays the
task to be completed. Instructions
remain visible during the main task**

**Completion Gauge shows
approximate progress for the user**

After running a trainer or evaluation, the **Training and Testing** screen
reappears. You can continue to run other trainers or evaluations for other
projects. When you are finished studying the whole book, you can also run
the trainers and evaluations for the final exams.

To view reports for each trainer or evaluation that you ran, click on the
Reports button (see the section "Running the MOUS PinPoint Software").

To exit from the **Launcher**, first move to the **Home** screen by clicking on
the **Home** button. Then click on the **Exit** button.

Viewing Reports

In the **Launcher**, you can view two kinds of reports after running a MOUS
PinPoint trainer or evaluation:

To display reports in the Launcher:

1. Start the **Launcher** and log on.

2. Click on the **Reports** button (see Figure I.23). This report displays a line (record) of data for each instance that you have run a MOUS PinPoint trainer or evaluation:

   ■ **Accuracy** is the number of tasks you performed correctly

   ■ **Maximum** is the total number of tasks that were configured to run

   ■ **Time** is the total elapsed time in minutes (from the moment you started running the trainer or evaluation to the moment that you exited the trainer or evaluation)

Figure I.23
The Reports screen appears, displaying the first kind of report.

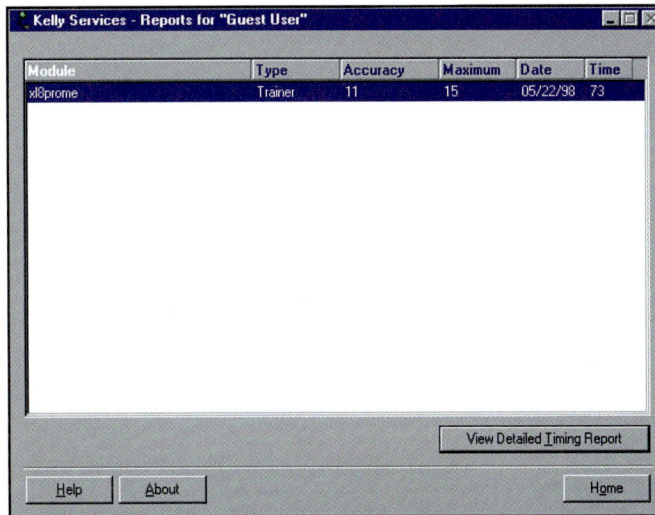

Module	Type	Accuracy	Maximum	Date	Time
xl8prome	Trainer	11	15	05/22/98	73

View Detailed Timing Report

Help About Home

3. The second kind of report is the **Detailed Timing Report** (see Figure I.25). If you wish to view this report, select the record for which you would like the timing report and click on the **View Detailed Timing Report** button.

Figure I.24
Select the specific record.

Module	Type	Accuracy	Maximum	Date	Time
xl8prome	Trainer	11	15	05/22/98	73

Figure I.25
The **Detailed Timing Report**.

Timing results of xl8prome for Guest User

Item No.	Item	Actual	Optimal	Correct	Did Show Me
1	Save Workbook	2	10	No	No
1	Save Workbook	8	10	Yes	No
2	Close Workbook	2	10	Yes	No
21	Header and Footer	130	30	No	No
21	Header and Footer	1	30	No	Yes (1)
26	Page Titles	23	25	No	No
26	Page Titles	21	25	No	Yes (1)
26	Page Titles	29	25	Yes	Yes (1)
35	Preview a Worksheet	8	20	No	No
35	Preview a Worksheet	24	20	No	Yes (1)
35	Preview a Worksheet	7	20	No	Yes (1)
35	Preview a Worksheet	7	20	No	Yes (1)
35	Preview a Worksheet	1	20	No	Yes (1)
36	Print a Worksheet	26	20	No	Yes (1)
41	Save as HTML	12	45	No	Yes (1)
44	Enter Text/Numbers	58	30	No	No
44	Enter Text/Numbers	66	30	Yes	No
45	Save As	12	30	Yes	No
49	Office Assistant	24	25	Yes	No
50	Help	13	30	Yes	No
51	Go To a Range	10	10	Yes	No
53	Page Orientation	12	15	Yes	No
54	Page Margins	27	20	Yes	No
55	Scale Worksheet	36	10	Yes	No

Close Print

4. To print the **Detailed Timing Report**, click on the **Print** button:

■ **Actual** is the time, in seconds, you used to complete the task. This time is considered the "involved time," the time that was taken from the moment that you clicked with the mouse (or entered something on the keyboard) to the moment that you clicked on the **Done** button. It does not count the "thinking time," before you first moved the mouse (or used the keyboard) and it does not count the time used to run and view a SHOW ME demonstration.

■ **Optimal** is a reasonable amount of time, in seconds, required to perform a task by an efficient method.

■ **Correct - Yes**, if the you performed the task correctly; **No** if you did not perform the task correctly.

■ **Did Show Me - Yes**, if you viewed a SHOW ME demonstration for the task; **No**, if you did not view a SHOW ME demonstration for the task. The **Did Show Me** column appears only if the timing report contains data for a **trainer** and not for an **evaluation**. (Evaluations do not have SHOW MEs.)

5. Close the **Detailed Timing Report** window by clicking on the **Close** button. The **Reports** screen of the **Launcher** returns.

Removing the MOUS PinPoint Training and Testing Software

When you are finished using the MOUS PinPoint training and testing software, you can remove it. Be sure to follow the procedure below.

To remove your MOUS PinPoint training and testing software:

1. Start the **Launcher**.

2. Click on the **Installer** button.

3. Select the exam module from the **Installed Modules** list.

Figure I.26
Choose from the **Installed Modules** available.

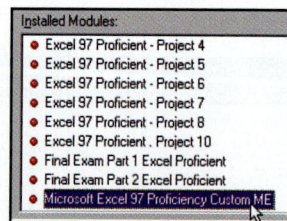

4. Click the **Remove** button.

5. When the **Confirmation** dialog box appears, click **Yes**.

6. When the **Remove** dialog box appears, click the **Yes** button.

7. An **"Uninstall complete"** message appears.

8. Find the MOUS PinPoint directory on your computer and delete it.

Troubleshooting

Table I.2 lists a few problems that can arise while running the MOUS PinPoint training and testing software. For each problem, a solution or explanation is given.

Table I.2 MOUS PinPoint Training and Testing Software Problems and Solutions	
Problem	Explanation or Action
A task is grayed out and not selected on the Training and Testing screen in the Launcher program (see Figure I.27).	A particular component has not been installed. Exit the Launcher and perform a full installation of Office 97 (see section "Installing Office 97").

Your computer crashes (locks up or exits ungracefully) while running the MOUS PinPoint training or testing.	Start you computer again and rerun the desired MOUS PinPoint training or testing. Exit the trainer or evaluation in the normal way. It is important to do this, even if you have no desire to run a trainer or evaluation. By running any trainer or evaluation, you will ensure that your computer's registry is reset to normal.
You see a message that says **"program was left in an unfinished state"** AND you have deleted the MOUS PinPoint directory (or one of its key components).	The problem is that your Windows Registry was changed by running the registry and needs to be set back to the state it was in before you started the MOUS PinPoint training and testing. Do the following: 1. Go to the **Windows** directory and find the following files: **OFC97.PIN** **OFC971.PIN** **OFC972.PIN** **OFC973.PIN** **OFC974.PIN** 2. Delete the **OFC97.PIN** file. 3. Rename the other four **.PIN** files so that they have a **.REG** extension. 4. Double-click on each of the **.REG** files to run them. This will reset your Registry.

Microsoft PowerPoint Expert Specialist User Skills

The skill areas covered in the exam and the required tasks for those skill areas are listed in Table I.3.

Table I.3	Expert User Skills		
Skill Set	Required Activity	Project	Lesson
Create a presentation	Create from a template	5	1
	Create from an existing presentation	2	7
	Delete slides	2	2
Add textual information	Enter text in Slide and Outline views	2	4
	Enter bulleted information	3	6
	Change the text alignment	3	3
Add visual elements	Add formatting	3	1
	Build a graph	4	2
	Draw an object	5	6
	Rotate and fill an object	5	7
		11	5
	Scale and size an object	5	7
	Add a table	9	2
	Add shapes	5	6
		11	3
	Animate objects	7	1-2
		12	6
	Add transitions	7	1
	Add an organizational chart	4	6
	Set custom options	7	3
	Check styles	8	3
Bring in data from other sources	Add clip art	5	8
		10	1-2
	Insert an Excel chart	12	1
	Import text from Word	9	1, 4
	Add scanned images	10	3
	Add sound and movies	10	4-5
	Export an outline to Word	9	5
Modify a presentation	Change the sequence of a slide	2	3
	Find and replace text	8	5
	Modify the slide master	5	4
	Modify sequence in outline mode	2	3
	Change tabs	3	4
	Change fonts	3	1
		8	2
	Change the alignment of text	3	3

Skill Set	Required Activity	Project	Lesson
Prepare for distribution	Spell check	8	4
	Add speaker notes	6	1
	Set automatic slide timing	7	5
Customize a presentation	Create a custom background	5	3
	Customize a color scheme	5	2
	Customize clip art and other objects	10	1
	Recolor and edit objects	5	7
		10	1
	Apply a template from another presentation	5	5
	Add links to other slides within the presentation	13	2
	Hide slides	7	4
Deliver presentations	Start a slide show on any slide	1	5
	Use onscreen navigation tools	1	5
	Generate meeting notes	7	8
	Electronically incorporate meeting feedback	7	8
	Print slides in a variety of formats	6	4
	Print color presentations	2	6
	Export to overhead	2	6
	Export to 35mm slides	2	6
	Present with presentation conferencing	7	10
	Save presentation for use on another computer	7	9
	Save for Internet	14	3

Table of Contents at a Glance

Table of Contents

Conventions Used in This Book

The *MOUS Essentials* series uses the following conventions to make it easier for you to understand the material:

- Text that you are to type or that appears onscreen appears in a special font and color.

- Underlined letters in menu names, menu commands, and dialog box options are the shortcut keys. Examples are the File menu, the Open command, and the File name list box.

- Key terms appear in *italic* the first time they are discussed and are defined in the margin as soon as they are introduced.

Project 1

One

Getting Started with PowerPoint 97

Learning the Basics

In this project you will learn the following objectives and their associated Microsoft Exam required activities.

Objectives	Required Activities

➤ Start PowerPoint

➤ Create a New Presentation

➤ Change the View

➤ Move among Slides in a Presentation

➤ Run an Electronic Slide Show ... ... Start a Slide Show on Any Slide

➤ Use Onscreen Navigation Tools

➤ Save and Close Your Presentation

➤ Get Help

➤ Exit PowerPoint

Presentation graphics program

A software application that helps you structure, design, and present information—such as graphs or bulleted lists—to an audience so that it is visually appealing.

Presentation

A group of related slides you can create using PowerPoint.

Electronic slide show

A predefined list of slides displayed sequentially onscreen or using a projection device such as an LCD panel/overhead projector combination.

LCD projection panel

A flat-screen device that you can use to project computer images to a large screen.

Why Would I Do This?

PowerPoint 8 for Office 97 (sometimes called PowerPoint 97) is a powerful *presentation graphics program*. Its primary purpose is to help you create a presentation on your computer. A *presentation* is simply a series of slides that contain visual information designed to persuade an audience. Using PowerPoint, you can effectively and efficiently create professional-looking handouts, overheads, charts, and other types of visual aides for use in a presentation to a group.

Whether you are creating a marketing plan, reporting progress on a project, or simply conducting a meeting, PowerPoint will help you create powerful presentations. After you create the presentation, you can add and modify text, charts, clip art, and drawn objects to strengthen your arguments. PowerPoint lets you edit and refine your presentation until it's just right.

You can deliver PowerPoint presentations in all the traditional ways—as printed handouts, 35mm slides, or overhead transparencies. One of the most popular and effective ways to use PowerPoint, however, is to create an *electronic slide show*. You can run a PowerPoint slide show on a computer monitor, or you can use an *LCD projection panel* or other projection device to cast the image from your computer onto a large screen.

Lesson 1: Starting PowerPoint

You can start PowerPoint a number of ways. An easy method is to use the Windows 95 taskbar, as you learn in this lesson.

To Start PowerPoint

1 **Move the mouse pointer to the Start button at the left edge of the taskbar; then click the left mouse button.**

The Start menu appears, as shown in Figure 1.1.

2 **Point to Programs.**

A list of available programs is displayed. The exact list depends on the programs that are installed on your system.

3 **Move the mouse pointer to Microsoft PowerPoint and click the left mouse button.**

Random access memory (RAM)

The temporary storage space where the computer places a program you are using.

PowerPoint is loaded into the computer's working area—*random access memory (RAM)*—and appears on your screen (see Figure 1.2). Note that PowerPoint's screen components are similar to those in other Windows programs and include a menu bar, a title bar, and toolbars.

If you have problems...

If you don't see Microsoft PowerPoint as a program listing, move the mouse pointer to the Microsoft Office folder. Then click the PowerPoint icon from the displayed list.

Additionally, unless the feature has been turned off, the Office Assistant (a cartoon paper clip with eyes) is displayed in its own window. In Lesson 7, you learn how to use the Office Assistant to get help while you work. For now, you can turn off the Office Assistant.

Figure 1.1
You can start PowerPoint from the Start menu.

Click here to display the Start menu

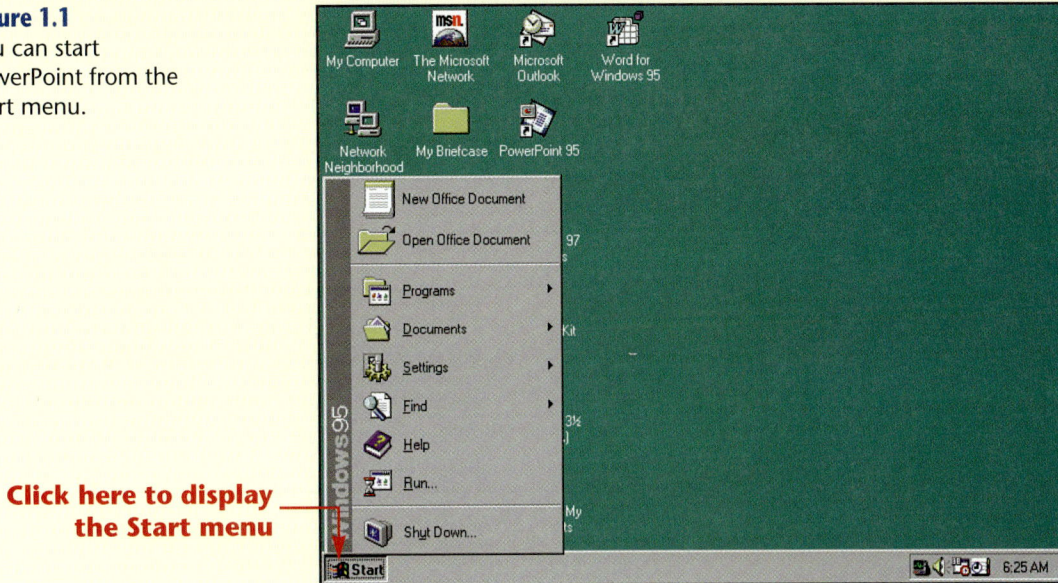

Menu bar   **Title bar**   **Minimize button**   **Restore button**   **Close button**

Figure 1.2
PowerPoint displays the startup dialog box and Office Assistant when you initially start the program.

Standard toolbar

Formatting toolbar

PowerPoint startup dialog box

Drawing toolbar

Office Assistant   Office Assistant Close button

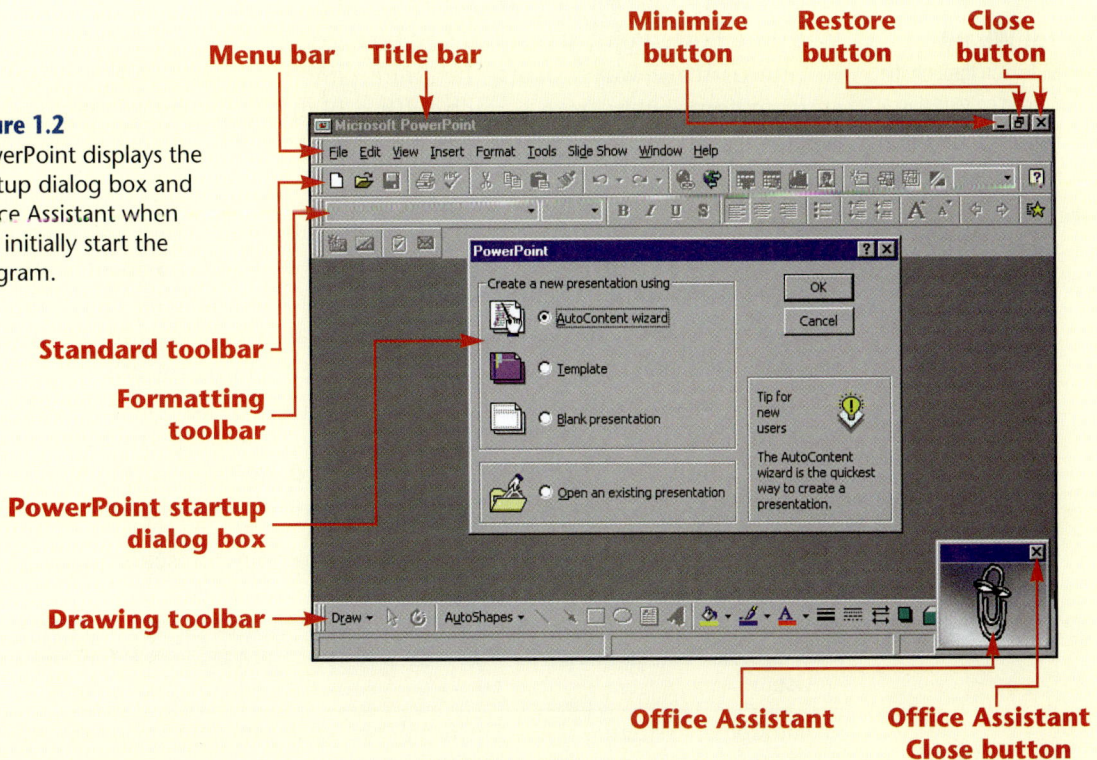

continues

4 **Click the Close button on the Office Assistant.**

The Office Assistant window closes, but the PowerPoint startup dialog box remains in the PowerPoint window. This dialog box helps you either create a new presentation or open one that was created and saved earlier (an existing presentation).

Leave the screen as it is and leave PowerPoint running for the next lesson, in which you use the AutoContent Wizard to create a presentation.

Inside Stuff

If a shortcut icon for PowerPoint is displayed on your Windows 95 desktop, you can also start PowerPoint by double-clicking the icon. Alternatively, you can right-click the shortcut icon and then choose Open from the displayed menu. Either method is faster than using the Start menu.

If Office 97 is installed on your computer, the Office 97 shortcut bar may be visible on your screen. If so, simply click the PowerPoint button in the shortcut bar to start the program.

Lesson 2: Creating a New Presentation

AutoContent Wizard
A tool that guides you through the steps of a proposed presentation and includes suggested content.

Template
A predefined design that includes formatting for a presentation.

With the PowerPoint startup dialog box, you can create a new presentation in one of three ways: using the *AutoContent Wizard*, using a *template*, or starting completely from scratch with a blank presentation. It's also possible to use an existing presentation as the basis for your new one (as discussed in Project 2).

To make creating presentations a snap, PowerPoint includes built-in presentations and templates. PowerPoint's templates, sometimes called presentation designs, include preset colors and designs but no content. The AutoContent Wizard, however, is a tool that contains sample content for commonly used presentation topics as well as an underlying template. Using the AutoContent Wizard, you can quickly create presentations to help you when recommending a strategy, conducting training, reporting progress, and so on. The AutoContent Wizard guides you through the planning stages by suggesting slide types, formatting, and contents.

Table 1.1 summarizes the methods for creating new presentations.

Table 1.1 Methods for Creating New Presentations	
Use	**To**
AutoContent Wizard	Create a presentation with the sample content already included.
Template	Create a presentation using a predesigned set of slide layouts formatted for a particular "look." Templates are also referred to as presentation designs.

PowerPoint

Use	To
Blank presentation	Create a presentation from scratch using a blank slide and default font settings.
An existing presentation	Open a presentation that was previously created and saved.

In this lesson, you use the AutoContent Wizard to create a presentation to recommend that your entire organization upgrade to PowerPoint 97.

If you have problems...

If you accidentally close PowerPoint's startup dialog box, you can still use the AutoContent Wizard to create a presentation. Choose File, New to display the New Presentation dialog box. Click the Presentations tab and then double-click AutoContent Wizard.

To Create a New Presentation

1 In the PowerPoint startup dialog box (which should still be open from Lesson 1, Figure 1.2), click the AutoContent wizard option and choose OK.

The first of six AutoContent Wizard dialog boxes is displayed, as shown in Figure 1.3. Notice that the diagram on the left side of the dialog box helps chart your progress as you create a presentation. The buttons at the bottom of the dialog box help you move between AutoContent dialog boxes or even cancel the wizard.

Figure 1.3
The AutoContent Wizard leads you step-by-step through the process of creating a presentation.

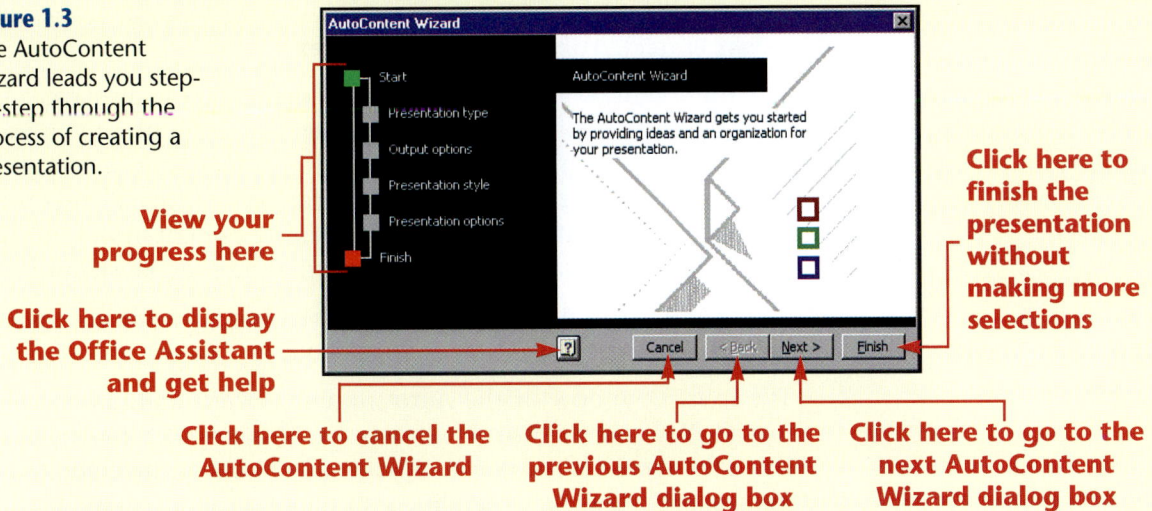

View your progress here

Click here to display the Office Assistant and get help

Click here to cancel the AutoContent Wizard

Click here to go to the previous AutoContent Wizard dialog box

Click here to go to the next AutoContent Wizard dialog box

Click here to finish the presentation without making more selections

2 Choose Next.

The next window of the AutoContent Wizard dialog box is displayed, as shown in Figure 1.4.

continues

Figure 1.4
You can select a category of presentation types, then a specific presentation from that category.

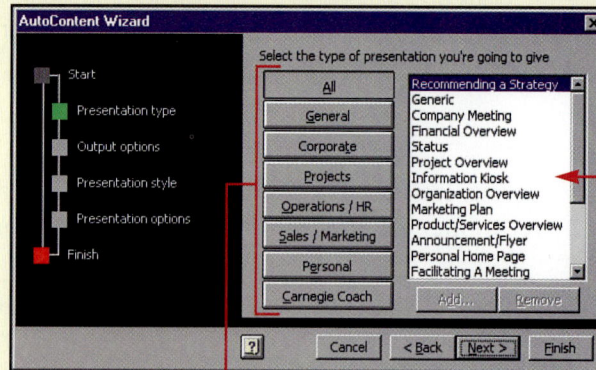

Choose a specific presentation topic here

Click a category button to limit the presentation types displayed

You can use this window to determine the presentation type that best fits your needs. By default, all presentation types are shown in the list on the right side of the dialog box. You can limit the number of presentation types listed by clicking one of the category buttons.

3 **Click several of the category buttons and take a look at the list to see what types of presentations each category contains.**

4 **When you're finished experimenting, choose the _P_rojects category button.**

In the list box, you should see all the presentations associated with this category.

5 **Select `Project Overview` and choose _N_ext.**

The third window of the AutoContent dialog box is displayed. You can use this window to choose the general type of output you want. If you plan to show the presentation to others (in a meeting, for example), you can select the _P_resentations, informal meetings, handouts option. If you want to publish the presentation for others to view in your absence, you can select the _I_nternet, kiosk option.

6 **Select the _P_resentations, informal meetings, handouts option button, if necessary; then choose _N_ext.**

The fourth window of the AutoContent Wizard dialog box is displayed. You use this window to choose the output type you want. PowerPoint selects the best template and color scheme combination to display your work, depending on the output you choose. You can also decide whether to print handouts as part of your presentation.

7 **Select On-_s_creen presentation and choose _Y_es; then choose _N_ext.**

The fifth window of the AutoContent Wizard dialog box is displayed, as shown in Figure 1.5. You can use this window to enter information for the first slide of your presentation—the title slide. If your computer is set up specifically for you, you are designated as the user, so your name and company probably already appear in the bottom two text boxes. If not, you can type them when you type the title.

Figure 1.5
You can automatically
create a title slide.

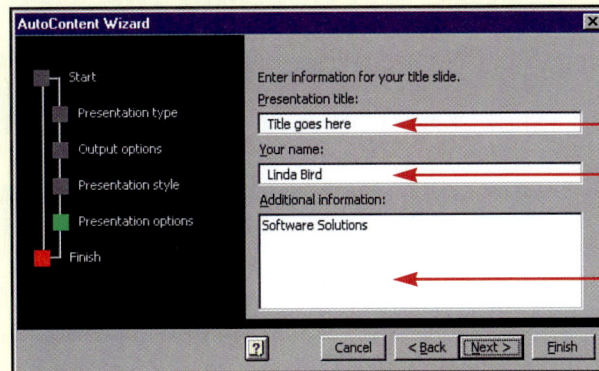

Type the title of your presentation here

Type your name here

Type your company or school here

8 **In the Presentation title box, select the text** Title goes here **by dragging the mouse pointer over it; then type** Project Proposal.

The text you type replaces the selected text.

9 **If necessary, select the text in the Your name and Additional information boxes, and type your name and the name of your company or school.**

10 **Choose Next to advance to the final window of the AutoContent Wizard dialog box.**

11 **Read the displayed information and then choose Finish to view your presentation.**

The AutoContent Wizard creates the presentation and displays it as an outline (see Figure 1.6). Outline view is often the easiest to use when revising content. The information you typed is included in the title slide. The rest of the presentation is created as a series of slides with major topics and subpoints. These suggested topics serve as a blueprint for your presentation. Additionally, a miniature color slide, or thumbnail picture, is displayed so that you can see how the presentation will look when viewed in Slide view. Notice that PowerPoint also includes a special toolbar—the Outlining toolbar—along the left edge of the screen.

Figure 1.6
The AutoContent Wizard creates a presentation in Outline view.

The information you entered is displayed in the title slide

Outlining toolbar

Slide number

Slide icon

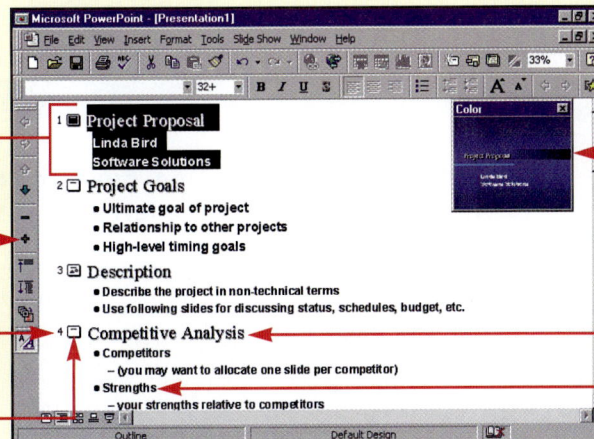

The Slide Miniature shows how the slide looks in Slide view

Main topic

Subpoint

Keep this presentation open for the next lesson, in which you learn how to use different views.

Lesson 3: Changing the View

After you've created a presentation, you can view it a number of different ways: Slide view, Outline view, Slide Sorter view, Notes Page view, and Slide Show. Table 1.2 describes the purpose of each of the views.

Table 1.2 Available Views in PowerPoint	
Use	To
Slide view	Work with one slide at a time, add or change text and graphics, or draw shapes.
Outline view	Work with the slide title and text in traditional outline form. Graphics cannot be inserted or modified.
Slide Sorter view	Display miniature versions of all slides, including text and graphics. Use this view to change the slide order, add transitions, and set timings for electronic slide shows.
Notes Page view	Display a page where you create speaker notes for each slide.
Slide Show	Display your presentation as an onscreen electronic slide show.

The two most commonly used screen views, especially as you develop the presentation, are Outline view and Slide view. Outline view displays text only, enabling you to make quick and easy changes to the presentation's text content. Outline view is also handy for making text changes because several slides are shown at once. Additionally, you can use Outline view to change text or reorder your slides.

In contrast to Outline view, Slide view displays only one slide at a time, but displays graphics and charts as well as text. This makes Slide view a good choice when you want to modify those elements on a slide.

The sample presentation should currently be in Outline view. You can change the view by using the View menu or clicking a view button. In this exercise, you practice using both methods. Now try changing the view of the presentation.

To Change the View

ScreenTip
A description box that is displayed whenever you rest the mouse pointer on a button.

1 **In the open presentation, move the mouse pointer to any of the view buttons on the left side of the status bar (see Figure 1.7).**

In a second or two, a *ScreenTip* is displayed, indicating the view button's name.

Figure 1.7
You can use the view buttons to switch to another view.

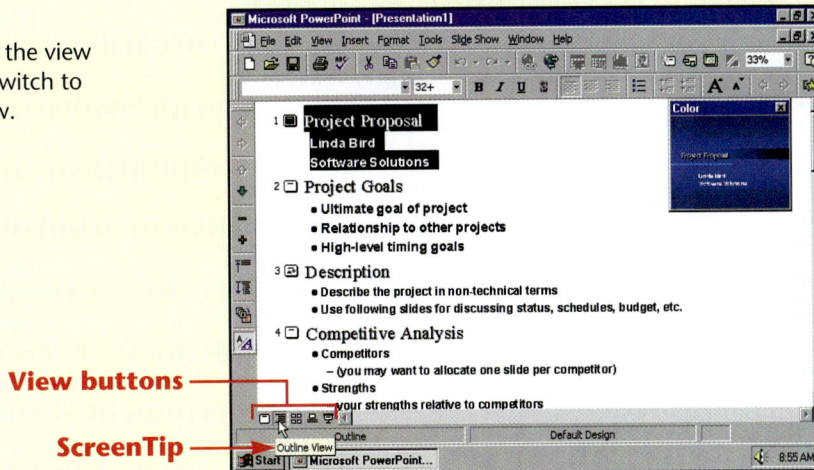

View buttons

ScreenTip

If you have problems...

If the ScreenTips are turned off, choose View, Toolbars, Customize. In the Customize dialog box, click the Options tab and select the Show ScreenTips on toolbars check box. Choose Close when you're finished.

---

2 **Place the mouse pointer on each of the other view buttons.**

A ScreenTip identifies each button.

3 **Click the Slide View button.**

The current slide appears onscreen, displaying the color, text, and graphics (see Figure 1.8). If the horizontal and vertical rulers are displayed on your screen, you can turn them off by choosing View, Ruler.

Figure 1.8
You can use Slide view to display a slide's color, text, and graphics.

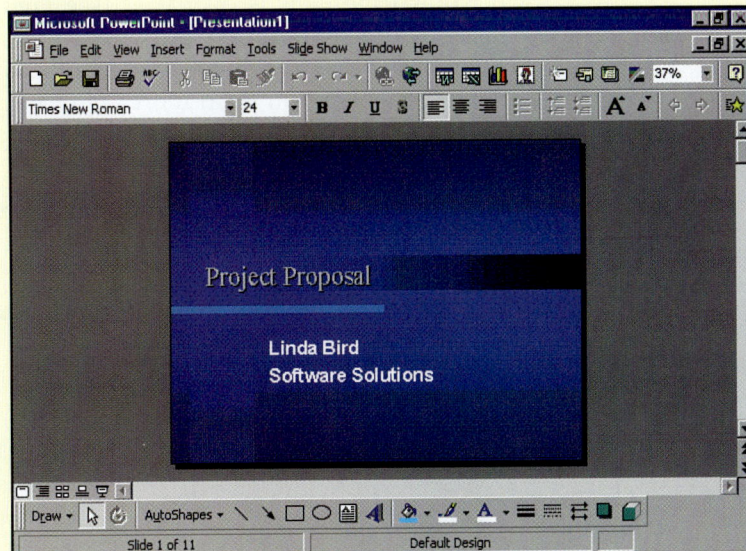

continues

❹ Click the Slide Sorter View button.

You can view the first six slides of the presentation on-screen (see Figure 1.9). Notice that the Slide Sorter displays its own toolbar. Slide Sorter view is used to add, delete, or rearrange slides. Additionally, you can add slide transitions and animation effects in this view by using the Slide Sorter toolbar. You learn more about transitions and animation effects in Project 7, "Automating Electronic Slide Shows."

Figure 1.9
You can use Slide Sorter view to display your presentation as miniature slides.

Slide Sorter toolbar

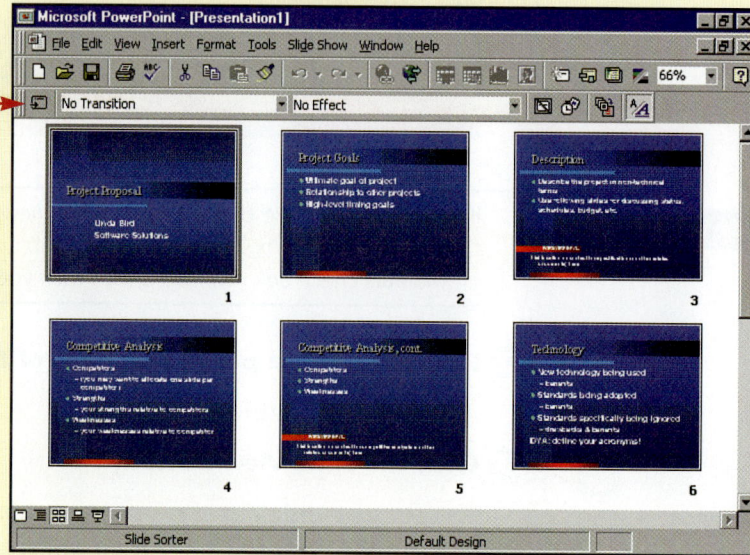

❺ Click the Notes Page View button.

Notes Page view is displayed (see Figure 1.10). This view includes miniature slides along with space for speaker notes. You can print the notes and use them to remember key points while giving your presentation. You learn more about using speaker notes in Project 6, "Using Speaker Notes and Handouts."

Figure 1.10
You can use Notes Page view to type speaker notes.

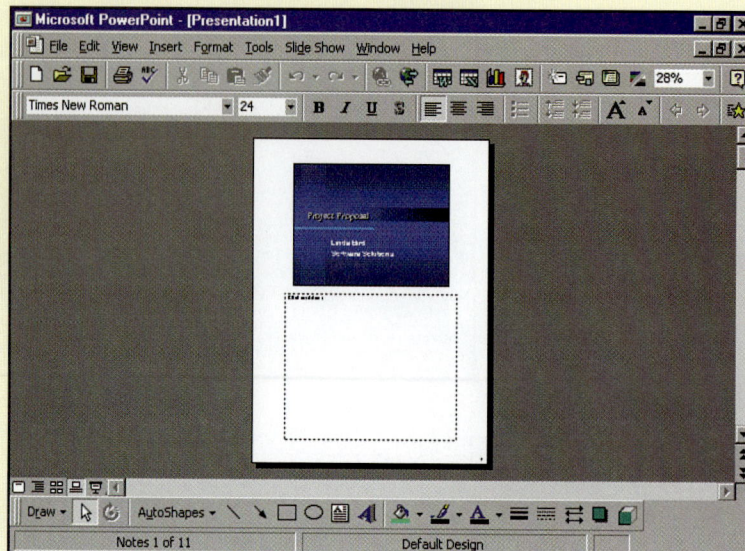

6 Click the Slide Show button.

The presentation is displayed as a full-screen electronic slide show.

7 Click the left mouse button several times to advance through the slides.

Once you have viewed the entire presentation, PowerPoint displays Notes Page view, which was the last view you used before starting the slide show.

Keep this sample presentation open for the next lesson, in which you learn to move among slides in Outline and Slide views.

If you have problems...   You can end a slide show at any time by pressing Esc.

Lesson 4: Moving among Slides in a Presentation

After you create the presentation, you need to move around in it efficiently. In this lesson, you learn to move among slides in both Outline and Slide views.

To Move among Slides in a Presentation

1 In the open presentation, click the Outline View button.

Alternatively, you can choose View, Outline.

The presentation returns to Outline view. Notice that not all the text is displayed onscreen at once. Note also that PowerPoint provides a vertical scroll bar on the right side of the screen that you can use to move among the slides (see Figure 1.11).

Figure 1.11
You can use the vertical scroll bar to move among slides.

Vertical scroll bar up arrow

Vertical scroll box

Vertical scroll bar

Vertical scroll bar down arrow

Horizontal scroll bar

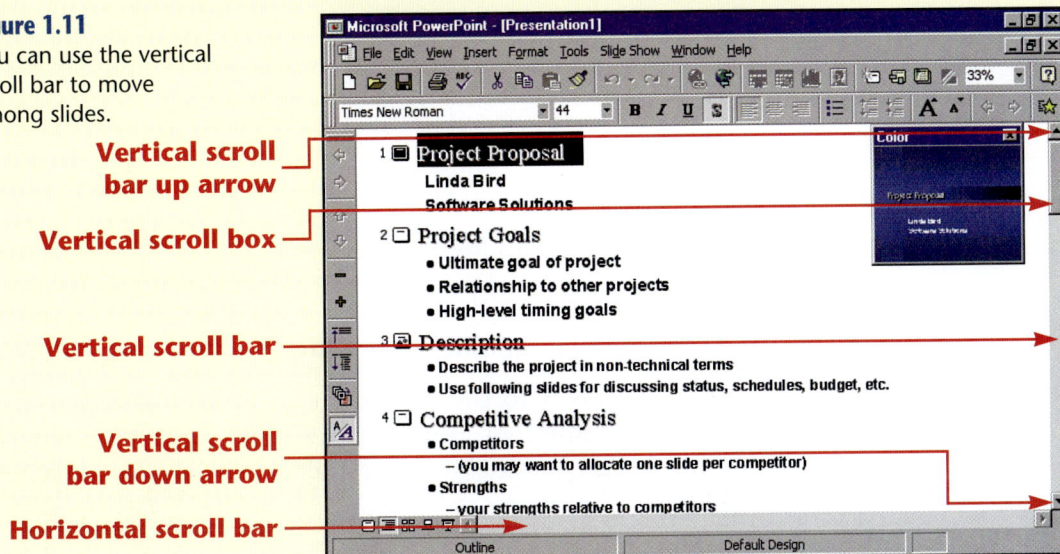

continues

To Move among Slides in a Presentation   (continued)

2 **Click the down arrow located at the bottom of the vertical scroll bar several times.**

Clicking the down arrow advances your view through the presentation one line at a time. In the same way, clicking the up arrow moves upward in the presentation one line at a time. You can also scroll continually by holding down the left mouse button while pointing to either arrow.

3 **Press and hold down the mouse button while pointing to the up arrow.**

The scroll box moves to the top of the scroll bar, indicating that you have moved to the top of the presentation.

4 **Press ⬇ on the keyboard several times.**

The *insertion point* advances one line at a time through the presentation text. In the same way, pressing ⬆ moves the insertion point backward through the presentation. You can also use keyboard shortcuts to move among presentation slides.

5 **Press Ctrl+Home.**

PowerPoint moves the insertion point to the first slide. Using Ctrl+Home is relatively easy to remember because most Windows programs use it to move to the beginning of a document. Likewise, you can press Ctrl+End to move to the end of a document.

Now try moving among slides in Slide view.

6 **Choose View, Slide.**

The presentation is displayed in Slide view. You can use the vertical scroll bar to move among slides in this view as well. In addition to displaying the scroll bar elements used for Outline view, Slide view displays the Next Slide and Previous Slide buttons just below the vertical scroll bar. You can use these buttons to quickly move through the presentation.

7 **Click the Next Slide button.**

The second slide in your presentation is displayed.

8 **Click the Previous Slide button.**

The first slide is now displayed.

9 **Click the vertical scroll box; then drag it up and down slowly.**

A ScreenTip appears to the left of the scroll bar. This ScreenTip shows the slide number and title (see Figure 1.12). When you release the mouse button, the slide indicated by the ScreenTip will be displayed.

Insertion point
The blinking vertical bar that shows where text will appear when you type.

PowerPoint

Figure 1.12
You can use the Next Slide and Previous Slide buttons to quickly move among slides.

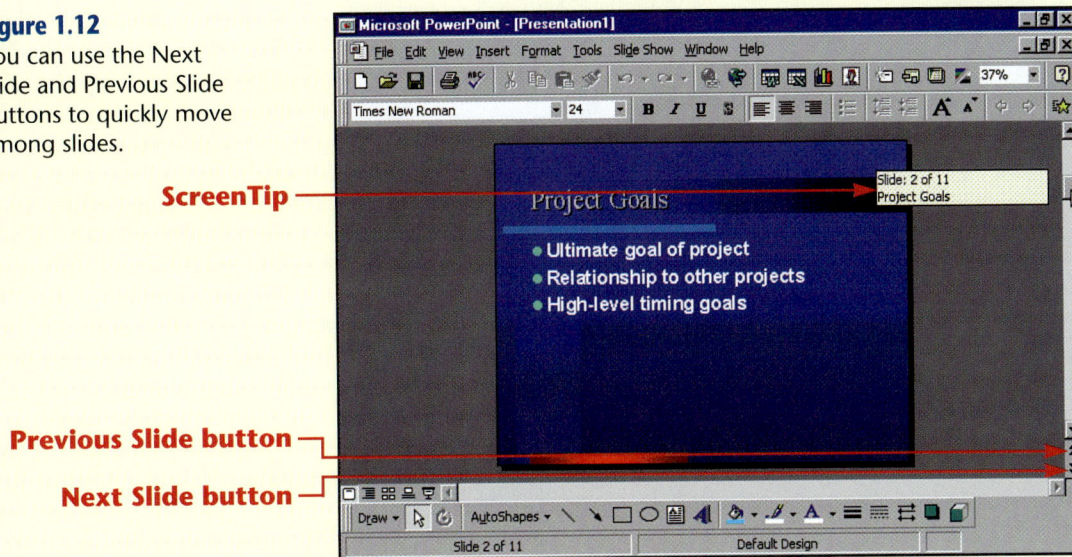

ScreenTip

Previous Slide button

Next Slide button

10 **Stop at Slide 4,** `Competitive Analysis`**, and release the mouse button.**

The slide indicated in the ScreenTip becomes the active slide, shown in Slide view.

11 **Press** PgUp **three times.**

Each time you press PgUp, the previous slide is shown. Likewise, pressing PgDn moves through the presentation one slide at a time.

Leave this presentation open for the next lesson, in which you move among slides in an electronic slide show.

Table 1.3 lists the different mouse and keyboard commands you can use to move around in a presentation in Slide view.

Table 1.3 Mouse and Keyboard Commands for Moving around in Slide View		
To Move To	Use This Keyboard Command	Use This Mouse Command
First slide	Ctrl+Home	Drag the vertical scroll box to the top of the scroll bar.
Last slide	Ctrl+End	Drag the vertical scroll box to the bottom of the scroll bar.
Next slide	PgDn	Click the Next Slide button.
Previous slide	PgUp	Click the Previous Slide button.

Inside Stuff

When you are in Outline view and you want to view a specific slide in Slide view, double-click the slide icon to the right of the title of the slide you want to see. PowerPoint switches you to the Slide view of that slide.

When you are in Slide Sorter view and you want to view a specific slide in Slide view, double-click the miniature of the slide you want to see. PowerPoint switches you to the Slide view of that slide.

Lesson 5: Running an Electronic Slide Show

Shortcut menu
A context-sensitive menu activated by right-clicking the mouse on an object or screen area.

In Lesson 3, you learned how to activate an electronic slide show using the Slide Show button. In this lesson, you learn special commands to help you move around in a slide show. These commands are especially useful when you are conducting a presentation using an LCD display and overhead projector. One efficient way to control a running slide show is to use PowerPoint's *shortcut menu*—a context-sensitive menu you activate by right-clicking the mouse on an object or screen area.

To Run an Electronic Slide Show

❶ Make sure that Slide 1 is displayed in Slide view.

❷ Click the Slide Show button.

The electronic slide show begins. Notice that the first slide displayed is the one that was active when you began the show—Slide 1. (Any time you want to start the slide show from the beginning, you must start from Slide 1; otherwise, the slide show starts with the currently displayed or selected slide.) The slide now fills the entire screen, as it would during an actual electronic presentation.

❸ Click the left mouse button.

The next slide in the presentation appears. If you prefer to use the keyboard, you can press ←Enter or PgDn to advance to the next slide. You can press ←Backspace or PgUp to move back one slide.

Pop-up menu
Another term for shortcut menu.

You can also use the shortcut menu, sometimes called a *pop-up menu*, to move effectively in a slide show.

❹ Click the right mouse button.

The slide show shortcut menu appears (see Figure 1.13). This menu includes commonly used commands that help you control a running slide show. Although you activated the shortcut menu by clicking the right mouse button, you choose commands with the left mouse button.

Figure 1.13
You can control a running slide show by using the shortcut menu.

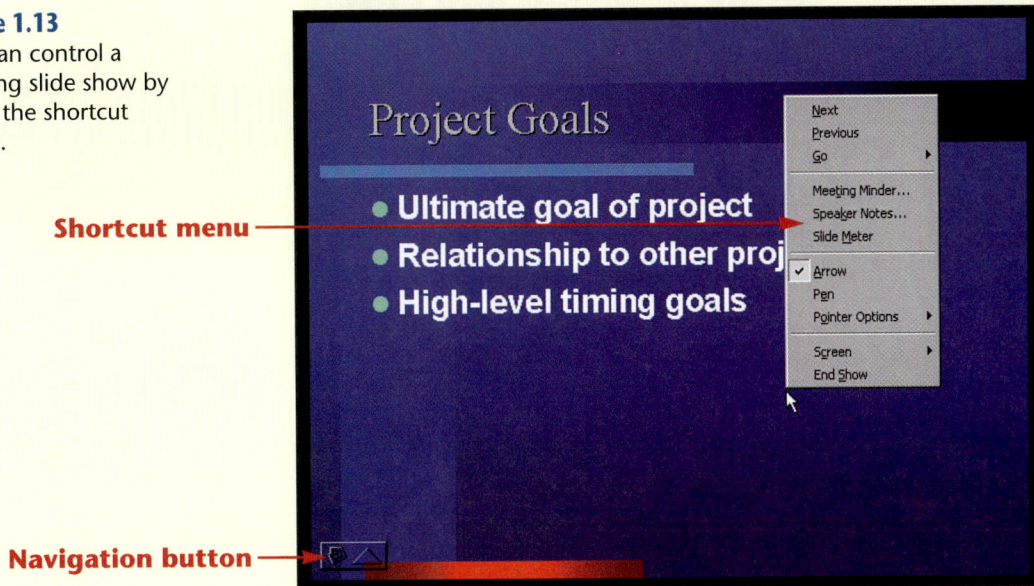

Shortcut menu

Navigation button

5 Choose Previous from the shortcut menu.

Slide 1 is displayed. Notice that you can also move forward in a presentation by choosing Next from the shortcut menu.

Inside Stuff

You can see the same menu choices that appear on the shortcut menu when you click the Navigation button with the left mouse button. The Navigation button appears after you move the mouse in the Slide Show screen.

6 Right-click the mouse to display the shortcut menu; then choose Go, Slide Navigator.

The Slide Navigator dialog box is displayed. Because this dialog box shows all the slide titles, you can use it to move quickly to any slide in your presentation.

7 Double-click Slide 7, Team/Resources.

The presentation jumps to Slide 7.

8 Right-click the mouse and choose End Show from the shortcut menu.

PowerPoint displays the presentation in Slide view—the one you used most recently before you started the electronic slide show. You can also end a slide show by pressing Esc.

Keep this presentation open for the next lesson, in which you save the presentation.

If you have problems...

If the shortcut menu isn't displayed when you right-click the mouse, choose Tools, Options; then click the View tab in the Options dialog box. In the Slide show section, check the box for Popup menu on right mouse click, and then choose OK.

Lesson 6: Saving and Closing Your Presentation

So far, your presentation exists only in random access memory (RAM)—the working area of the computer. RAM retains its contents only as long as power is supplied to your computer. If power is interrupted to your computer, you lose everything in RAM.

However, when you save the presentation from RAM to one of the computer's permanent storage areas (the floppy disk, the hard drive, or a network drive), you have a stored copy. This saved file can be opened, used, and revised at a later time.

When you initially save a file, you must tell PowerPoint the name and storage location for the presentation, just as you label a file before placing it in a filing cabinet. PowerPoint 97 allows you to use long filenames so that you can accurately describe a file's contents. You can use up to 255 characters, including spaces. This means that you can give a presentation a descriptive name such as Annual Meeting, 1997 or Presentation to Stockholders. However, you cannot use the following characters:

/ \ > < * ? " | : ;

You use the File, Save or File, Save As command to save a presentation. Use File, Save As when you first save a presentation or when you change the name, drive, or folder of a saved presentation. You can use File, Save to quickly update a file that was previously saved. You can also click the Save button on the Standard toolbar.

After you save a presentation, you can close it—just as you clear your desk at work to make room for another project. If you made any changes since the presentation was last saved, PowerPoint prompts you to resave it. If you haven't made any revisions to a saved presentation, PowerPoint closes it. You can also close an open presentation without saving it—just as you throw away papers on your desk you no longer need.

In this lesson, you save the sample presentation to a new, formatted disk using your floppy disk drive—usually drive A. After the presentation is saved, you close it. Before starting the tutorial, make sure you have a formatted disk in your floppy disk drive. (You should also check with your instructor in case he or she wants you to save the presentation to your hard disk or a network drive.)

To Save and Close Your Presentation

❶ In the open presentation, choose File, Save As from the menu bar.

The Save As dialog box is displayed (see Figure 1.14). You use this dialog box to indicate the name and location for your file.

Click to select a storage location for your file

Figure 1.14
You use the Save As dialog box when you first save a file.

Possible storage locations

Enter the filename here

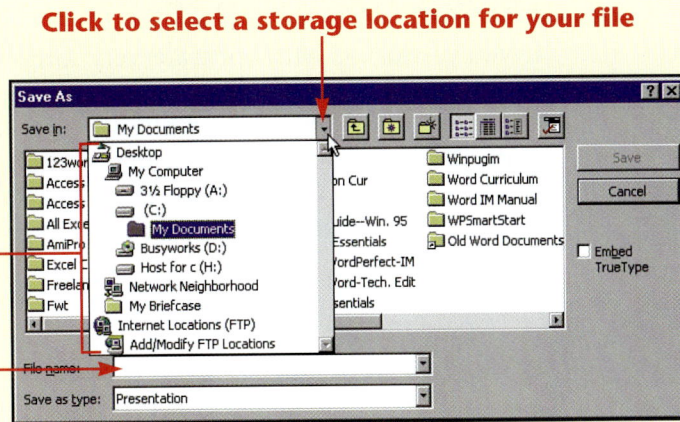

② Click the Save in drop-down list arrow (see Figure 1.14).

PowerPoint displays a list of available storage locations for your computer. This list may vary from computer to computer, depending on which drives are installed.

③ Click $3\frac{1}{2}$ Floppy (A:).

Drive A is selected as the storage location for your presentation.

④ Move the mouse pointer into the File name text box area.

The pointer changes to an I-beam, indicating that this is an area that can accept text. However, before you can enter text, you must "set" the I-beam.

⑤ Click in the text box area.

This changes the I-beam to an insertion point so that you can type your filename.

⑥ Type New Project Proposal **and click the Save button.**

That's all there is to it! Your presentation is saved as New Project Proposal on the floppy disk. You now have a permanent copy stored for later use.

If you make changes to the presentation (either now or later), you can choose File, Save or click the Save button to update the stored file. The file is automatically updated with the same name and location. In other words, you replace the existing file instead of creating a second copy.

Now that you have a permanent copy of the presentation, you can close the copy in memory. You can close the presentation by choosing File, Close or clicking the document's Close button.

⑦ Choose File, Close.

The presentation closes from memory, but you have a permanent copy—the one you just saved to the floppy disk. In Project 2, "Modifying Presentations," you open an existing presentation so that you can revise it.

The next lesson focuses on using PowerPoint's help system to quickly find information about the program. Keep PowerPoint running for this lesson.

Lesson 7: Getting Help

If you've worked with software very long, you know that sooner or later you need information about a particular feature. Fortunately, PowerPoint can provide you with help while you work. You can use the Help Topics dialog box to research a particular subject, or you can display ScreenTips using the What's This? feature. You can also use the Office Assistant to display help, tips, and messages related to the work you're performing.

In this lesson, you learn the basics of getting help in PowerPoint.

Using the Help Topics Dialog Box

One of the most straightforward methods of getting help is to use the Help Topics dialog box. You can access this dialog box by choosing Help, Contents and Index.

To Use the Help Topic Dialog Box

1 **From the menu bar, choose Help, Contents and Index.**

The Help Topics: Microsoft PowerPoint dialog box appears, as shown in Figure 1.15. The tabs represent different ways of researching your topic. You can click any tab to display the associated help page.

Figure 1.15
You can get help on general topics.

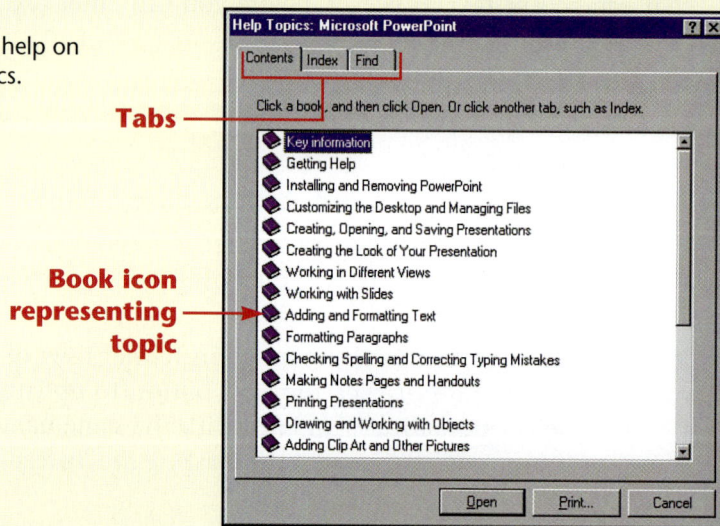

Tabs

Book icon representing topic

2 **Click the Contents tab, if necessary.**

The Contents page shows subjects topically—just like a table of contents in a book. Each topic is represented by a book icon. You can double-click the book to display subtopics related to the main topic.

3 **Double-click the Getting Help book icon.**

A list of subtopics appears, as shown in Figure 1.16. You can double-click any of these to show information about the topic. Alternatively, you can click to select the icon and then choose the Display button.

Figure 1.16
You can double-click a main topic to display its subtopics.

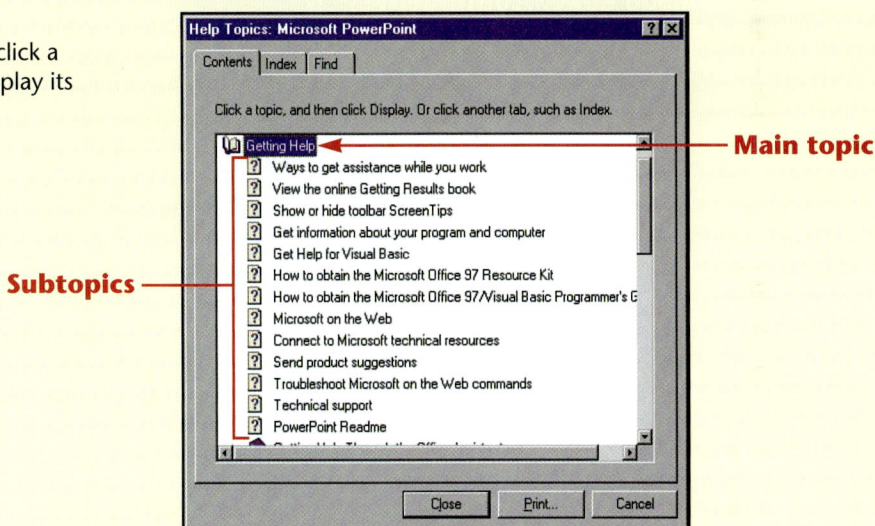

Main topic

Subtopics

4 **Click Ways to get assistance while you work; then choose Display.**

Hyperlinks
Areas of the screen that you can click to display related information.

PowerPoint displays a dialog box that graphically depicts the ways you can get assistance (see Figure 1.17). This screen contains *hyperlinks*. You can find a hyperlink by moving the mouse pointer until a hand pointer appears. When you click a hyperlink, information related to that topic appears in a pop-up box near the hyperlink.

Figure 1.17
You can use PowerPoint's graphical screens to get assistance.

Click this button to return to the Help Topics dialog box

You can activate a hyperlink by clicking the hand pointer

Hyperlink

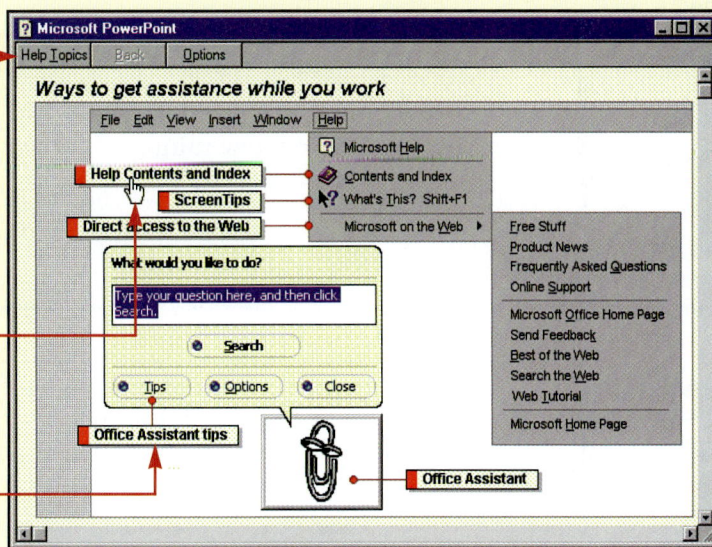

5 **Move the mouse pointer to the Help Contents and Index hyperlink and then click.**

Information related to this topic is displayed as a ScreenTip. You can clear the tip by clicking anywhere in the dialog box.

continues

6 Click in the dialog box to clear the tip; then click the Help Topics button (see Figure 1.17).

The Contents page of the Help Topics dialog box appears again. Now try using the Index page, which includes an alphabetical list of topics. Using the Index, you can search for a topic you want, and then display information about it.

7 Click the Index tab.

The Index page appears. Notice that the insertion point is already in the Type the first few letters of the word you're looking for text box. You can use this text box to indicate the topic you want.

8 Type `creating presentations` in the Type the first few letters of the word you're looking for text box.

PowerPoint highlights the topic you indicated. You can choose Display to view the subtopics associated with this subject.

9 Click Display.

The Topics Found dialog box is displayed, with a list of subtopics. You can double-click any topic to display specific help about it.

10 Double-click `Create a new presentation`.

PowerPoint displays information about creating a new presentation.

11 Read the displayed information and then click the Close button in the upper-right corner of the dialog box.

PowerPoint closes the dialog box and displays the presentation. If you want, take a few minutes to research other topics by using the Help Topics dialog box.

In the next tutorial, you learn how to use the Office Assistant to get tips and help while you work.

Inside Stuff

PowerPoint provides ScreenTips to give you information about different items onscreen. In any dialog box, click the question mark (?) and then click the dialog box command you want to research. To find information about a toolbar button, menu command, or screen area, choose Help, What's This? and then click the object.

Using the Office Assistant

Did you ever wish for a personal computer trainer—someone to personally guide you through a new software program? Fortunately, PowerPoint 97 includes an electronic version of such a person: the Office Assistant. Although not a substitute for a personal trainer, the Office Assistant can display tips related to the feature you're using. Additionally, the Office Assistant can provide a list of subjects related to a question you type.

PowerPoint

You can choose <u>H</u>elp, Microsoft PowerPoint <u>H</u>elp to display the Office Assistant. Alternatively, you can click the Office Assistant button on the Standard toolbar. When the Assistant is displayed, you can type the question you want, or display a tip. When you're finished, you can close the Office Assistant window by clicking its Close button.

To Use the Office Assistant

1 Choose <u>H</u>elp, Microsoft PowerPoint <u>H</u>elp.

The Office Assistant is displayed in its own window (see Figure 1.18). The bubble shows how to use the Assistant to get help.

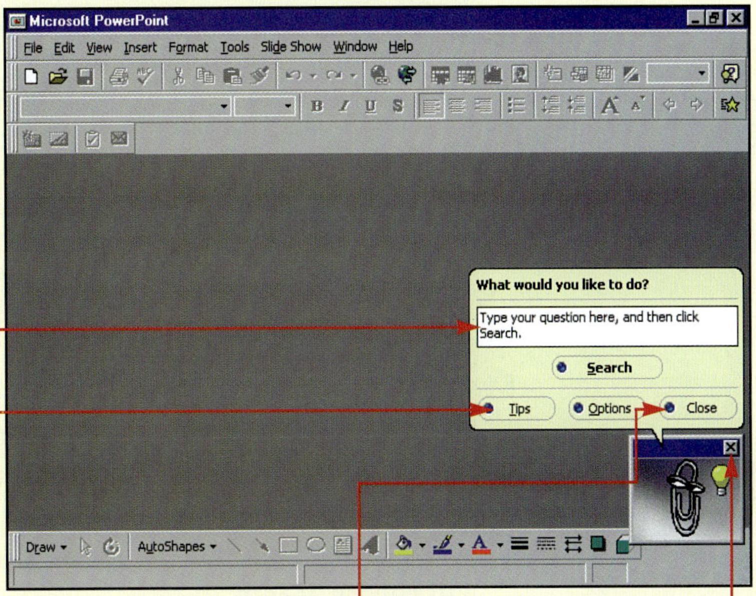

Figure 1.18
You can use the Office Assistant to get help.

Type your question here and then choose Search

Click here to view tips

Click here to close the bubble

Click here to close the Office Assistant

2 Click the Office Assistant window to display the bubble; then click <u>T</u>ips.

The Assistant displays a tip (see Figure 1.19). You can also click the <u>N</u>ext or <u>B</u>ack button to scroll through a list of tips. When you're finished, you click Close in the tip bubble.

continues

To Use the Office Assistant   (continued)

Figure 1.19
You can display tips using the Office Assistant.

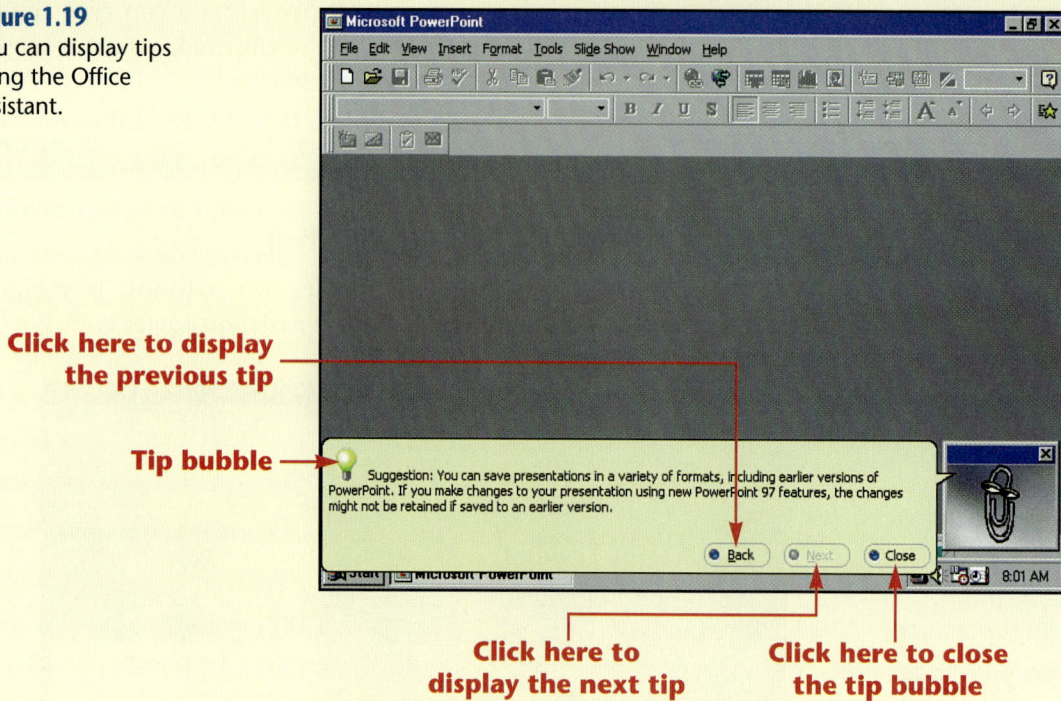

Click here to display the previous tip

Tip bubble ────→

> Suggestion: You can save presentations in a variety of formats, including earlier versions of PowerPoint. If you make changes to your presentation using new PowerPoint 97 features, the changes might not be retained if saved to an earlier version.

Click here to display the next tip

Click here to close the tip bubble

3 **Click Close to close the tip; then click the Office Assistant to display the bubble.**

Besides displaying tips, the Assistant can list topics related to a question you type.

4 **In the Office Assistant's text box area, type** How can I get help? **and choose Search.**

A list of related topics is displayed (see Figure 1.20). You can click the topic for which you want help.

Figure 1.20
The Office Assistant answers your question by displaying related topics.

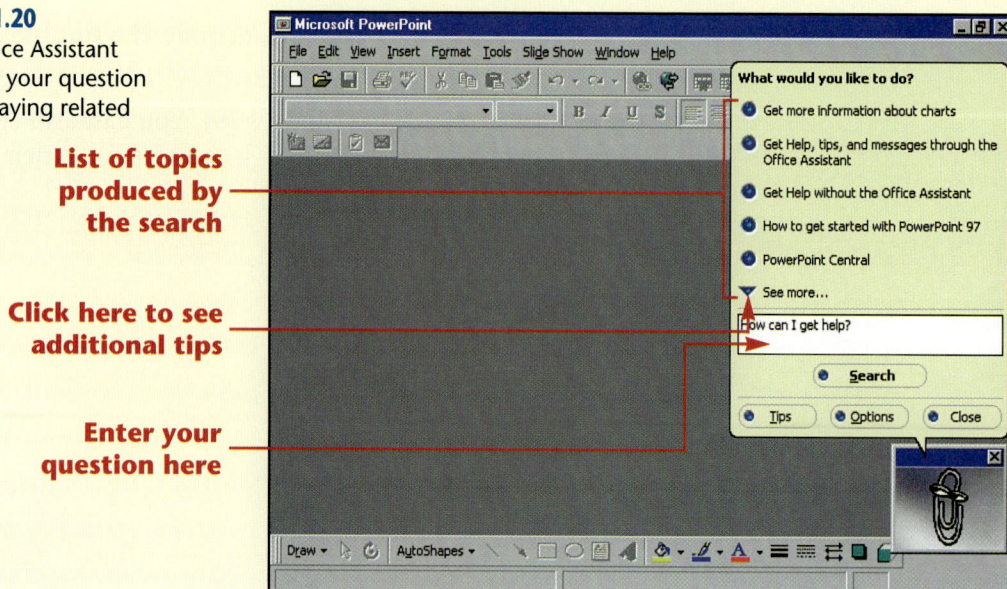

List of topics produced by the search

Click here to see additional tips

Enter your question here

What would you like to do?
- Get more information about charts
- Get Help, tips, and messages through the Office Assistant
- Get Help without the Office Assistant
- How to get started with PowerPoint 97
- PowerPoint Central
- See more...

How can I get help?

Search

Tips   Options   Close

PowerPoint

⑤ From the list, choose Get Help, tips and messages through the Office Assistant.

The help dialog box about this topic is displayed.

⑥ Read the information in the dialog box and then click the Close button in the upper-right corner.

You can leave the Office Assistant displayed onscreen while you work with your presentations, or you can close it and then reopen it just when you need it. The easiest way to close the Office Assistant is to click its Close button.

⑦ Click the Office Assistant's Close button.

The Office Assistant window closes.

Keep PowerPoint running for the next lesson, in which you learn how to exit the program correctly.

Inside Stuff

The default Office Assistant is displayed as a personified paper clip, called "Clippit." However, you can change the Office Assistant's appearance to suit your personality. Insert your Office 97 CD in the CD-ROM drive. In the Assistant's bubble, choose Options to display the Options dialog box, and then click the Gallery tab. Click the Next and Back buttons to scroll through the available Assistants. When you see the Assistant picture you want to use, click OK.

Lesson 8: Exiting PowerPoint

Closing a presentation, as you did in Lesson 6, is like clearing a project from your desk. Exiting the entire program is like leaving your office. When you exit PowerPoint, you clear the program from memory and return to the Windows 95 desktop.

You can exit PowerPoint by clicking the application's Close button (on the right side of the application title bar) or choosing File, Exit from the menu. Once you've exited the program, you can start it again, especially if you plan to complete the "Applying Your Skills" exercises at the end of this project. However, if you're finished working, you should also shut down Windows 95 and turn off the computer. Try exiting PowerPoint and Windows 95 now.

To Exit PowerPoint

❶ Click the PowerPoint application's Close button (see Figure 1.21).

Alternatively, you can choose <u>F</u>ile, E<u>x</u>it from the menu. If you don't have any unsaved presentations, PowerPoint is cleared from RAM, and the Window 95 desktop is displayed. If you have a presentation in memory that contains unsaved work, PowerPoint prompts you to save it before exiting the program.

Figure 1.21
PowerPoint is easy to exit.

Click this button to exit the PowerPoint application ——

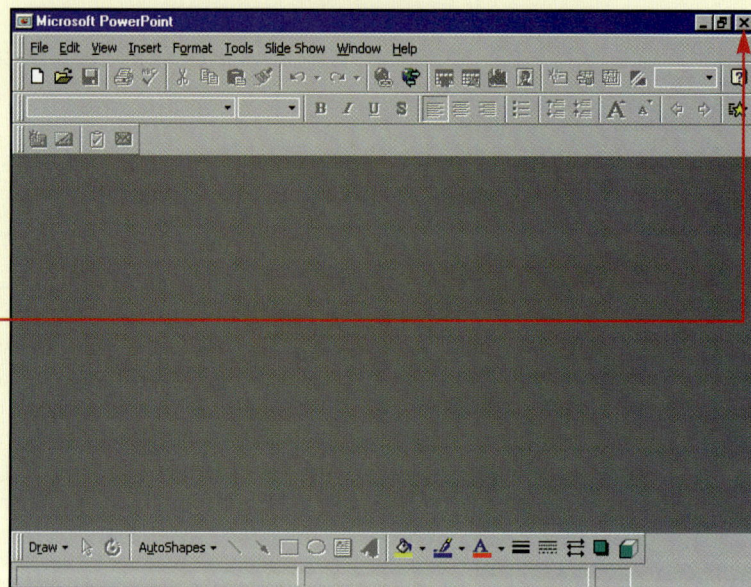

It's also important to exit Windows correctly before turning off the computer. The best way to do this is to use (ironically enough) the Start button.

❷ Click the Start button and choose Sh<u>u</u>t Down from the menu.

The Shut Down Windows dialog box is displayed (see Figure 1.22). You use this dialog box to control how to shut down or restart Windows.

Figure 1.22
Be sure to shut down Windows correctly.

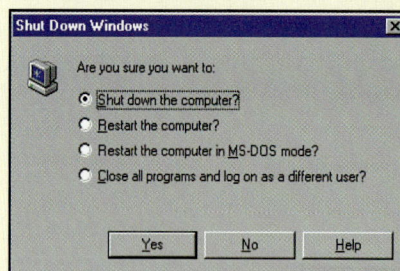

3 **Make sure that the Shut down the computer? option button is selected; then click Yes.**

Windows closes temporary files and is cleared from memory. This process generally takes a few seconds, so be patient. It's important to wait until Windows indicates that you can turn off the computer.

4 **Wait until the It's now safe to turn off your computer message appears.**

When you see the message, you can turn off your computer.

5 **Turn off your computer monitor, main unit, and any other hardware (such as speakers or a printer).**

If you have finished your work session, exit PowerPoint and shut down Windows before turning off your computer. Otherwise, complete the "Checking Your Skills" and "Applying Your Skills" exercises at the end of this project.

Project Summary

To	Do This
Start PowerPoint	Choose the Start button, Programs, Microsoft PowerPoint.
Use the AutoContent Wizard	Choose File, New; then click the Presentations tab and double-click AutoContent Wizard.
Use different views	Click the PowerPoint view buttons.
Move to the first slide	Drag the scroll box to the top of the vertical scroll bar.
Move to the last slide	Drag the scroll box to the bottom of the vertical scroll bar.
Move to the next slide	Click the Next Slide button.
Move to the previous slide	Click the Previous Slide button.
End a running slide show	Press Esc.
Use the Slide Navigator	Right-click in the slide show screen and choose Go, Slide Navigator.
Display general help topics	Choose Help, Contents and Index.
Display the Office Assistant	Click the Office Assistant button.
Save a presentation	Choose Save or Save As from the File menu.
Close a presentation	Choose File, Close.
Exit PowerPoint	Choose File, Exit.
Shut down Windows 95	Choose the Start button, Shut Down.

Checking Your Skills

True/False

For each of the following, check *T* or *F* to indicate whether the statement is true or false.

__T __F **1.** You can view a presentation using one of ten views.

__T __F **2.** The Slide Sorter View button automatically sorts the slides alphabetically.

__T __F **3.** Outline view, Slide view, and Slide Show are just different ways of viewing the same set of slides.

__T __F **4.** The AutoContent Wizard creates the structure and suggested content based on choices you make.

__T __F **5.** You can get help by using the PowerPoint Window Assistant.

__T __F **6.** The first time you save a presentation, you must name it.

__T __F **7.** Closing a presentation and exiting PowerPoint are the same.

__T __F **8.** You shut down Windows 95 by using the Start button.

__T __F **9.** To move among PowerPoint slides in Slide view, you must use the mouse.

__T __F **10.** If power is interrupted to your computer you lose everything in random access memory (RAM).

Multiple Choice

Circle the letter of the correct answer for each of the following questions.

1. Which of the following views is the best to view only the text contained in a presentation?

   a. Slide view

   b. Slide Sorter view

   c. Outline view

   d. Notes Page view

2. Which of the following can you use to quickly create a presentation that already contains sample content?

   a. Template Wizard

   b. AutoContent Wizard

   c. Outline view

   d. Answer Wizard

3. Which of the following describes an LCD panel?

   a. A device used with an overhead projector to display images from the computer to a screen

   b. Another name for a toolbar

   c. A list of special effects for transition from one slide to another

   d. The Learning Center Display panel shown when you use the Office Assistant

4. One way to move among slides is to use which of the following?

    a. The Search feature on the Help menu

    b. The Office Assistant

    c. The horizontal scroll bar

    d. The vertical scroll bar

5. You can use the Office Assistant to do which of the following?

    a. To display tips

    b. To automatically create a presentation with sample content

    c. To move among slides

    d. To end an electronic slide show

6. A presentation you create using the AutoContent Wizard initially displays in which of the following?

    a. Slide view

    b. Outline view

    c. AutoContent Wizard view

    d. Slide Sorter view

7. You can quickly move to the first presentation slide in Slide view by doing which of the following?

    a. Clicking the First Slide button on the vertical scroll bar

    b. Pressing Ctrl + Home

    c. Pressing Home

    d. Dragging the scroll box to the bottom of the vertical scroll bar

8. Which of the following views does PowerPoint provide?

    a. Outline

    b. Slide Sorter

    c. Notes Page

    d. All of the above

9. When you initially save a new presentation, which of the following is true?

    a. You can use only eight characters in the file name.

    b. You must save to the hard drive.

    c. You indicate a file name and location for the presentation.

    d. You can use characters such as < > ? : .

10. When you're finished working with PowerPoint, you should do which of the following?

    a. Simply turn off the computer.

    b. Choose File, Exit from the menu.

    c. Click the Application Close button.

    d. Both b and c.

Completion

In the blank provided, write the correct answer for each of the following statements.

1. The temporary working area that the computer uses to run programs is called _____.

2. _____ view shows six slides onscreen at once.

3. You can use _____ view to add notes to your presentation.

4. A group of related slides you can create using PowerPoint is called a _____.

5. A software application that helps you structure, design, and present information (such as graphs) to an audience so that it is visually appealing is called _____ software.

6. A predefined list of slides displayed sequentially onscreen or using an LCD panel and overhead projector is called a _____.

7. The _____ is a tool that guides you through the steps of a proposed presentation and includes suggested content.

8. A _____ is a predefined design that includes formatting for a presentation.

9. The _____ is the blinking vertical bar that shows where text will appear when you type.

10. You can right-click the mouse in a slide show to display a _____.

Matching

In the blank next to each of the following terms or phrases, write the letter of the corresponding term or phrase. (Note that some letters may be used more than once.)

a. AutoContent Wizard

b. RAM

c. ScreenTip

d. shortcut menu

e. presentation

f. hard drive

g. insertion point

h. template

i. Office Assistant

j. LCD projection panel

_____ **1.** A series of related slides

_____ **2.** A flat-screen device used to project computer images on a screen

_____ **3.** The computer's temporary memory

_____ **4.** A permanent storage location on your computer

_____ **5.** A PowerPoint feature you can use to find information

_____ **6.** A tool for creating a new presentation with sample content already included

_____ **7.** A presentation design that contains formatting but no content

_____ **8.** A description box that is displayed when you rest the mouse pointer on a button

_____ **9.** The result of right-clicking the mouse

_____ **10.** A blinking vertical bar that shows where text will next appear

Applying Your Skills

Practice

The following exercises enable you to practice the skills you have learned in this project. Take a few minutes to work through these exercises now.

Creating a Presentation

Because you have attended a PowerPoint class, everyone in your department now considers you a PowerPoint expert. For this reason, your coworkers want you to convince management to buy the latest and greatest computers for them. You decide to use PowerPoint to present your ideas at tomorrow's meeting to show that purchasing new computers would be cost-effective. Because you need to prepare the presentation by tomorrow, you decide to use the AutoContent Wizard. After creating the presentation, you can practice displaying it in different views and running an electronic slide show.

To create and run a presentation, follow these steps:

1. Start PowerPoint, if necessary.

2. Choose AutoContent Wizard in the startup dialog box. (If this dialog box is not displayed, choose File, New, click the Presentations tab, and double-click AutoContent Wizard.)

3. Choose Selling Your Ideas as the presentation type.

4. Choose an onscreen presentation for an informal meeting. Also indicate that you'd like PowerPoint to produce handouts.

5. Type Improving Productivity as your presentation title. Enter your name and company, if necessary.

6. Use the view buttons to observe the presentation in each of the five views.

7. Use the methods listed in Table 1.3 to move among slides in Slide view and Outline view.

8. Run the electronic slide show. Use the shortcut menu to move to the previous and next slides as well as to end the show. Then run the presentation from the second presentation slide.

9. Save the presentation as Our Plan for Getting New Computers and then close it.

Creating a Marketing Plan Presentation

As Marketing Manager, you've just found out that your boss wants you to present your new marketing plan at the upcoming annual company meeting. Because the meeting is only two days away, you decide to use the AutoContent Wizard to quickly create an on-screen presentation.

To create a marketing plan presentation, follow these steps:

1. Start PowerPoint, if necessary, and choose the AutoContent Wizard from the startup dialog box. (If this dialog box is not displayed, choose File, New, click the Presentations tab, and double-click AutoContent Wizard.)

2. Choose `Marketing Plan` as the presentation type and click the Finish button.

3. View the text contents of the presentation in Outline view; then choose View, Slide to switch to Slide view.

4. Use the vertical scroll bar to move through the slides in Slide view.

5. Run the electronic slide show starting with various slides. Use the shortcut menu to move among the slides and end the show.

6. Save the presentation as `Marketing Plan for the Annual Meeting` and then close it.

Creating a Presentation with the AutoContent Wizard

You are working for a company that deals in computer ergonomics products—products designed to help people work more effectively at the computer. You want to create a presentation to promote your products for a sales meeting. You decide to use the AutoContent Wizard to create the basic framework and suggested slide content.

To create a presentation with the AutoContent Wizard, follow these steps:

1. Start PowerPoint, if necessary, and choose the AutoContent Wizard from the startup dialog box. (If this dialog box is not displayed, choose File, New, click the Presentations tab, and double-click AutoContent Wizard.)

2. Choose `Product/Services Overview` as the presentation type and choose Finish.

3. Click the Slide Show button to run the presentation as an electronic slide show.

4. Press ⏎Enter to advance through the presentation one slide at a time.

5. Press Esc to end the show.

6. Save the presentation as `Company Products` and close it.

Using the Office Assistant

You stay late one night at the office to learn a few new features in PowerPoint. In order to use your time efficiently, you decide to use PowerPoint 97's Office Assistant to find the information you need.

To use the Office Assistant, follow these steps:

1. In the open PowerPoint screen, click the Office Assistant button on the Standard toolbar.

2. Click the Tips button to view a tip.

3. In the tip bubble, scroll through the available tips by clicking the <u>N</u>ext and <u>B</u>ack buttons.

4. Close the tip bubble by clicking the Close button.

5. Display the Assistant's bubble by clicking the Office Assistant window.

6. Type `How do I create a presentation?` in the text box area; then choose <u>S</u>earch.

7. Choose a subject from those displayed. When you're finished reading the information, close the help dialog box.

8. Close the Office Assistant window by clicking the Close button.

Using the AutoContent Wizard

As part of one of your business classes you need to give a speech on a software program. Because you are familiar with PowerPoint 97, you decide to create a PowerPoint presentation to use along with your speech.

To use the AutoContent Wizard, follow these steps:

1. Start PowerPoint if necessary; then choose <u>F</u>ile, <u>N</u>ew to display the New Presentation dialog box.

2. Click the Presentations tab to display that page.

3. Double-click the AutoContent Wizard icon to start the AutoContent Wizard.

4. Read the opening AutoContent Wizard dialog box; then click <u>N</u>ext.

5. Choose <u>G</u>eneral as the type of presentation and choose `Generic` from the list; then click <u>N</u>ext.

6. Click the <u>P</u>resentations, informal meetings, handouts option button and then click Next.

7. Click the On-<u>s</u>creen presentation and <u>Y</u>es option buttons in the Presentation style step; then click <u>N</u>ext.

8. In the Presentation options screen, type `PowerPoint 97` in the Presentation title text box. Press (Tab⁺) to move to the <u>Y</u>our name text box and enter your name. Also enter the school you attend in the <u>A</u>dditional information text box. When you're finished entering text, click <u>N</u>ext.

9. Click <u>F</u>inish in the last AutoContent screen to view your presentation as an outline.

10. Save the presentation as `PowerPoint 97 Speech`; then close it.

Challenge

The following challenges enable you to use your problem-solving skills. Take time to work through these exercises now.

Using the AutoContent Wizard

You are president of your university's Biking Club. As such, you are frequently asked to give presentations on the activities in which your club participates. To quickly develop a presentation of this type, you decide to use the AutoContent Wizard.

To use the AutoContent Wizard, follow these steps:

1. Start PowerPoint and display the New Presentation dialog box.

2. Launch the AutoContent Wizard.

3. Choose the `Product/Services Overview` as the Presentation type.

4. Choose the option that creates a presentation for meetings. Also choose to create an onscreen presentation.

5. Enter `University Biking Club` as the Presentation title. Also enter your name and school in the appropriate locations in the AutoContent Wizard screens.

6. View the presentation in Outline, Slide, Slide Sorter and Slide Show views.

7. Save the presentation as `Biking Club Presentation`; then close it.

Using Different PowerPoint Views

You are helping a friend create a presentation for the first time and learn the basics of using the PowerPoint views. To do so, you use the AutoContent Wizard.

To use different PowerPoint views, follow these steps:

1. Start PowerPoint and display the New Presentation dialog box.

2. Start the AutoContent Wizard.

3. Choose whichever presentation type you wish; then click <u>F</u>inish.

4. Click PowerPoint's view buttons to display the presentation in Outline, Slide Sorter, Slide, Notes Page, and Slide Show views. Run the presentation as a slide show starting with Slide 2. Use the screen navigational tools to move among slides.

5. Use the <u>V</u>iew menu to display the presentation in the various views.

6. Close the presentation without saving it.

Using the AutoContent Wizard to Create an Announcement

You're planning a birthday party for a friend. To create the invitations in a snap, you decide to use the AutoContent Wizard.

To use the AutoContent Wizard to create an announcement, follow these steps:

1. Start PowerPoint and display the New Presentation dialog box.

2. Launch the AutoContent Wizard.

3. Choose the `Announcement/Flyer` presentation type in the Personal category.

4. Choose the Presentations, informal meetings, handouts option in the Output options screen.

5. Choose to display the presentation onscreen and to print handouts.

6. In the Presentation options screen, type `Birthday Party!` in the Presentation title text box. Delete entries in the other text boxes.

7. View the presentation in Outline, Slide, Slide Sorter, and Slide Show views.

8. Save the presentation as `Birthday Party`.

9. Close the presentation.

Using Help and the Office Assistant

You have some extra time after class and decide to research a few PowerPoint topics. You use PowerPoint's help system and Office Assistant to do so.

To use help and the Office Assistant, follow these steps:

1. Start PowerPoint if necessary, then choose Help, Contents and Index to display the Help Topics: Microsoft PowerPoint dialog box.

2. Double-click the Key information book icon; then research the following topics:

   a. What's new in PowerPoint 97

   b. How to get started with PowerPoint 97

3. Write down at least one new thing you learned for each topic.

4. On the Contents page of the Help Topics: Microsoft PowerPoint dialog box, double-click the Working in Different Views book icon.

5. Double-click the PowerPoint Views sub-topic; then click each of the hyperlink buttons to display information about the views.

6. Click the Close button in the Microsoft PowerPoint dialog box to close it.

7. Click the Office Assistant button on the Standard toolbar.

8. Type `How do I run a slide show?` in the text box area of the Assistant's bubble; then choose Search.

9. Click the Ways to run a slide show option button and read the displayed information. Close the Microsoft PowerPoint dialog box.

10. Close the Office Assistant.

Moving Among Presentation Slides

Because you have learned PowerPoint so quickly, your instructor has hired you as a tutor for those students who are struggling. To brush up on your skills before a tutorial session, you work through the following steps:

To move among presentation slides, follow these steps:

1. Create a new presentation using the AutoContent Wizard.

2. Use the view buttons to display the presentation in Outline, Slide Sorter, Slide, and Notes Page views.

3. Display the presentation in Slide view.

4. Use the mouse and keyboard commands listed in Table 1.3 to move among slides.

5. Move to Slide 1 in the presentation; then start the electronic slide show.

6. Click the left mouse button several times to move through the entire presentation.

7. Click the right mouse button to display the slide show shortcut menu; then use its commands to move forward and backward through the slide show.

8. Choose End Show from the shortcut menu to stop the slide show.

9. Start the slide show beginning on slide 2. Run the slide show in its entirety; then press Esc to end it.

10. Close your presentation without saving it.

PinPoint Assessment

You have completed the project and the associated lessons, as well as the "Checking Your Skills" and "Applying Your Skills" sections. Now use the PinPoint software Evaluation mode to assess your comprehension of the specific exam tasks you have just learned. You can also use the PinPoint Trainer mode and the SHOW ME tutorials to practice these specific exam tasks.

Project

Two 2

Modifying Presentations

Working with Existing Presentations

In this project you will learn the following objectives and their associated Microsoft Exam required activities.

Objectives   ## Required Activities

➤ Open an Existing Presentation

➤ Add and Delete Slides … … … … … … … … … … …   Delete Slides

➤ Change Slide Order … … … … … … … … … … … …   Change the Sequence of a Slide
                                                            Modify Sequence in Outline Mode

➤ Add, Demote, and Promote Text … … … … … …   Enter Text in Slide and Outline Views

➤ Select and Move Text

➤ Print Outlines and Slides … … … … … … … … …   Print Color Presentations
                                                            Export to Overhead
                                                            Export to 35mm Slides

➤ Create a Presentation from an … … … … … … …   Create from an Existing
   Existing File   Presentation

Why Would I Do This?

In Project 1, you created a presentation by using the AutoContent Wizard. However, the product of this wizard is only a basis for your presentation. With PowerPoint, you can edit and enhance the existing presentation in various ways for more impact.

Whenever you are presenting your ideas, you want to make a powerful impression. In this project, you develop a business plan for a small business you are starting that provides computer training. You are speaking at the area Chamber of Commerce next week and need to outline the main services your business can provide. To develop the presentation, you open an existing presentation, add and delete slides, and change text and slide order. You also print your presentation. Through this process, you customize the presentation so that it is truly your own and makes the greatest possible impression on your audience.

Lesson 1: Opening an Existing Presentation

If you want to work with a file in your office, you might get the file from a file cabinet, make a copy, and put it on your desk so that you can work on it. In the same way, opening an existing presentation in PowerPoint simply creates a copy from one of the computer's storage areas and places it in memory so that you can work with it.

With PowerPoint, you can open an existing presentation in a number of ways. One method is to choose the Open an existing presentation option in the PowerPoint startup dialog box. You can also click the Open button on the Standard toolbar. Alternatively, if you use the same presentations frequently, you can use the recently used files list displayed at the bottom of the File menu.

After you open a file, it's sometimes advantageous to create immediately a "clone" of the file by saving it with a new name. You can then work with the copy and keep the original file intact. You use this method for the tutorials in this book.

To create a copy of an existing file, you open it and then choose File, Save As. In the Save As dialog box, you enter a new name for the file and choose Save. This effectively creates a copy of the original file with a new name.

In the following tutorial and in later projects, you will need to use the student data files supplied on the CD that accompanies this book. For information about where these files are located and how you can access them, see your instructor.

Now try opening an existing presentation by using the PowerPoint startup dialog box.

To Open an Existing Presentation

1 **Start PowerPoint (and close the Office Assistant window by clicking the Close button, if necessary).**

The PowerPoint startup dialog box is displayed in the PowerPoint window. You can use this dialog box to open a presentation.

2 **Click the Open an existing presentation option button, as shown in Figure 2.1, and choose OK.**

Figure 2.1
You can quickly open an existing file by using the PowerPoint startup dialog box.

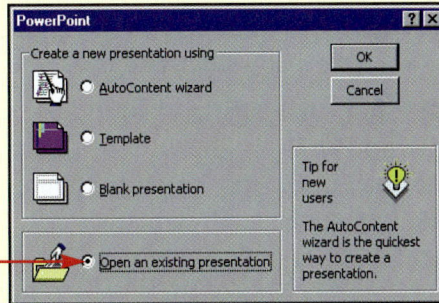

Click here to open an existing presentation

The Open dialog box is displayed (see Figure 2.2). This dialog box shows the folders and files on your computer. In this dialog box are several buttons that enable you to access different views of your files.

Figure 2.2
The Open dialog box lists files and folders on your computer.

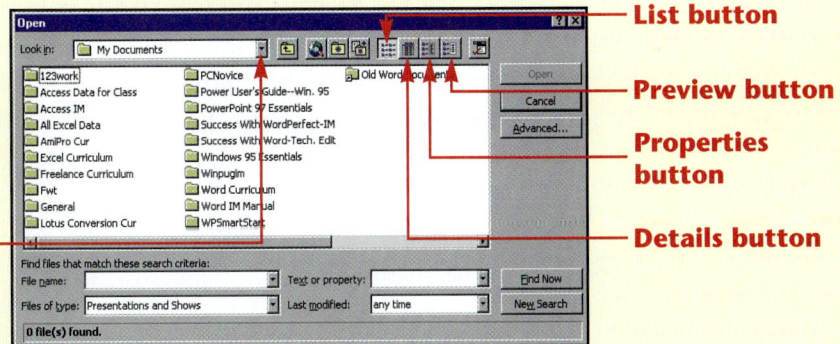

List button

Preview button

Properties button

Click here to display storage locations on your computer

Details button

If you have problems...
If PowerPoint is already started, choose File, Open to display the Open dialog box.

3 **Insert the CD containing the student data files for this project in your CD-ROM drive; then click the Look in drop-down list arrow and select the CD-ROM drive. Select the Project-01 folder on that drive.**

The list of folders and files on the CD is displayed. The list includes folders for each project in this book and the data files you'll use to complete the tutorials.

Before you actually open the file into memory, you can learn quite a bit of information about the file. This information is especially helpful because it is easy to forget the name or contents of a presentation created some time ago.

continues

To Open an Existing Presentation   (continued)

Before you preview a file, list information about it, or open it, you must first select it. You can select a file from the list by pointing to it and clicking the left mouse button.

If you have problems...

Your instructor may have copied the PowerPoint files for this book to your hard drive or to a network drive. Check with your instructor if you are unsure where the data files are located for this class.

4 **Point to Proj0201 in the list of files and then click the left mouse button to select the file.**

Proj0201 is highlighted to show that it is selected. After this file is selected, you can display information about it.

Additionally, the way your files are displayed in the center of the dialog box depends on which view button is selected—List, Details, Properties, or Preview (refer to Figure 2.2). The view button currently selected on your system is the last one that was used.

5 **Click the List button near the top of the dialog box.**

Only the presentation's file names are shown. Because of this, List view enables you to see more files or folders in the dialog box than when you choose the Details, Properties, or Preview button.

6 **Click the Details button to show your files in Details view.**

The size, type, and modification date of the files are now shown in addition to the file name.

7 **Click the Properties button.**

Pertinent information related to the selected file is shown, including the title, author, last modification date, and so on. You can also click the vertical scroll bar's down arrow to view more information (see Figure 2.3).

Location of selected file   **Properties button**

Figure 2.3
You can click the Properties button to display valuable information about a file.

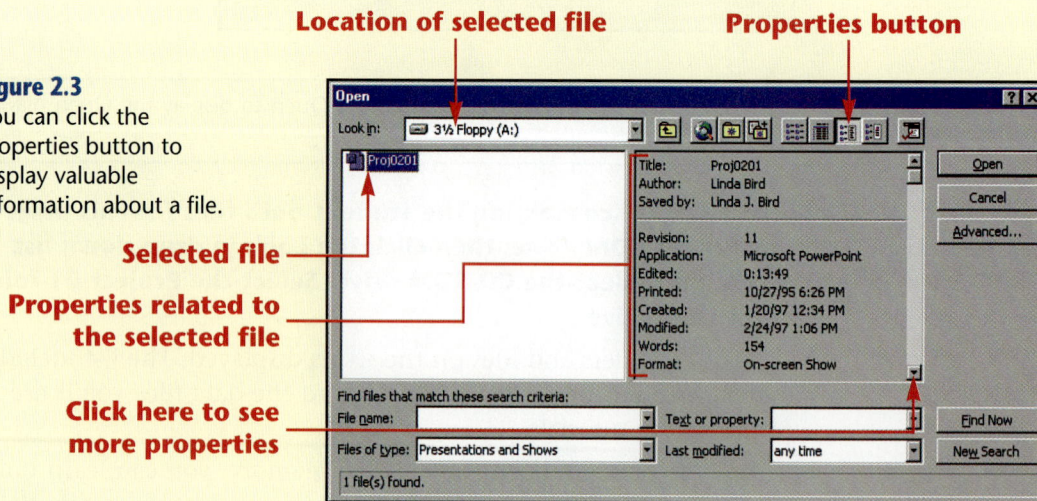

Selected file

Properties related to the selected file

Click here to see more properties

Title:	Proj0201	
Author:	Linda Bird	
Saved by:	Linda J. Bird	
Revision:	11	
Application:	Microsoft PowerPoint	
Edited:	0:13:49	
Printed:	10/27/95 6:26 PM	
Created:	1/20/97 12:34 PM	
Modified:	2/24/97 1:06 PM	
Words:	154	
Format:	On-screen Show	

Open
Look in: 3½ Floppy (A:)
Proj0201

Find files that match these search criteria:
File name: Text or property: Find Now
Files of type: Presentations and Shows   Last modified: any time   New Search
1 file(s) found.

You can also use the Preview view to quickly determine whether a presentation is the one you want to open.

8 Click the Preview button.

The title slide for the selected presentation is shown in miniature. This helps you identify the correct file.

After you locate the file you want, you can double-click its filename to open it. Alternatively, you can select the file and click Open.

9 With Proj0201 still selected, click the Open button.

PowerPoint opens the selected file. Notice that the name of the presentation (Proj0201) is displayed in the title bar, as shown in Figure 2.4. PowerPoint automatically displays the presentation in Outline view.

Figure 2.4
The presentation opens in Outline view.

Title of presentation

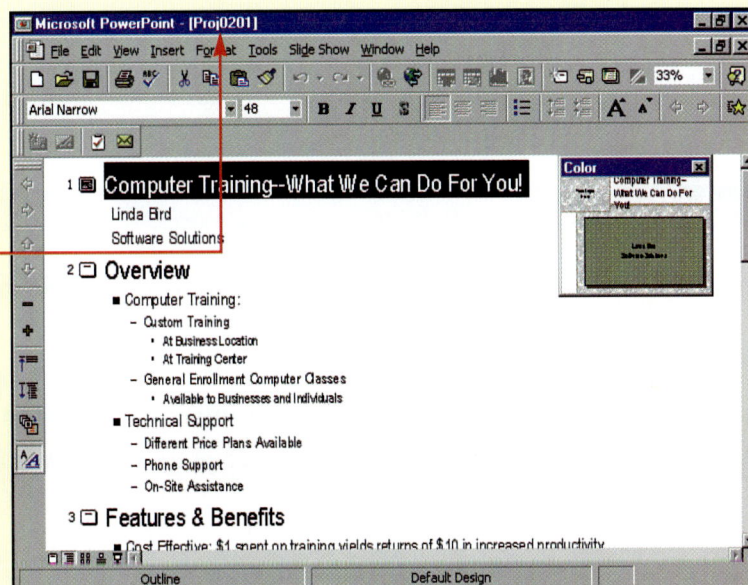

After the file is opened in memory, you can use the Save As dialog box to copy and rename the file. This keeps the original file unaltered.

10 With Proj0201 onscreen, choose File, Save As.

The Save As dialog box is displayed. You can save the file with the new name (Chamber of Commerce) in the drive location your instructor specifies.

11 In the File name text box, type Chamber of Commerce **and choose Save.**

Proj0201 is copied and renamed Chamber of Commerce. Notice that the title bar displays the new name. You work with this file throughout the rest of this project, so leave it open.

Inside Stuff

PowerPoint automatically adds a three-character extension to each file (.ppt) to uniquely identify it as a PowerPoint file. However, depending on how your system is set up, the extension may or may not be displayed.

Lesson 2: Adding and Deleting Slides

Whether you rely on the AutoContent Wizard to create your presentations or you create them from scratch, you want the flexibility of adding and deleting slides. Table 2.1 lists the methods you can use to add and delete a slide.

Table 2.1 Methods for Adding and Deleting Slides	
To add a slide	Choose Insert, New Slide from the menu bar.
	Click the New Slide button on the Standard toolbar.
	Press Ctrl+M.
To delete a slide	In Outline or Slide Sorter view, click to select the slide and then press Del.
	In Slide view, choose Edit, Delete Slide.

In this lesson, you add and delete slides in Outline and Slide Sorter views because you can see more easily what you are doing. Try adding and deleting slides now.

To Add and Delete Slides

1 Make sure the Chamber of Commerce presentation is onscreen in Outline view.

2 Scroll down until you can see Slide 6, Pricing.

3 Place the mouse pointer on the slide icon for Slide 6.

The mouse pointer changes to a four-sided arrow. When the pointer is displayed in this manner, you can click the slide icon to select instantly an entire slide.

4 Click the Slide 6 slide icon.

The slide icon is selected, as shown in Figure 2.5. If the selected slide contains subpoints, they will be selected as well.

Figure 2.5
You can select a slide in Outline view by clicking the slide icon.

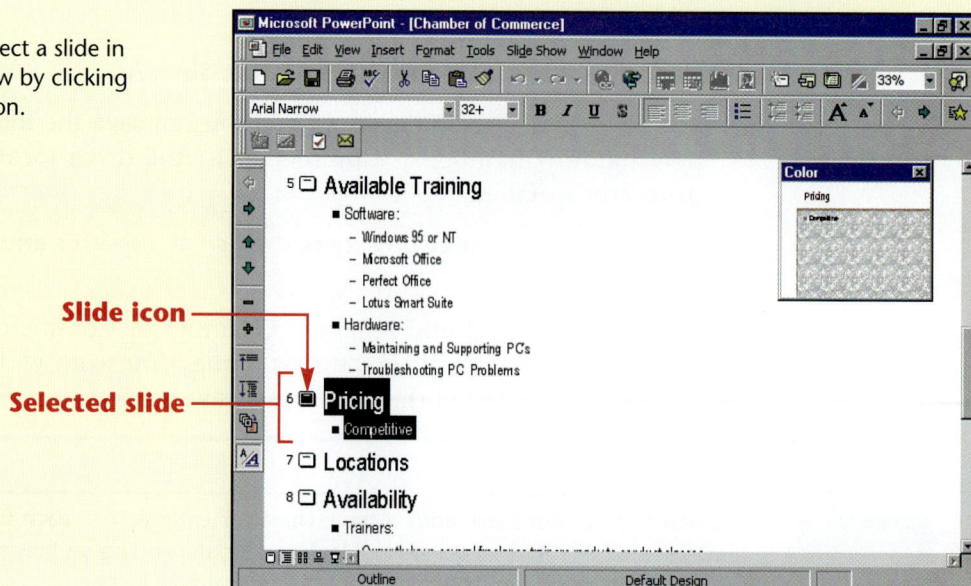

⑤ Press Del.

The selected slide—Slide 6—is deleted from the presentation. PowerPoint automatically renumbers the remaining slides.

You can reverse this (or any other) deletion by using Undo, a handy feature that PowerPoint provides to reverse your last action.

⑥ Click the Undo button.

Slide 6 is reinserted in the presentation.

You can also delete slides in Slide Sorter view.

⑦ Click the Slide Sorter View button and then click Slide 7, Locations.

The presentation is shown in Slide Sorter view with a double border surrounding Slide 7. This indicates that it is the selected slide.

⑧ Press Del.

The selected slide is deleted. The black line between Slides 6 and 7 indicates that the location of the insertion point is between the two slides. This is where you want to add a new slide.

⑨ Click the New Slide button on the Standard toolbar.

Placeholder
On a PowerPoint slide, an area that can accept text, graphics, or objects (such as charts).

PowerPoint displays the New Slide dialog box. This dialog box contains 24 predefined layout options, called AutoLayouts. Each one contains *placeholders* for text, graphics, charts, and drawn objects. Using the AutoLayouts takes considerably less time than defining the format each time you add a slide. Notice that as you single-click an AutoLayout, its name is displayed in the lower-right corner of the dialog box (see Figure 2.6).

Figure 2.6
You can quickly add a slide with preset formatting.

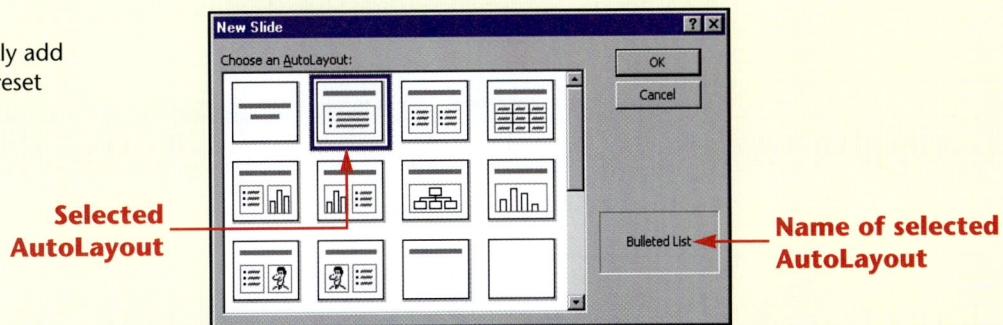

Selected AutoLayout

Name of selected AutoLayout

⑩ Double-click the AutoLayout for Bulleted List (the second layout in the first row).

A bulleted list slide is inserted into your presentation between Slides 6 and 7.

⑪ Click the Save button to save your changes.

Keep this presentation open for the next lesson, in which you change the slide order.

Inside Stuff

You can also add a new slide to a presentation by choosing Insert, New Slide from the menu. Alternatively, you can press Ctrl+M.

When you add a slide to a presentation, the new slide is inserted after the slide where the insertion point is currently positioned. You can add slides in any view except Slide Show view.

In Outline view, you can delete several slides simultaneously. Click the first slide you want to delete, press ◆Shift, and click the last slide to be deleted. All the intervening slides are selected. Then press Del to remove them all.

If you accidentally delete a slide, immediately choose Undo from the Edit menu or click the Undo button. The slide will be reinserted in your presentation.

Lesson 3: Changing Slide Order

Drag-and-drop

To perform a move on a PowerPoint slide icon by selecting and dragging it to another location and then releasing the mouse button.

You will often find that you need to rearrange the slides in your presentation to create a more logical sequence. You can use Slide Sorter view to immediately see the move's effect on the entire presentation. To move a slide using this view, select the slide and then drag it to the new location. This method is sometimes referred to as *drag-and-drop*. Try moving slides by using this technique now.

To Change Slide Order

❶ **Make sure the Chamber of Commerce presentation is displayed in Slide Sorter view on your screen.**

Before you move a slide, you must first select it.

❷ **Click Slide 4, Applications, to select it.**

A double border surrounds Slide 4, indicating that it is selected (see Figure 2.7).

Figure 2.7
You can click in the middle of a slide to select it in Slide Sorter view.

Selected slide →

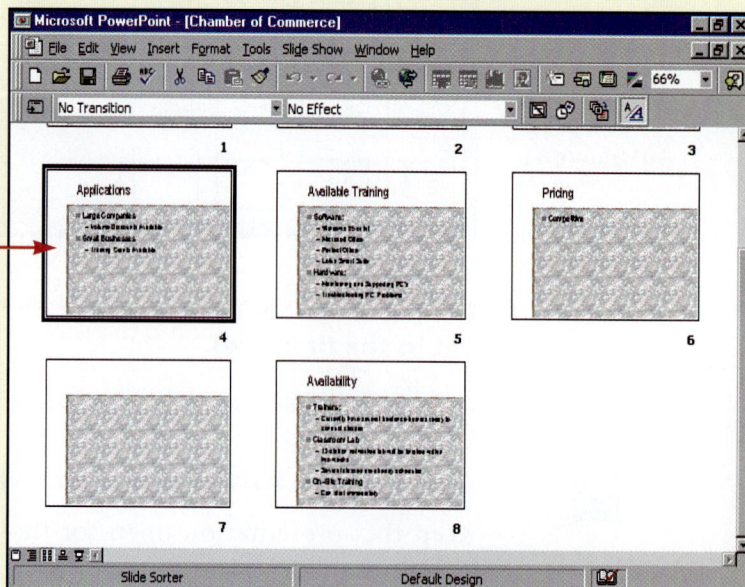

❸ Move the mouse pointer to the middle of the selected slide; then click and drag the line indicator to the space between Slides 5 and 6.

The new location for the slide is indicated by the inserted line between Slides 5 and 6 (see Figure 2.8).

Figure 2.8
You can drag a selected slide to the new location.

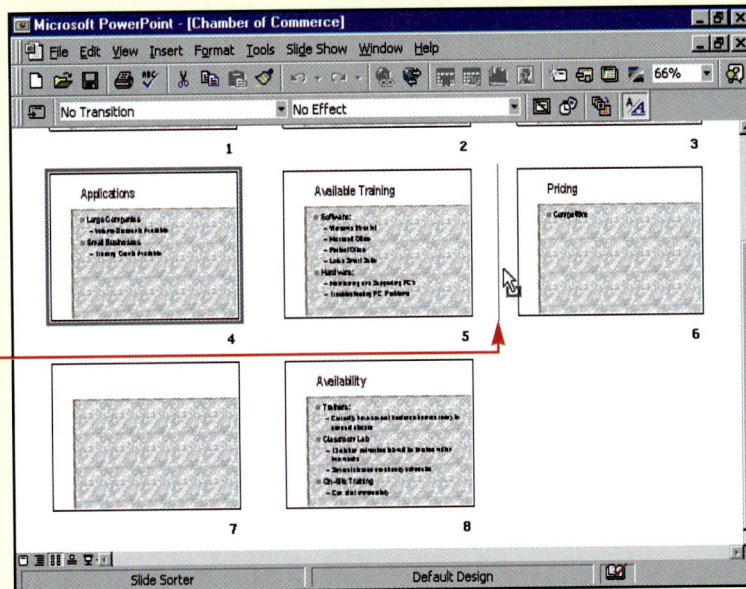

The indicator line shows the new location for your slide

❹ Release the mouse button.

The selected slide is moved to the position between Slides 5 and 6. Because PowerPoint automatically renumbers your slides, the Applications slide is now Slide 5, and Slide 5 becomes Slide 4.

You can also select multiple slides and then move them. To move two or more slides simultaneously, press ⬆Shift as you click to select the slides. Release ⬆Shift; then click and drag the group of slides to the new location. Try moving multiple slides now.

❺ With the newly renumbered Slide 5, `Applications`, still selected, press ⬆Shift while clicking Slide 4, `Available Training`.

Double borders encompass both slides, indicating that you've successfully selected them (see Figure 2.9). Now you can move them to a new location by dragging, just as you did earlier in this tutorial. If you drag one of the selected slides, both will move. As before, the indicator line shows the new location for the selected slides.

continues

To Change Slide Order (continued)

Figure 2.9
You can select and move multiple slides.

Select multiple slides by pressing ◆Shift as you click the slides

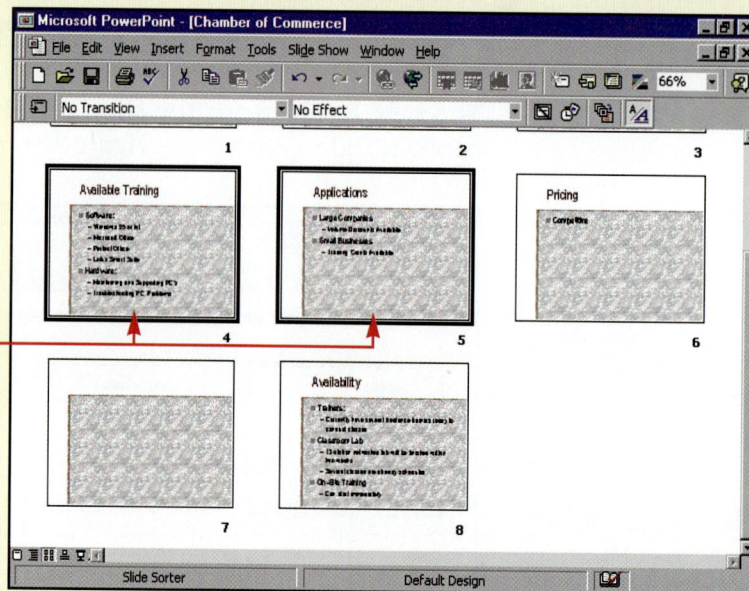

6 **Move the mouse pointer to the middle of Slide 4,** Available Training; **then click and drag the indicator line between Slides 2 and 3.**

If you have problems...

Moving the slides with drag-and-drop is easier if you can see the new location as well as the slides you're moving. If necessary, click the vertical scroll bar arrows to readjust your view.

7 **Release the mouse button to drop the slides into their new location.**

Both slides are moved to the specified location. Again, PowerPoint renumbers the slides.

8 **Choose Edit, Undo Drag and Drop to reverse the most recent move.**

The last move is reversed.

9 **Save your changes.**

Keep the presentation open for the next lesson, in which you add, demote, and promote text.

Inside Stuff

The drag-and-drop method works well in the Slide Sorter view if you can see where you are dragging the slides. This is more difficult in a larger presentation. If you need to move slides to a position in the presentation you can't see on your screen, you should cut and paste the slides instead. First, select the slides you want to move and click the Cut button on the Standard toolbar. Then select the slide that will appear just before the slide you're moving. Click the Paste button on the Standard toolbar.

Exam Notes

You can use drag-and-drop to modify sequence in Outline view. Click the slide icon for the slide you want to move, drag it to a new location in your outline (indicated by a horizontal line), and release the mouse button.

Drag-and-drop has one drawback in Outline view—you need to see the destination point when you drag. In Lesson 5, "Selecting and Moving Text," there are alternatives for moving text—and slides—within the outline.

Lesson 4: Adding, Demoting, and Promoting Text

When you first create a presentation, you have only a framework for adding text and graphics. In previous lessons, you focused on changing the basic structure so that your presentation would flow in a more logical manner. You did this by adding, deleting, and rearranging slides. After the framework is in place, you can use a number of ways to enter and modify the text itself so that the presentation becomes your own. Being able to manipulate text in a presentation is an important skill.

Demote

To indent a line of text more than the preceding line, indicating a lower level of importance.

Promote

To indent a line of text less than the preceding line, indicating a greater level of importance.

This lesson focuses on ways to enter, *demote*, and *promote* text in Slide view. You demote or promote text to arrange it logically or to increase or decrease the relative importance of your points. In this lesson, you use the blank slide you inserted in Lesson 2. Because you can easily add and revise text in Slide view, you should switch to it before working with text.

To Add, Demote, and Promote Text

❶ Make sure the Chamber of Commerce presentation is displayed in Slide Sorter view; then double-click Slide 7 to switch to Slide view.

Slide 7 is displayed in Slide view with placeholders for adding a title and a bulleted list (see Figure 2.10). The placeholders that are displayed depend on the AutoLayout you choose. For this slide, you have title and bulleted list placeholders. (If the horizontal and vertical rulers are displayed on your screen, you can turn them off by choosing View, Ruler.)

continues

To Add, Demote, and Promote Text (continued)

Figure 2.10
You can enter text in the slide's placeholders.

Placeholder for title text

Placeholder for bulleted text

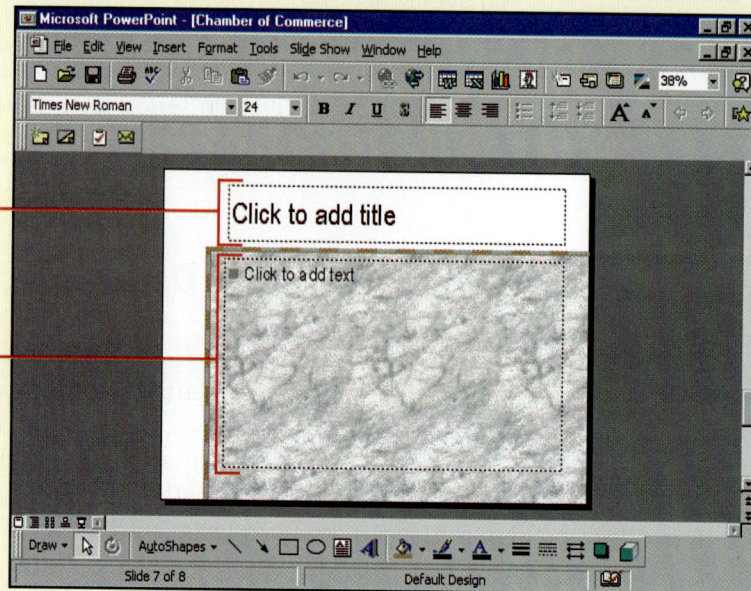

❷ **Click the upper placeholder,** Click to add title.

The placeholder words are replaced by an insertion point so that you can enter text.

❸ **Type** Experienced Trainers **and then click the lower placeholder,** Click to add text.

The title is fixed in the upper placeholder, and the insertion point is moved to the bulleted list placeholder. Because this slide is based on the Bulleted List AutoLayout, you can quickly create a list with bullets. Bulleted lists are generally used when you want to emphasize each subpoint, but the order of the items is not particularly important.

❹ **Type** Rebecca Bell **as the first bullet point and press** ⏎Enter.

Rebecca Bell is listed as the first bullet point, and a second bullet is automatically created.

❺ **Type** Sarah Hitt **as the second bullet point and press** ⏎Enter.

Sarah Hitt is entered as the second point. Now you can create subpoints that support or enhance your main point. One way you can create subpoints is by pressing Tab to indent a line. Alternatively, you can click the Demote button on the Formatting toolbar.

If you have problems...

Don't worry if you see a red, wavy line beneath the name Hitt. This mark just indicates that PowerPoint's spell checker doesn't recognize the word. To eliminate this mark, right-click on the word and choose a correction or choose Ignore All from the displayed list.

6 Press `Tab`, **type** `10 years corporate training experience`, **and press** `Enter`.

Pressing `Tab` demotes this line, indenting it to show that it has less importance than the preceding line. Additionally, every time you press `Enter`, another subpoint at the same level is created.

7 Type `Writes books for Que Education and Training` **as the second subpoint and press** `Enter`.

You can also promote a line so that it is indented less. You can do this by pressing `Shift`+`Tab` or clicking the Promote button on the Formatting toolbar.

8 Press `Shift`+`Tab` **to promote the bullet on the current line; then type** `Lonnie Stegall`.

Your slide should now look similar to Figure 2.11.

Figure 2.11
You can increase or decrease the relative importance of your points.

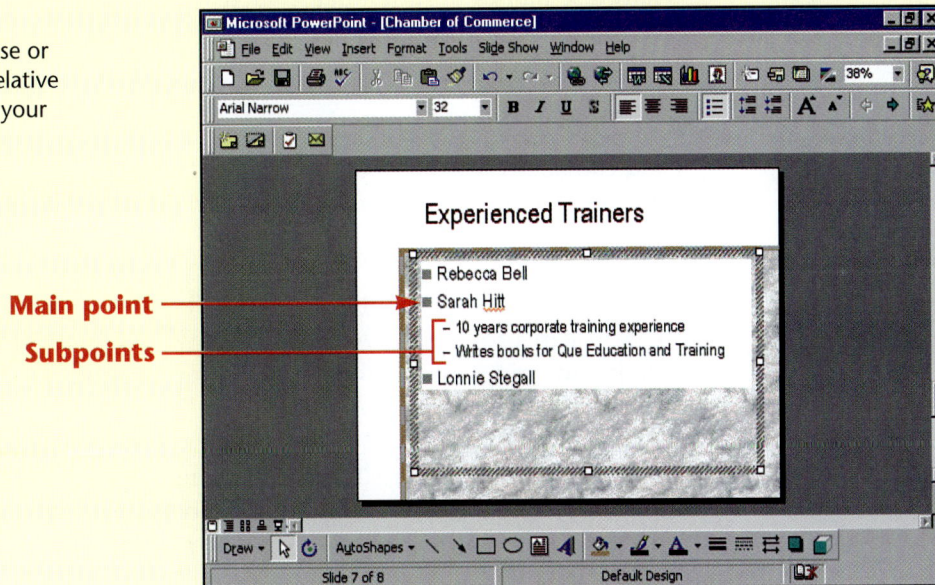

Main point
Subpoints

9 Save your changes to the presentation.

Keep the Chamber of Commerce presentation open for the next lesson, in which you select, copy, and move text.

Inside Stuff

You delete text in PowerPoint the same way that you do in a word processing program. Press `Del` or `Backspace` to erase one character at a time. You can also select larger sections of text with the mouse and then press `Del`. If you accidentally delete too much text, click the Undo button on the Standard toolbar.

You can also enter and edit text in Outline view. You position the insertion point on the slide and then type the text. You can press `Tab` to demote a point or `Shift`+`Tab` to promote a point—just as in Slide view—or use the Demote or Promote buttons on the Formatting or Outlining toolbar. In Outline view, you can promote a bullet point into a slide title if you want.

Lesson 5: Selecting and Moving Text

In addition to entering text in a presentation, you can easily change the order of the bullet points. The tasks of copying and moving text are facilitated by the *Clipboard*. Before you cut or copy text, however, you must first select it. After it is selected, you can click the Cut (or Copy) button to move (or copy) the selected text to the Clipboard. You move the insertion point to where you would like to place the text, and then click the Paste button. You can also drag selected text to a specified location. You can move text more easily in Slide view or Outline view. For this tutorial, you use Outline view.

Clipboard

A temporary area of memory that holds material that is cut (or copied) so that it can be pasted elsewhere.

To Select and Move Text in Outline View

❶ In the open presentation, choose <u>V</u>iew, <u>O</u>utline.

The presentation is displayed in Outline view. Again, don't be concerned if PowerPoint places red, wavy lines under words, especially the names of individuals. Such words are not in PowerPoint's dictionary.

❷ Use the vertical scroll bar so that you can view Slide 4, Available Training.

You can select a word, a subpoint, or the entire slide contents. The quickest way to select a single word is to double-click it.

❸ Double-click the word Available.

The word Available highlighted to indicate that you have selected it. You can move this word by cutting it, which sends it to the Clipboard, and then pasting it to another location. Try this now.

❹ Choose <u>E</u>dit, Cu<u>t</u>.

Alternatively, click the Cut button. The selected word is removed from the screen and sent to the Clipboard. Now you can position the insertion point where you want to place the text and then choose <u>E</u>dit, <u>P</u>aste.

❺ Position the insertion point to the right of the word Training **and choose <u>E</u>dit, <u>P</u>aste.**

Alternatively, you can click the Paste button or press Ctrl+V. The word is pasted at the location you indicated.

In Outline view, you can also select a subpoint and then move it by using the Move Up or Move Down button on the Outlining toolbar. Try this now.

❻ On Slide 4, position the mouse pointer on the bullet for the subpoint Windows 95 or NT; when the pointer changes to a four-sided arrow, click once.

The entire subpoint is selected (see Figure 2.12). Now you can use the Move Down button to position the subpoint where you want it.

Figure 2.12
You can use the Move Up and Move Down buttons in Outline view.

Move Up button →

Move Down button →

Click a bullet to select its text →

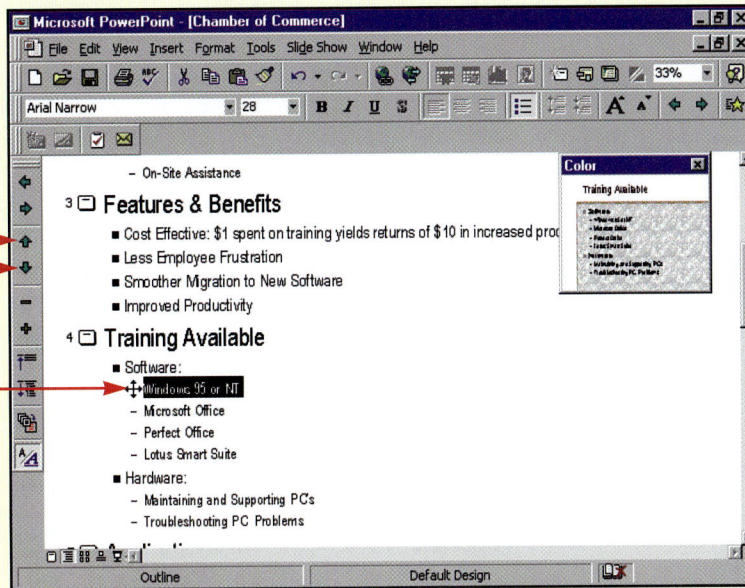

⑦ **With the subpoint still selected, click the Move Down button on the Outlining toolbar.**

The subpoint moves down one line in the presentation. Likewise, you can move the subpoint up.

⑧ **Click the Move Up button on the Outlining toolbar.**

The subpoint moves back to its previous location.

You can also select a main point and then move it. When you select a main point, all the subpoints are automatically selected as well.

⑨ **On Slide 4, click the bullet for** Software.

The main point, Software, and all the related subpoints are selected (see Figure 2.13).

Figure 2.13
When you select a main point, all subpoints are also selected.

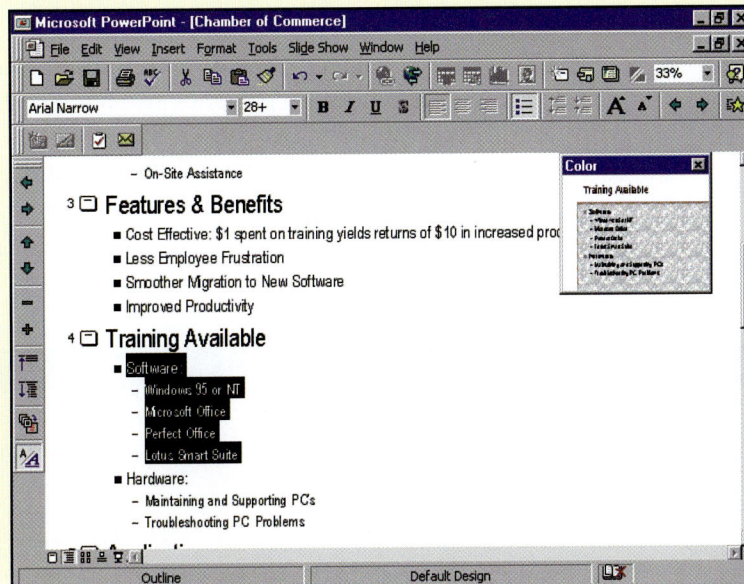

continues

To Select and Move Text in Outline View (continued)

10 **Click the Move Down button three times.**

The information about software programs is moved down three lines.

11 **Save the changes to your presentation.**

Leave the presentation open for the next lesson, in which you print the presentation outline and a slide.

Inside Stuff

The drag-and-drop method can also be applied to moving selected bullet text or selected slides. Click the bullet or the slide icon to select the bullet text or slide text. Then drag up or down in the outline, using the horizontal line that appears as your placement guide. When the horizontal line is in the position where you want to put the selected text, release the mouse button.

This same method also works with moving bullet points in the Slide view.

Lesson 6: Printing Outlines and Slides

One of the main ways you can output, or produce, a presentation is to print it. PowerPoint provides a variety of ways to print your presentation. This lesson focuses on two of the most basic ways: printing the main outline and printing the slides. (In Project 6, you learn how to print speaker notes and handouts.)

Printing an outline is useful, especially when you are working on a long presentation, because a printed outline helps you see the overall flow and sequence of the presentation. Because the main purpose of the outline is to view the content, the printout shows only the text that has been typed—no graphics are shown.

In contrast, you can print the presentation as a series of slides. Slides show not only text but also graphics and backgrounds. Printing a slide or series of slides is done in much the same manner as printing an outline. However, you need to consider two additional factors when printing in Slide view: color, and which slides should be printed.

In the following tutorial, you print the presentation as an outline, and then you print one of the slides. Try your hand at printing now.

To Print an Outline and a Slide

1 **With the** Chamber of Commerce **presentation open, choose File, Print.**

The Print dialog box is displayed (see Figure 2.14).

If you have problems... You can't display the Print dialog box by clicking the Print button on the Standard toolbar. Clicking the Print button automatically sends the current presentation or selection to the printer with no further confirmation from you! Make sure that you choose File, Print so that you can access the Print dialog box.

Figure 2.14
You make choices about output in the Print dialog box.

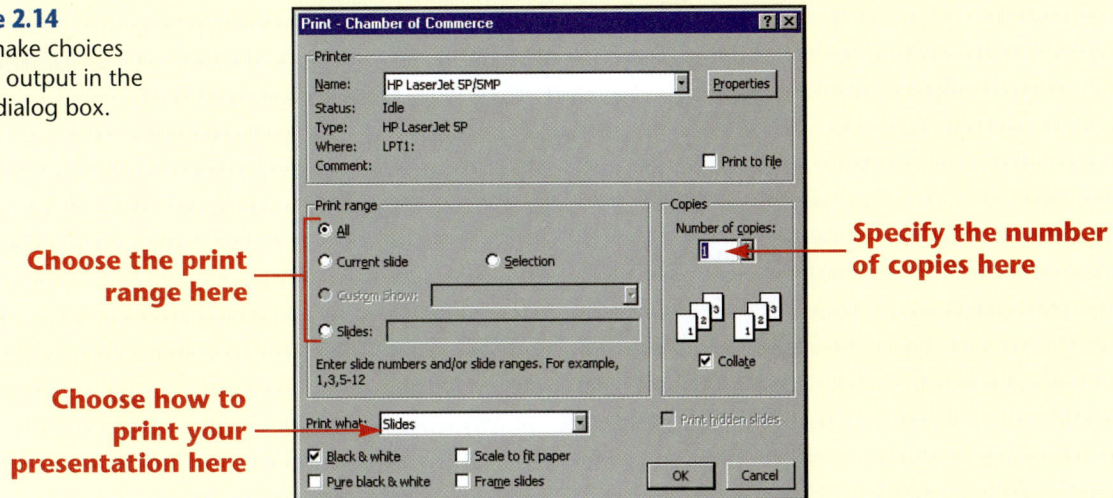

Choose the print range here

Choose how to print your presentation here

Specify the number of copies here

You can use the Print dialog box to make choices about the type of output (slides or outline, for example), the number of copies, and the print range.

2 Click the drop-down arrow to the right of the Print what text box.

A drop-down list displays various ways you can print your presentation.

3 Select Outline View.

Outline view is shown as the current selection in the Print what text box. Next, you want to make sure that the correct settings are selected so that the entire presentation will print as an outline.

4 In the Number of copies text box, make sure that the number of copies is set to 1.

5 In the Print range area, make sure that the All option button is selected.

6 Choose OK.

This accepts the print settings and prints the outline.

You can also print your presentation as slides. When printing slides, it's usually best to choose the Black & white check box. This selection optimizes the appearance of color slides when printed on a black and white printer by substituting gray shades for the variation of colors (be careful not to select Pure black & white, as it changes all the gray shades to either black or white). Of course, if you have a color printer, the slides will print nicely without your choosing this option.

continues

To Print an Outline and a Slide   (continued)

If you want to print only one slide (rather than the entire presentation), you must also move the insertion point to the text of the slide you want so that PowerPoint can identify it as the current slide (or select the slide by clicking the slide number) before you open the Print dialog box.

Try printing a slide now.

7 In the open presentation, press Ctrl+Home to move the insertion point to the first slide, the Title slide.

Moving the insertion point to this slide makes it the current slide. Now change options in the Print dialog box so that the slide prints correctly.

8 Choose File, Print.

The Print dialog box is displayed.

9 In the Print range area, click the Current slide option button so that only one slide will print.

Next, you need to confirm that you are printing a slide and that it will print in black and white, not color.

10 Make sure that Slides is displayed in the Print what text box and that the check box for Black & white is selected.

11 Click OK to print the current slide.

This accepts the print settings and prints the slide.

12 Save the presentation file.

Inside Stuff

Before you print a presentation, it's a good idea to make sure that the correct printer is selected. The Name text box in the Printer area of the Print dialog box shows the current printer. If the printer listed is not the one you want, click the drop-down arrow to the right of the Name box and select a printer. This makes it easy to change printers, especially if you are working on a network and have a variety of printers available.

You can also select a specific slide to print by typing the slide number in the Slides text box of the Print range area. This text box also enables you to "pick and choose" slides by entering the slide numbers separated by commas. For example, entering 1–3,5,8 in the Slides text box would print those slides. If you start the print job from the Slide Sorter and select the slides you want printed, click Selection in the Print range area to print only those slides.

Exam Notes

Printing color presentations on paper is nice, but using transparency film with a color printer produces excellent overheads for use with your overhead projector. The whole group sees the projected slide show in color, although it is static. You need an LCD panel with an overhead projector (or other projection device) to use movement and animation as well as color.

To optimize printing of color transparencies, choose File, Page Setup from the menu. Choose Overhead from the Slides sized for drop-down list to set the page size and print margins correctly for overhead transparencies.

If you have a film recorder, you can print 35mm slides. First, choose File, Page Setup from the menu. Choose 35mm Slides from the Slides sized for drop-down list to set the page size and print margins correctly for 35mm slides. Then you print the slides as if you were printing on paper, except that you specify the name of the film recorder in the Name text box of the Print dialog box.

You don't have to purchase a film recorder or a color printer to get 35mm slides or color transparencies. You can send your files to a service bureau that will print the 35mm slides or color transparencies directly from your PowerPoint presentation file. Some service bureaus may ask you to prepare a special print file, which you create by choosing File, Print and then selecting Print to file. After you click OK, you enter a filename for the print file.

If you decide to use a service bureau, follow their instructions for preparing the file for their use.

Lesson 7: Creating a Presentation from an Existing File

When you need to create a new presentation, you don't always have to start from scratch. In the previous lessons, you were working on a presentation to be given for the Chamber of Commerce. However, next week the Home and School Association would like a presentation on computer training for adults. In this new presentation, you could use some of the slides you prepared for the Chamber of Commerce.

In this lesson, you learn how to take an existing presentation and use it as the basis for a new presentation.

To Create a Presentation from an Existing File

1 **With the** Chamber of Commerce **presentation open, choose File, Save As from the menu.**

You start with a presentation file that has many similar slides that you can easily modify to fit your needs. Then you save the file with a different name and/or location in the Save As dialog box (see Figure 2.15).

Figure 2.15
Assign a new location and/or name to the file to use it as the basis of a new presentation.

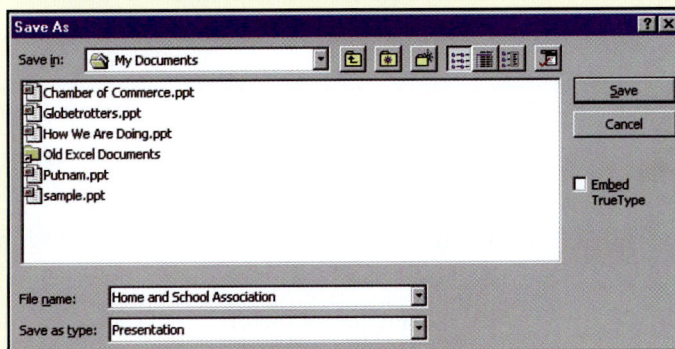

continues

PowerPoint (side tab)

To Create a Presentation from an Existing File   (continued)

2 **Select the location where you want to store the new file from the Save in drop-down list.**

3 **In the File name text box, enter** Home and School Association. **Choose Save.**

By saving the current file with a different name, you create a duplicate file.

4 **Switch to the Slide view and press** Ctrl + Home.

You see the title slide of the presentation.

5 **Click in the title text** Computer Training—What We Can Do For You!

Your insertion point is now in the title.

6 **Delete** What We Can Do For You **and type** Where to Get What You Need.

You may need to select the title text and reduce the size so it all fits in the title area.

7 **Select the title text by dragging across it. Then click the Decrease Font Size button on the Formatting toolbar as many times as necessary to make the text fit the title area.**

Now that you've changed the title page, you are able to add or delete slides and modify text to customize it for the group that will see it.

8 **Save the file and close it.**

If you have finished your work session, exit PowerPoint and shut down Windows before turning off your computer. Otherwise, complete the "Checking Your Skills" and "Applying Your Skills" exercises at the end of this project.

Project Summary

To	Do This
Open an existing presentation	Choose File, Open from the menu bar.
Add a slide to a presentation	Click the New Slide button on the Standard toolbar.
Delete a slide	Select the slide and choose Edit, Delete Slide from the menu.
Demote a point (indent more)	Click the Demote button on the Formatting toolbar or press Tab.
Promote a point (indent less)	Click the Promote button on the Formatting toolbar or press Shift + Tab.

Move text	Select the text and choose Edit, Cut; position the insertion point at the new location and choose Edit, Paste.
Change slide order	In Slide Sorter view, click to select the slide and drag it to the new location.
Print	Choose File, Print.
Use an existing presentation to create a new one	Open the existing presentation and then choose File, Save As. Give the file a new name and choose Save.

Checking Your Skills

True/False

For each of the following, check *T* or *F* to indicate whether the statement is true or false.

__T __F **1.** You can preview presentations before opening them.

__T __F **2.** Demote means to decrease the size of your text.

__T __F **3.** You can print a presentation as an outline or as a series of slides.

__T __F **4.** You can use Slide Show to change slide order.

__T __F **5.** You add a new slide to a presentation by clicking the Promote button.

__T __F **6.** The Details button enables you to see a miniature slide of the selected presentation in the Open dialog box.

__T __F **7.** The extension for PowerPoint files is .ppt, but may or may not display depending on how the computer is set up.

__T __F **8.** You can drag-and-drop slides to reorder them in Slide view.

__T __F **9.** You promote a bulleted point when you click the Move Up button on the Outlining toolbar.

__T __F **10.** You can click the Print button on the Standard toolbar to display the Print dialog box.

Multiple Choice

Circle the letter of the correct answer for each of the following questions.

1. Which of the following is not a method of moving text?

    a. Cut selected text and then paste it in the new location.

    b. Drag selected text to a new location.

    c. Use the Preview button to move text up in Outline view.

    d. Use the Move Down button to move text down in Outline view.

2. To promote a point means to do which of the following?

    a. Make the text larger.

    b. Select a subpoint.

    c. Indent it less.

    d. Indent it more.

3. Printing a presentation as an outline allows you to do which of the following?

    a. Check logical flow and content.

    b. View graphics.

    c. Check the colors and backgrounds of a slide.

    d. None of the above.

4. To delete a slide, you do which of the following?

    a. Click the Move Out button.

    b. Show the presentation in Slide Show view and then press (Del).

    c. Select a slide in Slide Sorter view and then press (Del).

    d. Choose Insert, Delete Slide from the menu bar.

5. To add a slide, you do which of the following?

    a. Click the Slide Sorter View button and then press (←Enter).

    b. Press (PgDn) when in Slide view.

    c. Click the Get the New Slide button on the Slide Sorter toolbar.

    d. Click the New Slide button on the Standard toolbar.

6. Which of the following buttons in the Open dialog box displays information about the file such as revision date, author, and title?

    a. List button

    b. Properties button

    c. Preview button

    d. Details button

7. To save an existing file with a new name or location, you do which of the following?

    a. Click the Save button on the Standard toolbar.

    b. Choose File, Save.

    c. Choose File, Save As.

    d. Choose Tools, Save As.

8. Which of the following occurs when you delete a slide?

    a. PowerPoint automatically renumbers the remaining presentation slides.

    b. PowerPoint prompts you before removing the slide.

    c. You must be in Slide view.

    d. All of the above.

9. You can select more than one slide in Slide Sorter view by pressing which of the following as you click the slides?

    a. (Ctrl)+(✦Shift)

    b. (Ctrl)

    c. (Ctrl)+(F1)

    d. (✦Shift)

10. How can you tell when a slide is selected in Slide Sorter view?

    a. It displays in reverse view.

    b. Its text is highlighted.

    c. A double border surrounds the slide.

    d. None of the above.

PowerPoint

Completion

In the blank provided, write the correct answer for each of the following statements.

1. To move a point up one level in importance is to _____ it.

2. Printing the _____ results in a printout with text only.

3. You can move a slide in Slide Sorter view by _____ it to the new location.

4. The _____ and _____ buttons are used to create various indent levels.

5. When text is cut or copied, it is sent to a temporary area in memory known as the _____.

6. If you accidentally delete a slide, you can click the _____ button to restore it.

7. Before you can preview information about a file in the Open dialog box, you must first _____ it.

8. To insert a new slide, you can click the _____ button on the Standard toolbar.

9. The area on a slide that can accept text, graphics, or objects is called a _____.

10. You can press _____ from the keyboard to indent a line more.

Matching

In the blank next to each of the following terms or phrases, write the letter of the corresponding term or phrase. (Note that terms may be used more than once.)

a. Clipboard

b. Slide view

c. Slide Sorter view

d. Demote

e. Promote

f. File, Save

g. File, Save As

h. cutting

i. pasting

j. drag-and-drop

_____ 1. The command used to save a copy of a presentation with a new name or location

_____ 2. The command used to update the current presentation with the same name and location

_____ 3. Placing the Clipboard's contents on a slide

_____ 4. Removing text from the presentation and placing it in the Clipboard

_____ 5. Selecting a slide and dragging it to a new location

_____ 6. The PowerPoint view used to select multiple slides for deletion

_____ 7. The PowerPoint view used to promote or demote bulleted points

_____ 8. The temporary area in memory used to hold material to be pasted

_____ 9. To indent a line of text less than the preceding one

_____ 10. To indent a line of text more than the preceding one

Applying Your Skills

Practice

The following exercises, found in the Project-02 folder on the CD, enable you to practice the skills you have learned in this project. Take a few minutes to work through these exercises now.

Using the Open Dialog Box

You need to locate a specific presentation. To find information about your files, you use the Open dialog box.

To use the Open dialog box, follow these steps:

1. Choose File, Open to display the Open dialog box.
2. Use the Look in drop-down list to locate the drive where your data files are located.
3. Make sure the first presentation on the list is selected; then click the List and Details buttons. Compare how the file information is displayed for each.
4. Click the Properties button. Write down the displayed information.
5. Click the Preview button to show a miniaturized slide.
6. Double-click the filename to open the file.
7. Close the open presentation without saving it.

Creating a New Presentation from an Existing One and Moving and Deleting Slides

You are in charge of new employee orientation at your company. You have previously created a presentation for this purpose, but some benefits have recently changed. You decide to revise the presentation. To do so, you create a new presentation from the existing one. You then revise the presentation by deleting and rearranging slides.

To create a new presentation from an existing one and to move and delete slides, follow these steps:

1. Open the presentation Proj0202 and choose the File, Save As command to rename it New Employee Orientation.
2. Display the presentation in Slide Sorter view. Delete Slide 3, History of Company, and Slide 4, Who's Who.
3. Move the new Slide 4, Benefits Review, between Slides 2 and 3 so that it becomes Slide 3.
4. Display the presentation in Outline view and make the following changes to Benefits Review (Slide 3):

   The fitness center has closed down, so it is no longer a benefit. Eliminate the point associated with it.

Change the text to show that you now get 3/4 sick day per month instead of 1/2.

Move the point for the 401(k) plan to just below the point for the two-week vacation benefit.

5. Save and close the New Employee Orientation presentation.

Printing Your Presentation in Color

To make sure that your New Employees Orientation presentation is showing information in a logical sequence, you decide to print it in Outline view. You also print the presentation in color.

To print your presentation in color, follow these steps:

1. Open Proj0203 and save it as Printing Practice.

2. Choose File, Print to display the Print dialog box.

3. Print the entire presentation as an outline.

4. Choose File, Print to redisplay the Print dialog box. Print the entire presentation in color.

5. Save and then close the Printing Practice presentation.

Moving Text and Slides and Deleting Slides

You need to present a short pep talk to your sales force about how to work with different types of people. To prepare for your talk, you revise a presentation you already created.

To move text and slides and delete slides, follow these steps:

1. Open Proj0204 and save it as People Skills.

2. Display the presentation in Outline view; then move Slide 3 between Slides 1 and 2.

3. Display the presentation in Slide Sorter view; then delete Slide 2, Summary, from the presentation.

4. Show the new Slide 2, Skills, in Outline view. Promote the last point listed, Communication Skills, so that it is the same level as the other major points.

5. Move the bulleted point for Communication Skills to the first point on Slide 2. Then delete the text associated with this point.

6. Demote the four points listed under Understanding Personality Types (the Lion, the Beaver, the Golden Retriever, and the Otter.)

7. Save and then close the People Skills presentation.

Creating a Presentation from an Existing One and Entering Text in It

As president of the University Biking Club, you must present information to prospective members. You decide to revise an existing presentation in order to do this effectively.

To create a presentation from an existing one and to enter text in it, follow these steps:

1. Open Proj0205 and save it as `Biking Club`.

2. Display the `Biking Club` presentation in Slide Sorter view.

3. Use drag-and-drop to move Slide 3, `Officers`, to between Slide 1 and Slide 2.

4. Display the presentation in Outline view.

5. Click the bulleted subpoint on Slide 3, `Trip to watch Virginia "Race of Champions."`

6. Click the Move Up button twice on the Outlining toolbar to move the subpoint up two lines.

7. Display Slide 3 in Slide view and then click the New Slide button. Choose Bulleted List as the AutoLayout.

8. Enter the following text on the newly inserted slide:

   Title placeholder: `How to Join`

   Text placeholder: `Fill out membership form`

   `Fill out proof of insurance form`

   `Pay dues to David Reams (Treasurer)`

9. Print an outline of your presentation. Then size and print the presentation in color. Finally, size and export the presentation to 35mm slides and to color overheads.

10. Save, and then close the `Biking Club` presentation.

Challenge

The following challenges, found in the Project–02 folder on the CD, enable you to use your problem-solving skills. Take time to work through these exercises now.

Creating a Presentation from an Existing One

As president of the College Horseback Riding Club, you're in charge of an upcoming horse show. To publicize the event, you decide to revise an existing presentation to show during the next club meeting.

To create a presentation from an existing one, follow these steps:

1. Open Proj0206 and save it as `Horseback Riding Club`.

2. On Slide 2, demote the three points under `Classes`.

3. On Slide 2, move the location (Indoor Arena) to the first line on the slide.

4. Add a slide at the end of the presentation with the Bulleted List AutoLayout. Enter the following information in Outline view:

Title placeholder: How to enter:

Text placeholder: Bring proof of club membership

Sign up for classes at entry stand

Pay club treasurer

5. Print the presentation as a series of color slides and as color overheads. Then print the presentation as an outline.

6. Save the Horseback Riding Club presentation; then close it.

Using the Open Dialog Box

You have lost track of where you saved a certain presentation. To find it, you explore the properties associated with each of the files listed in the Open dialog box.

To use the Open dialog box, follow these steps:

1. Display the drive where your student files are located in the Open dialog box.

2. Select at least three PowerPoint files on your list. For each file, click the List, Details, Properties, and Preview buttons.

3. Write down the author, title, and number of slides for each presentation on a piece of paper.

4. Find the last modification date for the files. Write down what you find.

5. Open a presentation of your choice and view it in Outline and Slide Sorter views. When you're finished, close the presentation without saving it.

Working with Presentation Text

As part of one of your business classes, you need to give a speech on a software program. Because you know PowerPoint 97, you decide to revise a presentation that you previously created.

To work with presentation text, follow these steps:

1. Open Proj0207 and save it as My PowerPoint Presentation.

2. Using the following outline as a guide, revise the presentation by adding, demoting, and promoting text. You also delete and reorder slides. Use whichever PowerPoint view (Outline, Slide, or Slide Sorter) is appropriate for the action you are performing.

1 ▭ **PowerPoint 97**
   Linda Bird
   University of Rio Grande

2 ▭ **PowerPoint 97**
   ▪ Microsoft's new presentation graphics program
   ▪ Improved features

3 ▭ **Topics**
   ▪ What's New in PowerPoint 97
   ▪ Disadvantages of PowerPoint 97

4 ▭ **What's New:**
   ▪ Office Assistant
      ◆ User-friendly help
   ▪ World Wide Web Support
   ▪ Expanded Multimedia
   ▪ Improved Speaker Notes

5 ▭ **Disadvantage:**
   ▪ Increased memory requirements

3. Print a copy of your presentation as an outline. Then export the presentation as 35mm slides.

4. Save the presentation and then close it.

Working with Presentation Text

To earn extra money, you work part-time in the office of a local company. Your boss asks you to revise a presentation he needs to give at an upcoming Chamber of Commerce meeting. To do this, you add and demote text, and print an existing presentation.

To work with presentation text, follow these steps:

1. Open Proj0208 and save it as Country Food Producers.

2. Using the following outline as a guide, revise the presentation by adding and demoting text. Work in either Outline or Slide view to perform these actions.

1 ▭ Hickory Grove Foods
   Producers of
   Good Ole'
   Country Foods

2 ▭ Our Objectives
   ▪ Produce High-Quality Foods
      – Cheeses
      – Sausages
   ▪ Unparalleled Customer Satisfaction
   ▪ Service to Community
      – Donate money to country park
      – Donate money to Habitat for Humanity
   ▪ Well-Trained and Compensated Employees

3 ▭ Our Customer's Needs
   ▪ High Quality, Fresh Foods
      – Wide Choice of Products
   ▪ Down-Home Atmosphere
      – Located in rural America on a working farm
      – Country-style ambience
   ▪ Competitive Price

3. Print a copy of your presentation as an outline.

4. Print your presentation as color slides. Export the presentation as 35mm slides and as color overheads.

5. Save the presentation and then close it.

Adding, Deleting, and Rearranging Slides

You work part-time for a manufacturing company. You need to revise a presentation for the company by adding, deleting, and moving slides.

To add, delete, and rearrange slides, follow these steps:

1. Open Proj0209 and save it as Cory Glass Manufacturing.

2. In Outline view, perform the following actions:

   a. Delete Slide 7, Training Session Evaluations.

   b. Move Slide 6, The Bad News, between Slide 3 and Slide 4.

   c. Move the newly renumbered Slide 6, Sick Days—1994 vs. 1995, between Slide 4 and Slide 5.

   d. Delete Slide 2, Overall Status of Safety Campaign.

   e. Add a new slide between Slide 1 and Slide 2 using the Bulleted List AutoLayout.

3. In Slide view, add the following text to the new Slide 2:

   Title placeholder: Our Goals:

   Bulleted list: To decrease sick days by 5% from 1994

   To decrease incidents of lost-time accidents by 10% from 1994

4. Print an outline of the presentation; then print the presentation as color slides.

5. Save, and then close the presentation.

PinPoint Assessment

You have completed the project and the associated lessons, as well as the "Checking Your Skills" and "Applying Your Skills" sections. Now use the PinPoint software Evaluation mode to assess your comprehension of the specific exam tasks you have just learned. You can also use the PinPoint Trainer mode and the SHOW ME tutorials to practice these specific exam tasks.

Project 3

Three

Formatting Text and Bullets

Customizing Text Appearance

In this project you will learn the following objectives and their associated Microsoft Exam required activities.

Objectives	Required Activities
➤ Change Text Appearance … … … … … … … … …	Change Fonts Add Formatting
➤ Use the Format Painter	
➤ Change Alignment … … … … … … … … … … …	Change Text Alignment
➤ Change Tabs and Indents … … … … … … … …	Change Tabs
➤ Adjust Paragraph Spacing	
➤ Add and Remove Bullets … … … … … … … …	Enter Bulleted Information
➤ Modify Bullets	

Why Would I Do This?

n earlier projects, you created and revised presentations. Most of the modifications you made involved changing the overall structure of a presentation, such as changing slide order or moving text. With PowerPoint, you can also customize text appearance—how individual characters look. For example, you can format text to change color, size, and style. Once you've changed text appearance, you can quickly apply your text *formatting* to other sections of text by using the Format Painter. You can also change text alignment and paragraph spacing, and you can add, remove, and modify bullets.

The Formatting toolbar provides quick and easy access to the most commonly used formatting commands (see Figure 3.1). Additionally, for more specific control over formatting, you can use commands from the Format menu.

Formatting
The way your presentation (including text, alignment, bullets, margins, and so on) is set up to display.

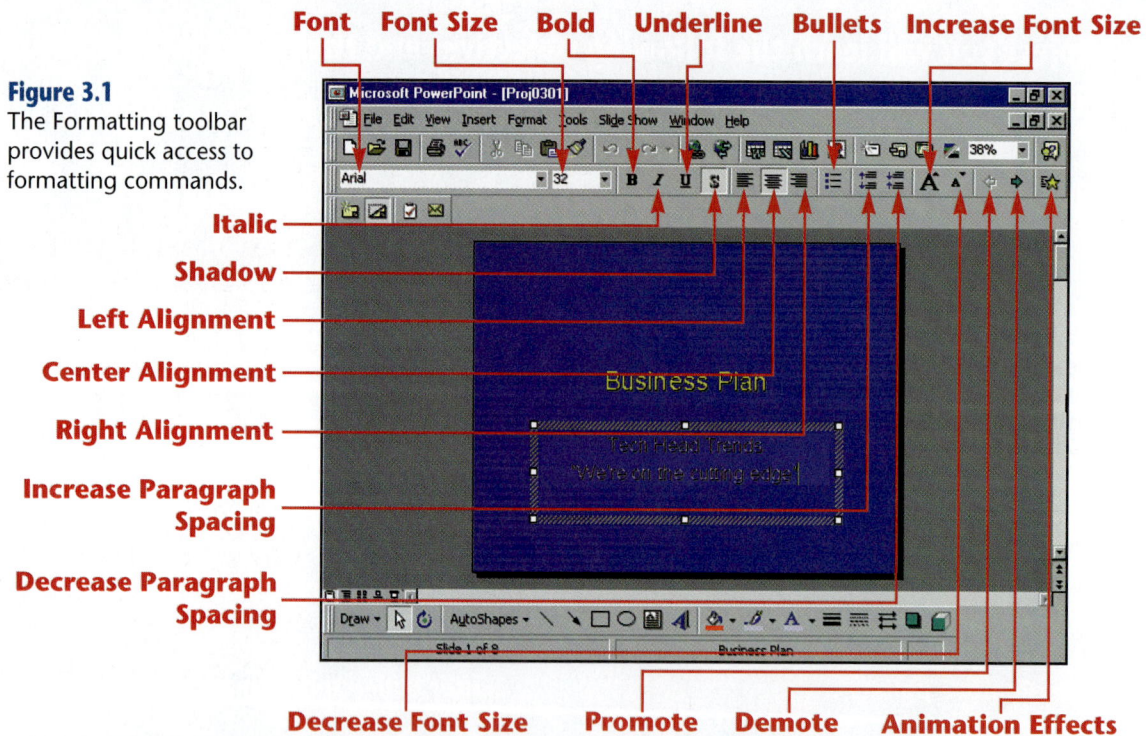

Figure 3.1
The Formatting toolbar provides quick access to formatting commands.

Lesson 1: Changing Text Appearance

The **font**, or typeface, displayed on a slide depends on the template you used to create the slide and the placeholder. For example, the title placeholder for the New Project Proposal presentation you created in Project 1 is automatically displayed in Times New Roman, 44-point text because of the template and placeholder used (see Figure 3.2). However, these settings are only a starting point. You can add *character attributes*, such as bold, italic, or underline, to emphasize information. You can also change the font face or **point size**, and apply color and shadow.

Character attribute
An enhancement you add to a font, such as bold, italic, or underline, to change the appearance of the characters.

> **Jargon Watch**
>
> A number of terms are used in relation to computer text. Most of the terms originated in the printing industry. A **font** (sometimes referred to as a typeface or font

face) is a collection of characters (letters, numbers, and special symbols) that have a specific appearance. A large number of alphabet fonts have been developed for use on the computer. **Point size** is the unit of measurement typically used to designate character height. Because 1 point is equivalent to 1/72", the larger the point size, the larger the text. A typical size for PowerPoint title text is 44 points.

Figure 3.2
The placeholder helps determine the default font and font size.

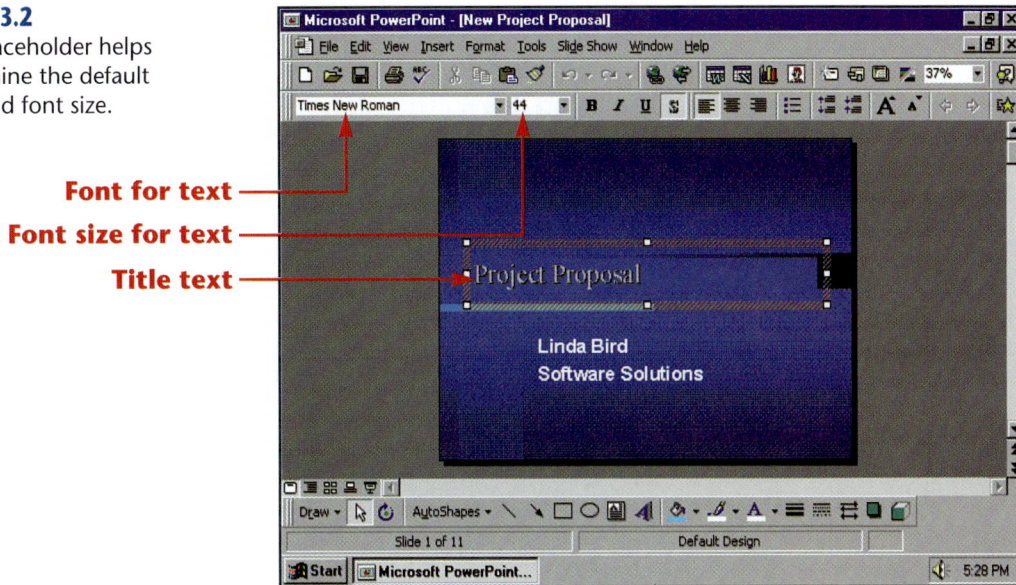

To change the appearance of text, you must first select it. You select text by clicking in the appropriate placeholder and then dragging over the text with the mouse. You can also double-click to select a word, or click a bullet to select all the text associated with it. Once the text is selected, you apply formatting by clicking buttons on the Formatting toolbar, or by using menu commands. Try enhancing a presentation by changing its text now.

To Change Text Appearance

❶ **Start PowerPoint, if necessary. Open Proj0301 from the Project-03 folder on the CD, and save it as** Business Plan.

❷ **Display the first slide of the Business Plan presentation in Slide view, if it isn't already displayed.**

❸ **Double-click the word** cutting **in the subtitle.**

This selects the word so that you can change the formatting.

❹ **Click the Bold, Italic, and Underline buttons on the Formatting toolbar.**

Italic, bold, and underline effects are added to the selected word. You can also add these effects from the Font dialog box (choose Format, Font) or by using keyboard shortcuts. For example, you can press Ctrl+I for italic, Ctrl+B for bold, and Ctrl+U for underline.

continues

To Change Text Appearance   (continued)

5 Select the text in the title placeholder, Business Plan.

Notice that the Font and Font Size boxes on the Formatting toolbar indicate that this text is currently 44-point Arial, as shown in Figure 3.3. Notice also that the word displays a shadow effect, as indicated by the activated Shadow button on the Formatting toolbar. The shadow effect was applied automatically by the template and placeholder chosen when this presentation was created.

Font face of selected text   **Font size of selected text**

Figure 3.3
You can view the current font settings on the Formatting toolbar.

Click here to choose another font face

Click here to choose another font size

Selected text

Activated Shadow button

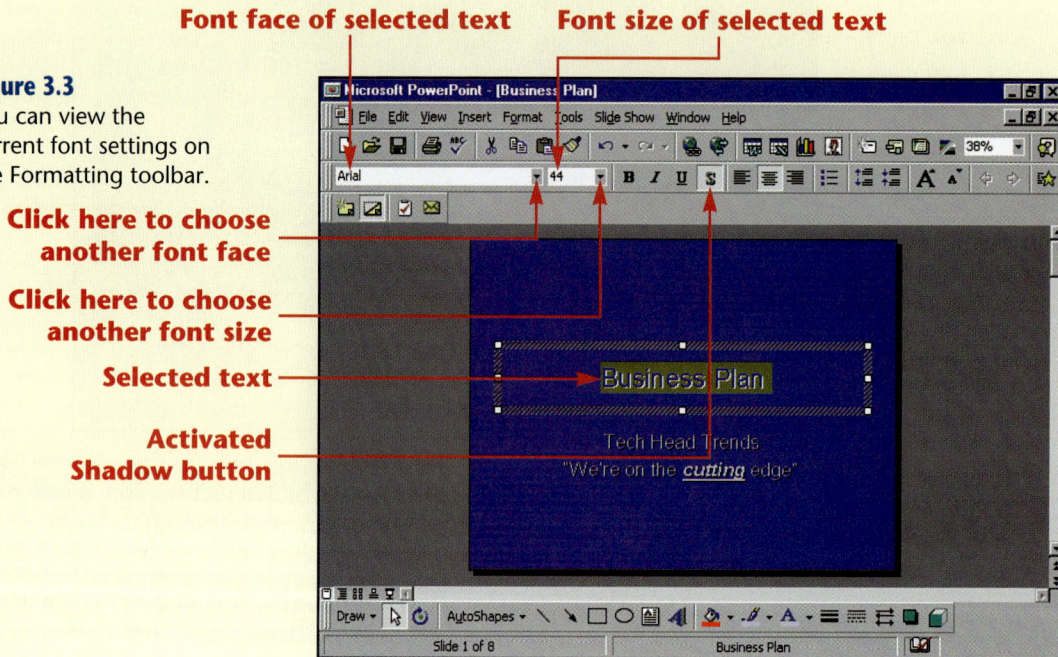

You can also change the current font settings with the Formatting toolbar. The easiest way to do this is to click the drop-down list arrows associated with the Font and Font Size boxes.

6 Click the drop-down arrow to the right of the Font Size box on the Formatting toolbar; then click 66 **to select it as the new point size.**

The selected text changes to the larger point size. Now try changing the font, or typeface.

7 With the text still selected, click the Font box drop-down list arrow and select Brush Script. (If Brush Script is not available, select another script type font.)

The selected text is shown in the Brush Script font.

You can also change the color for selected text. One way to do this is to use the Font dialog box. Additionally, you can use this dialog box to make more specific choices not available on the Formatting toolbar, such as adding subscript and superscript text.

8 Click and drag the mouse pointer to select the entire line Tech Head Trends **in the lower placeholder.**

The selected text is highlighted to show that it is selected.

PowerPoint

9 **Choose For̲mat, F̲ont to display the Font dialog box (see Figure 3.4).**

Figure 3.4
You can change text color in the Font dialog box.

Choose a font here →

Choose special effects here →

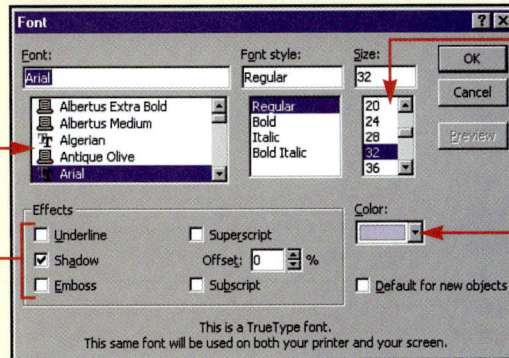

Choose a font size here

Click here to display a palette of compatible colors

10 **Click the C̲olor drop-down list arrow to display a palette of colors.**

PowerPoint displays eight colors on a color palette (see Figure 3.5). These colors are those most compatible with your template's color scheme.

Figure 3.5
You can choose a compatible color from the list.

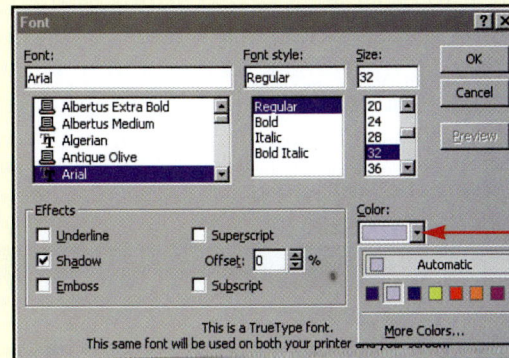

Click the drop-down list arrow to display the color palette

11 **Click Red on the color palette (the fifth from the left) and choose OK to close the Font dialog box.**

The color is applied to the text you selected. However, because the text is still selected, you don't see the change immediately. To see the color change, you must deselect the text.

12 **Click anywhere else on the slide to deselect the text.**

As the text is deselected, you see the color change.

If you have problems... ▶

As you click outside the selected text, you might inadvertently click a Slide Master object and activate the Office Assistant. Don't worry about the Slide Master right now—just click the Thanks for the tip option button in the bubble to close the Assistant. You learn about Slide Masters in Project 5, "Changing the Appearance of a Presentation."

13 **Save the Business Plan presentation.**

Keep the presentation open for the next lesson, in which you use the Format Painter.

Inside Stuff

Most slide text should be at least 18 points to be readable—especially if you plan to create overhead transparencies or show the presentation using an LCD panel and overhead projector.

If you don't see the color you want on the color palette, you can click More Colors to display the Colors dialog box. Click the color you want and then choose OK in the Colors and Font dialog boxes.

If you don't want to use the Font dialog box to change text color, you can instead click the Font Color button on the Drawing toolbar.

If you're in a hurry, you can change font size quickly by selecting text and then clicking the Increase Font Size or Decrease Font Size button. Using these buttons also helps you select a font size without knowing the exact point size you want.

Lesson 2: Using the Format Painter

Text formatting (including font, point size, and color) can be copied to other sections of text. This method of formatting text is efficient, because you can create the font and color combination you want once, and then copy it to other areas of text. Think of the text that has the style you want to apply as a paint can. To "paint" formatting, you use the Format Painter. By clicking the Format Painter button, you dip your "paintbrush" into the can. You "paint" the formatting to other text by dragging over it—just as you paint a wall by dragging a paintbrush over it.

Try using the Format Painter now.

To Use the Format Painter

❶ Select the Business Plan **text on Slide 1.**

It is important that you select the text from which you want to copy formatting *before* you choose the Format Painter. If you don't, PowerPoint won't apply the correct formatting.

❷ Click the Format Painter button on the Standard toolbar.

The mouse pointer changes to the Format Painter I-beam pointer (see Figure 3.6).

Figure 3.6
You can quickly apply formats with the Format Painter.

Format Painter button ───

Format Painter pointer ───

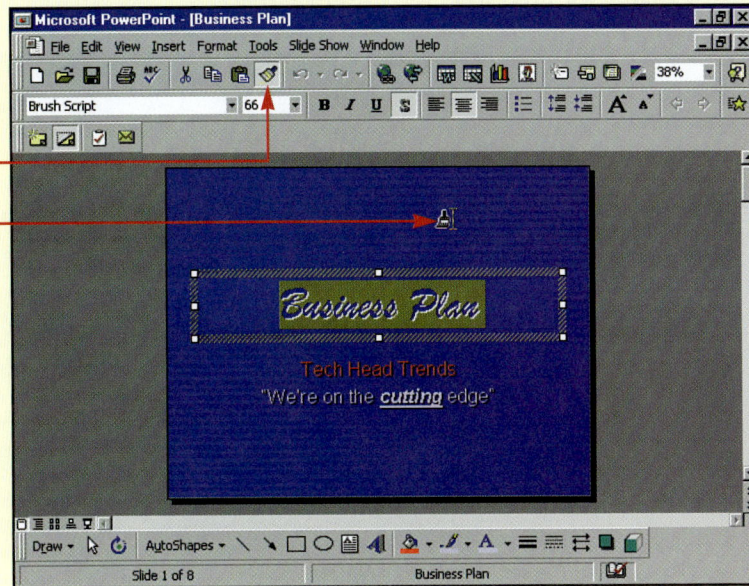

③ Click and drag the pointer over Tech Head Trends.

The formatting styles associated with Business Plan are applied to Tech Head Trends. Also notice that the Format Painter button is turned off as soon as you "paint" the format to the new text. To keep the Format Painter active so that you can format multiple text sections, double-click the Format Painter button.

④ Select the Business Plan **text in the title placeholder and double-click the Format Painter button.**

The Format Painter is activated so that you can copy formatting to several sections.

⑤ Drag over "We're **in the subtitle placeholder.**

The formatting is copied to the selected word, and the Format Painter is still active.

⑥ Drag over edge" **in the subtitle placeholder.**

The formatting is applied to the selected word. To turn off the Format Painter, you click the Format Painter button again.

⑦ Click the Format Painter button.

The Format Painter is turned off.

⑧ To see the formatting better, click outside the lower place-holder.

Your slide should now look similar to Figure 3.7.

continues

To Use the Format Painter   (continued)

Figure 3.7
You can easily change text appearance with PowerPoint.

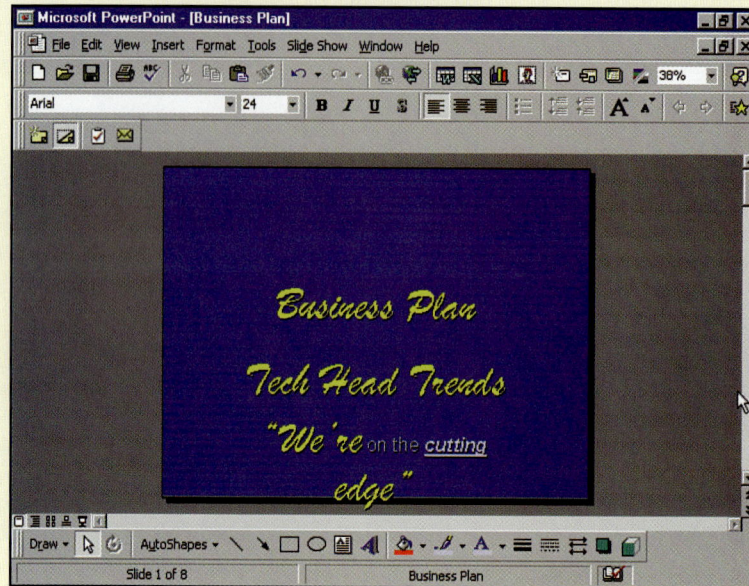

9 **Save your changes to the Business Plan presentation.**

Keep the presentation open for the next lesson, in which you change text alignment.

If you have problems...

Make sure that the text containing the desired format is selected before you click the Format Painter button. Then click the text for which you want to apply the format.

Lesson 3: Changing Alignment

In addition to changing the text appearance on slides, you can change text alignment—how the text displays horizontally in the placeholder. In the presentation you are using, titles and subtitles are centered, whereas lists with *bullets* are left-justified. However, you can easily change text in any placeholder to left, center, or right alignment. The easiest way to do this is to use the alignment buttons on the Formatting toolbar. Alternatively, you can use the F̲ormat, A̲lignment command.

Bullet
An object, such as a circle or square, that is used to set off items in a list.

Now try changing the alignment of text in the Business Plan presentation.

To Change Alignment

1 **Display the first slide of the Business Plan presentation in Slide view, if necessary.**

2 **Click the first line on the slide,** Business Plan.

Notice that the Center Alignment button on the Formatting toolbar is "pushed in," indicating that it is turned on. When you choose another alignment, Center Alignment will be turned off.

3 **Click the Left Alignment button on the Formatting toolbar.**

The first line of the slide becomes left-justified.

4 **Press** PgDn **twice.**

This moves you to Slide 3, Company Introduction and Background. This slide has both title and bulleted list placeholders. To change alignment for more than one line, you must first select them.

5 **Select all bulleted text in the lower placeholder on Slide 3.**

6 **Click the Center Alignment button on the Formatting toolbar.**

All the lines you selected are centered (see Figure 3.8).

Figure 3.8
You can align text within a placeholder.

Select your text

Then click an
Alignment button

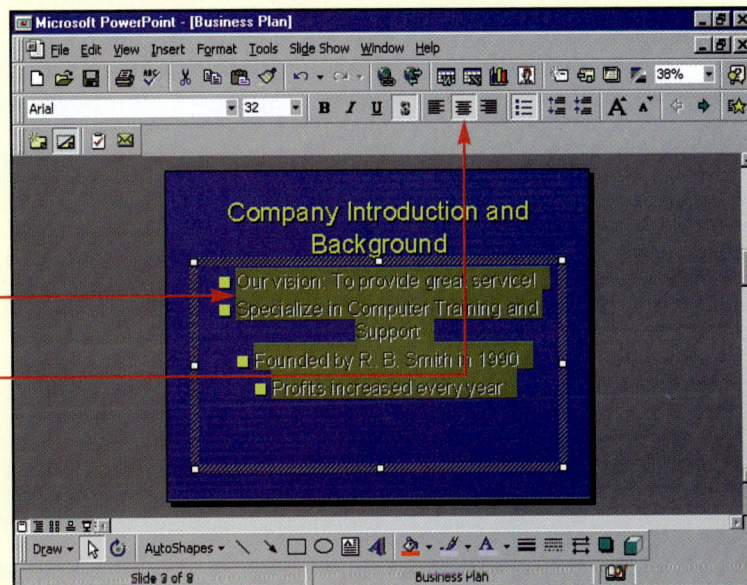

Leave the presentation open for the next lesson, in which you change tab and indent settings.

Inside Stuff

You can also use the Format menu to change alignment. Choose Format, Alignment; then choose Left, Center, Right, or Justify from the submenu.

Exam Notes

Using the Center Alignment button puts the bullets out of alignment. When you are working with bullet text, you should change the text anchor instead of using text alignment. The text anchor sets where the entire set of bullet text fits within the placeholder box. Click the border of the placeholder box to select it (small boxes called handles appear on the corners and in the middle of each side). Choose Format, AutoShape. Click the Text Box tab. From the Text anchor point drop-down list, select the position in the box where you want to anchor the text, such as Top Centered or Middle Centered. Choose OK. If you selected Top Centered, all the bullet text starts at the top of the placeholder box but is centered horizontally within the box. However, all the bullets are still aligned on the left.

Lesson 4: Changing Tabs and Indents

Because text is such an important element in a presentation, PowerPoint has a great number of text handling capabilities. These are very similar to what you use in a word processor such as Microsoft Word, but are geared toward the short paragraphs typical of presentations.

Occasionally, you need to use features you would think only belonged in a word processor. One of those features is the capability to set tabs. Not all text in a presentation is bulleted, but even in bulleted text you may sometimes need a second column. This is especially true in lists, where amounts follow names or items.

In bulleted text, you may also want to adjust the spacing between the bullet and the text. To do this, you need to set the indent amounts for the paragraph.

In this lesson, you create a slide that lists the basic history of the firm followed by the dates in another column. Therefore, you need to set tabs.

To Change Tabs and Indents

❶ **With Slide 3 of the Business Plan presentation displayed, click the New Slide button on the Standard toolbar.**

The New Slide dialog box appears.

❷ **Select the Bulleted List AutoLayout (second AutoLayout in row 1) and choose OK.**

A new bulleted list slide appears.

❸ **Click in the** Click to add title **placeholder. Type** Company History.

❹ **Click in the** Click to add text **placeholder. Type** Founding, **press** Tab, **and type** 1990. **Press** Enter.

❺ **Type** Desktop publishing classes, **press** Tab, **and type** 1991. **Press** Enter.

❻ **Type** Network basics, **press** Tab, **and type** 1993. **Press** Enter.

❼ **Type** Authorized training center, **press** Tab, **and type** 1996.

You have entered the text for the slide, but the years don't line up.

❽ **Choose View, Ruler if the ruler isn't currently displayed.**

To set tabs, you need to be able to see the ruler. You may need to change the Zoom amount to better see the ruler and the text (select a higher percentage from the Zoom drop-down list on the Standard toolbar).

❾ **Select all the bulleted text. Point to the 7 inch mark on the horizontal ruler and click to place a tab marker there.**

A small "L" appears at 7 inches on the ruler (see Figure 3.9). If your marker is not exactly at 7 inches, drag it to the correct position. If you accidentally clicked twice and got an extra tab marker, drag the extra one straight down off the ruler.

Figure 3.9
All the years line up at the tab you set at 7 inches.

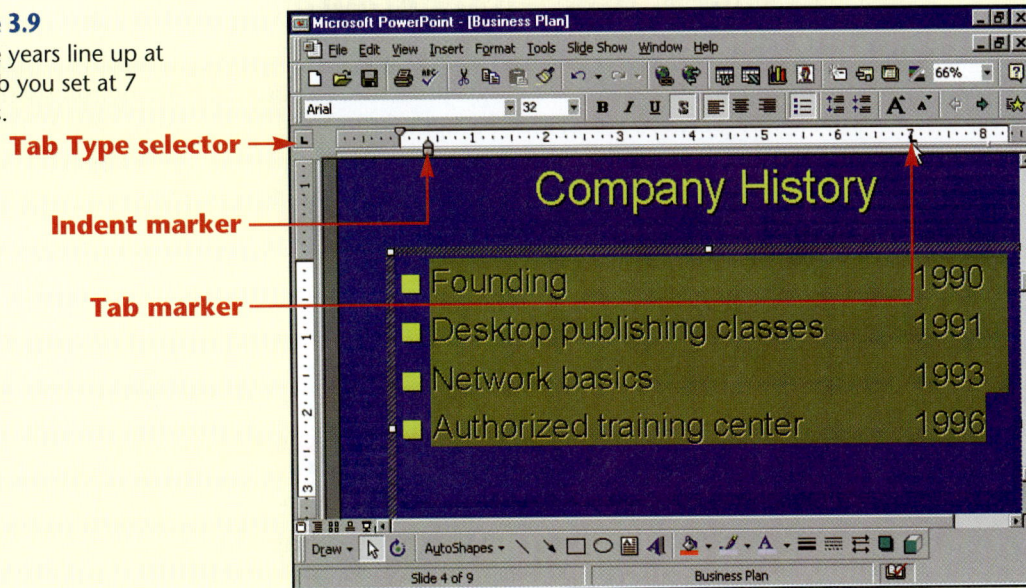

Tab Type selector →

Indent marker →

Tab marker →

Now that you have set the tab, you need to create a little more space between the bullet and the text in each bulleted paragraph.

⑩ With the bulleted paragraphs still selected, drag the indent indicator on the ruler about a quarter of an inch to the right.

Drag the triangle on top, and not the box beneath, which changes the position of both triangles at once. The triangle on the top of the ruler moves the position of the bullet relative to the edge of the placeholder box, so you don't want to move that either.

⑪ Deselect the text by clicking outside the text box.

If you changed the Zoom on the Standard toolbar, you may want to return it to the original percentage. Also, if you no longer need the ruler, choose View, Ruler to remove it from the screen.

⑫ Save the presentation and leave it open for the next lesson.

Exam Notes

Tabs can be set with different alignments—left, right, center, and decimal. Before you set the tab, click the Tab Type button as many times as needed to select the type of tab you want to set. Then click the ruler to insert the tab marker.

The most commonly used tab is the left-aligned tab, which is represented as an "L" on the ruler. With a left-aligned tab, the first character of each word or item lines up at tab. A right-aligned tab (represented by a backward "L") is used to line up words or items by the last character. When you use a center-aligned tab (represented by an upside-down "T"), all the words or items are centered under that tab. You use a decimal tab (represented by an upside-down "T" with a dot next to it) to line up the decimal points in numbers.

Lesson 5: Adjusting Paragraph Spacing

You can also improve the appearance of a slide by expanding or compressing the space between paragraphs (such as bulleted list items) so that they display evenly. Select the paragraphs whose spacing you want to change, and then click the Increase Paragraph Spacing or Decrease Paragraph Spacing button on the Formatting toolbar. For more specific control, you can select paragraphs and then use the Format, Line Spacing command to indicate a number of lines or points to space.

Try to adjust paragraph spacing now.

To Adjust Paragraph Spacing

1 **In the open Business Plan presentation, press** PgUp **to switch to Slide 3, then select all the bulleted points on the slide.**

2 **Click the Increase Paragraph Spacing button on the Formatting toolbar six times.**

The spacing between the bulleted points increases each time you click the mouse (see Figure 3.10).

Figure 3.10
You can easily increase paragraph spacing with the Increase Paragraph Spacing button.

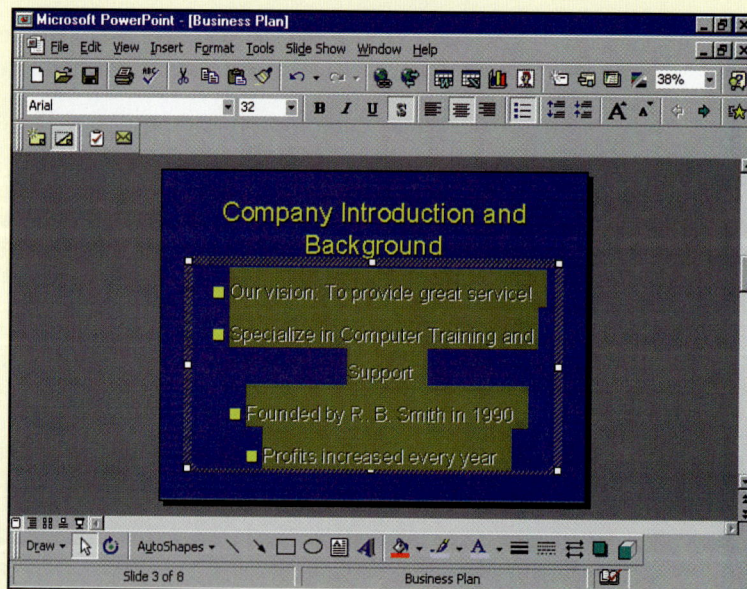

3 **With the text still selected, click the Decrease Paragraph Spacing button twice.**

The spacing between the bulleted points decreases. Now try adjusting paragraph spacing for a specific paragraph.

4 **Move to Slide 5,** Market Conditions, **and position the insertion point on the line** Top competitors.

This is the paragraph for which you want to adjust spacing.

5 **Choose F̲ormat, Line S̲pacing.**

The Line Spacing dialog box is displayed (see Figure 3.11). You use this dialog box to change *line spacing* or the space between paragraphs. You can specify the spacing in lines or points.

Line spacing
The space between each line within the paragraph. This differs from paragraph spacing, which is the space before or after a paragraph.

Figure 3.11
You can use the Line Spacing dialog box to change spacing.

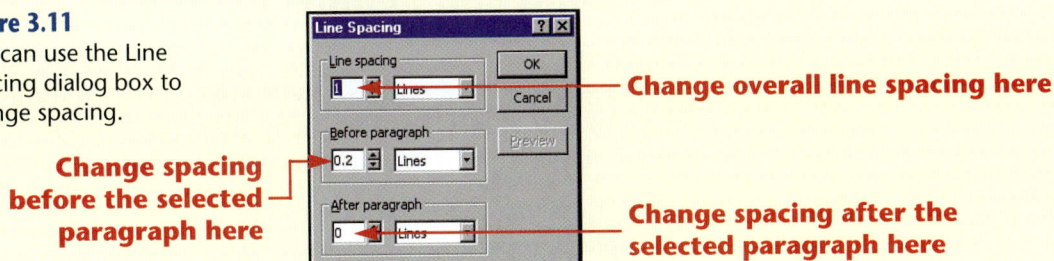

Change spacing before the selected paragraph here

Change overall line spacing here

Change spacing after the selected paragraph here

6 **Click the down-arrow spin button in the <u>B</u>efore paragraph section to change the spacing to** `0.2` **lines or select the current value in the text box and type** `0.2`**.**

This adjusts the space before the paragraph you selected so that it is closer to the preceding one. Now increase the space following it.

7 **In the <u>A</u>fter paragraph section, click the up-arrow spin button to change the spacing to** `0` **lines.**

This expands the space following the paragraph.

8 **Click OK to close the dialog box and view your changes.**

Your completed slide should look similar to Figure 3.12.

Figure 3.12
Your completed slide should display several changes.

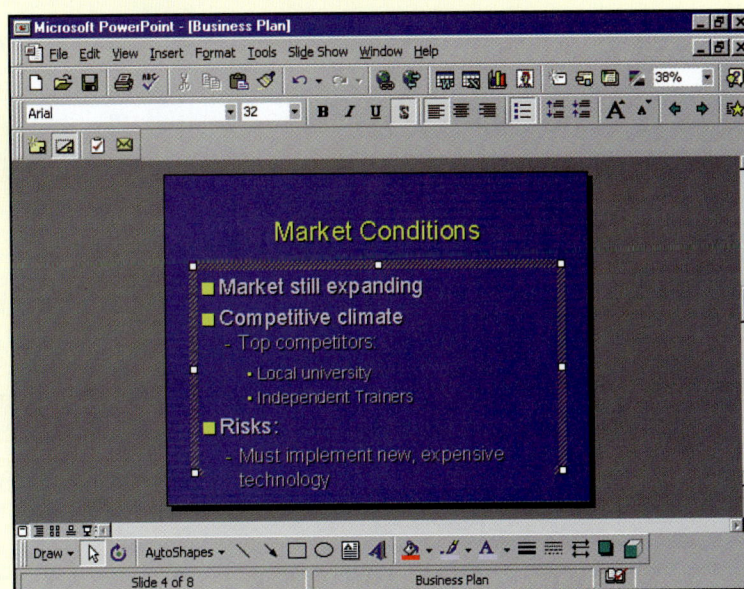

9 **Save your presentation.**

Keep the presentation open for the next lesson, in which you add and remove bullets.

Inside Stuff

You can preview any changes you make in the Line Spacing dialog box. Simply make your changes and then click the <u>P</u>review button. Most likely, you'll also need to move the Line Spacing dialog box (by dragging its title bar) so that you can see the revisions onscreen. If you're satisfied, click OK to accept the changes.

Lesson 6: Adding and Removing Bullets

Bullets are markers that make a list of items more readable. By default, PowerPoint displays bullets as circles, diamonds, squares, and so on. However, you can modify bullets to almost any shape. Bullets are also usually combined with indentation so that the related text wraps properly.

PowerPoint makes it easy to add bullets to a slide, because it includes them as part of the text placeholders in its AutoLayouts. To add bullets, just click in a text placeholder and begin typing. When you're finished typing a line, you can press ↵Enter to create a new bulleted paragraph. You can also start a new line without a bullet by pressing ⇧Shift+↵Enter.

Alternatively, you may want to remove bullets from a line of text. Click in the line from which you want to remove the bullet; then click the Bullets button on the Formatting toolbar. If you want to remove bullets from several paragraphs at once, first select the paragraphs and then click the Bullets button. You use the same button to add bullets to text again—just select the text and click the Bullets button a second time.

Because it's easiest to make changes to bulleted items in Slide view, you use that view for this lesson. Try working with bullets now.

To Add or Remove Bullets

1 **In the open Business Plan presentation, move to Slide 2,** Agenda.

This slide contains a text placeholder. By default, a text placeholder displays bullets. You can easily remove the bullets by selecting the associated text and then clicking the Bullets button.

2 **Position the insertion point at the beginning of the bulleted list, press** ⇧Shift, **and click at the end of the list.**

All the bulleted text is selected. Now you can remove the bullets.

3 **Click the Bullets button.**

Bullets are removed from all the paragraphs you selected. You can also add bullets by clicking the Bullets button again.

4 **With the paragraphs still selected, click the Bullets button again.**

Bullets are added to the selected paragraphs. Keep the presentation open for the next lesson, in which you modify the appearance of bullets.

Lesson 7: Modifying Bullets

The appearance of a bullet is determined by each presentation's template. However, if you don't like the way a bullet looks, you can always change it. First, select the paragraphs with the bullets you want to change; then choose Format, Bullet from the menu bar to display the Bullet dialog box. You use this dialog box to change the color, size, or appearance of your bullets.

Try modifying some bullets now.

To Modify Bullets

1 **In the open presentation, make sure the bulleted list in Slide 2 is still selected.**

2 **Choose Format, Bullet.**

The Bullet dialog box is displayed (see Figure 3.13). You use this dialog box to make revisions to your bullets.

Click here to display different character sets

Figure 3.13
You modify your bullets
in the Bullet dialog box.

**Click here to turn
bullet display on or off**

**Choose a different
bullet character here**

**Click here to change
bullet size**

**Click here to
choose a color
for your bullet**

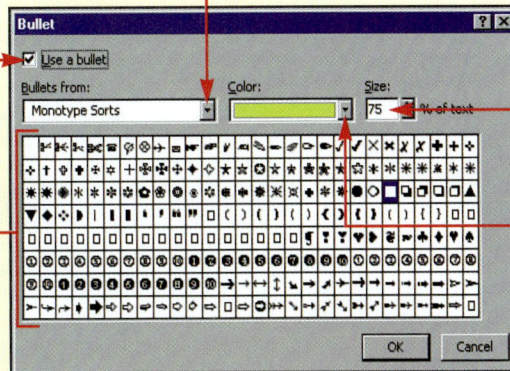

To change color, you can click the Color drop-down list arrow to display a palette of colors that coordinate with your template. If you're good at combining colors (or simply adventuresome), you can click More Colors from the palette and then select a color from the Colors dialog box that appears. Try changing bullet color now.

3 **In the Bullet dialog box, click the Color drop-down list arrow to display the color palette (see Figure 3.14); then choose the orange color—the third box from the right.**

Figure 3.14
You can change the
bullet color to jazz up
your presentation.

**Click here to display
the palette**

**Then choose
this color**

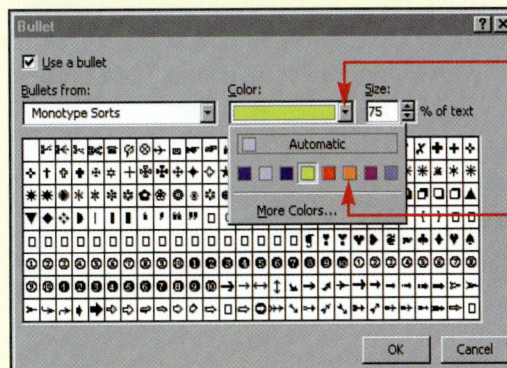

You can also use the Bullet dialog box to change the size of your bullet. You determine how large the bullet should be displayed relative to the text (from 25%–400%) in the Size text box, or you use the spin button to change the percentage in 5 percent increments. Try changing bullet size now.

continues

4 **In the Bullet dialog box, double-click in the Size text box.**

The current percentage (75%) is selected. This means that the bullets are displayed at 75 percent of text height. After the information in a text box is selected, you can simply type to replace it.

5 **Type** 125 **and choose OK to close the dialog box.**

The slide displays your changes (see Figure 3.15). Notice that the text is still selected.

Figure 3.15
You can change bullet size and color.

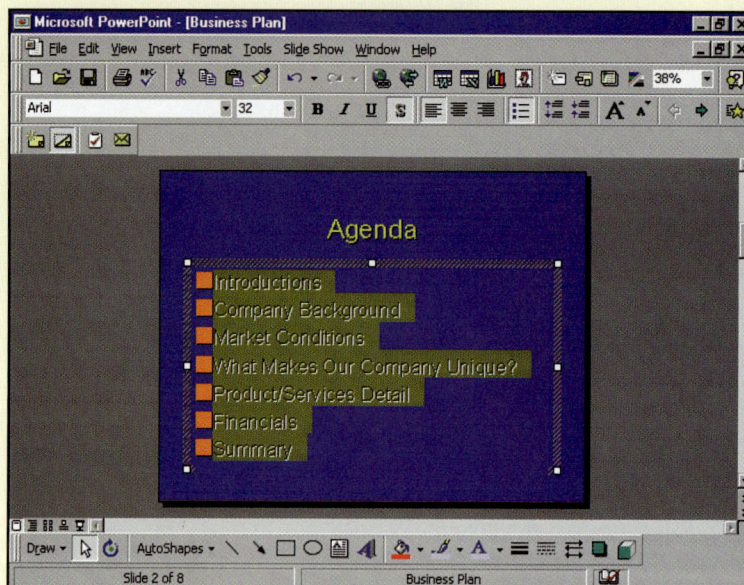

You can also use a wide variety of symbols for bullets. The Bullet dialog box includes a number of font and character sets from which you can choose bullet symbols. Try changing bullet symbols now.

6 **With the bulleted list still selected, right-click in the list to display a shortcut menu (see Figure 3.16).**

PowerPoint

Figure 3.16
You can use the
shortcut menu to open
the Bullet dialog box.

**Right-click in the
selection to display
this shortcut menu**

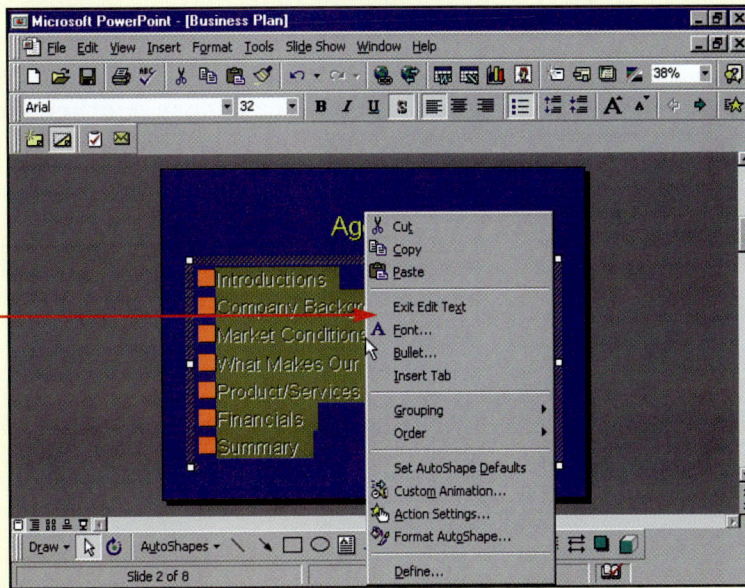

7 **Left-click Bullet from the shortcut menu.**

The Bullet dialog box is displayed.

8 **In the Bullet dialog box, click the Bullets from drop-down list
arrow to display a list of font and character sets (see Figure
3.17).**

Figure 3.17
You can use a variety of
symbols for bullets.

**Click this drop-
down list arrow**

**Then choose a character
or font set from the list**

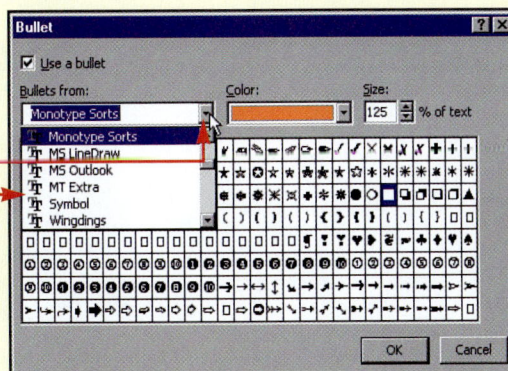

Each set contains a number of symbols. For example, Wingdings
includes computer, arrow, and clock symbols. Likewise, Botanical
has symbols for flowers, leaves, and trees. You can experiment by
choosing different sets to see which symbols they include.

9 **Choose Wingdings from the list. (If this character set is not
available on your computer, choose another set.)**

The symbols associated with this character set are displayed in the
dialog box. You can click any symbol to magnify it for better viewing.

continues

To Modify Bullets   (continued)

⑩ Click the computer symbol (the second one from the right on the first row), or choose another symbol if the Wingdings character set is not available.

The selected symbol enlarges so that you can see it better (see Figure 3.18).

Figure 3.18
You can click any symbol to enlarge its view.

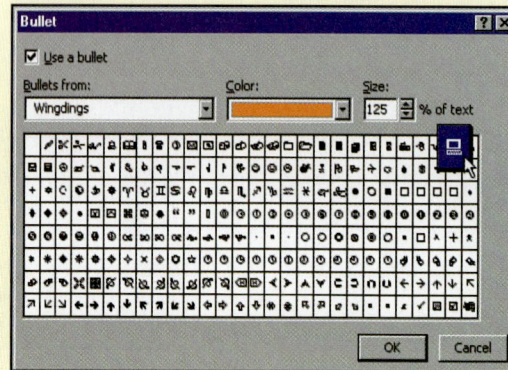

⑪ With the computer symbol still selected, choose OK.

The default bullets are replaced by the symbol you choose. Customizing bullets in this way helps to spice up your presentation for greater impact.

⑫ To see your changes better, click outside the text placeholder.

Your slide should look similar to Figure 3.19.

Figure 3.19
You can enhance your presentation by using bullet symbols.

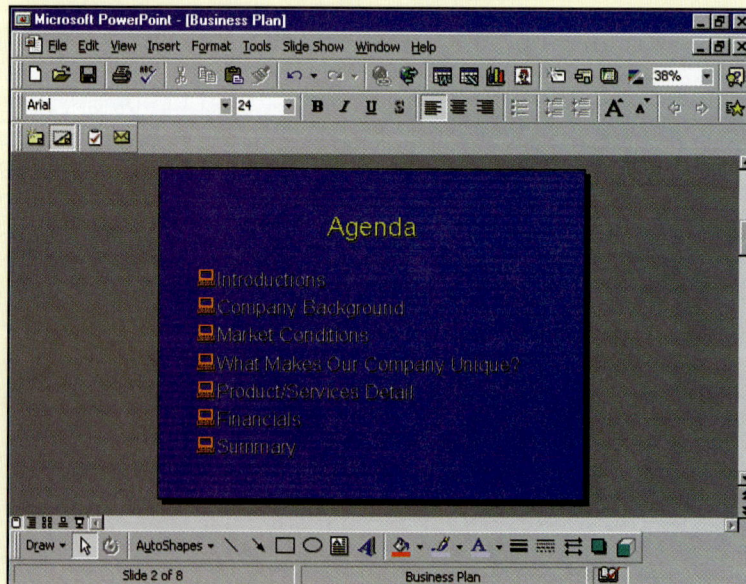

⑬ Save the Business Plan presentation and then close it.

If you have finished your work session, exit PowerPoint and shut down Windows before turning off your computer. Otherwise, complete the "Checking Your Skills" and "Applying Your Skills" exercises at the end of this project.

Project Summary

To	Do This
Change character attributes	Select the text and click the Bold, Italic, or Underline button on the Formatting toolbar.
Change font size	Select the text and choose a size from the Font Size drop-down list.
Change font	Select the text and choose a font from the Font drop-down list.
Change text color	Select the text and choose Format, Font; then choose a color from the Color drop-down palette.
Apply formatting	Select the text from which you want to copy formatting, click the Format Painter, and drag over the text to which you want to apply the formatting.
Change alignment	Select the text and click the alignment buttons on the Formatting toolbar.
Adjust paragraph spacing	Select the paragraphs and click the Increase Paragraph Spacing or Decrease Paragraph Spacing button on the Formatting toolbar.
Add or remove a bullet	Select the text and click the Bullets button on the Formatting toolbar.
Modify a bullet	Select the text and choose Format, Bullet to display the Bullet dialog box.

Checking Your Skills

True/False

For each of the following, check *T* or *F* to indicate whether the statement is true or false.

__T __F **1.** You can toggle bullets on or off by clicking the Bullets button.

__T __F **2.** PowerPoint provides a variety of symbols you can use for bullets.

__T __F **3.** You can double-click the Format Painter button to keep it active.

__T __F **4.** In general, the larger the point size, the smaller the font.

__T __F **5.** You increase point size automatically when you increase paragraph spacing.

__T __F **6.** You can use the Formatting toolbar to view the font size for selected text.

__T __F **7.** You can change selected text to italic by pressing Ctrl+I.

__T __F **8.** You can increase or decrease paragraph spacing between bulleted points.

__T __F **9.** Most of the buttons you use to format text are found on the Font toolbar.

__T __F **10.** You can only use left-aligned tabs in PowerPoint.

Multiple Choice

Circle the letter of the correct answer for each of the following questions.

1. You can change character attributes such as bold, italic, and underline by using which of the following?

   a. the Font dialog box

   b. toolbar buttons

   c. keyboard shortcuts, such as Ctrl+B for bold

   d. all of the above

2. Which of the following describes a point?

   a. a quick method of applying formatting from one text section to another

   b. the unit of measurement typically used to designate character height

   c. a button used to promote and demote text

   d. a button used to change text alignment

3. Which of the following are ways that you can change text appearance?

   a. increasing font size

   b. applying bold

   c. applying italic

   d. all of the above

4. When you use the Format Painter, which of the following is true?

   a. You must first select the text that contains the formatting you want to copy.

   b. You can change text appearance for a text placeholder only (not for title placeholders).

   c. Changes are made to the entire presentation.

   d. All of the above.

5. Which of the following is true regarding bullets?

   a. They are usually combined with indention so that the related text wraps properly.

   b. They can be added or removed.

   c. Their appearance can be changed.

   d. All of the above.

6. You can use the Font dialog box to do which of the following?

   a. change text color

   b. change font size

   c. italicize

   d. all of the above

7. Which of the following is true regarding default bulleted lists?

   a. They are usually left-justified.

   b. They always include a square bullet marker.

   c. They cannot be center-justified.

   d. None of the above.

PowerPoint

8. Before you add text enhancements such as bold or underline to existing text, you must do which of the following?

    a. Select the text.

    b. Double-click the Bold or Underline button to activate it.

    c. Display the Bold or Underline dialog boxes by choosing Format, Bold or Underline.

    d. None of the above.

9. To change a series of bulleted points to center-alignment, you should do which of the following?

    a. Click anywhere in the bulleted list placeholder; then click the Center Alignment button.

    b. Select all the bulleted points; then click the Center Alignment button.

    c. Choose Format, Bullet to display the Bullet dialog box.

    d. None of the above.

10. You can change a bullet's color by doing which of the following?

    a. using the Fill Color drop-down list arrow on the Standard toolbar

    b. using the Color drop-down list arrow in the Bullet dialog box

    c. right-clicking the bullet; then choosing Color

    d. all of the above

Completion

In the blank provided, write the correct answer for each of the following statements.

1. A _____, or typeface, is a collection of characters that have a specific appearance.

2. A _____ is the unit of measurement typically used to designate character height.

3. A _____ is an enhancement you add to a font, such as bold, italic, or underline.

4. A _____ is an object, such as a square or circle, which is used to mark items in a list.

5. You can view and change font settings on the _____ toolbar.

6. You can quickly copy formatting from one text section to another using the _____.

7. You can start a new line of text without a bullet by pressing _____.

8. _____ refers to the way your presentation is set up to display.

9. You can expand the space between bulleted list items by using the _____ button.

10. _____ refers to how text displays horizontally in the placeholder.

Matching

In the blank next to each of the following terms or phrases, write the letter of the corresponding term or phrase. (Note that some letters may be used more than once.)

a. typeface

b. Format Painter

c. 18 points

d. font

e. point

f. left

g. center

h. bullet

i. template

j. formatting

_____ **1.** A circle or square that marks items on a list

_____ **2.** The default alignment for most title placeholders

_____ **3.** The default alignment for most text placeholders

_____ **4.** Another name for font

_____ **5.** 1/72"

_____ **6.** A way to copy formatting

_____ **7.** Largely determines the default font and font size

_____ **8.** The smallest font size you should use on a slide

_____ **9.** The toolbar that includes the Bullets, Shadow, and Underline buttons

_____ **10.** The dialog box used to change text appearance, such as changing font color

Applying Your Skills

Practice

The following exercises, found in the Project–03 folder on the CD, enable you to practice the skills you have learned in this project. Take a few minutes to work through these exercises now.

Adding Formatting to a Presentation

You have previously created a presentation to promote your company, which sells ergonomic products. To enhance the presentation, use some of the formatting features PowerPoint provides.

To add formatting to a presentation, follow these steps:

1. Open Proj0302 and save it as `Ergonomics in the Workplace`.

2. Display Slide 1 in Slide view and format `Ergonomics` with italic, bold, and underline. Increase point size for `Ergonomics` to 60 and change text color to orange.

3. Use the Format Painter to apply the formatting from `Ergonomics` to the word `healthy` on Slide 1.

4. Display Slide 2 and select all the bulleted text. Center the text and increase paragraph spacing so that the text fills up the slide area.

5. Save and close the Ergonomics in the Workplace presentation.

Changing Text Appearance

You decide to jazz up a new employee orientation presentation. To do so, you use the Formatting toolbar, Font dialog box, and Format Painter.

To change text appearance, follow these steps:

1. Open Proj0303 and save it as `Orientation`.

2. In Slide 1, change `New Employee Orientation` to bold, italic, and underline. Then remove the underline.

3. Use the Font dialog box to change the text color of `New Employee Orientation` to a color compatible with the template.

4. Increase the font size of the date text (`October 5, 1997`) to 36 points. Then change the font to one of your choosing, using the Formatting toolbar.

5. Use the Format Painter to apply the formatting from the date line to the presenter's name (`Mr. P. Senter`).

6. In Slide 2, `Agenda/Topics to Be Covered`, select the bulleted list.

7. Remove the bullets and then center the text.

8. Save the Orientation presentation and close it.

Changing Paragraph Alignment and Spacing

You represent a small company that specializes in children's clothing. To present an overview of your company to potential investors, you develop a presentation. You decide to change the paragraph alignment and spacing in an existing paragraph for a better appearance and greater readability.

To change paragraph alignment and spacing, follow these steps:

1. Open Proj0304 and save it as `Creative Kids`.

2. Go to Slide 2, `Our Goals`, and select the bulleted text in the lower placeholder.

3. Center the bulleted points.

4. Reduce the font size of the bulleted text to 32.

5. Use the Increase and Decrease Paragraph Spacing buttons to display the bulleted points effectively.

6. Modify the bullets using the Wingdings font set in the Bullets dialog box.

7. Save the Creative Kids presentation and close it.

Working with Bullets

To spice up a presentation and make your points more effectively, you can add bullets to an existing presentation. You can also modify the bullets by changing their color, size, and appearance.

To work with bullets, follow these steps:

1. Open Proj0305 and save it as `Hickory Hill Nurseries`.

2. On Slide 2, `Our Objectives`, add bullets to the list in the lower placeholder.

3. Evenly space the bulleted points.

4. Use the Bullet dialog box to change the bullet color to red (one of the compatible colors) and the bullet size to 125 percent.

5. Change the bullets to a symbol from the Botanical character set.

6. Change the font size for the list text to 28 points.

7. On Slide 1, `Hickory Hill Nurseries`, select the title placeholder text. Change the font color for the selected text to red.

8. View your changes in Slide view. Then save and close the Hickory Hill Nurseries presentation.

Changing Text Appearance

You work for a company that conducts seminars on how to give presentations. You decide to revise some of your publicity materials by using PowerPoint's formatting features.

To change text appearance, follow these steps:

1. Open Proj0306 and save it as `ABC Training`.

2. Select the title text on Slide 1, `ABC Training Company Presents...`

3. Using the Font and Font Size drop-down list arrows on the Formatting toolbar, change the font to Rockwell, 48 points. (If you don't have this font on your system, choose another one.)

4. Press Ctrl+B and Ctrl+I to add bold and italic to the title text.

5. With the title text still selected, choose Format, Font to display the Font dialog box.

6. Click the Color drop-down list arrow and choose the red color (second from the right); then click OK.

7. Click outside the selected text to view your changes.

8. Save, and then close the ABC Training presentation.

Challenge

The following challenges, found in the Project–03 folder on the CD, enable you to use your problem-solving skills. Take time to work through these exercises now.

Modifying Bullets and Changing Alignment

You work part-time at a sports store. To help recruit quality workers, you have put together a presentation that shows the company's commitment to its employees. To add interest to the presentation, you decide to modify the bullets. You also decide to space and align the bullets so that they are more readable.

To modify bullets and change alignment, follow these steps:

1. Open Proj0307 and save it as Company Culture.

2. Select the first bulleted line of text on Slide 2, Provide a great work environment; then display the Bullet dialog box.

3. Choose Wingdings as the character set; then choose the number 1 symbol (the fourteenth symbol in the fourth row). Increase the bullet size to 100 percent of the text. When you're finished, click OK.

4. Select the second bulleted line of text on Slide 2, Pay Competitive Wages; then display the Bullet dialog box. Repeat Step 3 (above), but choose the number 2 symbol (the fifteenth symbol in the fourth row).

5. Modify the remainder of the bullets on Slide 2 by choosing the appropriate number symbols in the Bullet dialog box. Also resize each bullet so that it displays as 100 percent of text.

6. Select all bulleted points on the list; then center them.

7. Change the paragraph spacing so that the bulleted points display more evenly within the placeholder.

8. Save the Company Culture presentation; then close it.

Formatting a Presentation

For a speech, you develop a short presentation on the advantages and disadvantages of Windows 95. You decide to jazz up the formatting, but it needs to be ready in five minutes. To change text appearance efficiently, you use the Formatting toolbar buttons. Then, to apply the formatting to other areas of text quickly, you use the Format Painter.

To format a presentation, follow these steps:

1. Open Proj0308 and save it as Speech Presentation.

2. On Slide 1, format the title, Windows 95, in blue and bold.

3. On Slide 2, change the title, Advantages, to red.

4. Using the Format Painter, apply the formatting from the word Advantages to Friendly User Interface, Support for 32-bit software, and Multitasking/Multithreading.

5. Apply the same formatting to the word Disadvantages on Slide 3. (Hint: Double-click the Format Painter to keep it active.)

6. Save the presentation; then close it.

Adding Additional Formatting Features

Because you have learned PowerPoint so well, you freelance by revising presentations for various businesses. You're currently working on a production report for one of your clients. You decide to spice it up using PowerPoint's formatting features.

To add additional formatting features, follow these steps:

1. Open Proj0309 and save it as `Production Report`.

2. Improve the appearance of the title on Slide 1 by changing it to another color and font. Also increase the font size for the title.

3. Add italic to the subtitle text on Slide 1.

4. Using the Format Painter, copy the formatting from the Slide 1 title (`Production Report`) to the titles on Slides 2–4. (Hint: Double-click the Format Painter so that it remains active.)

5. Change the bullet color on Slide 2 to match that of the slide title.

6. Modify the bullets on Slide 2 to right-pointing arrows.

7. Increase the spacing between bulleted points on Slide 2 for better readability and appearance.

8. Save the presentation; then close it.

Changing Alignment and Spacing

You are head of the research and development department in your company. Because you are experienced at giving presentations, your boss has asked you to give a short talk to share your "tips and tricks" with other employees. To enhance the presentation, you change text alignment and paragraph spacing.

To change alignment and spacing, follow these steps:

1. Open Proj0310 and save it as `Presenting a Technical Report`.

2. Left-align the bulleted text on each slide.

3. Adjust paragraph spacing for the bulleted text on each slide so that the points display properly in the text placeholders.

4. Remove the bullets on Slide 6, `Close`.

5. Change the bullets on Slides 3–5 to one of the check marks from the Monotype Sorts character set. (If this character set is not available on your computer, choose another character set and symbol.)

6. View the presentation as a slide show.

7. Save, and then close the presentation.

Formatting Text and Bullets

As the outgoing president of the Biking Club, you develop a presentation to help the new club officers learn how to facilitate meetings. To make the presentation more appealing, you change bullet and text appearance using PowerPoint's formatting features.

To format text and bullets, follow these steps:

1. Open Proj0311 and save it as `Facilitating a Meeting`.

2. Increase the font size for the Slide 1 title to 60 points. Then add italic and shadow to the text.

3. Display Slide 3 and change the bullet's symbol for the four subpoints to check marks.

4. Increase paragraph spacing for the bulleted text on Slide 4. Then change the bullets to check marks.

5. Modify Slide 5 and Slide 6 so that the bulleted points display similar to the bullets on Slide 4.

6. View the presentation as a slide show.

7. Save, and then close the presentation.

Entering Bulleted Information and Changing Tabs

You're presenting a safety report at an upcoming meeting. To create an easy-to-read presentation, you enter text in a bulleted list on a slide. You also change tabs and enter text on another slide.

To enter bulleted information and change tabs, follow these steps:

1. Open Proj0312 and save it as Safety Meeting.

2. Display Slide 2, What We've Done, in Slide view. Enter the following items as bulleted points on the slide:

   Conducted safety meetings (by department)

   Held a safety contest (by shift)

   Posted safety signs throughout plant

   Hired a safety consultant

3. Display Slide 3, Results of Safety Emphasis. If the ruler is not displayed, choose View, Ruler.

4. Set the insertion point at the beginning of the first line of text in the lower placeholder (305 days without a lost-time accident!); then press Tab⇥. Repeat the process for the second and third lines in the lower placeholder.

5. Select all the text in the lower placeholder. Set a left-aligned tab stop at 1.5".

6. Save the Safety Meeting presentation; then close it.

PinPoint Assessment

You have completed the project and the associated lessons, as well as the "Checking Your Skills" and "Applying Your Skills" sections. Now use the PinPoint software Evaluation mode to assess your comprehension of the specific exam tasks you have just learned. You can also use the PinPoint Trainer mode and the SHOW ME tutorials to practice these specific exam tasks.

Project 4

Four

Working with Charts

Presenting Information with Charts

In this project you will learn the following objectives and their associated Microsoft Exam required activities.

Objectives   Required Activities

➤ Select an Appropriate Chart Type

➤ Create a Data Chart ... ... Build a Graph

➤ Edit Chart Data

➤ Change Chart Types

➤ Resize and Move Charts

➤ Choose a Chart Sub-Type and Format a Chart

➤ Create an Organization Chart ... ... Add an Organization Chart

➤ Modify an Organization Chart

Why Would I Do This?

Have you ever longed for a way to convey complicated data in a clear, concise manner to business clients, stockholders, or colleagues? One of the best ways to do this is to present your data as a PowerPoint *chart*, or graph. As you create your presentations, keep in mind that people are usually convinced more by a well-presented chart than by words. Business users want to know the bottom line—so use PowerPoint's capability to create pictorial charts to your advantage. For example, Figure 4.1 shows information as text. Figure 4.2 displays the same information graphically as a chart.

Chart
A pictorial representation of data. A chart is sometimes referred to as a graph.

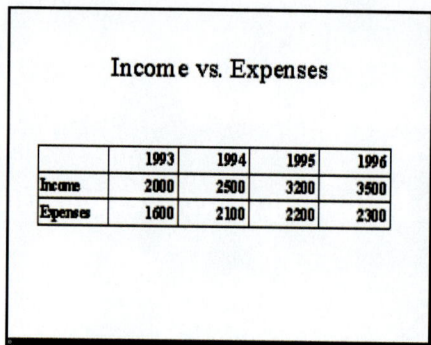

Figure 4.1
Data presented as text can be dull and hard to read.

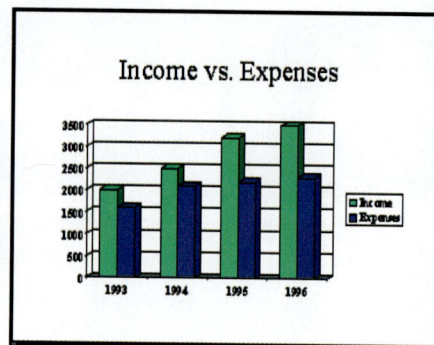

Figure 4.2
A chart makes the same data attention-getting and easier to read.

In this project, you learn the basics of creating and formatting charts so that you can emphasize specific information, such as your company's market share. You learn also how to create and revise organization charts. First, however, it's important to select the appropriate chart type for your presentations.

Lesson 1: Selecting an Appropriate Chart Type

You have a choice of several standard chart types to present your data clearly and effectively. Additionally, each chart type includes several sub-types—variations on the main type. As you develop your presentation, make sure you format your data with the best chart type for what you're trying to convey. Because the most commonly used chart types include line, bar, column, pie, and organization, the lessons in this project emphasize these types. Table 4.1 summarizes the most-used chart types.

Table 4.1	Available PowerPoint Chart Types	
Chart Type	Main Use	Example
Column chart	Shows data changes over time or illustrates a comparison of items. The values are organized vertically, and categories are shown horizontally to emphasize variation overtime.	Sales by quarter for the year.

Bar chart	Shows comparison of individual items. Categories are arranged vertically and values horizontally, placing more emphasis on categories than values.	Sales by region, with region on the vertical axis and sales on the horizontal axis.
Line chart	Shows trends in data at equal intervals.	Monthly production over a twelve-month period.
Pie chart	Illustrates the relationship of parts to the whole. Pie charts can show only one data series.	Market share held by your company versus the competitors.
XY (Scatter) Chart	Shows the relationship between values in several chart series.	The relationship between quantity and price.
Area chart	Shows the magnitude of change over time.	Cumulative sales from several divisions.
Doughnut chart	Similar to a pie chart because it shows the relationship of parts to the whole. However, it can show more than one data series, each "ring" representing a series.	Expenses broken down by category for several departments.
Radar chart	Shows frequencies of changes in data relative to each other and to a center point.	Analysis of how well several products did in comparison with each other.
Surface chart	Shows where the result of combining two sets of data produces the greatest overall value.	A chart showing the greatest combination of cold and wind (windchill).
Bubble chart	Shows data similar to a scatter chart, but also shows (by size of the bubble) the result of the data.	A chart showing the effect of temperature and humidity on soda sales.
Stock chart	Shows high, low, and closing values for stock.	A chart that shows stock performance.
Cylinder, Cone, and Pyramid charts	Shows data similar to that in bar and column charts but displays it as cylinders, cones, or pyramids.	A chart using pyramids to graphically show the height of mountains.

In addition to the chart types listed in Table 4.1, PowerPoint has the capability to produce organizational charts. In Lesson 6, you learn to create an organizational chart using PowerPoint.

Lesson 2: Creating a Data Chart

PowerPoint has the capability to create different types of charts so that you can illustrate your points effectively. PowerPoint uses Microsoft Graph 97, a peripheral program, to create charts. *Peripheral programs* are started every time you access a feature within the main program and place an object within the primary program. You can think of the object as a doorway leading to the peripheral program, which gives you access to its features and capabilities. PowerPoint shares Microsoft Graph 97 with other Microsoft Office programs. This makes chart development more uniform and efficient when working with PowerPoint and the various Office 97 products.

With PowerPoint, you can add charts in a variety of ways. You can use the chart placeholder on an existing or new slide, or you can use the Insert Chart button on the Standard toolbar. Because you actually start Microsoft Graph 97 from within PowerPoint, you can choose the Insert, Chart command to start the program. After you start Microsoft Graph, a *datasheet* is displayed so that you can input information. The datasheet consists of columns and rows. The intersection of a column and row is called a cell. Cells are always named by the column heading, followed by the row number (for example, A1).

When you are finished entering your data, you close the peripheral program, and your chart is embedded as an object within the slide.

In this lesson, you use PowerPoint's peripheral program charting capability to add a chart to your presentation. Try creating a chart now.

Peripheral program

Sometimes called an applet, this is a program with a specific function that is started every time a feature is accessed.

Datasheet

A grid of columns and rows that enables you to enter numerical data into a PowerPoint chart.

To Create a Data Chart

1 Open the file **Proj0401** from the Project-04 folder on the CD, and save it as `Bell Manufacturing`.

2 Display Slide 3, `Revenue`, **in Slide view and click the New Slide button on the Standard toolbar. The New Slide dialog box is displayed. As you recall from earlier lessons, you can choose one of 24 AutoLayouts to produce a slide with preset formatting quickly. Three of the AutoLayouts include a chart placeholder, so you can use these to create a chart. For this lesson, you choose the AutoLayout with the largest chart placeholder.**

3 Click the Chart AutoLayout (the fourth AutoLayout in the second row).

The Chart AutoLayout is selected. This AutoLayout includes placeholders for a title and the chart (see Figure 4.3).

Figure 4.3
You can use a Chart AutoLayout as the basis for your chart.

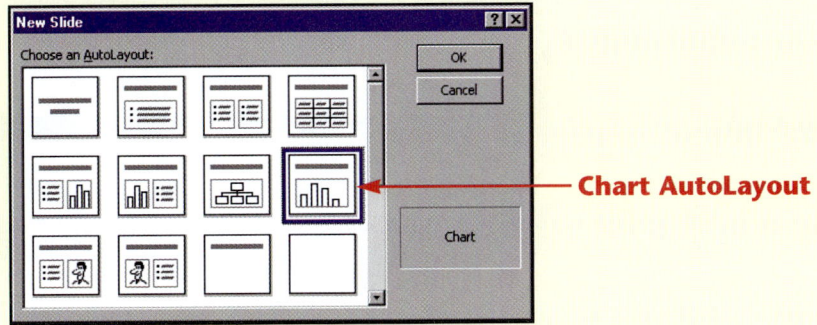

Chart AutoLayout

4 **Choose OK.**

A new slide is inserted with placeholders for a title and a chart (see Figure 4.4).

Figure 4.4
You can use the Chart AutoLayout to help create a chart on your slide.

Title placeholder

Chart placeholder

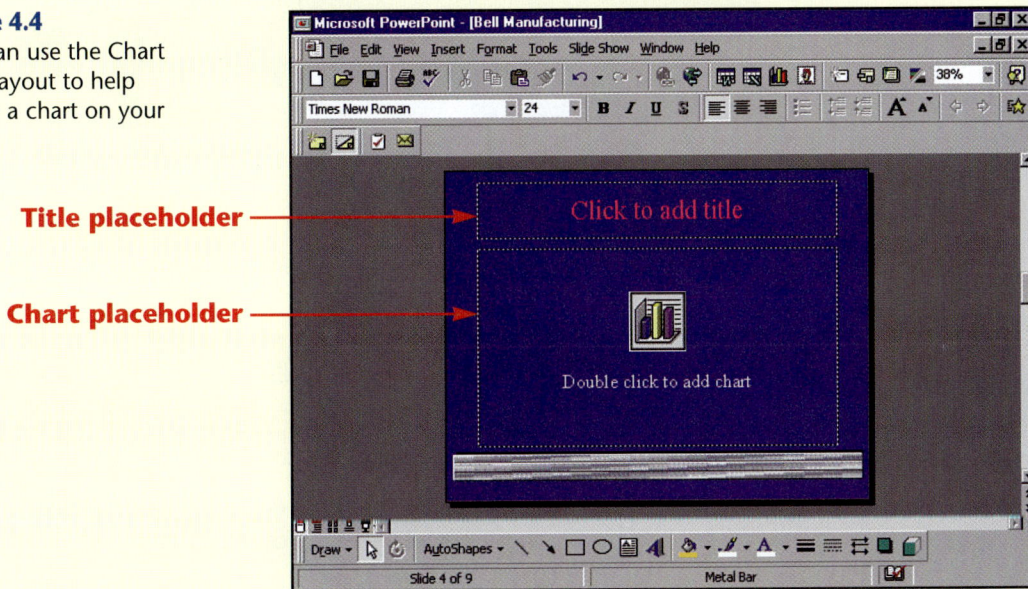

5 **In the title placeholder, type** Revenues—1996 vs. 1997.

This is the title for the chart. Now you're ready to create your chart. You start Microsoft Graph 97 by double-clicking the chart placeholder.

6 **Double-click the chart placeholder.**

If you are successful, Microsoft Graph 97 starts, and a datasheet is displayed with sample data. And, because you are using Microsoft Graph, the Microsoft Graph Standard and Formatting toolbars are activated so that you can use charting commands (see Figure 4.5).

continues

To Create a Data Chart   (continued)

Row Heading   Select All button   Column heading

Figure 4.5
A sample chart and
datasheet are displayed
when you activate
Microsoft Graph.

Microsoft Graph
menu bar

Microsoft Graph
standard toolbar

Microsoft Graph
Formatting toolbar

Active Cell

Datasheet

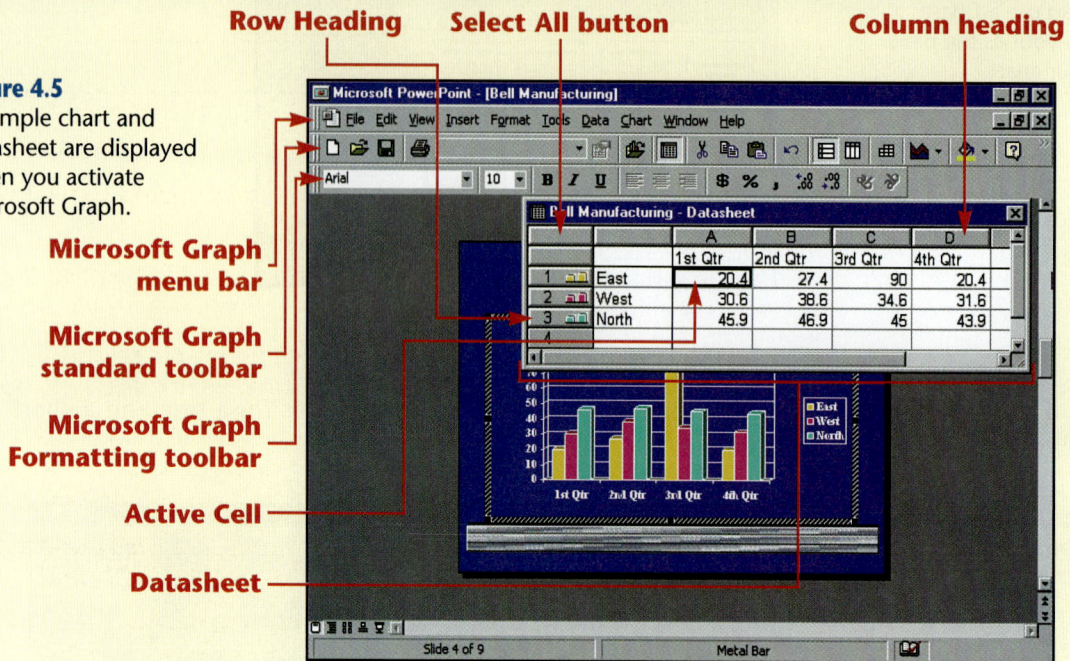

The sample data is simply a guide and is easily replaced with your own data. Each time you open Microsoft Graph, the same sample data appears. To enter your own data, click the cell and type your entry. When finished, you press ↵Enter or an arrow key (or use Tab↹) to move one cell to the right and ⇧Shift+Tab↹ to move one cell to the left).

❼ Click the cell containing the word East.

The darkened border around the cell, called the cell pointer, indicates that this is the active cell—ready for an entry.

❽ Type 1996 **and press** ↓.

This enters 1996 in the cell and moves the cell pointer down one cell.

❾ Click the row 3 heading (North).

The entire row is selected.

❿ Press Del.

The sample data from the entire row 3 is deleted.

⓫ Enter the data shown in Figure 4.6 into your datasheet.

PowerPoint

Figure 4.6
You can easily replace sample data with your own.

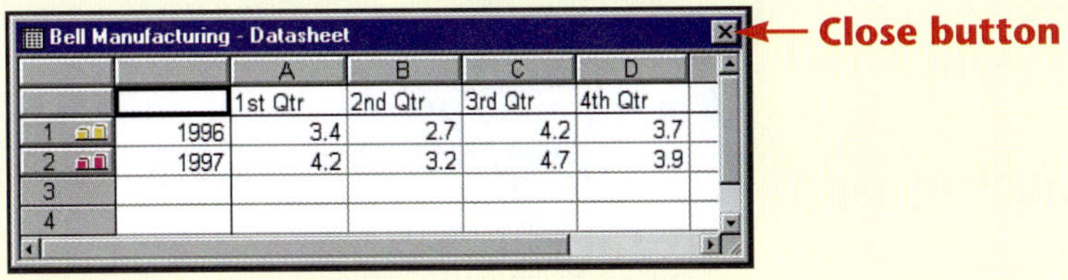

		A	B	C	D
		1st Qtr	2nd Qtr	3rd Qtr	4th Qtr
1	1996	3.4	2.7	4.2	3.7
2	1997	4.2	3.2	4.7	3.9
3					
4					

Bell Manufacturing - Datasheet

← Close button

⑫ **Click the Close button in the datasheet's upper-right corner.**

The datasheet view closes, and a column chart is created (the default chart type). The chart is embedded into the slide as an object. Black selection handles encompass the chart, indicating that it is still activated—Microsoft Graph is still active in memory.

⑬ **Click outside the chart to deselect it.**

The selection handles are removed, indicating that you have closed Microsoft Graph.

Keep the presentation open for the next lesson, in which you learn to edit chart data.

Inside Stuff

You can also click a column heading to select an entire column for deletion. Clicking the Select All button selects the entire datasheet so that you can delete all the sample data at once.

Choosing a Chart AutoLayout as you create a new slide is probably the easiest way to make a chart. However, when you want to place a chart on a slide without a Chart AutoLayout, you can choose Insert, Chart or click the Insert Chart button.

Lesson 3: Editing Chart Data

After you create a chart, you may want to edit its data. For example, you may want to update sales or production figures as they become available. In this lesson, you learn how to activate Microsoft Graph 97 for an existing chart, and you learn ways to edit your data.

Before you make changes to a chart, you must first activate it. Clicking one time on a chart object selects it and places white selection handles around it. You use these handles in the next lesson to move and resize the chart and an entire object. In contrast, double-clicking the chart activates it and opens Microsoft Graph so that you can again use its commands and features. When the chart is activated, you see a rope-like border and black selection handles.

Try activating your chart and editing its data now.

To Edit Chart Data

1 **In the open presentation, double-click the chart object you created on Slide 4.**

The chart is activated, as shown by the rope-like border and black selection handles (see Figure 4.7).

Figure 4.7
An activated chart displays a rope-like border and clock selection handles.

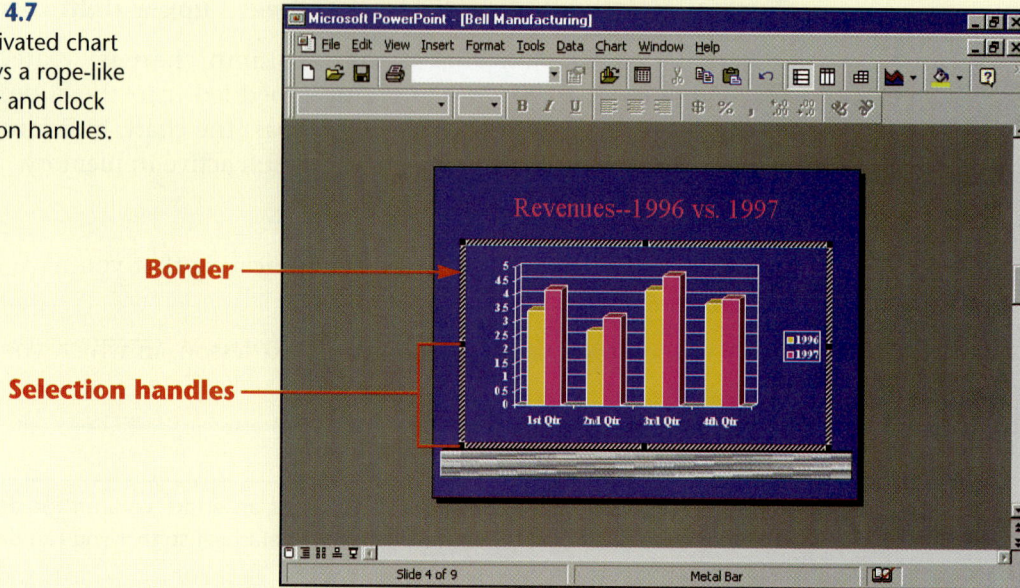

Border

Selection handles

If you have problems...

It's sometimes tricky to activate the chart, rather than simply select it. If your chart doesn't look like the one in Figure 4.7, double-click the chart again. Make sure to click in fairly rapid succession and to hold the mouse steady between clicks. Also, be sure to click an element of the chart and not a background area. Alternatively, you can single-click the chart and then press ↵Enter.

Now try opening the associated datasheet so that you can revise the chart's data.

2 **Click the View Datasheet button on the Standard toolbar.**

The datasheet is displayed, enabling you to revise the data it contains.

3 **Click the Select All button in the upper-left corner of the datasheet.**

The entire datasheet is highlighted to show that it is selected (see Figure 4.8).

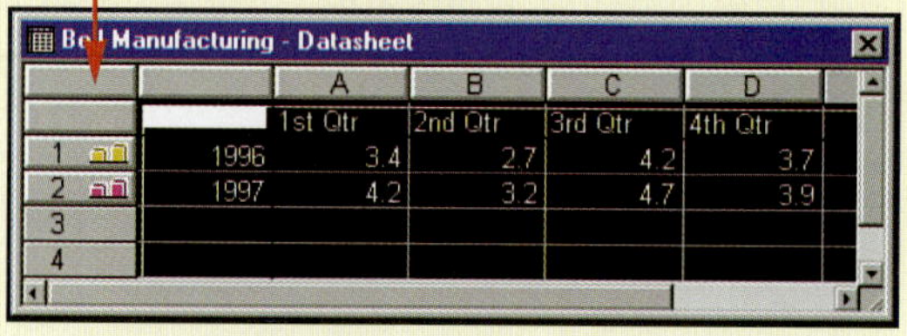

Click here to select the entire datasheet

Figure 4.8
You can select the entire datasheet and then delete its contents.

④ **Press** Del.

The datasheet contents are deleted. Now you can enter new data.

⑤ **Enter the information shown in Figure 4.9 into your datasheet.**

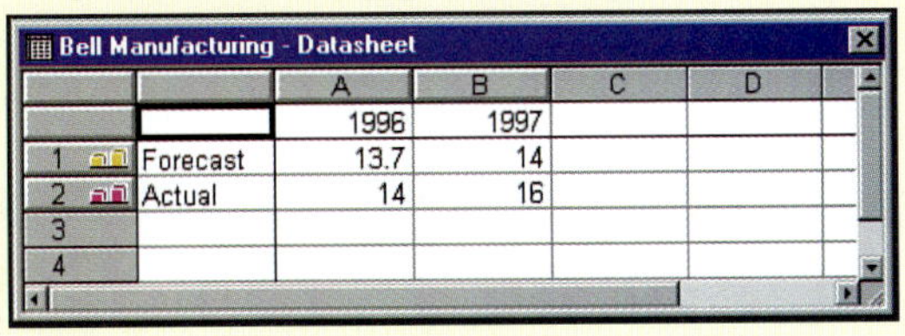

Figure 4.9
You can easily revise your chart by editing data.

Bell Manufacturing - Datasheet		A	B	C	D	
		1996	1997			
1	Forecast	13.7	14			
2	Actual	14	16			
3						
4						

⑥ **When you have finished entering the data, click the Datasheet Close button.**

The Datasheet window closes, but the chart remains active. Keep your presentation open for the next lesson, in which you learn to change chart type, move, and resize your chart.

Lesson 4: Changing Chart Types, Resizing, and Moving Charts

After you create a chart and enter data, you can change the chart type to see the data displayed in various ways. The easiest way to do this is to click the drop-down list arrow next to the Chart Type button. Keep in mind that the underlying data remains the same—the chart types simply display the data differently. Because you don't affect the data when you change chart type, you can experiment freely to see which chart is best for your information.

Because Microsoft Graph places a chart as an object on your slide, you can resize, move, and delete the chart like any other object. Most of the time, you use the mouse along with the white resizing handles to perform these commands.

To Change Chart Types and Resize and Move Charts

① **In the open presentation, make sure the chart in Slide 4 is active.**

Black selection handles indicate that the chart is still active. If your chart isn't displayed in this manner, double-click the chart object to activate it.

continues

To Change Chart Types and Resize and Move Charts   (continued)

2 **On the Microsoft Graph Standard toolbar, click the Chart Type drop-down list arrow.**

The types of charts available on your system are displayed on a palette (see Figure 4.10). Notice that some of the charts are simply variations of other types. For example, the palette shows both 2-D and 3-D bar and column charts.

Figure 4.10
You can easily change chart type.

Click this drop-down list arrow to display chart types

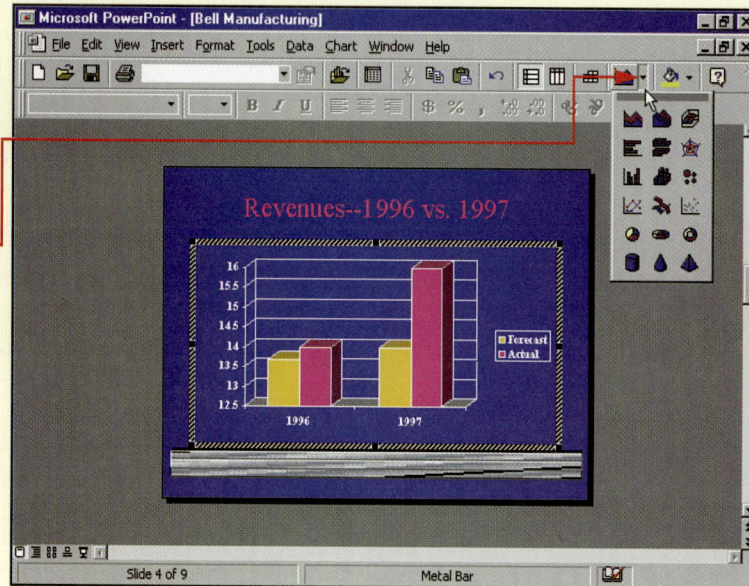

3 **Place the mouse pointer momentarily on any chart type on the palette.**

A ScreenTip is displayed to indicate the type of chart (see Figure 4.11).

Figure 4.11
A ScreenTip is displayed when you rest your mouse pointer on the palette.

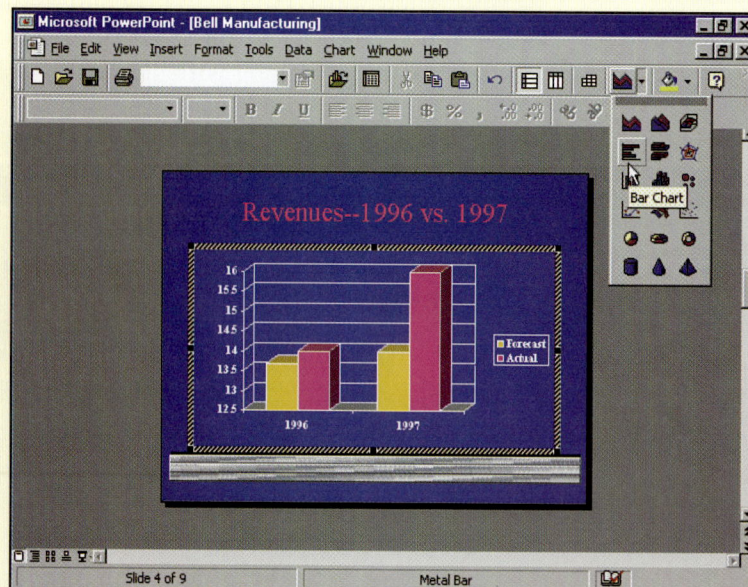

PowerPoint

4 **Move the mouse pointer to the 3-D Bar Chart type on the palette; then click to select it.**

The chart is displayed as a bar chart (see Figure 4.12). For practice, change to other chart types. When you're finished experimenting, choose the 3-D bar chart before continuing with the lesson.

Figure 4.12

You can quickly change to a 3-D bar chart.

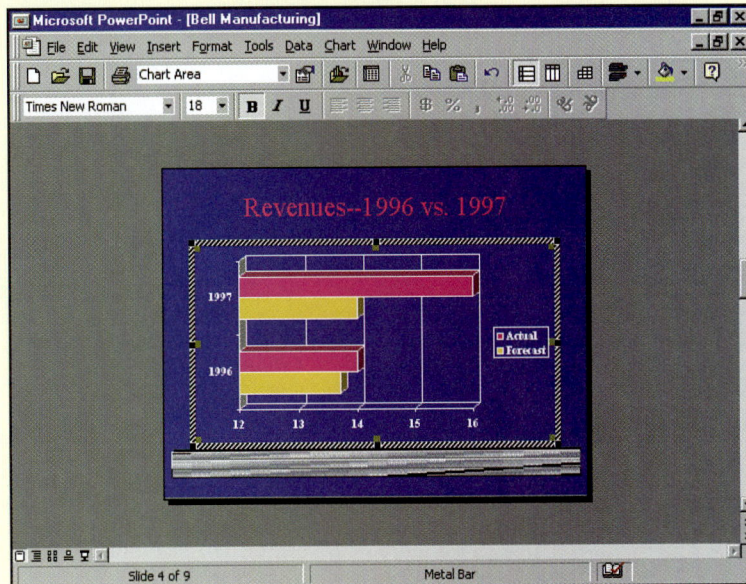

Besides changing chart type, you may also want to resize or move your chart on the slide. PowerPoint makes this task easy.

5 **Click outside the chart to embed it as an object on the slide.**

The selection handles disappear because the chart is not selected or activated.

6 **Select the chart by single-clicking it.**

White selection handles surround the chart object. This indicates that the chart is selected as an object, but that the Microsoft Graph program is not activated.

Now try resizing the chart object.

7 **Move the mouse pointer to the white selection handle on the upper-right corner of the object so that the pointer is displayed as a resizing arrow (see Figure 4.13).**

continues

To Change Chart Types and Resize and Move Charts **(continued)**

Figure 4.13
You can resize a chart object.

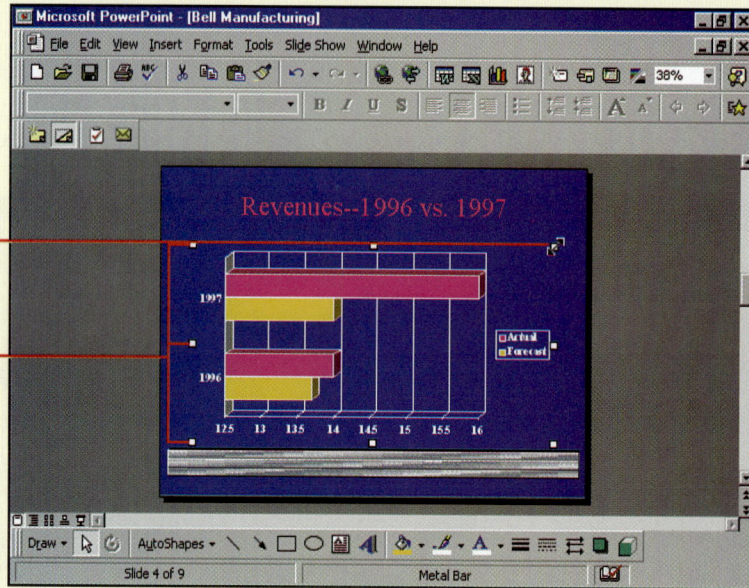

Use this resizing arrow to enlarge or shrink your object

White selection handles indicate the chart is selected

8 **Drag toward the middle of the chart until it is approximately half the original size; then release the mouse button.**

The object is resized on the slide. Now try moving the object to the middle of the available space.

9 **Move the mouse pointer to the middle of the chart object until a four-sided arrow is displayed (see Figure 4.14).**

Figure 4.14
You can move a selected chart object.

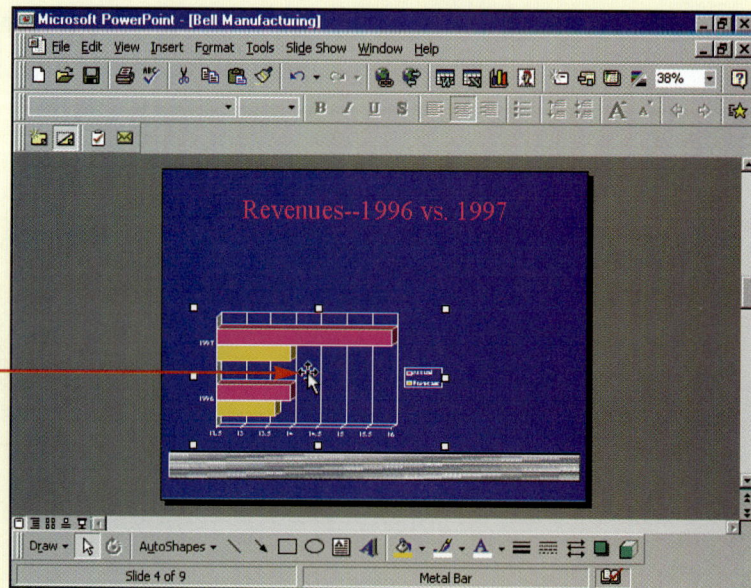

Make sure the mouse pointer is displayed before dragging the object

10 **Drag the chart object so that it is displayed in the middle of the slide.**

11 **Click outside the chart object to deselect it.**

The slide should now look similar to Figure 4.15.

Figure 4.15
You can resize and
move charts for a better
appearance.

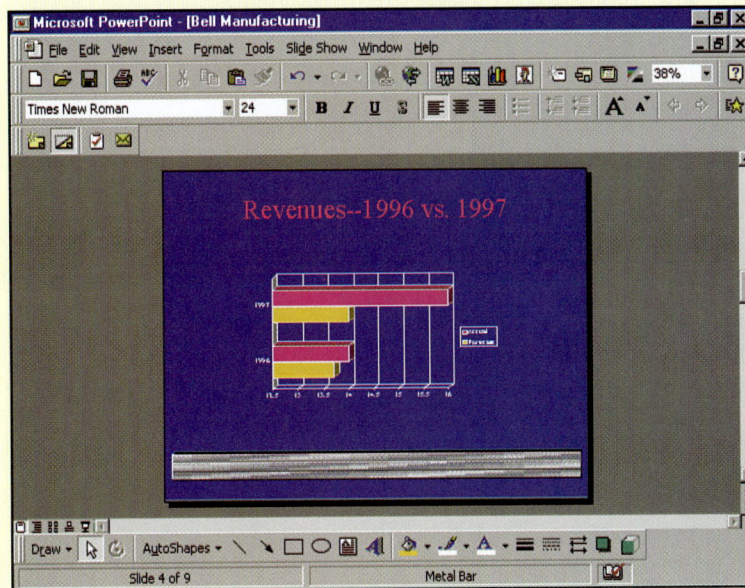

⓬ **Save your changes and close the Bell Manufacturing presentation.**

Keep PowerPoint running for the next lesson, in which you format charts.

Lesson 5: Choosing a Chart Sub-Type and Formatting a Chart

So far in this project, you have learned how to create charts within a PowerPoint slide. To make your charts more readable and understandable, you can format them in various ways.

Choosing a Chart Sub-Type

In this lesson, you learn how to choose a chart sub-type and how to change the text and color associated with a chart. You work with a safety campaign presentation, which includes a column chart. Try some formatting options on this chart now.

To Choose a Chart Sub-Type

❶ **Open Proj0402 from the Project-04 folder on the CD, and save it as** Safety.

❷ **Double-click the chart in Slide 4,** Total sick days per facility, **and close the datasheet.**

Microsoft Graph 97 is activated, as shown by the black handles around the chart. The chart is currently a 3-D column chart; however, you now want to view the information in a stacked column chart.

continues

To Choose a Chart Sub-Type   (continued)

3 **Choose Chart, Chart Type.**

The Chart Type dialog box is displayed, as shown in Figure 4.16. You use this dialog box to select a variation, or sub-type, of the main chart type.

Figure 4.16
You select and preview chart types in this dialog box.

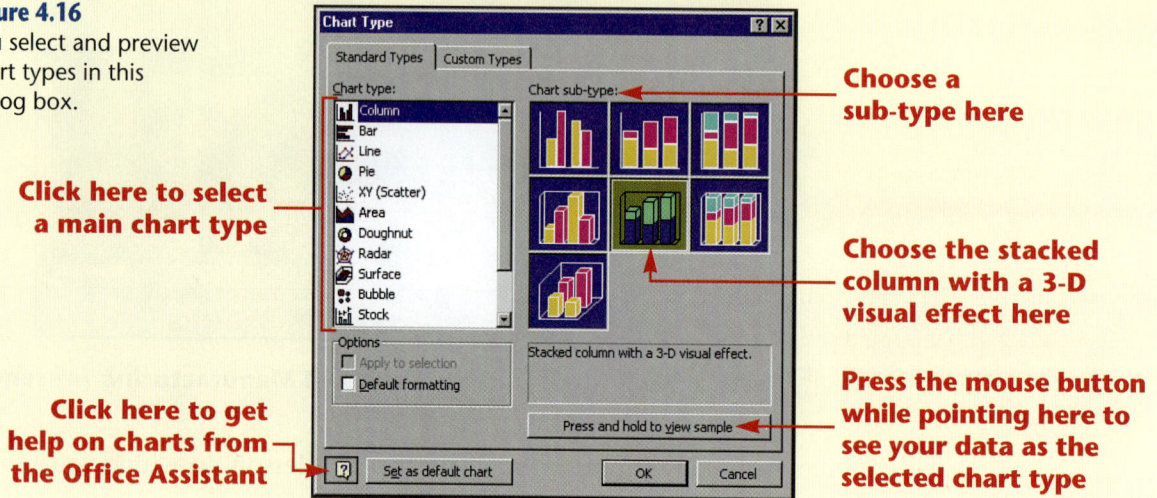

Click here to select a main chart type

Click here to get help on charts from the Office Assistant

Choose a sub-type here

Choose the stacked column with a 3-D visual effect here

Press the mouse button while pointing here to see your data as the selected chart type

4 **Click the stacked column with a 3-D effect visual effect sub-type—the middle chart on the second row.**

You can also preview the chart type with your data by using the special preview button that PowerPoint provides.

5 **Move the mouse pointer to the Press and hold to view sample button. Click and hold down the mouse button for a few seconds before releasing it.**

PowerPoint displays your data with the selected chart's format. If you want, select and preview several other chart types and sub-types. Choose the stacked column with a 3-D visual effect sub-type before proceeding.

6 **Click OK in the Chart Type dialog box.**

The selected chart type is applied to your chart. Keep your chart activated for the next tutorial, in which you explore some other methods of formatting your chart.

Inside Stuff

You can use the Office Assistant to learn more about chart types and sub-types. In the Chart Type dialog box, choose the chart type you want to learn about, and then click the Office Assistant button in the lower-left corner of the dialog box. Click the Example of the selected chart type option button. You can then use the Help dialog box that is displayed to view information about chart types. Click the Close button in the Help dialog box when you're finished. Click the Office Assistant's Close button to close the Office Assistant.

Formatting and Deleting Chart Objects

A chart is made up of several objects, such as the data series, graph walls, legend, and so on. Before you can format an individual chart object, you must first select it. In PowerPoint 97, the easiest way to select a chart object is to use the Chart Objects drop-down list on the Formatting toolbar (see Figure 4.17). After you select the chart object, you can format it. You can also delete a selected chart object.

Figure 4.17
You must select an object before you format it.

Click here to display a list of chart objects you can select

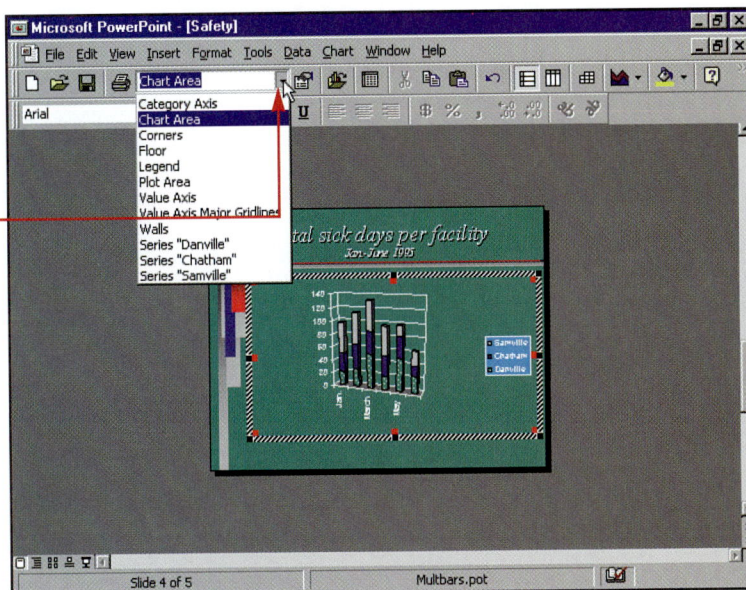

To Format and Delete Chart Objects

Data Series
A group of bars or columns that shares the same color, a line, an area, or a set of data points that represent the data in a row of a datasheet.

1 **In the activated chart, click the drop-down list arrow to the right of the Chart Objects box and choose** Series "Danville."

The *data series* that represents the Danville factory is selected. Selection handles are displayed around the series so that you can identify your selection. Now you can format the chart object.

2 **Choose Format, Selected Data Series from the menu.**

The Format Data Series dialog box is displayed, as shown in Figure 4.18. Notice that PowerPoint includes several formatting categories—such as Patterns and Shape—each on a separate, tabbed page.

continues

To Format and Delete Chart Objects   (continued)

Figure 4.18
You can change many formatting features by using the Format Data Series dialog box.

Choose a formatting category by clicking a tab

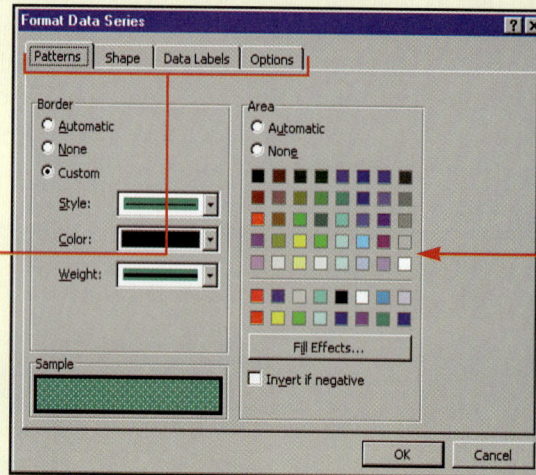

Choose colors and patterns on this page

3 **In the Area section of the Patterns page, click the white color box.**

The Sample box displays the result of your choice. Now try changing the pattern associated with the data series.

4 **Click the Fill Effects button.**

The Fill Effects dialog box is displayed (see Figure 4.19). You can choose a gradient, pattern, or texture for the data series.

Figure 4.19
You can choose a variety of fills for your data.

Click a tab to display another page

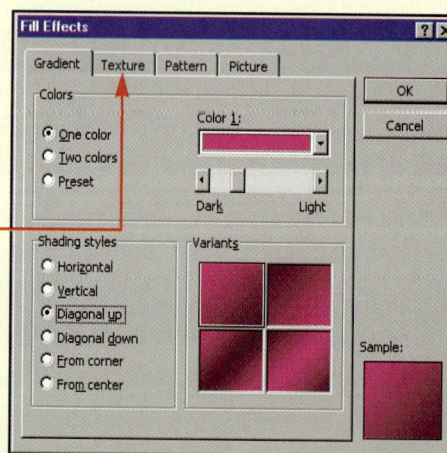

5 **Click the Texture tab to display its page and then click several fill textures.**

Each texture you choose is shown in the Sample box. Now try viewing available patterns.

6 **Click the Pattern tab and choose the second pattern from the left on the fifth row (the black background with white dots).**

Your selected pattern is shown in the Sample box.

7 **Click OK in the Fill Effects dialog box and in the Format Data Series dialog box to accept your changes.**

The color and pattern you chose is applied to the data series. You can format any chart object in a similar way: Use the Chart Objects drop-down list to select an object; then choose the Selected (name of object) command from the Format menu.

You can also double-click a chart object to open an associated Format dialog box. Try using this method to change the *legend's* appearance now.

Legend
A set of color boxes or markers with labels that indicate which series of data the colors or markers represent.

❽ Double-click the legend to display the Format Legend dialog box.

You use this dialog box to modify the colors, font, and placement for the legend.

If you have problems...

Make sure you double-click the legend background, and not one of the legend entries (such as Danville).

❾ In the Area section of the Patterns page, choose red for your legend color and then click OK.

The legend's background is formatted with the new color. You can also delete a chart object by selecting it and pressing Del. Try deleting a data series now.

❿ Click the drop-down list arrow to the right of the Chart Objects box and choose `Series "Samville."`

The series is selected, and you can delete it.

⓫ Press Del.

The selected series is removed from the chart. Notice that the legend entry for Samville is deleted simultaneously (see Figure 4.20).

Figure 4.20
You can select and then delete a chart object.

The Samville data series is deleted

The legend entry is deleted

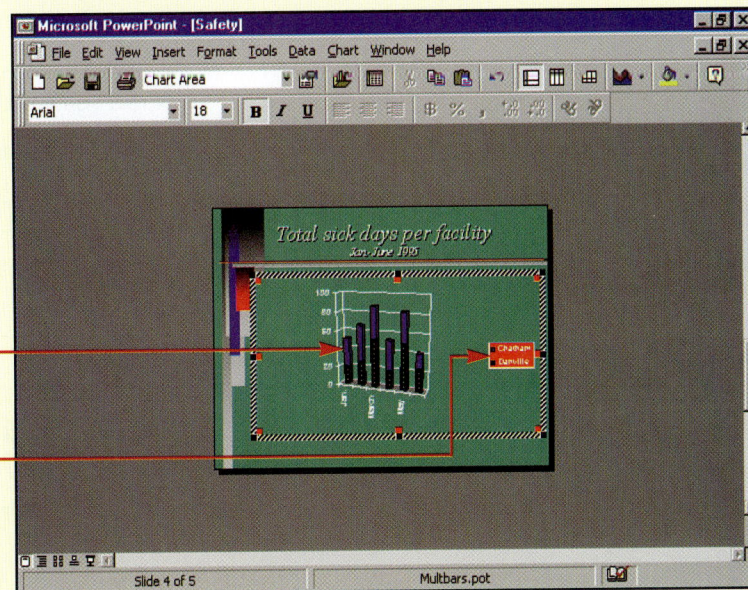

⓬ Click outside the chart to embed it in the slide; then save and close the Safety presentation.

Leave PowerPoint running for the next lesson, in which you create an organization chart.

Inside Stuff

If you incorrectly format or delete a chart object, you can click the Undo button to reverse your change. However, Undo reverses only the most recent change, so you must use it before you execute any other commands.

To select and format an element of a chart, you can also right-click the element and select the Format (name of element) command from the shortcut menu.

Table 4.2 is a handy reference guide showing common ways to use the Microsoft Graph program.

Table 4.2 Summary of Microsoft Graph 97 Charting Features	
To	Use
Start Microsoft Graph 97	Insert, Chart from the menu.
	Click the New Slide button and select an AutoLayout with a chart placeholder.
	Click the Insert Chart button on the Standard toolbar.
Change the chart type	Click the Chart Type drop-down list arrow.
	Choose Chart, Chart Type.
Resize a chart	Place the mouse pointer on a selected chart handle until the pointer changes to a double-sided arrow; then drag to resize.
Move a chart	Move the mouse pointer to the middle of a selected chart and drag to new location.
Delete a chart object	Click to select the chart object and press Del.
Change data in a datasheet	Click the View Datasheet button.
Delete data from a chart	View the datasheet and select the cells, column, or row you want to erase; then press Del.
Change color or pattern	Select the chart object and choose Format, Selected (name of object).
	Double-click the object to display the associated formatting dialog box.
Change chart options	Choose Chart, Chart Options.

Lesson 6: Creating an Organization Chart

Organization charts show the structure and relationship between people or functions in an organization. PowerPoint creates organization charts by using a peripheral program, called Microsoft Organization Chart, in its own window. You can start this program and create the chart in two ways. First, you can choose the Organization Chart AutoLayout in the New Slide dialog box. On the slide, you double-click the chart placeholder to start Microsoft Organization Chart. Second, you can choose Insert, Object to display the Insert Object dialog box, and then choose MS Organization Chart from the Object Type list. The second method automatically starts the chart program for you. In either case, Microsoft Organization Chart displays a menu bar at the top of its window. Additionally, you can use the box tools displayed on the program's icon bar.

In this lesson, you create and enter information in an organization chart. In Lesson 7, you change the organization chart structure and format the chart. Try working with an organization chart now.

If you have problems...

If, when trying to start Microsoft Organization Chart, you get a message that PowerPoint can't start the program, you may have one of the following problems:

- Your computer doesn't have enough memory to run another program. To free up more memory on the computer, make sure that only PowerPoint and the current presentation are running.

- You get a message saying that Microsoft Organization Chart can't be started. The reason may be that it wasn't installed or that it has been deleted or relocated so that PowerPoint can't find it. See your instructor to troubleshoot the problem.

To Create an Organization Chart

1 **Create a new presentation by clicking the New button on the Standard toolbar.**

The New Slide dialog box is displayed, with available AutoLayouts. The Organization Chart AutoLayout is on the second row, second from the right.

2 **Double-click the Organization Chart AutoLayout.**

A new slide is created with a placeholder for the organization chart in the lower portion of the slide (see Figure 4.21).

Figure 4.21
You can use the Organization Chart AutoLayout to create an organization chart quickly.

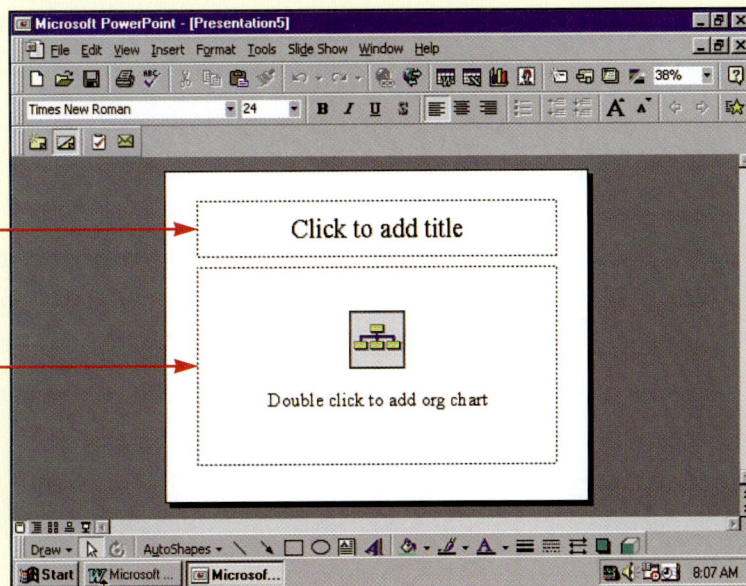

Title placeholder

Organization Chart placeholder

continues

To Create an Organization Chart (continued)

3 **In the title placeholder, type** `Team Structure` **and double-click the Organization Chart placeholder to activate Microsoft Organization Chart.**

The chart program is started, and the Microsoft Organization Chart window is displayed (see Figure 4.22). When you create an organization chart, you're actually using a peripheral program that comes with PowerPoint—Microsoft Organization Chart—as an embedded object on a slide. When Microsoft Organization Chart is activated, it also displays box tools (on an icon bar) and a menu bar so that you can use its commands.

Figure 4.22
Microsoft Organization Chart is displayed in its own window.

Microsoft Organization Chart menu bar

Microsoft Organization Chart box tools on the icon bar

Enter your information here

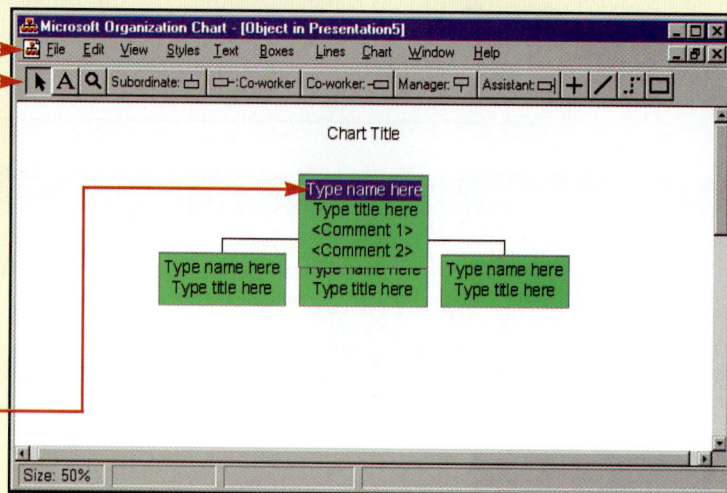

Notice that when you first open a new chart, the chart template is displayed with four boxes. The field names, such as name or title, act as placeholders for information you type. You can enter information the same way as in a word processor—by typing and revising text. Just click the box, type data, and press Tab↹ or ↵Enter to move to subsequent fields. Click outside the box when you're finished. Try entering information now.

4 **Type** `Lonnie Stegall`, **press** ↵Enter, **and then type** `President`.

This enters the name and title into the top-level box.

5 **Click the lower-level boxes and enter the information shown in Figure 4.23; then click outside the boxes.**

Figure 4.23
Enter the information shown to create an organization chart.

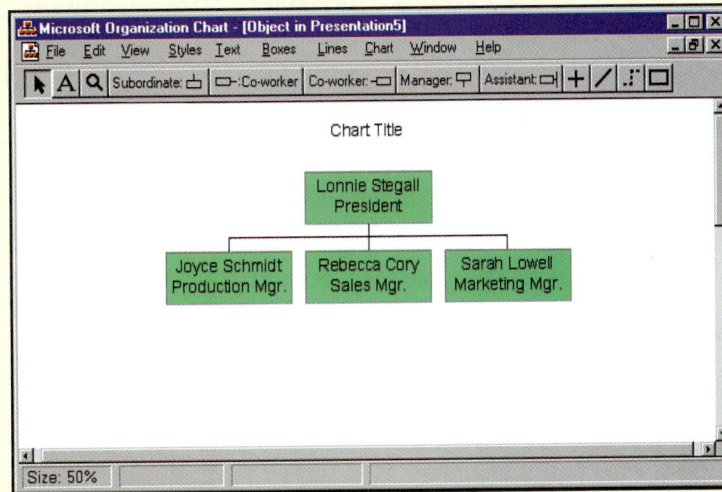

Notice that clicking outside a selected box (either in the background or another box) deselects it.

After you enter text, you can select the text and then format it with commands from the Text menu. Click a box to select all the text it contains, or drag over just the characters you want. Then choose Text, Font or choose Text, Color to change the selected text's appearance. Try formatting text now.

6 In the top box, select Lonnie Stegall and choose Text, Font.

The Font dialog box is displayed. You can use this dialog box to choose font or point size.

7 Choose Impact, 16-point font and then click OK. (If this font isn't available on your system, choose another font.)

The selected text is formatted with the new font and point size. You can also select a box and then change formatting for all the text included in the box. Try this now.

8 Click the lower-left box, Joyce Schmidt, and choose Text, Color.

The Color dialog box is displayed. The color you select will apply to all the text in the selected box.

9 Click the red color, choose OK, and click outside the box to deselect it.

The text in the selected box is formatted in red. Leave your presentation open for the next lesson, in which you change the structure of your organization chart and format boxes.

Inside Stuff

You can select multiple boxes and then apply formatting commands (such as changing text color) to the boxes simultaneously. To select more than one box, press and hold down ⬆Shift) while clicking the boxes you want.

Additionally, you can change alignment for selected text by choosing Left, Right, or Center from the Text menu.

To move from box to box using the keyboard quickly, hold down Ctrl) and press an arrow key.

Lesson 7: Modifying an Organization Chart

When you first create an organization chart, PowerPoint provides a Manager box and three Subordinate boxes. However, this four-box organization chart is just a starting point. Unless your organization fits the default setup, you'll need to add, delete, and generally restructure the chart. Luckily, you can add Subordinates, Coworkers, Managers, and Assistants as needed by using the box tools on the icon bar.

To add new boxes, you click the appropriate box tool and then click the parent—the existing box to which you want to attach the new one. For example, you can add an assistant to a manager by clicking the Assistant box tool and then clicking the Manager box.

You can also revise your chart by moving, formatting, and deleting boxes.

Try modifying your chart using these features now.

To Modify an Organization Chart

| Assistant: ☐|

1 **In the open organization chart window, click the Assistant box tool and then click the Manager box** (Lonnie Stegall, President).

An Assistant-level box is added (see Figure 4.24). You enter information in this box in the same way as for the other boxes.

Figure 4.24
You can easily add boxes to change your chart's structure.

You can add an Assistant box →

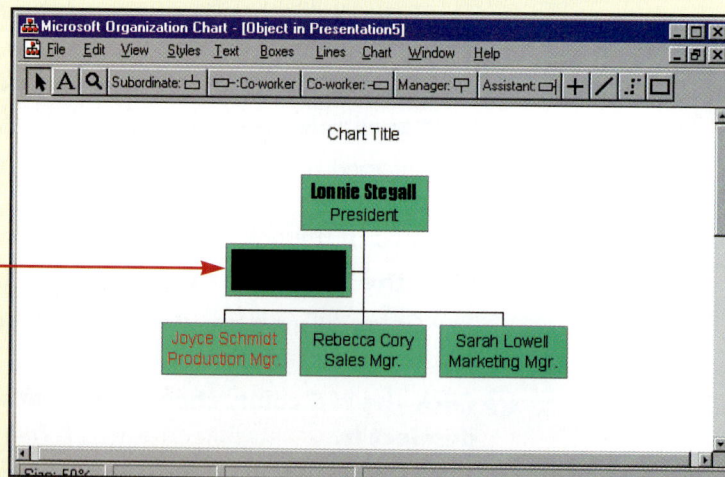

2 **Type** Betty Rivers **in the Assistant box and click outside of it.**

You can also select boxes and then format them by choosing Color or Shadow from the Boxes menu. When you're finished, you can click in the background area to see the effects of your changes.

One quick way to select every box is to choose Edit, Select, All. Alternatively, you can press Ctrl+A.

3 **Choose Edit, Select, All.**

Your entire organization chart is selected (see Figure 4.25).

Figure 4.25
You can quickly select an entire organization chart.

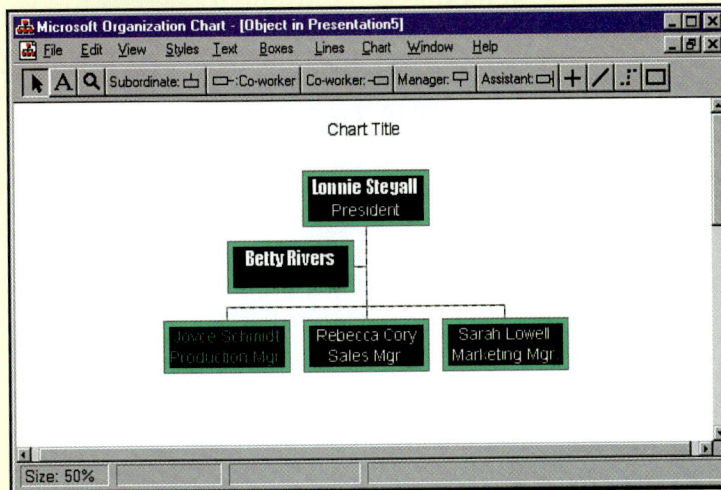

The boxes are highlighted, and the lines show light gray dashes to indicate that they are selected. After the boxes are selected, you can format them to highlight information or for greater overall impact.

4 Choose Boxes, Color.

The Color dialog box is displayed. You can choose a color from this dialog box and then click OK to apply the color to the selected boxes.

5 Click the blue color box (the fourth from the left in the first row) and choose OK.

The boxes are displayed in blue but are still selected. Now try adding a shadow to the boxes.

6 With all the boxes still selected, choose Boxes, Shadow to display a submenu (see Figure 4.26).

Figure 4.26
You can enhance your chart by adding box shadows.

Choose this shadow style

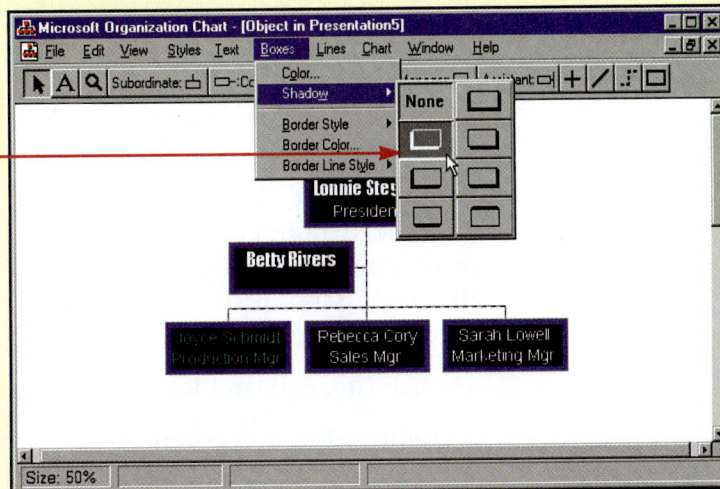

continues

To Modify an Organization Chart   (continued)

7 **Click the shadow style indicated in Figure 4.26 and then click outside the boxes.**

The selected shadow is applied to the boxes.

You can also move a box by dragging it to another location. Select the box you want to move; then drag its border until it is on top of the box to which you want it attached. You can't simply drop it next to the box, because the program doesn't understand where you want to place it. Try moving the Assistant box from its current location and attach it to Joyce Schmidt's box now.

8 **Select the Assistant box (Betty Rivers) and drag it on top of the Joyce Schmidt box until you see the subordinate icon (see Figure 4.27); then release the mouse.**

Figure 4.27
You can drag and drop boxes to other locations.

Drag the Assistant box until you see this icon →

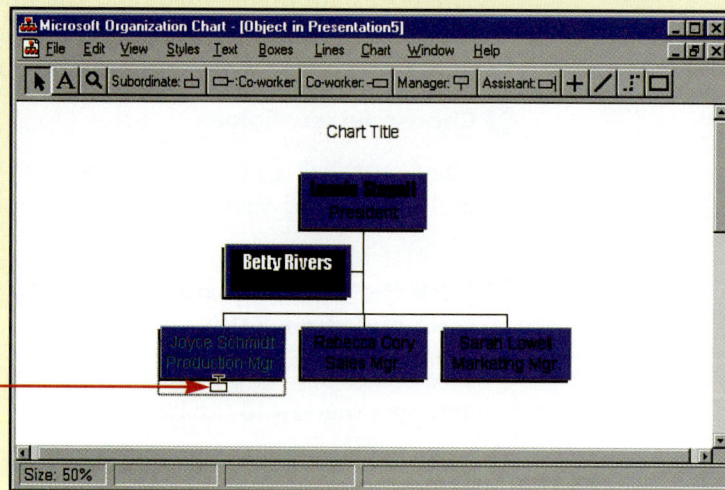

The Assistant box attaches to Joyce Schmidt's box as a subordinate.

You can also modify a chart's structure by deleting unwanted boxes. To remove a box, you select it and press Del.

9 **Select the Betty Rivers box, if it isn't already selected, and press Del.**

The box is removed from your chart. As usual, if you want to reverse the action, you can choose Edit, Undo. For now, you leave the chart in its present state and close Microsoft Organization Chart to return to the presentation.

10 **Choose File, Exit and Return to Presentation.**

A confirmation box prompts you to update the organization chart in the presentation with the changes you made in the Microsoft Organization Chart program.

PowerPoint

⑪ Choose <u>Y</u>es to update the object; then click outside the chart object.

Congratulations! You have just added an organization chart to the presentation. If you later want to revise the chart, simply double-click the organization chart object to re-enter the Microsoft Organization Chart program.

⑫ Save the presentation as `My Organization` and then close it.

If you have finished your work session, exit PowerPoint and shut down Windows before turning off your computer. Otherwise, complete the "Checking Your Skills" and "Applying Your Skills" exercises at the end of this project.

Inside Stuff

If you want to use a box tool a number of times, press `◆Shift` as you click it. You can deselect the box tool when you're finished by clicking the Select tool on the icon bar.

Table 4.3 summarizes the tools available on Microsoft Organization Chart's icon bar. Use this as a quick reference when working with organization charts.

Table 4.3   Microsoft Organization Chart Icon Bar Tools

Icon Bar Tool	Function
▶	Selects objects
A	Adds a text object to the organization chart
🔍	Zooms the chart to larger or reduced views
Subordinate:	Adds a box directly below the selected (parent) box
:Co-worker	Adds a box to the left and at the same level of the selected (parent) box
Co-worker:	Adds a box to the right and at the same level of the selected (parent) box
Manager:	Adds a box directly above the selected (parent) box
Assistant:	Adds a box below and to the left of the selected (parent) box

Project Summary

To	Do This
Create a data chart	Click the New Slide button on the status bar and select an AutoLayout containing a chart placeholder.
Edit a data chart	Double-click a chart object to activate Microsoft Graph.

continues

To	Do This
View a datasheet	Click the View Datasheet button.
Change chart type	Click the drop-down list arrow next to the Chart Type button; then select a chart.
Change a chart object's pattern or color	Select object to change within a chart; then choose Format, Selected (name of object).
Resize a chart	Place the mouse pointer on a white selection handle to display a two-headed arrow; then drag to resize.
Move a chart	Move the mouse pointer to the middle of a selected chart until the pointer is displayed as a four-sided arrow; then drag to a new location.
Delete data from a chart	View the datasheet and select the cells, column, or row you want to erase; then press Del.
Delete a chart	Click the chart object to display the white selection handles; then press Del.
Create an organization chart	Use the Organization Chart AutoLayout when creating a new slide.
Edit an organization chart	Double-click the organization chart object.
Add a job position to an organization chart	Click the job position box tool; then click the box to which it will be attached.
Add box color	Select box(es) and choose Boxes, Color.
Add box shadowing	Select the box and choose Boxes, Shadow.
Delete a box	Select the box and press Del.
Move a box	Drag the box to the box where you want it attached.

Checking Your Skills

True/False

For each of the following, check *T* or *F* to indicate whether the statement is true or false.

__T __F **1.** PowerPoint uses a peripheral program to create charts.

__T __F **2.** Before you can change chart data, you must first activate the chart.

__T __F **3.** You can create an organization chart by using Word, a peripheral program.

__T __F **4.** You enter or edit data in a chart by using a datasheet.

__T __F **5.** After you create a chart, you cannot change the chart colors.

__T __F **6.** Charts are embedded as objects on a slide.

__T __F **7.** You cannot modify individual chart objects.

__T __F **8.** You choose Format, Organization Chart to modify an organization chart.

__T __F **9.** You can start Microsoft Graph by double-clicking a data chart object.

__T __F **10.** A chart subtype is a variation of a main chart type.

Multiple Choice

Circle the letter of the correct answer for each of the following questions.

1. Which of the following is the peripheral program that PowerPoint uses to create or revise data charts?

    a. Microsoft Datasheet

    b. Microsoft Organization Chart

    c. Microsoft Graph

    d. Microsoft PowerGraph

2. To add an Assistant box to a Manager box, you do which of the following?

    a. Click the Manager box tool and drag it to the Assistant box.

    b. Drag the Assistant box from the icon bar to the Manager box in the chart.

    c. Click the Assistant box on the icon bar and then click the Manager box to which you want the Assistant box attached.

    d. Choose Boxes, Attach Assistant from the menu bar, and then click the Manager box to which you want to attach the Assistant box.

3. Which of the following changes can you make to a chart once it is created?

    a. Change the color of the data series.

    b. Change the chart type.

    c. Change the data itself.

    d. All of the above.

4. How do you activate Microsoft Graph to edit an existing data chart?

    a. Double-click the placeholder object that contains the chart.

    b. Click the Graphing Programs button on the Standard toolbar.

    c. Choose File, Graph from the menu bar.

    d. None of the above.

5. To select more than one box in an organization chart, you do which of the following?

    a. Press Ctrl while clicking the boxes you want.

    b. Press ◆Shift while clicking the boxes you want.

    c. Double-click each box you want.

    d. All of the above.

6. Which of the following chart types can you create with PowerPoint?

    a. bar chart

    b. line chart

    c. area chart

    d. all of the above

7. A pie chart is best used for showing which of the following?

    a. the relationship of parts to the whole

    b. data changes over time

    c. trends in data at equal intervals

    d. the magnitude of change over time

8. Which of the following is true regarding an organization chart?

    a. It is used to show changes over time.

    b. It is created by clicking the Create Org Chart button.

    c. It shows comparisons of individual items.

    d. None of the above.

9. Which of the following is one way to create a data or organization chart?

    a. Click the Create Chart button on the Formatting toolbar.

    b. Choose the appropriate AutoLayout in the New Slide dialog box.

    c. Choose Format, Create Chart from the menu bar.

    d. None of the above.

10. Which of the following represents methods of selecting cells on a datasheet?

    a. Click the Select All button to select all cells.

    b. Click the column heading to select a column.

    c. Click a row heading to select a row.

    d. All of the above.

Completion

In the blank provided, write the correct answer for each of the following statements.

1. The grid of columns and rows that PowerPoint provides for entering chart data is called a _____.

2. The intersection of a column and row in a datasheet is called a _____.

3. A group of related information in a chart is called a data _____.

4. A type of chart that shows the relationship of one part to the whole is called a _____ chart.

5. A program with a specific function that is started every time a feature is accessed is called a _____ program.

6. By default, Microsoft Graph initially creates a _____ chart.

7. You can click the _____ button to select all cells in the datasheet.

8. You can insert a data chart using the chart placeholder or the _____ button.

9. You can use a _____ tool to add a job position to an organization chart.

10. The peripheral program PowerPoint uses to create an organization chart is called _____.

Matching

In the blank next to each of the following terms or phrases, write the letter of the corresponding term or phrase. (Note that some terms may be used more than once.)

a. chart object

b. cell

c. peripheral

d. datasheet

e. chart

f. Microsoft Organization Chart

g. chart sub-type

h. organization chart

i. Chart Type

j. Microsoft Graph

_____ 1. A grid of columns and rows

_____ 2. A chart to show how a business is structured

_____ 3. The intersection of a column and row

_____ 4. The program used to create data charts

_____ 5. A variation of a main chart type

_____ 6. A pictorial representation of data

_____ 7. The program used to create organization charts

_____ 8. The type of program that starts when you access a feature within a main program

_____ 9. The item you double-click to edit a chart

_____ 10. The button used to display various types of graphs

Applying Your Skills

Practice

The following exercises, found in the Project–04 folder on the CD, enable you to practice the skills you have learned in this project. Take a few minutes to work through these exercises now.

Creating Data Charts and Organization Charts

You need to create a presentation that includes sales data and the structure of your organization. Because PowerPoint excels at creating great-looking charts, you decide to use it for your presentation.

To create a data chart and organization chart, follow these steps:

1. Create a new, blank presentation and select the Chart AutoLayout.

2. Create a column chart with the title `Five Year Summary`, using the following data:

	1993	1994	1995	1996	1997
Sales	104	135	125	140	150
Expenses	65	89	67	60	88

3. Change the chart type to line and then to a 2-D horizontal bar chart.

4. Change the color for the Expenses data series to red.

5. Add a new organization chart slide and enter the following data:

   Title Placeholder: Lowell Manufacturing

   Joseph Lowell, President

   Ann Luther, Admin. Assistant to the President

   Rebecca Cory, Sales Manager

   Eugene Stegall, Production Manager

6. Delete any extra boxes.

7. Change the box color to white.

8. Save the presentation as Sales Summary and then close it.

Creating a Line Chart

You need to show your boss that the cost of living is constantly rising, while your wages (adjusted for inflation, of course!) are falling. Create a line chart to emphasize your point.

To create a line chart, follow these steps:

1. Create a new presentation and select the Chart AutoLayout.

2. Add the title I need a raise! in the title placeholder.

3. Double-click the chart placeholder to activate Microsoft Graph. Enter the following information in the datasheet:

	Jan	Feb	March
Income	2000	1980	1967
Cost of Living	2000	2100	2150

4. Close the datasheet to show the chart as a column chart.

5. Change the chart type to a line chart.

6. Save the file as Living Expenses and then close it.

Changing Data Series

You have previously created a stacked column chart that shows expenses as a percentage of income. To enhance the chart, you want to change colors and patterns.

To change data series, follow these steps:

1. Open Proj0403 and save it as Income.

2. Activate the Microsoft Chart program by double-clicking the chart placeholder; then close the datasheet.

3. Choose Series "Income" from the Chart Object drop-down list to select the data series representing income.

4. Choose F̲ormat, S̲elected Data Series to display the Format Data Series dialog box.

5. Change the Income data series to red.

6. Change the Expenses data series to a pattern of your choice.

7. Save the file and then close it.

Working with a Pie Chart

You have created a chart that shows your company's percentage of market share. You would like to change the chart to emphasize how well your organization is doing.

To work with a pie chart, follow these steps:

1. Open Proj0404 and save it as `Market Share`.

2. Double-click the chart placeholder area to activate the Microsoft Graph program; then close the datasheet.

3. Use the Chart Type button on Microsoft Graph's Standard toolbar to change the pie chart to 3-D.

4. Change the background color for the legend to red.

5. Select the wedge for Bell Mfg. and then drag to separate it from the rest of the pie.

6. Save the file and then close it.

Building a Chart

Due to rising costs, you need more money for college expenses. To illustrate this, you prepare a PowerPoint graph to take with you on your next visit home.

To build a chart, follow these steps:

1. Create a new, blank presentation and select the Chart AutoLayout.

2. Add the title, `College expenses are increasing!` in the title placeholder.

3. Double-click the chart placeholder to activate Microsoft Graph. Enter the following information in the datasheet:

	1st year	2nd year	3rd year
Tuition	10000	11500	13000
Room/Board	4000	4500	4800
Books	400	450	475
Misc.	300	300	300

4. Close the datasheet to view the chart.

5. Click the Chart Type drop-down arrow to display the various chart types; then choose each to see how your data displays.

6. Choose C̲hart, Chart T̲ype to display the Chart Type dialog box.

7. In the Chart type column, choose Column. Choose the Stacked column with a 3-D visual effect as the Chart sub-type; then click OK.

8. Save the presentation as Rising College Expenses.

9. Print one copy of the presentation; then close it.

Challenge

The following challenges, found in the Project–04 folder on the CD, enable you to use your problem-solving skills. Take time to work through these exercises now.

Editing Data and Formatting a Chart

You are preparing a financial report for your company's annual meeting, using charts to make the data more understandable. You decide to enhance one of the charts using Microsoft Graph's formatting features.

To edit data and format a chart, follow these steps:

1. Open Proj0405 and save it as Financial Report.

2. Activate the chart object on Slide 4, Revenue by Division.

3. Change the division names as follows:

    Division A   Southern

    Division B   Atlantic

    Division C   International

    Division D   Western

4. Select the wedge for International; then drag to separate it from the rest of the pie.

5. Display the Format Data Point dialog box for the International pie slice. Click the Fill Effects button; then choose a Shading style. Close all dialog boxes.

6. Add shading styles to the other three data points (Southern, Atlantic, and Western).

7. Save the presentation; then close it.

Choosing Chart Sub-Types

You want to display the relationship of income to expenses for your company. In order to find the best chart type to display the data, you experiment by viewing various chart types in the Chart Type dialog box.

To choose chart sub-types, follow these steps:

1. Open Proj0406 and save it as Income and Expense Comparison.

2. Activate Microsoft Graph; then choose Chart, Chart Type to display the Chart Type dialog box.

3. Choose each chart sub-type that PowerPoint provides. After you choose a sub-type, click the Press and hold to view sample button to see how each chart sub-type displays your data.

4. When you finish viewing all chart sub-types, choose Pyramid on the Chart type list. Then choose Stacked column with a pyramid shape as the Chart sub-type and click OK.

5. Print your graph.

6. Save, then close your presentation.

Building a Chart

As treasurer of the Biking Club you track how club dues have been spent over the last two years. Because you want to share this information in an understandable way at your next meeting, you create and format a column chart using PowerPoint.

To build a chart, follow these steps:

1. Create a new, blank presentation in PowerPoint.

2. Create a new slide using the `Title Only` AutoLayout.

3. Enter `Dues...where do they go?` in the title placeholder.

4. Start Microsoft Graph by clicking the Insert Chart button.

5. Delete the sample data in the datasheet; then enter the following:

	1995	1996
Club Activities	1200	1350
Newsletter	350	375
Advertisements	89	125
Contributions	500	400

6. Close the datasheet to view your chart.

7. Click outside the chart object to close Microsoft Graph. Then resize and move the chart object so that it displays attractively on the slide.

8. Print one copy of your graph.

9. Save the presentation as `Club Dues`; then close it.

Changing Chart Type

You are the Biking Club treasurer. To prepare for an upcoming meeting, you want to show how club dues have been spent over the past year. Because the best way to compare each spending category to the entire amount spent is to use a pie chart, you change an existing chart to this type. You also format the chart.

To change chart type, follow these steps:

1. Open Proj0407 and save it as Spending Categories.

2. Activate Microsoft Graph and view the datasheet. Delete the information for 1995; then close the datasheet.

3. Use the Chart Type button to change the chart to a 3-D Pie Chart.

4. Click the By Column button to display the data properly.

5. Select and then double-click each of the pie wedges to display the associated Format Data Point dialog box. Change the color for each wedge for greater contrast.

6. Click outside the chart object to close Microsoft Graph.

7. Print one copy of your graph.

8. Save the presentation; then close it.

Creating an Organization Chart

As secretary for the Biking Club you want to show how the club is structured. You decide to use an organization chart to do so.

To create an organization chart, follow these steps:

1. Open a new, blank presentation in PowerPoint.

2. Create a new slide in your presentation using the Organization Chart AutoLayout.

3. Enter Biking Club in the title placeholder.

4. Activate Microsoft Organization Chart; then enter the following data in the boxes:

    Lucinda Samual, President

    Heather Parks, Vice President

    Grace Stegall, Treasurer

    David Reams, Secretary

5. Modify the boxes by changing the color to gray and adding a shadow effect.

6. Print the chart.

7. Save the presentation as Club Organization; then close it.

PinPoint Assessment

You have completed the project and the associated lessons, as well as the "Checking Your Skills" and "Applying Your Skills" sections. Now use the PinPoint software Evaluation mode to assess your comprehension of the specific exam tasks you have just learned. You can also use the PinPoint Trainer mode and the SHOW ME tutorials to practice these specific exam tasks.

project

Five

5

Changing the Appearance of a Presentation

Enhancing Presentation Color and Design

In this project you will learn the following objectives and their associated Microsoft Exam required activities.

Objectives	Required Activities
➤ Use Templates … … … … … … … … … … … … … …	Create from a Template
➤ Work with Color Schemes … … … … … … … … …	Customize a Color Scheme
➤ Change the Slide Background … … … … … … … …	Create a Custom Background
➤ Work with a Slide Master … … … … … … … … …	Modify the Slide Master
➤ Save a Template … … … … … … … … … … … …	Apply a Template from Another Presentation
➤ Create Drawn Objects … … … … … … … … … …	Draw an Object Add Shapes
➤ Select and Modify Drawn Objects … … … … … …	Rotate and Fill an Object Scale and Size an Object
➤ Use Clip Art … … … … … … … … … … … … …	Add Clip Art Recolor and Edit Objects

Why Would I Do This?

You can strengthen the impact of your presentations by enhancing the color and design. PowerPoint contains a number of color schemes and design layouts created by graphic artists to make your presentation truly outstanding. You can use these preset color schemes or create your own. You can also use PowerPoint's Slide Master to add design elements, such as date and time, to every slide in your presentation.

Another way to spice up a presentation is to include drawings and illustrations. PowerPoint comes with a set of electronic pictures, called clip art, that you can add to emphasize parts of your presentation. You can also use PowerPoint's drawing tools to create simple or complex illustrations. By combining these features, you can produce an impressive presentation quickly and easily. Try using these features to create an exciting presentation now.

Lesson 1: Using Templates

Template
A blueprint that PowerPoint uses to create slides. The template includes the formatting, color, and graphics necessary to create a particular look for a presentation.

PowerPoint provides an extensive group of predesigned *templates* (sometimes called design templates) that you can use for your presentation. Because they have been created by professional graphic artists, these templates can help you create a presentation with a consistent, well-designed look. By using the templates, you can concentrate on content rather than on layout and design.

You can use a template at any time while working with a presentation. You can choose a template when you initially create the presentation, or you can apply a template later. For example, if you have already created a presentation but want to see some other "looks," you can apply various templates until you find one you like. Try working with templates now.

To Use Templates

❶ Start PowerPoint, if necessary, and choose Template from the PowerPoint startup dialog box. If PowerPoint is already open, choose File, New.

The New Presentation dialog box is displayed, as shown in Figure 5.1.

You can click the General, Presentations, Presentation Designs, or Web Pages tab to display the associated page and create that type of presentation.

Figure 5.1
You use the New Presentation dialog box to start a new presentation.

Choose a blank presentation on this page

Choose a design template on this page

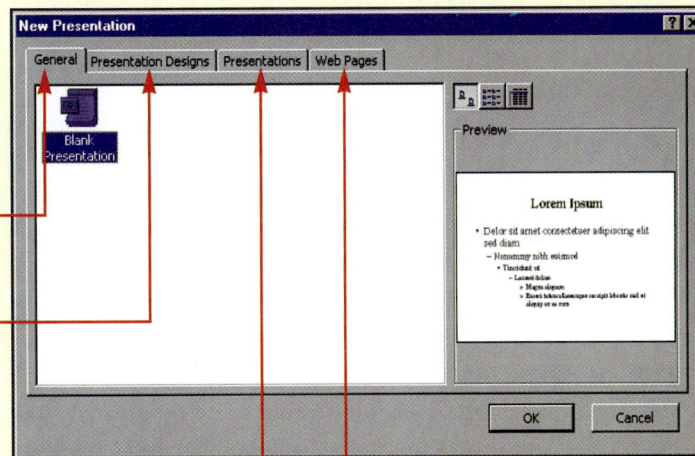

Choose an AutoContent presentation on this page

Choose a Web Page presentation on this page

The General tab, used to create a blank presentation, has no particular template associated with it. The Presentations tab provides a list of files that the AutoContent Wizard uses to make presentations with sample content already included. The Web Pages tab helps you design a home page for the World Wide Web. Finally, the Presentation Designs tab includes a list of available templates. You use this page to select a template.

2 Click the Presentation Designs tab.

This brings the Presentation Designs page to the front. The templates available are shown (see Figure 5.2). You can use this page to preview and choose a template for your presentation.

If you have problems...

If your templates look different from those shown in Figure 5.2, don't worry—your system probably is showing the files in List view or Details view rather than in Large Icons view. You can click the Large Icons button to display the templates in Large Icons view.

continues

To Use Templates (continued)

Figure 5.2
You can preview and
choose a template in
the New Presentation
dialog box.

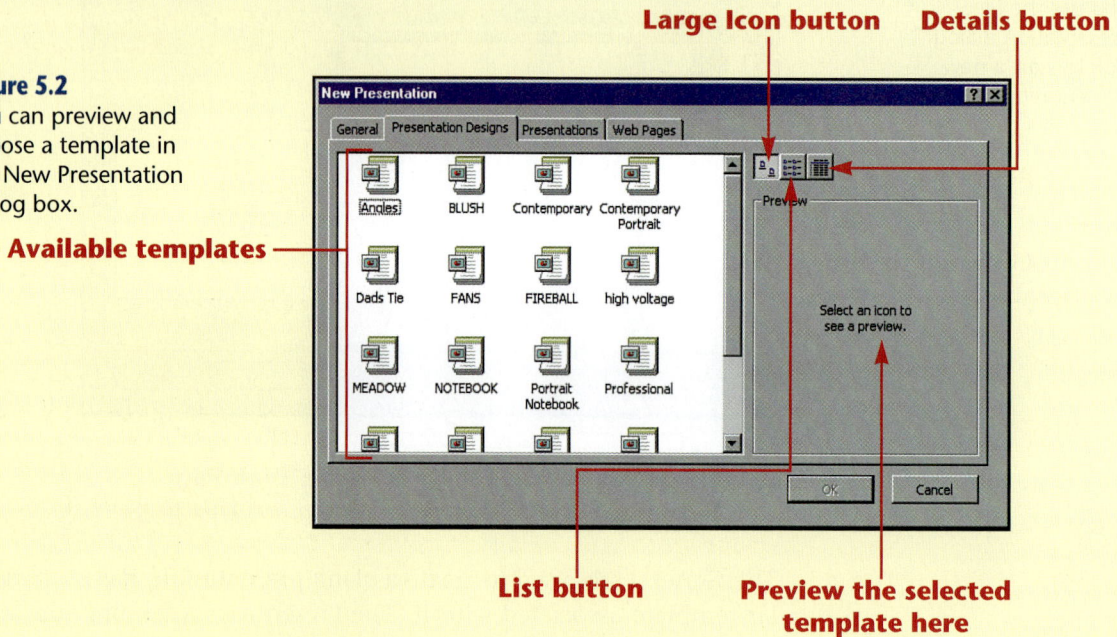

Large Icon button   Details button

Available templates

List button

Preview the selected
template here

❸ **Click the Angles template icon.**

The preview area displays an example of the selected template. If
you want, click several templates to preview them and then proceed
with the tutorial.

❹ **Choose the FIREBALL template and click OK.**

The New Slide dialog box is displayed so that you can select an
AutoLayout.

❺ **Make sure the Title Slide AutoLayout is selected; then
choose OK.**

A title slide with the selected template is created. All slides that you
add to this presentation will use the same template.

❻ **In the title placeholder, type your company name and enter
your own name in the subtitle area.**

You can choose a template when you initially create a presentation,
or you can apply another template to an existing presentation. Try
changing design templates now.

❼ **Right-click the mouse on the slide, and from the shortcut
menu, choose Apply Design.**

The Apply Design dialog box is displayed, showing a list of all available templates (see Figure 5.3). Notice that this is the same list of
templates you saw in the New Presentation dialog box. Additionally,
you can preview a template by clicking it, just as you did earlier.

PowerPoint

Figure 5.3
You can apply a template to a presentation at any time.

Selected template

Preview of selected template

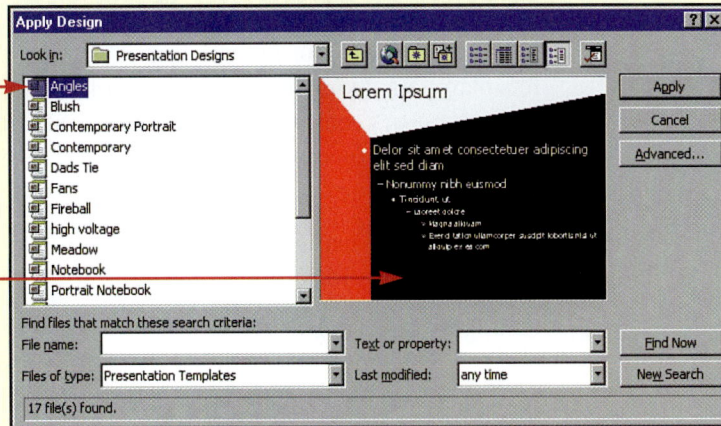

❽ Choose the Notebook template and click Apply.

The new template design is applied to the presentation (see Figure 5.4). If you want, try applying other templates. When you're finished, close the presentation without saving it.

Figure 5.4
You can change design templates for a different appearance.

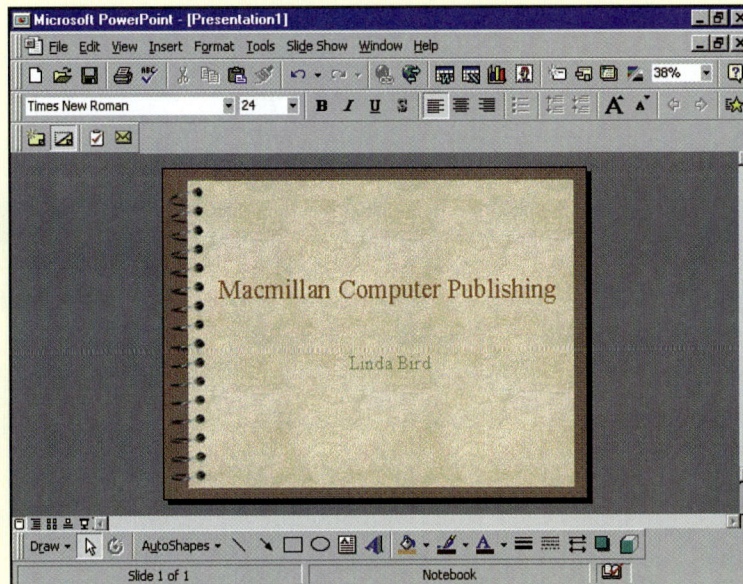

Keep PowerPoint running for the next lesson, in which you work with color schemes.

Inside Stuff

You can apply design templates by choosing Format, Apply Design or by clicking the Apply Design button on the Standard toolbar.

If you are artistically inclined (or just want to create a custom look for your presentations), you can design your own template. To create your own template, change whatever slide features you'd like—such as color, font style, and graphics—of a presentation. Choose File, Save As and enter a name for your new template. Then choose `Presentation Template` from the Save as type drop-down list so that it will be saved as a template and not a file. You'll learn more about this in Lesson 5.

Color Scheme

A set of eight coordinated colors you can use in your presentation.

Lesson 2: Working with Color Schemes

A *color scheme* is the underlying set of eight colors in a presentation. Each template that you use includes a color scheme to ensure that new objects you create or recolor will match those already in place. For example, when you change font color, the colors initially displayed are from the underlying color scheme.

In addition to using the color scheme in place, you can change the color scheme for all slides in a presentation or for just the current slide.

Changing color schemes for the entire presentation is handy for a couple of reasons. You might be about to give a presentation on the road, and the LCD or computer screen doesn't have the same contrast as your office computer. Being able to change the color scheme could create a better contrast and literally save your presentation (or job)!

You may also have similar presentations but have added customized slides for different audiences—one set for sales, one for marketing, one for advertising, and so on. By changing the color scheme for each audience, you can instantly tell that you are running the correct version of your presentation.

You can also change the color scheme for only one slide in order to highlight certain information. For example, you might want to highlight a new proposal or agenda. Changing color schemes for that slide is a subtle but effective attention-grabber.

Try customizing the color scheme of an existing presentation now.

To Work with Color Schemes

1 **Open Proj0501 from the Project-05 folder on the CD, and save it as** Hickory.

2 **Display the presentation in Slide Sorter view.**

Color schemes are easy to see in Slide view or Slide Sorter view.

3 **Choose F̲ormat, Slide C̲olor Scheme.**

The Color Scheme dialog box is displayed, as shown in Figure 5.5. If you are working in Slide view, you can also open this dialog box by choosing Slide C̲olor Scheme from the shortcut menu.

Figure 5.5
You can quickly change color schemes in the Color Scheme dialog box.

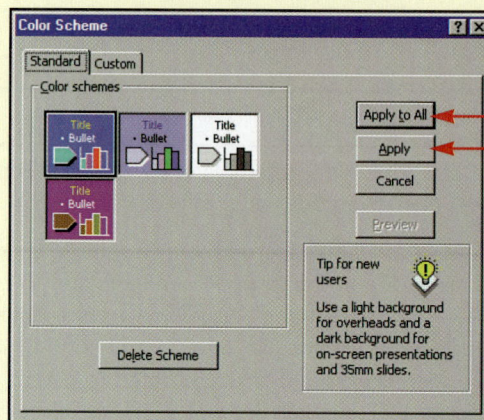

Click here to apply a new color scheme to all presentation slides

Click here to apply a new color scheme to current slide only

In general, you should select a scheme with a light background and dark text for overheads. Select a dark background with contrasting text for onscreen display and 35mm slides. Try selecting a color scheme for onscreen display now.

4 Select the dark maroon color scheme on the second row; then choose Apply to All.

The presentation is shown with the dark maroon color scheme applied to all slides. However, if you chose Apply, the color scheme for only the displayed slide would change. Try changing the color scheme for just one slide now.

5 Select Slide 3, Our Customer's Needs, and choose Format, Slide Color Scheme.

6 In the Color Scheme dialog box, choose the light blue color scheme (the middle box) on the first row and then choose Apply.

The selected color scheme is applied to only the selected slide. Notice that the slide elements, such as graphics and font style, remain consistent on all slides (because they are created by the underlying template) but that the color combinations are different.

7 Save the Hickory presentation and then close it.

Keep PowerPoint running for the next lesson, in which you change the background color.

If you have problems...   Make sure you choose Apply rather than Apply to All if you want to change the color scheme for the current slide only.

Inside Stuff   If you like the overall color scheme but want to change color for one color element, click the Custom tab in the Color Scheme dialog box to display the colors that make up the scheme. Click the Scheme color you want to change; then choose Change Color. Choose a color in the Color dialog box and then choose OK. You can choose Apply to place the modified color scheme on the currently displayed slide, or Apply to All to change the color scheme on all slides.

Lesson 3: Changing the Slide Background

You can also change the slide background. By changing the background, you add pizzazz to your presentation and get your audience's attention. You can customize your background by adding shadow effects, textures, and patterns. Try changing the slide background now.

To Change the Slide Background

1 **Open Proj0502 from the Project-05 folder on the CD, and save it as** Appalachian Logging Company.

2 **With Slide 1,** Business Overview**, in Slide view, choose Format, Background.**

The Background dialog box is displayed, as shown in Figure 5.6.

Figure 5.6
You can choose a new background for your presentation in the Background dialog box.

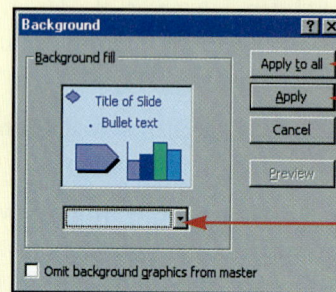

Click here to change the background for all slides

Click here to change the background of the current slide

Click here to list background fills

3 **In the Background fill area of the dialog box, click the drop-down list arrow and choose Fill Effects.**

The Fill Effects dialog box is displayed, as shown in Figure 5.7. You can use this dialog box to choose a variety of background styles.

Figure 5.7
You can choose a variety of gradient patterns.

Choose a color or color combination here

Choose a shading style here

Choose a variation of the shading style here

View a sample here

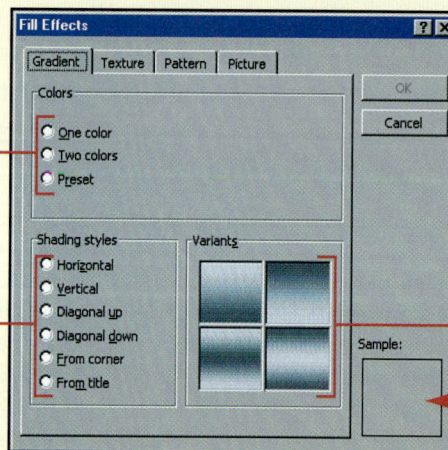

4 **Click the Gradient tab, if necessary, and then click the Preset option button in the Colors area. Choose a color selection from the Preset colors drop-down list.**

You can also choose variations of the pattern.

5 **Click the Diagonal up option button and preview your choice in the Sample box.**

6 **Choose OK and then choose Apply to all in the Background dialog box.**

The new background style is applied to all slides.

PowerPoint also provides a number of textures you can use as a background. Try using these now.

7 **Right-click Slide 1,** `Business Overview`, **to display the shortcut menu; then choose Back̲ground.**

The Background dialog box is displayed.

If you have problems... Make sure you right-click on the slide background and not on a placeholder area so that the correct shortcut menu is displayed.

---

8 **Choose F̲ill Effects from the drop-down list of available backgrounds.**

The Fill Effects dialog box is displayed.

9 **In the Fill Effects dialog box, click the Texture tab.**

The Texture page is displayed with a number of natural-looking backgrounds, such as wood and stone, that you can use. If you want, click several of the textures to preview them in the Sample box before proceeding with the next steps.

10 **Scroll through the available textures and choose Oak, as shown in Figure 5.8; then click OK to close the Fill Effects dialog box.**

Figure 5.8
You can choose a texture for your slide background.

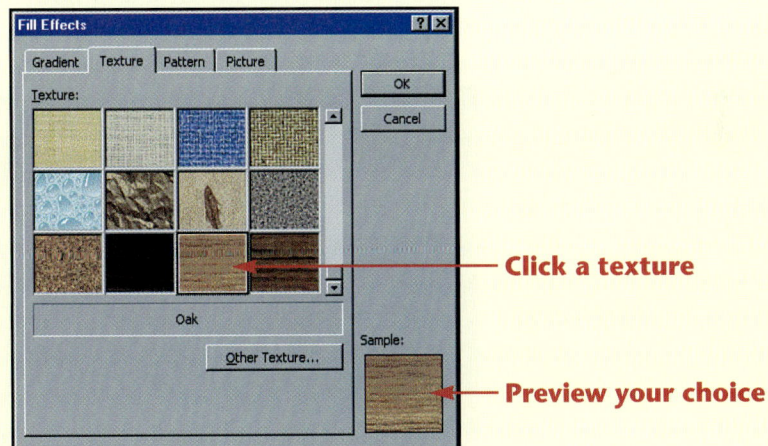

Click a texture

Preview your choice

11 **Choose Apply t̲o all in the Background dialog box.**

The textured oak wood background is applied to all slides in the presentation.

12 **Save and close the file.**

Keep PowerPoint running for the next lesson, in which you work with a Slide Master.

Lesson 4: Working with a Slide Master

Slide Master

A framework slide that controls how a slide will look, and enables to you place items such as date, name, and logo on each slide automatically.

The *Slide Master* controls the elements displayed on each slide. Every presentation that you create automatically includes the Slide Master. This master works "behind the scenes" and contains instructions so that the same objects are included on every presentation slide. You can change the Slide Master so that different elements are included in a specific presentation. For example, once you place a logo or the date on the Slide Master, that element is displayed on all slides in the presentation.

You can use four masters in PowerPoint: Slide Master, Title Master, Handout Master, and Notes Master. Each dictates the elements included on the associated slide type. In this lesson, you use and modify a Slide Master. Try working with a Slide Master now.

To Work with a Slide Master

1 **Open Proj0503 from the Project-05 folder on the CD, and save it as** Star Manufacturing.

2 **Choose View, Master, Slide Master.**

The master slide for the presentation is displayed (see Figure 5.9). It contains a title object and a body object that you can use to specify the default format for the title and body text. You can also add other objects, such as the date, to the Slide Master to be included on all slides.

Figure 5.9
You can control which slide elements are displayed by changing the Slide Master.

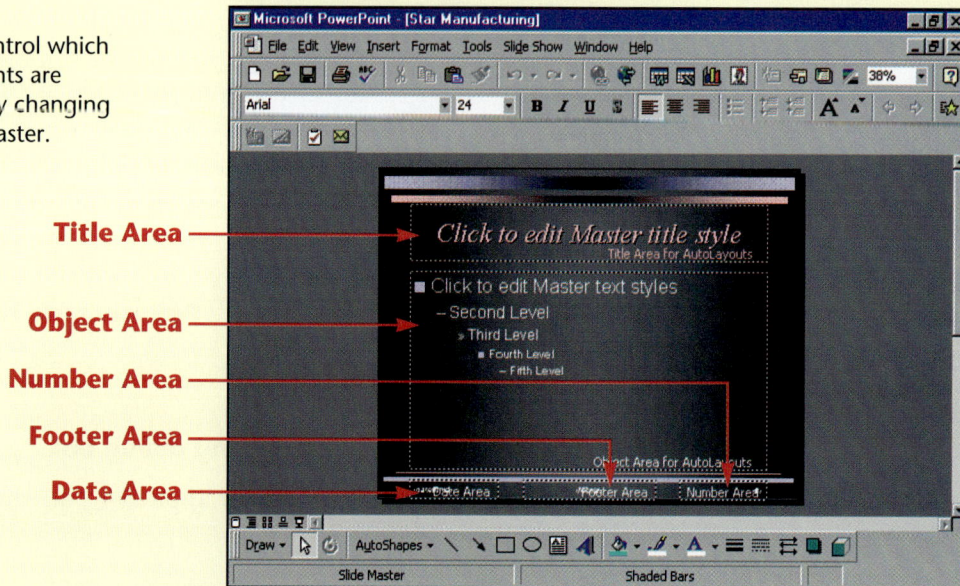

3 **Click the object** Click to edit Master title style.

The title area is selected, as indicated by the thickened border. The text in this area is currently formatted in italic.

4 **Click the Italic button.**

Italic is removed from the title area text. Because you made this change on the Slide Master rather than on an individual slide, the change affects all the presentation slides.

You can also customize the presentation by including information such as your name, department, or company name in the footer area of the Slide Master. When you place this information on the Slide Master, the information is automatically placed on all slides.

To work more effectively with the Slide Master, you can use the Zoom button on the Standard toolbar to enlarge the view.

42%

5 **Click the Zoom button drop-down list arrow and choose** 66%.

Your view is enlarged, enabling you to see the Slide Master objects more easily.

6 **Use the vertical scroll bar to scroll to the bottom of the Slide Master; then click the footer area object.**

The footer area is selected (see Figure 5.10). You also see a field for footer text. You can select this field and then enter your own text.

Figure 5.10
You can enter your own text in the Slide Master.

Drag over this field and type your text

Selected area

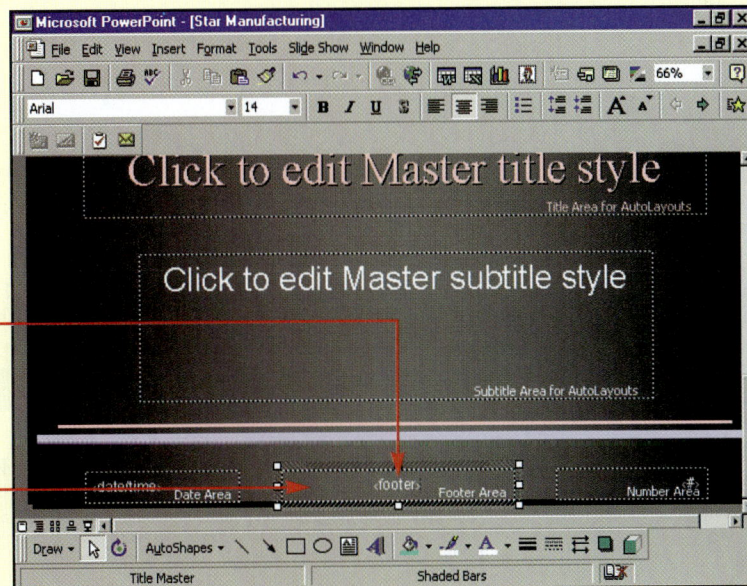

7 **Drag over the** <footer> **field and type** Joyce Parks, Management.

The text that you type is entered in the footer area so that it can be included on every slide. Before you switch to Slide view, change the view percentage so that you can see an entire slide onscreen.

8 **Click the Zoom button drop-down list arrow and choose** Fit.

The entire Slide Master is displayed onscreen. Switch to Slide view so that you can see the change on your presentation slides.

9 **Choose** **View, Slide.**

The footer text is inserted on each slide in the presentation. Scroll through the slides to see the text at the bottom of each slide.

10 **Save and close the presentation.**

Keep PowerPoint running for the next lesson, in which you save a template.

Inside Stuff

To toggle quickly between the Slide Master and Slide view, rest the mouse pointer on the Slide View button. Press and hold down ⬆Shift) and click the Slide View button. The Slide Master is displayed. You can click the Slide View button again to return the presentation to Slide view.

To set a header and footer for the presentation without opening the Slide Master, choose View, Header and Footer. Click the Slide tab in the Header and Footer dialog box, if it's not already selected. To have a date or time appear in the Date area on your slides, select Date and time. Click Update automatically to have the current date appear and then select the date/time format from the drop-down list; click Fixed to use a specific date and type the date in the text box. To have the slide number automatically appear in the Number area of the slides, select Slide number. To enter text for the Footer area, click Footer and type the text in the text box. Click Don't show on title slide if you want to prevent the header, footer, and slide number from appearing on the title slide of the presentation. Choose Apply to have the changes only appear on the current slide; choose Apply to All to have them displayed on all the slides.

Lesson 5: Saving a Template

After you've made changes to the Slide Master, the color scheme, or the slide background of a presentation, you may decide that you want to use that same formatting again for later presentations. Or, to create a template that is unique to you or your company, you may want to start with a blank presentation and create a custom template. In either case, you must save the presentation as a template so it can be reused.

To Save a Presentation as a Template

1 With PowerPoint open, choose File, New.

If you are starting PowerPoint, choose Blank presentation and skip to step 3.

2 In the New Presentation dialog box, select the General tab and double-click the Blank Presentation icon.

The New Slide dialog box appears.

3 Select the Title Slide AutoLayout and choose OK.

The title slide appears. The background and text are fairly plain.

4 Choose Format, Background.

The Background dialog box appears.

5 From the drop-down list, select Fill Effects.

The Fill Effects dialog box opens (see Figure 5.11).

Figure 5.11
Select a fill type and
select appropriate colors
and variations to make
your background.

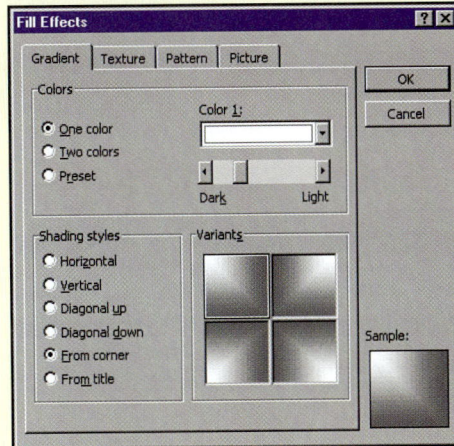

6 **In the Colors area, click Qne color. Then from the Shading styles, select From corner. Click one of the Variants, then choose OK.**

7 **Choose Apply to all.**

All the slides in the presentation share the gradient background. Now you need to set the style of the title text.

8 **Choose View, Master, Slide Master.**

9 **Click in the** Click to edit Master title style **placeholder.**

10 **Choose Format, Font. Set the font to 48-point Times New Roman, Bold Italic. Select Shadow. Set the Color as yellow (click More Colors to select yellow). Choose OK.**

Now you need to set the style of bullet for the body text. This establishes the style of bullet used throughout the presentation.

11 **Click in the text** Click to edit Master text styles. **Choose Format, Bullet.**

12 **Change the Bullets from character set to** Wingdings **or another appropriate symbol set. Select a bullet symbol and make the Color yellow. Choose OK.**

The yellow color choice is available on the color palette after you chose it for the text.

13 **Choose View, Slide to return to the Slide view.**

Now that you have established a "look" for your presentation, it's time to save it as a template.

14 **Choose File, Save As.**

The Save As dialog box appears (see Figure 5.12).

continues

To Save a Presentation as a Template   (continued)

Figure 5.12
You must change the Save as type to Presentation Template to create a template for later use.

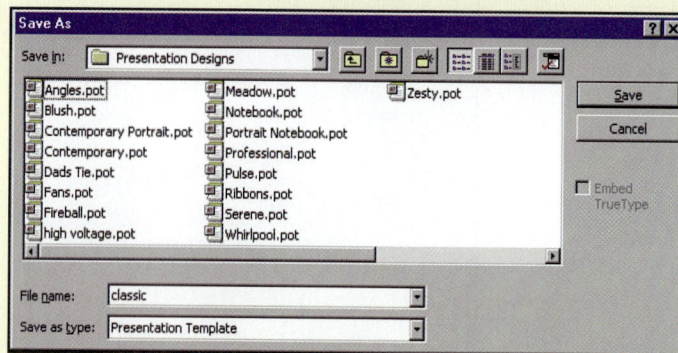

15 **From the Save as type drop-down list, select** Presentation Template.

This automatically switches you to the Template folder on your hard drive, where the Microsoft Office templates are stored. If it doesn't, ask your instructor for directions to switch to that folder.

16 **Double-click the Presentation Designs folder to open it. Enter the name** Classic **for the template in the File name box and then choose Save.**

The Classic template is now available when you start a new presentation.

17 **Close the current file.**

You start a new presentation by selecting the Classic template.

18 **Choose File, New. Click the Presentation Designs tab in the New Presentation dialog box. Double-click** Classic.

The new presentation opens using the Classic template you designed.

19 **Close the file without saving it, but leave PowerPoint open for the next lesson.**

Lesson 6: Creating Drawn Objects

With PowerPoint, you can add drawn objects—such as rectangles, ovals, lines, and arrows—to your presentation. PowerPoint has a variety of drawing tools that enable you to create simple to complex illustrations. You can use these tools to jazz up a slide or emphasize specific information (see Figure 5.13). Once the objects are created, you can move, resize, and modify them. By using graphics in your presentation, you make it a cut above the rest and help get your audience's attention.

Figure 5.13
You can jazz up a slide with drawn objects.

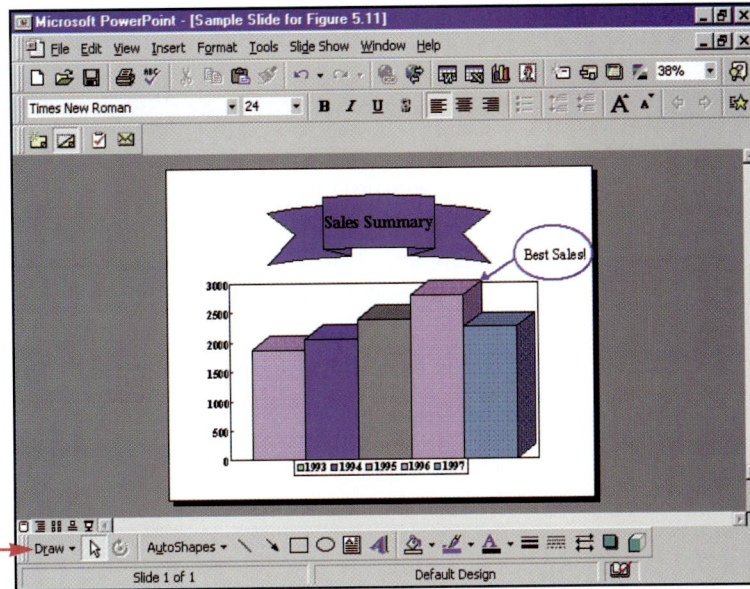

Drawing toolbar →

In this lesson, you learn how to create basic objects by using the tools on the Drawing toolbar. Table 5.1 describes these tools. You can use this table as a handy reference when you create and modify drawings.

Table 5.1	The Drawing Tools	
Tool	Name	Use
	Select Objects	Select drawn objects
	Free Rotate	Rotate a selected object
AutoShapes ▾	AutoShape	Display menu options for inserting a pre-designed shape
	Line	Draw a line
	Arrow	Draw an arrow
	Rectangle	Draw rectangles and squares
	Oval	Draw ellipses and circles
	Text Box	Draw a text box where you click and drag so that you can enter text
	Insert WordArt	Start the WordArt program
	Fill Color	Add, remove, or modify the texture, color, or pattern for a selected object
	Line Color	Add, remove, or modify the line color for a selected object
	Font Color	Change font color for a selected object
	Line Style	Change line thickness
	Dash Style	Change line appearance
	Arrow Style	Change arrowhead appearance
	Shadow	Add, remove, or modify shadow formatting for a selected object
	3-D	Add, remove, or modify 3-D formatting for a selected object

To Create Drawn Objects

1 Start a new presentation and display a blank slide.

You can use PowerPoint's horizontal and vertical rulers in order to help you accurately place drawn objects. You can turn the rulers on or off by choosing View, Ruler. When turned on, the rulers appear in Slide view and Notes Page view, at the top and left side of the slide window. The 0" marks on the horizontal and vertical rulers represent the center of the slide. When you draw an object, the movement reflects on the rulers to show your exact location on the slide.

2 Choose View, Ruler.

The rulers are displayed (see Figure 5.14).

Figure 5.14
You can draw objects precisely by using the rulers.

Horizontal ruler →

Vertical ruler →

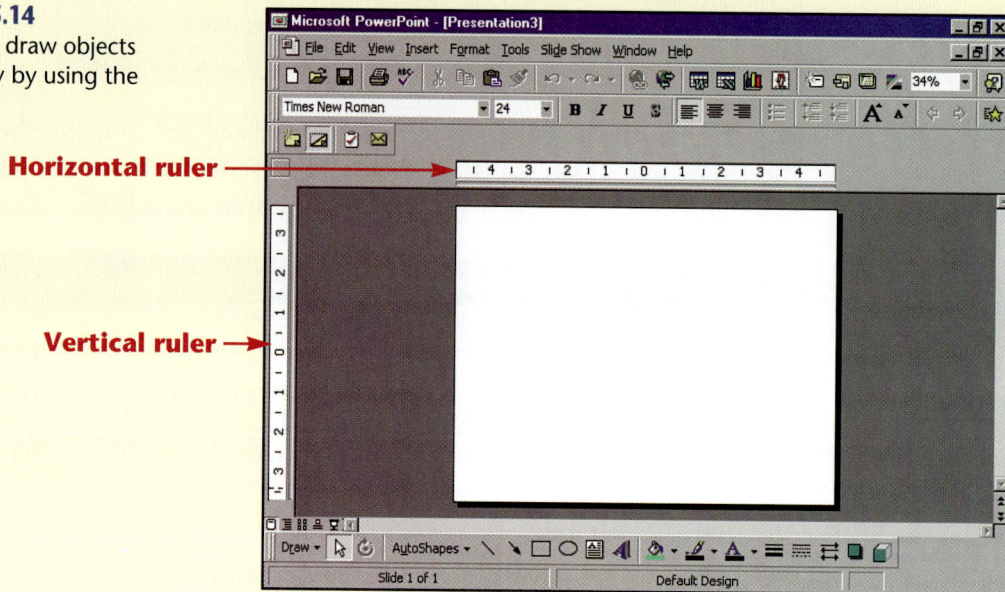

3 Click the Rectangle tool on the Drawing toolbar and move the mouse pointer to the slide area.

The mouse pointer changes to a crosshair so that you can accurately place the drawn object.

4 On the slide, position the crosshair where the two 0" marks intersect; then click and drag until the lower-right corner of the rectangle is at the place where the 3" horizontal ruler mark and the 2" vertical ruler mark intersect.

A rectangle is added to your presentation (see Figure 5.15). The fill color and line colors used for the object are assigned based on the color scheme used by the current template; they can be changed. Additionally, white selection handles appear around the object to indicate that it is selected. When you click on the slide or draw another object, the rectangle is deselected. (You learn more specifically how to select and modify drawn objects in Lesson 7.)

Figure 5.15
You can add drawings to your presentation.

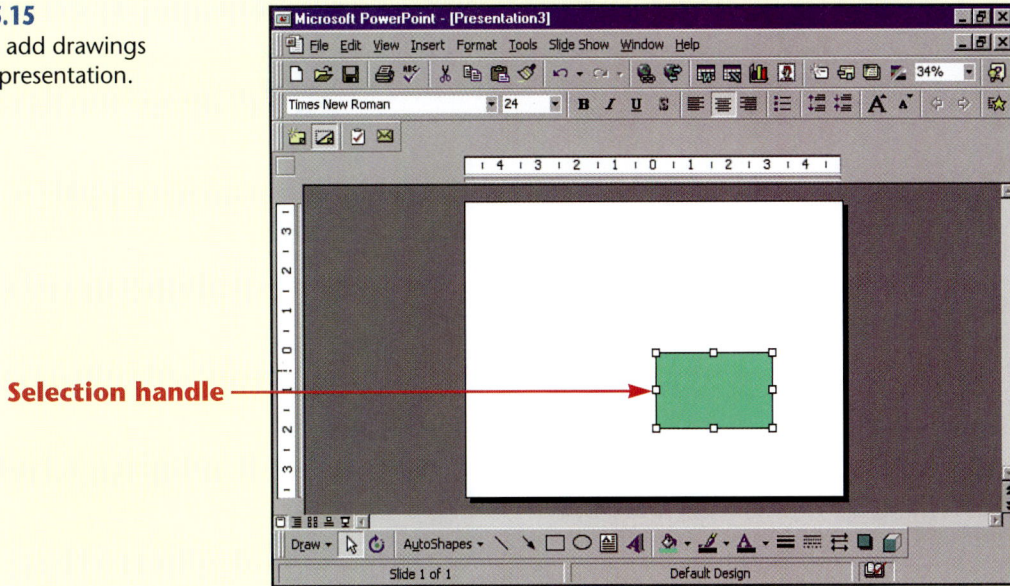

Selection handle

You can use other tools in the same manner. You click the tool and then drag to draw the object on the slide. Try drawing an oval, or an ellipse, now.

5 **Click the Oval tool and drag to draw an oval in the upper-left corner of the slide.**

You can also make an object symmetrical by pressing ⬥Shift as you draw it. For example, pressing ⬥Shift while using the Rectangle tool produces a perfect square; pressing ⬥Shift while using the Oval tool creates a perfect circle. To draw an object from the center out, hold down Ctrl while you draw. Try drawing a circle now.

6 **Click the Oval tool, press ⬥Shift, and drag to draw a circle in the lower-left corner of the slide.**

If you have problems... Make sure you release the mouse button before you release ⬥Shift, or your object may skew into an oval.

You can also use the Line tool to create lines. To make a straight horizontal or vertical line or force a diagonal line to be drawn at a 15-degree interval, press ⬥Shift while you draw it.

7 **Click the Line tool and draw a line from the oval to the rectangle (see Figure 5.16).**

continues

To Create Drawn Objects   (continued)

Figure 5.16
You can draw lines on your slide.

Select the Line tool and drag from here...

...to here

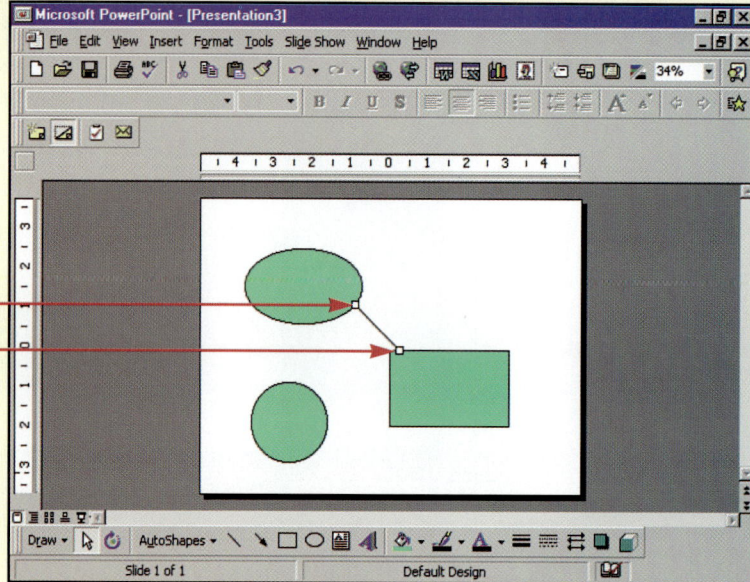

A drawing tool is automatically turned off once you draw an object with it. However, you can double-click the tool to keep it active so that you can draw multiple objects. You turn the tool off by clicking it a second time or pressing Esc. Try drawing multiple ovals now with the Oval tool.

8 Double-click the Oval tool and draw several small ovals in the upper-right corner of the slide.

Your slide should look similar to that in Figure 5.17.

Figure 5.17
You can double-click a tool to keep it active and draw multiple objects.

Ovals

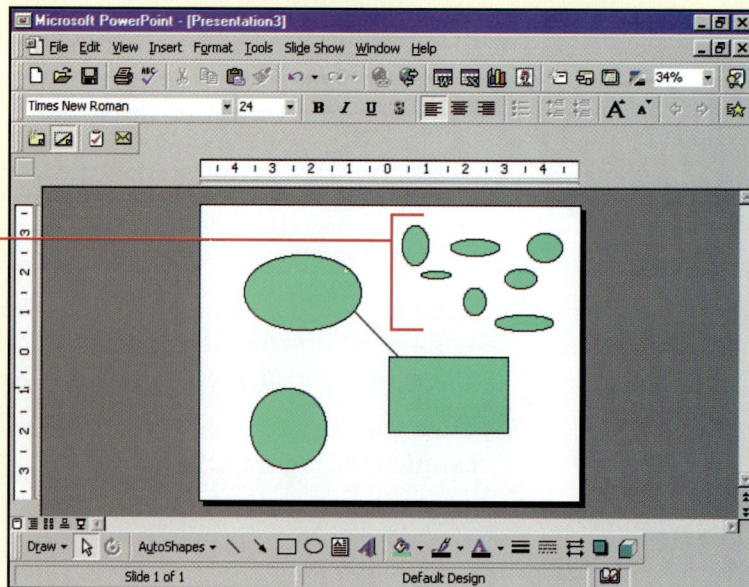

PowerPoint

9 Click the Oval tool to turn it off.

If you want, practice using the various drawing tools.

10 When you're finished, close your presentation without saving it. Keep PowerPoint open for the next lesson, in which you select and modify objects.

Inside Stuff

If you're not very artistic, or you simply want some help when you create drawings, you can use PowerPoint's AutoShapes feature to create professionally designed shapes. Click the AutoShapes tool on the Drawing toolbar to display the AutoShapes menu. Move your mouse pointer to a menu item to display a graphical submenu; then click the shape you want—arrows, triangles, stars, flowchart shapes, and more. You drag to draw the shape on a slide, just as you created rectangles, ovals, and lines in the preceding lesson.

Lesson 7: Selecting and Modifying Drawn Objects

After you have created drawn objects, you can modify them in a number of ways. You can move, resize, recolor, or delete objects. However, before you modify an object, you must first select it. You can use Table 5.2 as a handy reference for selecting and deselecting objects.

Table 5.2 Methods of Selecting Objects	
To	Do This
Select an object	Click the object.
Select multiple objects	Press and hold down ◆Shift while clicking objects.
	Using the Select Objects tool, draw a box around all objects.
Deselect one object	Hold down ◆Shift, click the object, and release ◆Shift.
Deselect all objects	Click outside selected objects.

Selecting, Resizing, Moving, Rotating, and Deleting Drawn Objects

In this lesson, you learn how to select drawn objects by using some of the techniques listed in Table 5.2. Once the objects are selected, you can modify them in various ways. Try selecting and modifying objects now.

To Select, Resize, Move, Rotate, and Delete Drawn Objects

1 **Open Proj0504 from the Project-05 folder on the CD, and save it as** Drawing.

2 **Click the diamond object.**

The diamond is selected, as indicated by the white selection handles that surround it.

3 **Press and hold down** ⬆Shift, **click the rectangle object, and then release** ⬆Shift.

The rectangle is selected in addition to the diamond.

4 **Click the Select Objects tool on the Drawing toolbar, if necessary, and drag from above and to the left of the diamond object down to the lower-right corner of the slide.**

A dashed border indicates the area being selected (see Figure 5.18).

Figure 5.18
You can select multiple objects.

Drag a box
around objects
to select them

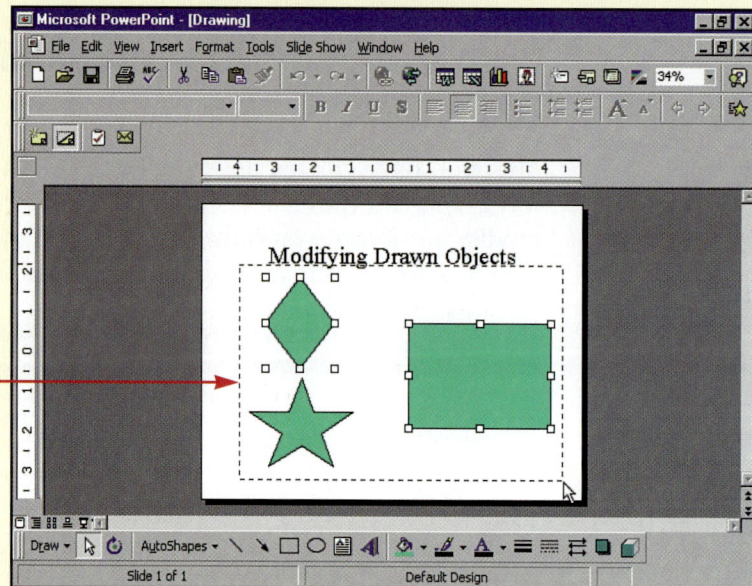

5 **Release the mouse button.**

When you release the mouse button, all the objects within the area are selected, indicated by white selection handles.

If you have problems...

Make sure you start drawing the selection box above and to the left of all the objects. If you start in the middle of an object, that object won't be selected.

6 **Click outside the objects.**

All objects are deselected. Next, you learn to resize an object.

7 **Click the rectangle to select it and then move the mouse pointer across the top-center handle until it becomes a two-sided resizing arrow (see Figure 5.19).**

PowerPoint

Figure 5.19
You can resize a
selected object.

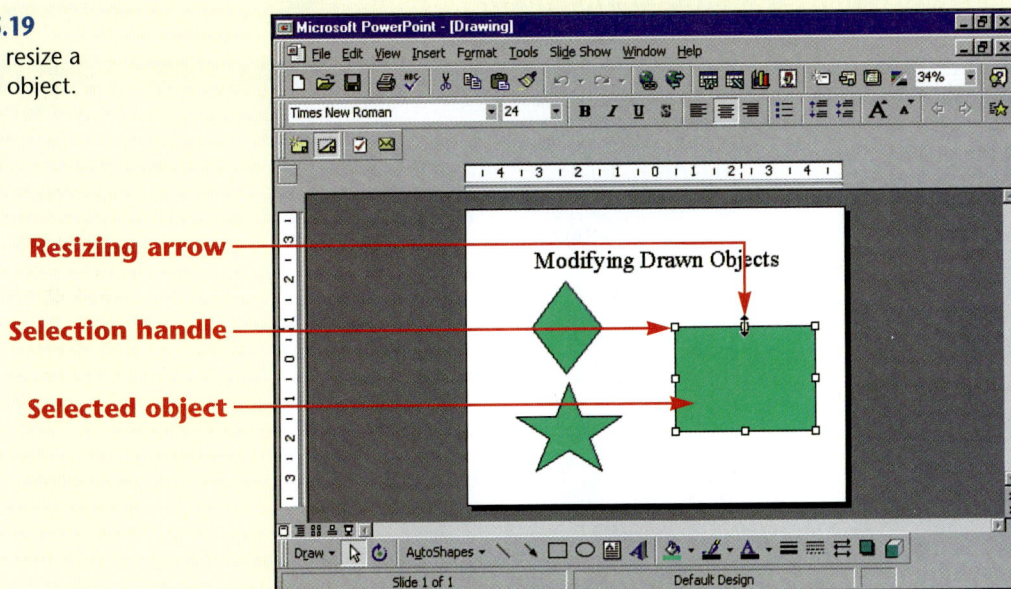

Resizing arrow

Selection handle

Selected object

8 **Drag the upper border of the rectangle downward to resize it to about half the original size; then release the mouse button.**

The rectangle is resized. You can also move a selected object.

9 **With the rectangle still selected, move the mouse pointer inside the rectangle until the pointer changes to a four-sided arrow.**

10 **Click and drag the rectangle object until it touches the bottom border of the slide; then release the mouse button.**

The drawn object is moved. If you make a mistake as you move or resize an object, choose Edit, Undo to reverse the action. You can also delete objects.

11 **Select the rectangle if it isn't already selected and press Del.**

The selected object is deleted. Selecting several objects before pressing Del erases all the objects at once. If you accidentally delete an object, click the Undo button.

12 **Click on the diamond to select it and then click the Free Rotate button on the Drawing toolbar.**

The selection handles disappear and are replaced by four round rotation handles (see Figure 5.20). The mouse pointer becomes a circular arrow.

continues

To Select, Resize, Move, Rotate, and Delete Drawn Objects (continued)

Figure 5.20
You use the Free Rotate tool to change the angle of the object.

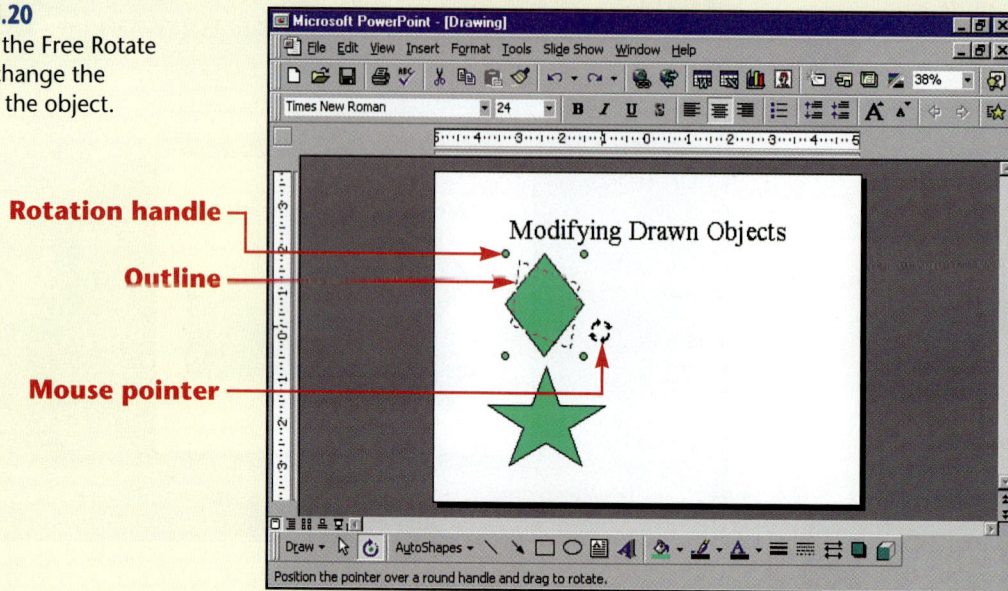

Rotation handle

Outline

Mouse pointer

13 **Position the mouse pointer over one of the rotation handles so the handle appears in the center of the mouse pointer.**

14 **Hold down the left mouse button and drag in a clockwise or counter-clockwise direction.**

The mouse pointer becomes four small arrows in a circle. As you drag, you see a dashed-line outline of the diamond showing the position the diamond will take when you release the mouse button.

15 **Release the mouse button when you have rotated the diamond about 90 degrees.**

When you wish to return the object back to its original position, you undo the rotation.

16 **Click the Undo button on the Standard toolbar to return the diamond to its original position.**

Keep the presentation open for the next tutorial.

Inside Stuff

If you hold down Shift while rotating, you force the object to turn in 15-degree increments (15°, 30°, 45°, 60°, and so on). If you hold down Ctrl, you can rotate the object around a point outside the object. PowerPoint uses as the center the round handle opposite the handle you select to rotate. With Shift+Ctrl pressed, the object rotates in 15-degree increments about the external center.

Changing Lines and Colors on a Drawn Object

After the objects are selected, you can change the color and lines associated with them. Changing lines and colors helps to emphasize certain information in your presentation or to create a different "look." Try changing lines and colors now.

To Change Lines and Colors on a Drawn Object

1 In the Drawing presentation that you revised in the preceding tutorial, select the star object.

As usual, you must first select an object before you can modify it.

2 Click the Fill Color tool drop-down arrow.

A color palette is displayed (see Figure 5.21). You can use this palette to select a coordinating color or a fill effect. You can also click the More Fill Colors button to see additional colors.

Figure 5.21
You can quickly change fill color or effect.

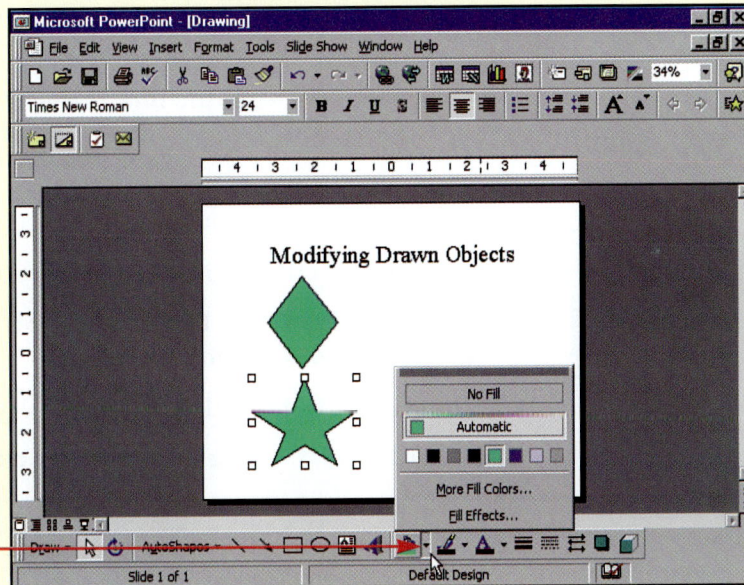

Click this arrow to display a palette of color and fill effects

3 Click the blue color (the third box from the right).

The Fill Color palette closes, and the selected color is applied to the star.

4 With the star object still selected, click the Line Style tool.

A palette of line styles is displayed (see Figure 5.22). You can choose a line style from this palette to apply to the selected object.

continues

To Change Lines and Colors on a Drawn Object   (continued)

Figure 5.22
You can select a new line style for your object.

Choose this line style

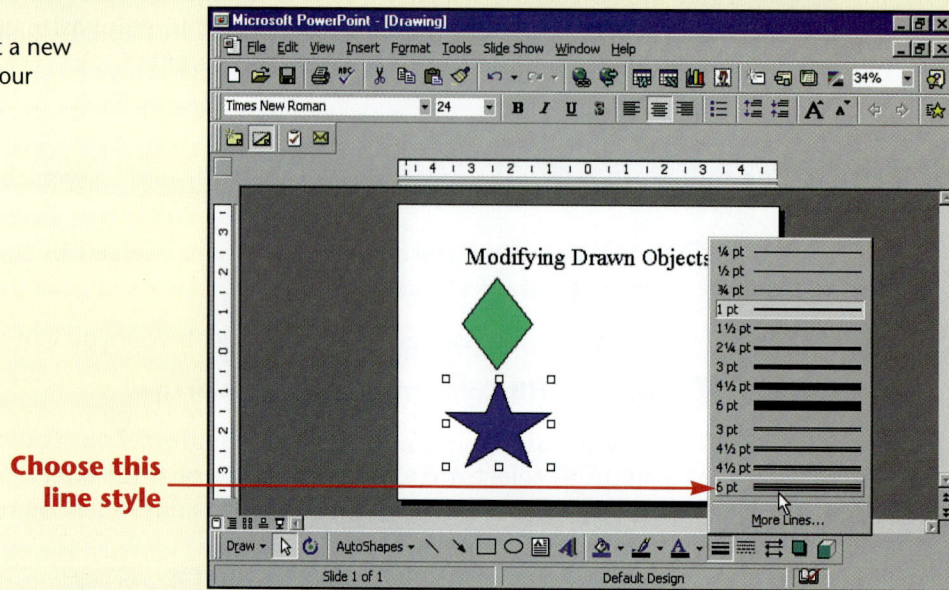

5 Click the 6-point triple line (refer to Figure 5.22).

The selected line style applies to the star. (If you want to see the effect better, choose <u>V</u>iew, <u>Z</u>oom, <u>6</u>6%. When you're finished viewing your changes, choose <u>V</u>iew, <u>Z</u>oom, <u>F</u>it to see the entire slide.)

You can also change the line color.

6 Click the Line Color tool drop-down arrow and choose gray (the third color from the left).

The star's outline border appears in gray.

7 Save the Drawing presentation and close it.

Inside Stuff   You can apply color and line options to several objects at once by selecting them and then applying the attributes to the entire group.

Lesson 8: Using Clip Art

The PowerPoint program includes a good selection of electronic *clip art* in its Clip Gallery that you can use to enhance your presentation. Including clip art on a slide can help hold audience attention and reinforce your main points. The Clip Gallery that comes with PowerPoint includes a variety of pictures for personal and business use. You can also purchase additional clip art if you want more choices.

Clip art
A collection of electronic pictures, stored on disk and available for use by PowerPoint.

After clip art is placed on a slide, you can change its location, size, and appearance. Clip art can also be ungrouped into its component parts so that you can work with each part as an individual object. For example, you can recolor parts of a map to highlight data associated with it. Try your hand at clip art now.

PowerPoint

To Use Clip Art

① **Open Proj0505 from the Project-05 folder on the CD, and save it as** Clip Art Examples.

② **Display Slide 2,** Financial Stability, **in Slide view, and click the New Slide button.**

③ **In the New Slide dialog box, click the Text & Clip Art AutoLayout (the first layout on the third row) and choose OK.**

A new slide is inserted with a clip art placeholder (see Figure 5.23). You can double-click this placeholder object to display the Clip Gallery then choose a picture.

Figure 5.23
You can use the clip art placeholder to access the Clip Gallery.

Clip art placeholder

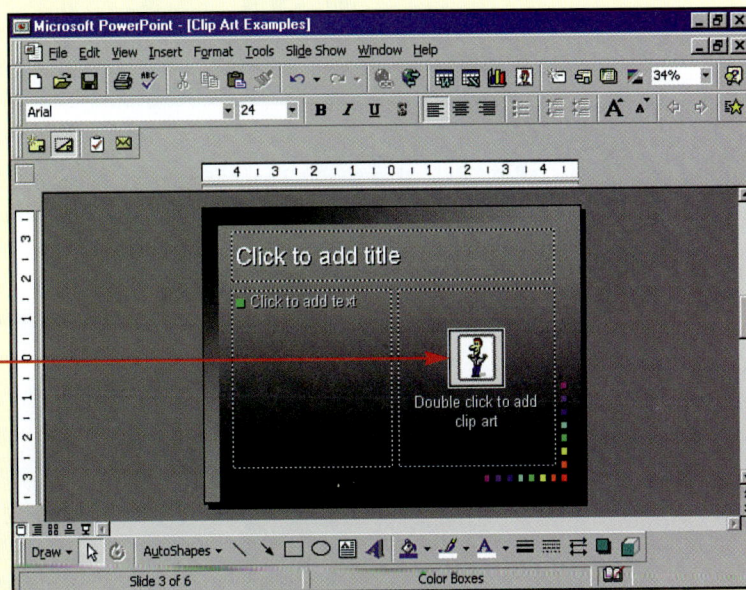

④ **Double-click the clip art placeholder.**

The Microsoft Clip Gallery dialog box is displayed, with a graphical list of available images, as shown in Figure 5.24. (The Clip Gallery on your computer may list different pictures from those illustrated in this project, depending on what art has been installed.) Once you are in the Clip Gallery, you can view all the available clip art or select a specific category to limit the display.

continues

To Use Clip Art   (continued)

Figure 5.24
The Microsoft Clip Gallery dialog box displays the available images.

Click here to display all pictures

Click a category to limit the display

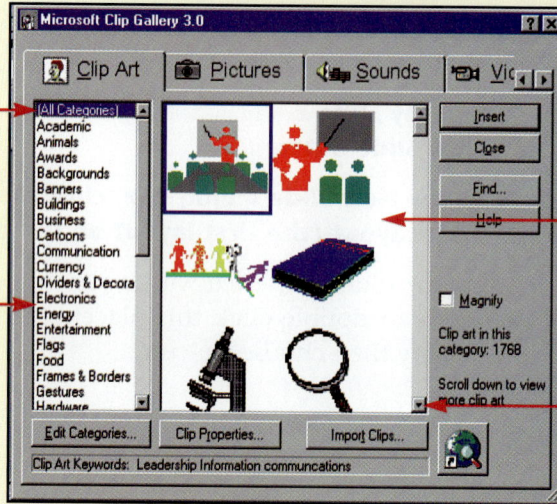

Select a picture here and click Insert

Scroll here to see more pictures

5 **Click the** `Buildings` **category, select the image indicated in Figure 5.25, and choose** Insert **(if that image isn't available, select a similar one).**

Figure 5.25
You can choose from a variety of clip art.

Selected category

Selected picture

The selected image is placed on the slide. The white selection handles indicate that the image can currently be resized, moved, or deleted in the same way as the drawn objects in Lesson 7.

You can easily replace the clip art on your slide with another clip art image. Just double-click the clip art to access the Clip Gallery; then choose another image. Try replacing the picture now.

6 Double-click the clip art on your slide.

The Clip Gallery is displayed.

7 Choose any category and picture you want; then choose Insert.

The clip art you originally selected is replaced by the new image.

You can also insert clip art on a slide that doesn't have a clip art placeholder. To do this, you use the Insert Clip Art button. Try this now.

8 Move to Slide 2, Financial Stability, and click the Insert Clip Art button.

The Clip Gallery is displayed so that you can choose a picture. You can quickly insert the picture on your slide by double-clicking the picture.

9 In the Cartoons category, double-click to insert the Reward Agreeable picture—the man holding money—on your slide. (If this image isn't available on your computer, choose a similar one.)

The picture is placed on the slide. If you don't like the placement or size of the picture, you can easily move or resize it, just as you moved and resized the drawn objects. Click to select the picture; then drag it to a new location or use the resizing handles to change the size.

10 Move the picture so that it is displayed in a blank area of the slide.

You can also change the coloring of the clip art.

11 Click the Recolor Picture button on the Picture toolbar.

Although the Picture toolbar usually displays when you select the picture, choose View, Toolbars, Picture if the toolbar is not displayed.

The Recolor Picture dialog box appears (see Figure 5.26). You are going to change the man's hair color to gray.

Figure 5.26
In the Recolor Picture dialog box, you change the colors for parts of the clip art.

Select current color here

Choose replacement color here

Click to preview the clip art in the slide

See how your changes affect the clip art

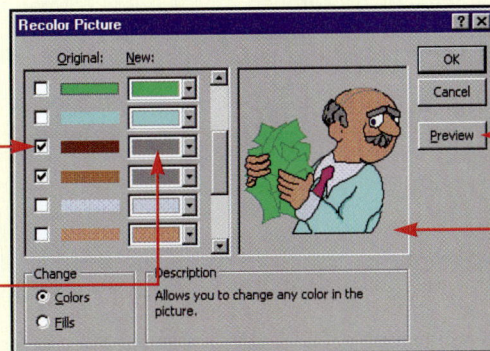

continues

12 **Scroll down the list of Original colors until you see the brown that matches the current hair color. Select that color by clicking the check box.**

13 **From the New drop-down list, select Gray (the first box on the left). Click Preview to see the result of your change.**

You may have to select another brown and change it to gray, until you finally get the hair color.

14 **Choose OK.**

15 **Save and close the presentation.**

If you have finished your work session, exit PowerPoint and shut down Windows before turning off your computer. Otherwise, complete the "Checking Your Skills" and "Applying Your Skills" exercises at the end of this project.

Inside Stuff

You can also recolor a picture by selecting the image and choosing Format, Picture. Click the Picture tab in the Format Picture dialog box and choose Recolor. In the New area, click the drop-down arrows for the colors you want to change; then choose a new color. You can preview your changes in the Recolor Picture dialog box. When you're satisfied with your choices, close the Recolor Picture and Format Picture dialog boxes.

Project Summary

To	Do This
Apply a template	Click the Apply Design button on the Standard toolbar.
Apply a color scheme	Select Format, Slide Color Scheme.
	Right-click a slide to activate the shortcut menu; select Slide Color Scheme.
Change the slide background	Choose Format, Background.
View the Slide Master	Choose View, Master, Slide Master.
Insert a footer into a Slide Master	Select the footer area placeholder on the Slide Master and then type the text.
Modify a Slide Master	Select the placeholder and then format or change the text.
Save a template	Choose File, Save As. Change the Save as type to Presentation Template. Choose Save.
Create a drawn object	Select the tool from the Drawing toolbar; then click and drag to draw.
Select a drawn object	Click the object.

PowerPoint

To	Do This
Select multiple objects	Hold down ⇧Shift while clicking objects.
	Use the Select Objects tool and draw a box around all objects.
Deselect one object	Hold down ⇧Shift, click the object, and release ⇧Shift.
Deselect all objects	Click outside selected objects.
Resize an object	Rest the mouse pointer on a selection handle until the pointer turns into a two-sided arrow; then drag to resize.
Move an object	Move the mouse pointer to the middle of the selected object; then drag to move.
Delete an object	Select the object and press Del.
Change an object's colors	Click the Fill Color tool drop-down arrow on the Drawing toolbar.
Change an object's line style	Click the Line Style tool on the Drawing toolbar.
Insert clip art	Double-click a clip art placeholder.
	Click the Insert Clip Art button on the Standard toolbar.
Replace clip art picture	Double-click a clip art object.
Recolor clip art	Select a picture and choose Format, Picture; then click the Picture tab and choose Recolor.

Checking Your Skills

True/False

For each of the following, check *T* or *F* to indicate whether the statement is true or false.

__T __F **1.** You create drawn objects in your presentation by using the Design toolbar.

__T __F **2.** Changes to the Slide Master, such as adding footer text, apply only to the current slide.

__T __F **3.** The design template enables you to select and print handouts for a presentation.

__T __F **4.** Customizing the template design before building your presentation is usually best because you can't change the template later.

__T __F **5.** You can add clip art to a slide even if it doesn't have a clip art placeholder.

__T __F **6.** You can preview a template before choosing it.

__T __F **7.** You can apply a color scheme to the current slide or to all slides in your presentation.

__T __F **8.** You should carefully draw any objects on a slide because they can't be resized later.

__T __F **9.** You can customize and save a template for later use.

__T __F **10.** You can double-click a drawing tool to keep it active and create multiple drawings.

Multiple Choice

Circle the letter of the correct answer for each of the following questions.

1. Which of the following is a good reason for changing color schemes?

  a. to change display contrast when using an LCD panel and overhead projector

  b. to emphasize a particular slide

  c. to keep track of similar but slightly different presentations you created for different audiences

  d. all of the above

2. Which of the following is true regarding Design templates?

  a. They are the same as a Slide Master.

  b. They are a "blueprint" that PowerPoint uses to determine the overall look of a presentation.

  c. They can't be changed once selected.

  d. None of the above

3. You can select multiple objects and then do which of the following?

  a. Apply the same color or line style to them at the same time.

  b. Apply AutoShapes to them.

  c. Delete them.

  d. Both a and c.

4. Using the Slide Master, you can change which of the following?

  a. the footer area text

  b. font sizes or styles

  c. the date area data

  d. all of the above

5. You can create a perfect square by doing which of the following?

  a. pressing ⬆Shift while using the Rectangle tool

  b. pressing Ctrl while using the Rectangle tool

  c. using the Square tool on the Drawing toolbar

  d. selecting an existing rectangle and then choosing Format, Square

6. When you draw an object on a slide, which of the following occurs?

  a. White resizing handles appear to indicate that the object is selected.

  b. You use the tools on the Formatting toolbar.

  c. You can hold down Ctrl while drawing to make an object symmetrical.

  d. All of the above.

PowerPoint

7. Drawn objects are usually used in a PowerPoint presentation to do which of the following?

    a. Create organization charts.

    b. Create data charts.

    c. Emphasize specific information.

    d. All of the above.

8. You can select multiple drawn objects by doing which of the following?

    a. double-clicking each of them

    b. pressing Ctrl while clicking them

    c. pressing ◆Shift while clicking them

    d. none of the above

9. Which of the following is true in relation to clip art?

    a. PowerPoint displays available pictures in the Clip Gallery.

    b. You can use a toolbar button or a placeholder to insert clip art.

    c. You can recolor clip art.

    d. All of the above.

10. Which of the following is true regarding the Slide Master?

    a. It controls the way elements on a slide display.

    b. It is the same as a Title Master.

    c. It cannot be changed.

    d. None of the above.

Completion

In the blank provided, write the correct answer for each of the following statements.

1. You can select several objects by pressing _____ while clicking them.

2. You can tell that a drawn object is selected because it has _____ around its borders.

3. The set of eight colors associated with a slide design is called its _____.

4. PowerPoint contains electronic pictures referred to as _____.

5. A blueprint or pattern for slide design is called a _____.

6. The _____ dictates the components that display on a slide.

7. You can change the slide _____ by adding various fill effects (such as wood and stone).

8. You can use vertical and horizontal _____ to help you draw objects precisely.

9. You can select objects by using the _____ tool to draw a box around them.

10. You can remove a selected object by pressing _____.

Matching

In the blank next to each of the following terms or phrases, write the letter of the corresponding term or phrase. (Note that some of the letters may be used more than once.)

a. AutoShapes

b. handles

c. Slide Master

d. clip art

e. Fill Color button

f. Rectangle

g. Oval

h. Line Color button

i. slide background

j. color scheme

_____ **1.** Electronic pictures

_____ **2.** The drawing tool used to create squares

_____ **3.** The drawing tool used to create circles

_____ **4.** Eight colors that coordinate with your template

_____ **5.** Using a shading style on an entire slide

_____ **6.** Enables you to place a logo or footer on each slide

_____ **7.** Professionally designed drawn shapes

_____ **8.** Indicates that an object is selected

_____ **9.** Changes fill color of selected object

_____ **10.** Changes line color of selected object

Applying Your Skills

Practice

The following exercises, found in the Project 5 folder on the CD, enable you to practice the skills you have learned in this project. Take a few minutes to work through these exercises now.

Working with Templates, Slide Masters, and Color Schemes

Your boss has asked that you revise a presentation she previously created and that you add some elements to jazz it up. To do this, you decide to apply a different design template. You also add clip art and add a footer to the Slide Master.

To work with templates, Slide Masters, and color schemes, follow these steps:

1. Open Proj0506 and save it as `Company Overview`.

2. Choose Format, Apply Design to view the Apply Design dialog box. Then preview how your presentation will look with different design templates such as Dad's Tie, Angles, and Meadow.

3. Apply the Ribbons template to the entire presentation.

4. Add a footer that reads `Report developed by B. Cory` to the Slide Master.

5. Add a clip art image to Slide 2, `Financial Stability`. Select the stacked coins picture from the Currency category (or a similar image).

6. Save and close the presentation.

Working with Drawn Objects

As the owner of a small company, you develop your own publicity materials. You decide to practice using PowerPoint's drawing tools so that you can easily create logos, flyers, and other publicity materials.

To work with drawn objects, follow these steps:

1. Create a new presentation with a blank slide.

2. Use the Rectangle tool on the Drawing toolbar to create a rectangle and a perfect square.

3. Use the Oval tool to create an ellipse and a perfect circle.

4. Use the Fill Color tool to change the color of each object to blue.

5. Change the line style of each object to a $4\frac{1}{2}$-pt single line. Change the line color of each object to gray.

6. Delete the circle.

7. Resize the rectangle so that it is approximately half the original size.

8. Close the presentation without saving it.

Selecting and Modifying Drawn Objects

Your boss has told you that she wants you to use PowerPoint to develop flowcharts and other diagrams for a training manual. In preparation for the project, you decide to practice selecting and modifying drawn objects.

To select and modify drawn objects, follow these steps:

1. Open Proj0507 and save it as Working with Objects.

2. Select each of the objects on the slide.

3. Click outside the objects to deselect them.

4. Use the Select Objects tool to select all the objects simultaneously.

5. Deselect the rectangle.

6. Change the fill color for the star and diamond to blue. Change the line style to a 6-point single line.

7. Click outside the objects to deselect them.

8. Save the presentation and then close it.

Using Clip Art

Your company gives a certificate to employees who successfully complete a safety training course. To make the certificate, you decide to insert and recolor clip art on a PowerPoint slide.

To use clip art, follow these steps:

1. Create a new presentation with a blank slide.

2. Click the Insert Clip Art button to display the Clip Gallery.

3. Choose the Academic category and double-click any picture that looks like a book.

4. Double-click the clip art picture on your slide to access the Clip Gallery again.

5. Select the picture that looks like a diploma and choose Insert.

6. With the clip art image selected on your slide, choose Format, Picture. Click the Picture tab and choose Recolor.

7. Change the red ribbon to blue (or change another item on your clip art image).

8. Close the Recolor Picture and Format Picture dialog boxes.

9. View your changes and close the presentation without saving it.

Applying Designs and Customizing Color Schemes

You need to create a presentation to convince management to buy new software. In order to do this, you use a predesigned presentation; then apply different templates and color schemes to it.

To apply a design and customize a color scheme, follow these steps:

1. Choose File, New to create a new presentation.

2. In the New Presentation dialog box, click the Presentations tab. Select the Selling Your Ideas—Dale Carnegie Training® presentation and click OK.

3. Choose Format, Apply Design to display the Apply Design dialog box. Preview each of the design templates PowerPoint provides.

4. Apply the Fans template to the entire presentation.

5. Choose Format, Slide Color Scheme to display the Color Scheme dialog box.

6. Choose the third color scheme in the third row; then choose Apply to All.

7. Close the presentation without saving it.

Creating Custom Backgrounds

You have a few minutes before leaving work and decide to experiment with PowerPoint. To become more familiar with applying custom backgrounds, you create a new presentation, and then apply various backgrounds to it.

To create custom backgrounds, follow these steps:

1. Create a new, blank presentation in PowerPoint. Choose the Title Slide AutoLayout in the New Slide dialog box.

2. Enter your name in the title placeholder; then enter your company's name in the subtitle placeholder.

3. Choose Format, Background to display the Background dialog box. Click the drop-down list arrow in the dialog box and choose Fill Effects.

4. Apply at least three different gradient fills to your slide. Then apply at least three different textured fills to your slide.

5. Close your presentation without saving it.

Challenge

The following challenges, found in the Project–05 folder on the CD, enable you to use your problem-solving skills. Take time to work through these exercises now.

Working with Design Templates

As president of the Biking Club you are preparing for an upcoming meeting. In order to find the best template for your presentation, you preview several before choosing one.

To work with design templates, follow these steps:

1. Open Proj0508 and save it as Revised Biking Club Presentation.

2. Preview the presentation with each of the design templates listed in the Apply Design dialog box.

3. Apply the High Voltage template to the presentation.

4. View the presentation as a slide show.

5. Save the presentation; then close it.

Modifying a Slide Master

To make the elements appear more uniform on your biking club presentation, you decide to change the Slide Master.

To modify a slide master, follow these steps:

1. Open Proj0509 and save it as Slide Master Changes.

2. Display the Slide Master.

3. Make the Master Title Style italic.

4. Add the current date in the Date Area.

5. Add the text May Meeting in the Footer Area.

6. Display the presentation in Slide view; then scroll through your presentation to see the changes.

7. Save the presentation; then close it.

Adding and Recoloring Clip Art

To spice up your presentation to the biking club, you add some clip art. Then, for added interest, you recolor it.

To add and recolor clip art, follow these steps:

1. Open Proj0510 and save it as `Adding Clip Art`.

2. Display Slide 1 in Slide view; then open the Clip Gallery.

3. In the Sports & Leisure category, choose the bicyclist clip art.

4. Move and resize the clip art picture so that it displays in the lower right corner of the slide.

5. Right-click the picture; then choose Format Picture.

6. In the Format Picture dialog box, click the Picture tab and choose Recolor.

7. Change the color of the clip art to dark maroon.

8. Display your presentation as an electronic slide show to see your changes.

9. Save your presentation; then close it.

Adding Clip Art, Recolor, Edit, Rotate, and Fill Objects

As part of your biking club presentation, you need to provide directions to the club activity. You decide to use PowerPoint's drawing tools and clip art to do so.

To add clip art, recolor, edit, rotate, and fill objects, follow these steps:

1. Open Proj0511 and save it as `Ride and Picnic`.

2. Using PowerPoint's drawing tools, clip art, and the following diagram as a guide, create a flyer for the upcoming club activity. (Hint: Use the Text Box tool to create the text.)

3. Print a copy of the slide.

4. Save the presentation; then close it.

Customizing Color Schemes

You arrive at the biking club meeting to give your presentation when you discover that the presentation's template and color scheme doesn't display properly using the LCD projector and overhead. Rather than panicking, you decide to quickly change to another color scheme so that the contrast onscreen is more marked.

To customize a color scheme, follow these steps:

1. Open Proj0512 and save it as `Color Scheme Changes`.

2. Displays the presentation using each of the color schemes available.

3. Apply the second color scheme on the first row of the Color Scheme dialog box to the entire presentation.

4. View the presentation as an electronic slide show.

5. Save the presentation; then close it.

Saving a Custom Template

Your boss has charged you with the task of creating and saving a custom template for your company. This template will then be used company-wide for all new presentations. To create the template, you draw on your knowledge of many PowerPoint features, including revising the Slide Master, changing slide background, and formatting text.

To save a custom template, follow these steps:

1. Create a blank, new slide in PowerPoint.

2. Modify the Slide Master to include your company's name in the Footer Area. Insert the current date in the Date Area. Format your company's name and the date using bold and italic.

3. Add a custom slide background to the slide. Choose a gradient fill or textured fill.

4. Save the presentation as a template with the name `Company Standard`.

5. Close the presentation.

6. Create a new presentation based on the Company Standard template. Enter information about your company (or school) in each slide you add to the presentation. When you're finished, close the presentation without saving it.

PinPoint Assessment

You have completed the project and the associated lessons, as well as the "Checking Your Skills" and "Applying Your Skills" sections. Now use the PinPoint software Evaluation mode to assess your comprehension of the specific exam tasks you have just learned. You can also use the PinPoint Trainer mode and the SHOW ME tutorials to practice these specific exam tasks.

Project 6 · Six

Using Speaker Notes and Handouts

Documenting and Distributing Slides

In this project you will learn the following objectives and their associated Microsoft Exam required activities.

Objectives	Required Activities
➤ Create Speaker Notes … … … … … … … … … … …	Add Speaker Notes
➤ View Speaker Notes	
➤ Use the Notes Master	
➤ Print Speaker Notes and Handouts … … … … … …	Print Slides in a Variety of Formats

Why Would I Do This?

Speaker notes and handouts are two beneficial features in PowerPoint. You use **speaker notes** to document your slides so that you have a ready reference when you give your presentation. You use handouts to print slides for your audience.

You can create speaker notes by using Notes Page view, and then use these notes to help you remember what you want to say when you're in front of an audience. For example, you might include supporting data, experiences, quotations, or anecdotes in your notes. Even though you can view your key points in Outline view, using speaker notes is more useful because they can hold as much text as you can fit on a page. In short, speaker notes help you make your presentation sound as polished as your slides look.

PowerPoint automatically provides a notes area for each presentation slide. You can view this area by using Notes Page view, and then add and revise text. Alternatively, you can add, revise, and view notes in a separate Speaker Notes window.

You can also customize the appearance of your notes pages by using the **Notes Master**. You can add a header, footer, and date text so that it is displayed on all notes pages. You can also resize the slide image or notes box on the Notes Master.

After you have finished the speaker notes and revised the Notes Master, you can print speaker notes. To help your audience follow and remember key points, you can print handouts—with two, three, or six slides to a page. Printed handouts differ from speaker notes in that handouts typically include only the slide content, but printed speaker notes include all the text you entered.

In this project, you learn how to create, revise, and print speaker notes. You learn also how to use the Notes Master to customize their appearance. Finally, you print notes and handouts.

Jargon Watch

Speaker notes are just notes that you create in PowerPoint to help you document and give your presentation. Speaker notes are created on special pages called notes pages. Each presentation slide has an associated notes page that you can view by choosing <u>V</u>iew, <u>N</u>otes Page or clicking the Notes Page View button.

You can also view your speaker notes in a special Speaker Notes window, which remains open as you move from slide to slide.

The way your notes are displayed and printed is determined by the **Notes Master**. The Notes Master contains elements, such as header, date, and footer areas, that are uniform for each note page. You can revise the Notes Master to change the items and control formatting for all pages.

Lesson 1: Creating Speaker Notes

You can prepare speaker notes as you prepare your presentation, or you can add them later. Additionally, you can use Notes Page view to add your notes, or you can create them "on-the-fly" in any view by using the Speaker Notes window. Try using both methods of preparing notes now.

To Create Speaker Notes

❶ Start PowerPoint, if necessary, and select <u>O</u>pen an existing presentation from the PowerPoint startup dialog box. If PowerPoint is already running, choose <u>F</u>ile, <u>N</u>ew.

❷ Open Proj0601 from the Project-06 folder on the CD, and save it as Safety Report.

You can easily add notes to a page by switching to Notes Page view. This view provides a miniature of the current slide and an area for your notes.

❸ Make sure Slide 1, Safety Report**, is displayed; then click the Notes Page View button.**

Alternatively, you can choose <u>V</u>iew, <u>N</u>otes Page. The current slide is shown in Notes Page view (see Figure 6.1). This view contains a small-scale version of the slide (the slide image) as well as an area where you can enter your notes—the notes box.

Figure 6.1
Use Notes Page view to
add notes.

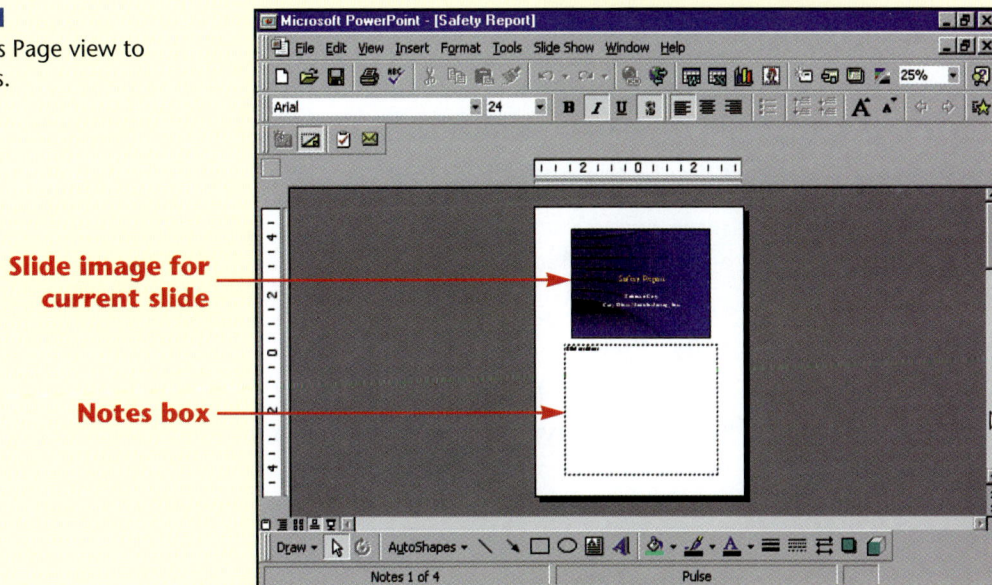

Slide image for
current slide

Notes box

To see the notes box better and to enter text, you can enlarge the view by using the Zoom button.

❹ Click the Zoom button's drop-down arrow and choose 75%.

42%

The view is enlarged so that you can enter your notes (see Figure 6.2). Because monitor displays may vary a little from one computer to the next, don't be concerned if your screen looks slightly different from that shown in Figure 6.2.

continues

To Create Speaker Notes   (continued)

Figure 6.2
You usually need to enlarge the view to enter notes.

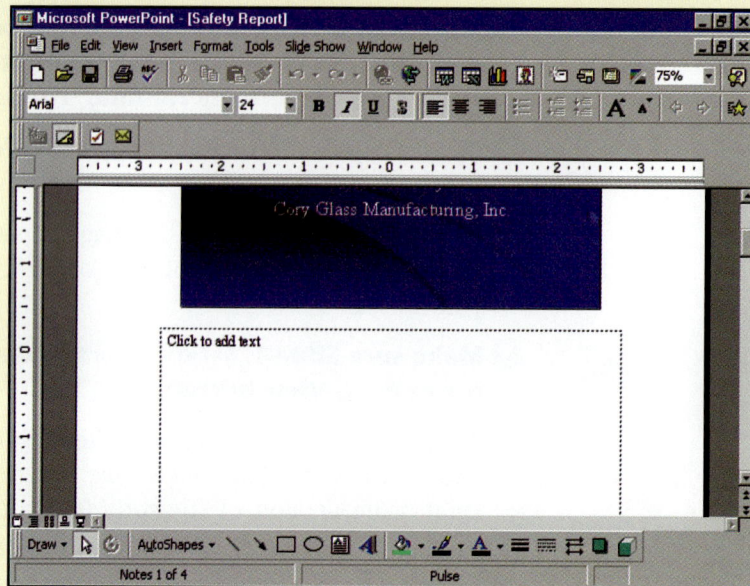

Now type some speaker notes. Remember that these notes are usually used as reminders for yourself—to keep you on track and to make sure you don't forget any critical information during a presentation.

⑤ Click in the notes box and type the following:

```
(Make sure to play Bach's Brandenburg Concerto #5 as people
arrive, then fade it out.)

"Welcome! I'm glad to be presenting this safety report to you
today. Here at Cory Glass Manufacturing we have some good news
about our safety record, as well as some challenges ahead."
```

The text you type is entered in the notes box and becomes part of the slide. Even when you switch to another view, the notes are still attached to the slide. Later in this project, you learn how to print these notes.

Another method of entering notes is to use the Speaker Notes window, which you can access from any view except Notes Page view. The Speaker Notes window remains open as you move from slide to slide so that you can easily document your entire presentation. Try using the Speaker Notes window now.

⑥ Click the Slide Sorter View button and select Slide 2, `Overall Status of Safety Campaign`.

This is the slide to which you want to add notes.

⑦ Choose View, Speaker Notes.

The Speaker Notes window is displayed for Slide 2 (see Figure 6.3). You can enter and revise text in this window just as you did in Notes Page view.

Figure 6.3
You can enter notes in the special Speaker Notes window.

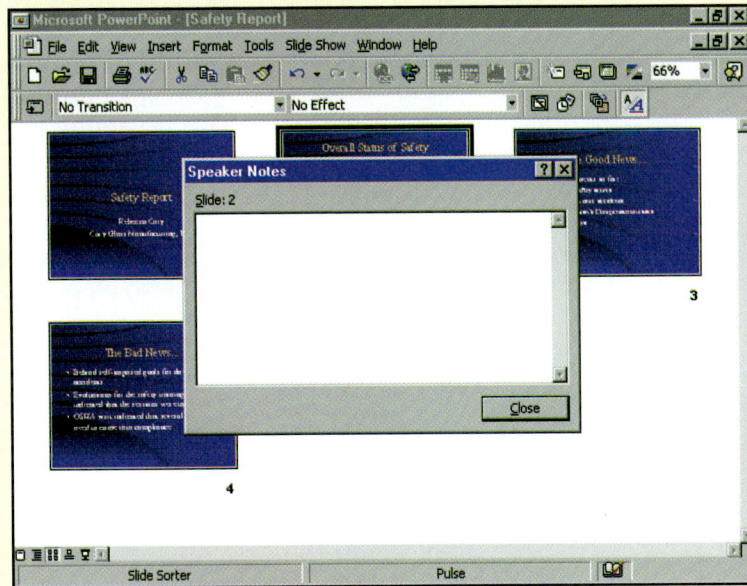

8 **Enter the following text in the Speaker Notes window:**

Safety Awareness Training: The 1-hour mandatory program was completed by all 275 employees during the last two months.

Safety Consultant: Used Safety Engineers, Inc. from Columbus, Ohio to work closely with employees and managers. The new workstations were designed with input from the employees, and surpass OSHA, state, and local regulations.

Safety Competition: We want to thank Lauren Clark for this idea! The competition is 2 months long, and measures safety criteria (lost time accidents, sick days, etc.) for the 3 teams. Each member of the winning team will receive an extra 1% salary bonus. The competition is still going on, and will finish at the end of the month.

9 **Choose Close in the Speaker Notes window.**

The notes you entered are now part of Slide 2. Keep the presentation open and keep PowerPoint running for the next lesson, in which you display the notes in different PowerPoint views.

Inside Stuff

You can leave the Speaker Notes window open as you move from slide to slide. This helps you quickly view your supporting material and notes. If there aren't any notes for a slide, a blank Speaker Notes window is displayed for that slide.

Also keep in mind that because Speaker Notes are attached to a slide, deleting the slide deletes the notes as well!

Lesson 2: Viewing Speaker Notes

With PowerPoint 97, you can use the Speaker Notes window to display a slide's notes in any view except Notes Page view—Slide, Slide Sorter, Outline, and Slide Show. This capability is handy when you want to check or revise notes for a presentation and don't want to switch to Notes Page view. Try displaying the Speaker Notes window in different views now.

To View Speaker Notes

1 In the open presentation, choose View, Outline to display Slide 2, Overall Status of Safety Campaign, **in Outline view.**

2 Choose View, Speaker Notes to open the Speaker Notes window for the slide.

The text you entered in the preceding lesson is displayed in the Speaker Notes window (see Figure 6.4). The content of your speaker notes remains the same whether you view the notes in Notes Page view or in the Speaker Notes window.

Figure 6.4
You can view your speaker notes in Outline view.

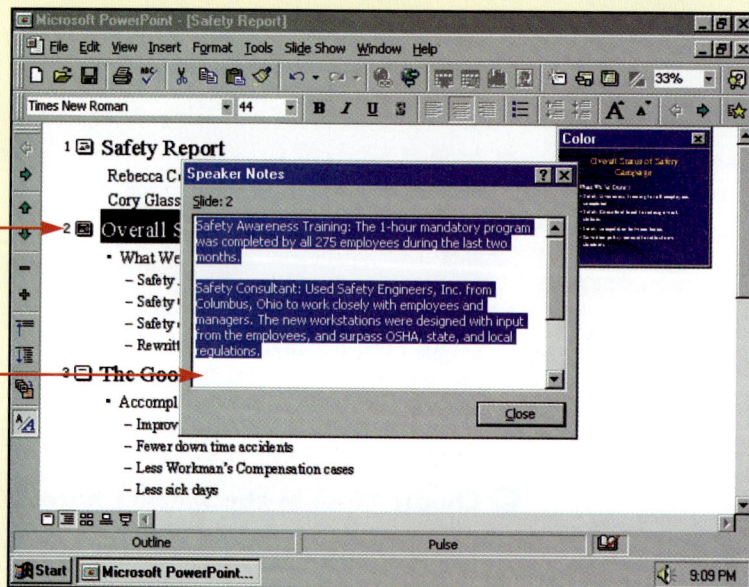

Selected slide in Outline view

Speaker Notes window

Now view the notes in Slide view.

3 With the Speaker Notes window still open, click the Slide View button.

Slide 2 is displayed in Slide view, with the Speaker Notes window displayed also. Drag the Speaker Notes window title bar to see more of the slide.

As you move between slides, the Speaker Notes window remains open. This enables you to scan your notes easily for an entire presentation. Experiment with this feature now.

4 **Press** PgUp **to move to Slide 1,** `Safety Report`.

The Speaker Notes window remains open and displays the notes for Slide 1. Now try viewing notes in Slide Sorter view.

If you have problems...

If you drag the Speaker Notes window, you must click the slide to reactivate it before pressing PgUp.

5 **Click the Slide Sorter View button.**

The presentation is displayed in Slide Sorter view. The Speaker Notes window remains open and continues to display notes for Slide 1 because it is selected. If the Speaker Notes window is open when you begin a slide show, the window remains open as you view presentation slides.

You can also view speaker notes in an electronic slide show. It's often handy to view your notes while running a slide show because you can see more of the slide's contents while preparing the notes. You normally use this feature when getting ready for a presentation—not when actually giving it.

You can also open the Speaker Notes window in a running slide show by right-clicking your mouse and then choosing Speaker Notes from the shortcut menu. Try viewing speaker notes in an electronic slide show now.

6 **With the Speaker Notes window still open, click the Slide Show button.**

The electronic slide show begins, and the Speaker Notes window is displayed for Slide 1 (see Figure 6.5). You can move the Speaker Notes window to see a slide's contents better by dragging the title bar.

Figure 6.5
You can use the Speaker Notes window—even when running a slide show.

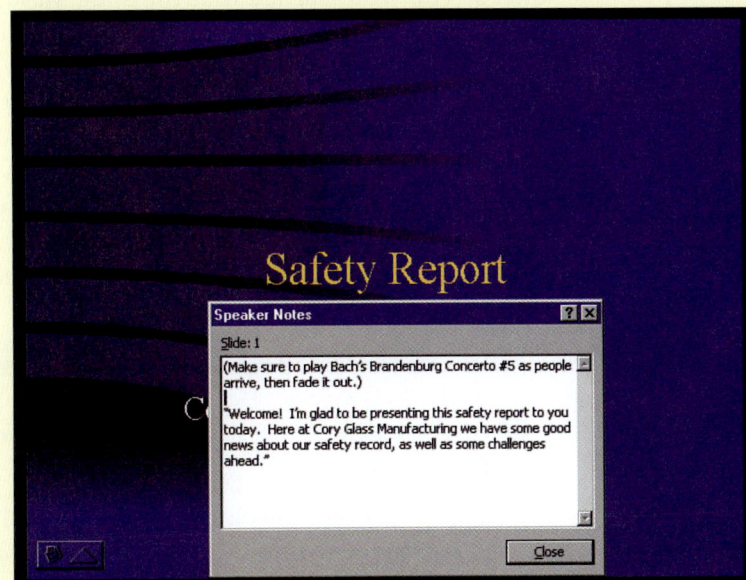

Safety Report

Speaker Notes

Slide: 1

(Make sure to play Bach's Brandenburg Concerto #5 as people arrive, then fade it out.)

"Welcome! I'm glad to be presenting this safety report to you today. Here at Cory Glass Manufacturing we have some good news about our safety record, as well as some challenges ahead."

Close

continues

To View Speaker Notes   (continued)

7 Double-click the slide (not the Speaker Notes window).

The slide show advances to Slide 2, and the Speaker Notes window remains open, showing the notes for Slide 2.

8 Click Close to close the Speaker Notes window.

Now try opening the Speaker Notes window again. The easiest way to display the Speaker Notes window in Slide Show view is to choose Speaker Notes from the shortcut menu.

9 Right-click anywhere on the slide and choose Speaker Notes from the shortcut menu.

The Speaker Notes window is again displayed so that you can view or revise notes.

10 Close the Speaker Notes window and press Esc.

This ends the slide show and returns you to Slide Sorter view.

Keep the Safety Report presentation open for the next lesson, in which you use the Notes Master.

Inside Stuff

You can format your notes text—with bold, italic, fonts, and so on. Formatting notes helps you more easily follow them when you're in front of a group and emphasizes key information. However, to format notes text you must use the notes area in Notes Page view. You cannot format text in the Speaker Notes window.

Lesson 3: Using the Notes Master

In Project 5, you learned that the Slide Master determines the elements displayed on a slide. In a similar way, the Notes Master controls the components, formatting, and layout for your notes. You can add or revise headers, footers, or date text in the Notes Master so that they are changed for all notes pages. For example, you can add your name, department, date, company logo, or page number to the Notes Master. You can also resize or move the slide image or notes box to suit your needs. The revisions you make to the Notes Master are displayed when you switch to Notes Page view or print the notes. Try working with the Notes Master now.

To Use the Notes Master

1 In the open Safety Report presentation, display Slide 1 in Notes Page view.

You can access the Notes Master from Slide, Slide Sorter, Outline, or Notes Page view. Notice that the notes page is still displayed with the previous Zoom percentage. To see the Notes Master better, change the Zoom to fit the entire page onscreen.

42% ▼

2 **Click the Zoom button's drop-down arrow and choose Fit; then choose View, Master, Notes Master.**

The Notes Master is displayed (see Figure 6.6). By default, the Notes Master includes placeholders for headers, footers, page number, and date/time. You can enter information in these placeholders so that it is displayed on every note page. You can also resize or format each area.

In addition, areas are displayed for the slide image and notes box (sometimes called the Notes Body Area). Later in this tutorial, you learn how to resize the slide image to create more room for your notes.

Figure 6.6
You can revise note items with the Notes Master.

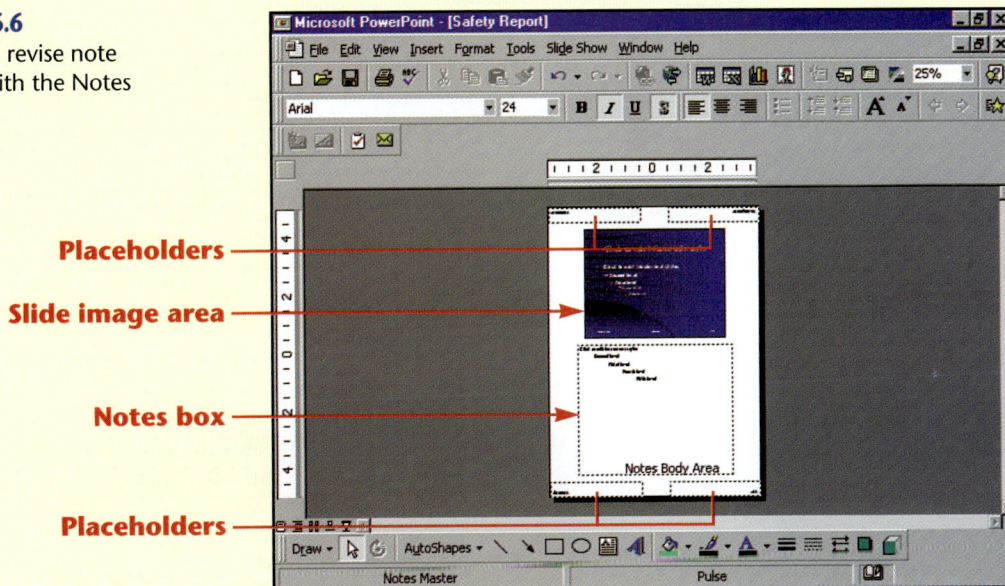

Placeholders

Slide image area

Notes box

Placeholders

If you have problems... ◄

If your Notes Master doesn't display the placeholders shown in Figure 6.6, choose Format, Notes Master Layout. In the Notes Master Layout dialog box, click the check boxes for all the placeholders listed and then choose OK.

42% ▼

3 **Use the Zoom button to enlarge the view to 75%; then scroll to the bottom of the Notes Master.**

You enlarge the view to see more clearly and to work with the placeholders.

4 **Click in the footer placeholder to select it and then drag over <footer>. Type** `Prepared by Eugene Stegall` **(see Figure 6.7).**

continues

To Use the Notes Master   (continued)

Figure 6.7
You can add a footer to
your notes.

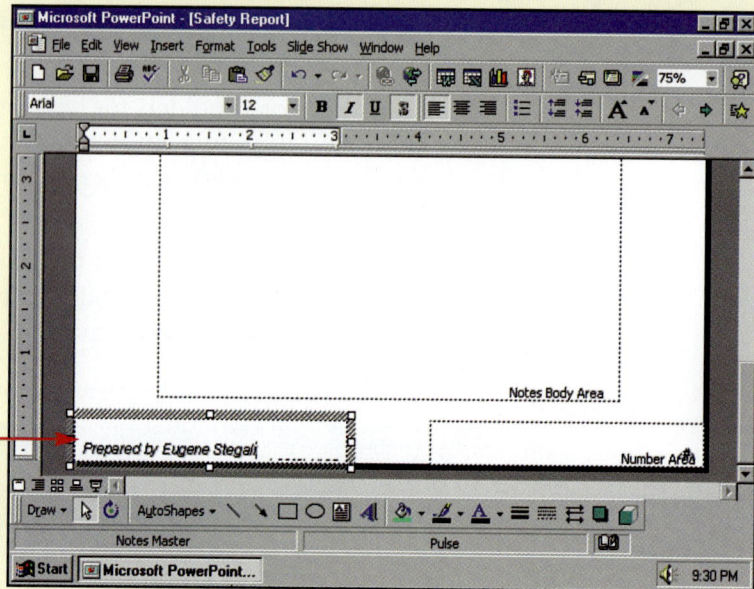

Select the footer placeholder and type the text you want

The footer text that you type is automatically added to each notes page. You can also format text in the Notes Master to change the text's appearance for all notes pages.

B

5 Drag over the text you typed (Prepared by Eugene Stegall**) and click the Bold button.**

The selected text is formatted in bold. Italic and shadow are already in effect because of the template used for this presentation. Now try adding a date in the date placeholder.

6 Scroll up to the upper-right corner of the Notes Master and drag over the date/time placeholder to select it; then type February 7, 1998 **(see Figure 6.8).**

Figure 6.8
You can enter a date
here so that it appears
on each notes page.

Select the date placeholder and type a new date

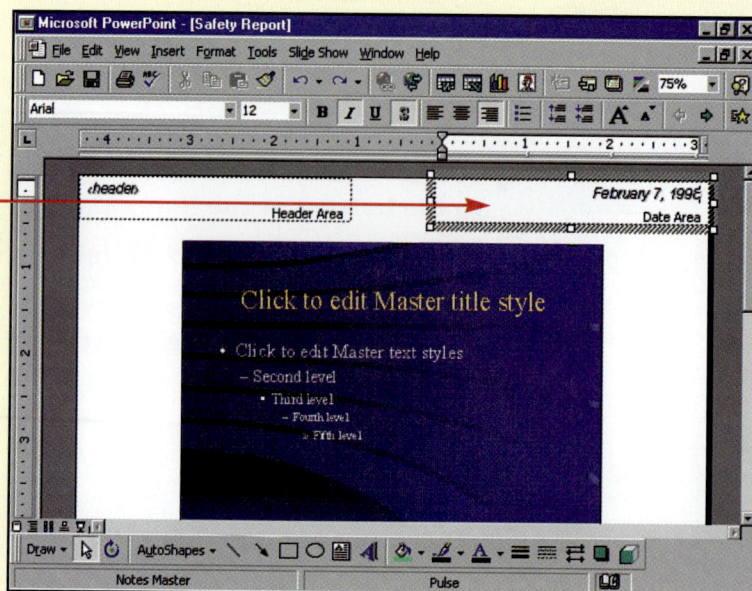

Because you have added the date to the Notes Master, and not to an individual slide, the date is added to each notes page.

You can also resize the slide image in the Notes Master. This is handy when you want more room for the notes themselves. You resize the slide image in the same way you resize other objects—by clicking to select the slide image and then using the resizing arrow to drag a handle.

To work effectively with the slide image, you need to change the view.

7 Choose View, Zoom to display the Zoom dialog box, choose Fit, and click OK.

The entire Notes Master is displayed onscreen. Now try resizing the slide image.

8 Click the slide image to select it; then place the mouse pointer on the selection handle in the upper-right corner.

A two-sided resizing arrow is displayed. You use this arrow to resize the slide image (see Figure 6.9).

Figure 6.9
You can resize the slide image.

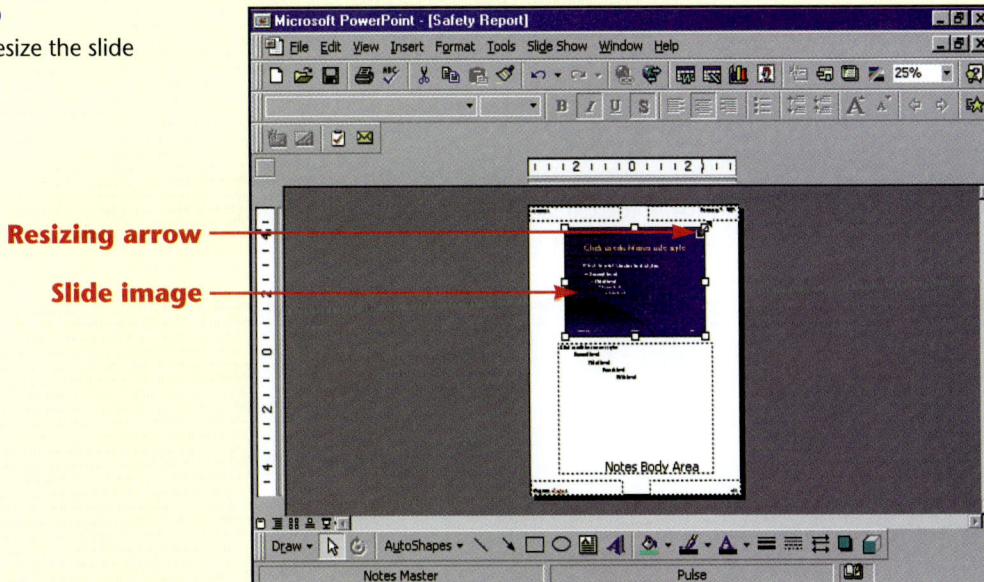

9 Drag toward the middle of the slide image until it is approximately half the original size; then release the mouse button.

The slide image is resized. If necessary, you can also move the slide by dragging it.

10 Drag the selected slide image so that it is displayed in the center of the available space (see Figure 6.10).

continues

To Use the Notes Master   (continued)

Figure 6.10
Move the slide image to center it.

New location

Four-sided arrow

Original location

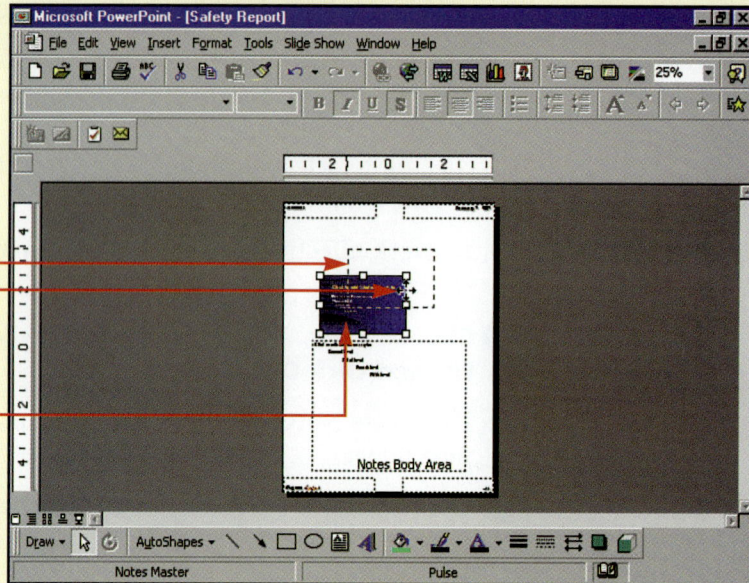

The slide image is moved. You can also select and then resize or move the notes box area. The Header Area, Date Area, Footer Area, and Number Area placeholders can also be sized or moved. For now, you switch back to Notes Page view to see your changes.

⑪ Choose View, Notes Page.

The presentation is displayed in Notes Page view. Notice that the footer and date text is changed and that the slide image is resized (see Figure 6.11).

Figure 6.11
The changes you made to the Notes Master are displayed in Notes Page view.

New date

Resized slide image

New footer

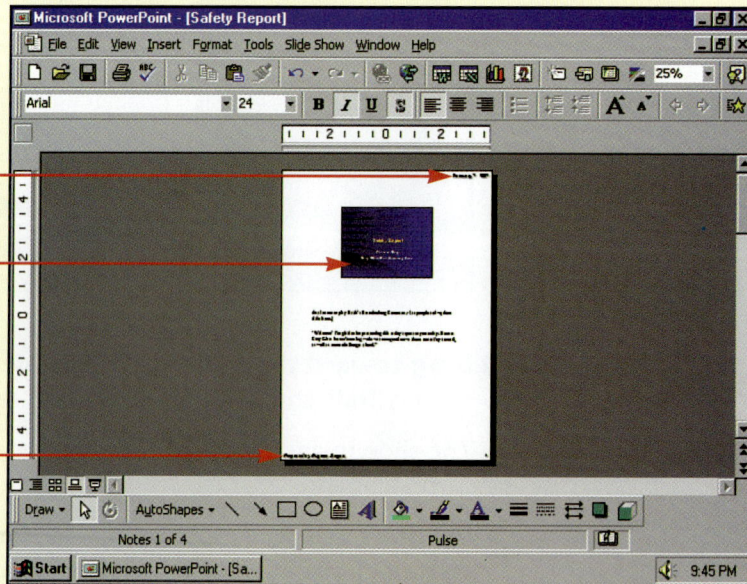

To confirm that each slide is affected by the changes you made, you can scroll through your presentation.

⓬ Press ⌨PgDn⌨ **several times to move through your presentation.**

Each slide is displayed in Notes Page view, with the changes you made to the Notes Master. Notice that PowerPoint also automatically adds page numbers to your notes pages.

⓭ Save the presentation.

Leave the presentation open for the next lesson, in which you print speaker notes and handouts.

Exam Notes

A quick way to add text to the Date, Header, Footer, and Number area is to open the Header and Footer dialog box (see Figure 6.12). Choose View, Header and Footer. Click the Notes and Handouts tab on the dialog box. Select the items you want included on your notes pages and handouts—Date and time, Header, Page number, Footer.

Figure 6.12
You use the Header and Footer dialog box to quickly enter text in all the placeholders.

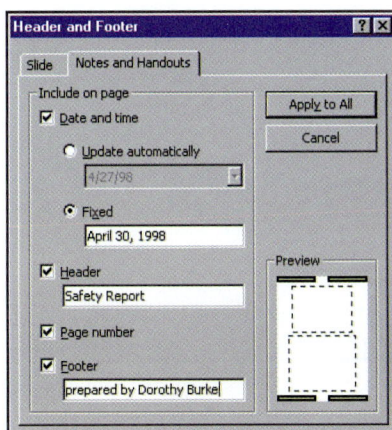

If you chose to add the date, select the Update automatically option to have PowerPoint use the current date and then choose a date format from the drop-down list. Otherwise, select Fixed and then type a date in the text box.

Type the text for the header or footer in the text boxes below the option. The page number is the slide number automatically generated by PowerPoint. Choose Apply to All to close the dialog box.

Lesson 4: Printing Speaker Notes and Handouts

After you create speaker notes, you can print them so that you have a ready reference during your presentation. Printing your notes is straightforward and relatively easy. To print your notes, choose File, Print and then choose Notes Pages in the Print what area of the Print dialog box.

You can also print handouts for your audience. By default, PowerPoint includes options to print two, three, or six slides per page as handouts. In contrast to the notes page, handouts include only the slides contents, and not the accompanying notes. You print handouts in the same way you print notes—by specifying the type of handouts you want in the Print what area of the Print dialog box.

Try printing speaker notes and handouts for your presentation now.

To Print Speaker Notes and Handouts

❶ In the open Safety Report **presentation, move to Slide 2,** Overall Status of Safety Campaign.

Slide 2 is displayed in Notes Page view because that is the view you most recently used. However, you can print notes from any view.

❷ Choose File, Print.

The Print dialog box is displayed (see Figure 6.13). You used this dialog box in Project 2 to print slides and outlines. In this lesson, you use it to print notes.

Figure 6.13
The Print dialog box provides ready access to printing options.

Choose which slides to print in this area

Click here to print in black and white

Click this arrow to choose Notes Pages or Handouts

Click here to add frames

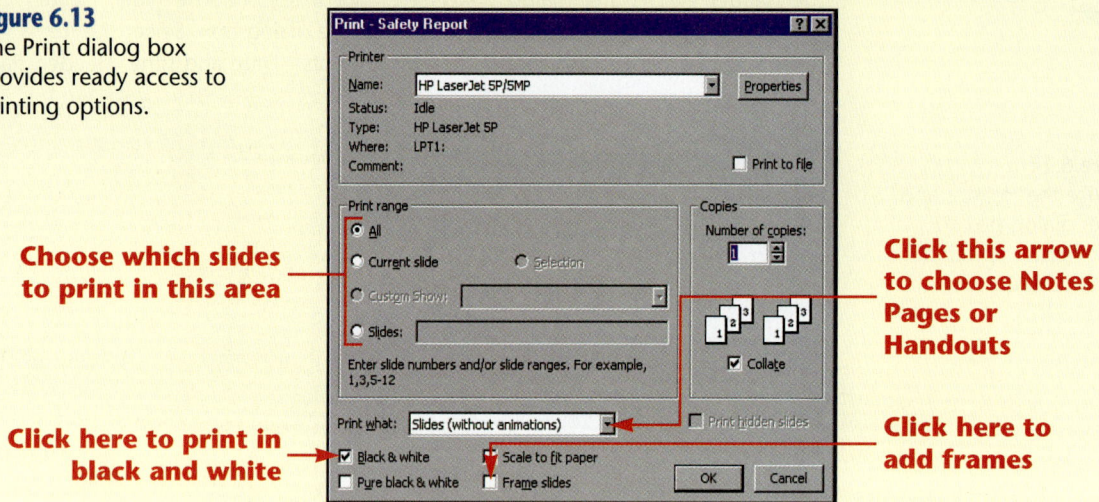

❸ Click the Print what drop-down list arrow and choose Notes Pages **from the list.**

This specifies to PowerPoint that you want to print the notes associated with the current presentation.

The notes generally print with a better appearance if you frame the slide image, notes box, and page. You add frames by checking the Frame slides box.

❹ Make sure the Frame slides box is checked.

You can print the current slide, print all presentation slides, or pick and choose those you want. You specify which slides PowerPoint should print in the Print range area of the dialog box.

❺ In the Print range area, choose the Current slide option button.

After selecting the options you want, you're ready to print.

❻ Make sure your printer is turned on, and then choose OK.

The Notes Page prints for your current slide. Now try printing handouts.

PowerPoint

7 **Choose File, Print to display the Print dialog box again.**

You use the Print what area of the dialog box to specify how PowerPoint should print your presentation.

8 **Click the Print what drop-down list arrow and choose** Handouts (6 slides per page) **from the list.**

Because the handouts print miniatures of each slide, it's a good idea to frame them so they look better.

9 **Make sure that the Frame slides box is still checked and that the Print Range is set to All.**

10 **Choose OK.**

PowerPoint prints your presentation as audience handouts.

11 **Save the** Safety Report **presentation and then close it.**

If you have finished your work session, exit PowerPoint and shut down Windows before turning off your computer. Otherwise, complete the "Checking Your Skills" and "Applying Your Skills" exercises at the end of this project.

Inside Stuff

You can modify the Handout Master, which controls how handouts print, in much the same way you modified the Notes Master. To view the Handout Master, choose View, Master, Handout Master. You can insert and format text just as you did in the Notes Master. However, you can't resize or move the slide images. When you're finished making revisions, choose View, Slide.

Project Summary

To	Do This
View a slide in Notes Page view	Choose View, Notes Page.
Create a note	Display a slide in Notes Page view and then enter text in the notes box area.
	Choose View, Speaker Notes.
View speaker notes in a slide show	Choose Speaker Notes from the slide show's shortcut menu.
View the Notes Master	Choose View, Master, Notes Master.
Add placeholders to the Notes Master	Display the Notes Master and choose Format, Notes Master Layout.
Resize placeholders or slide image	Select the placeholder or slide image and then use the resizing arrow.
Move placeholders or slide image	Drag a selected placeholder or slide image.
Print notes pages	Choose Notes Pages in the Print what area of the Print dialog box.

continues

To	Do This
Print handouts	Choose Handouts in the Print <u>w</u>hat area of the Print dialog box.
View the Handout Master	Choose <u>V</u>iew, <u>M</u>aster, Han<u>d</u>out Master.

Checking Your Skills

True/False

For each of the following, check *T* or *F* to indicate whether the statement is true or false.

__T __F **1.** You can change the elements that are displayed on every notes page by using the Notes Master.

__T __F **2.** To print handouts, switch to Handout view and choose <u>F</u>ile, Print <u>H</u>andouts.

__T __F **3.** You can add speaker notes in any view—Slide, Slide Sorter, Notes Page, Outline, or Slide Show.

__T __F **4.** You cannot format text in the Speaker Notes window—you must use Notes Page view.

__T __F **5.** You prepare speaker notes by using Speaker Notes view.

__T __F **6.** The Slide Master and the Notes Master are the same.

__T __F **7.** Speaker notes are mainly used for printing and handing out to your audience.

__T __F **8.** Printed speaker notes contain only a slide's contents.

__T __F **9.** You can modify the way handouts print by changing the Handout Master.

__T __F **10.** Printed speaker notes and a printed outline include exactly the same information.

Multiple Choice

Circle the letter of the correct answer for each of the following questions.

1. Which of the following is true regarding Speaker Notes?

a. They provide supporting data or documentation during a presentation.

b. They help you keep on track during a presentation.

c. They help you remember quotations or anecdotes.

d. All of the above.

2. When you type footer information (such as your company's name) in the Notes Master, which of the following results?

a. The footer information is displayed at the bottom of each slide when you run the electronic slide show.

b. The footer information appears at the bottom of each notes page you print.

c. The footer information is displayed at the bottom of each slide shown in Slide Sorter view.

d. None of the above.

3. Which of the following is true regarding the Speaker Notes window?

    a. It automatically closes when you advance to the next presentation slide in a slide show.

    b. It remains open until you close it or switch to Notes Page view.

    c. It can be displayed only in Slide view.

    d. It can be displayed only in Notes Page view.

4. Using the Notes Master, you can change which of the following?

    a. the footer area text for your notes

    b. text formatting for your notes

    c. the slide image's size

    d. all of the above

5. You can print handouts using which of the following layouts?

    a. 2, 3, or 6 slides per page

    b. 2, 4, or 8 slides per page

    c. 3, 4, or 8 slides per page

    d. none of the above

6. You can resize the notes box for all presentation slides by using which of the following?

    a. Handout Master

    b. Speaker Notes window

    c. Notes Master

    d. Title Master

7. You can use the Speaker Notes window to do which of the following?

    a. Add notes in Notes Page view.

    b. Format your speaker notes.

    c. Add notes in Slide view.

    d. All of the above.

8. The Footer, Header, and Date areas are all examples of which of the following on a Notes Master?

    a. placeholders

    b. views

    c. notes

    d. revision areas

9. Which of the following are two ways to view and add speaker notes?

    a. Notes Page view and the Handout Master

    b. Speaker Notes view and Notes Page view

    c. Handout view and Notes Page window

    d. Speaker Notes window and Notes Page view

10. Using PowerPoint, you can print which of the following?

    a. speaker notes

    b. handouts

    c. slides

    d. all of the above

Completion

In the blank provided, write the correct answer for each of the following statements.

1. The Notes Master contains footer and header _____ that you can use to enter text.

2. You use the _____ to change elements for every notes page in your presentation.

3. You can view speaker notes by choosing _____.

4. The _____ view displays a miniature slide as well as a box in which you can enter notes.

5. Information that you want to display at the bottom of each notes page is placed in the _____ area.

6. You can print audience _____ to distribute at a meeting.

7. You choose to print speaker notes in the _____ area of the Print dialog box.

8. Notes you use to document your presentation are called _____ notes.

9. You can format speaker notes using the _____ view.

10. You can choose to _____ slides so that each slide on a handout prints with a border around it.

Matching

In the blank next to each of the following terms or phrases, write the letter of the corresponding term or phrase. (Note that some letters may be used more than once.)

a. slide image

b. handouts

c. Zoom

d. placeholder

e. Notes Page view

f. Notes Master

g. notes box

h. speaker notes

i. Print dialog box

j. Speaker Notes window

_____ **1.** Controls formatting and elements of your printed notes

_____ **2.** Notes that help you document a presentation

_____ **3.** The PowerPoint view to use when you want to format speaker notes

_____ **4.** A miniature slide on the Notes Master

_____ **5.** What you can use to add notes when working in Slide view

_____ **6.** Slide miniatures you print for an audience

_____ **7.** A way to enlarge the view so you can more easily enter notes

_____ **8.** An area to enter notes in Notes Page view

_____ **9.** An area on the Notes Master you use to change the header or footer

_____ **10.** Where you choose to print handouts or speaker notes

Applying Your Skills

Practice

The following exercises, found in the Project–06 folder on the CD, enable you to practice the skills you have learned in this project. Take a few minutes to work through these exercises now.

Adding Speaker Notes

You're in charge of converting your company's network from Windows 3.1 to Windows 95. To present your progress to management at an upcoming meeting, you prepare speaker notes.

To add speaker notes, follow these steps:

1. Open Proj0602 and save it as `Migrating to Windows 95`.

2. Move to Slide 3, `Progress`, and click the Notes Page View button.

3. Enlarge the view to 75% and scroll down so that you can see the notes box.

4. Enter the following text in the notes box:

   `Workstation conversion from Windows 3.1 to Windows 95 began on time in early January. Independent contractors have been hired to help in the conversion.`

   `The original plan was to have trainers work with each employee within 2 weeks after the employee's workstation was converted. At this point, 68% have received the training within two weeks, while the remaining 32% have been trained within 3 weeks.`

5. Move to Slide 5, `Cost`, and type the following text in the notes box:

   `Make sure to emphasize that no additional cost overruns are anticipated.`

6. Save your presentation and close it.

Adding Speaker Notes

You're in charge of conducting new employee orientation at your company. To prepare for the meeting, you use the Speaker Notes window to add notes to your presentation.

To add speaker notes, follow these steps:

1. Open Proj0603 and save it as `Orientation Meeting`.

2. In the Speaker Notes window, add the following note to the Speaker Notes window of Slide 1:

   `Make sure to welcome them enthusiastically and make them feel part of the team.`

3. Add the following speaker note to Slide 3, `History of Company`:

   `Company was founded in 1990 to provide ergonomic computer equipment.`

   `Company has grown at a rate of 10% (average) per year.`

   `With increased interest in ergonomic workstation design, we antici-`
   `pate continued growth.`

   `Our motto: "To make working at a computer as comfortable as it is`
   `productive."`

4. Close the Speaker Notes window and move to Slide 1.

5. Start the electronic slide show.

6. Right-click the displayed slide and choose Speaker Notes from the shortcut menu.

7. Left-click the slide to advance the slide show and view notes in the Speaker Notes window.

8. Close the Speaker Notes window and press Esc to end the slide show.

9. Save the presentation and close it.

Modifying the Notes Master

You're preparing a presentation for an upcoming business meeting. Because you have many notes to add to each slide, you decide to use the Notes Master to resize the slide image and notes box to better accommodate the lengthy notes.

To modify the Notes Master, follow these steps:

1. Open Proj0604 and save it as `Working with the Notes Master`.

2. Display the Notes Master.

3. If necessary, choose Format, Notes Master Layout and check all place-holder boxes in the Notes Master Layout dialog box; then click OK.

4. Resize the slide image to approximately half its original size.

5. Center the slide image horizontally and move it to the top of the master.

6. Click the notes box and resize it to take advantage of the available space.

7. Scroll through your presentation in Notes Page view to see your changes.

8. Save your presentation and close it.

Printing Notes and Handouts

As head of the Management Information System Department, you're in charge of upgrading your company's computers to Windows 95. As a final step before presenting your progress report to management, you print your speaker notes and audience handouts.

To print notes and handouts, follow these steps:

1. Open Proj0605 and save it as `Printing Notes`; then display Slide 4, `Schedule`.

2. Display the Print dialog box.

3. In the Print <u>w</u>hat area of the dialog box, click the drop-down list arrow and choose Notes Pages.

4. In the Print range area, choose Curr<u>e</u>nt slide.

5. Click the check boxes for <u>B</u>lack & white and Fra<u>m</u>e slides; then choose OK to print your notes.

6. Display the Print dialog box again.

7. In the Print <u>w</u>hat area of the dialog box, click the drop-down list arrow and choose `Handouts (6 slides per page)`.

8. Make sure the boxes for Black & white and Frame slides are still checked; then choose OK.

9. Save the presentation and close it.

Adding Speaker Notes

As sales manager of your company, you conduct training for the sales team. To motivate your salespeople, you develop a presentation for an upcoming training session. To help you remember information, you add speaker notes to the presentation.

To add speaker notes, follow these steps:

1. Open Proj0606 and save it as `Sales Team Training Session`. Display the presentation in Slide view.

2. Move to Slide 1; then choose <u>V</u>iew, Spea<u>k</u>er Notes to display the Speaker Notes window.

3. In the Speaker Notes window, enter the following note:

   `Make sure to have the sales awards displayed at the front of the room and to have upbeat music playing.`

4. Close the Speaker Notes window.

5. Display Slide 2 and then click the Notes Page View button to switch to Notes Page view.

6. Click the Zoom drop-down list arrow and select `66%`. Scroll to view the notes box area.

7. Click in the notes box area; then enter the following note:

   `"People tend to support what they help create."—Betsy Hudson`

8. Click the Zoom drop-down list arrow and select `Fit`.

9. Click the Slide View button to switch to Slide view.

10. Print your speaker notes.

11. Save the presentation; then close it.

Challenge

The following challenges, found in the Project–06 folder on the CD, enable you to use your problem-solving skills. Take time to work through these exercises now.

Adding Speaker Notes

You are putting the finishing touches on the financial report that you will present at your company's annual meeting. As part of your final preparations for giving the presentation, you add and format speaker notes.

To add speaker notes, follow these steps:

1. Open Proj0607 and save it as Annual Meeting Financial Report.

2. On Slide 3, Income, add the following note in the Speaker Notes window:

   Make sure to point out the increase in each category over the past three years.

3. Move to Slide 4, Revenue by Division, then add the following note in the Speaker Notes window:

   Mention the division managers:

   Western: Lowell Schmidt

   Atlantic: Joseph Cory

   Southern: Eugene Jones

   International: Lonnie Smith

4. Close the Speaker Notes window and display Slide 4 in Notes Page view.

5. Format the note on Slide 4 so that each division name displays in bold and each manager's name displays in italic.

6. Save the presentation; then close it.

Modifying the Notes Master

To create more room for text on your notes pages for the Financial Report, you modify the Notes Master. You also add the current date and your company name to the Notes Master.

To modify the notes master, follow these steps:

1. Open Proj0608 and save it as Revisions to the Financial Report.

2. Display the Notes Master for the presentation.

3. Resize the slide image to approximately half of its original size. Then center it in the available space on the Notes Master.

4. Enlarge the notes box to create more room for notes.

5. Enter the current date in the date placeholder.

6. Enter the company name, Hickory Hills Company, in the footer placeholder.

7. Display the presentation in Notes Page view. Scroll through the presentation to view your changes.

8. Save the presentation; then close it.

Printing Speaker Notes and Handouts

To finish preparing for your financial report presentation, you print speaker notes and audience handouts.

To print speaker notes and handouts, follow these steps:

1. Open Proj0609 and save it as `Printing the Financial Report`.

2. Display Slide 4, `Revenues by Division`, then display the Print dialog box.

3. Print the speaker notes for the current slide.

4. Print audience handouts for the entire presentation (two slides per page). Make sure to frame the slides.

5. Save the presentation; then close it.

Adding and Printing Speaker Notes

To document a recruitment talk you are presenting to prospective members for the Biking Club, you add speaker notes to a presentation.

To add and print speaker notes, follow these steps:

1. Open Proj0610 and save it as `Biking Club Speaker Notes`.

2. Display Slide 2, `Officers`, then add the following speaker note to the slide:

   `Mention that officers are re-elected every September.`

3. Add the following speaker note to Slide 3, `Biking Club`:

   `Mention that Greg Schmidt, famous bicyclist, will be at the "Race of Champions."`

4. Format the speaker notes on Slide 3 as follows:

   Enlarge the font to 14 points

   Add bold to Greg Schmidt

   Italicize "Race of Champions"

5. Print the speaker notes for Slide 3.

6. Save the presentation; then close it.

Modifying the Notes Master

As part of your final preparation for your biking club presentation you modify the Notes Master and print speaker notes.

To modify the Notes Master, follow these steps:

1. Open Proj0611 and save it as `Printing the Biking Club Presentation`.

2. Modify the Notes Master as follows:

Reduce the size of the notes box and center it horizontally. Enlarge the slide image and center it horizontally. Add `Biking Club` to the header area.

3. Display the presentation in Notes Page view.

4. Print speaker notes for the presentation.

5. Save the presentation; then close it.

PinPoint Assessment

You have completed the project and the associated lessons, as well as the "Checking Your Skills" and "Applying Your Skills" sections. Now use the PinPoint software Evaluation mode to assess your comprehension of the specific exam tasks you have just learned. You can also use the PinPoint Trainer mode and the SHOW ME tutorials to practice these specific exam tasks.

Automating Electronic Slide Shows

Adding Automation to a Slide Show

In this project you will learn the following objectives and their associated Microsoft Exam required activities.

Objectives	Required Activities
➤ Add Slide Transitions	Add Transitions
➤ Animate Your Text ... ..., ,,, ...	Animate Objects
➤ Use Custom Animation Effects	Animate Objects Set Custom Options
➤ Hide Slides	
➤ Time the Slide Show Presentation	Set Automatic Slide Timing
➤ Use the Slide Show Shortcut Keys	
➤ Use the Annotation Pen	
➤ Use the Meeting Minder	Generate Meeting Notes Electronically Incorporate Meeting Feedback
➤ Save the Presentation for Use on Another Computer	Save Presentation for Use on Another Computer
➤ Present with Presentation Conferencing	Present with Presentation Conferencing

APPROVED COURSEWARE
Microsoft® Office
USER SPECIALIST

Why Would I Do This?

When you are presenting an electronic slide show to an audience, you want to make the best impression possible. Although your content should be center stage, you can use a number of techniques to enhance the content and command your audience's attention. One way to do this is to use PowerPoint's transition effects between slides. The transition effects vary how slides advance during a presentation. For example, you can add a transition effect to make one slide fade into another. Another way to create anticipation is to animate the text so that it displays your bulleted points one at a time.

You can also use techniques such as blackening the display or using the annotation pen to draw directly on a slide show slide. Both these techniques sharpen the audience's focus.

Finally, you can use the Meeting Minder to keep track of meeting minutes or action items onscreen. As you enter items in the Meeting Minder window, PowerPoint automatically creates a set of action items as a new slide and places it at the end of the presentation. You can even print this list and hand it out to participants as they leave.

PowerPoint also provides tools for sharing a presentation over a network, by setting up conferencing between the speaker and audience participants. All participants must have PowerPoint on their computers, be connected by phone, and be available at the same time. They all see the presentation on their own computer screens.

Another tool available with the PowerPoint program lets you share a presentation with someone who doesn't have the PowerPoint program. This tool, called the Viewer, includes enough of the PowerPoint program with the presentation file to allow the user to run the slide show on his or her own computer—without having the PowerPoint program installed!

Lesson 1: Adding Slide Transitions

In Project 1, you learned how to move through a presentation in Slide Show view. Chances are that by now you have run some other slide shows. When you clicked the left mouse button, or pressed ↵Enter to move to the next slide, you probably noticed that the new slide instantly replaced the previous one.

Slide transition
A special effect used to introduce a slide during an electronic slide show.

You can change the way one slide moves to the next by using *slide transitions*. The transition effects help you make more of an impact by varying the way one slide replaces another. For example, you can specify that a slide fade, wipe, or dissolve into another. Table 7.1 describes some popular transition effects.

Table 7.1	Popular Transition Effects
Transition Effect	Description
Blinds	Opens the screen in wide, even strips horizontally or vertically
Box In or Out	Redraws the screen from the center outward, or from the outside to the center, using a box shape

Transition Effect	Description
Checkerboard	Changes the screen with a checkerboard pattern, either across or down
Cover	Redraws the screen as the new slide covers the previous one
Fade Through Black	Fades away the old slide, shows black momentarily, and then fades in the new slide
Split	Redraws the screen by splitting it in different directions
Uncover	Opens the screen like a curtain, in a variety of directions
Wipe	Sweeps the screen in a choice of directions

The easiest way to add a transition is to use the Slide Sorter toolbar. Try adding some transition effects now.

To Add Slide Transitions

1 Start PowerPoint, if necessary; then open Proj0701 from the Project-07 folder on the CD and save it as Quality Children's Clothing.

2 Display the presentation in Slide Sorter view.

Notice the Slide Sorter toolbar that is automatically displayed when Slide Sorter view is used (see Figure 7.1). You can use the Slide Sorter toolbar to add or change transition effects.

Figure 7.1
You can use the Slide Sorter toolbar to add slide transitions.

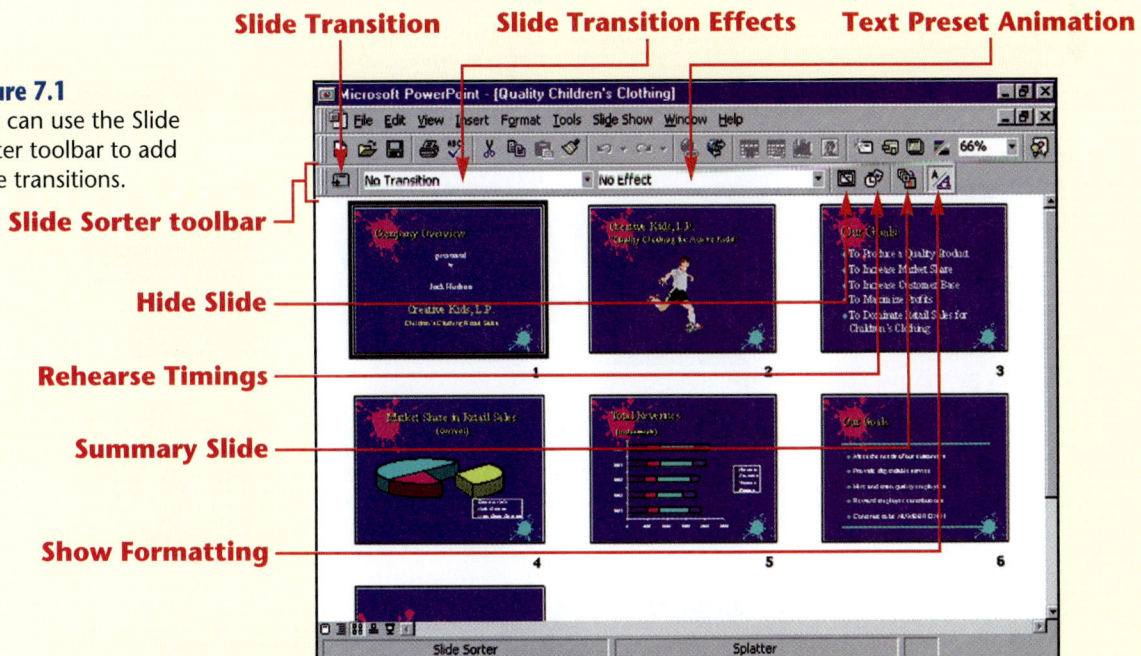

3 With Slide 1 selected, click the Slide Transition Effects drop-down list arrow.

A list of transition effects is displayed (see Figure 7.2). You can choose an effect and then preview it in Slide Sorter view.

continues

To Add Slide Transitions (continued)

Figure 7.2
PowerPoint provides a number of transition effects.

Click here to display a list of transition effects

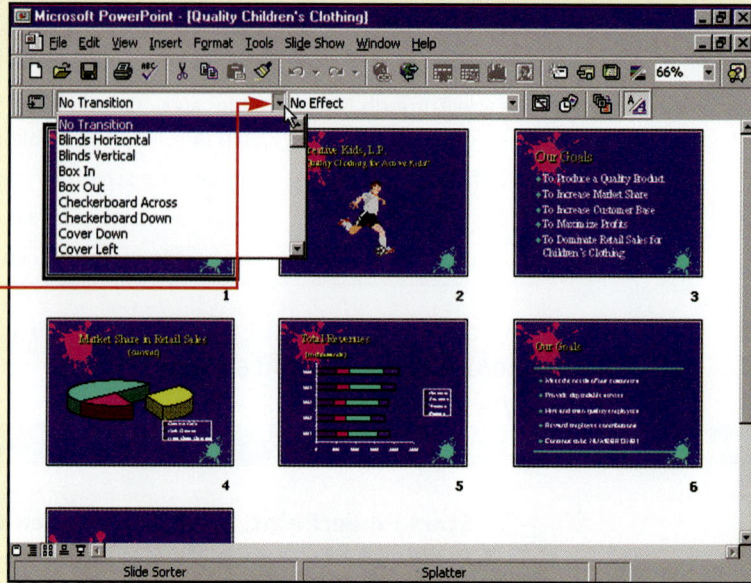

❹ **Choose Blinds Horizontal from the list.**

The transition effect is added for the selected slide, and a Slide Transition icon is added to the slide (see Figure 7.3). You can click this icon to preview the effect. This feature is handy because you don't have to go to the slide show to see how your transitions will look. Try using this technique now.

Figure 7.3
You can quickly preview the transition effect in Slide Sorter view.

Click the Slide Transition icon to preview the transition effect

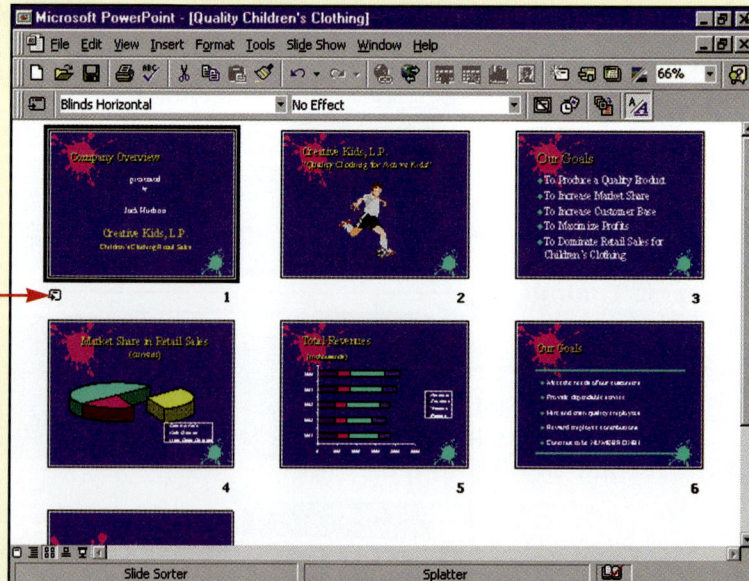

❺ **Click the Slide Transition icon for Slide 1.**

Slide 1 displays a preview of the transition effect.

If you want to apply the same effect to several slides, select the slides before selecting the transition. Now try changing the transition effect for several slides at once.

PowerPoint

6 **Click Slide 2, press** ⬆Shift⬆**, and click Slides 3 and 4.**

A thick black line is displayed around each slide, indicating that the slides are selected.

7 **Click the Slide Transition Effects drop-down list arrow and choose Checkerboard Across.**

The transition effect is applied to the selected slides. You can see the effect again by clicking the Slide Transition icon at the bottom of any slide that has a transition (refer to Figure 7.3). Now view the transitional changes in a slide show.

8 **Select Slide 1 and choose View, Slide Show.**

9 **Click the left mouse button several times to advance completely through the slide show.**

The transitions you specified are used as you move through the slides. When you finish the slide show, the presentation is displayed again in Slide Sorter view.

You can remove a slide transition by selecting the slide and choosing No Transition from the Slide Transition Effects drop-down list.

10 **Select Slide 3, click the Slide Transition Effects drop-down arrow, and choose** No Transition**.**

The transition is removed from the selected slide, and the Slide Transition icon is no longer displayed.

11 **Save the presentation.**

Keep the presentation open for the next lesson, in which you add text animation.

You can also preview your transition in Slide view or Outline view. From the menu bar, choose Slide Show, Animation Preview to display a miniature slide with the transition effect. To close the miniature slide, click its close button.

If you have a sound card and speakers, you can spice up your presentation even more by adding sound during the transition. Choose Slide Show, Slide Transition to display the Slide Transition dialog box. In the Sound area, click the drop-down list arrow and choose a sound. Choose Apply to associate the sound with the selected slide, or Apply to All to add the sound to all slides.

Clicking the Slide Transition button on the Slide Sorter toolbar also opens the Slide Transition dialog box. If you think the transition occurs too quickly, set a speed for the transition by selecting Slow, Medium, or Fast. Then click Apply (for just the selected slide) or Apply to All (for the entire presentation).

Lesson 2: Animating Your Text

Animate
To create the illusion of movement during an electronic slide show by controlling how text is displayed.

Another way to keep an audience's attention is to *animate* your text during a slide show so that you can focus on important points, control the flow of information, and add interest to your presentation. For example, you can have your bulleted points displayed one by one (usually called building or animating). This technique can prevent your audience from losing attention by reading ahead on a slide. You can animate your text so that it operates independently from transition effects, which you learned about in Lesson 1. Try using this attention-grabbing feature now.

To Animate Your Text

1 **Make sure that the** Quality Children's Clothing **presentation is open in Slide Sorter view, then select Slide 3, if necessary.**

Because Slide 3 has bulleted points, you can specify PowerPoint to build them separately.

2 **From the Slide Sorter toolbar, click the Text Preset Animation drop-down arrow.**

A list of available methods for building your text points is displayed (see Figure 7.4). When you select one of these methods, PowerPoint automatically builds the text one point at a time.

Figure 7.4
You can choose from a variety of text animation effects.

Click this arrow to display a listof text animation effects

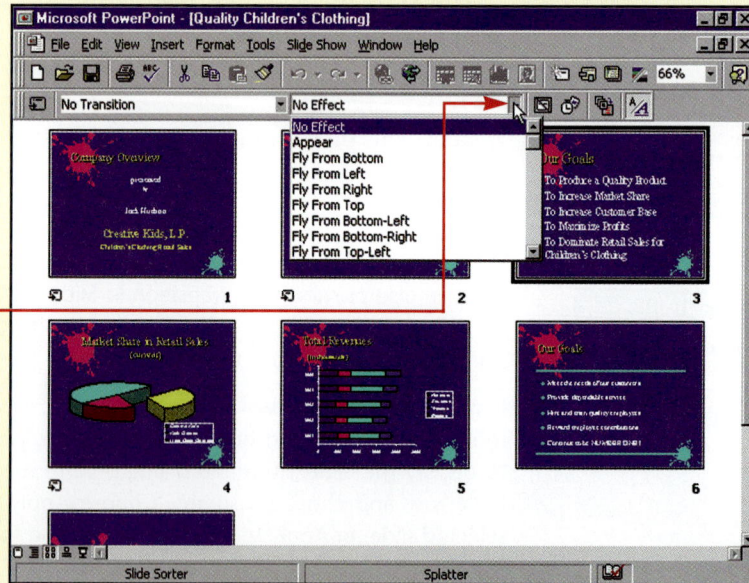

3 **Select Fly From Left.**

A special Text Animation icon is displayed at the bottom of Slide 3 (see Figure 7.5). This indicates that Slide 3 is a build slide.

PowerPoint

Figure 7.5
You can tell by the icon which slides have text animation.

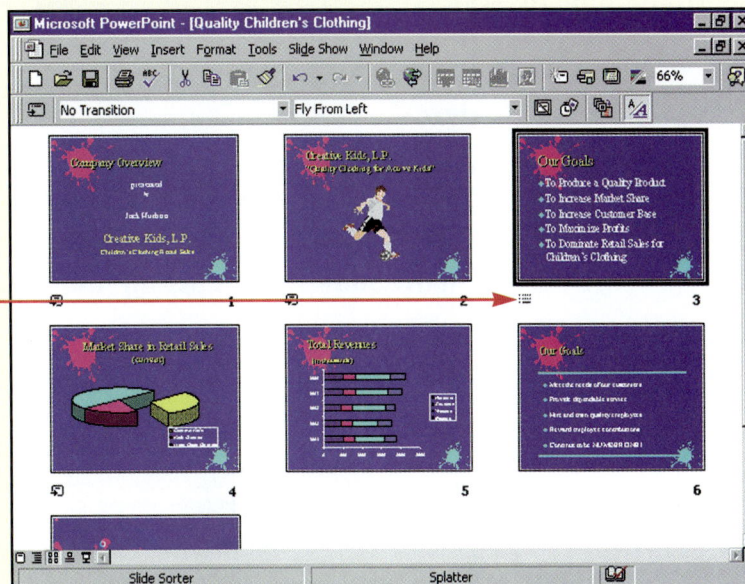

Text Animation icon ———→

4 Click the Slide Show button.

The slide show begins, starting with the selected slide (Slide 3). When you click the left mouse button or press ↵Enter, bulleted points are displayed one at a time.

5 Click the left mouse button several times.

PowerPoint builds the slide one bulleted point at a time. When all the slide text has been displayed, your next mouse click moves you to the next slide.

6 Press Esc.

This ends the slide show and returns you to Slide Sorter view.

7 Save the presentation.

Keep the presentation open for the next lesson, in which you learn to customize your animation effects.

Lesson 3: Using Custom Animation Effects

In Lesson 2, you saw how to add preset animation effects to text by using the Slide Sorter toolbar. However, you can create custom animation effects. Adding custom effects is a great way to grab your audience's attention. For example, you can have bulleted points that build progressively, with the previous point dimmed or even completely hidden. Such effects focus your audience's attention on the point at hand. Try using custom animation effects now.

To Use Custom Animation Effects

1 **In the open presentation, display Slide 6,** Our Goals**, in Slide view.**

You must select the slide for which you want to create custom effects, and then display it in Slide view before customizing animation.

2 **Choose Sli̲de Show, Custo̲m Animation.**

The Custom Animation dialog box is displayed (see Figure 7.6). You can use this dialog box to add a variety of special effects and then preview the effects.

Figure 7.6
You can customize your animation.

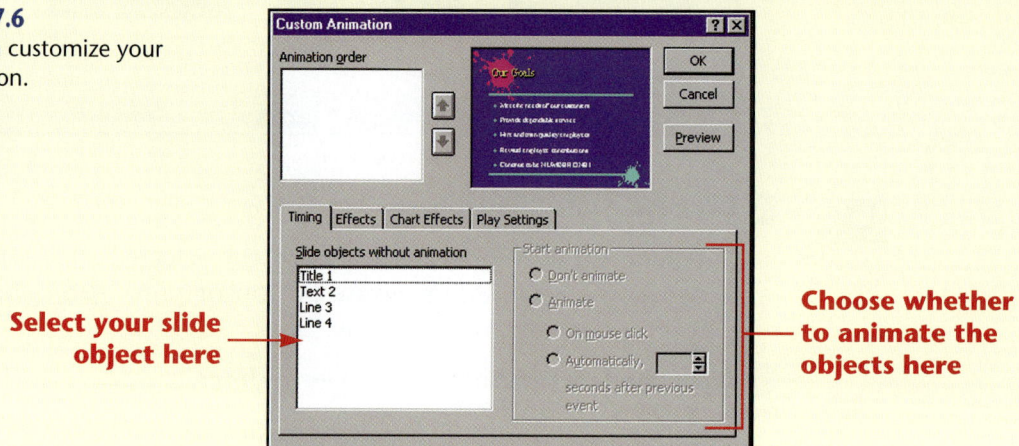

Select your slide object here

Choose whether to animate the objects here

Before you add special effects, you must first indicate which objects you want to animate. The easiest way to do this is to select the objects on the list and then choose A̲nimate.

3 **Click Title 1 from the S̲lide objects without animation list, press** ⬆Shift**, and click Text 2.**

The Title and Text objects are selected. Additionally, selection handles surround the object areas on the sample slide (see Figure 7.7). This helps you identify which object area you are choosing.

Figure 7.7
Select from the list the objects you want to animate.

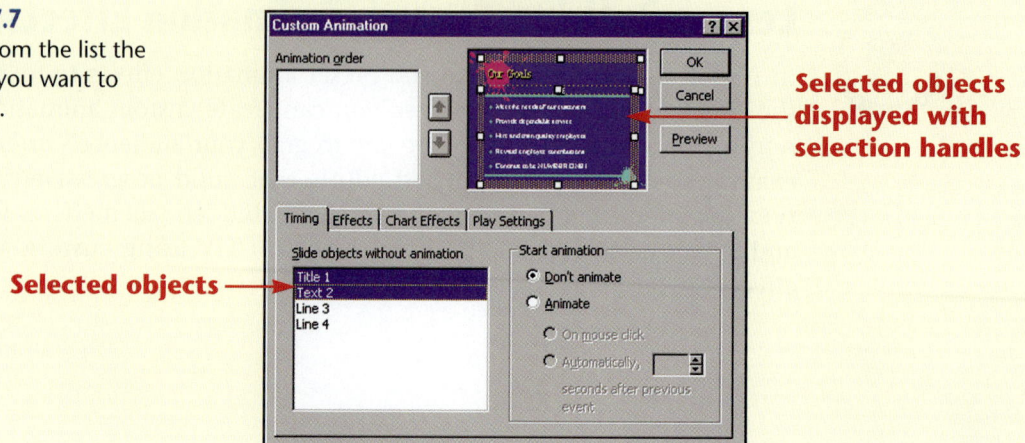

Selected objects

Selected objects displayed with selection handles

4 **Click the Animate option button.**

This places the selected objects in the Animation order list box (see Figure 7.8).

Figure 7.8
Objects to which you want to add custom animation should be displayed in the Animation order list box.

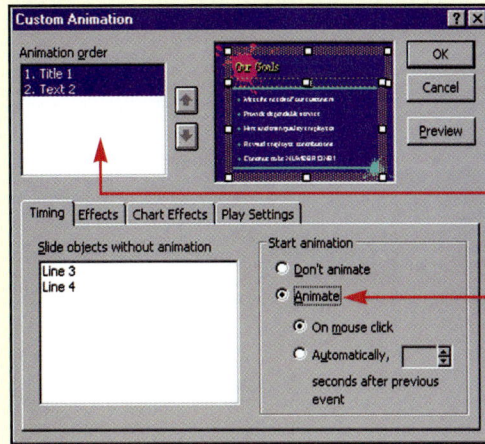

Click the Animate button to move selected objects to this list

Now you can add custom animation effects. You add these by using the Effects page.

5 **Click the Effects tab, and then click Text 2 in the Animation order list box.**

The Effects page of the Custom Animation dialog box is displayed (see Figure 7.9). Clicking Text 2 selects just that object.

Figure 7.9
You can add special animation effects by using the Effects page.

Choose the object here

Choose the entry animation here

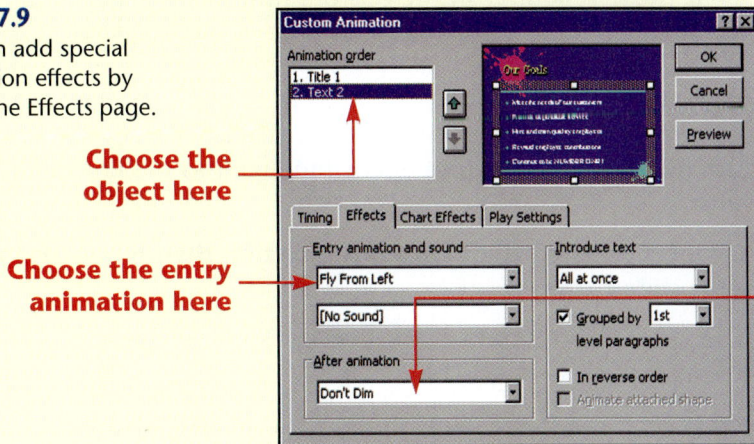

Choose how the object should be displayed when the next point is shown on the slide

PowerPoint automatically assigns the Fly From Left animation effect when the object is first displayed. However, you can change this entry effect.

6 **Click the first drop-down list arrow in the Entry animation and sound area, and then choose Spiral.**

The entry effect for the text is changed. You can also choose to dim any object when you move to the next point, or even hide the object completely.

continues

To Use Custom Animation Effects   (continued)

7 **Click the <u>A</u>fter animation drop-down list arrow.**

From the displayed palette, you can choose a color to dim the object as you move to the next object. You can also choose Hide After Animation to completely hide the point (see Figure 7.10).

Figure 7.10
You can choose to dim or hide an object after you move to the next bulleted point.

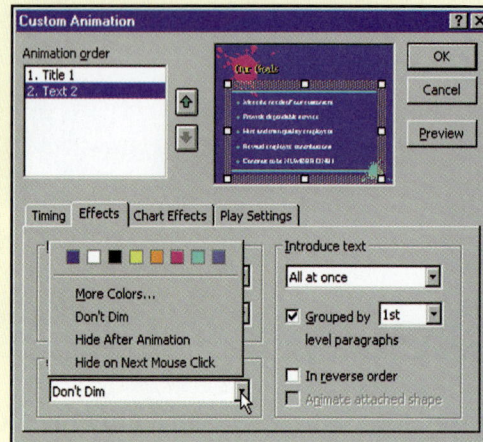

8 **Click the yellow color box (the fourth box from the left).**

This selects yellow as the dim color.

Once you have selected custom effects, you can preview them by using the sample slide in the Custom Animation dialog box.

9 **Click the <u>P</u>review button.**

Your custom animation is displayed in the sample slide area. If you want, experiment with other custom effects. When you're finished, choose yellow for the dim effect and Spiral as the entry animation effect.

10 **Click OK to close the Custom Animation dialog box and run your slide show.**

The special effects are displayed on Slide 6, including dimmed points.

11 **Press Esc to end the slide show, if necessary, and save your presentation.**

Keep the presentation open for the next lesson, in which you learn how to hide slides.

Inside Stuff

Custom animation can also be applied to objects such as clip art, shapes, and charts. When you open the Custom Animation dialog box, these objects are also listed in the <u>S</u>lide objects without animation list. You select the item, click <u>A</u>nimate, and then choose the appropriate animation effects on the Effects tab (or the Chart Effects tab for charts).

PowerPoint

Lesson 4: Hiding Slides

Before you give a presentation, you should try to anticipate any questions that your audience may have and be prepared to answer those questions. You might even want to create slides to support your answers to these questions, keeping the slides hidden until you need them.

Try creating a slide now that you are going to hide for your presentation.

To Hide a Slide

1 **Go to Slide 6,** Our Goals, **of the Quality Children's Clothing presentation. Display the slide in the Slide view.**

2 **Click the New Slide button on the Standard toolbar.**

3 **Choose the** Text & Clip Art **AutoLayout (first layout in third row) from the New Slide dialog box and click OK.**

You have added a blank slide that contains an area for bullets and an area for clip art.

4 **Double-click the clip art placeholder. Select the** Cartoons **category, then click the** Success **clip art (or clip art with a similar theme if you don't have this clip art). Choose** I**nsert.**

The Success clip art shows a business man placing a flag at the peak of a mountain (see Figure 7.11). Now add the text to accompany the picture.

Figure 7.11
The new slide shows bulleted text and clip art.

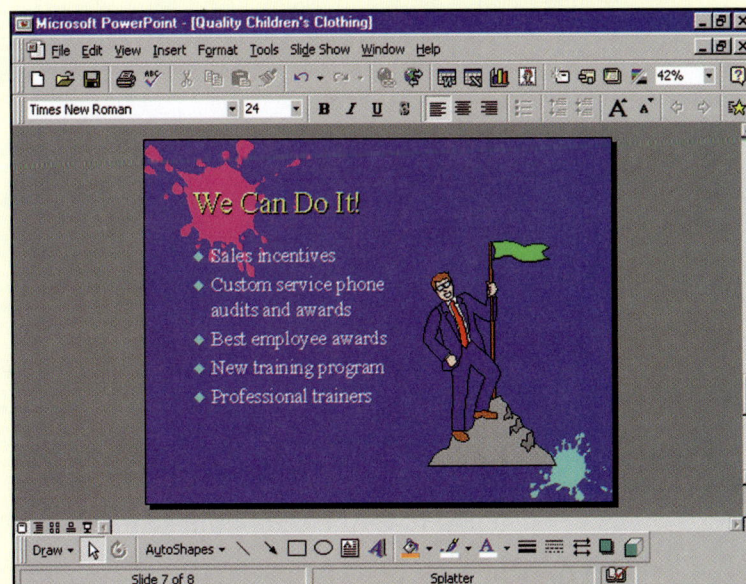

5 **Click in the title placeholder and type** We Can Do It!

6 **Click in the text placeholder and type the text you see in Figure 7.11.**

This is the slide you use in your presentation when the audience asks how you intend to accomplish your goals.

continues

To Hide a Slide   (continued)

7 Choose Sli_d_e Show, _H_ide Slide.

The slide is now hidden from the slide show, but you won't know that for certain unless you view the slide in the Slide Sorter view.

8 Click the Slide Sorter View button.

The slide number has a stroke through it that indicates it is hidden (see Figure 7.12).

Figure 7.12
When viewed in Slide Sorter view, the hidden slide has a stroke through its slide number.

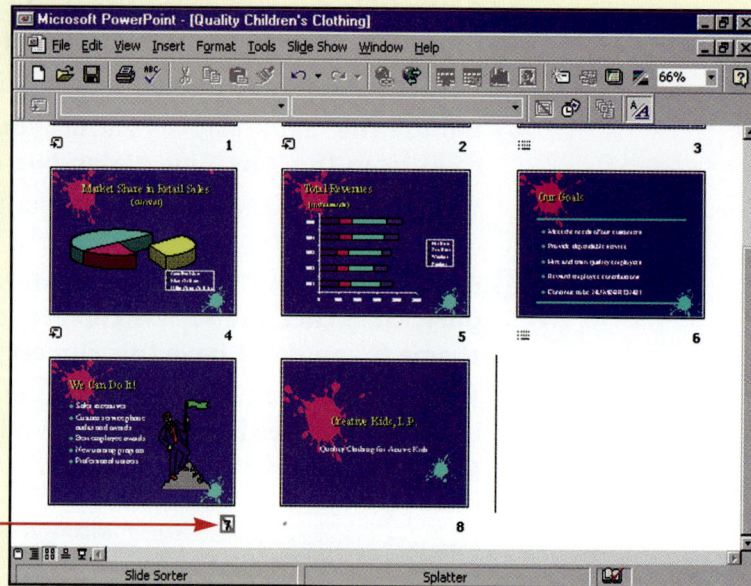

Slide number marked as hidden

9 Select Slide 6, Our Goals, and click the Slide Show view button.

10 Click the left mouse button until you move to Slide 8, Creative Kids. L.P.

You notice that the slide show skipped Slide 7, the slide you hid. In the next step, you display the slide.

11 Right-click the slide and choose _P_revious from the shortcut menu to return to Slide 6. Right-click that slide and select _G_o, _H_idden Slide.

You may have difficulty choosing the _H_idden Slide option unless you have the slide immediately before the hidden slide onscreen when you right-click (the choice of _H_idden Slide may be dimmed otherwise).

12 Press Esc to end the slide show and save the presentation.

The next time you show the slide show, the slide will again be hidden until you choose to display it.

Leave the presentation open for the next lesson, in which you learn to time an onscreen presentation.

PowerPoint

Inside Stuff

From the Slide Sorter view, you can hide and unhide slides by selecting the slide and clicking the Hide Slide button on the Slide Sorter toolbar.

Lesson 5: Timing the Slide Show Presentation

Because no one has unlimited time to give to a presentation, timing the slide show for the greatest impact is important. When developing your final presentation, you can decide whether PowerPoint should advance to a new slide automatically after a certain number of seconds, or whether slides should change only when the mouse is clicked. If you are presenting the show to a live audience, you certainly want to control the slide show by using the manual advance. The general rule when using manual advance is to allow 2–3 minutes per slide.

Even if you are planning to use manual advance, the slide timings are a good way of measuring the overall length of the presentation. To use them to practice and time your presentation, simply click the Rehearse Timings button. Talk as you would to the audience for the first slide, and then click to move to the next one. When you finish, you have a good idea of the overall length of the presentation, as well as the time needed for each individual slide.

In contrast, automatic advance is great if you have an onscreen show that you want to run continually (for example, at a trade show exhibit). When using automatic advance, you need to spend only as much time on a slide as the average person needs to read it. If the slide stays onscreen too long, people lose interest.

Try setting some timings now. Make sure you read and understand all steps before proceeding with the following tutorial.

To Time the Slide Show Presentation

1 **Display the Quality Children's Clothing presentation in Slide Sorter view.**

2 **On the Slide Sorter toolbar, click the Rehearse Timings button.**

The slide show begins—but with a difference. A Rehearsal dialog box is displayed that keeps track of how many seconds you show each slide. This dialog box also records the overall length of the presentation.

3 **After approximately 5 seconds, click the left mouse button to advance to Slide 2.**

The elapsed time for the current slide and the overall presentation length are displayed in the Rehearsal dialog box (see Figure 7.13).

continues

To Time the Slide Show Presentation   (continued)

Figure 7.13
You can use the Rehearsal dialog box to keep track of slide and overall presentation length.

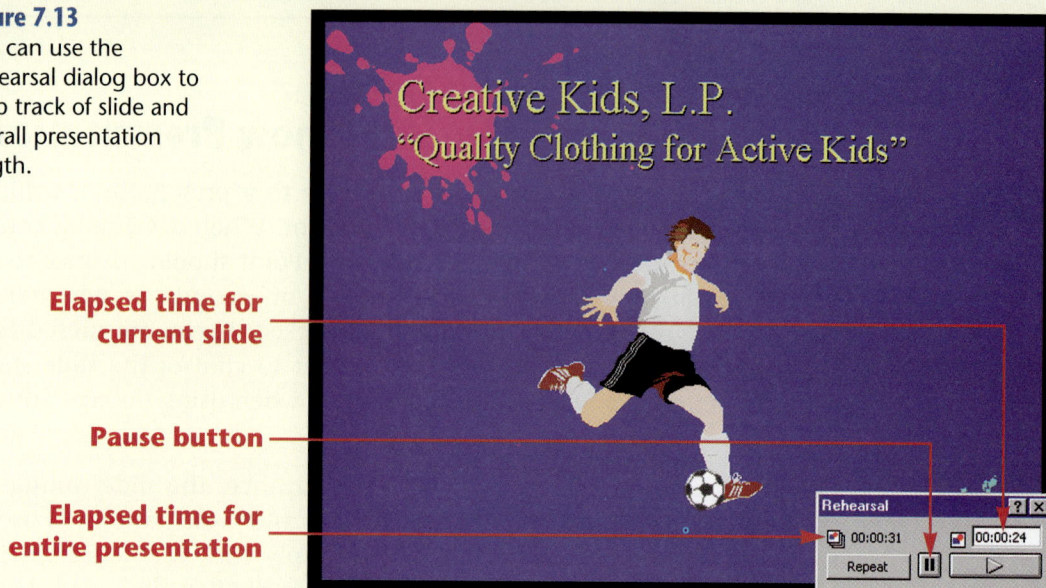

Creative Kids, L.P.
"Quality Clothing for Active Kids"

Elapsed time for current slide

Pause button

Elapsed time for entire presentation

Rehearsal   00:00:31   00:00:24   Repeat

4 In Slides 2–6, set timings of your choice, ranging from 3–10 seconds per slide or bulleted point.

When you are finished going through the entire show, PowerPoint displays a message box (see Figure 7.14). You can decide whether you want to keep the timings as part of your presentation.

Figure 7.14
PowerPoint confirms that you want to save the new timings.

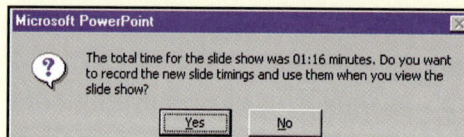

Microsoft PowerPoint

The total time for the slide show was 01:16 minutes. Do you want to record the new slide timings and use them when you view the slide show?

Yes   No

5 Choose Yes to accept the presentation timings; then choose Yes in the second message box to review the timings in Slide Sorter view.

The slides are displayed in Slide Sorter view, including the number of seconds after which each slide will advance (see Figure 7.15).

Figure 7.15
You can time your presentation and then display the number of seconds after each slide advances.

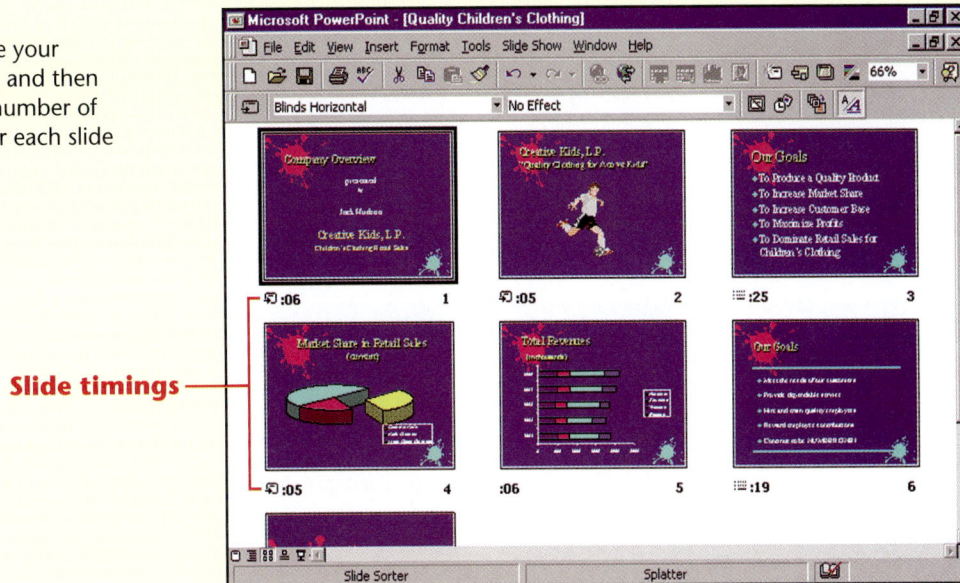

Slide timings

Now view your electronic slide show with the new timings.

6 Move to Slide 1 and click the Slide Show button to start the slide show.

The show advances through the slides, using the timings you specified. When the show is finished, the Slide Sorter view is again displayed.

7 Save the presentation and then close it.

Keep PowerPoint running for the next lesson, in which you learn efficient methods of moving among slide show slides.

Inside Stuff

If you want to run your slide show as a self-running presentation (such as at a trade show), set your slide timings just as you learned in this lesson. Then choose Slide Show, Set Up Show to display the Set Up Show dialog box. Choose Loop continually until 'Esc'. Make sure the Using timings option, if present option is selected. Click OK when you're finished.

If you don't want to use the Rehearse Timings method of setting timings for your slides, especially for a self-running show, select all the slides in Slide Sorter view, and then click the Slide Transition button on the Slide Sorter toolbar. In the Slide Transition dialog box, select Automatically after from the Advance area and then enter a number in the seconds box. Click OK. Then set up the show to loop continuously.

Lesson 6: Using the Slide Show Shortcut Keys

When you are presenting your slide show to a live audience, it's useful to know as many ways as possible to move among the slides. In Project 1, you learned some basic ways of moving among slides. For example, you learned that you could press ↵Enter or ↓ to advance to the next slide, and ↑ to move to the previous slide. You also used the shortcut menu to access the

Slide Navigator and end a show. In this lesson, you build on that knowledge to include additional methods of efficiently moving around in a slide show. You use shortcut keys that provide one-stroke access to common ways of moving in a slide show.

The shortcut keys have other functions in a slide show as well. For example, you can use special shortcut keys to blank out a current slide so that the audience's attention is redirected to you. Try using some keyboard shortcuts now.

To Use Slide Show Shortcut Keys

❶ Open Proj0702 from the Project-07 folder on the CD, and save it as Recruiting Technical Personnel.

❷ With Slide 1 displayed, choose <u>V</u>iew, Slide Sho<u>w</u>.

The presentation starts, and the first slide is shown.

❸ Press F1.

The Slide Show Help dialog box is displayed, with a list of available shortcut keys to help you get around the slide show (see Figure 7.16).

Figure 7.16
Press F1 to display a list of keyboard shortcuts for your slide show.

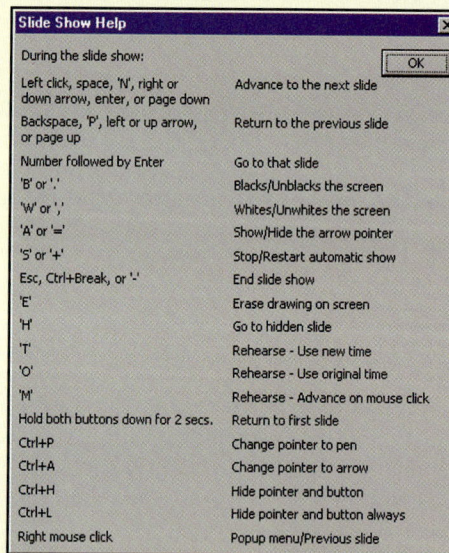

Slide Show Help	☒
During the slide show:	OK
Left click, space, 'N', right or down arrow, enter, or page down	Advance to the next slide
Backspace, 'P', left or up arrow, or page up	Return to the previous slide
Number followed by Enter	Go to that slide
'B' or '.'	Blacks/Unblacks the screen
'W' or ','	Whites/Unwhites the screen
'A' or '='	Show/Hide the arrow pointer
'S' or '+'	Stop/Restart automatic show
Esc, Ctrl+Break, or '-'	End slide show
'E'	Erase drawing on screen
'H'	Go to hidden slide
'T'	Rehearse - Use new time
'O'	Rehearse - Use original time
'M'	Rehearse - Advance on mouse click
Hold both buttons down for 2 secs.	Return to first slide
Ctrl+P	Change pointer to pen
Ctrl+A	Change pointer to arrow
Ctrl+H	Hide pointer and button
Ctrl+L	Hide pointer and button always
Right mouse click	Popup menu/Previous slide

❹ Click OK to close the Slide Show Help dialog box, and then press N.

The next slide is displayed. Likewise, pressing P moves you to the previous slide.

❺ Press P.

PowerPoint moves back one slide.

You can also use shortcut keys to clear the screen so that you can direct the audience's attention to yourself. You can press B to blacken the screen or W to white it out. The screen remains blank until you press B or W a second time to view the slide again. Try using this helpful feature now.

6 Press B to blacken the screen; then press B again.

The screen turns black when you press B, and then returns to normal when you press B again. If you want, try whiting out the screen before proceeding.

In Project 1, you learned that you could click the right mouse button on the slide show to display the shortcut menu, and then use the Slide Navigator to go to a certain slide. An even more seamless method of moving to a specific slide is simply to press the slide's number, followed by ⏎Enter. This method is quicker than using the Slide Navigator, and your audience doesn't see the command onscreen.

7 Press 4 and then ⏎Enter.

The presentation jumps to Slide 4.

8 Press Esc.

The slide show ends, and you are returned to Slide view.

Keep the presentation open for the next lesson, in which you use PowerPoint's electronic pen to emphasize your points.

Table 7.2 lists the shortcut keys for moving around in a slide show.

Table 7.2 Moving Around in a Slide Show	
To	Do This
Display a list of shortcut keys	Press F1.
Activate the shortcut menu	Right-click the mouse.
Go to the next slide	Left-click the mouse. Press ⏎Enter. Press N.
Go to the previous slide	Press ←Backspace. Press P.
Go to a specific slide	Type the slide number and press ⏎Enter Choose Go, Slide Navigator from the shortcut menu.
Blacken or unblacken the screen	Press B.
Whiten or unwhiten the screen	Press W.
Erase a screen drawing	Press E.
End the slide show	Press Esc. Choose End Show from the shortcut menu.

Lesson 7: Using the Annotation Pen

Annotate

To draw or write a comment. In a PowerPoint slide show, annotation refers to using the electronic pen to write or draw.

Have you ever wished that you could write or draw on a slide during a slide show? Maybe you want to draw attention to specific information or recapture your audience's attention. Luckily, PowerPoint provides an electronic pen you can use with the mouse to *annotate* the slide. Annotating is simply writing or drawing directly on the slide, and it's an effective method of emphasizing information.

The comments or objects that you draw are not permanent—once you move to another slide, they are erased automatically. You can also continue to display the slide, but erase the comments.

For even more impact, you can change annotation pen colors. For example, you might use white for most of the points you're trying to make, and then switch to orange for added emphasis. Try using the pen in a presentation now.

To Use the Annotation Pen

1 **In the open Recruiting Technical Personnel presentation, move to Slide 3 and click the Slide Show button.**

The slide show begins. To use the pen, you must first activate it.

2 **Right-click to display the shortcut menu, and then choose P̲en.**

The pointer changes into an annotation pen. You can use this pen to draw by holding down the left mouse button and dragging.

If you have problems...

When the annotation pen is active, clicking the left mouse button won't advance the slide show to the next screen, but just produces a dot onscreen. Press Ctrl+A to change the annotation pen back to an arrow, and then click to advance the slide show.

3 **Drag to draw a line that emphasizes the salary progression from the data series for Systems Support to Systems Analyst (see Figure 7.17).**

Figure 7.17
You can use the annotation pen to emphasize your points

Use the annotation pen to create this freehand drawing

Annotation pen

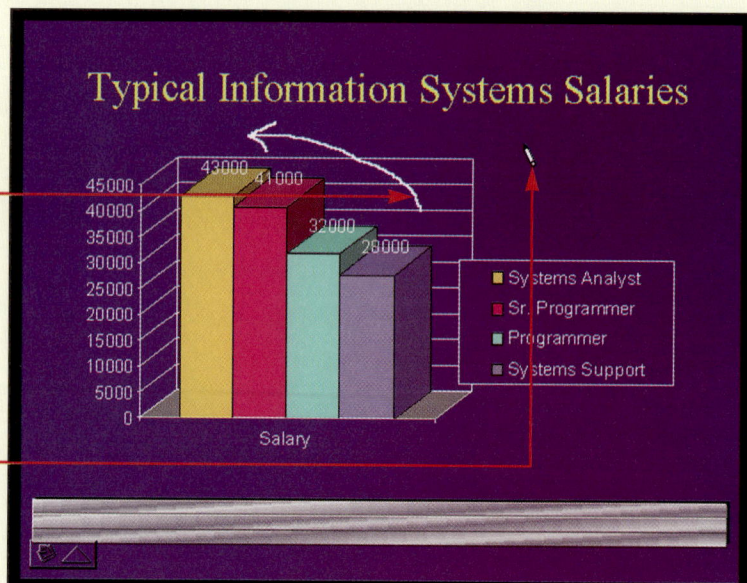

PowerPoint

The drawing is automatically erased whenever you move to another slide. Alternatively, you can erase the current slide's drawing by pressing E (for erase), which enables you to continue to display the slide. Try this now.

4 Press E.

The drawing is erased. Notice that your pen is still active so that you can create other comments. You can activate the arrow, which automatically turns off the pen. You must turn off the pen before advancing to the next slide by left-clicking the mouse.

5 Right-click to display the shortcut menu, and then choose Arrow.

The mouse pointer is displayed, and the electronic pen is turned off. You can quickly reactivate the pen again by pressing Ctrl+P. This method not only is quicker but also is preferred because the audience doesn't see the shortcut menu. Try activating the pen by using this technique.

6 Press Ctrl+P.

The electronic pen is activated. Now try changing pen color.

7 Right-click to display the shortcut menu; then choose Pointer Options, Pen Color.

A submenu is displayed with a list of available pen colors (see Figure 7.18).

Figure 7.18
You can choose from a variety of pen colors.

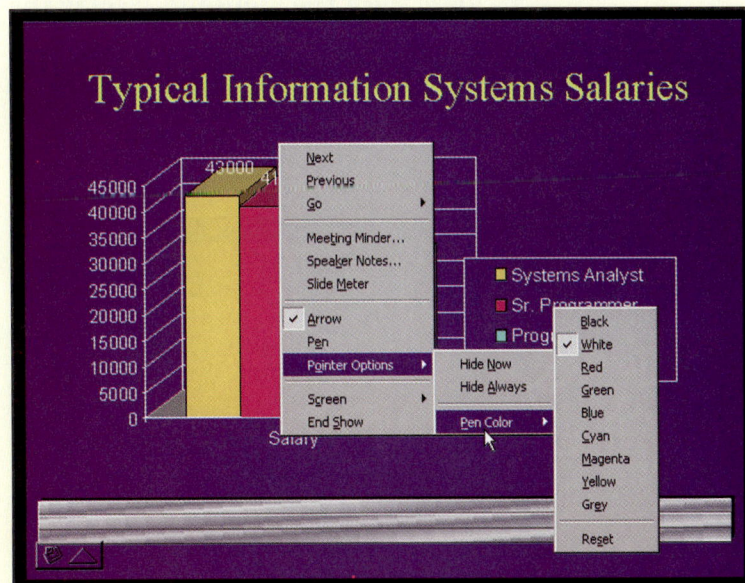

8 Choose Yellow and then draw on your slide to see the new color.

9 Press Ctrl+A.

The pen icon changes to a mouse pointer.

10 Press Esc and then close your presentation without saving the changes.

Keep PowerPoint running for the next lesson, in which you use the Meeting Minder.

Inside Stuff

To draw a perfectly straight line with the annotation pen, press (⬆Shift) while you draw.

Lesson 8: Using the Meeting Minder

The Meeting Minder is a feature that helps you take notes during a presentation. With the Meeting Minder, you can take minutes, record action items, and add to your notes pages during a slide show. Action items are displayed on a new slide at the end of your slide show.

The Meeting Minder is especially useful during an informal presentation such as a staff meeting or brainstorming session. Although you can use the Meeting Minder in any PowerPoint view, most people use it while running the electronic slide show. Try using the Meeting Minder now.

To Use the Meeting Minder

❶ **Open Proj0703 from the Project-07 folder on the CD, and save it as** Recruiting Plan.

❷ **Click the Slide Show button.**

This starts the presentation, beginning with the current slide.

❸ **Right-click the mouse to display the shortcut menu, and then choose Meeting Minder.**

The Meeting Minder dialog box is displayed with two tabs: Meeting Minutes and Action Items (see Figure 7.19). You can click the tab you want, and then enter information.

Figure 7.19
You can use the Meeting Minder to document your meeting and create action items.

Action Items tab

Meeting Minutes tab

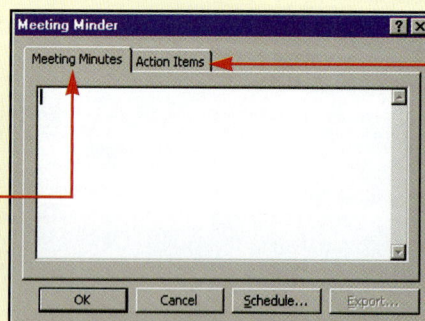

❹ **Click the Action Items tab to display the Action Items page (see Figure 7.20).**

PowerPoint

Figure 7.20
You can enter action items with the Meeting Minder.

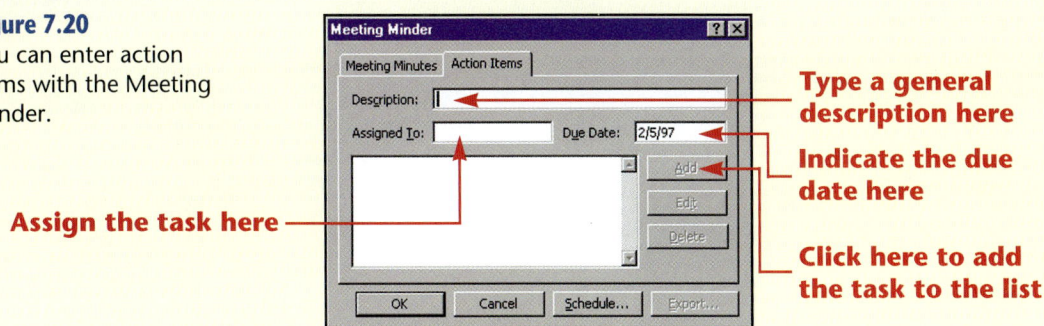

Type a general description here

Indicate the due date here

Assign the task here

Click here to add the task to the list

5 **In the Description text box, type** Attend job fairs at top colleges and universities to recruit employees **and press** Tab↹.

The text you typed is entered in the text box, and the insertion point moves to the Assigned To text box.

6 **Type** L. Schmidt **and press** Tab↹.

The insertion point moves to the Due Date text box. By default, this text box displays the current system date.

7 **Press** Del **as many times as necessary to erase the date, and then enter** 6/12/98.

After you create the basic information for an action item, you add it to the list.

8 **Click Add.**

The action item is displayed in the list, and the text boxes are cleared so that you can enter other tasks.

9 **Enter the following items in the Action Items page of the Meeting Minder dialog box:**

Description	Assigned To	Due Date
Coordinate advertising in national computer magazines	S. Black	2/7/98
Network with other businesses	J. Reams	3/24/98

10 **Choose OK to close the Meeting Minder dialog box.**

PowerPoint automatically creates a slide with the action items you entered and places the slide at the end of the presentation.

11 **Press** Esc **to end the slide show; then press** Ctrl+End.

The slide show ends, and the last slide, Action Items, is displayed in Slide view (see Figure 7.21). You can print this slide (using techniques you already know) to hand to your participants as they leave.

continues

To Use the Meeting Minder   (continued)

Figure 7.21
You can create an
Action Items slide.

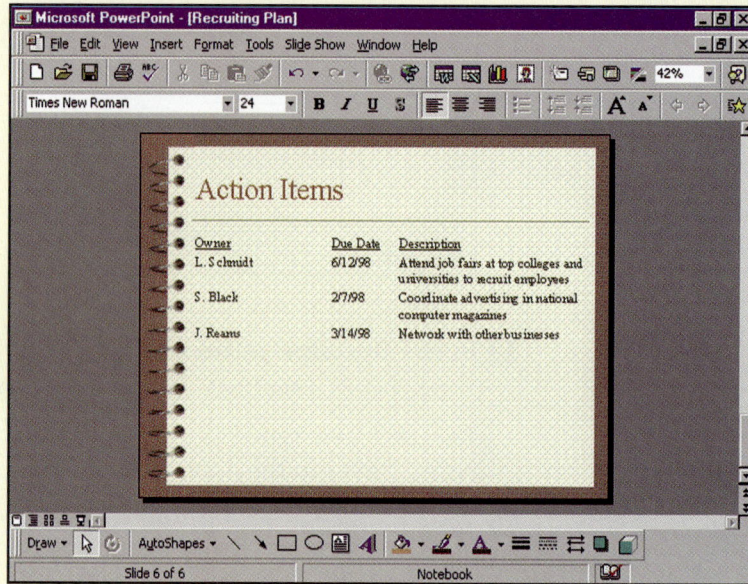

⑫ **With the Action Items slide displayed in Slide view, choose File, Print.**

The Print dialog box is displayed.

⑬ **Make sure Current slide is chosen in the Print range section, then choose OK.**

The Action Items slide is printed.

⑭ **Save the presentation, but leave it open for the next lesson where you save the presentation for use on another computer.**

Exam Notes

The Meeting Minder lets you take meeting minutes during the slide show or during a presentation conference. (Other users don't see the Meeting Minder during the presentation conference.) The minutes are kept together; you don't have different minutes for each slide. For each slide, you add to the existing text. When the minutes are complete, choose Export. Select Send meeting minutes and action items to Microsoft Word and then choose Export Now. If you have Microsoft Outlook and want to schedule a meeting, choose Schedule. This opens the Outlook Meeting Planner.

You can incorporate meeting feedback electronically by posting the Action Items you add during the slide show to the Microsoft Outlook task list. When viewing the Action Items tab of the Meeting Minder, choose Export. Select Post action items to Microsoft Outlook and then click Export Now. If you don't have Microsoft Outlook, export the action items to Microsoft Word. You can send the resulting document to a mail recipient or route it to several recipients using Microsoft Word's File, Send To command.

Lesson 9: Saving the Presentation for Use on Another Computer

Although you can copy a presentation file to another computer in order to show the slides there, you run the risk of forgetting any linked files needed for that particular presentation. And what if you send the file to someone who doesn't have PowerPoint?

The best way to pass along a presentation file, and all the linked files that go with it is to use the Pack and Go Wizard. The wizard not only copies all files and fonts used in the presentation to a disk, but includes the PowerPoint viewer if the destination computer doesn't have PowerPoint. The PowerPoint Viewer is a small program that has enough of the PowerPoint program to show the presentation slide show.

If you change the presentation after you run the Pack and Go Wizard, just run the wizard again to update the files.

Try storing the Recruiting Plan presentation on a floppy disk for use on another computer.

To Save a Presentation for Use on Another Computer

1 **Choose File, Pack and Go.**

The Pack and Go Wizard dialog box appears (see Figure 7.22). The Office Assistant also appears, offering help with this feature. Click No, don't provide help now to close the Office Assistant, if you don't need it.

Figure 7.22
The Pack and Go Wizard packages your presentation to show on another computer.

2 **Click Next.**

You now specify which file you want to package—the file you have open, or another file, or both. If you want to package another presentation, choose Other presentation and then enter the name and path of the file in the text box. Click Browse to select the file from a dialog box. In this case, however, you want to package the current file.

continues

To Save a Presentation for Use on Another Computer   (continued)

3 **Select Active presentation and then click Next.**

In the next dialog box, specify the destination to which you want to copy the files.

4 **Insert a floppy disk in your floppy disk drive and select A:\drive. Click Next.**

Choose B:\drive if your disk is inserted in that drive. If you can't use the floppy disk drive, select Choose destination and then ask your instructor where to store your files. Enter that destination in the text box.

If you have problems...

Presentation files that include graphics and animation can be quite large, especially if you choose to include linked files and to embed True Type fonts. If you try to copy a presentation file to a floppy disk, you may find the file is too large to fit on a floppy disk. However, when you use the Pack and Go Wizard, the wizard compresses the files. This may make it possible to put a large presentation on one floppy disk. If not, the wizard will prompt you to insert additional disks as needed.

5 **Select Include linked files and Embed True Type fonts. Click Next.**

If there are files linked to your presentation (such as spreadsheets or charts), you need to select the Include linked files option so that those files get copied along with the presentation file. Otherwise, an error message appears or a chart fails to appear because PowerPoint can't link up to the files when you run the presentation on another computer.

When you are using the presentation on another computer, you can't always guarantee that the fonts you used in the presentation are available on the other computer. By embedding the fonts in your file, you ensure that your presentation will look the same on whatever computer you use to run it.

6 **Select Viewer for Windows 95 or NT. Click Next.**

When you are going to run the presentation on a computer that doesn't have PowerPoint, you need to include the Viewer to have the few PowerPoint files necessary to make the slide show run. Select Don't include the Viewer if you know the computer the presentation will be run on does have PowerPoint.

7 **Click Finish.**

PowerPoint compresses your presentation file and stores it on the A: drive along with the PowerPoint Viewer. If the Viewer files weren't copied to your hard disk during the installation of PowerPoint, you may see a request to insert the Office CD. Insert the Microsoft Office CD and click Retry. Click Cancel if you don't have the CD, and PowerPoint will give you the option of not including the Viewer. Click OK to accept that option.

When PowerPoint has completed copying and compressing the necessary files, a dialog box appears saying that Pack and Go has successfully packed your presentation.

8 Click OK.

9 Save the presentation, but leave it open for the next lesson where you learn to present the slide show to a group of participants connected by a network.

Inside Stuff

When you or another user wants to use the presentation you packaged using the Pack and Go Wizard, insert the disk into the floppy disk drive of the computer where you want to run the show.

If the computer doesn't have PowerPoint installed, open the Windows Explorer. Then select the drive where the disk is located and double-click the Pngsetup icon. Enter the destination on the computer where you want the files copied. To run the show, open the folder where you copied the files and double-click the PowerPoint Viewer file `Ppview32`. Click the presentation to run.

On a computer where PowerPoint is installed, you simply open the presentation file from PowerPoint.

Lesson 10: Presenting with Presentation Conferencing

Trying to get a group of people together for a presentation is sometimes difficult. Presentation conferencing allows you to run a presentation over a network, or on the Internet.

All the participants (presenter and audience) use the Presentation Conference Wizard to participate in the meeting. The wizard supports users on a network or participants who connect directly to the Internet or who use a modem to dial in to an Internet service provider (ISP).

Some elements of a presentation can't be seen or heard by all the participants during a presentation conference. Only the presenter and any members of the audience who can see his monitor or a projection of his monitor can see the following:

■ Embedded objects, such as a Microsoft Graph chart.

■ The actual editing of linked or embedded objects.

■ Multimedia objects such as sound or video clips. (If a participant has the necessary hardware, the sound effects associated with transitions and animation can be heard.)

When you're getting ready for a presentation conference, you need to exchange some information with the participants, such as the names of the computers the audience is using or the address of the presentation (if you're using the Internet).

Before you begin a presentation conference, be sure to have your slides in the proper order and with the settings you want to use. The wizard uses the current slide show settings as the default.

If your classroom does not have a network, you may not be able to complete the presentation conference. Follow the directions of your instructor in that case.

To Deliver a Presentation Through Presentation Conferencing

1 With the Recruiting Plan presentation open, choose Tools, Presentation Conference.

The Presentation Conference Wizard dialog box appears. In this case, everyone participating in the conference should be connected to the network. If you were in different offices, you would also set up a conference call so that all the participants could hear instructions.

2 Click Next.

Select one member of the class to be the presenter; the others are the participants.

3 If you are the presenter, click Presenter. If you are a participant, click Audience.

PowerPoint automatically uses the current side show settings for the conference.

4 Click Next. If you are a member of the audience, select Local Area Network (LAN) or Corporate Network and then click Next. The presenter should click Next and then Next again to confirm you are connecting through a network.

Each member of the audience sees the name of his or her computer, which is shared with the presenter. The presenter must enter the computer name for each participant (see Figure 7.23).

Figure 7.23
The presenter must list the computer name or Internet address of each participant in the conference.

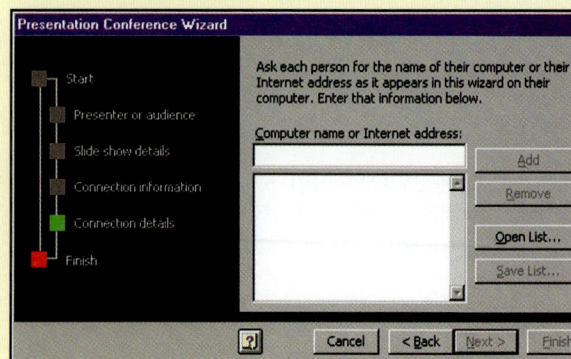

⑤ Click Next. Each audience member must click Finish. Then the presenter clicks Finish.

It takes quite a bit of time for the connections to be made, so the presenter and the audience all see `"Please wait"` messages for a while. Once the connection is made, the presentation appears full-screen to each member of the audience, but the presenter sees several windows (see Figure 7.24). Only the presenter can control the Slide Navigator, enter minutes, or view the speaker's notes (see Figure 7.25). The audience can use the pen to write on the slide, and the other participants in the conference can see the annotations.

Figure 7.24
The presenter sees several windows that help navigate the presentation and use the slide show tools.

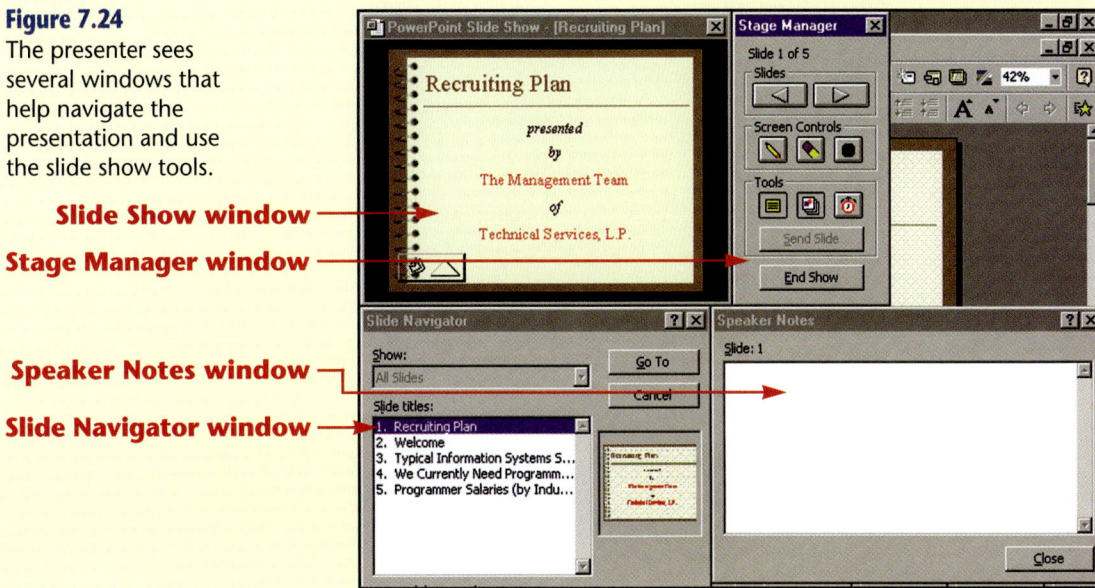

Slide Show window
Stage Manager window
Speaker Notes window
Slide Navigator window

Figure 7.25
The Stage Manager provides a set of tools for the presenter.

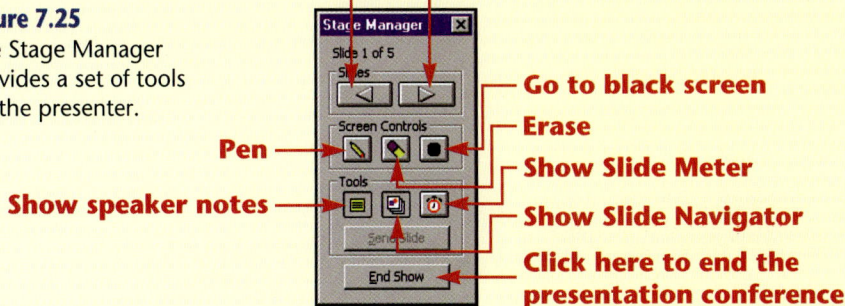

Previous slide   Next slide

Pen
Show speaker notes

Go to black screen
Erase
Show Slide Meter
Show Slide Navigator
Click here to end the presentation conference

⑥ When the presentation is complete, the presenter clicks End Show.

The slide show disappears from the audience monitors, the network connection is broken, and the presenter's screen returns to the PowerPoint view open before the conference began.

If you have finished your work session, exit PowerPoint and shut down Windows 95 before turning off your computer. Otherwise, complete the "Checking Your Skills" and "Applying Your Skills" exercises at the end of this project.

Project Summary

To	Do This
Add slide transitions in Slide Sorter view	Click the Slide Transition Effects drop-down list arrow.
View slide transitions	Click the Slide Transition button under the slide (in Slide Sorter view).
Remove slide transitions	Choose No Transition from the Slide Transition Effects drop-down list on the Slide Sorter toolbar.
Use preset animation	Click the Text Preset Animation drop-down list arrow.
Customize text animation	Display the slide in Slide view and choose Slide Show, Custom Animation.
Hide the current or selected slide	Choose Slide Show, Hide Slide.
Display a hidden slide during a slide show	Right-click and choose Go, Hidden Slide from the shortcut menu.
Rehearse slide timings	Click the Rehearse Timings button (in Slide Sorter view).
Run a slide show continually	Choose Slide Show, Set Up Show, and then check Loop continuously until 'Esc'.
Display slide shortcut keys	Press F1 (in Slide Show view).
Activate the slide show shortcut menu	Right-click the mouse.
Go to the next slide in a slide show	Left-click the mouse or press N.
Go to the previous slide in Slide Show view	Press P or ↑.
Go to a specific slide	Type the slide number and press Enter.
Blacken or unblacken the screen	Press B.
Whiten or unwhiten the screen	Press W.
Erase a screen drawing	Press E.
End the slide show	Press Esc.
Activate the annotation pen in a slide show	Press Ctrl+P.
Activate the mouse pointer in a slide show	Press Ctrl+A.
Change the pen color	Right-click and choose Pointer Options, Pen Color.
Use Meeting Minder	Right-click in the slide show and choose Meeting Minder.
Print action items	Display the Action Items slide and choose File, Print.
Prepare slide show for use on other computers	Choose File, Pack and Go. Follow the instructions in the Pack and Go Wizard.
Present over a network or the Internet	Choose Tools, Presentation Conference. Follow the instructions in the Presentation Conference Wizard.

PowerPoint

Checking Your Skills

True/False

For each of the following, check *T* or *F* to indicate whether the statement is true or false.

__T __F **1.** You can use the Meeting Minder to create action items.

__T __F **2.** You can hide slides in your slide show.

__T __F **3.** The only way to erase an annotation pen drawing is to advance to the next slide.

__T __F **4.** Slide transitions and text animation are just different names for the same feature.

__T __F **5.** You can animate individual objects on a slide, such as charts or text areas.

__T __F **6.** You can display a list of slide show shortcut keys by pressing F1.

__T __F **7.** You use the Presentation Conferencing feature to animate objects on a slide.

__T __F **8.** You can draw on a slide during an electronic slide show.

__T __F **9.** Annotation refers to the way bulleted points are displayed on a slide.

__T __F **10.** You can dim a bulleted point after it is displayed.

Multiple Choice

Circle the letter of the correct answer for each of the following questions.

1. One way to record action items during a presentation and create a slide with the items is to use which of the following?

  a. Minute Taker

  b. Meeting Minder

  c. Notes Page view

  d. Annotation pen

2. The annotation pen is used to do which of the following?

  a. Emphasize information during an onscreen presentation.

  b. Create a list of action items.

  c. Take meeting minutes.

  d. Draw objects in Slide view.

3. Which of the following occurs when you use the Action Items tab of the Meeting Minder?

  a. A printed list of action items results.

  b. The speaker notes are updated.

  c. A final slide of action items is produced.

  d. The action items are placed in the Slide Minder for future reference.

4. You can preview a slide transition in Slide Sorter view by doing which of the following?

    a. choosing Slide, View Transition

    b. pressing Ctrl+T

    c. clicking the Slide Transition icon beneath the slide in Slide Sorter view

    d. right-clicking on a slide and then choosing Show Transition from the shortcut menu

5. Which of the following is a command you can execute by using a keyboard shortcut?

    a. Press B to blacken or unblacken the screen.

    b. Press N to move to the next presentation slide.

    c. Press P to move to the previous presentation slide.

    d. All of the above.

6. Blinds, Checkerboard Across, and Box In are all examples of which of the following?

    a. annotation

    b. action items

    c. text animation

    d. slide transitions

7. You can activate the slide show shortcut menu by doing which of the following?

    a. right-clicking the mouse

    b. pressing Ctrl+A

    c. pressing F1

    d. pressing Ctrl+M

8. You can display the annotation pen in a slide show by doing which of the following?

    a. pressing Ctrl+P

    b. choosing Slide Show, Annotation Pen, Select from the menu

    c. choosing Pen from the Slide Show shortcut menu

    d. both a and c

9. To remove a transition effect, you do which of the following?

    a. Choose Slide Show, Remove Effect from the menu.

    b. Choose No Transition from the Slide Transitions Effect drop-down list.

    c. Press Ctrl+A.

    d. All of the above.

10. Which of the following is true with regard to action items?

    a. You create them using the Meeting Minder feature.

    b. You can print them.

    c. PowerPoint creates an action item slide and places it at the end of your presentation.

    d. All of the above.

PowerPoint

Completion

In the blank provided, write the correct answer for each of the following statements.

1. You can press _____ during an electronic slide show to display a list of shortcut commands.

2. You can use the Meeting Minder to create a list of _____ that appear as the last slide of your presentation.

3. You can change slide _____ to change the way one slide replaces another in an electronic slide show.

4. To add automatic slide timings to your presentation, click the _____ button on the Slide Sorter toolbar.

5. You can specify PowerPoint to _____ your text so that it is displayed one point at a time in the electronic slide show.

6. Slide _____ display below each slide in Slide Sorter view and show how long each slide displays.

7. You can draw, or _____ a slide during an electronic slide show.

8. You can use the _____ feature to save a presentation for use on another computer.

9. You can press _____ to end a running slide show.

10. You can press _____ to activate the mouse pointer in a slide show.

Matching

In the blank next to each of the following terms or phrases, write the letter of the corresponding term or phrase. (Note that some of the letters may be used more than once.)

a. presentation conferencing

b. P

c. F1

d. Ctrl+P

e. annotate

f. slide transition

g. animation

h. Slide Sorter

i. hide

j. Meeting Minder

_____ 1. Displays a list of slide show shortcut keys

_____ 2. A special effect used to introduce a slide during a slide show

_____ 3. A toolbar used to add slide transitions

_____ 4. Drawing on a slide during an electronic slide show

_____ 5. Used to create action items

_____ 6. Displays bulleted points one at a time

_____ 7. Used to share a presentation with people at several locations simultaneously

_____ 8. Displays the previous slide in a slide show

_____ 9. Displays the electronic pen

_____ 10. Not displaying a slide

Applying Your Skills

Practice

The following exercises, found in the Project–07 folder on the CD, enable you to practice the skills you have learned in this project. Take a few minutes to work through these exercises now.

Using Slide Show Commands Effectively

To get ready for an upcoming business presentation, you decide to practice using the Slide Show commands.

To use slide show commands effectively, complete the following steps:

1. Open Proj0704 from the Project-07 folder on the CD and save it as `Employee Information`.

2. Move to Slide 1, if necessary, and click the Slide Show button.

3. Press F1 to display a list of keyboard shortcuts. Read the list and then choose OK to close it.

4. Press N and then P to move to the next and previous slides, respectively.

5. Press 2 and then ⏎Enter to move to Slide 2.

6. Press B to blacken the screen and press B again to display the slide.

7. Right-click to display the shortcut menu, and then choose End Show.

8. Save and close the presentation.

Adding Transitions and Creating a Hidden Slide

You are slated to conduct an orientation meeting for new employees at your company. In preparation for this meeting, you create a presentation with hidden slides.

To add transitions and create a hidden slide, complete the following steps:

1. Open Proj0705 from the Project-07 folder on the CD and save it as `Revised Orientation Meeting`.

2. Display the presentation in Slide Sorter view.

3. Add the following transitions to the slides:

> Slide 1: Blinds Horizontal
>
> Slide 2: Box In
>
> Slide 3: Box Out
>
> Slide 4: Checkerboard Down
>
> Slide 5: Dissolve
>
> Slides 6–7: Fade Through Black
>
> Slides 8–10: Cover Left

4. Run the slide show to view your transitions.

5. In Slide Sorter view, select Slide 4 and then click the Hide Slide button.

6. Run the presentation as a slide show, practicing displaying and hiding the hidden slide.

7. Save and close the presentation.

Adding Transitions and Animation

You're preparing your PowerPoint presentation for the new employee orientation meeting. Because you're concerned that the information you must cover in the orientation session may be boring, you add slide transitions and animation to grab your audience's attention.

To add transitions and animation, complete the following steps:

1. Open Proj0706 from the Project-07 folder on the CD and save it as `Exciting Orientation Meeting`.

2. Display the presentation in Slide Sorter view and select Slide 1.

3. Click the Slide Transition Effects drop-down list arrow, and then choose `Box In` as the transition.

4. Select Slides 2–4, click the Slide Transition Effects drop-down list, and choose `Checkerboard Across`.

5. Select Slide 5, click the Text Preset Animation drop-down list, and choose `Crawl From Left`.

6. Double-click Slide 6 to display it in Slide view, and then choose Slide Show, Custom Animation.

7. Choose `Text 2` in the Slide objects without animation list; then choose Animate.

8. Click the Effects tab, click the After animation arrow, and choose blue to dim the text points.

9. Click the Preview button to see your effect, and then choose OK.

10. Run your slide show from Slide 1 to see your changes.

11. Save and close the presentation.

Generating Meeting Notes and Electronically Incorporating Meeting Feedback

You're conducting a brainstorming session with your company staff to explore possible product lines. To determine the feasibility of the new products, you use PowerPoint's Meeting Minder during the meeting. You enter, as action items, the staff assignments related to the project and then create an Action Items slide. Finally, you print a copy of the Action Items slide to distribute to staff members as they leave the meeting.

To generate meeting notes and electronically incorporate meeting feedback, complete the following steps:

1. Open Proj0707 from the Project-07 folder on the CD and save it as `Action Plan to Determine Feasibility`.

2. Move to Slide 3, `Why ergonomic workstations?`, and click the Slide Show button.

3. Right-click the mouse to display the shortcut menu, and then choose Meeting Minder.

4. Add the following to the action items list:

Description	Assigned To	Due Date
Conduct Market Survey	H. Schmidt	6/12/98
Research Competition	G. Sanders	6/15/98
Check Supplier Status	D. Hitt	6/20/98
Do Cost Analysis	R. Cory	7/1/98
Produce Marketing Materials	S. Lowell	8/18/98

5. Return to the slide show and end it.

6. View the Action Items slide and then print it.

7. Save and close the presentation.

Saving a Presentation for Use on Another Computer

You need to present information to employees at another office location. To save your presentation for use on a computer at the office, you use the Pack and Go Wizard.

To save a presentation for use on another computer, complete the following steps:

1. Open Proj0708 from the Project-07 folder on the CD and save it as `Office Meeting`.

2. Choose <u>F</u>ile, Pack and Go to launch the Pack and Go Wizard.

3. Save the presentation on your floppy disk. Accept all the other default options in the Pack and Go Wizard, and then click <u>F</u>inish.

4. Click OK in the message box that displays after PowerPoint has packaged your presentation.

5. Close the presentation.

Challenge

The following challenges, found in the Project–07 folder on the CD, enable you to use your problem-solving skills. Take time to work through these exercises now.

Adding Slide Transitions

For your speech class, you are giving a talk on how to do presentations. To help hold your audience's attention, you add slide transitions to the presentation.

To add slide transitions, complete the following steps:

1. Open Proj0709 from the Project-07 folder on the CD and save it as Presentation Guidelines.

2. Display the presentation in Slide Sorter view.

3. Add a transition of your choosing for each slide in the presentation.

4. Click the Slide Transition icon for each slide.

5. Display the presentation as an electronic slide show.

6. Remove slide transitions from Slides 3–4.

7. Save the presentation.

8. Keep the presentation open if you plan to complete the next exercise. If not, save and then close the presentation.

Using Automatic Slide Show Timings

To help you time your speech class presentation, you use PowerPoint's slide show timings.

To use automatic slide show timings, complete the following steps:

1. Display the Presentation Guidelines presentation open from the previous exercise in Slide Sorter view.

2. Set slide timings. Click the Rehearse Timing button and then discuss each slide just as you would for a live audience. Display each slide for a minimum of 10 seconds.

3. Accept the slide timings and view them in Slide Sorter view.

4. Run the slide show using the slide timings and manual advance.

5. Change the slide timings to those you prefer and run the slide show again.

6. Choose Slide Show, Set Up Show to display the Set Up Show dialog box. Choose Loop continually until 'Esc'. Make sure the Using timings, if present option is selected. Click OK when you're finished.

7. Launch your slide show. Let PowerPoint use the slide timings and automatic advance to display the show.

8. Keep the presentation open if you plan to complete the next exercise. If not, save and then close the presentation.

Adding Custom Text Animation

To keep people in your speech class interested in your presentation, you animate your text. You also dim each bulleted point after it is displayed.

To add custom text animation, complete the following steps:

1. Display the Presentation Guidelines presentation open from the previous exercise in Slide view.

2. Display Slide 4, Plan, and then choose Slide Show, Custom Animation.

3. Animate the Text 2 object associated with Slide 4 (the bulleted list). Choose Fly From Bottom-Left as the entry animation. Then choose to dim each point after it is displayed with a color of your choice. Finally, introduce the text grouped by 2nd Level Paragraphs.

4. Preview the animation in the Custom Animation dialog box.

5. Close the Custom Animation dialog box. Then display Slide 4 in Slide Show view.

6. Close the slide show.

7. Keep the presentation open if you plan to complete the next exercise. If not, save and then close the presentation.

Annotating Your Slide Show

To focus your audience's attention, you decide to use the annotation pen during your speech class presentation. To prepare for the presentation, practice using the pen.

To annotate your slide show, complete the following steps:

1. Display Slide 1 of Presentation Guidelines presentation open from the previous exercise.

2. Start the slide show and advance to Slide 4, Plan (con't).

3. Using the Annotation pen, draw an arrow to each of the subpoints listed on the slide.

4. Erase the drawing.

5. Change the pen color to blue.

6. Circle each of the subpoints on Slide 4.

7. End the slide show.

8. Save the Presentation Guidelines presentation, and then close it.

Electronically Incorporating Meeting Feedback

As president of the Biking Club, you want to make sure that club members follow through on assignments. To help them do this, you use the Meeting Minder to create and print action items.

To use the Meeting Minder, complete the following steps:

1. Open Proj0710 from the Project-07 folder on the CD and save it as `Biking Club Assignments`.

2. Display the presentation as an electronic slide show, and then use the Meeting Minder to enter the following action items:

Description	Assigned to	Due Date
Contact Sponsors	K. Luther	3/24/98
Check on tickets to the "Race of Champions"	J. Overby	4/17/98
Call Raccoon Creek Park to reserve shelter	G. Smith	5/4/98

3. Close the Meeting Minder window and the slide show.

4. View the Action Items slide.

5. Print the Action Items slide.

6. Save the presentation, then close it.

Presenting with Presentation Conferencing

You want to share the new employee orientation presentation with other Human Resource managers in your company and get their feedback on its effectiveness. Because they are at various locations, you decide to use PowerPoint's presentation conferencing feature to share the presentation with them.

To present with presentation conferencing, complete the following steps:

1. Open Proj0711 from the Project-07 folder on the CD and save it as `Conference`.

2. Choose Tools, Presentation Conference to start the Presentation Conference Wizard.

3. Work through the steps provided in the Presentation Conference Wizard to set up the presentation. (You need to coordinate this with others in your class, if you are using the local network.)

4. Participate in the presentation as either the presenter or an audience member.

5. Save and close the presentation.

PinPoint Assessment

You have completed the project and the associated lessons, as well as the "Checking Your Skills" and "Applying Your Skills" sections. Now use the PinPoint software Evaluation mode to assess your comprehension of the specific exam tasks you have just learned. You can also use the PinPoint Trainer mode and the SHOW ME tutorials to practice these specific exam tasks.

Project 8

Eight

Refining Your Presentation Text and Layout

Making a Professional-Looking Presentation

In this project you will learn the following objectives and their associated Microsoft Exam required activities.

Objectives   Required Activities

- ➤ Lay Out and Design Professional-Looking Presentations

- ➤ Replace Fonts Automatically … … … … … … … …Change Fonts

- ➤ Use the Style Checker to Ensure … … … … … … …Check Styles
  Design Consistency

- ➤ Use the Spelling Checker … … … … … … … … … …Spell Check

- ➤ Find and Replace Text … … … … … … … … … … …Find and Replace Text

Why Would I Do This?

Your goal for creating a PowerPoint presentation is to deliver a targeted, compelling message to an audience. In general, the more PowerPoint commands and tools you can effectively use to craft a well-designed presentation, the more convincing you can make the presentation. Luckily, PowerPoint provides a number of subtle but effective things you can do to refine a presentation and make it compelling. For example, you can quickly replace all the *fonts*, or typefaces, in your presentation with another for a better appearance. You can also use the Style Checker to ensure that your punctuation and text are consistent throughout the presentation. Finally, you can rely on the Spelling Checker to proof your text for errors. Also, if necessary, you can search for specific text and replace it with more appropriate text.

As you use these features, keep design and layout principles in mind so that your slides don't become cluttered and lose focus. You should avoid overwhelming a slide with PowerPoint elements just because they are available.

Now try using these principles and features to help you create a sophisticated and refined presentation.

Lesson 1: Laying Out and Designing Professional-Looking Presentations

You can develop a persuasive presentation by implementing a few design principles. Because PowerPoint 97 has so many impressive features, it's easy to overuse them and overwhelm or confuse your audience. The overall presentation layout needs to be carefully crafted to ensure a focused message as well as balance and uniformity. As you refine your presentations, use the following principles as a guide:

- **Simplify Your Presentation. Keep your message and slide show as concise as possible**. Don't inadvertently include too many slides, slide elements, or extraneous text. Irrelevant information tends to distract the audience from your main message.

- **Use text effectively**. To use text effectively and professionally in a presentation:

  - Avoid using too many typefaces, (including a mix of color, style, and sizes) or the presentation may lack uniformity. When you want to emphasize information, apply bold, italic, or shadow to text rather than introducing another font.

  - Use a font size of at least 18 points so that your audience can easily see the text.

  - Avoid using all uppercase letters because they are significantly harder to read than a mix of upper- and lowercase letters.

  - Use more *sans serif* than *serif fonts*.

Font
The distinctive design of a set of text characters, sometimes called the typeface.

Sans Serif font
The type of font used for headlines that doesn't include finish lines at the bottom or top of the text characters. Finish lines are the fine, ornamental cross strokes at the end of the main strokes of a character. Arial is a typical example of a sans serif font.

Serif font
The type of font typically used for body text. It includes finish lines at the top or bottom of text characters that lead the reader's eye to the next word. Times New Roman is an example of a serif font.

PowerPoint

- Don't include more than five bulleted points on a slide.

- Finally, use concise, targeted phrases rather than complete sentences for your text.

- **Keep the presentation balanced and uniform**. Rely on PowerPoint's templates, slide backgrounds, color schemes, and the Slide Master to keep a presentation balanced and uniform in appearance.

You can use Table 8.1 as a reference when designing presentations.

Table 8.1 Design Guidelines	
Design Guideline	How to Implement
Simplify	Plan three to five text slides per major concept in a presentation.
	Use just one main concept for each slide.
	Use the minimum number of elements on a slide that will effectively convey your message.
	Limit each slide to five or less bulleted points that support the main idea.
	Use five or fewer data series per chart.
	Avoid too many objects on a slide.
Emphasize your main point	Use clip art and drawn objects to emphasize the most important point.
	Explode a pie slice or change data series chart color to emphasize the most important data.
Make text readable	Limit the number of typefaces.
	Use sentence case (upper- and lowercase lettering), not all capital letters.
	Make text at least 18 points for onscreen display.
	Use proportionately more sans serif fonts.
	Use short, to the point phrases rather than complete sentences.
Keep slides uniform	Use the same slide background, color scheme, and template for all slides (except to emphasize a particular point).
	Use the same fonts, sizes, and attributes throughout the presentation.
	Limit slide transition effects.
Use color effectively	Keep the color contrasts high.
	Test the color combination on your final delivery system.
	Avoid juxtaposing red and green, especially in chart series. Approximately 4 percent of men are red/green color blind and may find this hard to read.

In the following tutorial, you fix a number of problems in a presentation to clarify the message. Try using layout and design principles now.

To Lay Out and Design Sophisticated Presentations

❶ Start PowerPoint, and then open Proj0801 from the Project-08 folder on the CD and save it as Design Principles.

This presentation slide contains a number of design flaws that you can quickly fix (see Figure 8.1). For example, you can eliminate extraneous objects to reduce clutter and focus the slide's message.

Figure 8.1
You eliminate extra objects to reduce clutter and make a slide more attractive.

Adjacent green and red colors

All caps used

Too many fonts and bulleted points used

Text too small

Extraneous chart and drawn object

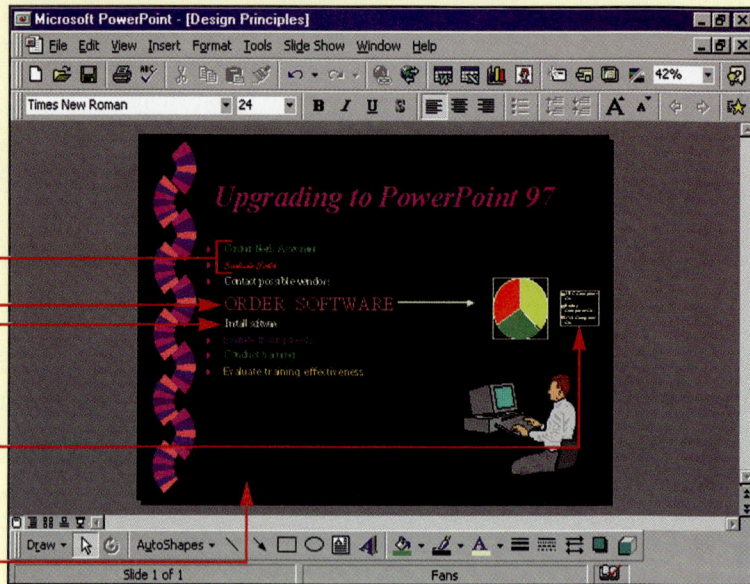

❷ Click the arrow to place selection handles around it and press Del**.**

The arrow is removed. Now you can remove the chart, which has no direct relation to the slide's main message.

❸ Click the chart placeholder to select it, and then press Del**.**

The chart is deleted from the slide. Notice that the slide already appears less cluttered.

You can also improve this slide by enlarging the text and using just one font. To do this, you select the bulleted points by dragging the mouse pointer over them, then choose a font from the Formatting toolbar.

Times New Roman

❹ Drag to select all bulleted points, and then click the Font drop-down list arrow on the Formatting toolbar and choose Arial**.**

Because Arial is a sans serif font, it is more readable than the mix of fonts originally used. (If Arial is not available on your computer, choose Univers or another sans serif font instead.)

Because text should be a minimum of 18 points for onscreen display, you should enlarge it.

`24` ▾

❺ With the bulleted points still selected, click the Font Size drop-down list arrow and select 24.

The font size increases so that text is easier to read. To make the slide even more cohesive, you should also limit the number of colors used—and preferably use those that coordinate with the presentation's template. The easiest way to change text color is to use the Font Color button on the Drawing toolbar.

If you have problems...

By default, the Drawing toolbar displays at the bottom of the PowerPoint screen. However, if you don't see this toolbar, choose View, Toolbars to display a submenu of available toolbars. Choose Drawing from the submenu to display the toolbar.

A ▾

❻ With the bulleted points still selected, click the Font Color button drop-down list arrow on the Drawing toolbar.

A palette of available colors is displayed (see Figure 8.2). The top row includes those that coordinate best with the current template and color scheme. Unless you are particularly artistic (or adventurous) you should choose from these colors. Also notice that as you rest the mouse pointer over a color box, a ScreenTip displays for which slide element the color is typically used.

Figure 8.2
Use the Font Color button to quickly change text color.

Colors that coordinate with the template

Custom colors

Click this arrow to display the color palette

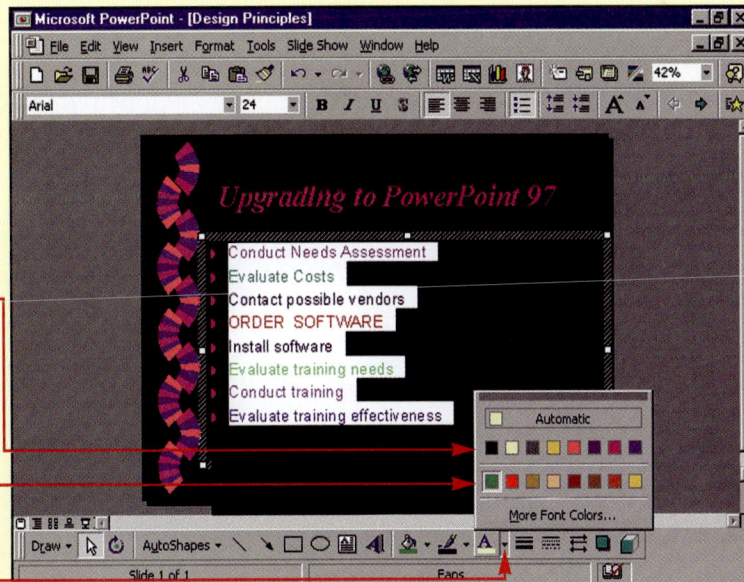

❼ On the top row of colors, rest the mouse pointer over the beige color (the second from the left) until the ScreenTip, `Follow Text and Lines Scheme Color`, displays. Click the color box.

The beige color is applied to the selected bulleted points. However, to see the effect, you must first deselect the text.

continues

To Lay Out and Design Sophisticated Presentations   (continued)

Case
The mix of upper- and lowercase letters used.

8 **Click outside the text placeholder to see your changes.**

Finally, to make the text more readable, you want to change the uppercase text to sentence *case* in which only the first letter of a phrase displays in uppercase. To quickly change case, you can use the PowerPoint's Change Case feature.

9 **Select the text for the fourth bulleted point,** ORDER SOFTWARE, **and then choose F**o**rmat, Change Ca**s**e**.

The Change Case dialog box is displayed (see Figure 8.3). Notice that each command actually shows an example of the type of case. For example, the command associated with the uppercase option button displays as UPPERCASE. You can use this dialog box to view and apply a case to selected text.

Figure 8.3
You can quickly change case using the Change Case dialog box.

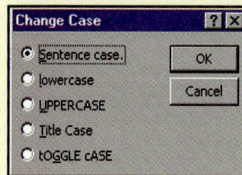

10 **Click the** **S**entence case option button (if not already selected) and click OK. Click outside the text placeholder to better see your changes.

The selected text displays using sentence case. Your finished slide shows marked improvement by reducing clutter and extraneous fonts (see Figure 8.4). (Times New Roman font displays in the Font box because you deselected the text box area that included the Arial font.)

Figure 8.4
You can improve a slide's appearance by implementing design principles.

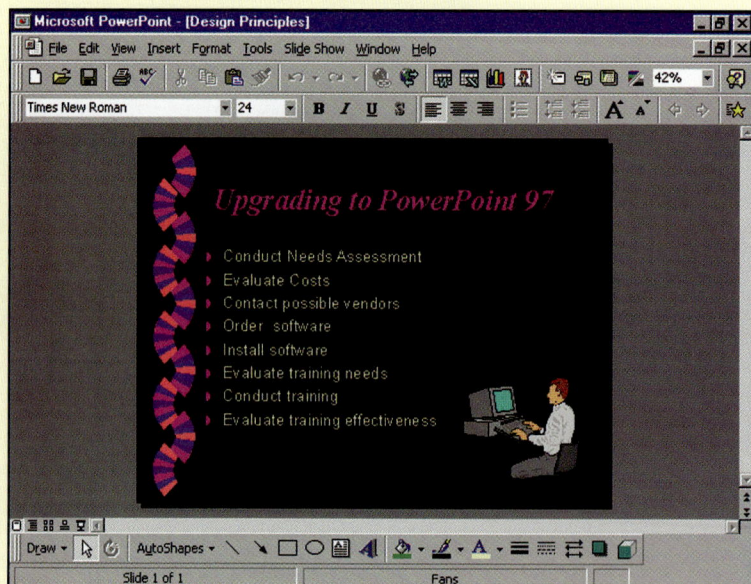

PowerPoint

⓫ Save the presentation, and then close it.

Keep PowerPoint running for the next lesson, in which you learn how to replace fonts automatically in a presentation.

Inside Stuff

You can further refine your overall presentation by expanding or compressing the information you include. For example, you can quickly expand a list of bulleted points into titles for individual slides so that you can include more information for each topic. To do this, display the slide and choose Tools, Expand slide. Once PowerPoint expands the bulleted points into slides, you can choose to view the result in Slide Sorter or Outline views.

Alternately, you can create a summary (sometimes called an agenda) slide that makes the titles of selected slides into bulleted points on one slide. If you want, you can print this summary slide to hand out to your audience as an agenda. To do this, select the slides you want to include in the Summary Slide in Slide Sorter view by pressing ◆Shift as you click the slides. Then click the Summary Slide button on the Slide Sorter toolbar.

Lesson 2: Replacing Fonts Automatically

One way to fine-tune your presentation is to replace a font with a more attractive one. However, performing this function manually would be laborious and time-consuming. Fortunately, PowerPoint includes an automation feature that enables you to quickly replace one font with another throughout your entire presentation. And, because this feature is so easy to use, you can experiment with replacing fonts until you find one that fits your needs. Try replacing fonts automatically now.

To Replace Fonts Automatically

❶ Open Proj0802 from the Project-08 folder on the CD, and save it as Replacing Fonts.

❷ Display Slide 2, Introduction; **then choose Format, Replace Fonts.**

The Replace Font dialog box is displayed (see Figure 8.5). You can use this dialog box to quickly replace an existing font with another one.

Figure 8.5
You can automatically replace one font with another throughout an entire presentation.

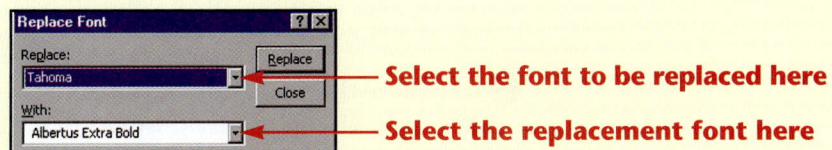

Replace Font

Replace:
Tahoma   — **Select the font to be replaced here**
Replace
Close
With:
Albertus Extra Bold   — **Select the replacement font here**

Don't worry if you see different fonts than those shown in Figure 8.5—your computer just has different fonts loaded.

continues

To Replace Fonts Automatically   (continued)

3 **Click the Replace drop-down list arrow to display a list of the fonts currently used in your presentation; then select Times New Roman.**

This is the font used for title text. Next, you designate the replacement font.

4 **Click the With drop-down list arrow.**

All the fonts available on your computer are displayed (see Figure 8.6). The fonts listed depend, in part, on the printer you use as well as which fonts have been loaded on your system. Because of this, you should expect some variation from one system to the next. However, choosing *TrueType* fonts (designated by the TT next to a font's name) will help you maintain consistency if you show your presentation on different computers than the one on which it was created.

TrueType font
A scalable font that prints the same as it displays onscreen.

Figure 8.6
Most systems have a variety of fonts from which you can choose.

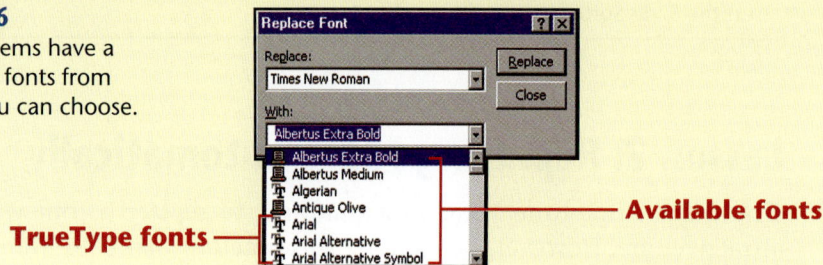

TrueType fonts

Available fonts

5 **Scroll down the list of available fonts and choose Impact. (If Impact isn't available on your system, choose another TrueType font or ask your instructor for assistance.)**

Even though you have designated the original and replacement fonts, you must click the Replace button to actually replace the fonts. The Replace Font dialog box remains open, so you can make additional changes. To best see the effect of your change, however, you should move this dialog box.

6 **Drag the title bar for the Replace Font dialog box so that you can view the slide's title and body text; then click the Replace button.**

The Impact font replaces the original one (Times New Roman). The change reflects in the title of Slide 2. Notice that the Replace Font dialog box is still open so you can replace other fonts. Try replacing the font used for body text (Arial) with another one.

7 **Choose Arial from the Replace drop-down list and Comic Sans MS from the With drop-down list, and then choose Replace. (If you don't have Comic Sans MS on your system, choose another font.)**

The new font replaces Arial and the result is displayed on Slide 2. To see the changes on all the slides, you must close the Replace Font dialog box.

PowerPoint

8 Click the Close button in the Replace Font dialog box, and then scroll through your presentation.

Notice that the fonts have been replaced on all slides. Using this method, you can maintain consistency as well as see how different fonts will look.

9 Save your presentation, and then close it.

Keep PowerPoint running for the next lesson, in which you use the Style Checker.

Inside Stuff

To check which fonts a particular presentation uses, choose File, Properties to display the Properties dialog box. Click the Contents tab to see a list of the fonts used.

Lesson 3: Using the Style Checker

You can refine your presentation and make sure it is uniform by using PowerPoint's Style Checker. *Style* refers to the way elements are used throughout a presentation. The Style Checker examines your presentation for spelling, consistent case, punctuation, and *visual clarity*, and then gives you the chance to fix any problems you might encounter. The Style Checker can analyze your presentation for the following:

Style
The way in which elements, such as text and graphics, are handled in a presentation.

Visual Clarity
The way in which fonts and other text elements are used. Visual clarity determines the legibility of a presentation.

- Spelling errors
- Visual clarity, which includes appropriate font usage and the legibility of your slide text
- Case and end punctuation, which includes consistency in capitalization and end punctuation for slide titles and body text

Using the Style Checker involves two steps: You set the options you would like for a particular presentation, and then check it.

First the Style Checker finds all spelling errors, and gives you the opportunity to change or ignore them. Then it checks for punctuation and case inconsistencies. When it finds a problem, it displays the Style Checker dialog box with a description of the inconsistency. You have several choices in this dialog box. For example, you can choose Change to correct this instance of the inconsistency, or Change All to correct all errors of the same type. The errors are corrected according to the settings you specified in the Style Checker Options dialog box. Likewise, you can choose Ignore to skip over the indicated inconsistency without correcting it, or Ignore All to skip over all errors of the same type.

Try using the Style Checker now to make your presentation consistent and professional-looking.

To Use the Style Checker

1 Open Proj0803 from the Project-08 folder on the CD, and save it as `Checking Styles`.

2 Choose Tools, Style Checker.

The Style Checker dialog box is displayed (see Figure 8.7).

Figure 8.7
You can turn Style Checker features on or off in this dialog box.

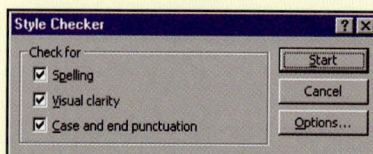

By default, all three check boxes are checked so that the Style Checker examines spelling, visual clarity, and punctuation. So that you perform a complete check, make sure that each feature is turned on. You can also use the Options button to set more advanced options.

3 Make sure each check box contains a check mark, and then click the Options button.

The Style Checker Options dialog box is displayed (see Figure 8.8). This dialog box includes two tabbed pages—Case and End Punctuation and Visual Clarity—so that you can make decisions regarding your check. The defaults include using title case for slide titles (without a period) and sentence case for body text (with a period). In addition, you can determine the maximum number of fonts, lines per title or bulleted point, and relative font size of title and body text.

Figure 8.8
You can set a variety of options related to checking style in this dialog box.

Use this page to set case and punctuation options

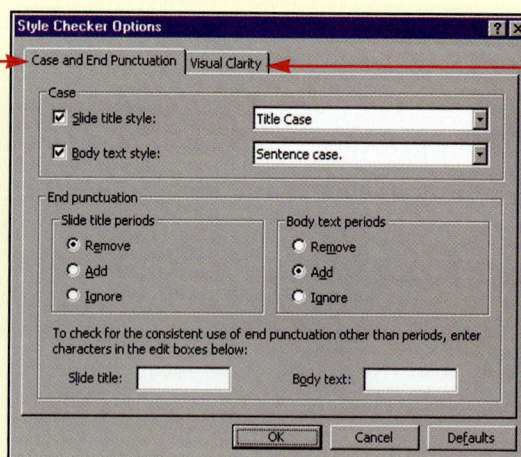

Click this tab to display options related to legibility and visual clarity

4 Read over the options on the Case and End Punctuation page, and then click the Visual Clarity tab.

The Visual Clarity page is displayed (see Figure 8.9). You use this page to make changes regarding the number of fonts allowed and the overall legibility.

Figure 8.9
You can set font and
legibility options using
the Visual Clarity page.

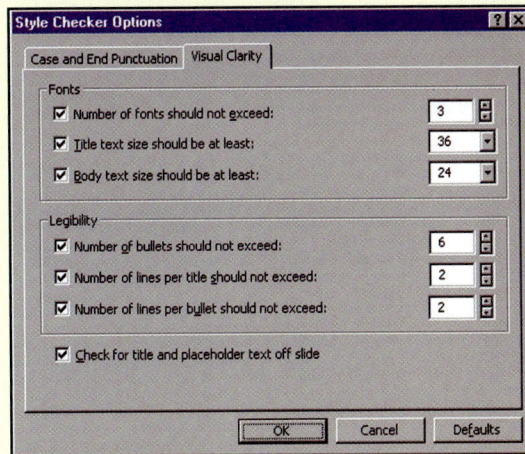

5 In the Fonts section, use the spin arrows to reduce the number of fonts to 2.

6 In the Legibility section, use the spin arrows to change the number of bullets to 5, and then click OK to close the Style Checker Options dialog box.

Once you set the options, you can begin your check.

7 Choose Start in the Style Checker dialog box.

The Style Checker examines your presentation until it finds a problem. In this case, it found a spelling error. The Spelling dialog box is displayed with possible replacements (see Figure 8.10). You can choose a word from the list of suggested words or ignore the error. Because the correct spelling for the word is already displayed in the Change to text box, you can simply choose Change.

Figure 8.10
The Style Checker
initially finds spelling
errors.

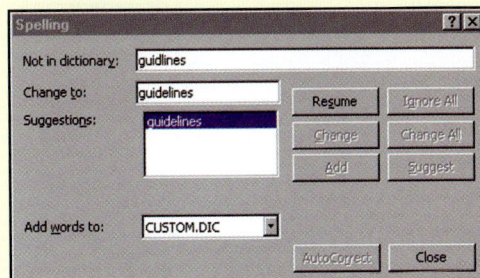

8 Choose Change to replace the incorrectly spelled word.

After the Style Checker finds all spelling errors, it checks for punctuation and case inconsistencies. When it encounters a problem, it displays the Style Checker dialog box (see Figure 8.11).

continues

To Use the Style Checker   (continued)

Figure 8.11
The Style Checker quickly finds punctuation and case inconsistencies.

Description of the inconsistency

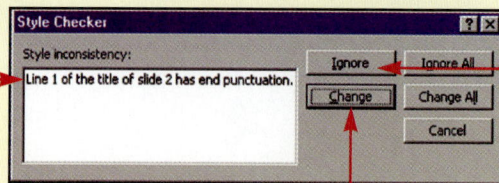

Click here to ignore the inconsistency

Click here to correct the inconsistency

9 **Choose Change All to correct the punctuation for all slide titles.**

The Style Checker fixes title text punctuation according to the options you specified earlier and then checks for other types of errors. The Style Checker dialog box displays again when it finds a problem with end punctuation for body text.

10 **Choose Change All to correct end punctuation for all body text.**

After the Style Checker fixes all spelling and punctuation inconsistencies, it displays a Style Checker Summary dialog box (see Figure 8.12). You can use this dialog box to get a quick list of other stylistic problems with your presentation. However, the Style Checker doesn't automatically fix these problems—you must manually do it because there are some changes you might not want the Style Checker to make. For example, you wouldn't want PowerPoint to automatically delete extra bulleted points just because there are too many on a slide. Nevertheless, the summary is handy because it marks problems you might otherwise overlook.

Figure 8.12
The Style Checker lists a summary of stylistic inconsistencies.

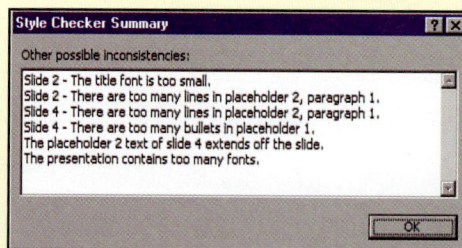

11 **Read through the list and then click OK to close the Style Checker dialog box.**

12 **Save the presentation, and then close it.**

Keep PowerPoint running for the next lesson, in which you work with the Spelling Checker.

Lesson 4: Using the Spelling Checker

PowerPoint provides a built-in Spelling Checker to help you put together an error-free presentation. If you want to check for only spelling (not style) errors, using the Spelling Checker is faster than using the Style Checker. When you use the Spelling Checker, PowerPoint checks all words in your presentation against its dictionary and shows discrepancies in the Spelling dialog box. You can then replace or ignore the unrecognized word, or even add it to the dictionary.

The Spelling dialog box displays a number of command buttons you can use to correct (or ignore) spelling errors. Notice that these commands are similar to those included in the Style Checker dialog box:

- **Ignore**. Click this button to skip over the highlighted word without making any changes.

- **Ignore All**. Click this button to skip over the highlighted word throughout the presentation.

- **Change**. Click this button to replace the original word with the one highlighted in the Change to text box.

- **Change All**. Click this button to correct every occurrence of the word in the presentation.

- **Add**. Click this button to add the word to PowerPoint's dictionary.

- **Suggest**. Click this button to display possible replacement words from the dictionary.

You can also turn on automatic spelling so that PowerPoint flags unrecognized words as you type with a wavy, red underline. You can then right-click the word and choose options from the spelling shortcut menu that displays.

To turn on automatic spelling, choose Tools, Options to display the Options dialog box. Click the Spelling tab. In the Check spelling as you type section, check the box for Spelling. If necessary, uncheck the Hide spelling errors check box. Choose OK when you're finished.

Try using PowerPoint's Spelling Checker feature now.

To Use the Spelling Checker

❶ Open Proj0804 from the Project-08 folder on the CD, and save it as Spelling.

When the automatic Spelling Checker is turned on, words that PowerPoint doesn't recognize are displayed with wavy, red underlines. This indicates that the words are not in PowerPoint's dictionary.

continues

2 On Slide 1, right-click the misspelled word, Seeling.

The spelling shortcut menu displays with suggested replacement words from which you can choose (see Figure 8.13). You can choose a replacement word from the list. Alternately, you can choose Ignore All if you want to skip over all incidences of the word in the presentation or Add if you want to place the word in the dictionary permanently. (You typically add a word to the dictionary that you might frequently use, such as company or personal names or technical terms related to your job.)

Figure 8.13
Right-click a misspelled word to view the spelling shortcut menu.

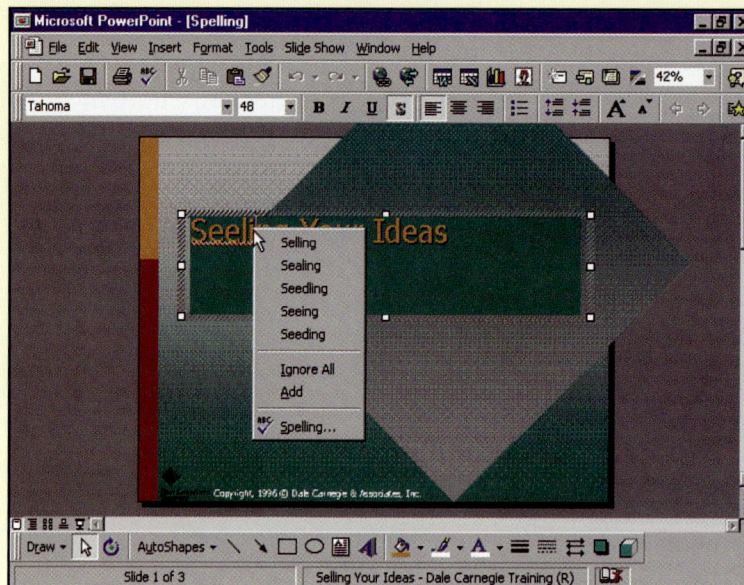

3 Select the word Selling **from the shortcut menu.**

PowerPoint replaces the misspelled word with the correct spelling. Now try using the automatic Spelling Checker as you type a word.

4 Click in the title placeholder area for Slide 1 below the Selling Your Ideas **title, and then type** By Rebecca Hitt **and press** Spacebar.

Because the personal name (Hitt) is not in PowerPoint's dictionary, a wavy, red underline appears beneath the word. If this name is one that you frequently use, you can choose to add it to the dictionary. If not, choose to skip over all occurrences of the word in this presentation.

5 Right-click the word Hitt, **and then choose Ignore All from the shortcut menu.**

The wavy, red underline disappears from the word.

Rather than spell checking individual words, you can also start the spelling checker to quickly proof the entire presentation. PowerPoint initially checks all slides for errors and then checks notes pages. Try checking an entire presentation now.

6 Click the Spelling button on the Standard toolbar.

PowerPoint's Spelling Checker begins and searches for unrecognized words. Any unrecognized words display in the Spelling dialog box and are highlighted on the slide so that you can readily identify them (see Figure 8.14).

Figure 8.14
The Spelling Checker displays unrecognized words in the Spelling dialog box.

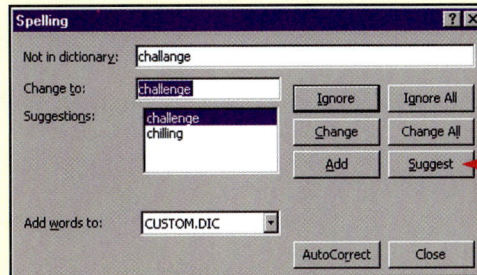

Click here to display a list of possible replacement words

7 Make sure challenge displays in the Change to text box, and then choose Change.

The Spelling Checker replaces the original word with the replacement one and then continues to check the presentation until it locates another spelling error (the word Evidance).

8 Choose Suggest to display a list of possible replacements for the misspelled word.

9 Make sure Evidence displays in the Change to text box, then choose Change.

Because the Spelling Checker didn't locate any more spelling errors, a message box displays informing you that the check is complete (see Figure 8.15).

Figure 8.15
PowerPoint informs you when the spelling check in finished.

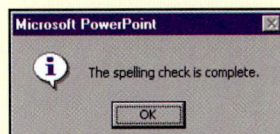

10 Click OK to close the message box, and then save and close the presentation.

Inside Stuff

Proper names or terminology related to your business probably don't appear in the spelling dictionary. PowerPoint will usually mark these words as possible misspellings. To add one of these words to the spelling dictionary, click the Add button when the word appears in the Spelling dialog box; or right-click the possibly misspelled word (indicated by the wavy underline) and choose Add from the shortcut menu. Just be sure the word is spelled correctly before you add it to the dictionary.

Lesson 5: Finding and Replacing Text

When you have a presentation, especially a long-established one that you use over and over again, a quick way of updating it is to change a few words to keep it accurate. For example, if you created it in 1997, you need to change the year to 1998. You also need to update names, if the people mentioned in the presentation have changed.

To Find and Replace Text

1 **Open Proj0805 from the Project-08 folder from the CD, and save it as** Sales Goals.

The Sales Goals presentation was developed for last year's annual sales meeting. Now you want to make changes to the presentation to use it as a sales orientation presentation for new employees. Before you get down to working with the individual slides, you want to make as many overall changes as possible.

2 **Display Slide 1,** Annual Sales Meeting. **Change the slide title to** Sales Orientation.

In the original presentation, there are references to San Francisco. You need to find the slide that has those references.

3 **Choose Edit, Find.**

The Find dialog box appears (see Figure 8.16).

Figure 8.16
Type the text you want to find in the Find what box.

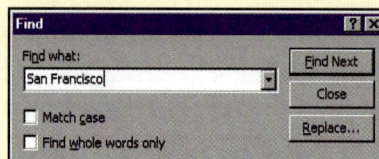

4 **Type** San Francisco **in the Find what text box. Click Find Next.**

The first reference to San Francisco is highlighted. You may have to drag the Find dialog box out of the way in order to see the reference.

If you have problems...

If you can't find text that you're sure is in the document, check the spelling of the Find what text and make sure unwanted search options are not enabled.

5 **Click in the slide text and change the first bullet paragraph to** Teamwork is important.

The Find dialog remains open while you edit the slide text.

6 **Click Find Next in the Find dialog box.**

PowerPoint finds the next instance of the San Francisco text.

7 **Click in the slide text and change** San Francisco **to** one city.

PowerPoint

8 **Click Find Next in the Find dialog box.**

PowerPoint can find no further instances of San Francisco, so a box appears saying the search item was not found (see Figure 8.17).

Figure 8.17
PowerPoint reports that it can't find the search item.

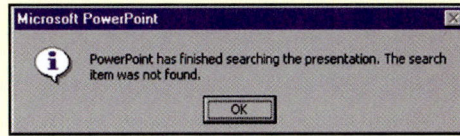

9 **Click OK. Then click Close in the Find dialog box.**

Now that you've set the presentation title, you need to change all the 1997 references to 1998 and the 1998 references to 1999.

10 **Press Ctrl+Home to return to Slide 1.**

11 **Choose Edit, Replace.**

The Replace dialog box appears (see Figure 8.18). The search item from the last search is still in the Find what box. The text is highlighted, so you can type the new search item and it will automatically replace the highlighted text.

Figure 8.18
Type the text you want to replace in the Find what box and then enter the new text in the Replace with box.

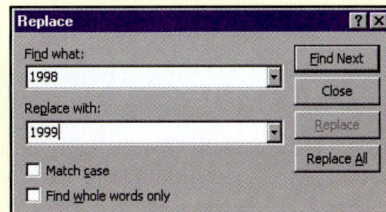

12 **Type 1998 in the Find what box. Type 1999 in the Replace with box. Click Find Next.**

PowerPoint finds the first instance of 1998. You click Replace to replace just that one instance with 1999. To replace all the occurrences of 1998 with 1999, click Replace All.

13 **Click Replace All.**

Figure 8.19
PowerPoint alerts you that the find and replace is complete and indicates how many occurrences of the text it replaced.

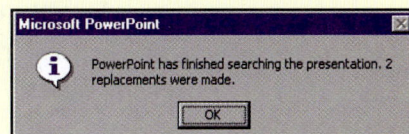

14 **Click OK.**

The Replace dialog box is still open.

15 **Type 1997 in the Find what box. Type 1998 in the Replace with box. Click Replace All.**

continues

To Find and Replace Text   (continued)

16 **Click OK when the replacements are complete. Then click Close in the Replace dialog box.**

The replacements have been made throughout the presentation.

17 **Save the presentation and close it.**

If you have finished your work session, exit PowerPoint and shut down Windows 95 before turning off your computer. Otherwise, complete the "Checking Your Skills" and "Applying Your Skills" exercises at the end of this project.

Inside Stuff

If you have the same word appearing in different cases ("The" and "the," for example) but want to replace the word in a specific case only, choose the Match case option in the Replace dialog box. This options requires an exact match for upper- and lowercase letters. By selecting this option, "The" will only match "The" and not "the" or "THE."

When finding words, PowerPoint also finds text that includes the search item. For example, if you are searching for "ten," PowerPoint might also find "tenuous" or "often." To find only the search item text, select the Find whole words only option.

Project Summary

To	Do This
Change font size	Select the text and click the Font Size drop-down list arrow on the Formatting toolbar.
Change the font	Select the text and click the Font drop-down list arrow on the Formatting toolbar.
Change font color	Select the text and then click the Font Color drop-down list arrow on the Drawing toolbar.
Change case	Choose Format, Change Case.
Expand a bulleted list	Choose Tools, Expand Slide into slide titles.
Create a summary slide	Select the slides in Slide Sorter view; then click the Summary Slide button.
Replace fonts automatically	Choose Format, Replace Fonts.
View a presentation's fonts	Choose File, Properties, and click the Contents tab.
Use the Style Checker	Choose Tools, Style Checker.
Use the Spelling Checker	Click the Spelling button on the Standard toolbar.
Check spelling as you type	Choose Tools, Options, click the Spelling tab; check the box for Spelling.
Find text in the presentation	Choose Edit, Find.
Replace text in the presentation	Choose Edit, Replace.

Checking Your Skills

True/False

For each of the following, check *T* or *F* to indicate whether the statement is true or false.

__T __F **1.** The Style Checker can examine a presentation for spelling.

__T __F **2.** To make a presentation interesting, you should include as many fonts as possible.

__T __F **3.** Body text should be at least 18 points to be readable for most audiences.

__T __F **4.** You can automatically replace one font with another throughout your entire presentation.

__T __F **5.** In PowerPoint you can put a maximum of three bulleted points on a slide.

__T __F **6.** You can replace fonts, but not text in a PowerPoint presentation.

__T __F **7.** PowerPoint indicates possible misspelled words with a red, wavy underline.

__T __F **8.** You can add words to the spelling dictionary.

__T __F **9.** You use the Search and Locate command to quickly find text in your presentation.

__T __F **10.** Serif and sans serif refer to the two main styles of typefaces.

Multiple Choice

Circle the letter of the correct answer for each of the following questions.

1. Which of the following is a design principle you should use when refining a presentation?

    a. Use as many font colors as possible to add interest.

    b. Use a maximum of four bulleted points per slide.

    c. Emphasize your main point.

    d. All of the above.

2. Which of the following can the Style Checker examine?

    a. visual clarity

    b. case and end punctuation

    c. spelling

    d. all of the above

3. Which of the following is true regarding a summary slide?

    a. It creates bulleted points from the titles of several slides.

    b. It creates titles for several new slides based on the bulleted points of the selected slide.

    c. It cannot be printed.

    d. None of the above.

4. Expanding a slide does which of the following?

   a. It creates subpoints under existing bulleted points.

   b. It makes the slide larger, so you can insert pictures.

   c. It creates an agenda slide.

   d. None of the above.

5. How can you spell check an individual word?

   a. Right-click the word.

   b. Double-click the word.

   c. Click the Word Check button on the Standard toolbar.

   d. Choose Tools, Check Word.

6. Which of the following are ways that you can format text?

   a. sentence case

   b. lowercase

   c. title case

   d. all of the above

7. Which of the following is true?

   a. You can find and replace text, but not fonts.

   b. You can replace fonts throughout your presentation.

   c. You must display your presentation in Outline view in order to find and replace text.

   d. None of the above.

8. Which of the following are command buttons in the Spelling dialog box?

   a. Ignore

   b. Change

   c. Add

   d. All of the above

9. What does a red, wavy line beneath a word indicate?

   a. that the word has formatting associated with it

   b. that there are too many bulleted points on a slide

   c. that the word is not in PowerPoint's dictionary and could be misspelled

   d. none of the above

10. Which dialog box do you use to turn on the check spelling as you type features?

    a. Spelling

    b. Options

    c. Tools

    d. Replace

Completion

In the blank provided, write the correct answer for each of the following statements.

1. The combination of upper- and lowercase letters is referred to as _____.

2. A _____ font is a scalable font that prints exactly as it displays onscreen.

3. The way in which slide elements are used throughout a presentation is called the presentation's _____.

4. You can quickly check for visual clarity and font usage with the _____ feature.

5. The distinctive design of a set of characters is called the typeface or _____.

6. Arial is an example of a _____ font.

7. Times New Roman is an example of a _____ font.

8. You choose _____ from the menu to display the Find dialog box.

9. _____ determines the legibility of a presentation.

10. You can choose _____ from the menu to replace fonts throughout a presentation.

Matching

In the blank next to each of the following terms or phrases, write the letter of the corresponding term or phrase. (Note that some of the letters may be used more than once.)

a. Find dialog box

b. visual clarity

c. Spelling short-cut menu

d. six

e. style

f. serif

g. Replace Fonts command

h. sans serif

i. Style Checker

j. automatic spelling

_____ 1. Maximum number of bulleted points per slide

_____ 2. Font without finish lines

_____ 3. Font with finish lines

_____ 4. Checks for spelling and visual clarity

_____ 5. Changes fonts throughout a presentation

_____ 6. The way elements display in a presentation

_____ 7. Legibility of a presentation

_____ 8. Used to spell check an individual word

_____ 9. Helps you locate text

_____ 10. Flags misspelled or mistyped words

Applying Your Skills

Practice

The following exercises, found in the Project–08 folder on the CD, enable you to practice the skills you have learned in this project. Take a few minutes to work through these exercises now.

Using Design Principles

Your boss is conducting a sales training session and wants you to format a presentation slide so that it is more readable. To do this, you implement design principles learned in this project.

To use design principles, complete the following steps:

1. Open Proj0806 from the Project-08 folder on the CD and save it as Positive Selling.

2. Select the bulleted points, and then change the font to 28 points.

3. Change the bulleted list to Arial font.

4. Click outside your bulleted points to better see your changes.

5. Select the word PROSPECTING, and then choose Format, Change Case. Choose OK to apply Sentence case to the text.

6. Delete the Money Bags clip art.

7. Delete the arrow.

8. Move the remaining clip art image (People) to the lower-right corner of the slide.

9. Print a copy of the slide.

10. Save the presentation, and then close it.

Changing Fonts

You want to improve a presentation's appearance. To do this, you replace and view several fonts in the presentation.

To change fonts, complete the following steps:

1. Open Proj0807 from the Project-08 folder on the CD and save it as Business Plan.

2. Display Slide 2, Mission Statement, and then choose Format, Replace Fonts.

3. Use the Replace and With drop-down list arrows to replace Times New Roman with Braggadocio.

4. Move the Replace Font dialog box to the lower half of the screen so that you can more easily view your changes.

5. Click the Replace button. Keep the Replace Font dialog box open so that you can make further font changes.

6. Use the Replace and With drop-down list arrows to replace Braggadocio with Brush Script; then choose Replace.

7. Use the Replace and With drop-down list arrows to replace Brush Script with Arial; then choose Replace.

8. Close the Replace Fonts dialog box. Scroll through your presentation to see that the fonts are replaced on all slides.

9. Save your presentation, and then close it.

Checking Styles

Because you are familiar with PowerPoint, your boss has asked you to *clean up* a presentation created by a coworker. Because the presentation has a number of case, punctuation, and font inconsistencies, you decide to use PowerPoint's Style Checker to quickly identify and fix the problems.

To check styles, complete the following steps:

1. Open Proj0808 from the Project-08 folder on the CD and save it as Upgrading to New Computers.

2. Choose Tools, Style Checker. Make sure all three check boxes (for spelling, visual clarity, and case and end punctuation) are checked.

3. Display the Style Checker Options dialog box.

4. On the End and Case Punctuation page, make sure that the Slide title style is Title Case. Make sure that the Body text style is Sentence case.

5. On the Visual Clarity page, reduce the number of allowable fonts to 2; then close the Style Checker Options dialog box.

6. Start the Style Checker. Correct all spelling errors and style inconsistencies that the checker indicates.

7. Read the list of inconsistencies in the Style Checker Summary dialog box; then close it.

8. Proof and manually fix any additional problems using the Style Checker Summary dialog box as a guide.

9. Save your presentation and close it.

Using the Spelling Checker

PowerPoint's Spelling Checker will help you produce an error-free presentation by checking your work for overlooked errors.

To use the Spelling Checker, complete the following steps:

1. Open Proj0809 from the Project-08 folder on the CD and save it as Producing an Error Free Presentation.

2. Choose Tools, Spelling to start the Spelling Checker.

3. Correct spelling throughout the presentation. Choose to ignore proper and company names. Correct misspelled words.

4. Click OK to close the message box.

5. Save the presentation; then close it.

Finding and Replacing Text

Your company has just been bought out by another company. Additionally, you have a new boss. To quickly update an existing presentation with the new information (and to impress your new boss) you use PowerPoint's Find and Replace feature.

To find and replace text, complete the following steps:

1. Open Proj0810 from the Project-08 folder on the CD and save it as Financial Performance.

2. Use the Edit, Find command to quickly locate the Revenue by Division slide. Close the Find dialog box.

3. Display the first presentation slide, and then choose Edit, Replace.

4. Type Ann Tyson in the Find what text box. Type Joyce Schmidt in the Replace with text box. Choose Replace All.

5. Click OK in the Microsoft PowerPoint message box.

6. In the Replace dialog box, type CompuConsult in the Find what text box. Type Becca Corporation in the Replace with text box.

7. Choose Replace All. Click OK in the Microsoft PowerPoint message box.

8. Close the Replace dialog box. Scan your presentation to view the changes.

9. Save the Financial Performance presentation, then close it.

Challenge

The following challenges enable you to use your problem-solving skills. Take time to work through these exercises now.

Changing Fonts Using a Set of Criteria

You arrive at your company's annual meeting, ready to give your presentation. Unfortunately, the font you've chosen for the presentation doesn't display well in the room. To quickly replace the font throughout the presentation, you use PowerPoint's Replace Fonts feature.

To change fonts, complete the following steps:

1. Open Proj0811 from the Project-08 folder on the CD and save it as Becca Corporation.

2. Use the Format, Replace Fonts command to make the following changes:

   Replace Bookman Old Style with Tahoma

   Replace Brush Script with Arial Black

   Replace Algerian with Times New Roman

3. Close the Replace Font dialog box.

4. View the font changes in your presentation.

5. Save the presentation, and then close it.

Checking Styles Using a Set of Criteria

You're putting together a promotional presentation that highlights information about your children's clothing company. To make sure the presentation is visually coherent, you use PowerPoint's Style Checker.

To check styles, complete the following steps:

1. Open Proj0812 from the Project-08 folder on the CD and save it as Creative Kids.

2. Choose <u>T</u>ools, St<u>y</u>le Checker to display the Style Checker dialog box.

3. Make sure all three boxes in the Style Checker dialog box are checked.

4. Display the Style Checker Options dialog box. Set the following options:

>Ignore Slide title periods

>Add Body text periods

>Make 2 the maximum allowable number of fonts

5. Start the Style Checker. Correct all spelling errors and style inconsistencies that the checker indicates.

6. Read the list of possible inconsistencies in the Style Checker Summary dialog box, and then close it.

7. Proof and manually fix any additional problems that the Style Checker flagged.

8. Save the presentation, and then close it.

Changing Fonts Using a Set of Criteria

You're working on a presentation you have to give at an upcoming meeting. To find out which fonts look the best for the presentation, you use PowerPoint's Replace Fonts feature to quickly swap one font for another.

To change fonts, complete the following steps:

1. Open Proj0813 from the Project-08 folder on the CD and save it as `Updated Presentation`.

2. Choose <u>F</u>ile, Proper<u>t</u>ies, and then click the Contents tab. View the fonts currently used in the presentation. Close the Properties dialog box.

3. Using the Replace Font dialog box, make the following replacements to the presentation:

>Replace Times New Roman with Albertus Extra Bold

>Replace Albertus Extra Bold with Algerian

>Replace Algerian with Century Schoolbook

>Replace Century Schoolbook with Comic Sans MS

4. Close the Replace Font dialog box.

5. Save your presentation, and then close it.

Finding and Replacing Text Using a Set of Criteria

You're helping to spearhead a major upgrade from Office 4.3 to Office 97. You have a presentation that outlines the major features for each software program that makes up Office 4.3. To quickly update the presentation, you use PowerPoint's Find and Replace feature.

To find and replace text, complete the following steps:

1. Open Proj0814 from the Project-08 folder on the CD and save it as Upgrading to Office 97.

2. Use the Find feature to locate all occurrences of Office 4.3. Close the message box and the Find dialog box.

3. Display the first presentation slide. Use the Replace feature to change Sarah Schmidt to Rebecca Lowell.

4. Use the Replace feature to change all occurrences of the following:

   Replace Office 4.3 with Office 97.

   Replace Word 6.0 with Word 97.

   Replace Excel 5.0 with Excel 97.

   Replace PowerPoint 4.0 with PowerPoint 97.

   Replace Access 2.0 to Access 97.

5. Close the Replace dialog box.

6. Save the changes to your presentation; then close it.

Using the Spelling Checker and Ignoring Proper Names

To fix misspellings and typos in your presentation you use PowerPoint's Spelling Checker.

To use the Spelling Checker, complete the following steps:

1. Open Proj0815 from the Project-08 folder on the CD and save it as Hickory Grove Foods.

2. Choose Tools, Spelling to start the Spelling Checker.

3. Correct spelling throughout the presentation. Choose to ignore proper names. Correct misspelled (or mistyped) words.

4. Click OK to close the message box. Proofread your presentation.

5. Save the presentation, and then close it.

PinPoint Assessment

You have completed the project and the associated lessons, as well as the "Checking Your Skills" and "Applying Your Skills" sections. Now use the PinPoint software Evaluation mode to assess your comprehension of the specific exam tasks you have just learned. You can also use the PinPoint Trainer mode and the SHOW ME tutorials to practice these specific exam tasks.

Project 9

Sharing Information between Programs

Using Features and Documents of Other Programs

In this project you will learn the following objectives and their associated Microsoft Exam required activities.

Objectives	Required Activities
➤ Copy and Paste Between Programs	
➤ Insert a Word Table	Add a Table
➤ Edit a Word Table	
➤ Import a Word Outline	Import Text from Word
➤ Export a Presentation	Export an Outline to Word

Why Would I Do This?

Because PowerPoint 97 is a Windows program, you can readily share information with other Windows software. Sharing information saves time because you don't have to re-create it, and helps ensure that original data is entered. For example, you might have sales or production information in a word processing program that you need to copy onto a PowerPoint slide.

You can use the Copy and Paste commands to select only the data you need, and then copy it to PowerPoint. Alternately, you can import an entire outline from Word to PowerPoint. You can even export a presentation from PowerPoint to Word. Finally, you can use one of Word's features—tables in your presentation to display your data in an organized manner.

Try sharing information between PowerPoint and Word now.

Lesson 1: Copying and Pasting Between Programs

You can copy text, charts, clip art, or other objects from PowerPoint to another Windows program. Alternately, you can copy text or objects from other Windows programs to PowerPoint.

The easiest way to share information between PowerPoint and other Windows programs is to use the **Clipboard** in conjunction with the Copy and Paste commands. Information that is copied (or cut) is placed on the Clipboard, where it can be pasted into any other Windows program.

To copy data, select the text or object in the original **(source) program**, then click the Copy button on the Standard toolbar. Alternately, you can choose the Edit, Copy menu command, or press Ctrl+C. The selected information is copied to the Clipboard. You can then switch to the **destination program** and click the Paste button. You can also paste the Clipboard's contents by choosing Edit, Paste or pressing Ctrl+V.

Of course, in order to share information between programs, each program must be installed on your computer system. For this exercise, you use both Word and PowerPoint, so make sure they are installed before starting the tutorial. Assuming you have access to both programs, try copying and pasting information between programs now.

Jargon Watch

The Windows **Clipboard** is a temporary storage area in memory where data that is cut or copied is stored. From the Clipboard, you can paste the material elsewhere. The material remains in the Clipboard until you cut or copy another item, or you exit Windows.

The application from which you cut or copy data is called the **source program** and the originating document (whether it's a word processing document, spreadsheet, graphic, and so on) is the source document.

The application into which you paste the material is the **destination program**, and the document into which the material is pasted is the destination document.

To Copy and Paste Between Programs

① Start PowerPoint, if necessary. Open Proj0901 from the Project-09 folder on the CD, and save it as Exchanging Information.

PowerPoint displays onscreen. In addition, a button appears on the Taskbar to indicate that PowerPoint is currently running in memory (see Figure 9.1).

Figure 9.1
A Taskbar button is displayed for each program in memory.

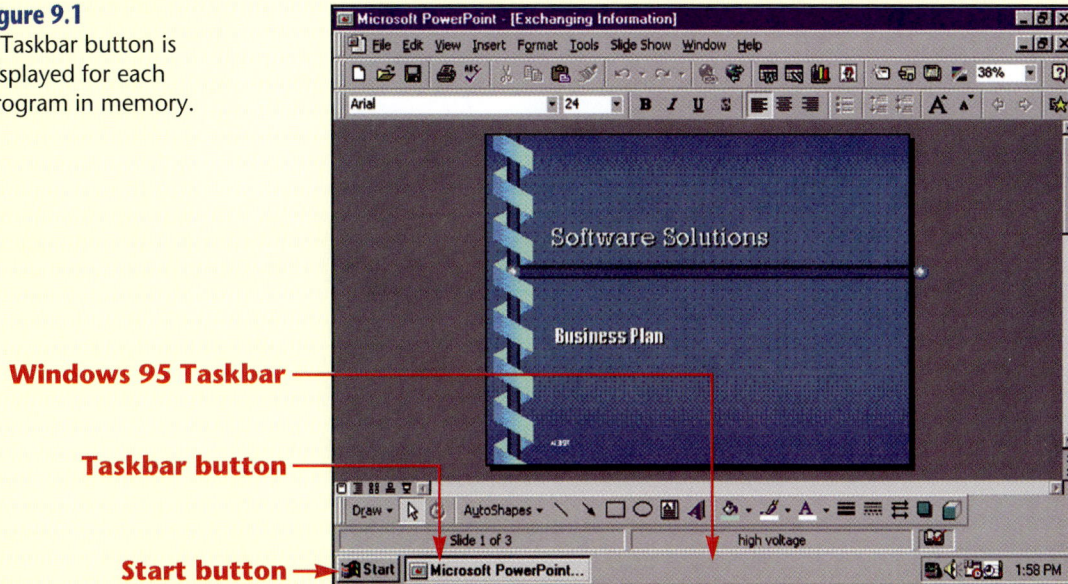

Windows 95 Taskbar

Taskbar button

Start button

② Click the Windows Start button, and then choose Programs, Microsoft Word to start Microsoft Word 97.

If you have problems...

If you have trouble finding or starting Microsoft Word 97, it may be located in a different folder, it may not be installed properly on your computer, or you may not have enough memory on your system to run both Word and PowerPoint. Ask your instructor for assistance.

Microsoft Word starts and its opening screen is displayed (see Figure 9.2). Notice the similarity of Word's toolbars to PowerPoint's, and the location of the Cut, Copy, and Paste buttons. Word also has a document area in which you can enter text. The insertion point indicates the location where the text you enter will appear.

Also notice that a Taskbar button is now displayed for Word as well as for PowerPoint. You use these buttons later to switch between the programs.

continues

To Copy and Paste Between Programs   (continued)

Figure 9.2
Word's screen appears
similar to PowerPoint.

Word's menu bar ——

Standard toolbar ——

Insertion point ——

Cut button ——

Copy button ——

Paste button ——

Document area ——

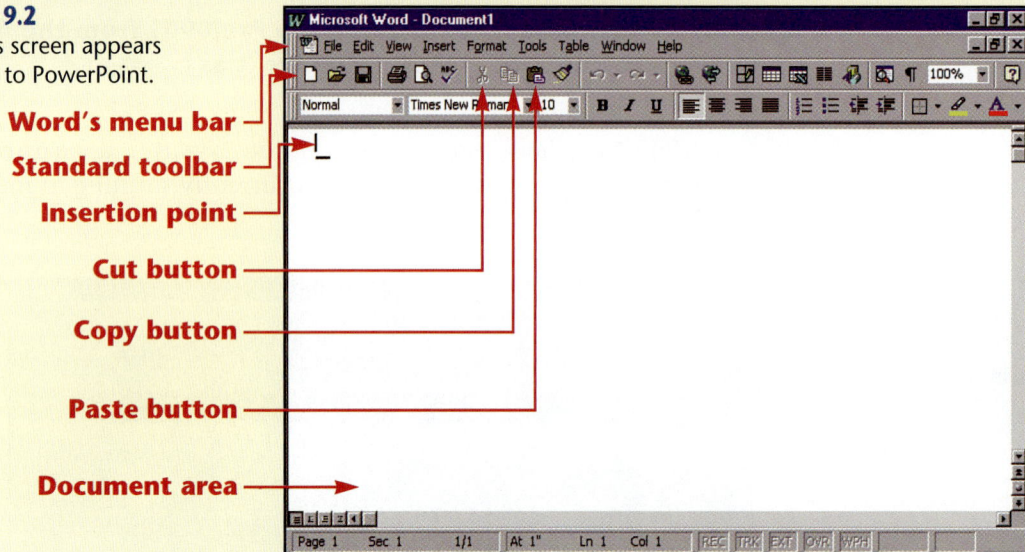

3 **In the document area, type** Our mission is to provide high-quality computer support for our clients.

4 **Drag the mouse pointer over the text to select it and click the Copy button.**

The text you selected is copied to the Clipboard. From the Clipboard, you can paste it into any other Windows program. First, however, you must switch to PowerPoint. The easiest way to do this is to click the Taskbar button for PowerPoint.

5 **Click the Microsoft PowerPoint Taskbar button.**

The Exchanging Information PowerPoint presentation displays onscreen. Before you paste the Clipboard's contents into PowerPoint, however, you must first designate a location within the presentation.

6 **Display Slide 2,** Mission Statement, **then click in the lower place-holder.**

You can click the Paste button to insert the text. You can also choose Edit, Paste or press Ctrl+V to perform the same function.

7 **Click the Paste button.**

The text you copied to the Clipboard is inserted on the slide.

You're now finished using the Word program, so you can close it to free up memory.

8 **Right-click the Taskbar button for Microsoft Word, then choose Close from the shortcut menu.**

The text you entered in Word has not been saved, therefore Word displays a message box so you can choose whether to save the document.

PowerPoint

9 **Choose No in the message box.**

The Word program is removed from memory and the PowerPoint screen is displayed. Notice that a Taskbar button for the Word program no longer displays. However, PowerPoint remains in memory.

10 **Save the Exchanging Information PowerPoint presentation.**

Keep the presentation open for the next lesson, in which you insert a Word table in PowerPoint.

Inside Stuff

Although clicking a program's Taskbar buttons is a quick and easy way to switch between programs, you can also press Alt+Tab↹ to do the same thing.

Lesson 2: Inserting a Word Table

Although PowerPoint can readily share information with any other Windows program through the Clipboard, it is most tightly integrated with other Office 97 Suite programs, especially Word and Excel. If you have Word installed on your computer, you can create and edit a Word table within PowerPoint as an *embedded object*.

Embedded object

An object embedded into a destination program created or edited by an application other than that which created the destination document. The object can be text, a chart, graphic, or even a sound or video clip.

Tables provide a good way of organizing information in PowerPoint. A table is simply a grid with columns and rows for entering data, similar to a worksheet. The intersection of a column and row is called a cell, and is the area in which you enter data. Using these cells, you can easily group related information together.

When you create a table in PowerPoint, you embed it as an object on a slide. An embedded object is an object created by one program (in this case, Word) within another program (PowerPoint). Whenever you access the embedded object—by double-clicking it—you can use the original program's commands to revise or format it.

It is not necessary to have Word running in memory before you create a table. PowerPoint automatically accesses Word when you create or edit the table, but closes it when you're done working with it.

In the following tutorial, you learn how to insert a Word table as an embedded object on a PowerPoint slide. Try inserting a table now.

To Insert a Word Table

❶ **In the open Exchanging Information presentation, display Slide 3, `The Team`.**

❷ **Click the Insert Microsoft Word Table button on the Standard toolbar.**

A drop-down palette displays (see Figure 9.3). You can use this palette to indicate the number of columns and rows you want. As you drag the mouse pointer down or to the right the grid squares are highlighted, indicating the number of columns and rows you will have in your finished table. You can create a table as large as six rows by 25 columns. For practical purposes, however, you will probably want a smaller, more readable table.

Figure 9.3
You can quickly create a Word table on a PowerPoint slide.

Click this button...

to display the table palette

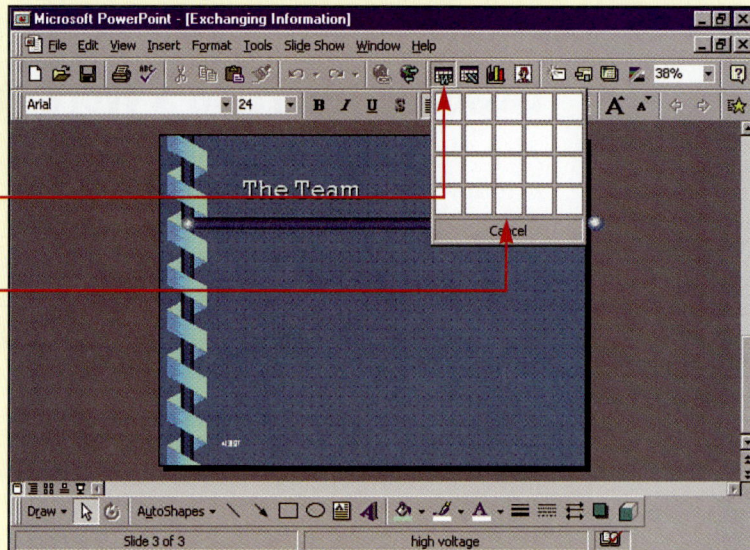

❸ **Drag over the palette to indicate a table two columns by three rows in size (see Figure 9.4).**

Figure 9.4
Drag over the palette to indicate table size.

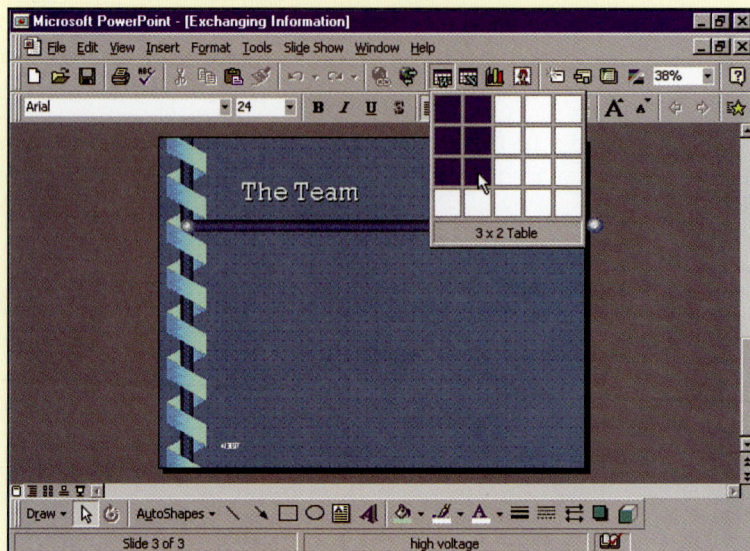

PowerPoint

❹ Release the mouse button.

A Word table of the indicated size is embedded on your slide (see Figure 9.5). Also notice that a dark, rope-like border and black selection handles surround the table, indicating that it is activated. Additionally, the Word toolbars and commands display because the table is an embedded Word object.

Figure 9.5
Word commands are available whenever the table is active.

Word menu bar
Word Standard toolbar
Word Formatting toolbar
Word rulers
Cell
Border
Word table

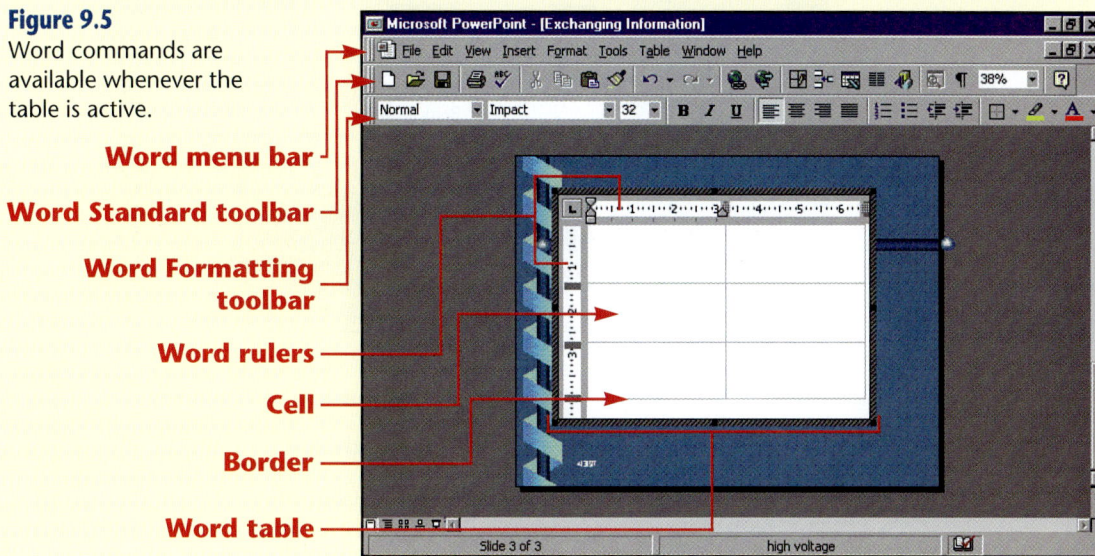

❺ Enter the following information into your table. Press Tab↹ **or** ⬆Shift+Tab↹ **to move forward or backward between cells.**

    Teams Members

    Sales

    Training

If you have text that you want to display on more than one line in a cell, you can press ↵Enter to expand the cell downward and create a new line. Alternately, if the text extends beyond the right border of the cell, it wraps to the next line automatically.

Try entering some text in your table now.

❻ Click in the cell to the right of Sales, type Lucinda Hitt, **then press** ↵Enter.

❼ In the same cell, type Lonnie Stegall **and press** ↵Enter, **then type** Betty Schmidt **and press** ↵Enter.

The cell expands downward when you press ↵Enter (see Figure 9.6). Word's capability to expand cells ensures that related information (in this case, Sales team members) stays together.

continues

To Insert a Word Table　(continued)

Figure 9.6
Cells expand downward when you press ↵Enter.

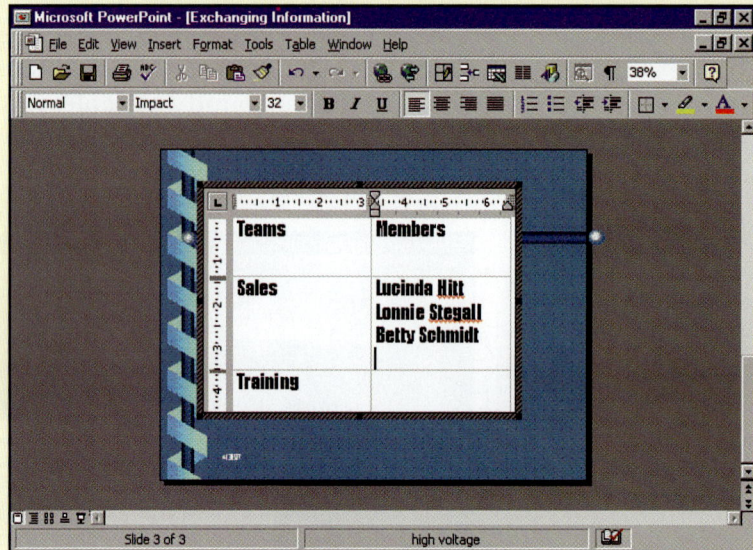

Now use the word wrap feature to expand a cell.

❽ Click in the cell to the right of Training and type The Training Team has yet to be determined.

The cell expands automatically to accommodate the new text (see Figure 9.7).

Figure 9.7
Word wraps automatically in a cell as you type.

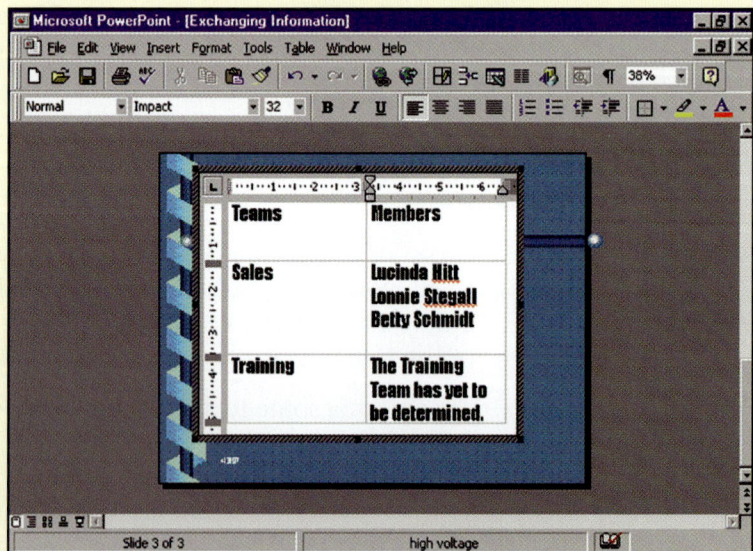

After you finish entering information in a table, you can deselect it and embed it on the slide as an object. You do this by clicking outside the object—in this case, clicking outside the table.

9 Click outside the table to deselect it.

The table appears as an embedded object on the slide. Notice the PowerPoint menu bar and toolbars again display. This indicates that the Word table is no longer active in memory.

10 Save your changes to the presentation.

Keep the presentation open for the next lesson, in which you learn how to edit the table.

Exam Notes

After you create the table, you can add more rows and columns if needed. You can also remove any unnecessary rows or columns.

To add a row at the bottom of the table, place your insertion point in the last cell on the right of the last row and then press Tab. To add a row in the middle of the table, place your insertion point in any cell of the row you want to appear after the new row. Then choose Table, Insert Row from the menu.

To add a column, you must first select the column that will appear to the right of the new column. To select the column, click in any cell of the column and choose Table, Select Column from the menu. Then choose Table, Insert Columns. When you want to add a column to the right of the last existing column in the table, click just to the right of the last cell in any row before selecting the column and inserting the new one.

To delete a row, or rows, you must first select the row you want to remove. To delete one row, click in any cell of the row and choose Table, Select Row; then choose Table, Delete Rows. When deleting more than one row, click in the first cell on the left in the first row you want to delete, hold down Shift, and then click in the last cell on the right of the last row you want removed. All cells between those you clicked in are selected. Then choose Table, Delete Cells. From the dialog box, select Delete entire row and choose OK.

To delete a column, or columns, you must first select the column you want to remove. To delete one column, click in any cell of the column and choose Table, Select Column; then choose Table, Delete Columns. When deleting more than one column, click in the first cell at the top of the first column on the left that you want to delete, hold down Shift, and then click in the bottom cell of the last column on the right that you want removed. All cells between those you clicked in are selected. Then choose Table, Delete Columns.

Lesson 3: Editing a Word Table

After you create a Word table, you can edit it. For example, you may need to add to or update the contents as new data becomes available. Additionally, you may want to resize, move, or reformat the table to make it easier to read.

Before you edit a table, you must first select or activate it. You can single-click the table object to select it and place white selection handles around it (see Figure 9.8). You can use these selection handles to resize or move the table.

Figure 9.8
You can select a table to move or resize it

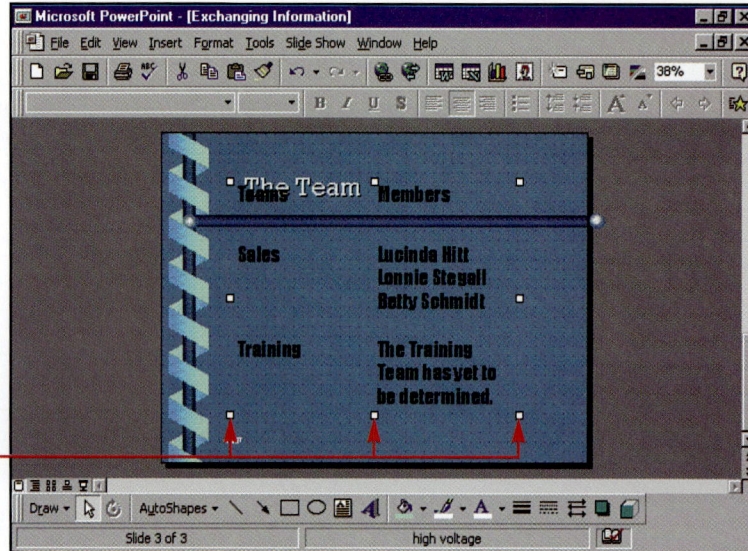

Click the table once to place these selection handles around your table

Alternately, you can double-click a table to activate it and place a rope-like border around it (see Figure 9.9). When an object is activated, you have complete access to the commands of the program that created it. In this case, double-clicking the table activates Word so that you can reformat or otherwise change the table with Word's commands.

Figure 9.9
You can double-click to activate a table object.

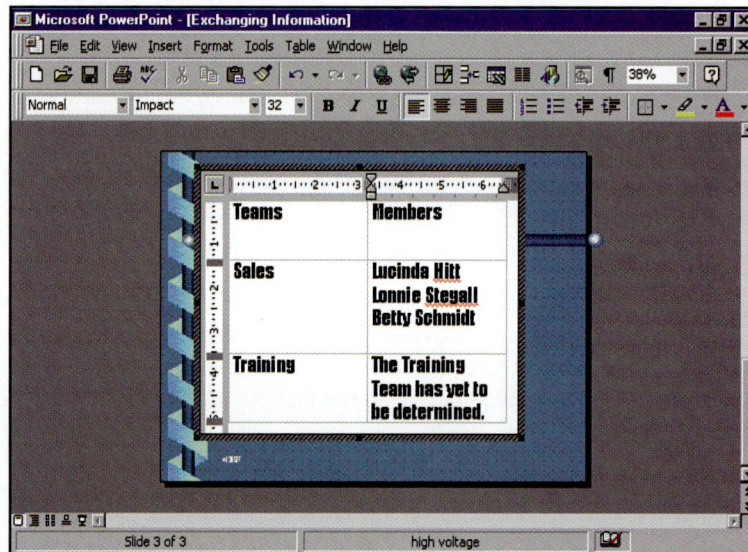

Try modifying the table now.

To Edit a Word Table

❶ In the open Exchanging Information presentation, single-click the table object on your slide.

White selection handles appear around the object's borders, indicating that it is selected (refer to Figure 9.8). When the table is selected, you can move or resize it.

2 **Move the mouse pointer to the middle of the selected table until it displays as a four-headed move arrow; then drag the table down on the slide so you can better see the slide title (**The Team**).**

You can also resize a selected table by resting the mouse pointer over a selection handle until a two-headed resizing arrow displays; then drag it. For now, you leave the table at its current size, but activate it so you have access to Word commands.

3 **Double-click the table to activate it.**

The dark, rope-like border appears around the table to indicate that it is activated (refer to Figure 9.9). When a table is activated, you can use Word's features to format the table.

Word automatically creates table columns with the same width. However, you may want to resize them to better fit your data.

4 **Rest the mouse pointer over the column divider on the Word ruler until a two-headed resizing arrow and ScreenTip display (see Figure 9.10).**

You can display and drag the resizing arrow to resize your columns.

Figure 9.10
You can resize column width by using the divider.

Resizing arrow —
Word ruler —
ScreenTip —
Column divider —

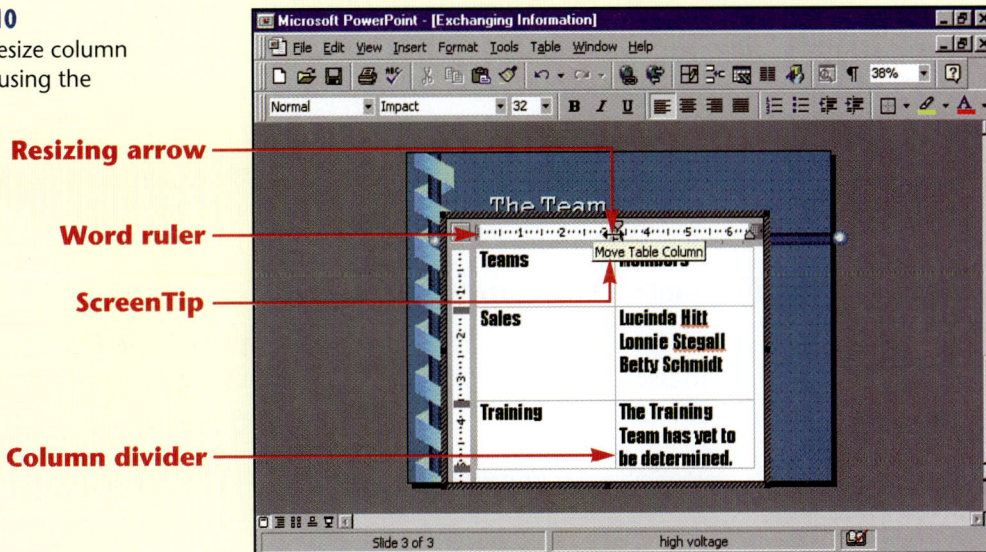

If you have problems... ► If the horizontal and vertical rulers don't display to the top and left of your table, choose View, Ruler from the menu bar.

5 **Click and drag the resizing arrow to the left until the number 1 on the ruler is no longer displayed, then release the mouse button.**

The columns are resized to better accommodate your text. You can also change row height in a similar manner—by using the resizing arrow in conjunction with the row dividers.

continues

To Edit a Word Table   (continued)

Figure 9.11
You can adjust row height with the resizing arrow.

6 **Move the mouse pointer over the top row divider until a resizing arrow and ScreenTip display (see Figure 9.11).**

Row divider with resizing arrow

ScreenTip

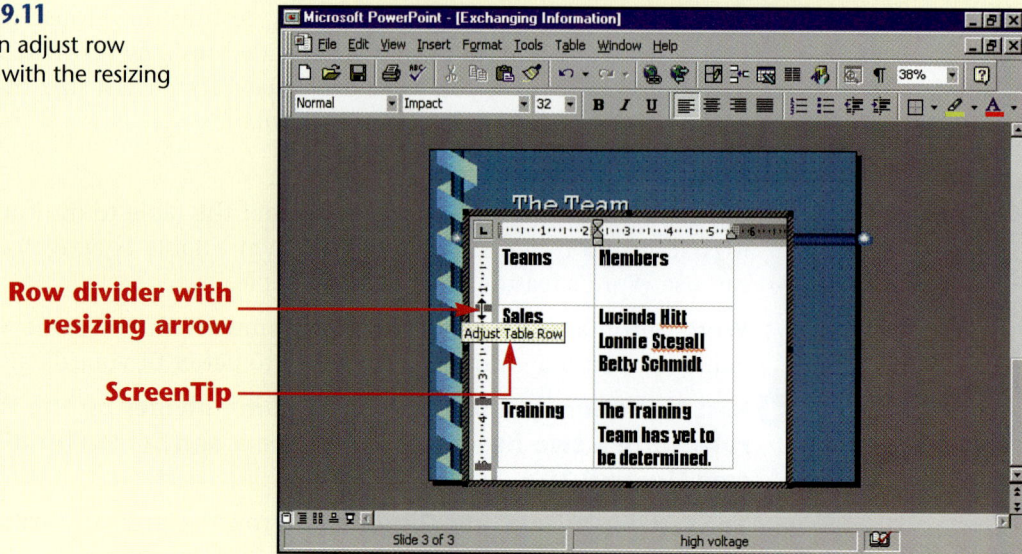

7 **Click and drag the resizing arrow upward until the divider line is below the text for** Team **and** Members**, then release the mouse button.**

The row height is modified to better display your table data. As you adjust column width and row height, remember that you can use the Undo button if you get unexpected results.

8 **Choose Table, AutoFormat.**

The Table AutoFormat dialog box is displayed (see Figure 9.12). You can use this dialog box to view and quickly apply a preset format to your table.

Figure 9.12
You can quickly apply a table format using this dialog box.

Choose a format here

Preview the selected format here

Choose formatting options here

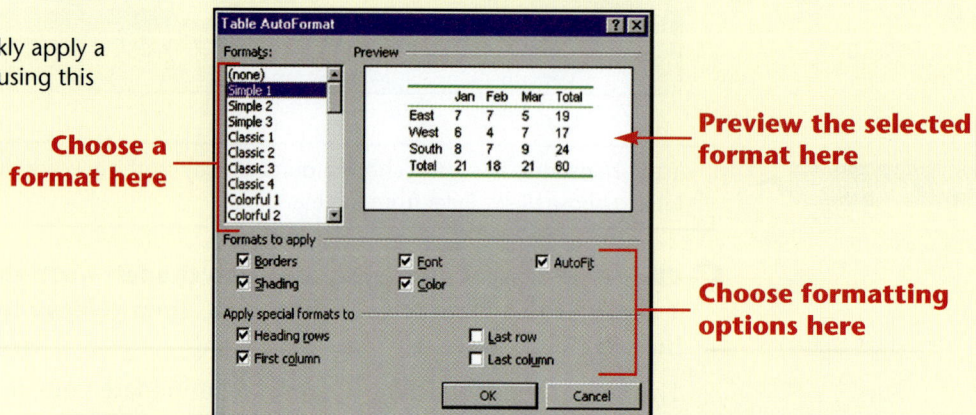

⑨ From the Formats list, select `Classic 4`.

A sample of the format displays in the Preview section. (If you want, view several other formats. Make sure you select Classic 4 before proceeding with the next tutorial step.)

Using the format you selected from the Formats list as a basis, you can refine the format by turning specific formatting features on or off. For example, you may like a format, but don't want shading or color. You toggle specific formatting features on or off using the check boxes in the Formats to apply and Add special formats to sections of the dialog box (refer to Figure 9.12). Try changing these formats now.

⑩ In the Formats to apply section of the dialog box, uncheck the box for Color.

The result of your choices displays in the Preview section (see Figure 9.13).

Figure 9.13
You can toggle formatting features on or off.

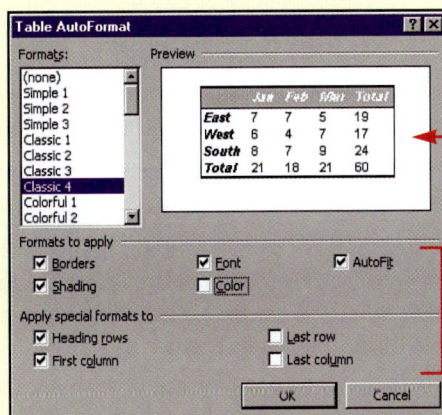

Preview your choices here

Turn formatting options on or off here

⑪ Choose OK.

The Table AutoFormat dialog box closes, and the format is applied to the table.

⑫ Click outside the table to embed it on your slide.

The formatted table should appear similar to Figure 9.14.

continues

To Edit a Word Table (continued)

Figure 9.14
You can format a table for a more appealing appearance.

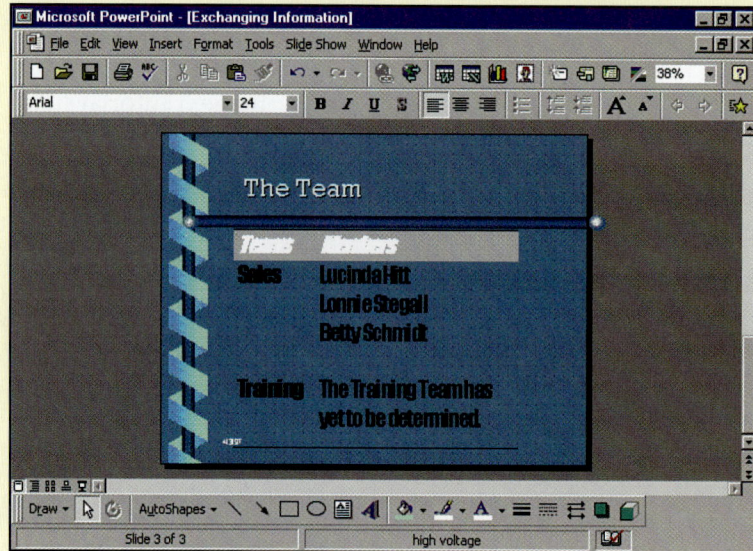

13 **Save and close the Exchanging Information presentation.**

Keep PowerPoint running for the next lesson, in which you import a Word outline into PowerPoint.

Inside Stuff

You can format table text just as you do in a Word document. Drag to select the text; then change the size, font, font color, and appearance using the Formatting toolbar buttons. You can also add bullets to selected text (to make it more readable) by clicking the Bullets button.

Lesson 4: Importing a Word Outline

If you have worked with Word and PowerPoint for a while, you have probably prepared an outline in Word, then wanted to use the same information as the basis of a PowerPoint presentation. Of course, you could copy and paste the information as you learned in Lesson 1. However, a better method is to *import* the outline. PowerPoint enables you to import an outline that you originally created in Word into a presentation. This saves reentering the same information or laboriously copying and pasting the entire outline.

Import
To load a file created by one program into a different program.

Style
In reference to Word, a group of formatting features that are applied to a paragraph.

PowerPoint formats the outline based on the *styles* used in Word. Heading 1 becomes a slide title, Heading 2 the first level bullet, Heading 3 the second level bullet, and so on. If you haven't used styles in the word processing document, PowerPoint uses paragraph indents or tabs to set the levels instead.

You can start a new presentation based on the imported outline, or import outline text into an existing presentation. Try working with this time-saving feature now.

To Import a Word Outline

❶ Click the Start button on the Windows Taskbar, then choose Programs, Microsoft Word.

After Word loads into memory, both Word and PowerPoint are running in memory and a Taskbar button appears for each.

To import a Word outline into PowerPoint, you must save it with a specific file format—either as rich text format (RTF) or plain text (TXT) format. Try opening and saving an outline in Word now.

❷ In Word, choose File, Open to display the Open dialog box. Open the Project-09 folder on the CD and double-click Proj0902 to open it. (If you can't find this file, ask your instructor for its location.)

By default, documents created in Word are saved as documents with the .doc extension. Now try saving it as a Rich Text Format file so that it can be exported to PowerPoint.

❸ In Word, choose File, Save As.

The Word Save As dialog box is displayed. You can use this dialog box to change the file's name and format.

❹ In the File name text box, type My Word Outline, then click the Save as type drop-down list arrow.

A list of file formats you can use to save your document displays (see Figure 9.15).

Figure 9.15
You can save a Word document as a specific text type.

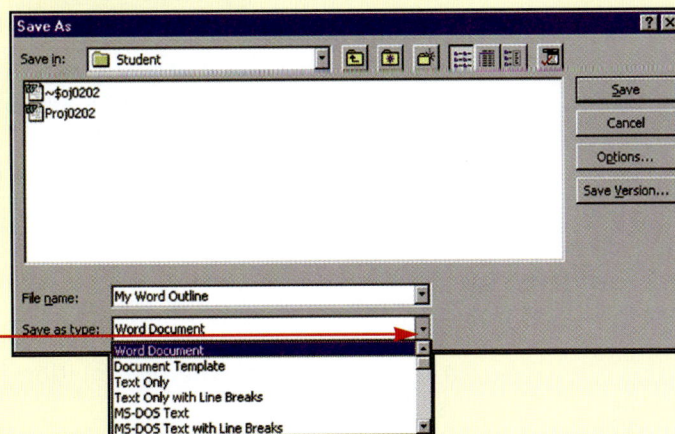

Click here to display a list of file formats

❺ Scroll through the list of file types, choose Rich Text Format and click Save.

Your Word outline is saved using the Rich Text Format.

❻ In Word, choose File, Close to close My Word Outline, then click the Microsoft PowerPoint Taskbar.

Now try importing the outline to PowerPoint.

continues

To Import a Word Outline   (continued)

7 In PowerPoint, click the Open button on the Standard toolbar.

The Open dialog box is displayed (see Figure 9.16). By default, only presentation files are listed. Because you want to access the Word outline you just saved, you need to list outline files. You use the Files of type drop-down list to do this.

Figure 9.16
You can list various file types in the Open dialog box.

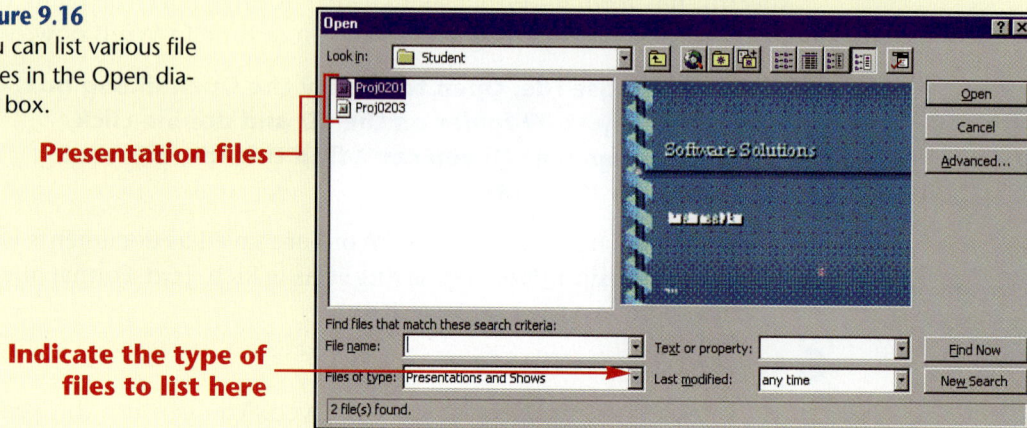

Presentation files

Indicate the type of files to list here

8 Click the Files of type drop-down list arrow, then choose All Outlines.

The My Word Outline file you saved using Rich Text Format displays on the list. When you open this file, PowerPoint automatically converts it to a presentation.

If you have problems...

If the outline file doesn't display on your file listing, you may have accidentally saved it to another drive or folder. Ask your instructor to help you locate the file.

9 Double-click the My Word Outline file to open it within PowerPoint.

PowerPoint automatically creates a presentation from the outline and displays it in Outline view (see Figure 9.17). Once created, you can modify and save the presentation just as you would any other presentation.

PowerPoint

Figure 9.17
Imported Word outlines display in Outline view.

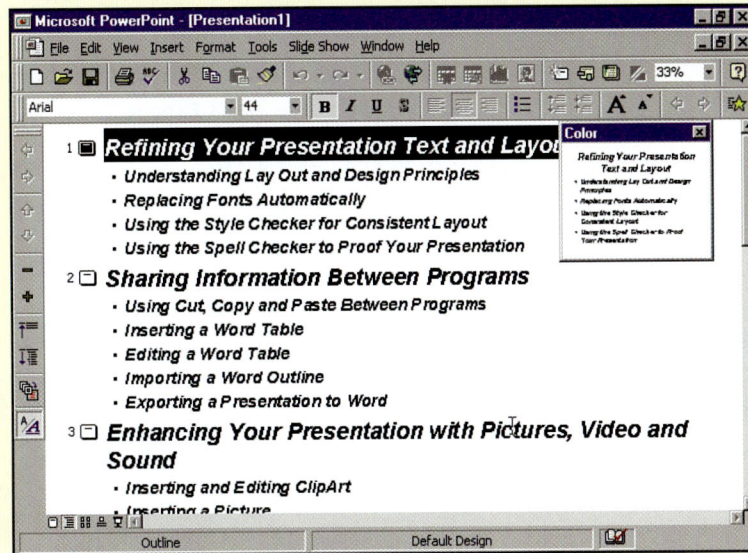

10 **Save the newly-created PowerPoint presentation as** Imported Outline, **then close it.**

Keep PowerPoint and Word running for the next exercise, in which you export a presentation to Word.

Inside Stuff

You can also import an outline into an existing presentation. Position the insertion point where you want to insert the outline, then choose Insert, Slides from Outline to display the Open dialog box. Choose All Outlines from the Files of type drop-down list, then select the drive and folder in which the file is stored. Double-click the file you want to use to export it. The imported file's text appears in Outline view at the insertion point.

Exam Notes

If you have set up your Word outline using the Word heading styles, there is an even quicker method of exporting your outline file to PowerPoint. You can do this even if you haven't started PowerPoint yet, and you don't need to convert your Word document to another file format.

With the Word outline document open, choose File, Send To, Microsoft PowerPoint. The Microsoft PowerPoint program opens in the Outline view with the outline text from your Word document displayed. Save the PowerPoint file and begin working on your presentation.

Lesson 5: Exporting a Presentation to Word

Export
To save a file in a specific format so that it can be sent to and read by another program.

Instead of importing a Word outline into PowerPoint, you may want to do just the opposite—*export* a PowerPoint presentation to Word. Luckily, PowerPoint includes a feature that enables an almost seamless transfer of information to Word. You can then modify and save the Word outline as any other Word document.

Try exporting, or sending, a presentation to Word now.

To Export a Presentation

1 In PowerPoint, open Proj0903 from the Project-09 folder on the CD and save it as Exporting a Presentation.

2 Choose File, Send To.

PowerPoint displays a submenu of potential locations to which you can send the presentation (see Figure 9.18).

Figure 9.18
You can export a PowerPoint presentation to a variety of locations.

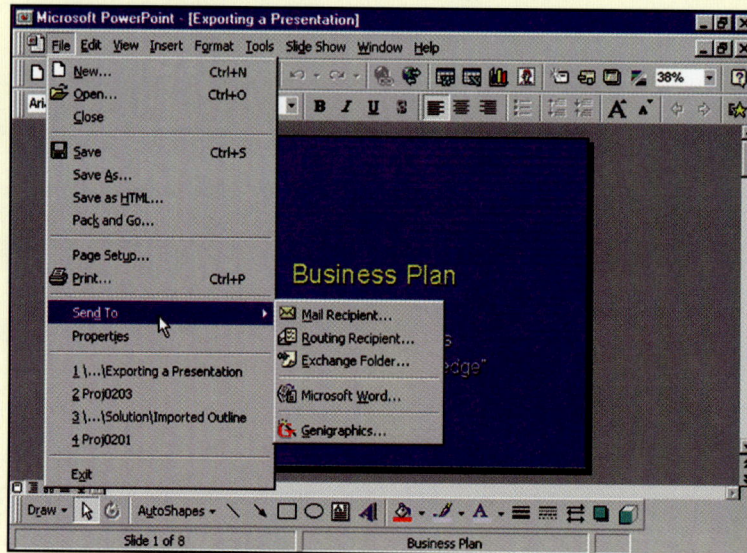

3 Choose Microsoft Word.

The Write-Up dialog box is displayed (see Figure 9.19). You can use this dialog box to designate the page layout for your outline.

Figure 9.19
You can choose from a variety of page layouts.

Choose main page layout here

Choose linking options here

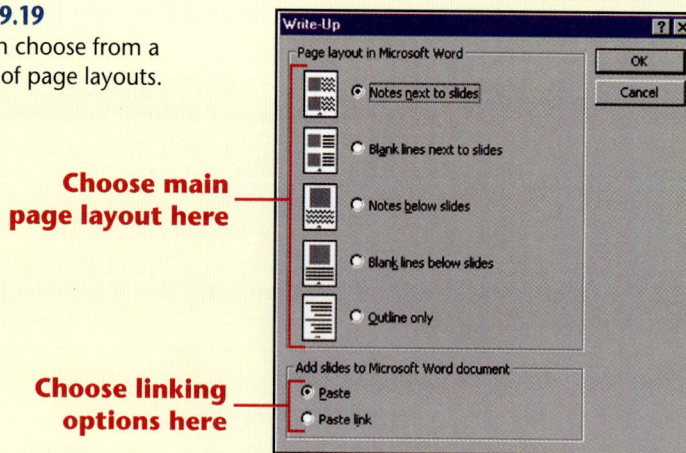

4 Click the option button for Outline only; then click OK.

PowerPoint exports the presentation to Word and creates a new Word file (see Figure 9.20). You can use this file as a basis for editing or formatting the outline. Also notice that the Word document has a generic name assigned (such as PPT1939), which displays in the title bar. This name is assigned based on the temporary file that Windows 95 uses for the new Word file and has no real significance. Also, don't be concerned if the name on other students' computers differs from yours.

Figure 9.20
PowerPoint can export a presentation to Word.

Style box—
Word document name

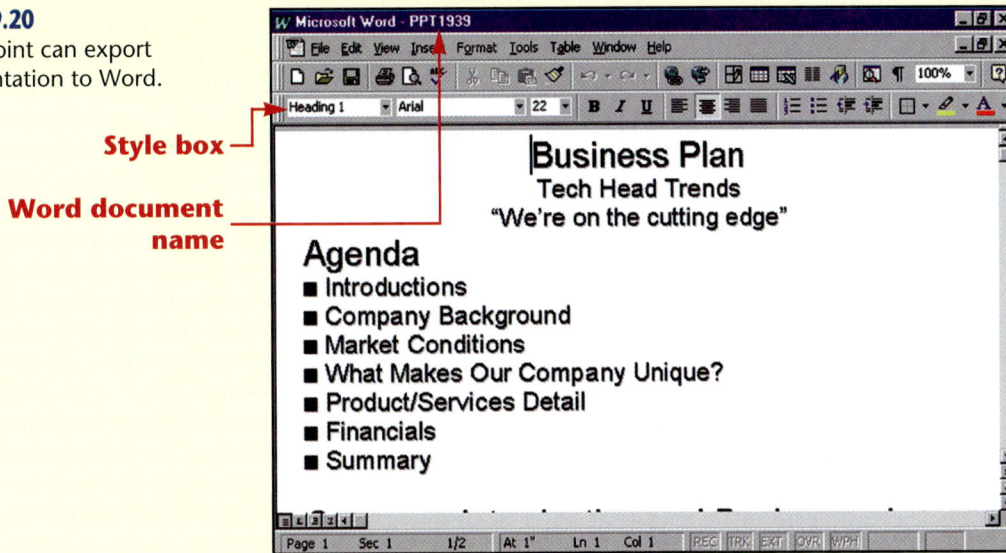

❺ Scroll through the document to view it.

Once you create an outline and view it, you can revise the outline text or formatting using any of Word's commands.

When PowerPoint exports a presentation to Word it automatically assigns a file name and saves the outline in C:\Windows\Temp folder. However, to save the file with a more descriptive name and in a folder you can more easily access the File, Save As command.

❻ In Word, choose File, Save As.

The Word Save As dialog box is displayed, and shows the current name and location for the outline (see Figure 9.21).

Figure 9.21
You can save your exported presentation in Word.

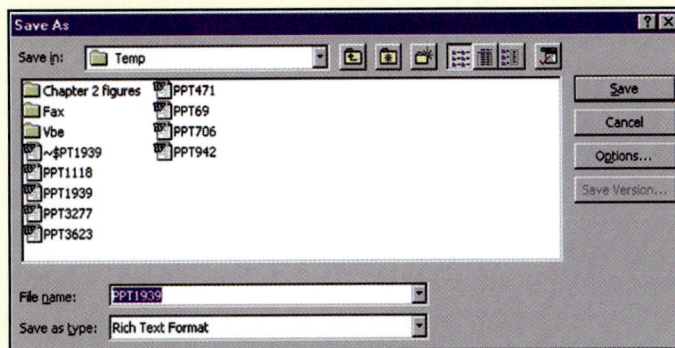

❼ In the File name text box, type Exported Presentation.

If your instructor indicates, also change the drive and folder location.

continues

To Export a Presentation   (continued)

8 Choose Save to save the Word file with the new name; then choose File, Exit to exit Word.

Your new outline is saved with the name and location you specified and Word clears from memory.

9 In PowerPoint choose File, Close to close the presentation.

If you have finished your work session, exit PowerPoint and shut down Windows 95 before turning off your computer. Otherwise, complete the Checking Your Skills and Applying Your Skills exercises at the end of this project.

Exam Notes

The Write-Up dialog box shown in Figure 9.19 also offers different document formats for exporting your presentation to Microsoft Word. If you have created speaker notes (notes pages), you can print those notes along with pictures of your slides. Your choices are to have the notes print next to the slides (the slides in one column and the notes in the second column) or to have the notes print below the slides. With the first choice, you print two slides per page with the notes; using the second choice, you print one slide per page. By using one of these options, you share your speaker notes as audience handouts.

You have two other options that enable you to print the slides with blank lines either next to the slides or below the slides. The first option prints two slides per page, with the slides in one column and the blank lines in a second column. The second option prints one slide per page with blank lines below the slide image. These options are useful for audience notes, making a handout with space for the audience members to write comments or take their own notes.

Project Summary

To	Do This
Copy text or objects	Select the text or object, then click the Copy button.
Cut text or objects	Select the text or object, then click the Cut button.
Paste text or objects	Set the insertion point to indicate the location, then click the Paste button.
Switch to another program	Click the program's Taskbar button.
Insert a Word table	Click the Insert Microsoft Word Table button on PowerPoint's Standard toolbar.
Move to the next table cell	Press Tab.
Move to the previous table cell	Press Shift+Tab.
Select an embedded object	Single-click the object.
Activate an embedded object	Double-click the object.

To	Do This
Resize a table column	Drag the column divider.
Resize a table row	Drag the row divider.
Use a preset table format	Choose Table, Table AutoFormat.
Prepare a Word document	In Word choose File, Save As, to import it to PowerPoint, then choose Rich Text Format from the Save as type drop-down list.
Import a Word outline into PowerPoint	In PowerPoint choose File, Open, then choose All Outlines from the Files of type drop-down list.
Export a PowerPoint presentation	In PowerPoint, choose File, Word Send To, Microsoft Word.

Checking Your Skills

True/False

For each of the following, check *T* or *F* to indicate whether the statement is true or false.

__T __F **1.** Information you cut or copy is sent to a temporary area in memory called the Exporter.

__T __F **2.** Exporting and importing are just different names for the same process.

__T __F **3.** You can run both Word and PowerPoint in memory at the same time.

__T __F **4.** To insert a table on a PowerPoint slide you must have Word loaded into memory.

__T __F **5.** A Taskbar button displays for each program in memory.

__T __F **6.** To export a PowerPoint presentation to Word, you can choose File, Send To, Microsoft Word.

__T __F **7.** You can use Word's menu bar and commands when you activate a table on a slide.

__T __F **8.** You can apply several preset formats to a table.

__T __F **9.** You can't resize a table's columns.

__T __F **10.** You press Tab to move to the next table cell.

Multiple Choice

Circle the letter of the correct answer for each of the following questions.

1. To share information between programs you can _____.

   a. insert one program within the other as an object

   b. use the Cut and Paste buttons

   c. use the Copy and Paste buttons

   d. all of the above

2. After you select an embedded object, you can _____.

   a. move it

   b. resize it

   c. access the source program's commands

   d. both a and b

3. As you create a table, you indicate the number of table columns and rows by _____.

   a. dragging over the table palette

   b. typing in the number of columns and rows in the AutoFormat Table dialog box

   c. dragging the column and row dividers

   d. all of the above

4. To import a Word outline into PowerPoint, you must save the document with the _____ file format.

   a. executable (.exe)

   b. Rich Text Format (.rtf)

   c. presentation (.ppt)

   d. command (.com)

5. Because Word and PowerPoint are both Microsoft programs, you can _____.

   a. use copy and paste to share information between them

   b. export a PowerPoint presentation to Word

   c. import a Word outline into PowerPoint

   d. all of the above

6. The keyboard shortcut for Cut is _____.

   a. Ctrl+C

   b. Ctrl+X

   c. Ctrl+T

   d. Ctrl+R

7. The keyboard shortcut for Paste is _____.

   a. Ctrl+X

   b. Ctrl+P

   c. Ctrl+V

   d. Ctrl+S

8. The feature used to format a Word table is _____.

   a. AutoTable

   b. Table AutoFormat

   c. WordFormat

   d. QuickFormat

9. Which of the following can be embedded objects?

   a. charts

   b. tables

   c. video clips

   d. all of the above

10. This is the area in memory where information that is cut or copied is placed.

    a. Clipboard

    b. Holdboard

    c. Importer

    d. Exporter

Completion

In the blank provided, write the correct answer for each of the following statements.

1. Information that is cut or copied is placed in the _____.

2. A _____ program is the original program from which data is cut or copied.

3. A _____ program is the program into which the Clipboard's contents are pasted.

4. You _____ an embedded object in order to resize or move it.

5. You _____ an embedded object to use the source program's commands.

6. The process of loading a file created by one program into another program is called _____.

7. A(n) _____ is a group of formatting features that are applied to a paragraph in Word.

8. The feature you use to apply formatting to a table is called _____.

9. The intersection of a column and row in a table is called a(n) _____.

10. Saving a file with a specific file format so that it can be sent to and read by another program is called _____.

Matching

In the blank next to each of the following terms or phrases, write the letter of the corresponding term or phrase. (Note that some of the letters may be used more than once.)

a. embedded object

b. cell

c. exporting

d. Ctrl+V

e. table

f. importing

g. Ctrl+X

h. style

i. Ctrl+C

j. Clipboard

_____ 1. A group of formatting features applied to a Word paragraph

_____ 2. Area in memory that holds items that are cut or copied

_____ 3. Keyboard shortcut for Copy

_____ 4. Keyboard shortcut for Cut

_____ 5. Keyboard shortcut for Paste

_____ 6. Way to display data in columns and rows

_____ 7. Intersection of a column and row

_____ 8. Sending a presentation from PowerPoint to Word

_____ 9. Bringing in a Word outline into PowerPoint

_____ 10. Table or chart on a slide that you can double-click to access another program

Applying Your Skills

Practice

The following exercises, found in the Project-09 folder on the CD, enable you to practice the skills you have learned in this project. Take a few minutes to work through these exercises now.

Copying and Pasting Information

Your supervisor has asked you (five minutes before a staff meeting) to give a quick update on a project you are spearheading. You have the information in a Word document, but need it in a PowerPoint presentation. Because you're in a hurry, you decide to copy and paste the data between the programs.

To copy and paste information, complete the following steps:

1. Open both Word 97 and PowerPoint 97.

2. In PowerPoint, open Proj0904 from the Project-09 folder on the CD and save it as `Project Status`.

3. Switch to Microsoft Word and open Proj0905 from the Project-09 folder on the CD.

4. Select all the text in the Proj0905 document, then click the Copy button.

5. In Word, choose File, Close. Don't save any changes to the document.

6. Display Slide 2, `Overall Status`, in your PowerPoint presentation. Make sure the slide displays in Slide view.

7. Click in the lower placeholder and then click the Paste button. Erase the extra bullet, if necessary.

8. Save and close the Proj0904 presentation. Leave both Word and PowerPoint loaded in memory if you plan to complete the next exercise.

Exporting a PowerPoint Presentation to Word

You have a safety report that you created as a PowerPoint presentation. So that you can make revisions to it in Word, you decide to export the presentation.

To export a PowerPoint presentation to Word, complete the following steps:

1. Make sure both Word and PowerPoint are loaded in memory.

2. In PowerPoint, open Proj0906 from the Project-09 folder on the CD and save it as `Cory Glass Safety Report`.

3. Choose File, Send To, Microsoft Word.

4. Choose Outline only in the Write-Up dialog box, then choose OK.

5. Save the Word document as New Cory Glass Safety Report.

6. Close the Word document and exit Word.

7. Save the PowerPoint presentation, and then close it.

Adding a Word Table

To make your safety report data more understandable, you decide to include a Word table in the presentation.

To add a Word table, complete the following steps:

1. In PowerPoint, open Proj0907 from the Project-09 folder on the CD and save it as Table.

2. Display Slide 4, Total sick days per facility, then click the Insert Microsoft Word Table button.

3. On the table palette, drag to select a 3 x 2 table (3 rows by 2 columns).

4. Enter the following information in the table:

Facility	Sick Days
Danville	45
Madison	38

5. Click outside the table to deselect it.

6. Save the Table presentation. Leave it open for the next exercise, in which you edit and format the table.

Editing and Formatting a Table

To make your safety report table more readable, you decide to move it and format it.

To edit and format a table, complete the following steps:

1. In the Table presentation you created in the preceding exercise, single-click the table on Slide 4.

2. Move the table down on the slide so that it is centered in the available space.

3. Double-click the table to activate it.

4. Choose Table, Table AutoFormat.

5. In the Table AutoFormat dialog box, preview several formats by clicking them on the Formats list.

6. Choose Grid 7 on the Formats list, then click OK.

7. Click outside the table to better see your changes.

8. Save and close the Table presentation.

Importing an Outline from Word

You have an outline in Word. Because you need to create a presentation based on the outline's information, you decide to import the text from Word.

To import an outline from Word, complete the following steps:

1. In Word, open Proj0908 from the Project-09 folder on the CD. Choose File, Save As.

2. In the Save As dialog box, click the Save as type drop-down list arrow and choose Rich Text Format (*.rtf). Change the file name to PowerPoint 97 Features.

3. Click Save to save the PowerPoint 97 Features file using Rich Text Format.

4. Start or switch to PowerPoint, then choose File, Open. In the Open dialog box, locate the folder where the PowerPoint 97 Features.rft file is saved.

5. Click the Files of type drop-down list arrow and choose All Outlines.

6. Double-click the PowerPoint 97 Features.rtf file to open it as a PowerPoint presentation.

7. Display the presentation in all views. If you wish, apply a design template to the presentation.

8. Save the PowerPoint presentation as New Features, and then close it.

Challenge

The following challenges, found in the Poject-09 folder on the CD, enable you to use your problem-solving skills. Take time to work through these exercises now.

Adding a Word Table Using a Set of Criteria

You're conducting a presentation about production at your plant. To quickly insert your production team leader's names in the report, you use a Word table.

To add a Word table, complete the following steps:

1. In PowerPoint open Proj0909 from the Project-09 folder on the CD and save it as Production Team Leaders.

2. Display Slide 3, Production Team Leaders, in Slide view.

3. Click the Insert Microsoft Word Table button. Drag over the table palette to indicate a table 4 rows by 3 columns in size.

4. Add the following information to the table:

Shift	Team Leader	Asst. Leader
1	Dane Black	Logan Schmidt
2	Lauren Stegall	Sarah Carpenter
3	Rebecca Bell	Eugene Byrd

5. Use the Table, Table AutoFormat command to apply the Grid 8 format to the table. Move the table so that it displays in the center of the available space.

6. Click outside the table to deselect it.

7. Save the presentation, and then close it.

Adding a Table Using a Set of Criteria

Your company provides computer software training for area businesses. You're scheduled to give a presentation at the next Chamber of Commerce meeting about the types of training you can conduct. To clearly show which types of software you support, you add a Word table to your presentation.

To add a table, complete the following steps:

1. In PowerPoint, open Proj0910 from the Project-09 folder on the CD and save it as `Computer Training`.

2. Display Slide 2, `Training Available`, in Slide view.

3. Click the Insert Microsoft Word Table button. Use the table palette to make a table 5 rows by 3 columns in size.

4. Add the following information to the table:

Software	Class
Excel 97	Sept. 12
PowerPoint 97	Sept. 15
Word 97	Sept. 17
Office Integration	Sept. 20

5. Use the Table AutoFormat command to apply the Simple 1 format to the table. Center the table in the available space.

6. Click outside of the table to better see your changes.

7. Save the Computer Training presentation, and then close it.

Exporting an Outline to Word

You have a presentation that you want to work with in outline form. So that you can use Word's features to revise the presentation, you export the presentation to Word.

To export an outline to Word, complete the following steps:

1. Open Proj0911 from the Project-09 folder on the CD and save it as `Tech Head Trends`.

2. Choose File, Send To, Microsoft Word.

3. In the Write-Up dialog box, choose Outline only. Click OK.

4. Save the newly-created Word document as `Tech Head Business Plan`.

5. Exit Word. Leave PowerPoint running for the next exercise.

Exporting Another Outline to Word

You work for a company that sells ergonomic equipment for computer users. To work with an existing presentation in Word (and use Word's features), you export the presentation from PowerPoint to Word.

To export an outline to Word, complete the following steps:

1. In PowerPoint, open Proj0912 from the Project-09 folder on the CD and save it as `Ergonomic Equipment`.

2. Choose File, Send To, Microsoft Word.

3. In the Write-Up dialog box, choose Outline only. Click OK.

4. Save the newly-created Word file as `Ergonomic Document`.

5. Close the Word document. Leave both Word and PowerPoint running for the next exercise.

Importing Text from Word

You work for the Information Technology Department at your company. Your boss suddenly informed you that he wants you to do a presentation to the staff on "Ways to work more effectively with PowerPoint." You have some tips and tricks listed in a Word document, but don't have a developed PowerPoint presentation on the subject. To save yourself time and effort, you import text from Word into PowerPoint, creating an (almost) instant presentation.

To import text from Word, complete the following steps:

1. In Word, open Proj0913 from the Project-09 folder on the CD. Choose File, Save As to display the Save As dialog box.

2. Change the file name to `PowerPoint Tips and Tricks`. Save the file using Rich Text Format.

3. In PowerPoint, choose File, Open. Click the Files of type drop-down list arrow and choose All Outlines.

4. Open the PowerPoint Tips and Tricks.rtf file in PowerPoint.

5. Save the newly created PowerPoint presentation as `Tips and Tricks`.

6. Close the presentation. Exit Word and PowerPoint

PinPoint Assessment

You have completed the project and the associated lessons, as well as the "Checking Your Skills" and "Applying Your Skills" sections. Now use the PinPoint software Evaluation mode to assess your comprehension of the specific exam tasks you have just learned. You can also use the PinPoint Trainer mode and the SHOW ME tutorials to practice these specific exam tasks.

Project 10

Ten

Enhancing Your Presentation with Pictures, Video, and Sound

Adding Sound, Movies, and Clip Art

In this project you will learn the following objectives and their associated Microsoft Exam required activities.

Objectives	Required Activities
➤ Insert and Recolor Clip Art	Add Clip Art Recolor and Edit Objects Customize Clip Art and Other Objects
➤ Use AutoClipArt	Add Clip Art
➤ Insert a Picture	Add Scanned Images
➤ Insert and Play Sounds	Add Sound and Movies
➤ Insert and Play Movies	Add Sound and Movies

Why Would I Do This?

The more unique and professional your presentation, the more convincing it will be. To make a powerful impression, you can enhance your presentation with PowerPoint's electronic clip art, pictures, sounds, and movies.

Clip art, pictures, sounds, and movies are collectively referred to as *clips*. You can view and choose clips in the *Clip Gallery*. You can also use the Clip Gallery to organize your clips by category or keyword so that it's easy to find the one you want.

You can insert *clip art* on your slides to emphasize main points or refocus attention. PowerPoint includes a couple of ways that you can insert these images in your presentation. You can scroll through the available art in the Clip Gallery and then choose what you want. However, PowerPoint also includes an easy-to-use feature, AutoClipArt, which selects clip art based on your presentation's text. And, if you want to use more realistic-looking images, you can add scanned photographic pictures to your presentation.

You can also use PowerPoint's **multimedia** capabilities to make a strong impact by inserting audio sound and movies. These multimedia features are especially effective when you use them as part of an interactive slide presentation (such as at a trade show). They can help you grab an audience's attention during an electronic slide show presentation. PowerPoint 97 includes improvements in multimedia support over earlier versions so that you can more easily insert and play sound files and movie (or video) clips in your presentation.

Because clip art and multimedia are powerful additions to a presentation, try working with them now.

Clip

A graphic, picture, sound, or video file you can use in a PowerPoint presentation.

Clip Gallery

The dialog box in which you can view or choose clips.

Clip art

Electronically reproduced graphic images you can insert into a presentation.

Jargon Watch

Communication media, such as the telephone, fax, and computer, are becoming more and more interwoven. Most personal computers, for example, are now equipped with sound and video capabilities. This means that you can use your computer to take phone messages, send faxes, or play your latest CD. The computer's capability to integrate various ways of communicating with others is called **multimedia**.

In order for your computer to be a multimedia machine, you must have certain equipment installed on it. An internal sound board is an adapter that adds digital sound reproduction capabilities to personal computers. Speakers are usually used with the sound board so that you can hear the sounds. And, because video and music files are usually too large for a 3 1/2-inch floppy disk, a CD-ROM disk, which can hold more data, is typically used instead in conjunction with a CD-ROM drive.

Lesson 1: Inserting and Recoloring Clip Art

You can jazz up almost any presentation by inserting clip art. Clip art refers to electronic graphic files you can purchase and use in your presentations. PowerPoint includes a number of pictures, or images, as part of the program. If you want more choices, however, you can purchase additional clip art packages or even download art from the World Wide Web.

PowerPoint provides two methods of inserting clip art into your presentation. You can insert clip art in a slide's clip art placeholder. Alternately, you can use the Insert Clip Art button on the Standard toolbar to insert an image onto any slide—whether or not it contains a clip art placeholder. In either case, PowerPoint displays the Clip Gallery so you can choose the image you want.

After you insert a clip art image, you may find that you don't like the colors PowerPoint provides for a clip. Luckily, it's easy to recolor the clip art image to colors that better suit your tastes or presentation.

Because including clip art is a quick and easy way to spice up a presentation, try inserting an image now.

To Insert and Recolor Clip Art

1 Start PowerPoint if necessary, and then open the Proj1001 file from the Project-10 folder on the CD and save it as Super Sports.

The open presentation displays onscreen so that you can insert clip art. Even though Slide 1 does not have a clip art placeholder, you can use the Insert Clip Art button on the Standard toolbar.

2 Display Slide 1 in Slide view, and then click the Insert Clip Art button.

The Clip Gallery dialog box displays (see Figure 10.1). You can scroll to see more images, or choose a category to limit the type of images displayed. When you find one you like, you can click the Magnify check box for a closer look, or click the Insert button to place it in your presentation.

Figure 10.1
You can choose clip art from the Clip Gallery.

Choose a category here

Choose a clip art image here

Click here to insert the selected image

Click here to toggle magnification on and off

Click here to browse the Web for images

continues

To Insert and Recolor Clip Art   (continued)

3 **In the category list, click** Sports and Leisure, **and then click the baseball player image and choose** **I**nsert. **(If you don't have this clip art image available on your system, choose another one.)**

The clip art image is inserted into your slide. Notice that white selection handles appear around the image. When it is selected, you can move or resize the object like any other object.

4 **Move the mouse pointer to the middle of the selected image until a four-headed move arrow displays, and then drag it to center it in the available space (see Figure 10.2).**

The image moves to the indicated location.

Figure 10.2
You can select, and then resize or move an image.

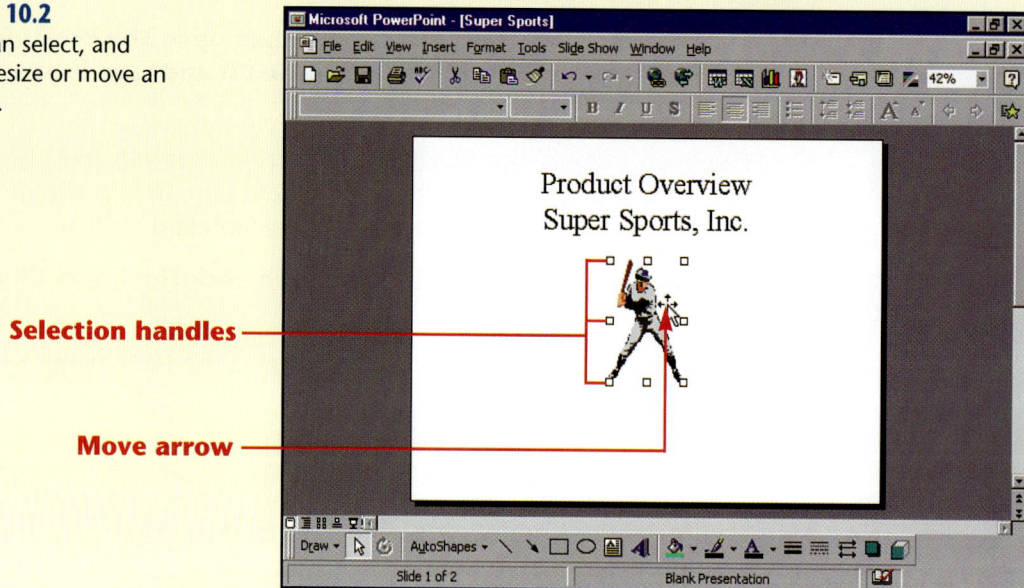

Selection handles

Move arrow

You can also insert clip art by double-clicking a clip art placeholder.

5 **Display Slide 2, and then double-click the clip art placeholder (see Figure 10.3).**

PowerPoint

Figure 10.3
You can double-click a clip art placeholder to access the Clip Gallery.

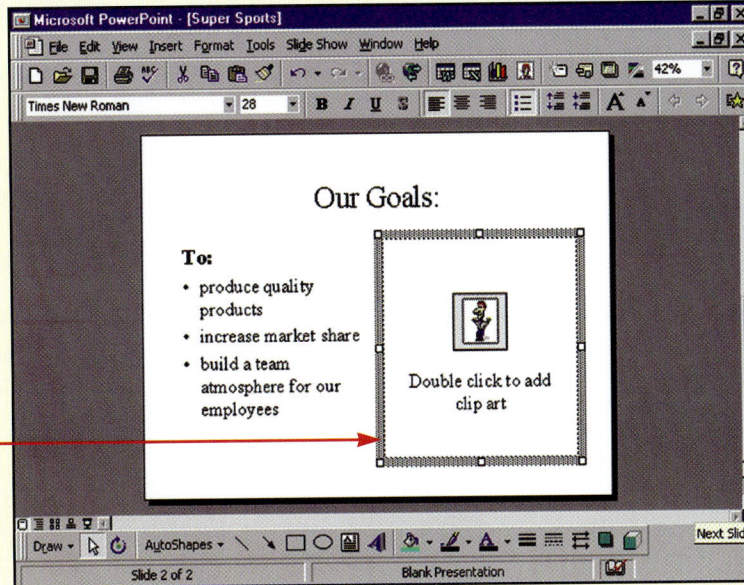

The Clip Gallery is displayed so you can view and select an image.

6 **Double-click the "bull's-eye" (target) image in the Sports and Leisure category.**

The clip art is inserted on the slide (see Figure 10.4).

Figure 10.4
You can double-click an image to insert it into a presentation.

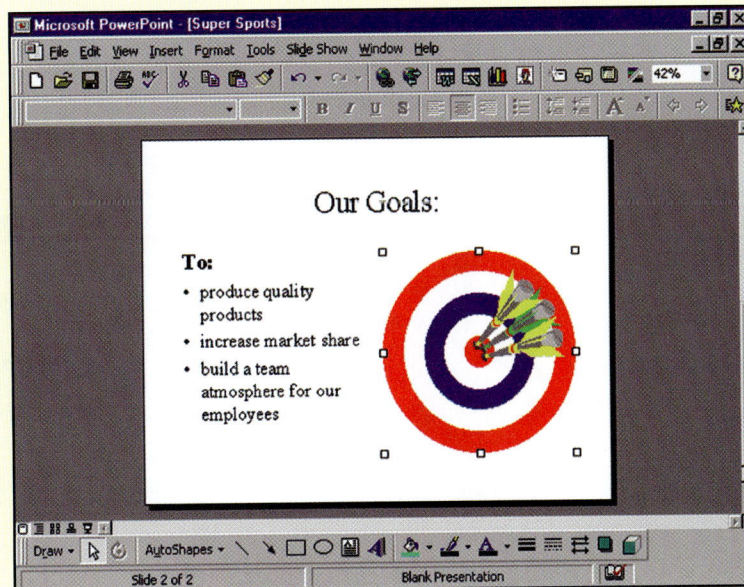

After a clip art image is inserted, you may want to modify it by changing its colors. For example, you may want to use corporate colors rather than those that PowerPoint provides. In order to recolor the image, you use the Format Picture dialog box.

continues

To Insert and Recolor Clip Art (continued)

7 **Right-click the clip art object on Slide 2, and then choose Format Picture.**

The Format Picture dialog box is displayed (Figure 10.5). Notice that this dialog box includes several tabbed pages.

Figure 10.5
The Format Picture dialog box provides several options for revising your image.

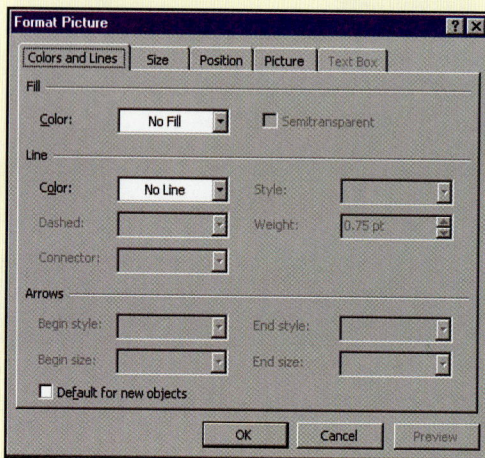

8 **Click the Picture tab, and then choose Recolor.**

The Recolor Picture dialog box is displayed (see Figure 10.6). You can change the original colors by clicking the appropriate drop-down list arrow in the New column, and then select another color from the palette that displays.

Figure 10.6
You can change clip art colors in this dialog box.

View the original colors here

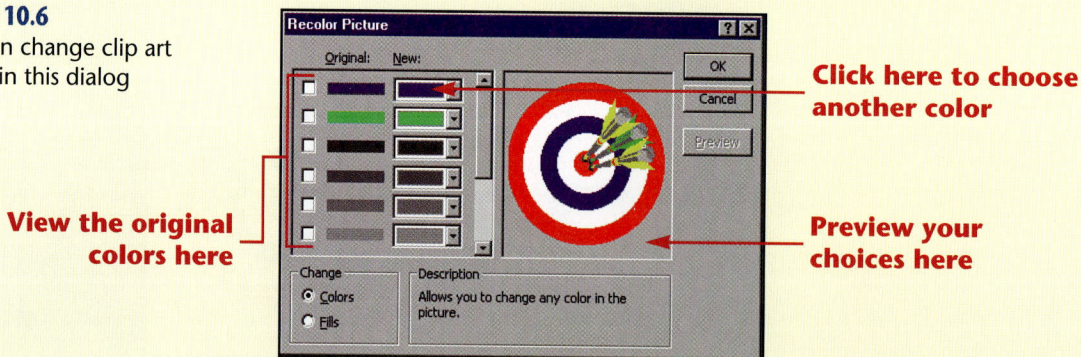

Click here to choose another color

Preview your choices here

9 **In the New column, click the blue color drop-down list arrow.**

A color palette is displayed with colors that coordinate with the presentation's colors (see Figure 10.7).

Figure 10.7
You can choose from a variety of colors in the color palette.

Click a drop-down list arrow...

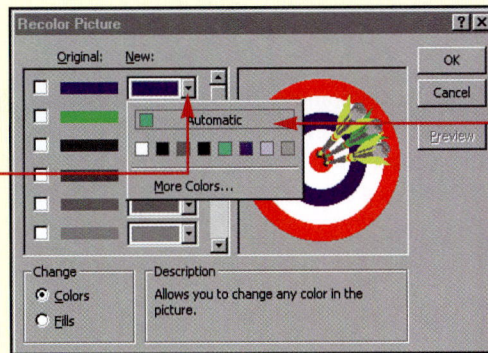

to display a palette of coordinated colors

⑩ Click the black color box (the fourth from the left).

You can see the effects of your changes in the Preview box.

⑪ Choose OK in both the Recolor Picture and Format Picture dialog boxes.

The new color is applied to your clip art image.

⑫ Save the Super Sports presentation, and then close it.

Keep PowerPoint running for the next lesson, in which you use AutoClipArt.

Inside Stuff

If you don't find a graphic you want in the Clip Gallery, look on PowerPoint's CD-ROM program disk. Also, assuming you have access to the World Wide Web and a Web browser, you can download clips from the Clip Gallery Live on the Web. To do this, click the Connect to the Web for Additional Clips button in the Clip Gallery. After you're connected to the Clip Gallery Live, you can find, preview, and download clips.

Exam Notes

Most of the clip art pictures available in PowerPoint are made up of several elements. The "bull's-eye" picture, for example, has several darts and rings of varying colors. You don't have to keep all these elements.

Draw ▾

To separate the elements of a clip art picture (or ungroup them), select the picture and then click Draw on the Drawing toolbar. Choose Ungroup from the menu. A warning appears stating that if you continue with the operation, you will lose all links (you can't double-click the art and return to the Clip Gallery); click Yes to continue. Selection handles appear around various elements that had composed the clip art. Deselect all the elements by clicking elsewhere on the slide. Then select any elements you want to eliminate from the slide and press Del. If ungrouping did not separate out the specific elements you wanted to eliminate, ungroup the portion of the clip art containing those elements. You can then eliminate the parts of the picture you don't want to include on your slide by selecting those elements and then pressing Del.

After you ungroup the elements in a clip art object, you can move, size, recolor, or delete any of the separate elements.

continues

To reunite the remaining elements of the clip art, you may be able to regroup them. Select any one of the elements, click the D̲raw button on the Drawing toolbar, and then choose Regr̲oup.

If the Regroup command is dimmed, you may have separated the clip art to the point that it could not be reunited. In this case, select all the remaining elements of the clip art, click D̲raw on the Drawing toolbar, and select G̲roup. This reunites all the selected elements so they act together as one object, or group.

Lesson 2: Using AutoClipArt

By now, you have probably discovered how easy it is to insert clip art from the Clip Gallery into your presentation. However, PowerPoint provides an even more effortless way to quickly add clip art to your presentation—AutoClipArt.

Viewing and Adding Keywords

The AutoClipArt feature searches your presentation text and suggests appropriate clip art based on keywords. A keyword is a word that helps you find a specific clip in the Gallery. For example, a picture of a person leading a meeting might have keywords such as leadership, communication, or goals. Keywords are assigned to images either by the program supplying the clip, or by you. You can view the keywords associated with each image. You can also add keywords to an image.

In the following tutorial, you use the Clip Gallery to view and change a clip's keywords and use the AutoClipArt feature. Try working with these features now.

To View and Add Keywords

1 **Open Proj1002 from the Project-10 folder on the CD, and save it as** Working with Clips.

Before you actually use AutoClipArt, it's helpful to see the keywords associated with clip art images. You can most easily do this in the Clip Gallery.

2 **Choose I̲nsert, P̲icture, C̲lip Art.**

The Clip Gallery is displayed so that you can view (and change) keywords.

3 **Click** Academic **on the category list, and then click the image indicated in Figure 10.8.**

The keyword associated with the image displays at the bottom of the dialog box (see Figure 10.8). (If you want, click other images to view their keywords. When you're finished, make sure to select the image shown in Figure 10.8.)

Figure 10.8
You can view keywords for an image.

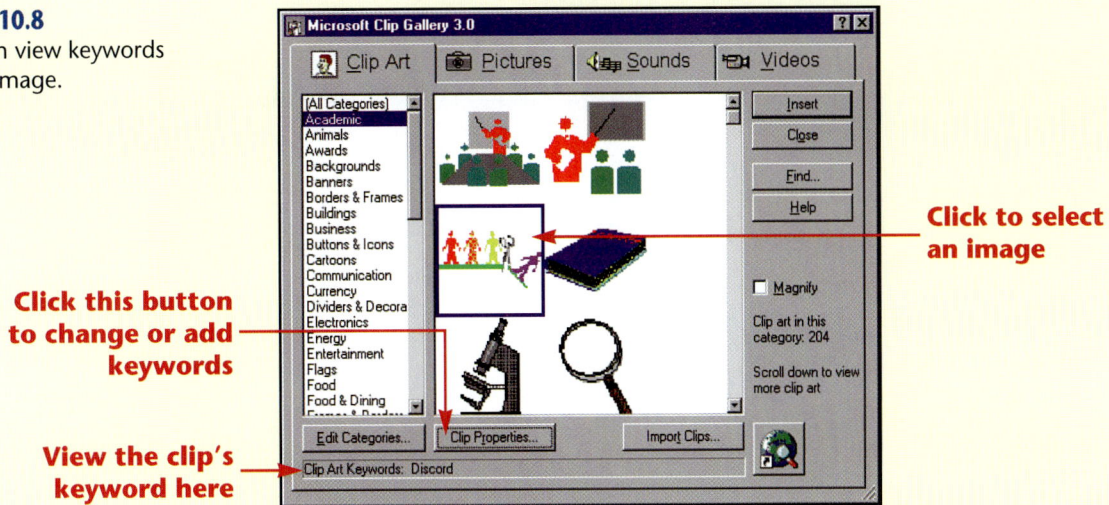

Click to select an image

Click this button to change or add keywords

View the clip's keyword here

❹ **Click the Clip Properties button.**

The Clip Properties dialog box displays so that you can change or add keywords for the image (see Figure 10.9).

Figure 10.9
Use this dialog box to view and change keywords.

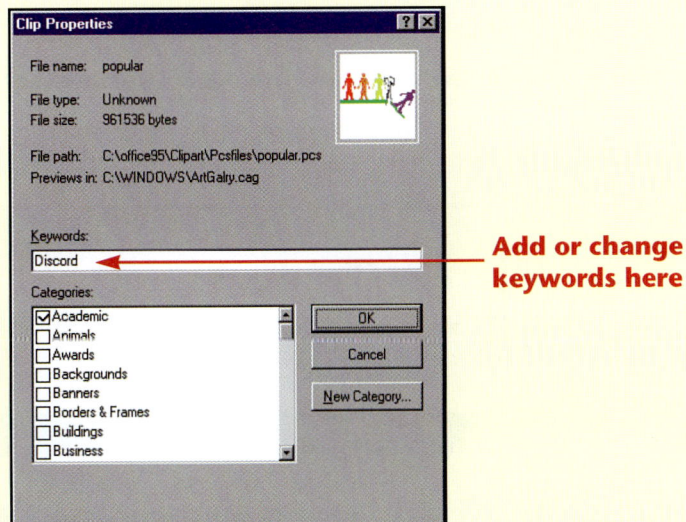

Add or change keywords here

❺ **Click in the Keywords text box after the word Discord and press** Spacebar.

You add keywords in this text box, separating each with a space.

If you have problems...

If you can't click in the Keywords text box, most likely the clip art you're using is used on a network or is a read-only file. In either case, you won't be able to make modifications to the keywords.

---

❻ **Type** Problem **in the text box, then click OK to close the Clip Properties dialog box.**

Notice that the keyword you added is now displayed in the Clip Gallery (see Figure 10.10).

continues

To View and Add Keywords   (continued)

Figure 10.10
Keywords you add display in the Clip Gallery.

New keyword →

Because you have finished working with keywords, you can close the Clip Gallery. Make sure to choose Close (not Insert) so that you don't accidentally insert a clip art image in your presentation.

7 Click Close to close the Clip Gallery.

8 Save the Working with Clips presentation.

Keep the presentation open for the next lesson, in which you use the AutoClipArt feature.

Using AutoClipArt

Now that you know how to view and add keywords, try using AutoClipArt to place clip art in your presentation.

To Use AutoClipArt

1 Display Slide 1 of the open presentation in Slide view, and then choose Tools, AutoClipArt.

PowerPoint scans your presentation's text to see which clip art keywords match it. When PowerPoint finishes the scan, the AutoClipArt dialog box is displayed (see Figure 10.11). You can use this dialog box to view and select clip art based on your presentation's text.

Figure 10.11
PowerPoint finds clip art based on a presentation's contents.

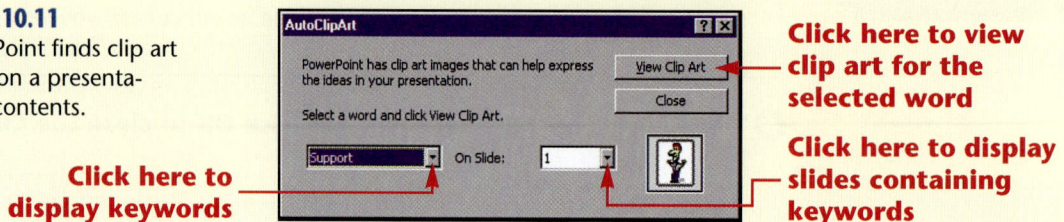

Click here to display keywords

Click here to view clip art for the selected word

Click here to display slides containing keywords

PowerPoint (side tab)

The first keyword found (Support) is displayed as well as the slide on which it was found. To see which clip art images are available for this keyword, you can click the View Clip Art button.

2 **Click the View Clip Art button.**

The Clip Gallery is displayed. Notice that a new category item (Results of Last Find) displays as well as all the images for the category (see Figure 10.12).

Figure 10.12
PowerPoint displays all images with the keyword.

New category

Keywords

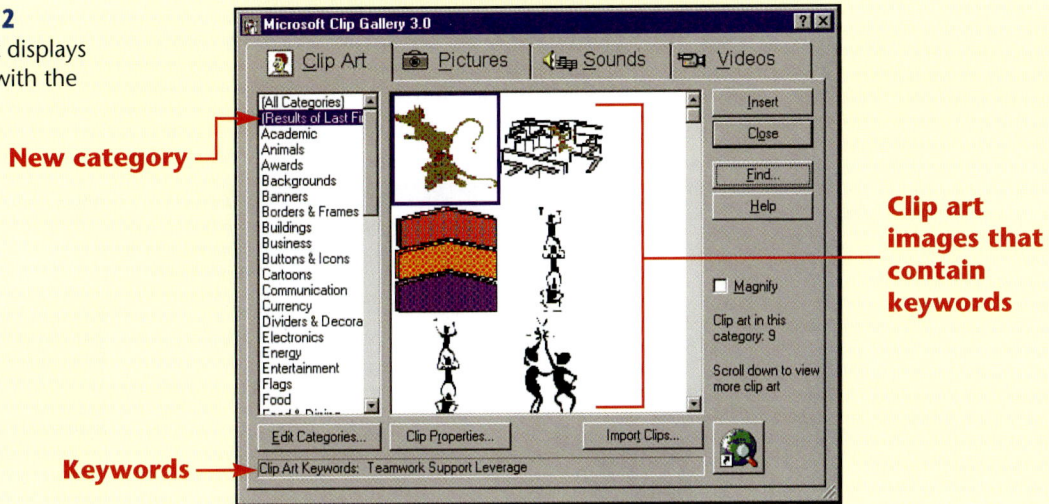

Clip art images that contain keywords

3 **Because none of the images are appropriate for Slide 1, click Close.**

The Clip Gallery closes and the AutoClipArt dialog box again displays. You can select other keywords and then view the keyword's clip art.

4 **Click the keyword drop-down list arrow, and then choose Problem from the list.**

When you select a keyword, the On Slide text box changes to reflect the slides in which the keyword is located. You can also click the On Slide drop-down list to designate a different slide on which to insert the clip art. (If you want, click the On Slide drop-down list arrow to display a list of all the slide locations where the word Problem was found, and then click again to close it.)

5 **Click the View Clip Art button to display the Clip Gallery and see all images associated with the word Problem.**

The clips that contain the keyword Problem display in the Clip Gallery. Notice that the image to which you added this keyword (in the previous exercise) is included on the list.

continues

To Use AutoClipArt   (continued)

6 **Scroll through the clip art images until you see the "screen bean with a question mark" image, and then choose Insert. (If you don't have this image on your computer, choose another.)**

AutoClipArt inserts the image on Slide 2. Additionally, the AutoClipArt dialog box remains open so that you can use it to insert other images if you want. For now, however, you can close AutoClipArt.

7 **Click Close in the AutoClipArt dialog box.**

The clip art image displays on Slide 2 (see Figure 10.13). (If you want, use the selection handles to resize and move the image.)

Figure 10.13
You can quickly insert appropriate images with AutoClipArt.

8 **Save the Working with Clips presentation, and then close it.**

Keep PowerPoint running for the next lesson, in which you learn to insert pictures.

Inside Stuff

You can also find images based on a keyword without using AutoClipArt. In the Clip Gallery, click Find to display the Find Clip dialog box. Type the keyword in the Keywords text box, and then choose Find Now. All images that contain the designated keyword display in the Clip Gallery.

Lesson 3: Inserting Pictures

In addition to using clip art in your presentation, you can also insert pictures. Pictures differ from clip art images in how they look, how they are created, and the type of file format used.

PowerPoint

Clip art images are created on the computer by graphic artists. They typically have file formats such as .cgm, .wmf, .drw., .pcs, and .wpg. In contrast, pictures are digital photographs, scanned images, and other bitmaps. Because they are scanned photographs, PowerPoint pictures usually look more realistic than clip art images. Typical picture file formats include .bmp, .tif, .jpg, .gif, and .pcx. (If you want to know the file format used for a selected image or picture in the Clip Gallery, select the image and then click the Clip Properties button.)

You insert pictures by using the Clip Gallery—much in the same way you insert clip art images. Try inserting pictures in a presentation now.

To Insert Pictures

1 Open Proj1003 from the Project-10 folder on the CD, and save it as Educational Opportunities.

2 Display Slide 2, Go to Japan, **and then choose Insert, Picture, Clip Art.**

The Clip Gallery dialog box is displayed with a tabbed page for pictures. You can click the Pictures tab to display pictures. By default, PowerPoint's pictures are available only on the program's CD-ROM disk. In order to easily access them, make sure that PowerPoint's CD-ROM disk is inserted in the CD-ROM drive, or ask your instructor where the files are located.

3 Click the Pictures tab.

The Pictures page of the Clip Gallery displays (see Figure 10.14). You use the Pictures page in a similar way as you did the Clip Art page earlier in this project. For example, you can click a category to limit the type of pictures that display.

Figure 10.14
Jazz up your presentation with scanned photographs.

Available pictures —

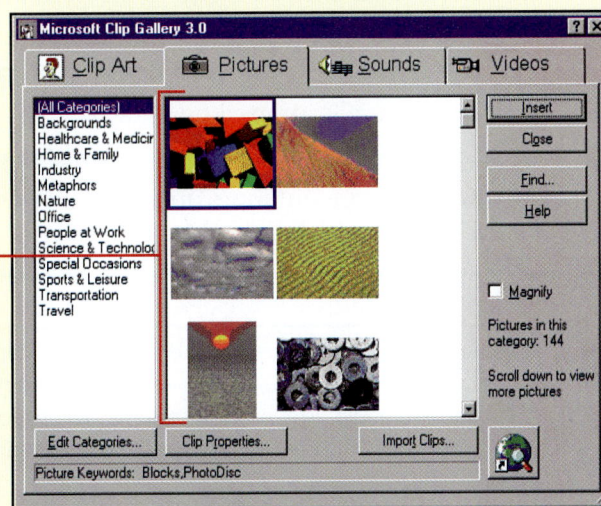

4 Click Travel **on the category list.**

Only those pictures associated with travel display.

continues

To Insert Pictures   (continued)

5 Make sure the first picture in the preview area is selected (Mt. Fuji in Japan); then choose Insert.

The selected picture is inserted on Slide 2 (see Figure 10.15). Notice that PowerPoint treats the picture as an object that you can resize or move, complete with selection handles.

Figure 10.15
PowerPoint inserts pictures as objects.

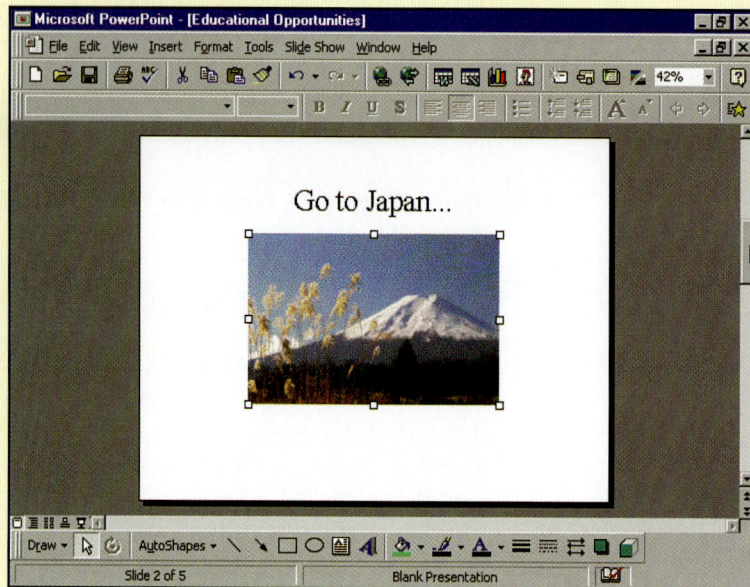

Now try inserting another picture in the presentation.

6 Display Slide 3; then click the Insert Clip Art button.

The Clip Gallery displays. Instead of using the Insert button, you can double-click a picture to insert it.

7 Click the Pictures tab; then double-click the first picture in the second column (the Great Wall of China).

The picture is inserted on Slide 3.

8 Save the Educational Opportunities presentation.

Keep the presentation open and PowerPoint running for the next lesson, in which you add sound to your presentation.

Inside Stuff

If the picture you want to include in your presentation is not one of the images contained in the Clip Gallery, you can still insert it in your slide. Choose Insert, Picture, From File. When the Insert File dialog box appears, specify the drive and folder where you stored the file, select the file, and then click Insert. Move and size the image to fit your slide.

To make your frequently used pictures (such as logos, pictures of buildings, portraits of management personnel, and so on) available from the Clip Gallery, open the Clip Gallery, select the Picture tab, and click Import Clips. The Add pictures to Clip Gallery dialog box opens. Specify the location of the file you want to add, and then select the file. Click Open. The Clip Properties dialog box appears. Select a category and enter any keywords for the image. Choose OK to close the Clip Properties box, and the picture appears in the Clip Gallery.

Lesson 4: Inserting and Playing Sounds

You can use sound in a variety of ways to "make or break" a presentation. You can use sound, for example, to indicate a *slide transition,* or to set a mood. You add sound to a slide by inserting a sound file, or clip. Once inserted, you can run an electronic slide show to actually play the sound clips.

Slide transition
The way in which one slide replaces another during an electronic slide show, including visual and sound effects.

PowerPoint includes two main ways to add sound to your presentation. The method you choose depends on the sound file you want to use and the effect you want.

- You can add sound as part of a slide transition so that the sound plays when one slide replaces another during an electronic slide show.

- You can add audio sound clips from the Clip Gallery or a file. The sound clip is inserted as an object on the slide. You play the sound by clicking the object during an electronic slide show presentation.

Because adding sound adds an air of professionalism and excitement to your presentation, try inserting and playing sound clips now.

If you have problems...

In order to fully use the multimedia features, such as the movie and sound clips, you must have the proper equipment on your system—usually a sound board and speakers. In addition, it's helpful (and usually standard in current systems) to have a CD-ROM drive. Before proceeding with Lessons 4 and 5, make sure you have the necessary equipment.

To Insert and Play Sounds

❶ In the open Educational Opportunities presentation, display Slide 1 in Slide view.

You can use music to set the tone for your presentation. This is most often done in conjunction with the opening presentation slide. Try inserting a sound file from the Clip Gallery for this purpose now.

❷ Choose Insert, Movies and Sounds; then choose Sound from Gallery on the submenu that displays.

The Sounds page of the Clip Gallery displays (see Figure 10.16). You can select a sound file from the preview area, and then play the sound or insert it into your presentation.

continues

To Insert and Play Sounds (continued)

Figure 10.16
You can preview a
sound before
inserting it.

Selected sound file

Click here to insert the sound on your slide

Click here to play the sound clip

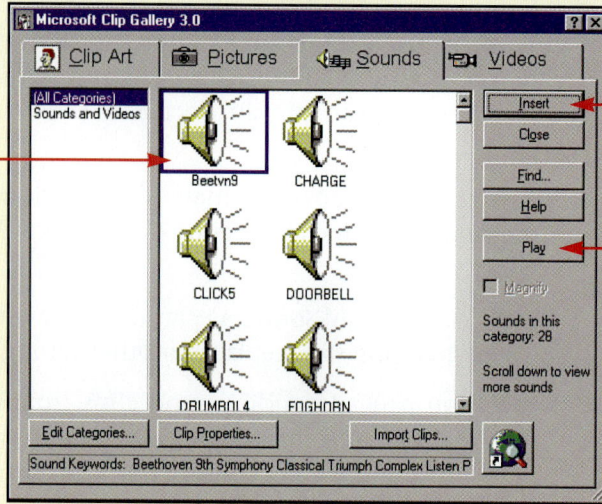

❸ **Make sure the** Beetvn9 **(Beethoven) file is selected, and then click the Play button.**

The sound clip plays. Now you can determine whether it is appropriate for your presentation.

If you have problems... ▸ Make sure you have a sound card and speakers installed on your system (and the speakers are turned on) or you won't be able to "preview" the sound.

❹ **After the sound clip finishes playing, click Insert.**

The sound clip is inserted on Slide 1 as an object (see Figure 10.17). You can select, move, and resize it like any other object. For now, you can leave it in its present location and add sound to a slide transition.

Figure 10.17
You can insert sounds
into your presentation.

Sound object

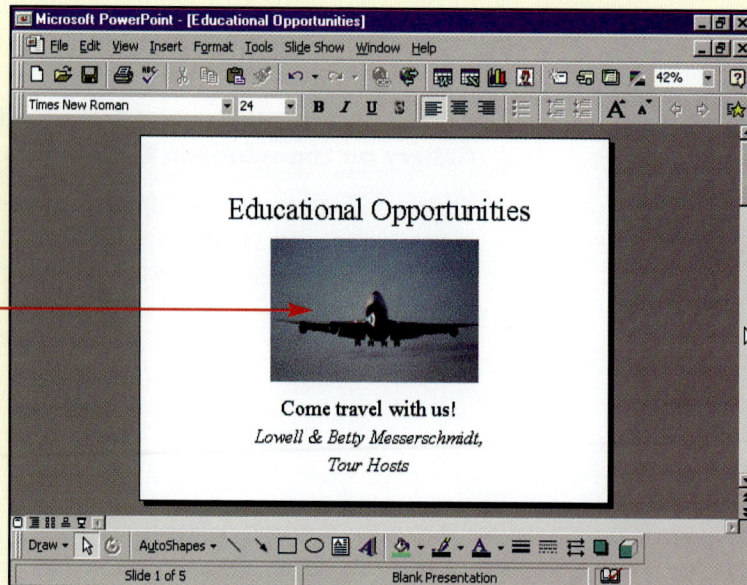

5 **Display Slide 2, and then choose Sli_de Show, Slide _Transition.**

The Slide Transition dialog box is displayed (see Figure 10.18). You can use this dialog box to add sound during the transition to Slide 2.

Figure 10.18
Get your audience's attention by adding sound to a slide transition.

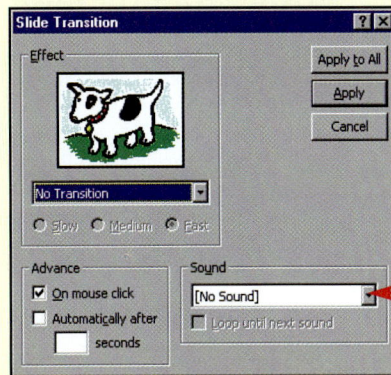

Click here to display and choose a sound

6 **Click the So_und drop-down list arrow to display sounds you can use for a transition.**

PowerPoint displays a list of sound files (such as applause and breaking glass) that are perfect for getting attention during a slide transition. You can select a sound clip, then add it to the current slide by choosing Apply, or to all presentation slides by choosing Apply _to All.

7 **Choose** Chime **from the list, and then choose _Apply. (If Chime is not available on your system, choose another sound file.)**

The sound effect is added to Slide 2. To hear the sound, you must view the presentation as an electronic slide show.

8 **In the open presentation, display Slide 1 and then click the Slide Show button.**

The slide show begins. Notice that the sound object displays on Slide 1, but doesn't automatically play. By default, PowerPoint doesn't play sound clips until you click the sound object. This gives you control over when (and if) the sound is played.

9 **Move the mouse pointer over the sound object until a hand pointer displays (see Figure 10.19).**

When the hand pointer displays, you can click the sound object to play it.

continues

To Insert and Play Sounds   (continued)

Figure 10.19
You click the hand
pointer on an object to
play a sound.

Hand pointer ━━━━━

Educational Opportunities

Come travel with us!
Lowell & Betty Messerschmidt,
Tour Hosts

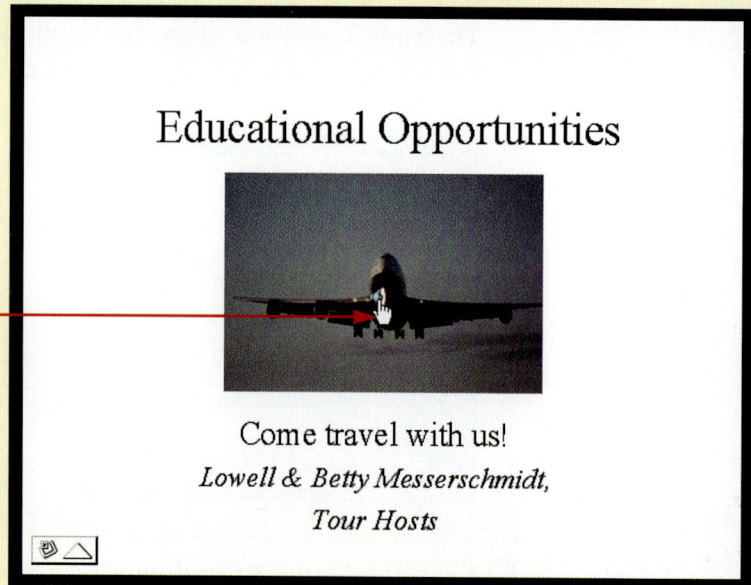

⑩ **Click the sound object.**

The sound associated with the object plays. You can play the sound as many times as you would like during a presentation (or skip playing it at all).

Next, you move to Slide 2. Because you have added a sound to the slide transition between Slides 1 and 2, the sound will play automatically as you move to Slide 2.

⑪ **Press ⏎Enter.**

The slide transition sound plays as Slide 2 replaces Slide 1.

⑫ **Press Esc.**

The slide show ends and the Educational Opportunities presentation displays in Slide view.

⑬ **Save the presentation.**

Keep the presentation open for the next lesson, in which you insert and play movie clips.

Inside Stuff

The Clip Gallery doesn't include many sound files. There are more sound files available on the Office 97 CD. When working with sound, insert the Office 97 CD in your CD-ROM drive so you can access these additional sound clips. You may also be able to download additional sound clips from the Microsoft Web site (click the Connect to Web for additional clips button in the bottom-right corner of the Clip Gallery dialog box).

PowerPoint

Lesson 5: Inserting and Playing Movies

PowerPoint can play movie clips (sometimes called video clips) during an electronic slide show. You insert the movies from the Clip Gallery or from a file on your hard disk. Once inserted, you can play the movies as part of your slide show. Movies are useful ways of catching an audience's attention, emphasizing information, explaining procedures, and so on.

Try inserting a movie clip now.

To Insert and Play Movies

❶ In the Educational Opportunities presentation, display Slide 4 in Slide view.

❷ Choose Insert, Movies and Sounds, and then choose Movie from Gallery.

The Video page of the Clip Gallery displays (see Figure 10.20). All videos on your CD display in the Gallery. You can select a video from the list to preview or insert it in your presentation.

Figure 10.20
You can choose video clips from the Gallery.

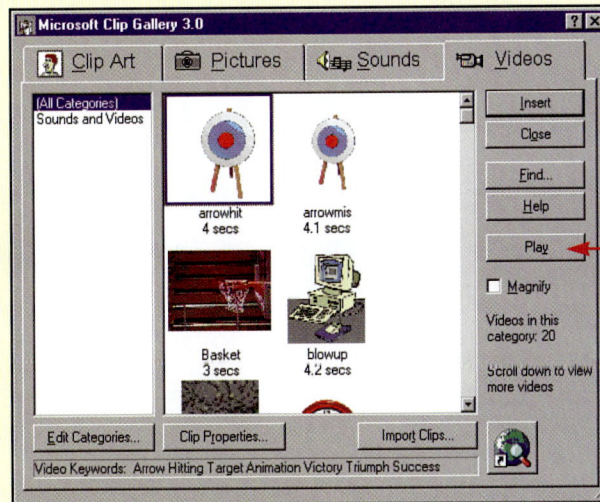

Click here to preview a movie

If you have problems...   If you don't see any movie files displayed, make sure you have the Office 97 CD in the drive or ask your instructor for assistance.

---

❸ Double-click the FIREWORK video clip.

The clip is inserted on Slide 4. Now try previewing a movie clip before inserting it in your presentation.

❹ Display Slide 5, then choose Insert, Movies and Sounds, Movie from Gallery.

❺ Click the GLOBE video clip, then choose Play.

The selected video plays in its own window so you can preview it (see Figure 10.21). PowerPoint uses the Media Player to automatically show the movie. When the movie finishes, the Media Player closes.

continues

To Insert and Play Movies   (continued)

Figure 10.21
You can preview movie clips in their own window.

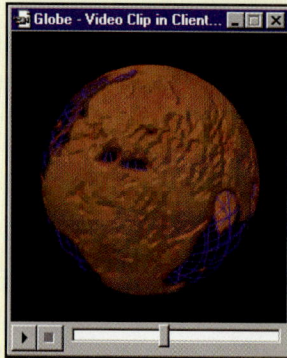
Globe - Video Clip in Client...

6 Double-click the GLOBE movie clip.

The movie clip is inserted on Slide 5. Now try playing the video clips during an electronic slide show.

7 Display Slide 4, and then click the Slide Show button.

The slide show begins, starting with Slide 4. To play a movie, you click the movie object with the hand pointer.

8 Rest the mouse pointer over the movie object until it displays as a hand pointer, and then click.

The movie plays. (You can play a movie clip as many times as you would like during a slide show before proceeding to the next slide.)

9 Press ⏎Enter to display Slide 5, and then click the movie object on Slide 5.

The movie for Slide 5 plays.

10 When the movie finishes playing, press Esc.

The slide show ends and Slide 5 displays in Slide view.

11 Save the Educational Opportunities presentation, and then close it.

If you have finished your work session, exit PowerPoint and shut down Windows 95 before turning off your computer. Otherwise, complete the "Checking Your Skills" and "Applying Your Skills" exercises at the end of this project.

Inside Stuff

If you decide you don't like a particular video clip, you can easily replace it. In Slide view, double-click the movie object to open the Clip Gallery. Double-click another movie clip to replace the original one.

PowerPoint

Project Summary

To	Do This
Insert clip art	Click the Insert Clip Art button.
Limit the clip images displayed	Choose a category in the Clip Gallery.
Increase the viewing size of an image	Click the Magnify check box in the Clip Gallery.
Recolor an image	Choose Format Picture from the object's shortcut menu; click the Picture tab and choose Recolor.
View a keyword	Select an image in the Clip Gallery; view the keyword at the bottom of the dialog box.
Add a keyword	Select an image, and then click the Clip Properties button in the Clip Gallery.
Use AutoClipArt	Choose Tools, AutoClipArt.
Display images based on a keyword	Click Find in the Clip Gallery; type the keyword in the Find Clip dialog box.
Insert a picture	Choose Insert, Picture, Clip Art, and then click the Pictures tab. Select the picture and click Insert.
Insert a sound clip	Choose Insert, Movies and Sounds, Sound from Gallery.
Preview a sound clip	Select a clip, and then click Play in the Clip Gallery.
Add sound to a slide transition	Choose Slide Show, Slide Transition.
Insert a movie clip	Choose Insert, Movies and Sounds, Movie from Gallery.
Preview a movie clip	Select a clip, and then click Play In the Clip Gallery.

Checking Your Skills

True/False

For each of the following, check *T* or *F* to indicate whether the statement is true or false.

__T __F **1.** Clip art images, videos, pictures, and sound files are collectively referred to as clips.

__T __F **2.** You use the Picture Art Gallery to insert clips.

__T __F **3.** You use the Media Player to change keywords.

__T __F **4.** You can find clips based on a keyword, such as *team* or *leadership*.

__T __F **5.** You can preview a movie before inserting it in your presentation.

__T __F **6.** You can add sound only during slide transitions.

__T __F **7.** PowerPoint includes a feature called Clipit, which automatically inserts appropriate clip art into your presentation.

__T __F **8.** Movies and videos are essentially the same thing.

__T __F **9.** You need a microphone attached to the computer in order to play sound clips.

__T __F **10.** You can find clips on the World Wide Web.

Multiple Choice

Circle the letter of the correct answer for each of the following questions.

1. In order to use PowerPoint's multimedia capabilities effectively, which of the following should your computer system include?

  a. a sound card

  b. speakers

  c. a CD-ROM drive

  d. all of the above

2. Using PowerPoint you can include _____ in your presentation.

  a. clip art

  b. scanned photographic images

  c. sound files

  d. all of the above

3. Clips are inserted on a slide as _____.

  a. objects

  b. sounds

  c. pictures

  d. none of the above

4. What are the four pages in the Clip Gallery?

  a. Clip Art, Pictures, Sounds, Videos

  b. Clip Art, Objects, Music, Movies

  c. Objects, Sounds, Videos, Movies

  d. Drawings, Pictures, Sounds, Movies

5. How do clip art images differ from pictures?

  a. They use different file formats.

  b. Clip art appears more realistic than pictures.

  c. Pictures are inserted using the Picture Gallery.

  d. You can add keywords to pictures but not to clip art.

6. After you insert clip art on a slide, you can _____.

  a. recolor it

  b. move it

  c. resize it

  d. all of the above

7. Which of the following is true regarding keywords?

  a. Keywords for a clip art image display when you select the image in the Clip Gallery.

  b. You can't make changes to keywords if you're running PowerPoint on a network.

c. You add or change keywords in the Clip Properties dialog box.

d. All of the above.

8. What is the name of the feature used to locate appropriate clip art based on a presentation's content?

   a. AutoComplete

   b. ClipImage

   c. AutoArt

   d. AutoClipArt

9. Where can you locate clips?

   a. on the Office 97 CD-ROM

   b. on the World Wide Web

   c. on your hard drive

   d. all of the above

10. What happens when you double-click a clip art placeholder on your slide?

    a. The Format Clip Art dialog box displays.

    b. The Recolor Clip Art dialog box displays.

    c. The Clip Gallery displays.

    d. The clip is deleted.

Completion

In the blank provided, write the correct answer for each of the following statements.

1. You use the _____ dialog box to view and insert clips.

2. A word that helps you find a certain type of clip is called a _____.

3. A _____ is the way one slide replaces another in a slide show.

4. Clips are inserted on slides as _____, which means that they can be selected, moved, or resized.

5. Changing a clip's color is called _____.

6. The computer's capability to integrate various ways of communicating with others is called _____.

7. You can _____ a video clip on a slide to display the Clip Gallery.

8. When a clip is selected on your slide, selection _____ appear around the border.

9. An image created by graphic artists is called _____.

10. Another name for a movie clip is a _____.

Matching

In the blank next to each of the following terms or phrases, write the letter of the corresponding term or phrase. (Note that some of the letters may be used more than once.)

a. recoloring

b. pictures

c. Clip Properties

d. keyword

e. sound clip

f. clip art images

g. AutoClipArt

h. Clip Gallery Live

i. Clip Gallery

j. video

_____ **1.** Feature used to locate appropriate clip art for a presentation

_____ **2.** Dialog box used to view and select clips

_____ **3.** Movie clip

_____ **4.** Where you can download clips from the Web

_____ **5.** Changing a clip's color

_____ **6.** Audio file

_____ **7.** Dialog box used to change a clip's keyword

_____ **8.** A word to help you find a specific clip in the Gallery

_____ **9.** Scanned photographic images

_____ **10.** Created by graphic artists

Applying Your Skills

Practice

The following exercises, found in the Project-10 folder on the CD, enable you to practice the skills you have learned in this project. Take a few minutes to work through these exercises now.

Inserting and Recoloring Clip Art

Your company gives a certificate to employees who successfully complete a safety training course. To make the certificate, you decide to insert and recolor clip art on a PowerPoint slide.

To insert and recolor clip art, complete the following steps:

1. Create a new presentation with a blank slide.
2. Click the Insert Clip Art button to display the Clip Gallery.
3. Choose the Academic category and double-click any picture that looks like a book.
4. Double-click the book clip art image to redisplay the Clip Gallery.
5. Select the picture that looks like a diploma and then choose Insert.
6. With the clip art image selected on your slide, choose Format, Picture. Click the Picture tab and then choose Recolor.
7. Change the red ribbon to blue. Change the other colors in the image to those that you feel look appropriate.
8. Close the Recolor Picture and Format Picture dialog boxes.
9. View your changes, and then close the presentation without saving it.

Adding and Recoloring Clip Art

As president of the University Biking Club, you are preparing for an upcoming meeting. To spice up your presentation, you add some clip art. Then, for added interest, recolor it.

To add and recolor clip art, complete the following steps:

1. In PowerPoint, open Proj1004 from the Project-10 folder on the CD and save it as `Biking Club`.

2. Display Slide 1 in Slide view, and then open the Clip Gallery.

3. In the Sports & Leisure category, choose the bicyclist clip art.

4. Move and resize the clip art picture so that it displays in the lower-right corner of the slide.

5. Right-click the picture, and then choose Format, Picture from the shortcut menu.

6. In the Format Picture dialog box, click the Picture tab and choose Recolor.

7. Change the color of the clip art to dark maroon.

8. Display your presentation as an electronic slide show to see your changes.

9. Save your presentation, and then close it.

Adding Scanned Images

You work for a scientific research facility and have been asked to represent the company at a trade show. In order to spiff up an existing presentation, you decide to add some pictures to it.

To add scanned images, complete the following steps:

1. Open Proj1005 from the Project-10 folder on the CD and save it as `ABC Research`.

2. Display Slide 1 in Slide view, and then display the Clip Gallery.

3. Click the Pictures tab, and then choose the Science & Technology category.

4. Click the Scope (microscope) picture, and then click the Magnify check box to enlarge the picture.

5. Insert the Scope picture onto your slide.

6. Resize and move the picture so that it displays in the center of the slide.

7. Display Slide 2, and then click the Insert Clip Art button. Click the Pictures tab in the Clip Gallery.

8. In the Science & Technology category, select the Chem (chemicals) picture, and then choose Insert.

9. Move the picture so that it displays in the center of the available whitespace.

10. Save the presentation. Keep it open for the next exercise.

Adding Sound

To further improve the ABC Research presentation open from the previous exercise, you decide to add sound.

To add sound, complete the following steps:

1. In the open ABC Research presentation, display Slide 1, and then choose Insert, Movies and Sounds, Sound from Gallery.

2. Click the Trngpnt sound file, and then choose Play to listen to the clip.

3. When the music stops playing, click Insert to place it on Slide 1.

4. Move the sound clip to the lower-right corner of Slide 1.

5. Display Slide 2, and then choose Slide Show, Slide Transition.

6. Click the Sound drop-down list arrow and choose Whoosh. Click Apply to apply the slide transition to the current slide.

7. Display Slide 1, and then click the Slide Show button.

8. When Slide 1 displays in the slide show, click the sound clip object to play the sound.

9. When the music finishes playing, move to Slide 2.

10. Press Esc to exit the slide show.

11. Save and close the ABC Research presentation.

Adding Sound and Movies

You are working on a presentation to motivate people to set goals. To help inspire them, you decide to insert both movie and sound clips in your presentation.

To add sound and movies, complete the following steps:

1. Open Proj1006 from the Project-10 folder on the CD and save it as Setting Goals.

2. With Slide 1 displayed, choose Insert, Movies and Sounds, Sound from Gallery.

3. Insert the CHARGE sound clip on your slide. Move it to the lower-right corner of the slide.

4. Display Slide 2, and then choose Insert, Movies and Sounds, Movie from Gallery.

5. On the Videos page of the Clip Gallery, double-click the arrowmis file.

6. Display Slide 3, and then choose Insert, Movies and Sounds, Movie from Gallery.

7. Click the arrowhit file on the Videos page, and then choose Insert.

8. Display Slide 1, and then click the Slide Show button. In the slide show, play the sound clip and videos you inserted.

9. Save the presentation, and then close it.

PowerPoint

Challenge

The following challenges, found in the Project-10 folder on the CD, enable you to use your problem-solving skills. Take time to work through these exercises now.

Adding Clip Art

Your boss (a brilliant, but unimaginative person) has asked that you help him jazz up a presentation. You decide to use one of the easiest, but most impressive ways to do so—adding clip art.

To add clip art, complete the following steps:

1. Open Proj1007 from the Project-10 folder on the CD and save it as Computer Clip Art.

2. Display Slide 1 in Slide view, and then click the Insert Clip Art button to display the Clip Gallery.

3. Select categories that you feel might have computer images (such as Business, Office, or Technology).

4. Click several clip art images and view their keywords.

5. Insert any computer image on your slide. Move and resize the image so that it displays in the center of the available space.

6. Repeat steps 2–5 for Slide 2.

7. Save the presentation, and then close it.

Adding and Recoloring Presentation Clip Art

To help raise money for your company's service project (helping underprivileged children in the area), you're in charge of a bake sale. To promote the bake sale, you develop a flyer using PowerPoint.

To add and recolor clip art, complete the following steps:

1. Open Proj1008 from the Project-10 folder on the CD and save it as Bake Sale.

2. Insert a clip art image from either the Food or Food & Dining categories.

3. Recolor the clip art so that the colors match that of the design template.

4. Print a copy of your flyer.

5. Save and close your presentation.

Inserting and Recoloring Presentation Clip Art

You're developing a presentation for your company, which helps clients set and reach financial goals. For the opening presentation slide, you insert and recolor a clip art image.

To insert and recolor presentation clip art, complete the following steps:

1. Open Proj1009 from the Project-10 folder on the CD and save it as Smith Financial Services.

2. Display Slide 1 in Slide view. Using the Clip Gallery, insert the clip art image of the money bags (the dollargb file). (Hint: You can use the Clip Properties dialog box to find this file.)

3. Resize and move the clip as necessary to display it in the center of Slide 1.

4. Recolor the image so that the dollar sign on the bag displays in white.

5. Save the presentation. Keep it open for the next exercise.

Adding Scanned Images to a Presentation

To further develop the Smith Financial Services presentation open from the preceding exercise, you add scanned images (pictures) to it.

To add scanned images to a presentation, complete the following steps:

1. In the open Smith Financial Services presentation, display Slide 2.

2. Insert the picture of the Matterhorn (file name: Mtn) on Slide 2. Move and resize the image as necessary to display it in the middle of the available space.

3. Display Slide 3.

4. Insert the Climb picture from the Pictures page of the Clip Gallery on Slide 2 (filename: Climb). Move and resize the image as necessary to display it in the middle of the available space.

5. View your presentation as an onscreen show.

6. Save your presentation. Keep it open for the next exercise.

Adding Presentation Sound and Movies

You finish developing your Smith Financial Services presentation by adding movies and sound.

To add presentation sound and movies, complete the following steps:

1. In the open Smith Financial Services presentation, display Slide 4.

2. Insert the Globe movie on Slide 4. Display the presentation as a slide show. Play the movie.

3. Insert the Handshke movie on Slide 5. Display the presentation as a slide show. Play the movie.

4. Insert the Beetvn9 sound on Slide 1. Move the sound object to the lower-right corner of the slide.

5. View the presentation as a slide show, starting at Slide 1. Play all the sounds and movies.

Save the Smith Financial Services presentation, and then close it.

PinPoint Assessment

PinPoint
Training

You have completed the project and the associated lessons, as well as the "Checking Your Skills" and "Applying Your Skills" sections. Now use the PinPoint software Evaluation mode to assess your comprehension of the specific exam tasks you have just learned. You can also use the PinPoint Trainer mode and the SHOW ME tutorials to practice these specific exam tasks.

Project 11

Eleven

Using Advanced Drawing Techniques

Illustrating Your Presentations

In this project you will learn the following objectives and their associated Microsoft Exam required activities.

Objectives	Required Activities
➤ Draw Freehand Objects	Draw an Object
➤ Use a Text Box	
➤ Use AutoShapes	Add Shapes
➤ Manipulate Objects	Rotate and Fill an Object
➤ Create 3-D Effects	
➤ Create Shadow Effects	
➤ Use WordArt	

Why Would I Do This?

When you need to include illustrations, logos, or other drawings in a presentation, you can turn to PowerPoint's Drawing toolbar for the tools you need. PowerPoint includes on this toolbar a wealth of drawing tools that help you quickly produce arrows, rectangles, circles, and other shapes. These shapes are useful to emphasize key information on a slide or to capture an audience's attention. For example, you might want to have an arrow point to the highest sales for the year, or to emphasize market share. Figure 11.1 shows how drawn objects can enhance a slide. The basics of drawing, selecting, and modifying objects was covered in Project 5, "Changing the Appearance of a Presentation."

Figure 11.1
You can use drawings to emphasize information.

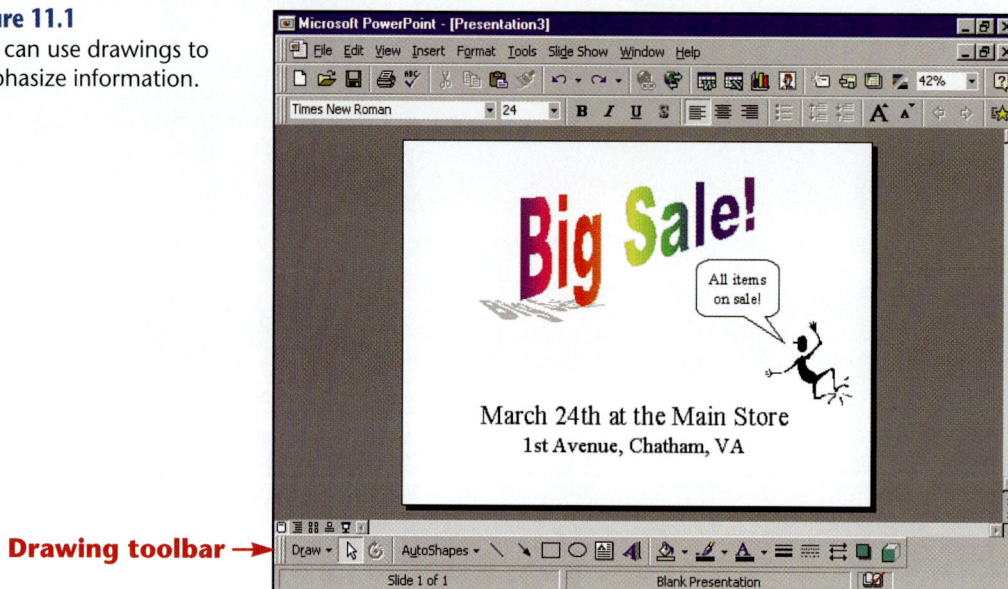

In addition to adding interest or emphasizing information, you can also use PowerPoint's drawing tools to create rather complicated drawings not available as predrawn clip art. For example, you may want to design a company, department, or personal logo and can't find clip art to fit the bill. If you're ambitious (and creative), you can use the drawing tools PowerPoint provides to design your own.

PowerPoint provides a wide variety of drawing tools. You can draw **freehand** shapes, such as arrows, circles, rectangles, and so on. You can also create text boxes to enter written information, or rely on PowerPoint's **AutoShapes** to quickly draw professionally designed shapes. After you draw an object, you can move, resize, and otherwise modify it. PowerPoint 97 also helps you quickly apply 3-D and shadow effects to objects. Finally, you can use WordArt to manipulate text in a variety of ways.

Because drawn objects can add so much pizzazz to a presentation, try working with them now.

Jargon Watch

In PowerPoint you can draw either freehand or AutoShape objects. **Freehand** objects, such as lines, rectangles, and ovals, are those that you draw from scratch with the mouse. In general, you must have good control of the mouse, a creative mind, and time in order to create complicated freehand shapes. In contrast, you can quickly reproduce professionally designed objects, such as stars, banners, bubble callouts, and so on, by using **AutoShapes**. These are predesigned shapes included in PowerPoint that you create using the AutoShapes tool.

Lesson 1: Drawing Freehand Objects

You can easily draw objects using PowerPoint's Drawing toolbar (see Figure 11.2). By default, this toolbar displays at the bottom of the PowerPoint screen. To draw a shape, click the tool you want, then drag to draw the shape on your slide.

Most of the tools, such as the line, rectangle, arrow, and oval tools, enable you to draw objects from one edge outward in the direction you drag. You learned to draw in this manner in Project 5. However, you can modify how a shape is drawn by using the following methods:

- Press ◆Shift while dragging to produce a straight line or arrow, and to create a perfect circle or square.

- Press Ctrl as you drag to make the point where you begin the center of your object.

- Press Ctrl + ◆Shift to create a symmetrical object (such as a perfect circle or square) from the point where you began.

Additionally, you can double-click a tool to keep it active to draw more than one object. When you're finished drawing objects, click the tool to turn it off.

Try using these techniques to draw some freehand objects now.

Figure 11.2
The Drawing toolbar gives you quick address to drawing tools.

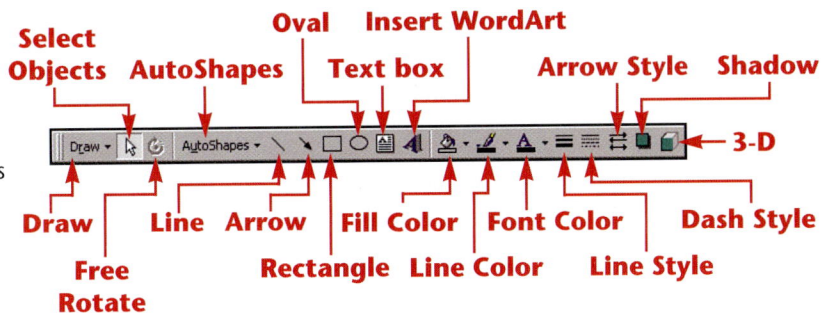

To Draw Freehand Objects

❶ Start a new presentation and display a blank slide.

You can use PowerPoint's horizontal and vertical rulers to help you accurately place drawn objects. You can turn the rulers on or off by choosing <u>V</u>iew, <u>R</u>uler. When turned on, the rulers appear in Slide view and Notes Page view, at the top and left side of the slide window. The 0" marks on the horizontal and vertical rulers represent the center of the slide. When you draw an object, the movement reflects on the rulers to show your exact location on the slide.

❷ If the rulers don't display on your screen, choose <u>V</u>iew, <u>R</u>uler.

The rulers display (see Figure 11.3).

If you have problems...

Because the <u>R</u>uler command is a toggle, don't complete step 2 if the rulers already display. Also, if the Drawing toolbar is not displayed, choose <u>V</u>iew, <u>T</u>oolbars, then choose Drawing from the submenu.

Figure 11.3
You can draw objects precisely using the rulers and guides.

Horizontal ruler

Inches from 0 and arrow showing direction display as you drag a guide

Vertical ruler

Horizontal guide

Vertical guide

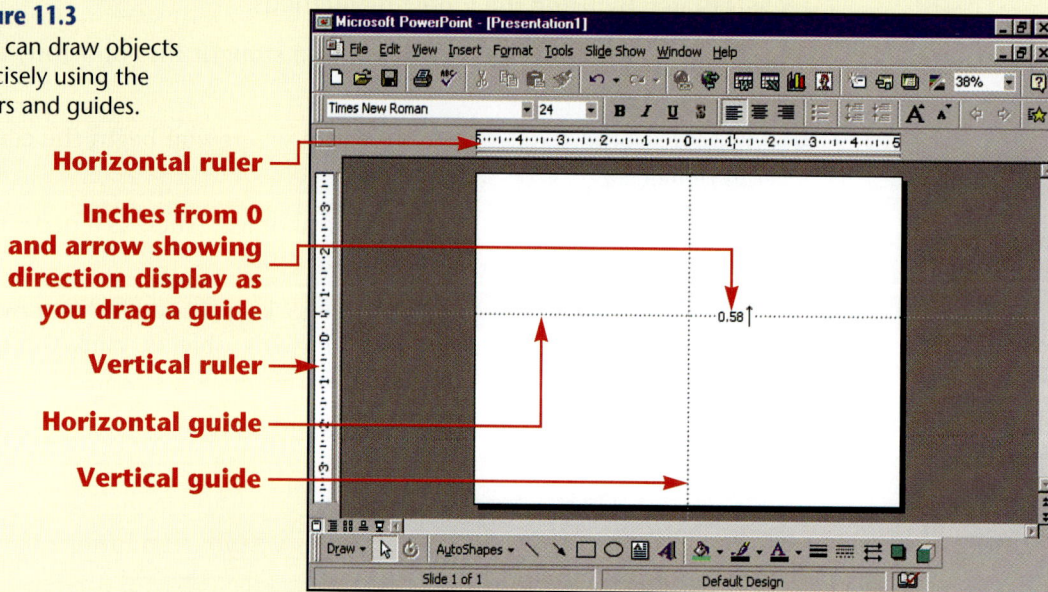

❸ Choose <u>V</u>iew, <u>G</u>uides to display the guides.

To help you know where you are onscreen in relation to the ruler, PowerPoint also provides nonprinting guides. The guides consist of a vertical line and a horizontal line that extend from 0" on each ruler across the slide. The lines cross at the center of the slide. To see the guides, choose <u>V</u>iew, <u>G</u>uides. The guides can also be positioned where you need them—just point at the guide line you want to move and drag it to another position. As you drag, the position of the guide in relation to the ruler appears and an arrow shows the direction you are moving in relation to the center (or zero point) of the slide. Choose <u>V</u>iew, <u>G</u>uides again to turn the guides off.

④ Click the Rectangle tool on the Drawing toolbar, then move the mouse pointer to the slide area.

The mouse pointer changes to a crosshair so that you can accurately place the drawn object. The mouse pointer's appearance changes depending on the type of tool you choose.

⑤ On the slide, position the crosshair where the two 0" marks intersect, hold down ◆Shift and Ctrl, then click and drag until the rectangle's lower-right corner is at the place where the 1.5" horizontal mark and the 1.5" vertical ruler mark intersect.

A square that is centered at the center of the slide is added to your presentation (see Figure 11.4). Holding down ◆Shift as you draw makes the rectangle a square; holding down Ctrl draws the object from the center out. The fill and line colors used for the object are whatever was used most recently for the Fill Color and Line Color tools. Additionally, white selection handles appear around the object to indicate that it is selected. When you click on the slide or draw another object, the rectangle is deselected. (You learn more specifically how to select and modify drawn objects in Lesson 4, "Manipulating Objects.")

You can use other drawing tools in the same manner; click the tool and then drag to draw the object on the slide.

Figure 11.4
You can add drawn objects using PowerPoint's tools.

Selection handles ———

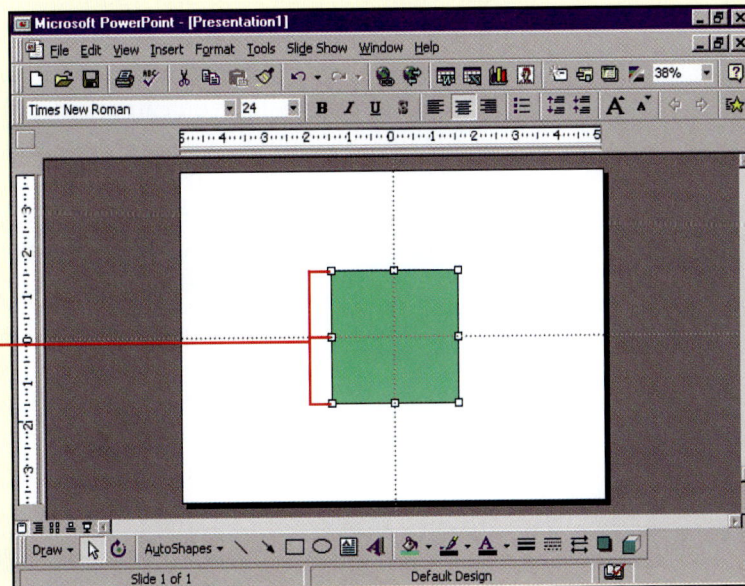

⑥ Click the Oval tool, then press ◆Shift as you drag to draw a 1" circle to the left of the square.

A perfect circle is added to your slide. Now try drawing an oval that originates from the center.

⑦ Click the Oval tool; then press Ctrl and draw a 1" oval to the right of the square.

The oval is drawn from the point where you first clicked the mouse.

continues

To Draw Freehand Objects   (continued)

8 Click the Arrow tool. Press ⬆Shift and drag from the center of the circle to the center of the oval.

The arrow is straight because you held down ⬆Shift as you drew the arrow.

Save the presentation as `Freehand Drawing`, then close it. Keep PowerPoint running for the next lesson in which you use PowerPoint to create a text box.

Inside Stuff

PowerPoint automatically fills ovals, rectangles, and so on, with the fill and line colors that were most recently used. Luckily, you can change an object's color. Click the object to select it, then click the arrow to the right of the Fill Color or Line Color buttons on the Drawing toolbar. Choose a new color from the palette that displays.

Lesson 2: Using a Text Box

Until now, you have probably relied on using the placeholders PowerPoint provides for text such as the title and bulleted lists. However, you may want more flexibility in creating your slides. Using text boxes, you can place all the text elements on a slide that you would like. In contrast with text placeholders, you can also dictate the exact location for the text box.

Drawing a text box is similar to drawing a rectangle, except that the box includes an area in which you can enter and edit text. In a sense, a text box is like a "mini document." To draw a text box, click the Text Box tool. Click at the beginning location on the slide, then drag the mouse until the text box is the size you want. Alternately, click the Text Box tool and then click once on the slide where you want the text to appear. In this case, the text box expands to accommodate your text.

Once you create a text box, you can enter and edit text as you would in a word processor. Click outside the box to deselect it. If you later decide to make text revisions, click inside the box to place the insertion point in it.

Because text boxes give you one more way to document a slide or place notes on it, try creating and using one now.

To Use a Text Box

1 Open Proj1101 from the Project-11 folder on the CD and save it as `Market Share`.

2 Click the Text Box tool, then click once in the lower-left corner of the slide.

PowerPoint creates a text box (see Figure 11.5). Notice that handles appear around the text box, indicating that it is currently selected. In addition, an insertion point displays in the box.

Figure 11.5
This text box will
expand as you type
text.

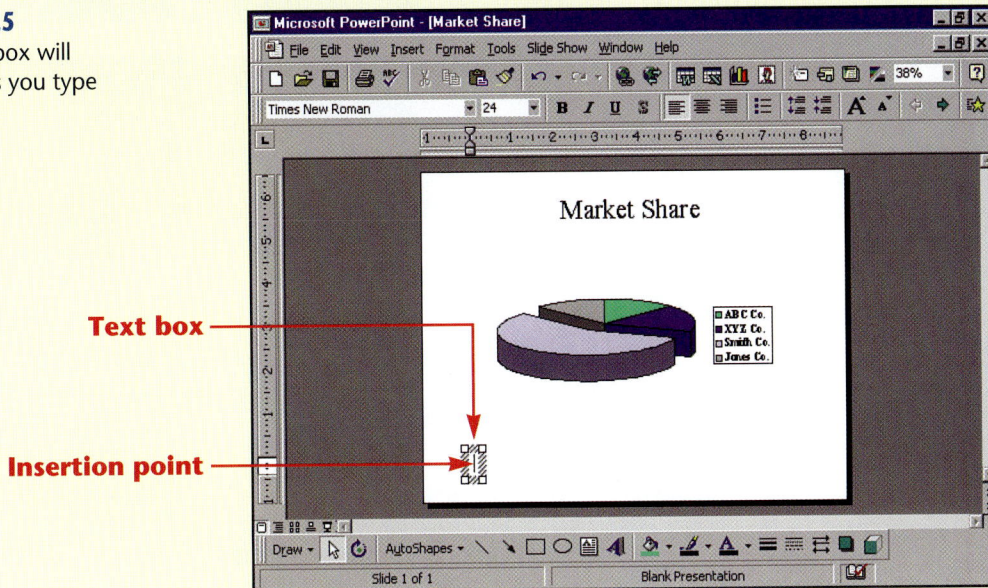

Text box

Insertion point

Don't be concerned that the text box won't accommodate the text you want to insert—it will expand to the necessary size as you type.

3 With the insertion point in the text box, type We need to increase our market share.

The text box expands to accommodate the new text.

4 Click outside the text box.

The text box is deselected. If you decide to revise the contents of the box, you can click inside it to select it. Once selected, you can edit and format text. Try this technique now.

5 Click inside the text box, then drag the mouse over the text to select it.

Selected text appears in reverse video. After text is selected, you can format it.

6 Click the Font Color drop-down list arrow.

A palette of colors that coordinate with the template displays. You can change text color by choosing a color from this palette.

7 Click the blue color (the sixth color from the left).

The text is formatted with the new color. Because the text is still in reverse video, you won't see the change until you deselect the text box. Before you deselect the box, however, try adding lines to the border.

8 Click the Line Style tool.

The Line Style palette displays (see Figure 11.6). You can select the thickness and appearance of the text box's border from this palette.

continues

To Use a Text Box (continued)

Figure 11.6
You can choose a border style for your text box.

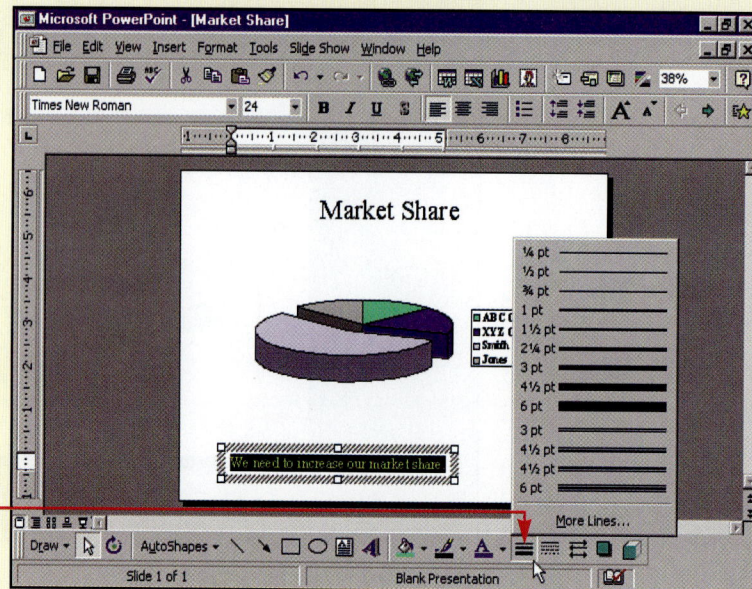

Click this tool to display line styles

⑨ **From the palette, select the 6 point triple line.**

A border is added to the text box. To better see your changes, deselect the text box.

⑩ **Click outside the text box.**

The text box is deselected so that you can see the new color and border (see Figure 11.7).

Figure 11.7
You can modify text boxes to suit your taste.

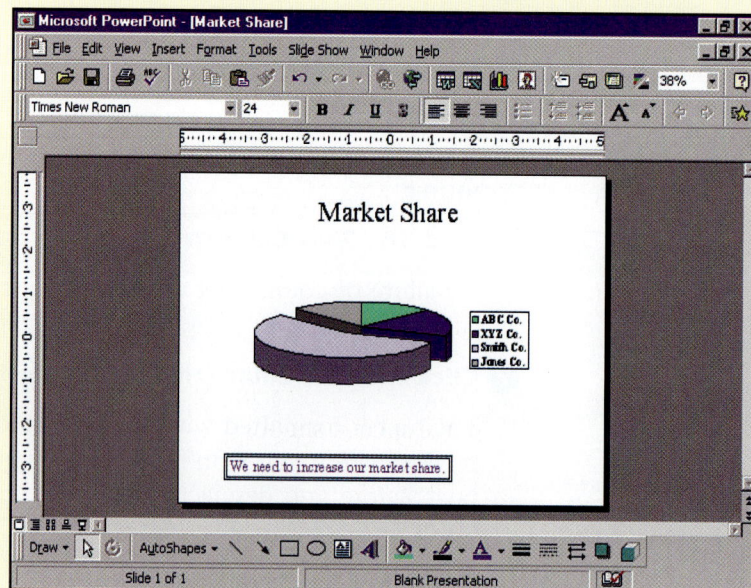

⑪ **Save the Market Share presentation, then close it.**

Keep PowerPoint running for the next lesson, in which you work with AutoShapes.

Inside Stuff

> If you click on the outside border of a text box (the selection border), you can make text attribute choices for all the text in the text box. You don't have to drag across the text to select it.

Lesson 3: Using AutoShapes

If you are not very artistic, or simply don't have a great deal of time, you will appreciate PowerPoint's AutoShapes when you want to quickly add drawn objects to a presentation. By using AutoShapes, you can easily insert professionally designed objects such as circles, rectangles, and arrows in your presentation to spice it up or emphasize certain information. Once inserted, you can move, color, resize, or even add text to an AutoShape. After you discover how easy it is to place AutoShapes into your presentation, you will probably find that it is quicker and more efficient to use them rather than drawing the same type of objects from scratch. Figure 11.8 shows how you can jazz up a slide by using AutoShapes.

Figure 11.8
Give a slide a snappy appearance with AutoShapes.

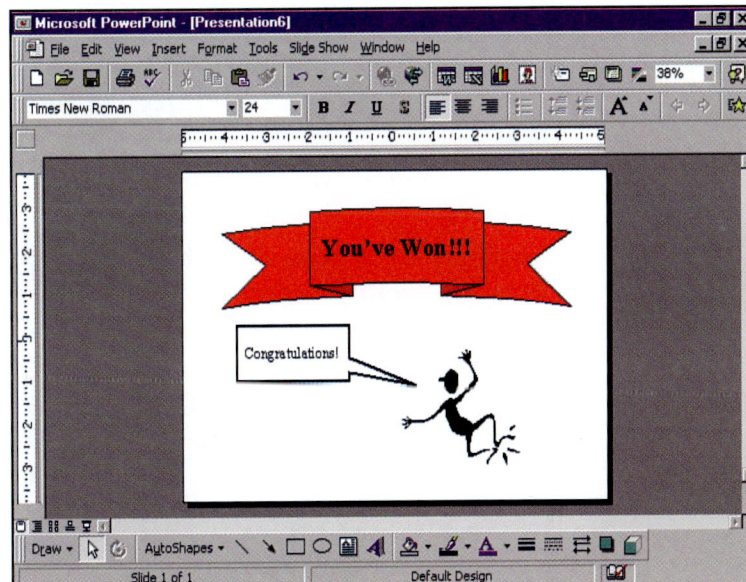

To give you plenty of variety, PowerPoint includes eight categories of AutoShapes:

- **Lines**. Six line tools to draw straight and curved lines freehand or make special shapes.

- **Connectors**. Nine connector tools that you can use to draw lines between other objects. Once connected, they stay connected, even if you move the objects. They are useful for flow charts, organizational charts, and so on.

- **Basic Shapes**. Thirty-two commonly-used shapes.

- **Block Arrows**. Twenty-eight block (thick) arrows.

- **Flowchart**. Twenty-eight shapes to help you build elements to create a flow chart or document processes.

■ **Stars and Banners**. Sixteen stars and banners that you can use to announce news, emphasize information, and otherwise add an element of excitement.

■ **Callouts**. Twenty ways to draw text annotations.

■ **Action Buttons**. Twelve button shapes that you can use as buttons on a slide. Once you draw the button, you can associate the action with a sound or movie file, or link it to the World Wide Web.

The basic process of creating an AutoShape is similar, no matter which type of shape you choose. Click the AutoShapes tool to display the AutoShapes menu. Choose a menu category, then click a shape from the submenu. Drag in the drawing area of the screen to create a shape.

To create a symmetrical shape, press ⬆Shift while drawing, just as you did earlier when you used the basic drawing tools. Likewise, you can press Ctrl to draw the shape from the center outward.

Because you can create such a variety of drawings using the AutoShapes, try using them now.

To Use AutoShapes

1 **Open Proj1102 from the Project-11 folder on the CD and save it as** Computer Training Procedures.

For this exercise, you use connector lines, a banner, and a callout. First, you create a banner for the Slide 2 title.

2 **Display Slide 2, then click the AutoShapes tool on the Drawing toolbar and move your mouse pointer to Stars and Banners.**

The Stars and Banners submenu displays (see Figure 11.9). You can rest your pointer over any of the AutoShapes on this submenu and a ScreenTip pops up to indicate the AutoShape's name. When you find the AutoShape you want, you can click to select it.

Figure 11.9
You can choose from a variety of AutoShapes.

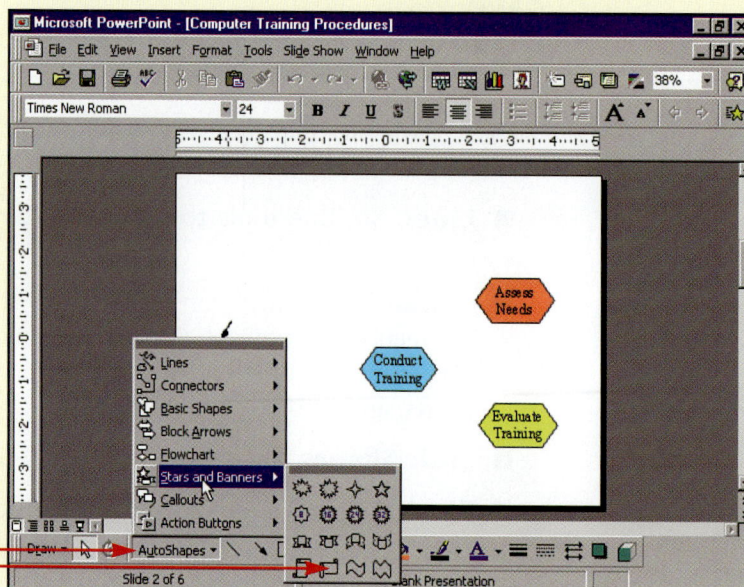

Click the AutoShapes tool to display a menu

Choose the Horizontal Scroll AutoShape

PowerPoint

3 **Rest the mouse pointer over the Horizontal Scroll AutoShape to display its ScreenTip, then click the shape.**

The AutoShape's tool is activated. Now you can draw the shape by dragging to indicate the size and location you want.

4 **Move the crosshair pointer to the intersection of the 3″ horizontal and vertical marks in the upper-left corner of the slide, then click and drag to the 3″ mark on the horizontal ruler and 2″ mark on the vertical ruler.**

Adjustment handle

A diamond-shaped handle you can use to change the appearance (not the size) of an AutoShape.

The banner is drawn using the dimensions you indicated (see Figure 11.10). Notice that the object has white selection handles that you can use to move or resize the object. However, it, like many AutoShapes, also has an *adjustment handle*. You use an adjustment handle to change the appearance of an AutoShape. For example, you can change the size of the point of an arrow. Some AutoShapes even contain more than one adjustment handle so that you can change several of the shape's elements. In this case, you use the adjustment handle to make the scroll's curve tighter or looser.

Figure 11.10

Many AutoShapes include an adjustment handle.

Use the adjustment handle to change the object's shape

Use the selection handles to move or resize the object's shape

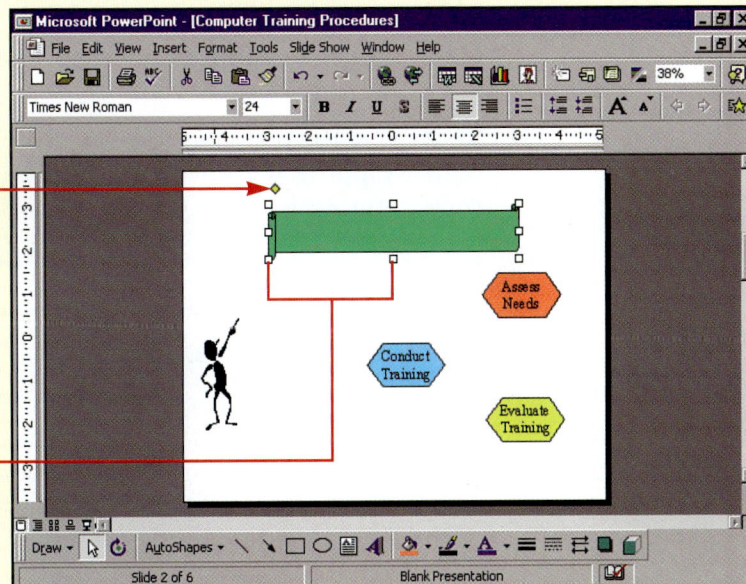

5 **Drag the adjustment handle to the right to increase the curve on the scroll, then release the mouse.**

The AutoShape's appearance changes. If you want, experiment by dragging the adjustment handle to the left and right until you are satisfied with the scroll's appearance. While PowerPoint lets you change the AutoShape's appearance, you can drag only a certain amount to the right or left for this particular shape. When you're finished, proceed with the next step.

continues

To Use AutoShapes   (continued)

You can add text to an AutoShape by clicking in the shape and typing. The text you add becomes part of the shape. For example, if you change the shape's size or location, the text moves with it. Try adding some text now.

6 Make sure the Banner is still selected, then type Computer Training Procedures.

The text is added to the AutoShape. You can select the text, then format it as in a text box. For now, however, you leave the text as it is and add another AutoShape to the slide.

AutoShapes ▾

7 Click the AutoShapes tool, then choose Callouts, Rounded Rectangular Callout.

8 Starting at 0" on the vertical ruler and 3" on the left side of the horizontal ruler, drag up and to the right to draw a callout approximately 1" high X 2" wide.

A callout bubble is added to your slide. Notice that you can use the adjustment handle to change the shape of the callout. You can also add text to the callout in the same way as you did to the banner.

9 Make sure the callout is selected, then type Make sure to follow the steps.

Notice that the text you type extends beyond the AutoShape rather than wrapping within it. You can adjust this text by using the Format AutoShape dialog box.

10 With the callout still selected, choose Format, AutoShape.

The Format AutoShape dialog box displays.

11 Click the Text Box tab.

The Text Box page of the Format AutoShape dialog box displays (see Figure 11.11). Notice that this text box contains options regarding how text should be handled. For example, you can wrap the text within the AutoShape (which makes the text fit in the AutoShape), or choose to have the AutoShape adjust to the text.

Figure 11.11
You can dictate how the AutoShape and text should combine.

Check this box to make the text fit to the AutoShape

Check this box to make the AutoShape fit the text

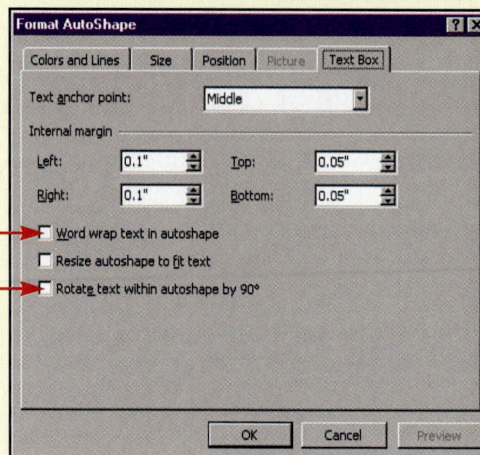

12 **Check the box for <u>W</u>ord wrap text in autoshape; then click OK.**

The text wraps to fit within the callout. Now try adding some connector lines between the three shapes on the right side of the slide. You can do this by using PowerPoint's connector lines to connect the objects. The connector lines are handy because they keep objects connected—even if you later move or resize them.

AutoShapes ▾

13 **Click the A<u>u</u>toShape tool, then choose Co<u>n</u>nectors, Straight Arrow Connector and draw a line from the Assess Needs object to the Conduct Training object.**

When you move the special connector pointer over an object, red handles display. This indicates that the object can be connected to another. When you drag to the second object, it also displays connector handles, indicating that it is connected to the first (see Figure 11.12). Now try using another connector line.

Figure 11.12
Connector lines are useful for keeping objects together.

Special connector pointer

Connector handles indicate an object is connected to another

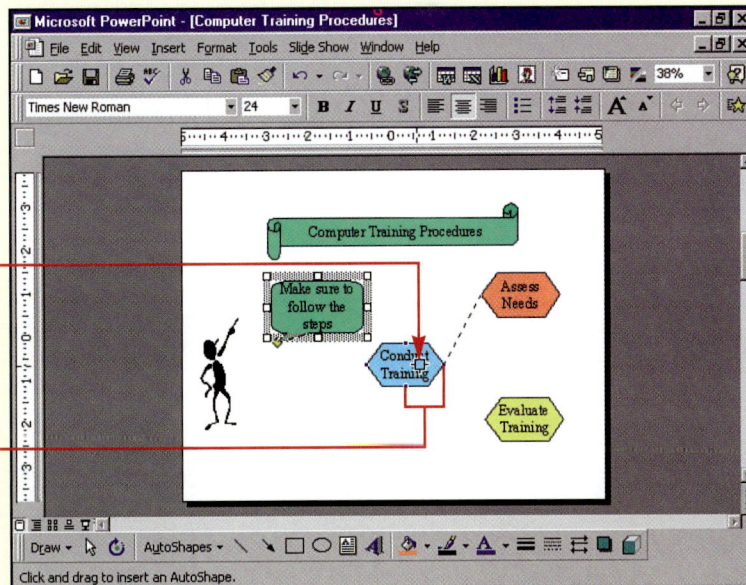

14 **Click the A<u>u</u>toShape tool, then choose Co<u>n</u>nectors, Elbow Arrow Connector, and draw a line from the Conduct Training object to the Evaluate Training object.**

The objects connect. Now try moving the Evaluate Training object.

15 **Click the Evaluate Training object to select it, then display the four-headed arrow over the object's border and move the object to the bottom of the slide.**

When you rearrange objects, the connectors remain attached.

16 **Save the Computer Training Procedures presentation.**

Keep the presentation open for the next lesson, in which you learn to manipulate objects by flipping, rotating, and aligning them.

Inside Stuff

If you have drawn an AutoShape and later decide it wasn't the shape you needed, you can change the shape. Click the shape you want to change to select it. Click the D̲raw button on the Drawing toolbar and choose C̲hange AutoShape from the menu. Select the category of shape you want and then choose the desired shape. The selected object will change to the new shape you chose.

Lesson 4: Manipulating Objects

If you are a typical PowerPoint user, you probably revise objects in various ways once you draw them. For example, you might draw several objects, then change your mind about how they are laid out. Luckily, you can flip, align, rotate, and otherwise manipulate objects to give you maximum flexibility in designing (or redesigning) your slide.

Use Table 11.1 as a reference when you want to manipulate your drawings.

Table 11.1 Methods of Selecting and Manipulating Objects	
To	Do This
Select a drawn object	Click the object.
Select multiple objects	Press ⬆Shift as you click the objects.
Deselect objects	Click outside the objects.
Resize an object	Select the object, then rest the mouse pointer over a selection handle until a two-sided arrow displays and drag to resize.
Move an object	Select the object; then move the mouse pointer to the middle of the object until a four-sided arrow displays and drag to the new location.
Duplicate an object	Select the object and choose E̲dit, Dupli̲cate.
Delete an object	Select the object and press Del.
Rotate an object	Select the object and click the Free Rotate button to place green rotate handles around the object. Move the mouse pointer over a handle and drag to spin the object.
Flip an object	Select the object and choose D̲raw, Rotate or Flip̲, Flip H̲orizontal, or Flip V̲ertical.
Align objects	Select the objects and choose D̲raw, A̲lign or Distribute.
Change the stacking order of objects	Select the object and choose D̲raw, Or̲der.
Group objects	Select the objects to group and choose D̲raw, G̲roup.
Ungroup an object	Select the object and choose D̲raw, U̲ngroup.

Many of the commands used to manipulate objects are located on the Drawing toolbar. In addition, you can click the D̲raw tool to display a menu with commands related to manipulating objects (see Figure 11.13).

Figure 11.13
You can execute many commands using the Draw menu.

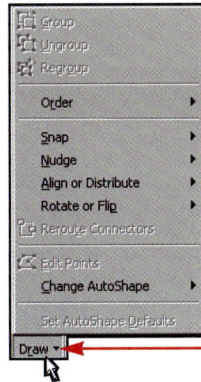

Group
Ungroup
Regroup

Order ▶

Snap ▶
Nudge ▶
Align or Distribute ▶
Rotate or Flip ▶
Reroute Connectors

Edit Points
Change AutoShape ▶

Set AutoShape Defaults

Draw ▾ ◄───── **Click the Draw tool to display this menu**

Because the capability to modify drawn objects is so critical to making a polished, professional-looking slide, try manipulating objects now.

To Manipulate Objects

❶ Display Slide 3 in the Computer Training Procedures presentation, then click the arrow, To be successful.

Before you can manipulate an object, you must first select it. As usual, white selection handles appear around any selected object.

Draw ▾

❷ Click the Draw tool on the Drawing toolbar, then choose Rotate or Flip, Flip Horizontal.

The object flips 180 degrees horizontally. Now try lining up multiple objects.

❸ Click outside the arrow to deselect it, then press ⬆Shift as you click the Plan, Present, **and** Evaluate **cube objects.**

Each object appears with white selection handles around the border (see Figure 11.14). Because you selected all the objects, any command you use will apply to all selected objects.

Figure 11.14
You can select multiple objects.

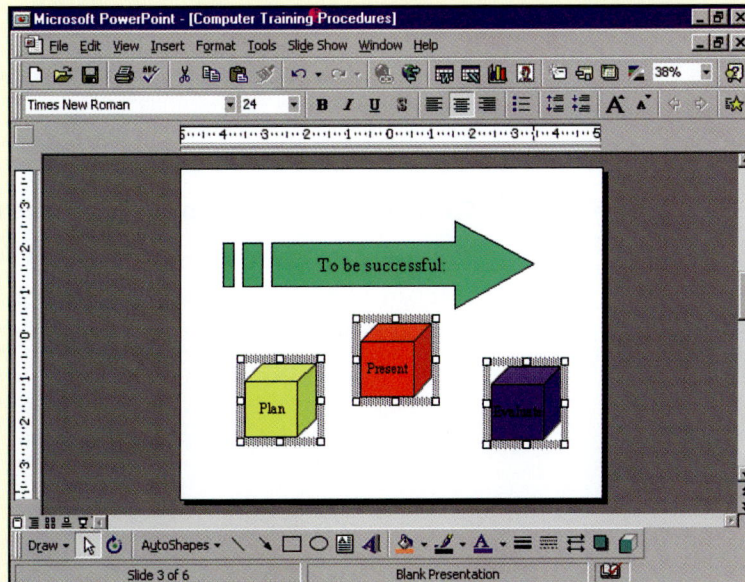

❹ **Click the D̲raw tool, then choose A̲lign or Distribute, Align Bottom.**

The bottom of the selected objects line up on an imaginary line. Now try using a command that spaces them evenly between the left and right objects.

❺ **Click the D̲raw tool, then choose A̲lign or Distribute, Distribute H̲orizontally.**

The objects rearrange so that an even amount of space is between each of them (see Figure 11.15).

Figure 11.15
You can space and align objects.

Objects are lined up at the bottom and evenly spaced

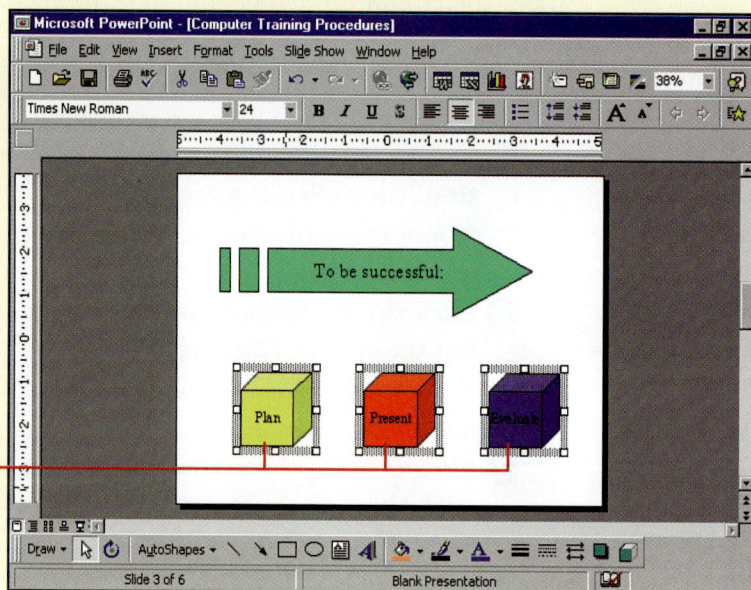

You can also manually rotate objects to the angle you want. Try this now.

❻ **Display Slide 4 in the open presentation, then click to select the arrow.**

This is the object you want to rotate.

❼ **Click the Free Rotate button on the Drawing toolbar.**

Green rotate handles appear around the object (see Figure 11.16). You can place the mouse pointer over any rotate handle, then drag to rotate the object.

Figure 11.16
You can rotate an object using the rotate handles.

Rotate handle ——————→

The mouse pointer changes appearance when you place it over a rotate handle ——————→

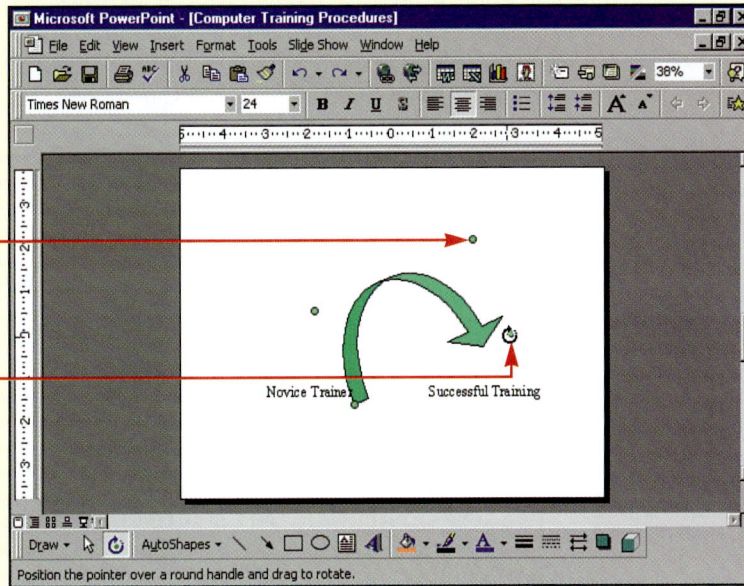

8 **Move the mouse pointer over the lower-right rotate handle.**

The mouse pointer changes appearance (refer to Figure 11.16).

9 **Drag downward to spin the object until it looks like that in Figure 11.17, then release the mouse button.**

The object rotates as you drag the mouse.

Figure 11.17
You can rotate the arrow for better appearance.

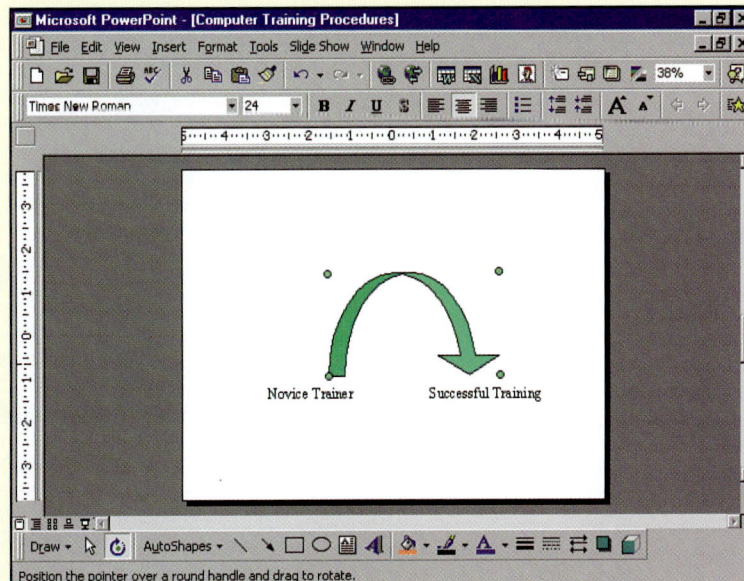

10 **Save the Computer Training Procedures presentation.**

Keep the presentation open for the next lesson, in which you create 3-D effects.

Exam Notes

Rotating an object 90 degrees can be difficult using the Free Rotate tool. To rotate a selected object 90 degrees, click the Draw button on the Drawing toolbar and then select Rotate or Flip from the menu. Choose Rotate Right to rotate the object 90 degrees clockwise or Rotate Left to rotate the object 90 degrees counterclockwise.

Lesson 5: Creating 3-D Effects

With PowerPoint 97, you can add a 3-D effect to lines, AutoShapes, and freeform objects. With 3-D settings, you can change the depth of the object and its color, rotation, angle, direction of lighting, and surface texture.

To add or change a 3-D effect for an object, select the object and then click the 3-D tool on the Drawing toolbar. Choose an effect from the palette. You can also change the 3-D settings for an object, or remove the 3-D effect altogether.

Try working with 3-D effects now.

To Create 3-D Effects

❶ In the open Computer Training Procedures presentation, display Slide 5, then choose Edit, Select All to select the objects.

You must select the objects that you want to effect with a command. In this case, you selected all objects in order to apply a 3-D effect to them simultaneously.

❷ On the Drawing toolbar, click the 3-D tool.

The 3-D palette displays (see Figure 11.18). You can display the name of a 3-D effect by momentarily resting your mouse pointer over it until a ScreenTip displays. Once you find a 3-D effect you like, you can apply it to selected objects by clicking it.

Figure 11.18
You can choose from a variety of 3-D effects.

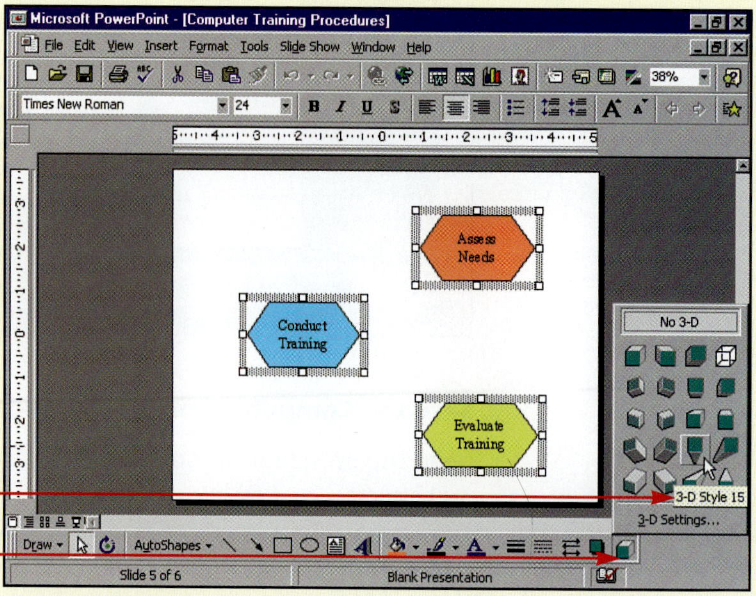

ScreenTip

Click this tool to
display 3-D effects

3 **Move your mouse pointer over the 3-D effects until a ScreenTip displays for 3-D Style 15, then click.**

The effect is applied to the selected objects (see Figure 11.19). (If you want, experiment by choosing other 3-D effects. Make sure you choose 3-D Style 15 before proceeding with the next step.)

Figure 11.19
The 3-D effect applies to all selected objects.

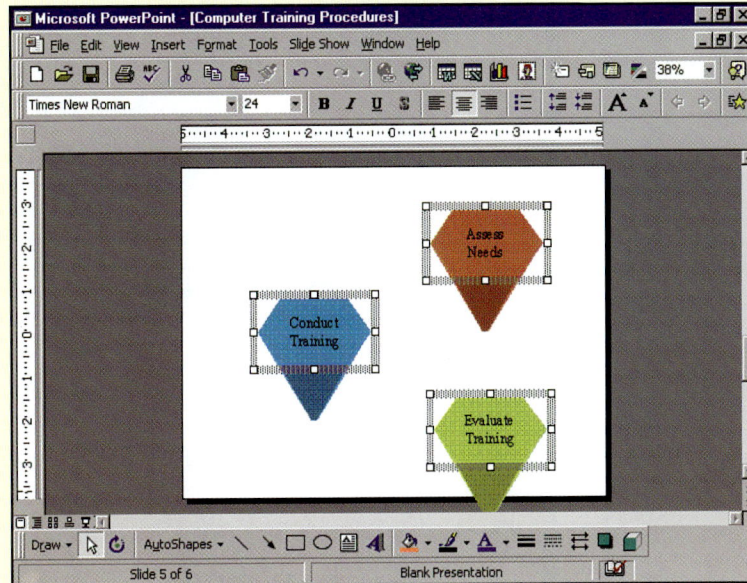

You can further modify the 3-D effect by changing its depth, perspective, surface appearance, and so on. You make these revisions by using the 3-D Settings toolbar. Try making some modifications to the effect now.

4 **With the objects still selected, click the 3-D tool and click the 3-D Settings button on the 3-D palette.**

The 3-D Settings toolbar displays (see Figure 11.20). You can use this toolbar to refine your 3-D effect.

continues

To Create 3-D Effects **(continued)**

Figure 11.20
PowerPoint provides a wealth of settings to apply to your 3-D objects.

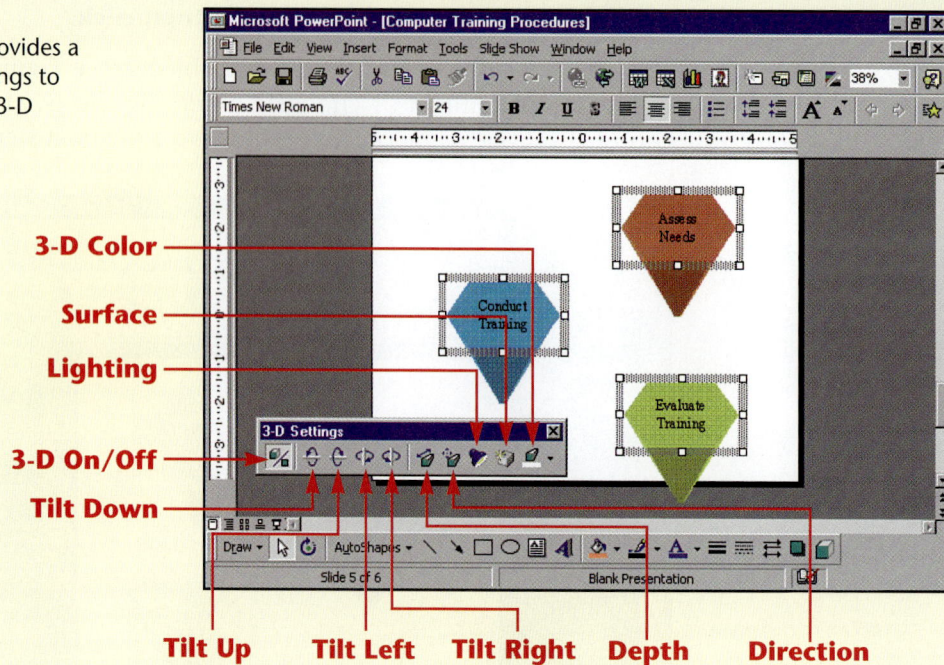

3-D Color
Surface
Lighting
3-D On/Off
Tilt Down

Tilt Up   Tilt Left   Tilt Right   Depth   Direction

5 Click the Tilt Left button three times.

The 3-D effect changes. Now try changing depth for the objects.

6 Click the Depth tool.

The Depth palette displays so that you can choose a depth (in points) for your effect (see Figure 11.21).

Figure 11.21
You can choose the depth of the 3-D effect.

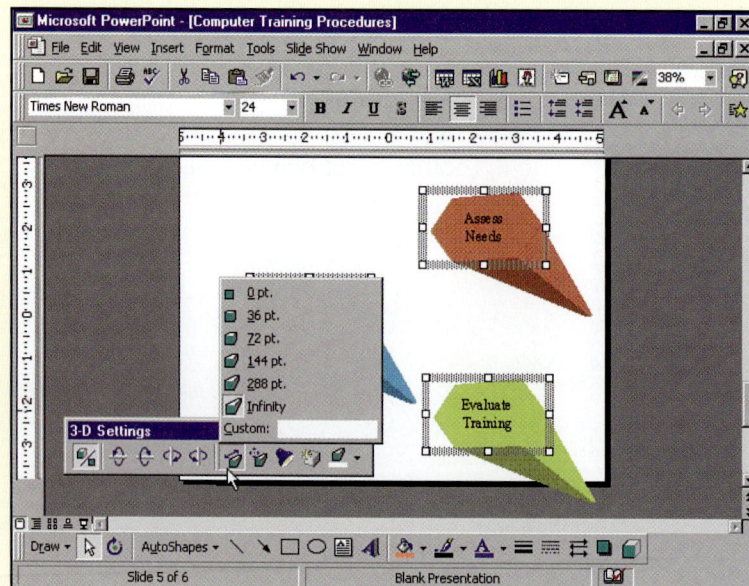

7 **Choose 144 pt.**

The new depth applies to the selected objects. You can also change the direction of the 3-D effect.

8 **Click the Direction tool and choose the third icon on the last row.**

The 3-D effect changes to the direction you choose. (If you want, experiment with other 3-D effects before proceeding to the next step.)

9 **On the 3-D Settings toolbar, click the Close button, then click outside the objects.**

The toolbar closes, and the effects you added are clearly seen onscreen.

10 **Save the Computer Training Procedures presentation.**

Keep the presentation open for the next lesson, in which you add shadow effects.

Inside Stuff   If you want to remove a 3-D effect, first select the object. Click the 3-D tool and choose No 3-D from the palette.

Lesson 6: Creating a Shadow Effect

PowerPoint also provides another great way to enhance objects—shadow effects. These effects give depth to an object and can make it appear more realistic. You can add a shadow to any object you create—even text boxes and AutoShapes.

To add or change a shadow effect to an object, select the object and then click the Shadow tool on the Drawing toolbar. Then choose a shadow style, or effect, from the palette that displays.

You can also use tools on the Shadow Settings toolbar to change the direction and angle of the shadow. Try working with 3-D effects now.

To Create a Shadow Effect

1 **Display Slide 6 in the open Computer Training Procedures presentation, then click the star object to select it.**

You must first select objects that you want to modify.

2 **Click the Shadow tool on the Drawing toolbar.**

A palette of shadow effects displays (see Figure 11.22). You can rest the mouse pointer over any palette icon to see a ScreenTip that identifies it. Once you locate the shadow effect you want, you can click to select it.

continues

To Create a Shadow Effect   (continued)

Figure 11.22
You can choose from a variety of shadow effects.

Click the Shadow tool
to see these effects

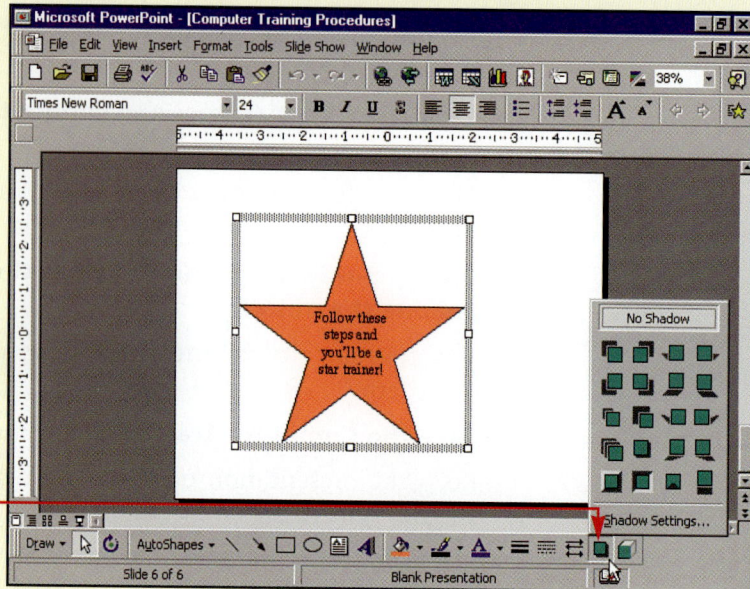

❸ Move your mouse pointer over the shadow effects until a ScreenTip displays for Shadow Style 4, then click.

The shadow effect is added to your object (see Figure 11.23). You can further modify the effect by using the Shadow Settings toolbar.

Figure 11.23
You can quickly add an shadow to your object.

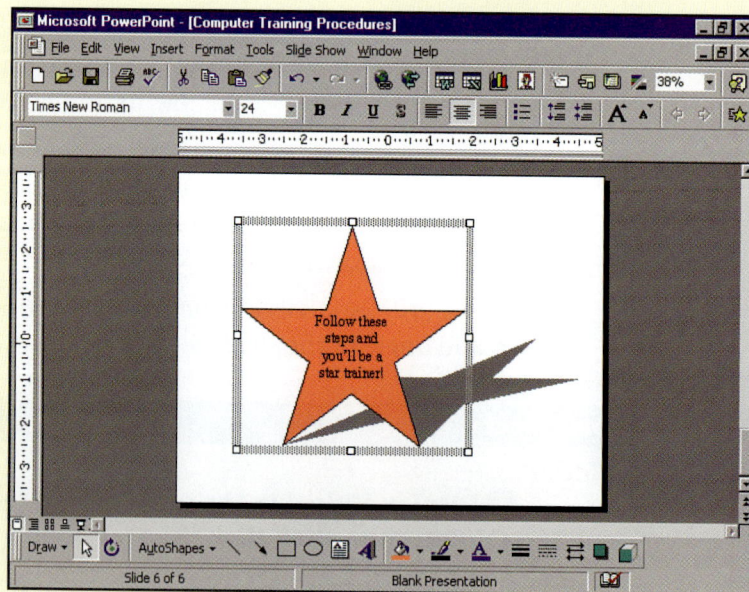

❹ Click the Shadow tool, then click the Shadow Settings button on the palette.

The Shadow Settings toolbar displays (see Figure 11.24). You can use these tools to move the shadow or change the shadow's color.

Figure 11.24
You can use the Shadow Setting toolbar to make adjustments to the shadow.

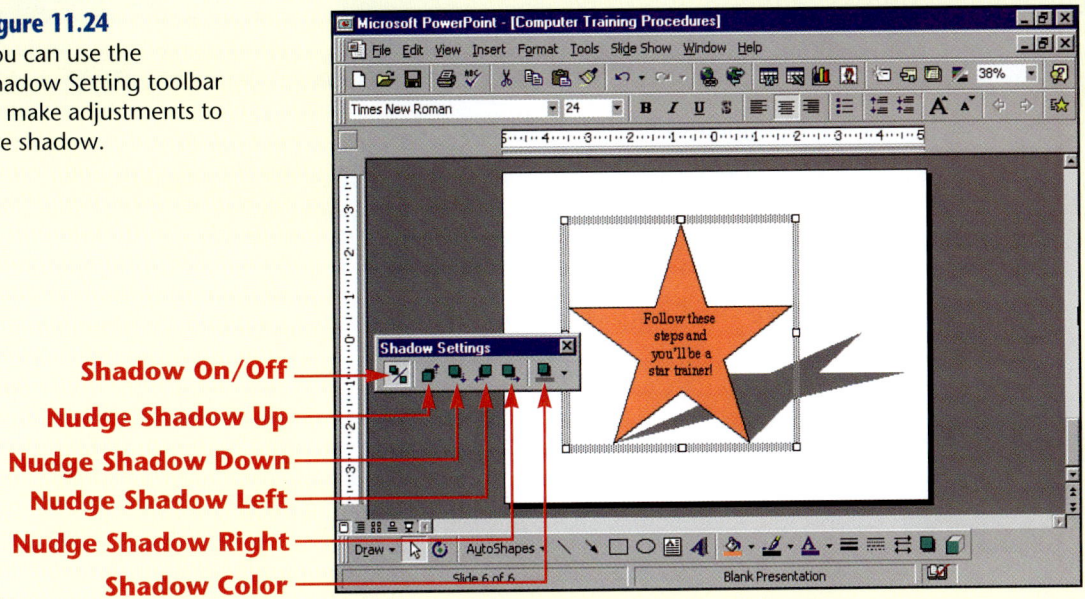

Shadow On/Off
Nudge Shadow Up
Nudge Shadow Down
Nudge Shadow Left
Nudge Shadow Right
Shadow Color

5 Click the Nudge Shadow Right tool five times.

The shadow moves slightly to the right (1 point) every time you click the mouse. (If you want to change the shadow effect in larger increments, press ⬆Shift while clicking the tool to move it 6 points at a time.) Now try changing the shadow's color.

6 Click the Shadow Color drop-down list arrow.

The Color palette displays (see Figure 11.25). The first row of colors are those that coordinate with the presentation's color scheme. The second row shows custom colors—those that are used in the presentation, but are not part of the color scheme. You can choose any of the colors shown, or click More Shadow Colors for additional choices.

Figure 11.25
You can easily change a shadow's color.

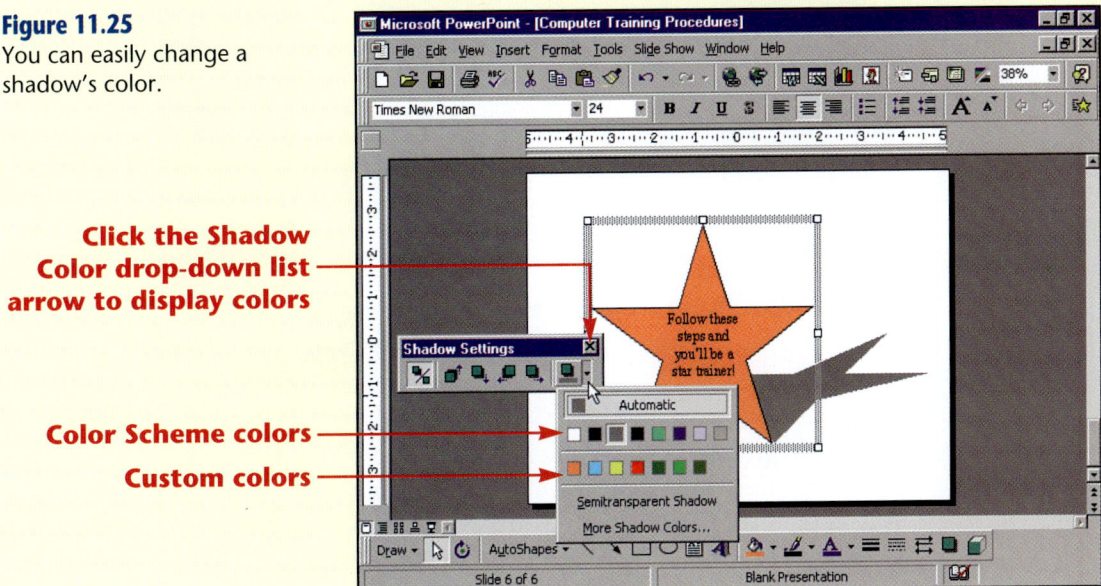

Click the Shadow Color drop-down list arrow to display colors

Color Scheme colors
Custom colors

continues

7 **Click the light gray color box (the last color in the first row).**

The shadow's color changes.

8 **Click the Close button on the Shadow Settings toolbar, then click outside the star object to deselect it.**

The effects you added are displayed.

9 **Save the Computer Training Procedures presentation.**

Keep the presentation open for the next lesson, in which you work with WordArt.

Inside Stuff

You can't add both a 3-D effect and a shadow effect to the same object. When you choose one effect for an object, the other is automatically removed.

Lesson 7: Using WordArt

One way to add exciting special text effects is to use the WordArt tool. With WordArt, you can stretch, emboss, and otherwise change the way text appears. This is because text you enter in WordArt is not really text at all—it's an object. Figure 11.26 shows examples of some of WordArt's special effects.

Figure 11.26
You can use WordArt to add special text effects.

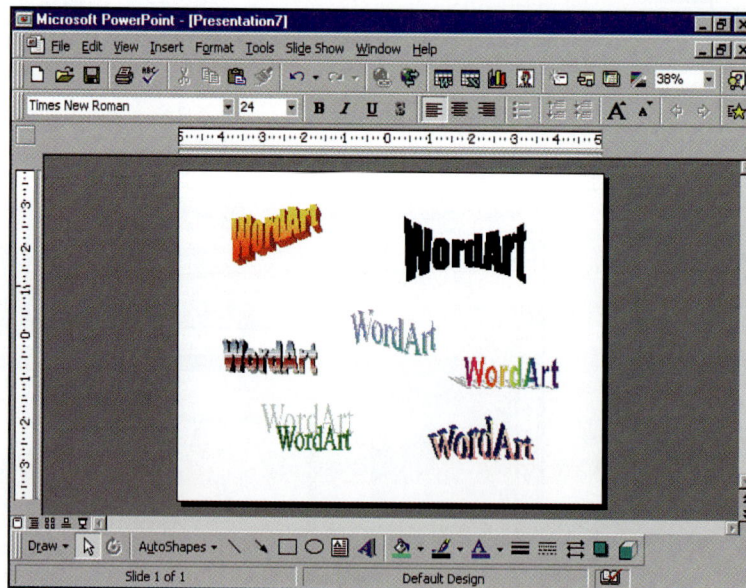

You activate WordArt by clicking the Insert WordArt tool on the Drawing toolbar. From the displayed WordArt Gallery, you can select a style to jazz up your text. If you want, you can further modify the style by using the WordArt toolbar.

Once you work with WordArt, you will probably find that you turn to it whenever you want to spiff up a text object. Try working with WordArt now.

PowerPoint

To Use WordArt

1 **Display Slide 1 in the open presentation.**

This blank slide is where you want to insert your WordArt object.

2 **Click the Insert WordArt tool on the Drawing toolbar.**

The WordArt Gallery displays, showing the available styles you can use for your text (see Figure 11.27).

Figure 11.27
You can choose a text style from the Gallery.

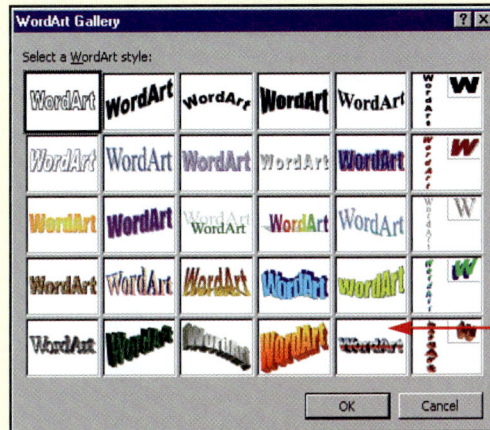

Choose this style

3 **Click the style fifth from the left on the bottom row, then choose OK.**

The Edit WordArt Text dialog box displays so that you can enter text (see Figure 11.28).

Figure 11.28
You enter your text in this dialog box.

Choose a font here

Text you type will replace this text

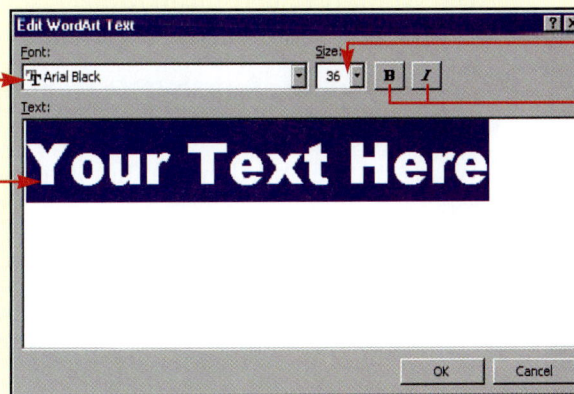

Choose the text size here

Select a font style

4 **Type** ABC Training, **then click OK.**

WordArt creates an object on your slide with the text and style you chose (see Figure 11.29). Notice that the object has both selection handles (to move and/or resize it) and an adjustment handle (to change the shape). Additionally, WordArt automatically displays the WordArt toolbar that you can use to make further modifications to the object.

continues

To Use WordArt   (continued)

If you have problems... If the WordArt toolbar doesn't display on your screen, right-click the Standard toolbar. Choose WordArt from the shortcut menu that displays.

Figure 11.29
WordArt places your text as an object.

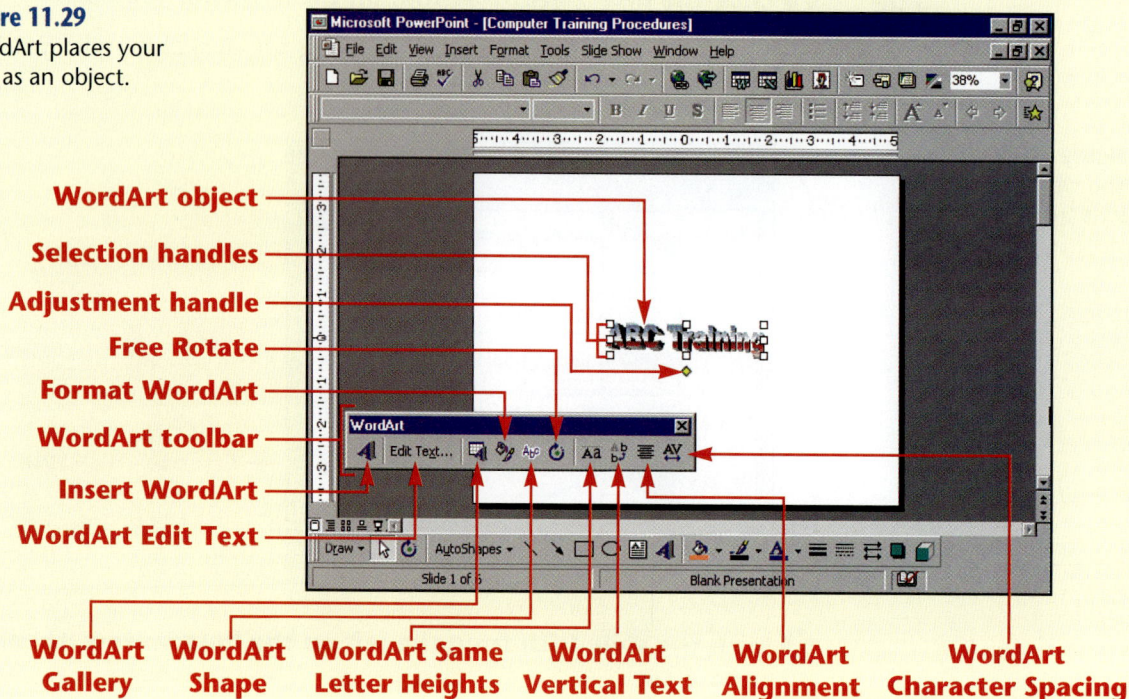

WordArt object
Selection handles
Adjustment handle
Free Rotate
Format WordArt
WordArt toolbar
Insert WordArt
WordArt Edit Text

WordArt Gallery   WordArt Shape   WordArt Same Letter Heights   WordArt Vertical Text   WordArt Alignment   WordArt Character Spacing

⑤ Click the WordArt Gallery tool on the WordArt toolbar.

The WordArt Gallery again displays so that you can choose another style.

⑥ Double-click the fourth style from the left on the third row.

The text displays using the new style. You can also select any WordArt style and then modify it further using the WordArt Shape tool.

⑦ Click the WordArt Shape tool on the WordArt Toolbar.

A palette of shapes you can apply to the WordArt style displays (see Figure 11.30). You can click a shape to quickly modify a WordArt style.

Figure 11.30
You can apply a number of shapes to your style.

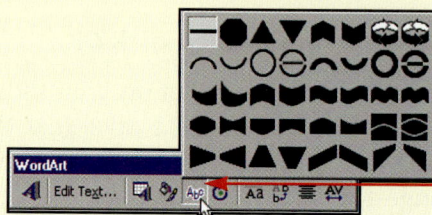

Click the WordArt Shape tool to display a palette of shapes

continues

8 Display the ScreenTip for the Wave 2 icon, then click.

The WordArt object displays with the new shape. (If you want, experiment with other shapes from the palette. Before you continue with the next step, make sure you choose Wave 2.)

Because the WordArt object has selection handles, you can resize (or move) it like any other object. Try increasing the object's size now.

9 Move the mouse pointer over the upper right selection handle, then drag upward and to the right until you double the object's size.

The object enlarges so you can see it better. Because you're done working with the object for now, you can deselect it.

10 Click outside the WordArt object.

The object is deselected. Notice that both the object's handles and the WordArt toolbar disappear when the object is deselected. (If you later decide to modify the object, you can click it to again display the handles and the toolbar.)

11 Save the Computer Training Procedures presentation, then close it.

If you have finished your work session, exit PowerPoint and shut down Windows 95 before turning off your computer. Otherwise, complete the "Checking Your Skills" and "Applying Your Skills" exercises at the end of this project.

Project Summary

To	Do This
Draw an object	Click the tool on the Drawing toolbar, then click and drag on the drawing area.
Draw a straight line or a symmetrical object	Select the tool, then press ◆Shift while drawing the object.
Make the starting point the center of an object	Select the tool, then press Ctrl while drawing the object.
Produce a symmetrical object that originates from the center	Select the tool, then press Ctrl+◆Shift while drawing the object.
Keep a tool active to draw multiple objects	Double-click the tool.
Display the Drawing toolbar	Choose View, Toolbars, Drawing.
Display the rulers	Choose View, Ruler.
Change an object's fill or line color	Select the object, then click the Fill Color or Line Color drop-down list arrows.

continues

To	Do This
Produce a text box	Click the Text Box tool, then click the starting location on the slide.
Change text color	Select the text, then click the Font Color drop-down list arrow.
Add a line style to a text box	Click in the text box, then click the Line Style tool.
Add an AutoShape	Click the AutoShapes tool, then choose a category and AutoShape. Drag to draw the shape on your slide.
Change an AutoShape's shape	Drag the yellow diamond adjustment handle.
Enter text in an AutoShape	Select the AutoShape, then type the text.
Make text wrap in an AutoShape	Select the AutoShape, then choose Format, AutoShape and check the Word wrap text in autoshape box.
Flip an object	Select the object, then choose Draw, Rotate or Flip.
Line up or space objects	Select the objects, then choose Draw, Align or Distribute.
Rotate an object	Select the object, then click the Free Rotate tool and drag a green rotation handle.
Add a 3-D effect	Select the object, then click the 3-D tool and choose an effect.
Revise a 3-D effect	Select the object, then click the 3-D tool and choose 3-D Settings.
Remove a 3-D effect	Select the object, then click the 3-D tool and choose No 3-D.
Add a shadow effect	Select the object, then click the Shadow tool and choose an effect.
Revise a shadow effect	Select the object, then click the Shadow tool and choose Shadow Settings.
Remove a shadow effect	Select the object, then click the Shadow tool and choose No Shadow.
Add a WordArt object	Click the WordArt tool, then select a style from the Gallery and click OK. Type your text and click OK.
Change a WordArt object's shape	Click the WordArt Shape tool on the WordArt toolbar.

Checking Your Skills

True/False

For each of the following, check T or F to indicate whether the statement is true or false.

__T __F **1.** AutoShapes are created using the WordDraw program.

__T __F **2.** You can add a shadow effect to an object to create a feeling of depth.

__T __F **3.** You must first select objects before you align them.

__T __F **4.** You can add text in a text box, but not in an AutoShape.

__T __F **5.** WordArt is a program you use to draw objects from scratch.

__T __F **6.** You drag a purple handle in order to change an AutoShape's appearance.

__T __F **7.** You can click the Flip Object button to rotate an object.

__T __F **8.** You can't add a 3-D and shadow effect to an object at the same time.

__T __F **9.** PowerPoint includes a variety of fills you can use to format an object.

__T __F **10.** You add a 3-D effect to a selected object by choosing Draw, 3-D, Effect from the menu.

Multiple Choice

Circle the letter of the correct answer for each of the following questions.

1. Using AutoShapes, you can create _____.

    a. connector lines between objects

    b. predesigned stars and banners

    c. callouts

    d. all of the above

2. Which type of handles do you use to modify the shape of an AutoShape?

    a. white, square handles

    b. red, square handles

    c. yellow, diamond handles

    d. green, rounded handles

3. Which of the following is true regarding 3-D effects?

    a. You must remove one effect before applying another.

    b. You make changes using the 3-D Drawing toolbar.

    c. They are the same as shadow effects.

    d. None of the above.

4. To draw a perfectly symmetrical circle, you can _____.

    a. double-click the Oval tool, then draw

    b. select the Oval tool, then press ⬆Shift while drawing

c. select the Oval tool, then press Ctrl while drawing

d. select the Circle tool, then press Ctrl while drawing

5. After you draw an object, you can _____.

a. flip it

b. rotate it

c. line it up with other objects

d. all of the above

6. What is the best use of the WordArt program?

a. drawing freehand shapes, such as circles and rectangles

b. inserting clip art on a slide

c. creating special text effects, such as on a title slide

d. adding fill color to freehand shapes

7. Which toolbar do you use to create AutoShapes?

a. WordArt

b. AutoArt

c. Tools

d. Drawing

8. How can you keep a drawing tool active so that you can draw multiple objects?

a. Choose Draw, Multiple Objects.

b. Right-click the tool, then choose Keep Active.

c. Double-click the tool.

d. None of the above.

9. How do you change a selected object's fill color?

a. Choose Draw, Fill Object.

b. Click the Fill Color button's drop-down list arrow.

c. Activate the ColorArt program.

d. None of the above.

10. Which of the following can you do with an AutoShape?

a. adjust its shape

b. enter text in it

c. make text wrap in it

d. all of the above

Completion

In the blank provided, write the correct answer for each of the following statements.

1. Predesigned shapes such as callouts, stars, and banners are called _____.

2. You can use the _____ tool to stretch, compress, and reshape a text object.

3. An object that is specifically designed to include text is called a(n) _____.

4. You can press _____ to draw an object that originates from the center.

5. Most of the tools you use for drawing are located on the _____ toolbar.

6. You can _____ a tool to keep it active and draw several objects of the same type.

7. You can press _____ to draw a perfectly straight line.

8. The program used to create special text effects is called _____.

9. You activate the rulers by choosing _____, _____.

10. When you first draw an object, white selection _____ appear around its borders.

Matching

In the blank next to each of the following terms or phrases, write the letter of the corresponding term or phrase. (Note that some of the letters may be used more than once.)

a. guides   _____ **1.** Indicate a selected object

b. shadow   _____ **2.** Adds a feeling of depth to an object

c. WordArt   _____ **3.** Display when you are rotating an object

d. red handles   _____ **4.** Predesigned shapes

e. green handles   _____ **5.** Used to create special text effects

f. white handles   _____ **6.** Used to adjust an AutoShape's shape

g. yellow handles   _____ **7.** Creates symmetrical object

h. AutoShapes   _____ **8.** Displays lines used to place objects on a slide

i. shift   _____ **9.** Used to create a circle

j. Oval tool   _____ **10.** Indicate an object is connected to another

Applying Your Skills

Practice

The following exercises, found in the Project–11 folder on the CD, enable you to practice the skills you have learned in this project. Take a few minutes to work through these exercises now.

Using a Text Box

As Production Manager for your organization, you have developed a presentation that charts waste. To help explain the chart's data, you decide to include and format a text box.

To use a text box, complete the following steps:

1. Open Proj1103 from the Project-11 folder on the CD and save it as Waste By Shift.

2. Click the Text Box tool, and then click in the lower-left corner of the slide.

3. Type Waste amounts have improved with increased management in the text box.

4. Make all the text in the text box blue.

5. Use the Line Style tool to add a 6-point, triple-line style border to the text box.

6. Deselect the text box to view your changes.

7. Save the presentation, then close it.

Using AutoShapes

You're in charge of the company picnic. To create an attention-getting flyer for the event, you decide to add some AutoShapes to the flyer. After you add them, you change the Fill Color.

To use AutoShapes, complete the following steps:

1. Open Proj1104 from the Project-11 folder on the CD and save it as Company Picnic.

2. Click the AutoShapes tool, then choose Stars and Banners. Display the ScreenTips for the various AutoShapes on the Stars and Banners submenu, then choose Up Ribbon.

3. Draw a banner across the top third of the slide, then enter the text Company Picnic!

4. Increase the font size for the AutoShape text to 36 points.

5. With the AutoShape still selected, click the Fill Color drop-down list arrow. Choose the blue color, then click outside the AutoShape to deselect it.

6. Add a bubble callout of your choice to the clip art figure. Use the adjustment handle to reshape the callout if necessary. Then enter the text Be sure to come!

7. With the callout still selected, click the Fill Color drop-down list arrow and choose No Fill.

8. Print one copy of the presentation.

9. Save the Company Picnic presentation, then close it.

Using Connectors and 3-D Effects

Because everyone at your company considers you a "computer guru," they have put you in charge of upgrading other computer users to PowerPoint 97. In order to outline the upgrade process, you decide to add connector lines to shapes on a PowerPoint slide. Then, to increase interest, you add 3-D effects to the objects.

To use connectors and 3-D effects, complete the following steps:

1. Open Proj1105 from the Project-11 folder on the CD and save it as Upgrade Process.

2. Click the AutoShapes tool, then choose Connectors.

3. Display ScreenTips for the connectors on the submenu, then choose Straight Arrow Connector. Connect the Evaluate Needs object to the Order Software object.

4. Connect the Order Software object to the Provide Training object using the same connector type.

5. Move the Provide Training object approximately two inches to the right. (Notice that the connector line resizes automatically to keep the two objects connected.)

6. Select all three of the objects.

7. Click outside the objects to better view your changes.

8. Save the presentation, then close it.

Using WordArt

You work in the Human Resources Department at your company, and are continually sending out flyers to company employees. To get their attention, you decide to use WordArt to help create an attention-getting flyer.

To use WordArt, complete the following steps:

1. Open Proj1106 from the Project-11 folder on the CD and save it as `Human Resource Flyer`.

2. Click the Insert WordArt tool. Choose the second style from the left on the third row of the WordArt Gallery, then choose OK.

3. In the Edit WordArt Text dialog box type `Don't Forget:`. Click OK.

4. Move the WordArt object to the center of the available space at the top of your slide. Then resize the object to fill the space.

5. Display the WordArt toolbar, if necessary. Click the WordArt Shape tool, then choose the Stop icon.

6. Click outside the WordArt object.

7. Print one copy of your presentation.

8. Save the Human Resource Flyer presentation, then close it.

Rotating and Flipping Objects

You're preparing a sales presentation to give at the next staff meeting. To do so, you add AutoShapes, then rotate and flip them so that they display as you want.

To rotate and flip objects, complete the following steps:

1. Open Proj1107 from the Project-11 folder on the CD and save it as `Sarah Candy Company`.

2. Display Slide 2, then add the Left Arrow AutoShape (in the Block Arrow category) in the title area of the slide. Enter the text `We've Come Far!` in the AutoShape.

3. Increase the font size of the AutoShape's text to 32 and apply bold.

4. With the AutoShape still selected, choose Dr̲aw, Rotate or Fli̲p, Flip H̲orizontal.

5. Select the arrow in the bottom half of Slide 2, then click the Free Rotate button.

6. Rotate the object so that it lines up properly with the two AutoShapes at the bottom of the slide (300,000 and Over 1 million). Move the arrow object, if necessary.

7. Recolor the arrow object to dark pink (one of the template's colors).

8. Print one copy of the presentation.

9. Save the presentation, then close it.

Challenge

The following challenges, found in the Project–11 folder on the CD, enable you to use your problem-solving skills. Take time to work through these exercises now.

Adding Shapes

Your store (and other stores) on Main Street are having a sidewalk sale. You decide to use PowerPoint to produce a promotional flyer for this event.

To add shapes, complete the following steps:

1. Create a new, blank presentation, and display a blank slide.

2. Add the Horizontal Scroll AutoShape from the S̲tars and Banners category to the top of the slide. Enter `Announcing...` in the AutoShape.

3. Format the text in the AutoShape to 40 point, bold.

4. Add a WordArt object (any style) immediately under the horizontal scroll AutoShape. Enter `Big Sidewalk Sale!` for the text.

5. Add a text box in the lower portion of the slide. Enter the following information in the text box:

       Date: July 4, 1998
       Time: 10:00 a.m.-5:00 p.m.
       Where: Main Street

6. Print one copy of the presentation.

7. Save the presentation as `Big Sale`, then close it.

Using WordArt

Your boss wants you to do a presentation at the next staff meeting. To get people's attention, you add a WordArt object as the title for the first slide.

To use WordArt, complete the following steps:

1. Open Proj1108 from the Project-11 folder on the CD and save it as `Tech Heads`.

2. Display Slide 1 and then click the Insert WordArt button. Choose the fifth style on the second row, then choose OK.

3. Enter `Business Plan` in the Edit WordArt Text dialog box.

4. Resize and move the WordArt object so that it displays in the middle of the available space.

5. Experiment by applying various 3-D effects to the WordArt object. When you're finished experimenting, choose 3-D Style 19.

6. Print a copy of Slide 1.

7. Save the presentation, then close it.

To Draw Objects

You want to draw attention to the fact that your company has the largest market share. To do so, you add a text box and arrow to a slide.

To draw objects, complete the following steps:

1. Open Proj1109 from the Project-11 folder on the CD and save it as `Our Company`.

2. Draw a text box in the upper-right corner of the slide, then enter `We're doing great!` in the box.

3. Add a 4 1/2-point line around the border of the text box.

4. Draw an arrow from the lower-left corner of the text box to the pie slice that represents your company.

5. Format the line with a width of 4 1/2 points. Also flip the arrowhead if necessary.

6. View the slide as a full-screen slide show. Make any necessary adjustments to the arrow and text box.

7. Print one copy of the slide.

8. Save the presentation, then close it.

Adding Connectors and Filling an Object

You work for a company that sells ergonomic products to computer users. To jazz up a slide, you add connectors and fill objects.

To add connectors and fill an object, complete the following steps:

1. Open Proj1110 from the Project-11 folder on the CD and save it as `Ergonomic Computer Products`.

2. Use the Straight Arrow Connector to draw connectors from each of the outside objects to the middle object (Increased Productivity).

3. Select the connectors, then apply the 3-point line style to them.

4. Select the oval objects, then apply the 3-D Style 3 to them.

5. Fill the oval objects with the white template color.

6. View your slide as a slide show.

7. Print a copy of the presentation.

8. Save the presentation, then close it.

Adding Shapes

You're working for the local library. To promote a summer reading program, you create a flyer to which you add a text box.

To add shapes, complete the following steps:

1. Open Proj1111 from the Project-11 folder on the CD and save it as Summer Reading Program.

2. Add a text box below the clip art image, then enter See information at front desk for more details! in the box.

3. Add a WordArt object to your slide.

4. Choose the first style on the third row.

5. Enter Reading Program! in the Edit WordArt dialog box, then click OK.

6. Resize and move the WordArt object so that it displays in the upper portion of your slide.

7. View your presentation as a full-screen slide show.

8. Print a copy of the presentation.

9. Save, then close your presentation.

PinPoint Assessment

You have completed the project and the associated lessons, as well as the "Checking Your Skills" and "Applying Your Skills" sections. Now use the PinPoint software Evaluation mode to assess your comprehension of the specific exam tasks you have just learned. You can also use the PinPoint Trainer mode and the SHOW ME tutorials to practice these specific exam tasks.

Project 12

Twelve

Beefing Up Your Presentation with Complex Charts

Working with Excel and PowerPoint for Better Charts

In this project you will learn the following objectives and their associated Microsoft Exam required activities.

Objectives   Required Activities

➤ Link an Excel Chart to a … … … … … … … … … … … Insert an Excel Chart
   PowerPoint Presentation

➤ Choose Chart Types and Sub-Types

➤ Add and Remove Chart Elements

➤ Format Chart Objects

➤ Use and Create Custom Charts

➤ Add Animation to a Chart … … … … … … … … … Animate Objects

Why Would I Do This?

Charts are great for visualizing data or statistics that might otherwise be difficult for people to comprehend or understand. Because charts can be used so effectively to help your audience interpret data, you can use them as tools to clarify information and drive home your ideas.

If you have worked with PowerPoint for a while, you already know that you can place a chart on a slide by double-clicking a chart placeholder or clicking the Insert Chart button on the Standard toolbar. Either command activates Microsoft Graph, a **peripheral program** that helps you create charts within PowerPoint. The charts you create with Microsoft Graph are **embedded objects** in your presentation.

However, you can also create charts in Excel and then **link** them to a PowerPoint slide. This helps you take advantage of Excel's powerful formulas to create charts based on complicated calculations and then insert them in PowerPoint presentations.

One of the best ways to place an Excel chart on a PowerPoint slide is to create a link. When you link the chart, you actively share information from a **source file** in Excel to a **destination file** in PowerPoint. When objects are linked, any changes made to the source file are automatically reflected in the destination file. Think of a **linked object** as a door between two rooms—an "Excel" room and a "PowerPoint" room. Creating the link opens the door between programs so that information can be freely shared from Excel to PowerPoint.

Using PowerPoint 97 you can also use advanced formatting features to enhance your chart and make it more appealing. For example, you can select from various chart types and sub-types, and add or remove chart elements. You can also change the color, lines, and other formatting associated with chart objects. And, after you format your chart, you can save it as a custom chart type so you can apply it to other charts in the future.

Finally, you can animate chart elements to focus on important points, control the flow of information, and add interest to your presentation.

Because PowerPoint charts are such powerful tools, try beefing up some presentations with them now.

Jargon Watch

Peripheral programs, like Microsoft Graph, are programs that are activated from within another program. When a peripheral program is activated, you have access to its commands and features to create a specific, specialized object. After you finish working with the peripheral program, you can usually click outside it to deactivate it and embed the object as an object in the destination program.

Embedded objects are those objects placed in the file of a destination program by another program. Once an object is embedded, it becomes part of the destination file. You can double-click an embedded object to reactivate the source program and make revisions to the object.

In contrast to embedded objects, **linked objects** are those created in a **source file**, then placed in the **destination file** while maintaining a connection—or **link**—between the two. The object in the destination file is automatically updated whenever you make changes to the source file. For example, you can link an Excel chart to a PowerPoint slide. Any changes you make on the Excel chart are reflected automatically on the PowerPoint slide. Changes to an embedded object are saved in the presentation and do not affect any source files.

Lesson 1: Linking an Excel Chart to a PowerPoint Presentation

In this lesson, you learn how to link a Microsoft Excel Chart to a PowerPoint presentation. Because Excel has the capacity to perform complicated calculations, you can create Excel charts based on this data and then link them to a PowerPoint slide.

In order to successfully create a link between Excel and PowerPoint, you need both programs loaded on your system. Make sure Excel 97 is available on your system and then try creating a linked chart.

To Create a Linked Chart

❶ Start a new PowerPoint presentation and display a blank slide.

This is the location to which you will link the Excel chart.

❷ Click the Start button, then choose Microsoft Excel from the Programs menu.

Excel 97 loads into memory and a blank worksheet displays.

If you have problems...

If Excel doesn't start, or you can't locate it on the Programs menu, it is most likely in a different folder on your system. Ask your instructor for help. Also, if the Office Assistant window displays in Excel, click its Close button.

❸ In Excel, open Proj1201 from the Project-12 folder on the CD and save it as Chart**.**

This worksheet file contains the chart that you want to link to a PowerPoint presentation. Because charts in Excel reflect underlying data, any time you change the data in the Excel worksheet, the chart changes as well.

The first step in creating a link is to select the object that you want to link.

❹ Click the chart object on the Excel worksheet.

The chart object is selected, as indicated by the black selection handles (see Figure 12.1). In addition, Excel places a border around the data used to create the chart. Any changes to this data are reflected on the chart.

If you have problems...

Make sure that the selection handles appear as shown in Figure 12.1, and not just around a chart object such as the chart title.

continues

To Create a Linked Chart   (continued)

Figure 12.1
You must select a chart before linking it.

Borders indicate the data used to create the chart

Black selection handles

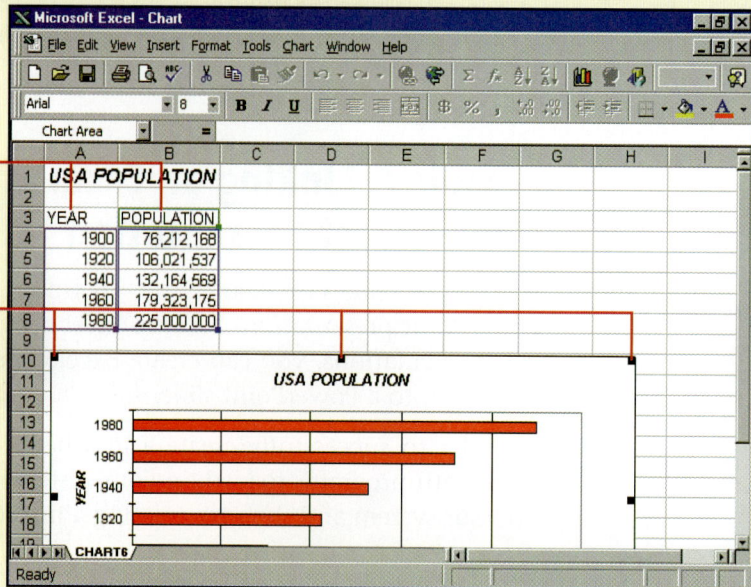

5 **Click the Copy button on the Standard toolbar.**

The chart is copied to the Clipboard. From the Clipboard, you can paste the chart into a PowerPoint presentation by clicking PowerPoint's Paste button (as you learned in Project 9). To create a link, however, you must choose the Edit, Paste Special command in PowerPoint. This command enables you to create an active link between the Excel chart and the PowerPoint presentation.

6 **Click the Microsoft PowerPoint button on the Taskbar, then Edit, Paste Special.**

The Paste Special dialog box displays (see Figure 12.2). You use this dialog box to create a link.

Figure 12.2
You can create an active link between programs using this dialog box.

Source program and file

Click here to create a link

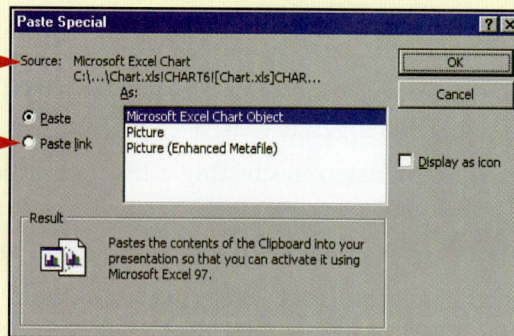

If you have problems... Don't cut corners by clicking the Paste button! You must use the Edit, Paste Special menu command to create a link. If you don't use this command, the chart you paste into your presentation won't automatically be updated when you make any changes back to the original chart or data in Excel.

PowerPoint

7 **Click the Paste link option button.**

This command creates a shortcut to the source file so that changes you make to it reflect on your presentation slide (the destination file).

8 **Choose OK.**

The Excel chart is placed in the presentation as an object (see Figure 12.3). Because the chart is linked to the source file, changes you make to the source file are updated in PowerPoint as well.

Figure 12.3
Use the Paste Special command to create a link.

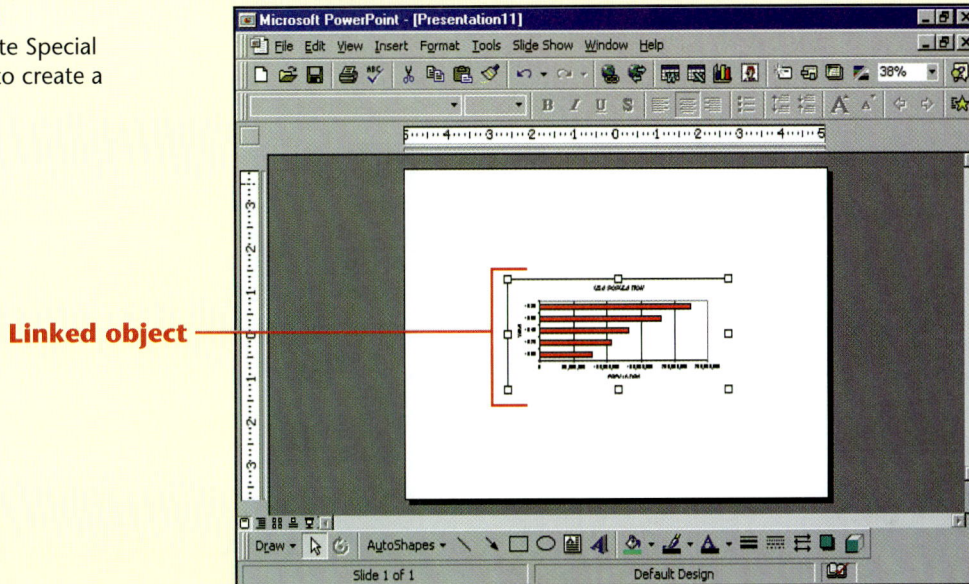

Linked object ———————

Before you change the data, use Zoom to see the linked object more clearly.

`42%`

9 **Click the Zoom drop-down list arrow, then choose 66%.**

The object enlarges for better viewing. Now try changing the information in Excel to see the change on your PowerPoint slide.

10 **Click the Microsoft Excel Taskbar button, then click in cell B8.**

Excel becomes the active program so that you can make changes to the source file. Additionally, clicking cell B8 places a dark border around it so that you can enter new information.

11 **In cell B8, type** 300,000,000 **and press** Enter.

The data changes on both the Excel worksheet and the chart. Now when you switch to PowerPoint, you see the change reflected in the destination file.

12 **Click the Microsoft PowerPoint Taskbar button.**

The chart object in PowerPoint updates to show the information you entered in Excel (see Figure 12.4).

continues

To Create a Linked Chart   (continued)

Figure 12.4
Linked files save time
and duplication

Changes made in the source file reflect in the destination file

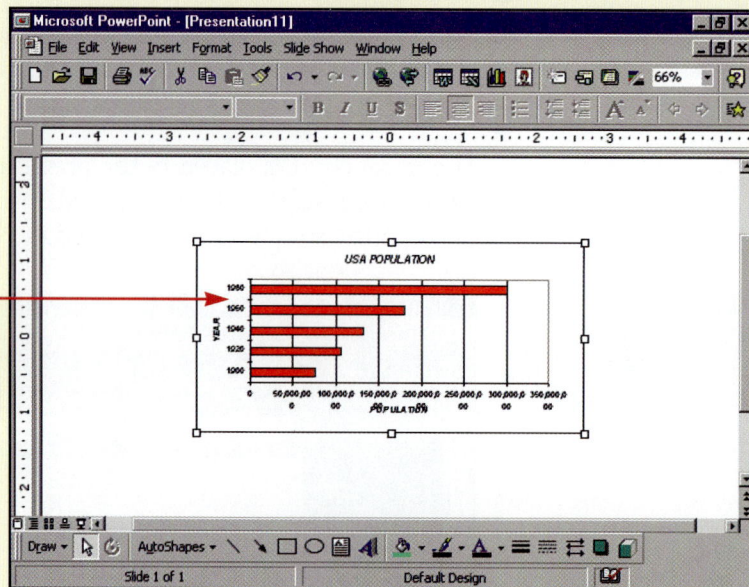

13 Save the PowerPoint presentation as `Linking Charts`, then close it.

Keep PowerPoint open for the next exercise where you change chart types.

14 Switch to Excel, save the Chart file, then exit the program.

Inside Stuff

You can also import an entire chart file into a PowerPoint presentation. Double-click a chart placeholder on the slide in which you want to import the file to activate Microsoft Graph. Then click the Import File button on the Standard toolbar to display the Import File dialog box. Specify the file name and location, then choose Open. In the Import Data Options dialog box that displays, choose whether to import the Entire sheet or just a specific Range. Finally, click OK to import the file.

Lesson 2: Choosing Chart Types and Sub-Types

By default, when you first create a chart, PowerPoint produces a column chart. However, you can always change to another chart type. PowerPoint makes it easy to select from 18 different chart types. Just click the Chart Type drop-down list arrow, then choose a type.

Additionally, you can further refine a chart type by choosing a chart sub-type. A sub-type is simply a variation of a main chart type. For example, a pie chart has sub-types such as exploded pie, 3-D pie, and so on. Try selecting a sub-type for a chart now.

To Change Chart Type

1 **Open Proj1202 from the Project-12 folder on the CD and save it as** Sample Chart.

2 **Double-click the chart object to activate it.**

Microsoft Graph starts, and its commands and toolbar buttons become available (see Figure 12.5). You can use the Chart Type button on the Standard toolbar to change the type of chart used. You can also select chart sub-types by choosing the Chart, Chart Type menu command.

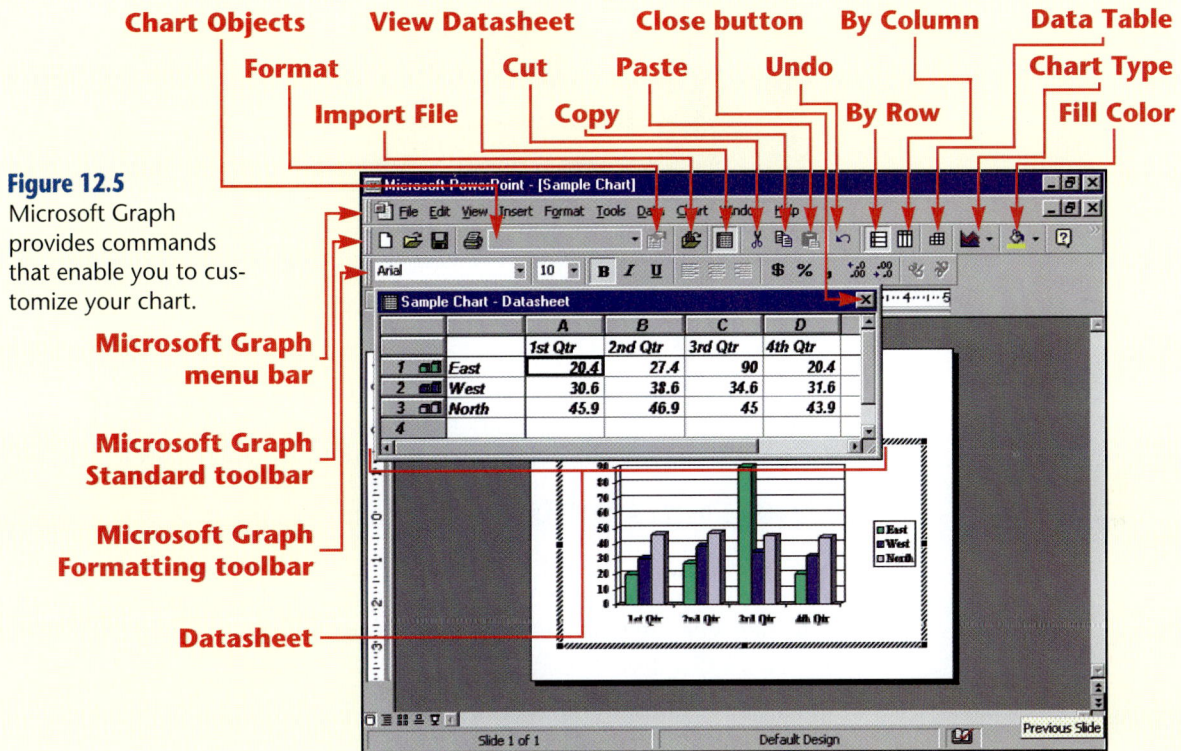

Figure 12.5
Microsoft Graph provides commands that enable you to customize your chart.

(Labels surrounding figure: Chart Objects, Format, Import File, View Datasheet, Cut, Copy, Paste, Close button, Undo, By Column, By Row, Data Table, Chart Type, Fill Color, Microsoft Graph menu bar, Microsoft Graph Standard toolbar, Microsoft Graph Formatting toolbar, Datasheet)

3 **Click the Datasheet Close button.**

The Datasheet closes.

4 **Click the Chart Type drop-down list arrow, then move the mouse pointer over any chart type on the palette.**

A ScreenTip displays to identify the chart type (see Figure 12.6).

continues

To Change Chart Type   (continued)

Figure 12.6
You can select from a variety chart types.

Click this arrow to display chart types

Rest your mouse pointer over any chart type to display the ScreenTip

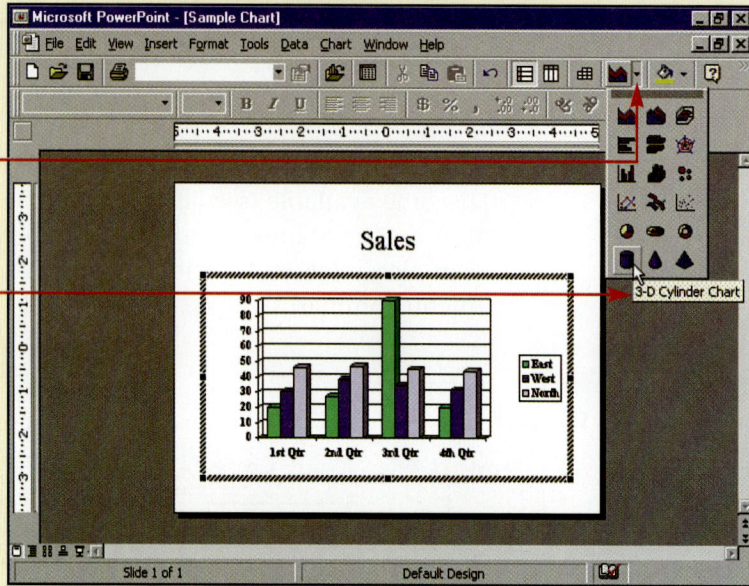

⑤ Click the 3-D Cylinder Chart icon on the palette (refer to Figure 12.6).

The chart type changes to reflect your choice. (If you want, experiment by selecting other chart types. Make sure you choose the 3-D Cylinder Chart type before proceeding with the next step.)

⑥ Choose Chart, Chart Type.

The Chart Type dialog box displays (see Figure 12.7). The main chart types display on the Chart type list, and variations of the selected type are shown in the Chart sub-type area.

If you have problems...

If the Office Assistant button on the Chart Type dialog box is selected, the Office Assistant window automatically displays. Click the Office Assistant's Close button to close the window.

Figure 12.7
You can choose from a variety of chart sub-types for each main chart type.

Choose a sub-type here

See a description of the selected sub-type here

Press and hold the mouse button here to preview a sample chart

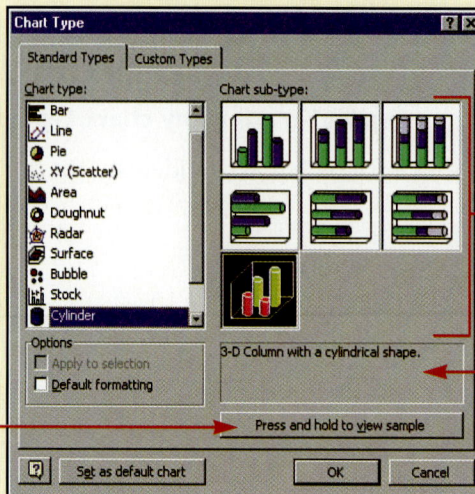

7 **Click the Stacked column with a cylindrical shape sub-type (the second sub-type in the first row).**

You can see the selected chart sub-type by pressing the mouse button while pointing to the Press and hold to view sample button.

8 **Point to the Press and hold to view sample button, then hold down the left mouse button for a few seconds.**

Your chart displays in the Sample area of the Chart Type dialog box (see Figure 12.8). When you release the mouse button, the chart sub-types again display.

Figure 12.8
You can display the chart data with the sub-type.

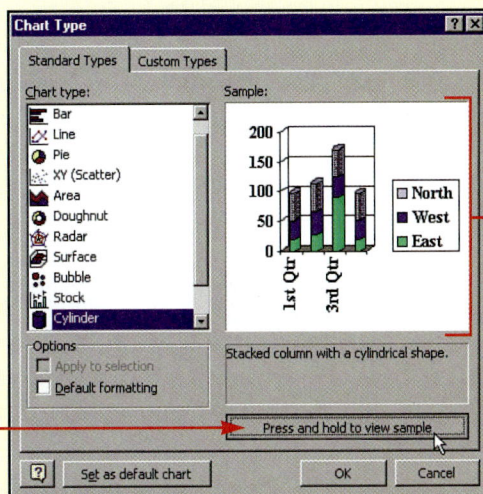

Chart sub-type with your data

Pressing this button toggles between sub-types and a sample chart

9 **Release the mouse button, then click OK to choose the Chart sub-type.**

The chart sub-type is applied to your data (see Figure 12.9).

Figure 12.9
You can change a chart's appearance by choosing a sub-type.

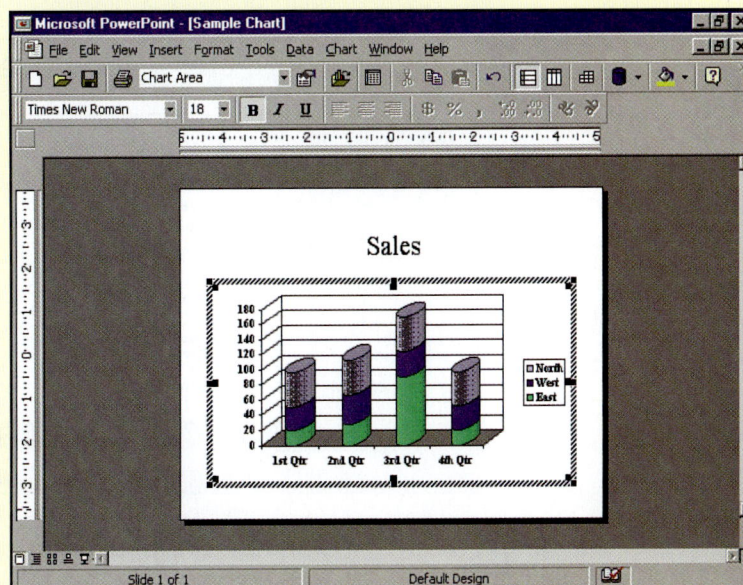

10 **Save the Sample Chart presentation.**

Keep the presentation open for the next lesson, in which you learn how to add and remove chart elements.

You can use the Office Assistant to learn about the various chart sub-types. In the Chart Type dialog box, click the Office Assistant button to display the Office Assistant window. In the bubble callout, click the option button for Example of the selected chart type. Click a chart type to display information and samples related to the type.

Lesson 3: Adding and Removing Chart Elements

Even if you're satisfied with the chart type you have chosen, you may want to add or remove specific chart elements. For example, you may want to display or remove a legend, data table, or data labels from a chart. Luckily, PowerPoint makes it easy to change which elements you use with a chart. In many cases, you can click a Microsoft Graph toolbar button to toggle the display of an object on or off. And, for more settings, you can choose Chart, Chart Options to display and use the Chart Options dialog box. You can also modify the way the chart displays data by arranging it by column or by row.

Try working with these features now to customize your chart.

To Add and Remove Chart Elements

1 **Make sure that the chart object in the Sample Chart presentation is selected, then click the Data Table button on the Standard toolbar.**

A data table is added to the chart (see Figure 12.10). This table shows the information on which the chart is based.

Figure 12.10
You can add a data table to your chart.

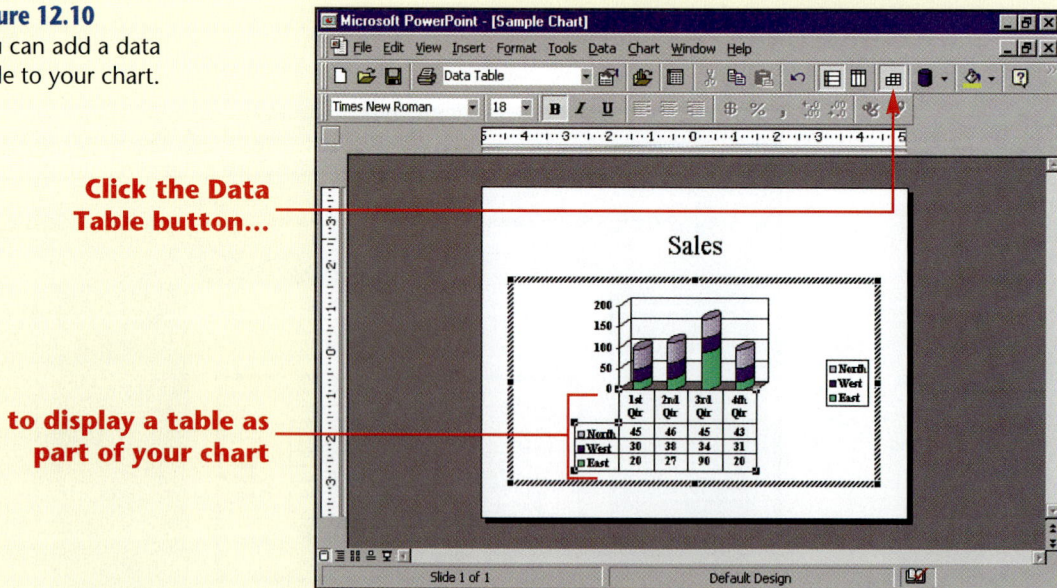

Click the Data Table button...

to display a table as part of your chart

2 **Choose Chart, Chart Options.**

The Chart Options dialog box displays (see Figure 12.11). You can use this dialog box to turn on or off the standard (default) settings for a chart. Notice that the dialog box has a series of tabs for different categories so that you can revise the settings for the Titles, Axes, Gridlines, and so on.

PowerPoint

Figure 12.11
You can easily revise the
default chart settings.

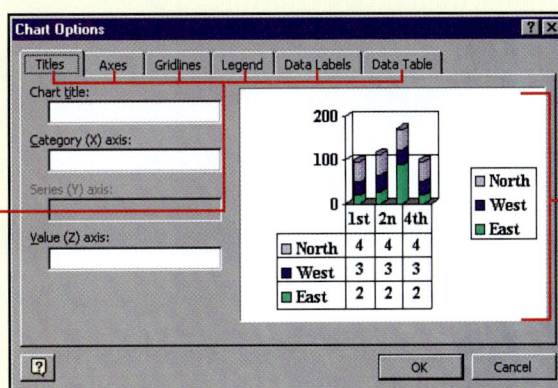

**Click a tab to display
a page of settings**

**Preview your
choices here**

If you have problems...

If the Office Assistant button is selected in this dialog box, the Office
Assistant window automatically displays. Click the Office Assistant Close button to close it.

**3 Click the Legend tab, then click to uncheck the Show legend
box.**

The legend is removed from the chart. Notice that your change displays in the preview area to help you find just the look you want.

Now try adding gridlines to your chart. Gridlines sometimes make it
easier to read chart data.

**4 Click the Gridlines tab, then check the box for Major grid-
lines.**

Vertical gridlines are displayed on the preview chart, extending up
from the Category axis. Horizontal gridlines are already displayed,
extending across the chart from the Value axis. Major gridlines
appear at the value or category label position on the axis; minor
gridlines appear between the major gridlines.

**5 Click the Data Table tab, then uncheck the Show data table
box.**

The data table is removed from your chart. Because you're finished
changing settings in the Chart Options dialog box, you can close it.

6 Click OK.

The Chart Options dialog box closes, and the new settings are
applied to your chart. Now try arranging your data by column and
by row (see Figure 12.12).

7 Click the By Column button on the Standard toolbar.

Your data displays by column, rather than by row.

continues

To Add and Remove Chart Elements (continued)

Figure 12.12
Try a different look—display your data by column or by row.

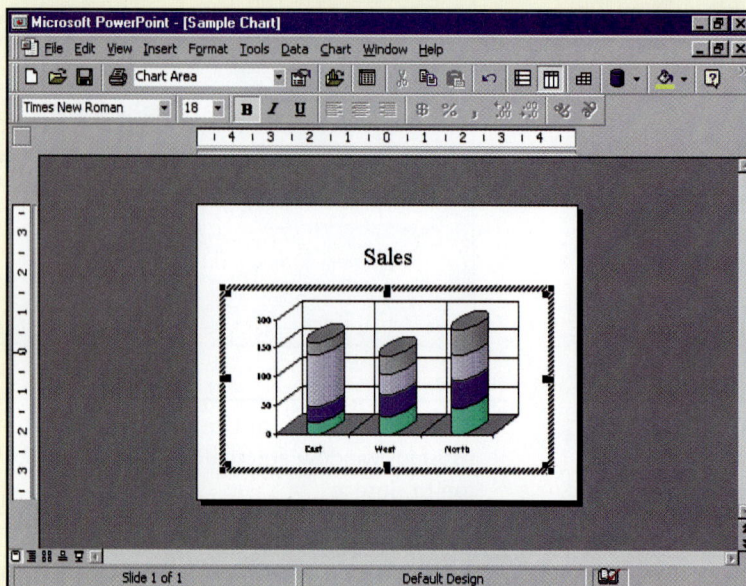

8 Click the By Row button on the Standard toolbar.

Your data displays by row.

9 Save the Sample Chart presentation.

Keep the presentation open for the next lesson, in which you format individual chart elements.

Inside Stuff

Once you've made changes to the chart elements, you may want to see how your modifications would look if you switch chart types. Double-click in the middle of the chart to activate the Microsoft Graph program.

Click the down arrow next to the Chart Type button on the Microsoft Graph Standard toolbar and then choose a different chart type.

Or, to see a larger range of chart types and sub-types, choose Chart, Chart Type from the menu to open the Chart Type dialog box. Then you can choose from the Chart type list and click a Chart sub-type. Click and hold down the Press and hold to view sample button to preview your choices and see how the changes you made to the chart elements look on different chart types. Choose OK when you decide to keep the selected chart and sub-type or Cancel to close the dialog box without making changes to the chart type.

Click outside the border around the chart to return to editing the PowerPoint slide.

Lesson 4: Formatting Chart Objects

Besides changing the chart type or settings, you may want to format individual chart elements. For example, you may want to change an object's color, border, or font to make it more readable or to emphasize specific information.

Before you can format a chart object, however, you must first select it. The easiest way to do this is to choose the object from the Chart Objects drop-down list. After an object is selected, you can use the Format button on the Standard toolbar to display a context-sensitive Format dialog box. For example, if you select a data series, clicking the Format button displays the Format Data Series dialog box.

Try formatting some chart elements with these commands now.

To Format Chart Objects

Value Axis ▾

❶ In the open Sample Chart presentation, click the Chart Objects drop-down list arrow.

A list of objects for your chart displays (see Figure 12.13). You can choose an object from this list to select it for formatting.

Figure 12.13
You must first select an object before formatting it.

Click this drop-down list arrow to display chart objects

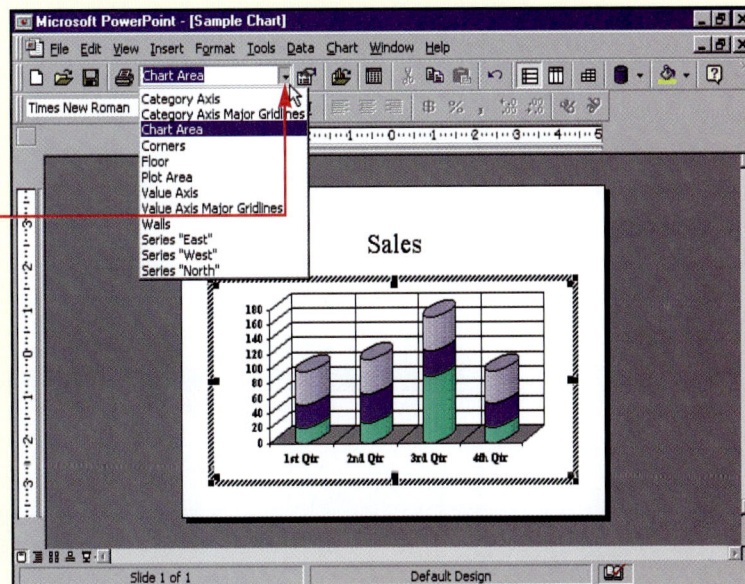

❷ From the list, choose Series "East."

Selection handles display around the data series for "East." After you have selected the object, you can display formatting commands related to it.

❸ Click the Format Data Series button.

The Format Data Series dialog box displays (see Figure 12.14) with the Patterns page in front. Notice that the formatting commands relate to the object that you selected.

continues

To Format Chart Objects   (continued)

Figure 12.14
PowerPoint displays formatting commands related to the objects.

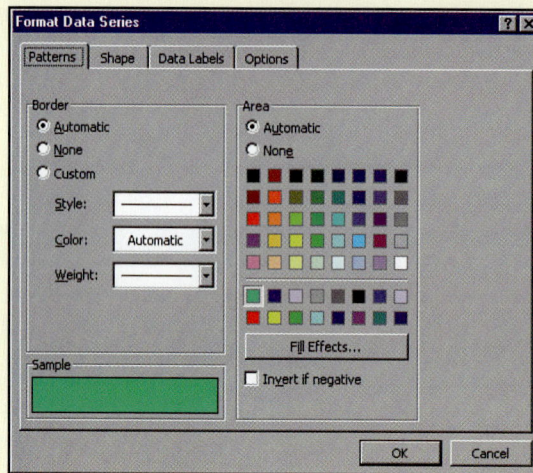

4 **In the Area section of the Patterns page, click the sixth color box on the bottom row (the Fuchsia color).**

The Sample box shows a preview of the new color. Now try changing other formatting options related to the data series.

5 **Click the Shape tab, then click the first Column shape box on the first row and choose OK.**

The formatting choices you made are applied to the chart (see Figure 12.15).

Figure 12.15
You can quickly format any chart.

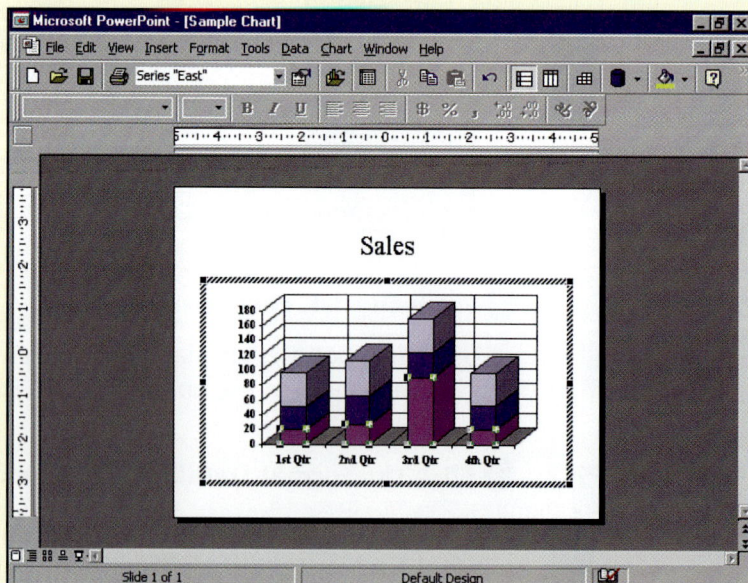

6 **Click outside the chart.**

The chart is deselected and Microsoft Graph's commands and toolbars are no longer available.

7 **Save the Sample Chart presentation, then close it.**

Keep PowerPoint running for the next lesson, in which you create a custom chart.

If you have problems...

Although Undo can undo the last 20 steps you did in PowerPoint, this does not apply to charts created by Microsoft Graph. When you're working with Microsoft Graph, you can undo only the previous step.

Once you've clicked outside the embedded chart and returned to normal slide editing in PowerPoint, clicking Undo or choosing the Edit, Undo command causes a dialog box to appear on your screen. The dialog box states that using undo may result in the loss of any changes you made to the chart since your last edit. Choose Cancel if you don't want to lose all your recent modifications.

Normally, if you choose OK, the last modification to the chart will be undone, but Microsoft Graph will be activated so you can undo other changes manually. However, in some cases, all the recent modifications to your chart are undone (including some you didn't want removed). If you click outside the chart border and use Undo again, the entire chart may disappear (click Redo to reinsert the chart on the slide).

Lesson 5: Using and Creating Custom Charts

PowerPoint provides a number of chart types that you can use for your charts. However, the default settings for the chart may not fit your needs or tastes. Luckily, you can format a chart with the type, colors, and other options you want, then save it as a custom chart type. Then, when you create new charts, you can quickly apply the custom chart formatting to them.

Try creating and using a custom chart type now.

To Create and Use a Custom Chart

❶ Open Proj1203 from the Project-12 folder on the CD and save it as Custom Chart Type.

❷ Double-click the chart object on Slide 1 to activate Microsoft Graph, then close the Datasheet.

After the chart is activated, you can make revisions to it using commands with which you are already familiar. You can then save the combination of features as a custom chart type.

One popular option is to change the color associated with the data series. For example, some presenters like to use corporate colors for their charts. Try changing a data series color now.

Value Axis ▾

❸ Choose Series "North" **from the Chart Objects drop-down list, then click the Format Data Series button.**

The Format Data Series dialog box displays (refer to Figure 12.14). You can change how the data series looks using commands that this dialog box provides.

❹ Click the Patterns page if necessary; then in the Area section, click the first color box on the second to the bottom row (the turquoise color).

The Sample box shows a preview of the new color.

continues

To Create and Use a Custom Chart   (continued)

5 **Click the Shape tab, then choose shape 4 (the Cylinder shape) and choose OK.**

The current chart displays the changes. Now try saving this combination of formatting features as a custom chart.

6 **Choose Chart, Chart Type, then click the Custom Types tab.**

The Custom Types page of the dialog box displays (see Figure 12.16). (If the Office Assistant also displays, click its Close button.)

Figure 12.16
You can create custom charts in this dialog box.

Built-in chart types

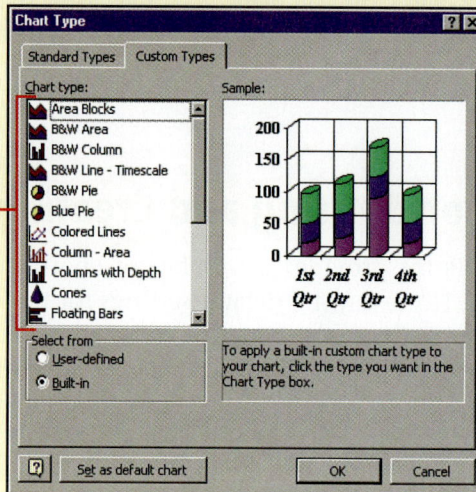

7 **In the Select from area, click the User-defined option button.**

A list of user-defined chart types displays (see Figure 12.17). Additionally, your current chart displays in the sample area of the dialog box to show you how the custom chart type will look.

Figure 12.17
You can click the User-defined button to add or remove a custom chart type.

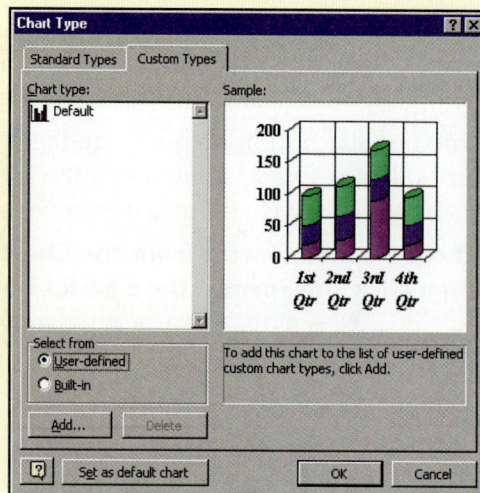

⑧ Click the Add button.

The Add Custom Chart Type dialog box displays (see Figure 12.18). You use this dialog box to give your custom chart type a name and (if desired) a description.

Figure 12.18
You identify a custom chart with a name and description.

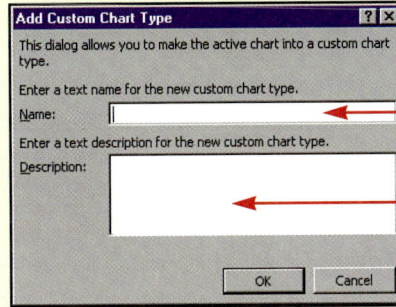

Type a name for your custom chart type here

Type a description for your custom chart type here

⑨ In the Name text box, type `Corporate Colors`, **and then click OK.**

The new custom chart type displays on your Chart type list (see Figure 12.19). You can now apply this chart type to other charts. (Click the Close button for the Office Assistant window if it displays.)

Figure 12.19
You can quickly create custom chart types to apply to other charts.

The new custom chart type appears on this list

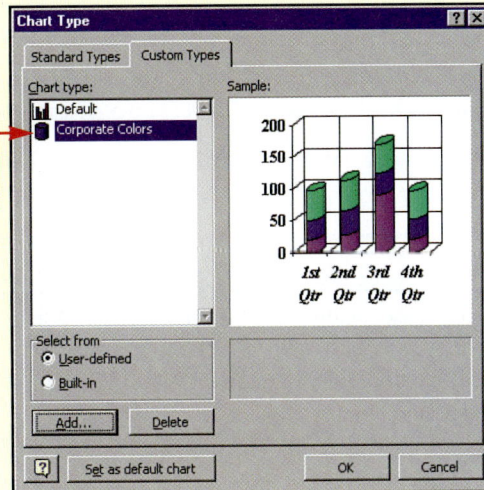

⑩ Click OK to close the Chart Type dialog box.

Now try applying the new custom chart to an existing chart.

⑪ Double-click the chart object on Slide 2 and close the Datasheet. Choose Chart, Chart Type.

The Chart Type dialog box displays.

⑫ Click the Custom Types tab and click the User-defined option button.

The custom chart type you previously defined displays on the Chart type list.

continues

To Create and Use a Custom Chart   (continued)

13 **Click the Corporate Colors chart type, then click OK.**

The chart on Slide 2 displays with the formatting for the custom chart type (see Figure 12.20).

Figure 12.20
You can quickly apply a custom chart type to an existing chart.

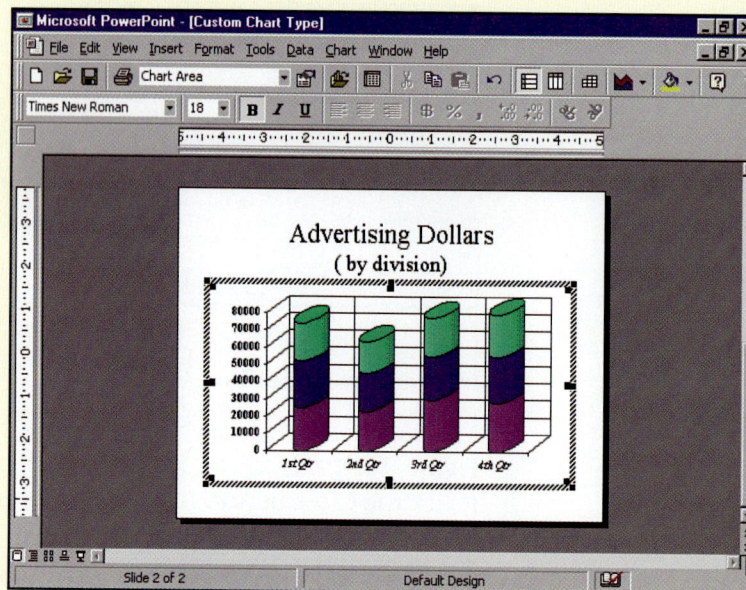

14 **Save the Custom Chart Type presentation, then close it.**

Keep PowerPoint running for the next exercise, in which you add animation to a chart.

Inside Stuff

You can also delete custom chart types. Display the Custom Types page of the Chart Type dialog box. Select the custom chart type you want to remove from the Chart type list, then click Delete. Choose OK in the message box to confirm the deletion.

Lesson 6: Adding Animation to a Chart

You can add *animation* to a chart. You create an animation effect by having chart elements display in sequence rather than all at once. For example, you can have slices of a pie chart display one at a time. This helps control the flow of information and keeps your audience's attention from wandering.

When you add animation to a chart, you can specify the following settings:

Animation
Displaying chart elements in sequence to create the illusion of movement.

- Select the level of the build. For example, you can have PowerPoint display a series of bars as a group, or show each one individually.

- Use a transition effect as you build chart elements. You can use 46 different effects such as Box Out, Fly from Right, and so on.

- Play a sound file as each element appears. PowerPoint provides 16 sound clips from which to choose.

In order to work with PowerPoint's chart animation feature, you must display your presentation in Slide view, then choose Slide Show, Custom Animation. Try adding animation to a chart now.

To Add Animation to a Chart

1 **Open Proj1204 from the Project-12 folder on the CD and save it as** Chart Animation.

2 **With the Chart Animation presentation in Slide view, choose Slide Show, Custom Animation.**

The Custom Animation dialog box displays (see Figure 12.21). You use this dialog box to specify how to animate your chart elements.

Figure 12.21
You can add custom animation to a chart.

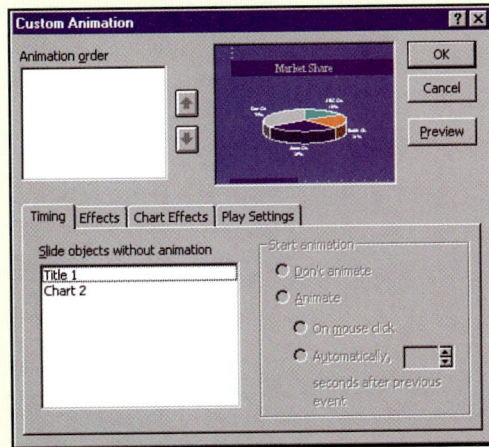

3 **Click the Chart 2 object from the Slide objects without animation list, then click the Animate option button.**

The Chart object is moved to the Animation order list (see Figure 12.22). This dictates that the entire chart is animated at once on the slide. You can see how this type of animation looks by clicking the Preview button.

Figure 12.22
You can animate the entire chart.

Select an object, then choose **A**nimate to move objects to this list

View the animation here

Click here to preview the animation

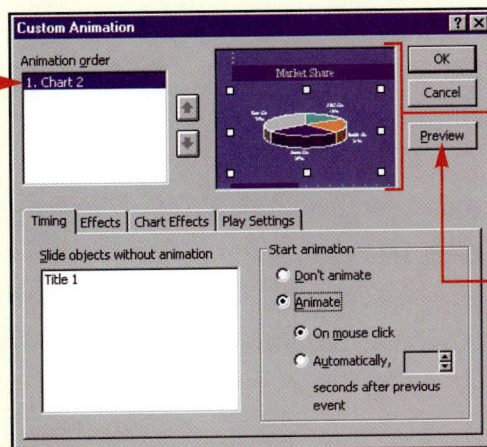

continues

To Add Animation to a Chart (continued)

4 **Click the Preview button.**

A preview of the animation effect displays in the dialog box. Notice that the entire chart appears at once. Now try animating the chart so that the individual pie slices display one at a time.

5 **Click the Chart Effects tab.**

The Chart Effects page displays (see Figure 12.23). You can use this page to determine how to introduce and draw chart elements on the slide.

Figure 12.23
You can control how chart elements are drawn during a slide show.

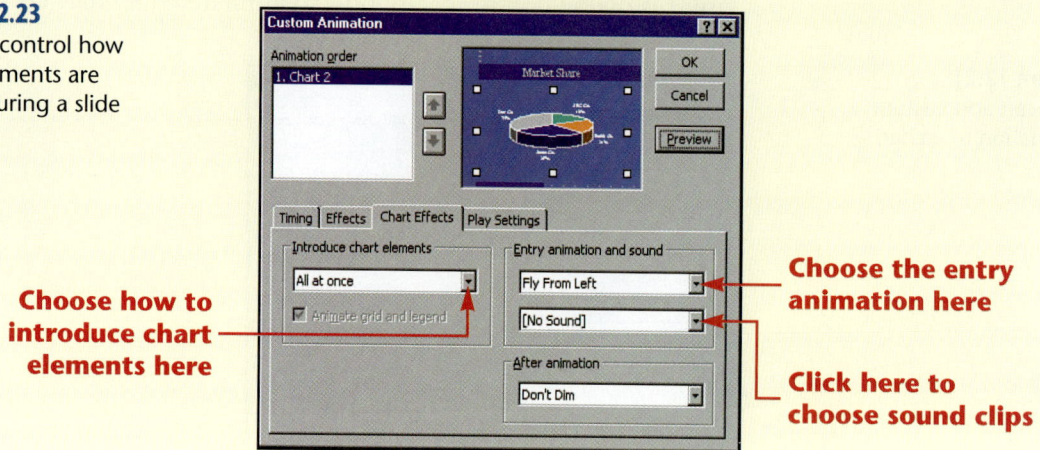

Choose how to introduce chart elements here

Choose the entry animation here

Click here to choose sound clips

6 **Click the Introduce chart elements drop-down list arrow, then choose by Category.**

This dictates that each slice of pie on your chart appears individually. Now try changing the animation transition—the transition effects that are added to each pie slide as it is drawn.

7 **Click the upper drop-down list arrow in the Entry animation and sound area, then choose Dissolve.**

Each pie slice is drawn using the Dissolve transition effect when you run the slide show. You can preview this effect.

8 **Click the Preview button to view your changes, and then choose OK.**

The custom animation settings are applied to your chart. Now try running a slide show to see the effects full-screen.

9 **Click the Slide Show button.**

The slide show begins, but only the slide title (Market Share) displays onscreen. To draw each chart element, you must click the left mouse button.

10 Click the left mouse button six times.

A chart element is drawn every time you click the mouse. After the entire chart is displayed, the slide show ends.

11 Save the Chart Animation presentation, then close it.

If you have finished your work session, exit PowerPoint and shut down Windows 95 before turning off your computer. Otherwise, complete the "Checking Your Skills" and "Applying Your Skills" exercises at the end of this project.

Project Summary

To	Use
Link a chart	Select the Excel chart and click the Copy button, then switch to PowerPoint and choose Edit, Paste Special. Click the Paste link option button and click OK.
Import a file	Double-click a chart placeholder, then click the Import File button.
Choose a chart type or sub-type	Choose Chart, Chart Type.
Add or remove a data table	Click the Data Table button.
Add or remove chart elements	Choose Chart, Chart Options.
Display chart data by row	Click the By Row button.
Display chart data by column	Click the By Column button.
Select a chart object	Click the Chart Objects drop-down list arrow, then click the object you want.
Format chart objects	Select the object, then click the Format button.
Create a custom chart type	Format a chart, then choose Chart, Chart Type and click the Custom Types tab. Click the User-defined option button, then click OK.
Animate an entire chart	In Slide view, choose Slide Show, Custom Animation. Choose the chart object, then click the Animate option button.
Animate a chart element	In Slide view, choose Slide Show, Custom Animation. Click the Chart Effects tab, then choose an element from the Introduce chart elements drop-down list.

Checking Your Skills

True/False

For each of the following, check *T* or *F* to indicate whether the statement is true or false.

__T __F **1.** Linking and embedding an object are the same thing.

__T __F **2.** You can remove chart elements, such as the data table, legend, or data labels, from a chart.

__T __F **3.** You must select chart objects before you can format them.

__T __F **4.** After you create a custom chart type, you can apply it to any other chart.

__T __F **5.** You can animate only bar and column charts.

__T __F **6.** You can link an Excel chart to a PowerPoint presentation.

__T __F **7.** You use a peripheral program, Microsoft Picture, to create charts in PowerPoint.

__T __F **8.** A chart sub-type is simply a variation on the main chart type.

__T __F **9.** PowerPoint is an example of a peripheral program.

__T __F **10.** PowerPoint includes 18 main chart types.

Multiple Choice

Circle the letter of the correct answer for each of the following questions.

1. To link an Excel chart to a PowerPoint slide, you copy the chart to the Clipboard, then switch to PowerPoint and choose which menu command?

    a. Edit, Paste

    b. Edit, Paste Special

    c. Insert, Paste Chart

    d. File, Insert

2. When you make changes to a chart in the source program, what happens to the linked object in the destination program?

    a. It doesn't reflect the changes.

    b. It is updated only when you choose Chart, Update Link.

    c. It cannot be updated.

    d. None of the above

3. You can select a chart sub-type by doing which of the following?

    a. clicking the Graph Sub-Type button

    b. choosing Insert, New Sub-Type from the menu

    c. choosing Chart, Chart Type from the menu

    d. any of the above

4. Which of the following modifications can you make to a chart?

    a. Change the data series color.

    b. Remove a legend.

c. Add data labels.

d. All of the above.

c. sub-family

d. none of the above

5. How do you select a chart object?

    a. Triple-click the object.

    b. Right-click the object twice.

    c. Choose the object from the Chart Objects drop-down list.

    d. All of the above.

6. How do you activate an embedded object and access the source program's commands?

    a. Choose File, Open Embedded Object from the menu.

    b. Click the Open Source Program button.

    c. Double-click the embedded object.

    d. None of the above.

7. A variation on a main chart type is called a _____.

    a. sub-type

    b. minor-type

8. What command do you use to animate a chart?

    a. Click the Animate Chart button.

    b. Choose Slide Show, Custom Animation from the menu.

    c. Double-click the chart.

    d. None of the above.

9. Objects placed in the file of a destination program are called _____.

    a. pasted objects

    b. embedded objects

    c. source objects

    d. none of the above

10. Objects that are created in a source file and then placed in the destination file while maintaining a connection between the two are called _____.

    a. linked objects

    b. original objects

    c. copied objects

    d. none of the above

Completion

In the blank provided, write the correct answer for each of the following statements.

1. _____ programs, such as Microsoft Graph, are those that are activated from within another program.

2. _____ objects maintain a connection between the program that created them and the file in which they are placed.

3. You can double-click a _____ object to activate the program that created it.

4. Each main chart type has several variations, or _____ associated with it.

5. A(n) _____ chart type is one that you can customize and then apply to existing charts.

6. You can arrange your chart data by column or by _____.

7. You can _____ chart elements in a sequence to create the illusion of movement.

8. You can click the _____ button to import a file.

9. You add animation to a chart in the _____ dialog box.

10. You can link charts created in _____ to a PowerPoint slide.

Matching

In the blank next to each of the following terms or phrases, write the letter of the corresponding term or phrase. (Note that some of the letters may be used more than once.)

a. column

b. linked object

c. animation

d. Microsoft Graph

e. Chart Objects

f. custom chart type

g. built-in chart type

h. Data Table

i. Chart Options

j. sub-type

_____ 1. A way to display chart elements one at a time

_____ 2. PowerPoint's default chart type

_____ 3. A variation of a main chart type

_____ 4. Program used to create charts in PowerPoint

_____ 5. A drop-down list used to select chart objects

_____ 6. Dialog box used to add or remove chart elements

_____ 7. Maintains a connection between the source and destination files

_____ 8. A user-defined chart type

_____ 9. A chart type that is already set up for you

_____ 10. Adds a table of information to your chart

Applying Your Skills

Practice

The following exercises, found in the Project-12 folder on the CD, enable you to practice the skills you have learned in this project. Take a few minutes to work through these exercises now.

Choosing a Chart Type and Sub-Type

You work for a government agency that tracks the population of the United States. To prepare for a talk, you decide to revise a chart by viewing and choosing sub-types.

To choose a chart type and sub-type, complete the following steps:

1. Open Proj1205 from the Project-12 folder on the CD and save it as USA Population.

2. Double-click the chart object to activate Microsoft Graph. Close the Datasheet.

3. Click the Chart Type drop-down list arrow to display the chart palette. Choose Bar Chart.

4. With the chart still activated, choose Chart, Chart Type to display the Chart Type dialog box.

5. Click the first sub-type shown in the Chart sub-type section, then hold down the left mouse button for several seconds while pointing to the Press and hold to view sample button. Repeat the process for each of the other bar chart sub-types.

6. Choose the Clustered bar with a 3-D visual effect sub-type, then click OK.

7. Save the USA Population presentation, then close it.

Adding and Removing Chart Elements

You are developing a presentation to show sales for the past year. To modify the presentation, you add and remove chart elements.

To add and remove chart elements, complete the following steps:

1. Open Proj1206 from the Project-12 folder on the CD and save it as `Yearly Sales`.

2. Double-click the chart object to activate Microsoft Graph. Close the Datasheet.

3. Choose Chart, Chart Options.

4. On the Titles page, click in the Chart title text box and type `Sales by State`.

5. Click the Legend tab, then check the Show data table box. Click OK to close the Chart Options dialog box.

6. Click the Data Table button to remove the table.

7. Save the presentation, then close it.

Creating a Custom Chart Type

As part of your job, you develop several presentations a month. Because you find yourself choosing the same formatting and chart options, you decide to create a custom chart type that you can quickly apply to other charts.

To create a custom chart type, complete the following steps:

1. Open Proj1207 from the Project-12 folder on the CD and save it as `Revenue vs. Expenses`.

2. Double-click the chart object on Slide 1 and close the Datasheet.

3. Click the By Column button to display the data by quarter.

4. Choose Chart, Chart Type. Choose Cylinder from the Chart type list.

5. Choose the 3-D Column with a cylindrical shape in the Chart sub-type area. Preview the chart sub-type, then choose OK.

6. Reopen the Chart Type dialog box. Click the Custom Types tab, then click the User-defined option button.

7. Click Add, then type `My Chart Type` in the Name text box. Close the Add Custom Chart Type and Chart Type dialog boxes.

8. Double-click the chart on Slide 2, then close the Datasheet.

9. Choose Chart, Chart Type, then click the Custom Types tab.

10. Click the User-defined option button, then double-click My Chart Type on the list.

11. Save the Revenue vs. Expenses presentation, then close it.

Adding Animation to a Chart

You are presenting sales figures at an upcoming meeting. In order to keep your audience's attention and control when information displays, you decide to add animation to a chart.

To add animation to a chart, complete the following steps:

1. Open Proj1208 from the Project-12 folder on the CD and save it as `Animated Chart`.

2. Display the presentation in Slide view, then choose Slide Show, Custom Animation.

3. Click Chart 2 on the Slide objects without animation list, then click the Animate option button.

4. Click the Chart Effects tab.

5. Click the Introduce chart elements drop-down list and choose by Element in Series.

6. Click the Preview button to see the effects, then choose OK.

7. Click the Slide Show button. Click the left mouse button as many times as necessary to view the chart's animation.

8. Press Esc if necessary to stop the slide show, then save and close the presentation.

Inserting an Excel Chart

As Sales Manager for your company, you use Excel heavily to track sales. However, for an upcoming meeting you need to use PowerPoint to present your information. To save yourself time and trouble, you insert an Excel chart with sales figures into a PowerPoint presentation.

To insert an Excel chart, complete the following steps:

1. Open Proj1209 from the Project-12 folder on the CD and save it as `Sales Meeting`.

2. Start Excel, then open Proj1210 from the Project-12 folder on the CD. Click the chart object on the Excel worksheet, then click the Copy button.

3. Switch to PowerPoint and display Slide 2 in the Sales Meeting presentation.

4. In PowerPoint click Edit, Paste Special to display the Paste Special dialog box.

5. Click the Paste link option button to create a link to the source file, then choose OK.

6. Resize and move the chart object on the PowerPoint slide so that it fills the available space.

7. Save the PowerPoint presentation, then close it. Close the Proj1210 worksheet without saving it. Exit Excel.

Challenge

The following challenges, found in the Project-12 folder on the CD, enable you to use your problem-solving skills. Take time to work through these exercises now.

Animating Objects

You have to conduct meeting for sales personnel. To keep their attention, you decide to animate objects on your slides.

To animate objects, complete the following steps:

1. Open Proj1211 from the Project-12 folder on the CD and save it as Motivational Sales Meeting.

2. Display Slide 2 in Slide view, then choose Slide Show, Custom Animation.

3. Click the Chart 2 object on the Slide objects without animation list, then click Animate.

4. Click the Chart Effects tab, then change the options so that chart elements are introduced by Element in Series.

5. Click the lower drop-down list arrow in the Entry animation and sound area, then choose Whoosh as the sound.

6. Preview your animation before closing the Custom Animation dialog box.

7. Test your animation in a slide show. Keep the presentation open for the next exercise.

Applying More Animation Objects

To further enhance the Motivational Sales Meeting presentation, you decide to animate more slide objects.

To apply more animation objects, complete the following steps:

1. In the Motivational Sales Meeting presentation open from the previous exercise, display Slide 3. Open the Custom Animation dialog box.

2. Drag to select all the objects on the Slide objects without animation list, then click Animate.

3. On the Animation order list, click Title 1 to select it. Click the Effects tab. In the Entry animation and sound section, click the upper drop-down list arrow and choose Fly From Bottom-Left.

4. Click Object 2 on the Animation order list (the clip art object). Display the Effects page if necessary. In the Entry animation and sound section, click the upper drop-down list arrow and choose Swivel.

5. Click Chart 3 on the Animation order list, then click the Chart Effects tab.

6. Introduce the Chart Elements by Element in Series.

7. Preview the animations in the Custom Animation dialog box, then click OK.

8. Test your animations in a slide show by viewing your presentation from Slide 1.

9. Save your presentation, then close it.

Animating a Chart

You are developing a presentation to show company employees. To emphasize your company's market share, you animate the chart.

To animate a chart, complete the following steps:

1. Open Proj1212 from the Project-12 folder on the CD and save it as Our Market Share.

2. With the slide displayed in Slide view, choose Slide Show, Custom Animation.

3. Animate the pie slices so they display in sequence by category.

4. Change the entry sound for each pie slice. Choose Laser as the sound.

5. Preview the animation in the Custom Animation dialog box.

6. Test the animation by displaying the slide in Slide Show view.

7. Save the presentation, then close it.

Inserting an Excel Chart

To create a sales presentation you insert an Excel chart with sales data into a PowerPoint presentation.

To insert an Excel chart, complete the following steps:

1. Start Excel. Open Proj1213 from the Project-12 folder on the CD and save it as Sales Data. Select the chart object and then click the Copy button.

2. Switch to (or start) PowerPoint. Open Proj1214 from the Project-12 folder on the CD and save it as Sarah's Sweets.

3. Display Slide 2 in the open presentation, then choose Edit, Paste Special. In the Paste Special dialog box, choose Paste link, then choose OK.

4. Resize and move the chart object on the slide so that it fills the available space.

5. Switch to Excel and change the data in cell B4 to $75,000.

6. Switch to PowerPoint and observe the change in the linked chart object (if the chart doesn't update automatically, right-click the chart and choose Update Link from the shortcut menu).

7. Save the Sales Data worksheet, then close it and exit Excel.

8. Save the PowerPoint presentation, then close it.

Animating Chart Objects

To spiff up your sales presentation, you add animation to a chart.

To animate objects, complete the following steps:

1. Open Proj1215 from the Project-12 folder on the CD and save it as Revenues.

2. Choose Slide Show, Custom Animation to display the Custom Animation dialog box.

3. Animate the slide title with a Fly From Bottom-Right entry animation.

4. Animate the chart object. Then set the options so that the chart objects display by each element in the category.

5. Animate the callout object so that it flies in from the right. Also change the entry sound to Drive By.

6. Preview your animations in the Custom Animation dialog box, then click OK.

7. Test the animations in a slide show.

8. Save your presentation, then close it.

PinPoint Assessment

You have completed the project and the associated lessons, as well as the "Checking Your Skills" and "Applying Your Skills" sections. Now use the PinPoint software Evaluation mode to assess your comprehension of the specific exam tasks you have just learned. You can also use the PinPoint Trainer mode and the SHOW ME tutorials to practice these specific exam tasks.

Project 13

Thirteen

Creating Interactive Slide Shows

Adding Features that Require User Involvement

In this project you will learn the following objectives and their associated Microsoft Exam required activities.

Objectives	Required Activities
➤ Create and Run Custom Slide Shows	
➤ Create Hyperlinks	Add Links to Other Slides Within the Presentation
➤ Create Action Buttons	
➤ Edit and Remove a HyperLink	
➤ Use Hyperlinks in a Slide Show	

Why Would I Do This?

PowerPoint includes a wide variety of ways you can create interactive slide shows—those that perform an action in response to user input. Interactive slide shows are useful when you want to involve the users (such as at a trade show or your company's **intranet**) or require input from them. Additionally, you can create interactive slide shows that branch to the information your audience wants.

Custom slide show

A PowerPoint feature that enables you to create several versions of a presentation from the same set of slides.

Using PowerPoint 97, you can create *custom slide shows*—presentations that have several variations based on which slides you choose. For example, you might have the same slides to begin a presentation, but then include one set of slides for sales, another for marketing, and so on.

You can also insert *hyperlinks* in your presentation. A hyperlink is text or an object in your presentation that provides a pathway, or link, to another slide, presentation, graphic, file, or **World Wide Web** location. You can place your mouse pointer over a hyperlink to display a pointing hand icon, then click to jump to the linked information. Additionally, some hyperlinks require you only to move the mouse pointer over the linked object. Hyperlinks enable you (or other users) to access additional information and display related slides or presentations. Figure 13.1 gives an example of a slide that contains hyperlinks to other locations.

Hyperlink

An object, text, or other graphic that you can click to access another slide, presentation, graphic, or Web location.

Figure 13.1
Hyperlinks help you access supporting or additional information.

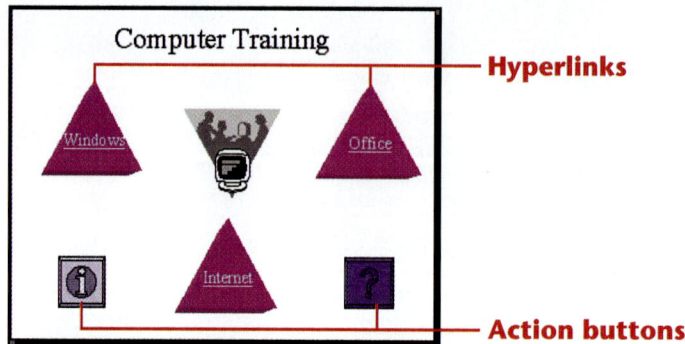

In this project, you learn how to create custom slide shows. You also learn how to create, edit, and remove hyperlinks in your document. Finally, you run an interactive slide show that contains hyperlinks.

Jargon Watch

You can publish presentations to your company's **intranet**, which is a network used within an organization. For example, you might distribute sales or production information through an interactive presentation that others in your company can access.

You can also publish presentations to the Internet. Originally designed as a way for government and university facilities to share information, the Internet has grown to become a loose association of thousands of networks worldwide. The Internet is an electronic city of sorts—through it you can access libraries, scientific, medical, or business information, and so on.

The **World Wide Web** (abbreviated WWW, or simply the Web) is the graphical, user-friendly way you can explore the Internet. To view the Web, you need a Web browser, software that helps you locate and view Web pages by clicking hyperlinks to move from one Web page to another. You can publish a presentation as a home page on the Web. A home page (sometimes called a start page) is the first screen displayed when you access a Web site. Most home pages have multiple hyperlinks so that the users can quickly jump to the information they want. Because so many people can access a home page, businesses (and individuals) can greatly increase their marketing leverage by publishing on the Web.

Lesson 1: Creating and Running Custom Slide Shows

You can use PowerPoint's custom slide show feature to create several subsets of the same presentation. Instead of developing several, almost identical presentations for different audiences, you can create a base presentation, and then jump to custom shows when appropriate.

Creating Custom Slide Shows

You might want to give similar presentations to different groups within your company. You can use the same slides to begin the show, then jump to one custom slide show for salaried employees, another for hourly workers, and so on.

You can jump to a custom slide show by choosing Go, Custom Show from the slide show's shortcut menu. Alternately, you can set up a hyperlink to the show (as you learn in Lesson 2). After you create the show, you can also edit it by adding or removing slides.

Because using this feature can be a time-saver and enable you to quickly customize a presentation, try creating custom shows now.

To Create Custom Slide Shows

1 **Open Proj1201 from the Project-12 folder on the CD and save it as** Promotional Information.

2 **Choose Slide Show, Custom Shows.**

The Custom Shows dialog box displays (see Figure 13.2). You use this dialog box to manage custom slide shows by adding, revising, or deleting shows.

Figure 13.2
You can create a variety of presentations from the same set of slides.

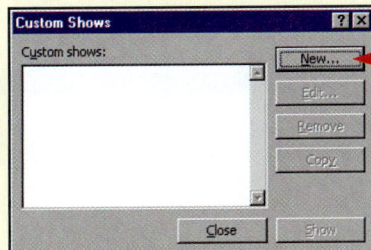

Click here to create a new custom slide show

continues

To Create Custom Slide Shows   (continued)

❸ Click the New button.

The Define Custom Show dialog box displays (see Figure 13.3). You use this dialog box to choose slides from your presentation that you want to include in your custom shows.

Figure 13.3
You can add any presentation slides to a custom show.

All presentation slides

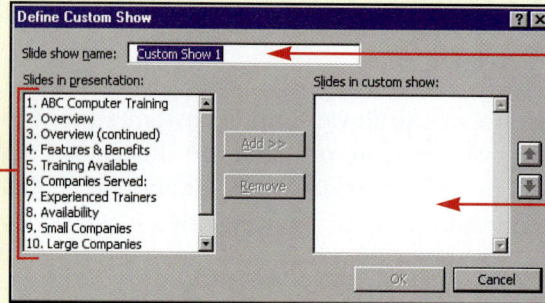

Enter the custom show's name here

Slides in the custom show

Notice that PowerPoint provides a way to name each custom show. It's useful to use descriptive names for each show. PowerPoint lets you use up to 31 characters for a custom show name.

❹ In the Slide show name text box, enter Large Co.

Now you're ready to choose slides from those in your presentation that you want for the custom show. The order they are listed on the Slides in custom show list is the order that they will display during a slide show.

PowerPoint provides a couple of ways to add slides to a custom show. You can click to select individual slides, then click the Add button to insert them in the custom show. Alternately, double-click the slides you want to add.

You can also select multiple, adjacent slides by pressing ⬆Shift while clicking the first and last slides you want. Alternately, you can click and drag the mouse over them.

In contrast, if you want to select non-adjacent slides, press Ctrl while clicking them. After you have selected the slides you want, click Add.

Try adding some slides to your custom show now.

❺ Click and drag over Slides 10–11, then click Add.

The specified slides are added to the custom slide show, and display on the Slides in custom slide show list (see Figure 13.4).

Figure 13.4
You can quickly create a custom slide show.

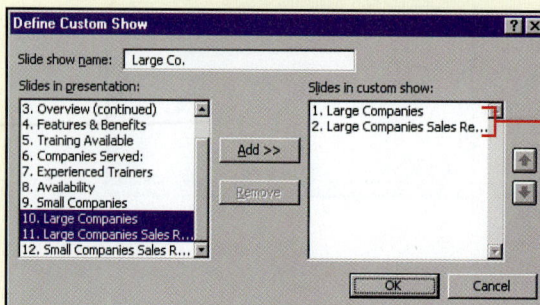

The slides you add to the custom show display here

6 **Click OK to close the Define Custom Show dialog box.**

The Custom Shows dialog box again displays. Notice that the Large Co. slide show you just created displays on the Custom shows list. Now try creating a second custom slide show—this time for Small Companies.

7 **In the Customs Shows dialog box click New, then type** Small Co. **in the Slide Show name text box.**

8 **Press** Ctrl **and then click Slide 9 and Slide 12 on the Slides in presentation list. Click Add.**

The selected slides are added to your Small Co. custom show.

9 **Click OK to close the Define Custom Show dialog box.**

The Custom Shows dialog box redisplays. Notice that both custom shows you developed display on the Custom shows list (see Figure 13.5).

Figure 13.5
You can create multiple custom shows based on the same set of slides.

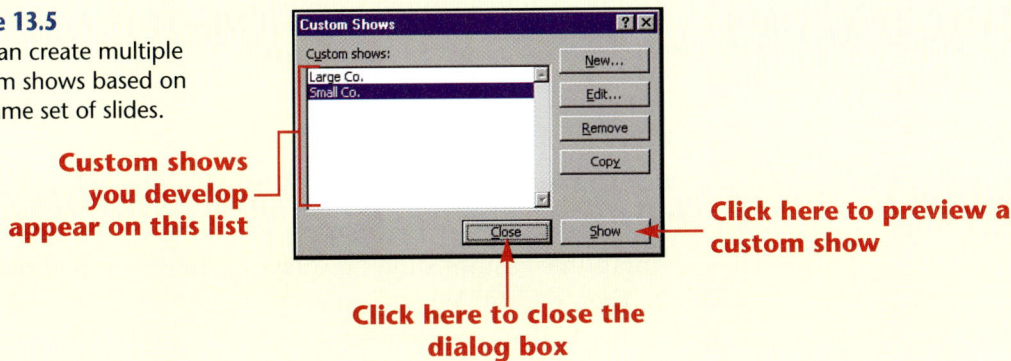

Custom shows you develop appear on this list

Click here to close the dialog box

Click here to preview a custom show

Keep the Custom Shows dialog box open for the next exercise, in which you learn two methods of running your custom shows.

Running a Custom Slide Show

After you define which slides you want in a custom show, you can run the show in two ways. First, you can click the Show button in the Custom Shows dialog box to get a preview of the show. Second, you can click the Slide Show button, then use the slide show shortcut menu to select a custom show. Try running a custom show now.

To Run a Custom Slide Show

1 **Make sure** Small Co. **is selected on the Custom shows list, then click the Show button.**

If you have problems...

If you have accidentally closed the Custom Shows dialog box, choose Slide Show, Custom Shows to reopen it.

continues

The custom slide show begins and the first slide displays full-screen. You can advance through a custom slide show by clicking the left mouse button.

2 **Click the left mouse button twice to advance completely through the custom show.**

When all the slides are shown, the Custom Shows dialog box redisplays. Now try using the second method of running a custom slide show—during a slide show. First, however, you must close the Custom Shows dialog box.

3 **In the Custom Shows dialog box, click Close.**

The presentation displays in Slide view. Now start the slide show.

4 **Make sure Slide 1 displays onscreen, then click the Slide Show button.**

The slide show begins. You can view the entire slide show in sequence, or branch to a custom show whenever you want.

5 **Click the left mouse button seven times.**

The slide entitled Availability should display on your screen. Now try showing the Small Co. custom show.

6 **Right-click the mouse on the slide show, then choose Go, Custom Show.**

The presentation's custom shows display on the Custom Show submenu (see Figure 13.6). When you select a custom show, the slide show branches to display the custom show's slides.

Figure 13.6
You can use the shortcut menu to branch to a custom show.

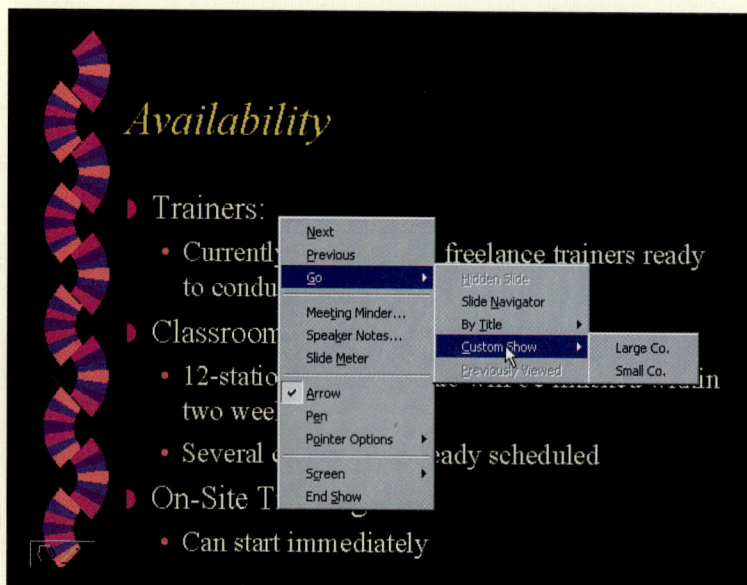

7 **Choose Small Co. from the submenu.**

The first slide for the Small Co. custom show displays.

8 Click the left mouse button twice.

PowerPoint advances through the remaining slides and redisplays the presentation in Slide view.

9 Save the Promotional Information presentation.

Keep the presentation open for the next lesson, in which you add hyperlinks.

Lesson 2: Creating Hyperlinks

One great way to make your presentations interactive is to add hyperlinks to them. Hyperlinks are text, graphics, or other objects to which you assign a mouse action. For example, you can jump to slides, presentations, files, or even a Web site when you click a hyperlink. You can also make a sound (such as a recorded message) play when you move the mouse over a hyperlink. Hyperlinks are effective when you add them to presentations at trade shows, on your company's intranet, or on a Web home page.

Creating a Hyperlink

One way to create a hyperlink is to use the <u>A</u>ction Settings command on the Sli<u>d</u>e Show menu to display the Action Settings dialog box. Using this dialog box, you can attach different actions to the same object, depending on whether you click the object or simply move the mouse pointer over it. For example, you might assign a sound to play when you move the mouse over an object, but require that users click the object to jump to another file or Web site. Hyperlinks become active when you run a slide show—not when you create them in Slide view.

Because hyperlinks enable you to create a truly interactive slide show, try adding some to your presentation now.

Inside Stuff Before you add hyperlinks, it's a good idea to save a presentation. Since you just saved the Promotional Information presentation at the end of the previous exercise, you don't need to save it again before creating a hyperlink.

To Create Hyperlinks

1 In the open Promotional Information presentation, display Slide 6 (Companies Served) in Slide view.

You must display your presentation in Slide view in order to create a hyperlink. You must also select the text (or object) to which you want to add the hyperlink.

2 Select the first bulleted point, Large Companies, then choose Sli<u>d</u>e Show, <u>A</u>ction Settings.

The Action Settings dialog box displays (see Figure 13.7). You use this dialog box to specify the object or file to which you want to create a link.

continues

To Create Hyperlinks (continued)

Figure 13.7
You set hyperlinks in
this dialog box.

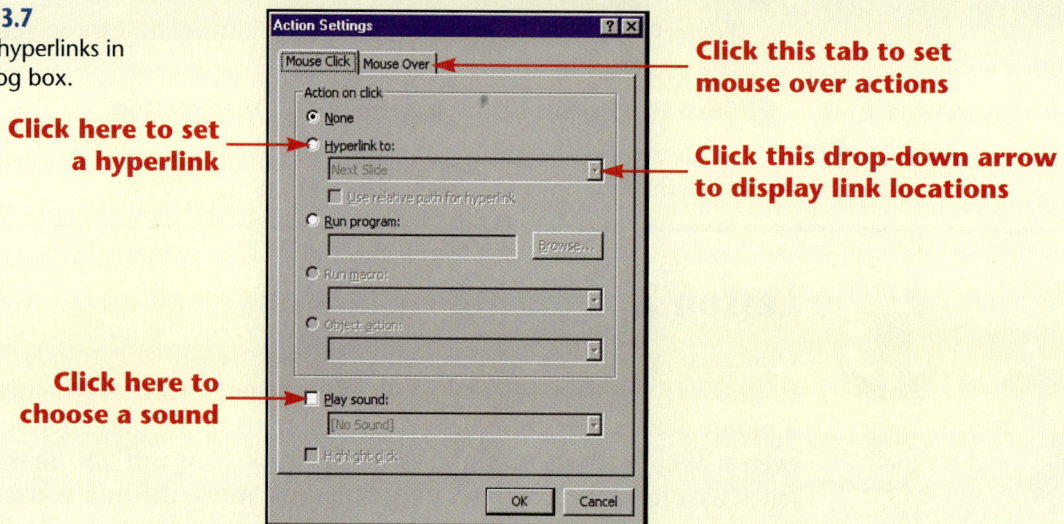

**Click here to set
a hyperlink**

**Click here to
choose a sound**

**Click this tab to set
mouse over actions**

**Click this drop-down arrow
to display link locations**

❸ **Click the Hyperlink to option button, then click its drop-down
list arrow.**

**URL (Uniform Resource
Locator)**
The address that you use to
locate a Web site.

A list of possible hyperlink sites displays (see Figure 13.8). Notice
that you can use the hyperlink to jump to other slides within the
current presentation, other files, custom shows, or even *URL* sites
(on the Web).

Figure 13.8
You can link to a variety
of locations.

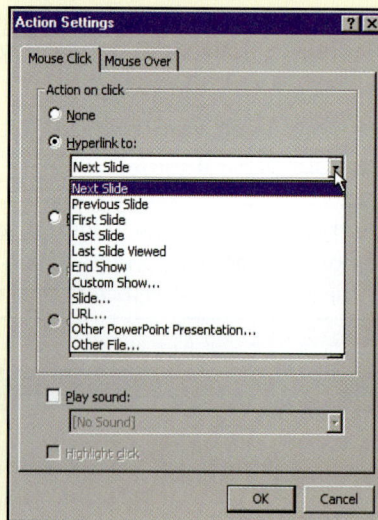

❹ **Click Custom Show.**

The Link to Custom Show dialog box displays (see Figure 13.9).
Notice that the custom shows you developed in the previous lesson
display on the Custom shows list. Additionally, you can check the
box for Show and return so that the current slide (Slide 6) is shown
when the custom show is finished.

Figure 13.9
You can link to
custom shows that you
previously created.

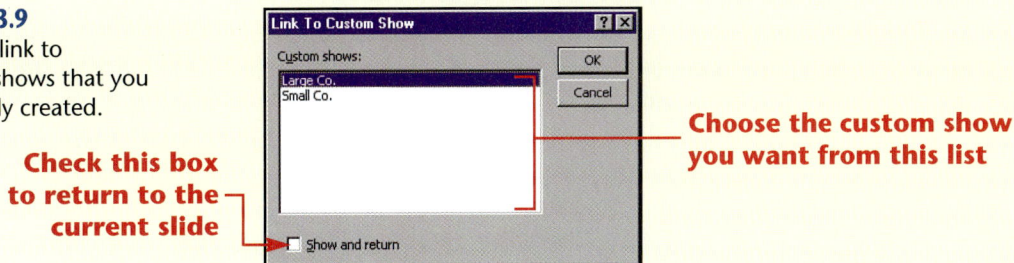

**Choose the custom show
you want from this list**

**Check this box
to return to the
current slide**

5 **Make sure** Large Co. **is selected in the Link to Custom Show
dialog box, then click OK in both the Link to Custom Show
and Action Settings dialog boxes.**

A hyperlink is created for the text, Large Companies, on Slide 6.
Notice that PowerPoint displays the hyperlink in a color that coordi-
nates with the presentation's color scheme. (You can click outside the
selected text to see the hyperlink's color if you want.) Remember,
however, the link is active in Slide Show view only—not in Slide view.

Now try setting a hyperlink to another presentation. Before you proceed with the next step, make sure your instructor has copied
Proj1302 (the file to which you are creating a link) from the Project-
12 folder on the CD to the same folder as your other student files.

6 **On Slide 4, Features & Benefits, select the words** Cost Effective
**within the first bulleted point, then choose Sli̲de Show,
A̲ction Settings.**

The Action Settings dialog box displays.

7 **Click the H̲yperlink to option button, then select Other File
from the H̲yperlink to drop-down list.**

The Hyperlink to Other File dialog box displays (see Figure 13.10).
You can select a file from this dialog box to link to your presenta-
tion. You can also browse your hard or network drives (or even the
Web) to locate the file you want.

Figure 13.10
You can link to other
files or presentations.

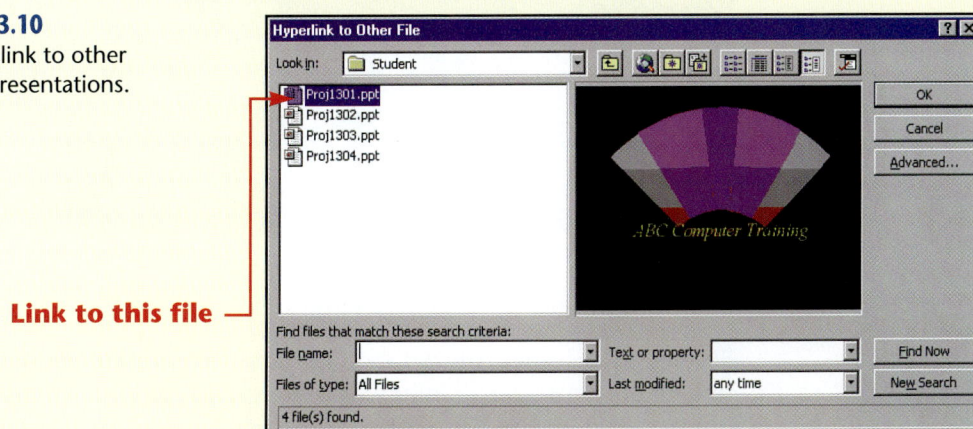

Link to this file

8 **Double-click Proj1302 to select it, then click OK in the Action
Settings dialog box.**

Now that you have set hyperlinks in your presentation, try using
them during a running slide show.

Using a Hyperlink in a Slide Show

As you are presenting the slide show, you can click any hyperlink you prepared when you need to jump to another slide, another presentation, or to
a custom slide show. Hyperlinks may not be obvious to the audience, so
you would have to use them only as needed in particular circumstances and
ignore them otherwise.

To Use a Hyperlink in a Slide Show

1 **With Slide 4 of the Promotional Information presentation still
displayed, click the Slide Show button.**

The slide show begins, starting with the current slide. Notice the
words to which you added a hyperlink (Cost Effective) display in a
different color. Now try using the hyperlink.

2 **Move the mouse pointer over the text, Cost Effective.**

A pointing hand icon displays (see Figure 13.11). PowerPoint
indicates a hyperlink by this special pointer. Whenever you see a
pointing hand icon, you can click the object to jump to the linked
location. In addition, PowerPoint displays the link location with a
ScreenTip.

Figure 13.11
You can identify
hyperlinks by the
special hand pointer.

Pointing hand icon —

ScreenTip —

Features & Benefits

▶ Cost Effective: $1 spent on training yields
returns of C:\My Documents\PPII97 Essentials\Project 6\Student\Proj0602.ppt y
▶ Less Employee Frustration
▶ Smoother Migration to New Software
▶ Improved Productivity

3 **Click the mouse on the hyperlink.**

Because this hyperlink is linked to another presentation file, the
linked presentation displays (see Figure 13.12). In this case, the
linked file contains supporting information for data in the main
presentation. When you're finished viewing the linked file, you can
return to your original presentation by pressing Esc.

Figure 13.12
You can jump to
another presentation to
display supporting data.

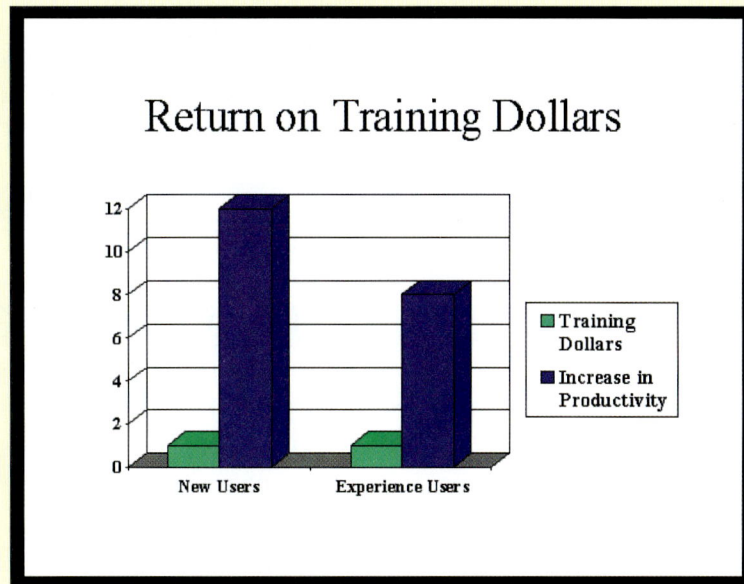

4 **Press** Esc **to return to the Promotional Presentation.**

Now try using the hyperlink on Slide 6 to jump to a custom slide show. By using hyperlinks to jump to a custom slide show, you create a smoother transition than when you use the slide show's shortcut menu.

5 **Press** ↵Enter **twice to display Slide 6,** Companies Served, **then click the hyperlinked text (**Large Companies**).**

The presentation jumps to the Large Co. custom slide show.

6 **Press** Esc **to end the slide show, then save the presentation.**

Keep the presentation open for the next lesson, in which you create hyperlinks with action buttons.

Inside Stuff

You can also add links to the World Wide Web. Select the text or object, then choose Slide Show, Action Settings. On the Hyperlink to drop-down list choose URL. Then type the Internet location in the Hyperlink to URL text box.

Alternately, select the text or object, then click the Insert Hyperlink button. Enter the Internet address (such as http://www.home.msn.com/) in the Link to file or URL text box and then choose OK.

Lesson 3: Creating Action Buttons

In the preceding lesson, you learned how to hyperlink text to custom slide shows or another file. However, you can also create action buttons, then link them to files, locations, or Web sites. Action buttons are used in much the same way as text hyperlinks, but because they are graphical, many people consider them easier to use.

You can add an action button from the AutoShapes menu on the Drawing toolbar, or by choosing Slide Show, Action Buttons from the menu. In either case, you can use action buttons to create links in much the same way as you learned in Lesson 2. For example, when you draw an action button, the Action Settings dialog box automatically displays so that you can view (and change) the default settings.

Try adding some action buttons to the Promotional Information presentation now.

To Create Action Buttons

1 **In the open presentation, display Slide 1 in Slide view, then choose Slide Show, Action Buttons.**

The Action Buttons submenu displays. Additionally, when you rest your mouse pointer over any button, a ScreenTip identifying the button appears (see Figure 13.13).

You can choose from a variety of action buttons. Most of the buttons contain default settings and are already linked to a particular action. For example, the second button in the second row contains a hyperlink to the next slide. You can use the preset action buttons, or choose the Custom button to designate your own hyperlink settings.

Figure 13.13
Choose an action button from this submenu.

Action Buttons submenu

ScreenTip

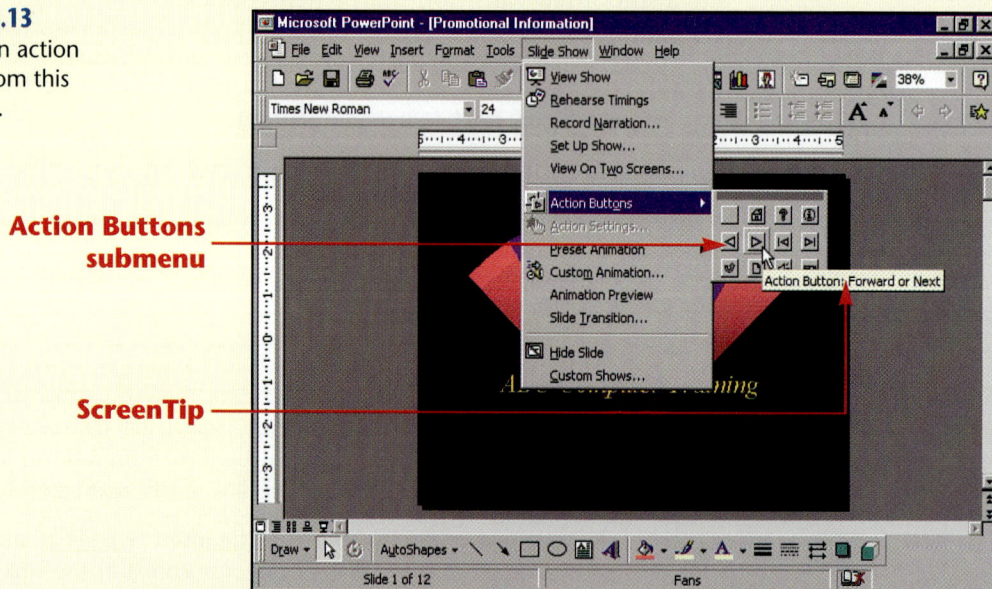

2 **Click the Action Button: Forward or Next (the second button from the left on the second row) from the submenu.**

The mouse pointer changes to a crosshair so that you can accurately place the button. You can drag to draw the size of button that you want. However, you can also just click the location for the button and PowerPoint automatically creates a button using the default size. When you click the mouse, PowerPoint not only creates the button, but also displays the Action Settings dialog box. Try creating the button now.

3 **Move the mouse pointer to the lower-right corner of the slide, then click once.**

PowerPoint automatically creates an action button and displays the Action Settings dialog box. Notice that this dialog box already contains hyperlink settings to the next slide (see Figure 13.14).

Figure 13.14
When you create an action button, the hyperlink location is already set.

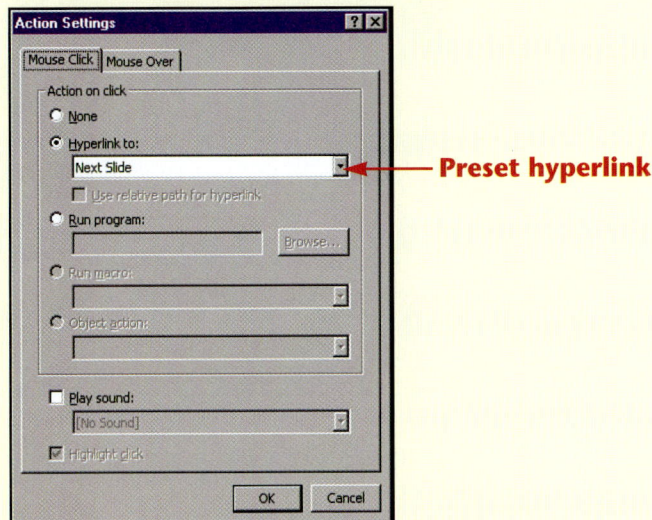

— **Preset hyperlink**

If you have problems...

Make sure you don't accidentally move (and drag) the mouse when you create your action button or you will create a small, hard-to-see button.

Even though PowerPoint automatically assigns a hyperlink location, you can change it (or other settings) if you want. For now, however, you can accept the predetermined settings that PowerPoint assigned to the button.

4 **Click OK in the Action Settings dialog box.**

The Action Settings dialog box closes, and the button you added displays on your slide (see Figure 13.15). Notice that the button has square selection handles so that you can move (or resize) the button—just like any other object. Additionally, the action button includes a yellow diamond adjustment handle so that you can modify its shape if you want (you learned about AutoShapes in Project 11).

continues

To Create Action Buttons   (continued)

Figure 13.15
Action buttons display
on your slide as objects.

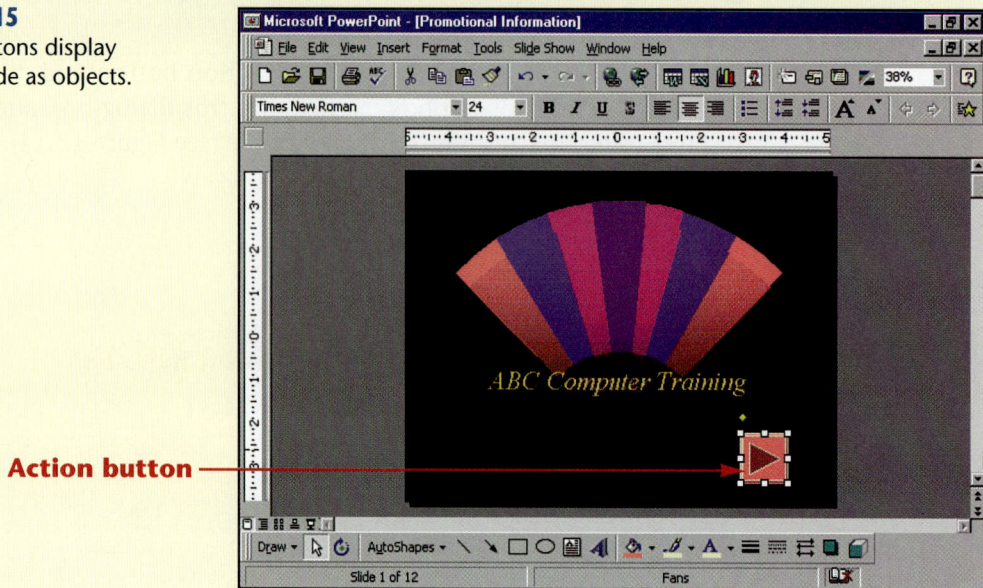

Action button

Now try adding a custom action button for which you specify the link location.

⑤ Display Slide 6, Companies Served, **then choose Sli̲de Show, Action Butto̲ns.**

⑥ Click Action Button: Custom (the first button on the first row), then drag to draw a button 6" wide by 2" deep in the bottom center of the slide and release the mouse button.

The action button is created and the Action Settings dialog box displays. Because the button is a Custom button, you must specify the hyperlink settings rather than rely on PowerPoint's default settings.

⑦ Click the H̲yperlink to option button, then click the drop-down arrow and choose Custom Show.

The Link to Custom Show dialog box displays.

⑧ Select Small Co. **in the Link to Custom Show dialog box, check the S̲how and return box, then choose OK.**

⑨ Click OK in the Actions Settings dialog box.

The button you created displays on your slide. You can add text to the button so users understand what action it performs.

⑩ Click the Text Box tool on the Drawing toolbar, then click in the custom button.

The insertion point appears in the button so that you can add text.

⑪ Type Click here for information on Small Bus.

Text is added to the button (see Figure 13.16).

Figure 13.16
Document action
buttons with text.

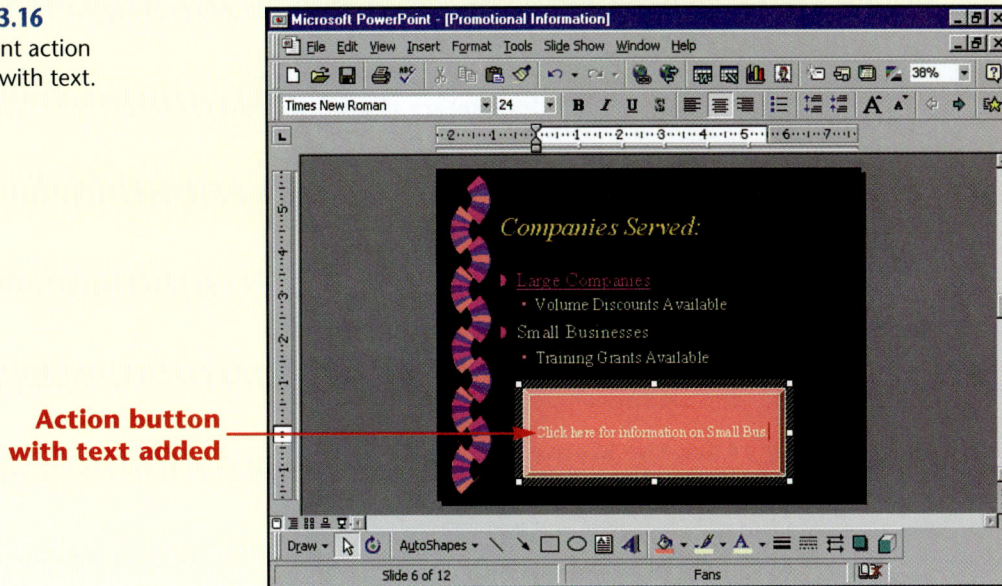

Action button
with text added

⑫ **Save the Promotional Information presentation.**

Keep the presentation open for the next lesson, in which you edit
and remove hyperlinks.

Inside Stuff

Action buttons are technically AutoShapes. Because of this, you can change their
colors, lines, and otherwise format them. To do this, double-click an action button
in Slide view to display the Format AutoShape dialog box. Choose the formatting
settings you want and click OK.

Lesson 4: Editing and Removing a Hyperlink

You can modify any hyperlink you want. For example, you might want to
add sound, a mouse over action, or change the object to which it is linked.
To change a hyperlink's settings, you can select it, then choose Slide Show,
Action Settings to display the Action Settings dialog box. You can then
make the modifications you want, using commands and options with
which you are now familiar.

You can also remove a hyperlink. Select the hyperlinked text or object, then
choose the None option button in the Action Settings dialog box.

Try editing and removing a hyperlink now.

To Edit and Remove a Hyperlink

❶ Make sure Slide 1 is displayed in the Promotional Information presentation, then select the action button object.

Because this object has a hyperlink associated with it, selecting the object selects the hyperlink as well. Likewise, when you select text that has a hyperlink, you select the hyperlink as well.

❷ Choose Slide Show, Action Settings.

The Action Settings dialog box displays, and shows the settings for the selected hyperlink. You can revise the hyperlink by changing the settings.

❸ Click the Mouse Over tab.

The Mouse Over page displays (see Figure 13.17). You can set options on this page so that an action occurs whenever the mouse pointer moves over the hyperlink.

Figure 13.17
You can set actions to occur when the mouse moves over a hyperlink.

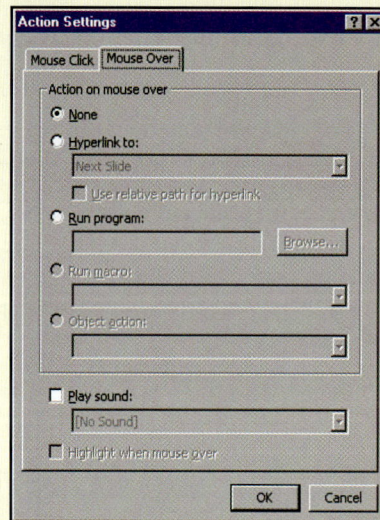

❹ On the Mouse Over page, check the Play sound box.

The Play sound command becomes active.

❺ Click the Play sound drop-down list arrow, then choose Drum Roll and click OK. (If this sound file is not available on your system, choose another.)

The action settings are modified. When you run a slide show, a drum roll will sound when the mouse pointer moves over the hyperlink.

Now try deleting a hyperlink that you added earlier in this project.

❻ On Slide 6, select the `Large Companies` hyperlink text, then choose Slide Show, Action Settings.

The Action Settings dialog box displays with the settings for the selected hyperlink.

7 **Click the Mouse Click tab, then choose the <u>N</u>one option button and click OK.**

This removes the hyperlink from the text.

8 **Save the Promotional Information presentation.**

Keep the presentation open for the next lesson, in which you run the slide show and use the hyperlinks.

Inside Stuff

If you have the proper equipment, you can record and save a message as a sound file, then associate it with a hyperlink.

Lesson 5: Using Hyperlinks in a Slide Show

After you add hyperlinks to text and objects, you can use them in a slide show. When you run the slide show, you have the option of clicking the hyperlinks or not. For example, you may create a hyperlink to a file or Web site that supports your position. Depending on the audience, however, you can opt whether or not to use it.

Try using the hyperlinks you created in your presentation now.

To Use Hyperlinks in a Slide Show

1 **In the open presentation, press Ctrl+Home to display Slide 1, then click the Slide Show button.**

The slide show displays, starting on Slide 1. Notice that this slide contains an action button. You previously added both Mouse Click and Mouse Over actions to this button.

2 **Move the mouse pointer over the object.**

Assuming you have the computer's speakers turned on, the drum roll sound clip plays. Now try clicking the button to perform the associated action.

3 **Click the action button.**

The slide show advances to the next slide according to the settings you specified earlier in this project.

4 **Press ←Enter twice to advance to the Features and Benefits slide, then click the Cost Effective hyperlink.**

Because this hyperlink is associated with another file, clicking it opens the file. This type of hyperlink is handy when you need to quickly access supporting information during a talk.

continues

5 Right-click, then choose G̲o, P̲reviously Viewed from the shortcut menu that displays.

The Features & Benefits slide redisplays.

6 Press ⏎Enter twice.

The Companies Served slide displays. This slide has an action button with a hyperlink to a custom show. Clicking the button launches the slides in the custom show.

You can associate action buttons with custom shows.

7 Click the action button.

The Small Co. custom show begins.

8 Press ⏎Enter twice to advance through the custom show.

The Companies Served slide reappears after you view the custom show.

9 Press Esc to end the slide show.

10 Save the Promotional Information presentation, then close it.

If you have finished your work session, exit PowerPoint and shut down Windows 95 before turning off your computer. Otherwise, complete the "Checking Your Skills" and "Applying Your Skills" exercises at the end of this project.

Project Summary

To	Use
Create a custom show	Choose Sli̲de Show, C̲ustom Shows.
Preview a custom show	Select the custom show you want in the Custom Shows dialog box, then click S̲how.
Branch to a custom show	Right-click during a slide show, then choose G̲o, C̲ustom Show.
Create a hyperlink	Select the text or object, then choose Sli̲de Show, Action Settings and select the link location from the H̲yperlink to drop-down list.
Create an action button	Choose Sli̲de Show, Action Butto̲ns, then click on the slide where you want the button.
Add text to an action button	Click the Text Box tool, then click in the action button and type the text.
Edit a hyperlink	Select the hyperlink text or object, then choose Sli̲de Show, A̲ction Settings and modify the settings.

PowerPoint

To	Use
Remove a hyperlink	Select the hyperlink text or object, then choose Slide Show, Action Settings, and choose None.
Use a hyperlink	Depending on settings, move your mouse pointer over or click the hyperlink during a slide show.

Checking Your Skills

True/False

For each of the following, check *T* or *F* to indicate whether the statement is true or false.

__T __F **1.** You can create hyperlinks only by using action buttons.

__T __F **2.** A Web home page typically contains a number of hyperlinks to other locations.

__T __F **3.** A custom slide show must contain hyperlinks.

__T __F **4.** You cannot modify hyperlinks after you create them.

__T __F **5.** Internet and intranet are just two terms for the same thing.

__T __F **6.** You can link to another presentation.

__T __F **7.** The type of software used to view Web pages is called Viewer Software.

__T __F **8.** You can link within a presentation, but can't link to another file.

__T __F **9.** Action buttons are technically AutoShapes.

__T __F **10.** You can't remove hyperlinks from a presentation.

Multiple Choice

Circle the letter of the correct answer for each of the following questions.

1. You can create a hyperlink to which of the following?

    a. a custom show

    b. another slide in the same presentation

    c. another file

    d. all of the above

2. When you develop a custom slide show _____.

    a. you must create a hyperlink in order to launch it

    b. it cannot be revised

    c. you can display it by choosing Go, Custom Show from the Slide Show shortcut menu

    d. none of the above

3. You can make a presentation interactive by doing which of the following?

    a. adding action buttons

    b. creating hyperlinks to text

c. developing custom shows

d. all of the above

4. Which of the following is a good use of an interactive slide show?

    a. an onscreen presentation at a trade show

    b. printing a presentation to hand out to your audience

    c. printing a presentation as overhead transparencies

    d. all of the above

5. A worldwide association of hundreds of computer networks used to distribute information is called the _____.

    a. home page

    b. intranet

    c. Internet

    d. hyperlink

6. To view the Web, you need which of the following?

    a. a sound card

    b. a CD-ROM disk drive

    c. browser software

    d. all of the above

7. In which dialog box do you set up hyperlinks to other presentation slides?

    a. Action Buttons

    b. Hyperlinks

c. Set Up Show

d. Action Settings

8. If you don't have a hyperlink set up to your custom show, how can you access it during a slide show?

    a. Right-click in the show, then choose Go, Custom Show.

    b. Click the Go To button.

    c. Choose Slide Show, Go To Custom Show from the menu.

    d. Press Ctrl+C.

9. Which of the following are slides to which you can create a hyperlink?

    a. a specific slide number in the presentation

    b. the first presentation slide

    c. the last slide viewed

    d. all of the above

10. URL refers to

    a. Universal Resource Links

    b. Uniformed Reliable Links

    c. Uniform Resource Locator

    d. None of the above

Completion

In the blank provided, write the correct answer for each of the following statements.

1. You can use a(n) _____ to create several versions of a presentation from the same set of slides.

2. A(n) _____ is an object, text, or other graphic that you can click to access another slide, presentation, graphic or Web location.

3. A network used within an organization is called a(n) _____.

4. The _____ is a user-friendly, graphical way to explore the Internet by using hyperlinks.

5. _____ is software designed to help you browse and view the Web.

6. A(n) _____ is address you use to locate a Web site.

7. The loose association of thousands of networks worldwide is called the _____.

8. The first screen that displays when you access a Web site is called the _____.

9. To add a hyperlink to selected text, choose _____ from the menu.

10. When the mouse pointer rests over a hyperlink in Slide Show view, it changes to a(n) _____.

Matching

In the blank next to each of the following terms or phrases, write the letter of the corresponding term or phrase. (Note that some of the letters may be used more than once.)

a. custom show

b. URL

c. WWW

d. hyperlink

e. home page

f. Action Settings

g. intranet

h. Internet

i. browser

j. action button

_____ 1. Start page of a Web site

_____ 2. World Wide Web

_____ 3. Type of software needed to use the Web

_____ 4. Text, graphic or other object to which you assign a mouse action

_____ 5. Branches to a presentation within a larger presentation

_____ 6. A button to which you can assign a mouse action

_____ 7. Dialog box used to set up hyperlinks

_____ 8. Uniform Resource Locator

_____ 9. First began as a way for government to share information

_____ 10. The network used within a company

Applying Your Skills

Practice

The following exercises, found in the Project-13 folder on the CD, enable you to practice the skills you have learned in this project. Take a few minutes to work through these exercises now.

Creating Hyperlinks

You are developing a presentation for your sales force that you plan to distribute over your company's intranet. To help your sales team quickly access the information they need, you develop a presentation with hyperlinks to data about your product lines.

To create hyperlinks, complete the following steps:

1. Open Proj1303 from the Project-13 folder on the CD and save it as Product Information.

2. Click the Workstations object, then choose Slide Show, Action Settings.

3. Click the Hyperlink to option button, then click its drop-down list arrow and choose Slide.

4. In the Hyperlink to Slide dialog box, choose Slide 4, Workstations.

5. Click OK in both the Hyperlink to Slide and Action Settings dialog boxes.

6. Repeat steps 2–5 for the Keyboards, Monitors, and Chairs objects. Create a hyperlink for each to the appropriate slide in the presentation.

7. Save the Product Information presentation and keep it open for the next exercise.

Creating Action Buttons

You want your sales team to be able to return to the first slide in your presentation (the start page) after they have jumped to another slide. To enable them to do this, you create an action button on each of Slides 2–5.

To create action buttons, complete the following steps:

1. In the open Product Information presentation, display Slide 2, Monitors.

2. Choose Slide Show, Action Buttons to display the submenu.

3. Choose the Action Button: Home (the second button on the first row), then click in the lower-right corner of the slide.

4. Look over the settings in the Action Settings dialog box, then click OK to accept them.

5. Repeat steps 2–4 for each of Slides 3–5.

6. Save the presentation and keep it open for the next exercise.

Creating a Hyperlink to Another File

To help your sales team quickly access ordering information, you create a link from the Product Information presentation to another file.

To create hyperlinks, complete the following steps:

1. In the open Product Information presentation, display Slide 1.

2. Select the text, Ordering Information, then choose Sli<u>d</u>e Show, <u>A</u>ction Settings.

3. Choose the Hyperlink to option button.

4. Click the Hyperlink to drop-down list arrow, then choose Other File.

5. In the Hyperlink to Other File dialog box, choose Proj1304 and click OK.

6. Click OK in the Action Settings dialog box.

7. Save your Product Information presentation and keep it open for the next exercise.

Using Hyperlinks in a Slide Show

Before you place your presentation on your company's intranet, you decide to test it out by running it as a slide show. For this exercise, locate the Proj1304 file in the Project-13 folder on the CD.

To use hyperlinks in a slide show, complete the following steps:

1. Display Slide 1 in the open Product Information presentation, then click the Slide Show button.

2. Click the Ordering Information object to jump to the Proj1304 (linked) file. In Proj1304, right-click the mouse to display the Slide Show shortcut menu. On the shortcut menu choose <u>G</u>o, <u>P</u>reviously Viewed.

3. Click the Monitors hyperlink to jump to the Monitors slide. Click the action button to return to Slide 1.

4. Click each of the other hyperlinks on Slide 1. Use each slide's action button to return to the first slide.

5. Press Esc to end the slide show.

6. Save the Product Information presentation, then close it.

Creating Links to Other Slides in the Presentation

You are presenting a talk on your company's finances. So that you can quickly display slides in your presentation, you create hyperlinks to them.

To creat links to other slides in the presentation, complete the following steps:

1. Open Proj1305 from the Project-13 folder on the CD and save it as Bell Manufacturing.

2. Display Slide 2 in the open presentation, then select the text for the first bulleted point (Revenue).

3. Display the Action Settings dialog box, then create a hyperlink to the Revenue slide (Slide 4). Close the Action Settings dialog box.

4. Repeat the procedure outlined in Steps 2 and 3 for the other bulleted items on Slide 2.

5. Test the hyperlinks by displaying the presentation as a slide show. Use the <u>G</u>o, <u>P</u>reviously Viewed command on the Slide Show shortcut menu to redisplay Slide 2 after viewing each slide.

6. Save the Bell Manufacturing presentation, then close it.

Challenge

The following challenges, found in the Project-13 folder on the CD, enable you to use your problem-solving skills. Take time to work through these exercises now.

Adding Links to Other Slides in the Presentation

You are conducting new employee orientation for your company. So that you can quickly display whichever slide you need, you add action buttons to your New Employee presentation.

To add links to other slides in the presentation , complete the following steps:

1. Open Proj1306 from the Project-13 folder on the CD and save it as Company Orientation.

2. Display Slide 2 in Slide view. Create a hyperlink for each of the topics listed that has an associated slide (such as, link the History of Company text to the History of Company slide in the presentation).

3. Test your links by displaying your presentation as a slide show. Use the <u>G</u>o, <u>P</u>reviously Viewed command on the Slide Show shortcut menu to redisplay Slide 2 after viewing each slide.

4. Save the Company Orientation presentation. Keep it open for the next exercise.

Adding Action Buttons to Link to Slides

To further refine the Company Orientation presentation, you add action buttons so you can redisplay the Agenda slide.

To add action buttons to link to slides, complete the following steps:

1. In the Company Orientation presentation open from the preceding exercise, display Slide 3, History of Company.

2. Create an action button in the lower right corner that you can use to display Slide 2, Agenda. Start by choosing Sli<u>d</u>e Show, <u>A</u>ction Buttons, Custom.

3. In the Action Settings dialog box, click the Hyperlink to option button and drop-down list arrow.

4. Choose Slide to display the Hyperlink to Slide dialog box. Select Slide 2, Agenda/Topics to be Covered, then click OK in all open dialog boxes.

5. Create custom action buttons in the lower-right corner of each of Slides 4–8 using the same procedure. Set up the action buttons so you can click them to redisplay Slide 2, Agenda.

6. Test your action buttons by running your presentation as a slide show. Make sure the hyperlinks from Slide 2, Agenda, to other slides (and back to Slide 2) work.

7. Save your presentation. Keep it open for the next exercise.

Adding Text to Your Action Buttons

After looking over your Company Orientation presentation, you decide that the action buttons should be labeled. To do this, you add text to each button.

To add text to your action buttons, complete the following steps:

1. In the Company Orientation presentation open from the previous exercise, display Slide 3, History of Company.

2. Click the action button to select it, then type Click here to see, then press ↵Enter. Finish typing your entry by typing Agenda slide.

3. Resize the action button so that the text fits in it.

4. Repeat steps 2 and 3 for the other action buttons in your presentation.

5. Test your action buttons by running your presentation as a slide show.

6. Save your Company Orientation presentation, then close it.

Adding Hyperlinks to a Presentation

As a member of the Information Technology Department at your plant, you're in charge of upgrading 500 users to Windows 98. To report to plant management about the progress your department has made, you develop a presentation, complete with hyperlinks.

To add hyperlinks to a presentation, complete the following steps:

1. Open Proj1307 from the Project-13 folder on the CD and save it as Project Report.

2. On Slide 2, Agenda, create hyperlinks from each of the bulleted points to the appropriate slide in the presentation.

3. Test each of the hyperlinks by running the presentation as a slide show. Use the Go, Previously Viewed command on the Slide Show shortcut menu to redisplay Slide 2 after viewing each slide.

4. Save the Project Report presentation. Keep it open for the next exercise.

Adding Action Buttons that Link to Other Presentation Slides

You decide that it's too awkward to use the Slide Show shortcut menu to redisplay Slide 2, Agenda. To make moving within the presentation more seamless, you add action buttons to your slides.

To add action buttons that link to other presentation slides, complete the following steps:

1. In the Project Report presentation open from the previous exercise display Slide 3, Status Summary.

2. Create a custom action button in the lower-right corner of the slide that links to Slide 2, Agenda.

3. Type Click here to return to the Agenda slide on the action button. Resize (and move) the action button as necessary to accommodate the text.

4. Repeat the procedure outlined in steps 2–3 to add an action button to each of Slides 4–9.

5. Test your action buttons and hyperlinked text by running the presentation as a slide show.

6. Save the Project Report presentation, then close it.

PinPoint Assessment

You have completed the project and the associated lessons, as well as the "Checking Your Skills" and "Applying Your Skills" sections. Now use the PinPoint software Evaluation mode to assess your comprehension of the specific exam tasks you have just learned. You can also use the PinPoint Trainer mode and the SHOW ME tutorials to practice these specific exam tasks.

PowerPoint

Project 14

Fourteen

Preparing Your Presentation for the World Wide Web

Using PowerPoint to Create Web Pages

In this project you will learn the following objectives and their associated Microsoft Exam required activities.

Objectives   ## Required Activities

➤ Install Web Authoring Tools

➤ Create a Web Home Page

➤ Save a Presentation as Web Pages   … … … … … … Save for Internet

World Wide Web

The graphical component of the Internet; a collection of documents accessible through the Internet that you view using Web browser software and navigate by clicking hyperlinks.

Internet

An international system of over 100,000 networks, linking every kind of information.

Intranet

A network used within an organization.

Figure 14.1

A Web page provides access to additional information with hyperlinks.

Why Would I Do This?

PowerPoint provides many choices for presenting the materials you produce with it—35mm slides, overhead transparencies, printed handouts, and slide shows onscreen. However, one of the most exciting mediums you can use to share your presentations is as a document on the *World Wide Web*.

PowerPoint 97 has built-in Web support so that anyone who uses the Web can view your presentations. As a result, publishing your presentation as a Web page enables you to share it with an extremely large audience—virtually any person connected to the *Internet* (or even a company *intranet*) who has a *Web browser*. Because of the almost unlimited audience that the Internet provides, most businesses (and many individuals as well) now have their own home page on the Web. Figure 14.1 shows a typical Web *home page*, with hyperlinks to related information.

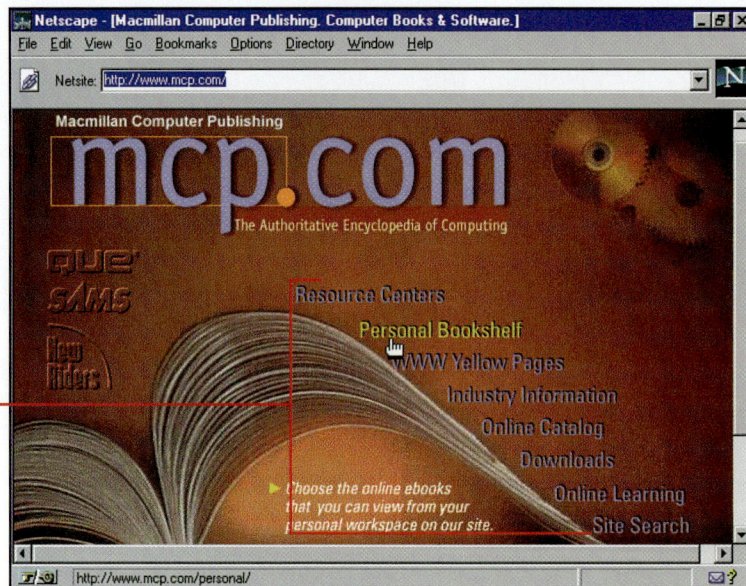

Hyperlinks

Web browser

Software designed to help you find and display Web pages.

Home page

A document on the World Wide Web dedicated to a certain subject, or product or company information. A home page typically contains a number of hyperlinks to related information.

Web authoring tools

Programs or utilities designed to help you ready documents for the Web.

The first step in publishing to the Web is to make sure that the proper *Web authoring tools* are installed on your system. Two such tools, Save As HTML Wizard and the Web Publishing Wizard, are extremely useful if you plan to publish to the Web. However, they are not included in the default PowerPoint installation and must be added if you plan to use them.

After you make sure all the Web tools you need are properly installed, you can create the presentation you want to use as your home page. You can use three methods to produce a Web presentation. First, you can rely on the AutoContent Wizard to create a home page. Second, you can use PowerPoint's online presentation templates. Finally, you can create the presentation totally from scratch, adding hyperlinks as you learned to do in Project 13, "Creating Interactive Slide Shows." Probably the most flexible approach, however, is to use a presentation template or the AutoContent's home page as a basis for the presentation, and then create additional hyperlinks where necessary.

Wizard

An interactive utility program that guides you through each step of a multi-step process by giving helpful hints and context-sensitive help.

HTML (Hypertext Markup Language)

The code used by Web browsers to display Web pages.

FTP (File Transfer Protocol) program

A utility program that transfers presentations over the Internet to a Web server.

Web site

A computer connected to the Internet and set up so that users can access its information.

HTTP (Hypertext Transport Protocol)

The Internet standard that supports the exchange of information on the Web through use of hyperlinks.

After you create the presentation, you must save it with a format that Web browsers can use—HTML, which stands for *Hypertext Markup Language*. HTML controls the display of graphics, formatting, and hyperlinks that are the hallmarks of the World Wide Web.

The final step in publishing to the Web is to copy the presentation to a Web server. In order to copy the presentation from your hard drive to the Web server, you need to know the server's location and how to access it. Additionally, you are usually required to have a User ID and password before you can post files to a server. You usually rely on the administrator of the Web server to handle this or help you with it.

Assuming you have access to a Web server, you can use an *FTP program* to transfer your files. While you can use this type of program to copy your files, the process is made considerably easier by using an add-on feature— the Web Publishing Wizard. You can use the Web Publishing Wizard to quickly convert your presentation into a series of linked Web pages and then post it on the Web server.

In this project, you learn how to install Web authoring tools, such as the Save As HTML and Web Publishing Wizards. You also prepare a presentation to use on the Internet or your company's intranet. Finally, you work with the Web Publishing Wizard. Because publishing a presentation to the Web has such widespread applications, try working with PowerPoint's Web features now.

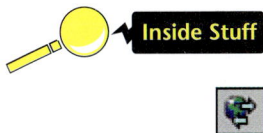

Inside Stuff

PowerPoint provides a wealth of built-in Web features. For example, you can display PowerPoint's Web toolbar by clicking the Web Toolbar button on the Standard toolbar, then use it to browse presentations on your intranet or Internet from within PowerPoint.

PowerPoint also includes direct Web support to features such as PowerPoint Central, which provides information on PowerPoint features. Additionally, you can connect to the Web and download clip art, photographs, video clips, and sound files from PowerPoint Central. To use PowerPoint Central, choose Tools, PowerPoint Central from PowerPoint's menu bar.

You can also use a free Internet browser—PowerPoint Animation Player to create or view animated PowerPoint Web pages. Your Web audience can also download it from Microsoft's *Web site* and use it to view animated PowerPoint presentations. This may be necessary if you want others to view or animate presentations because most animation features don't survive the transfer to Web format. The Web address for the PowerPoint Animation Player is http://www.microsoft.com/powerpoint/internet/player.

Microsoft also maintains a home page for PowerPoint, where you can find tips on using the product as well as information about add-ons and technical support. The address for PowerPoint's home page is http://www.microsoft.com/powerpoint/default.asp.

Lesson 1: Installing Web Authoring Tools

To properly publish a presentation to the Web, you need to save it in HTML format and post it to a Web server. Two add-on features, the Save As HTML Wizard and the Web Publishing Wizard, help you perform these tasks. Collectively, these add-on features (and others like them) are referred to as Web authoring tools because they help you prepare documents for the Web.

If you selected the default PowerPoint installation, these add-ons are not loaded on your system. Before you create a Web presentation, you should first install these features.

Ask your instructor if the Web authoring tools are already installed on your system. If they are, just read through Lesson 1. If not, try installing them now.

To Install the Web Authoring Tools

1 Make sure all programs on your computer are closed, then click Start on the Windows 95 taskbar and choose Settings, Control Panel.

The Control Panel window displays (see Figure 14.2). Windows 95 provides the Add/Remove Programs feature so that you can add software components that may not have been installed originally. You use this Windows 95 feature to install the Save As HTML Wizard.

Figure 14.2
Windows 95 provides a way to add program components.

Double-click this icon to add or remove program components

2 Double-click the Add/Remove Programs icon.

The Add/Remove Programs Properties window displays (see Figure 14.3). Make sure you have the CD for Office 97 inserted in your CD-ROM drive (usually the D: drive), then proceed with the next step.

PowerPoint

Figure 14.3
You can change the way a program is set up.

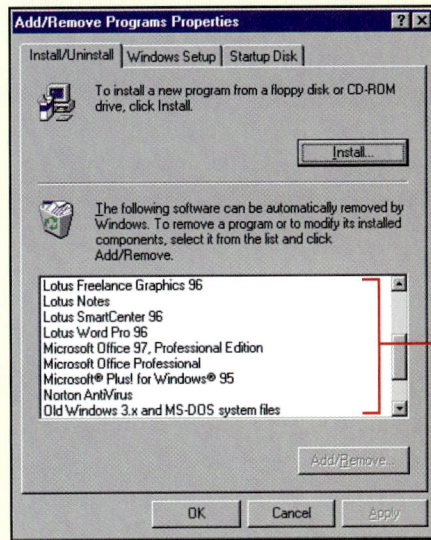

Choose a program to add or remove from this list

❸ On the listing of programs, click Microsoft Office 97, then click Add/Remove.

Windows displays a Setup message box telling you that you must insert the Microsoft Office 97 CD in your CD-ROM Drive.

❹ Click OK to close the message box.

Microsoft Setup loads into memory, and checks for which software components are already installed on your system. When it finishes, the Microsoft Office 97 Setup dialog box displays.

❺ Click Add/Remove.

The Microsoft Office 97-Maintenance dialog box displays (see Figure 14.4). You use this dialog box to specify which elements you want to install on your system. Unchecked boxes indicate that no components are installed for a program or add-on, while black check marks show that all the features have been installed. In contrast, gray check marks indicate that only some of the available features are installed.

Figure 14.4
You can indicate which features you want to add.

Gray checked box shows that some of the features are installed

Check this box to install the Save As HTML Wizard

Unchecked box indicates a feature is not installed

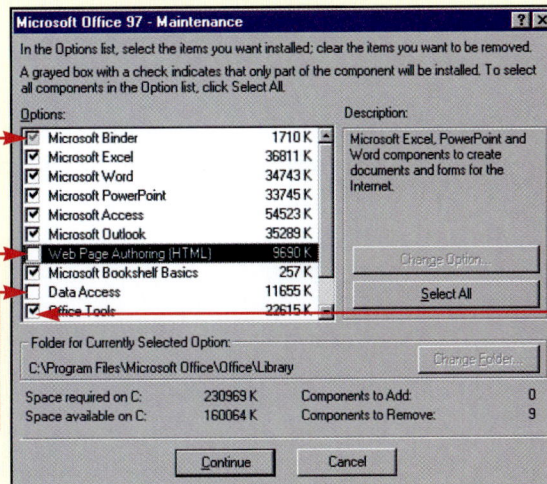

Black checked box indicates that all features are installed for a program

continues

You can check the box for Web Page Authoring (HTML) to install the Save As HTML Wizard. If you have other Office 97 programs on your computer, adding this feature adds Web Page Authoring capability to Word and Excel as well as PowerPoint.

6 Check the Web Page Authoring (HTML) box and click the Continue button.

The Setup program displays a series of message boxes as it checks for necessary disk space, copies the files, and updates your system. When completed, the Microsoft Office 97 Setup dialog box informs you that the installation was successfully completed.

7 Choose OK to close the dialog box, then click OK in the Add/Remove Programs Properties dialog box.

Both dialog boxes clear. Now try installing the Web Publishing Wizard. In contrast to the Save As HTML Wizard, the Web Publishing Wizard isn't actually part of PowerPoint, or even the Office 97 suite. Instead, it's a separate utility that Microsoft distributes with several of its programs. You can also download it from Microsoft's Web site. The Web Publishing Wizard is installed as a Windows 95 accessory—not as part of the PowerPoint program.

Microsoft supplies the Web Publishing Wizard on the Office 97 CD-ROM in the Valupack folder. Try finding and installing this handy add-on program now. (Before proceeding, make sure the CD for Office 97 is in Drive D or the appropriate CD-ROM drive on your computer.)

8 On the Windows 95 desktop, double-click My Computer icon, then double-click the icon for your CD-ROM drive and the Valupack folder.

Windows displays the contents of the Valupack folder. This folder contains a number of add-on items and features you can use with PowerPoint (or other Office 97 programs).

9 In the ValuPack folder, locate the Webpost subfolder and double-click it.

The Webpost icon displays in the subfolder (see Figure 14.5). You can double-click this icon to automatically install the Web Publishing Wizard on your system.

Figure 14.5
Installing the Web Publishing Wizard is almost effortless.

Double-click the Webpost icon to install the Web Publishing Wizard

⑩ Double-click the Webpost icon, then choose Yes to accept the license agreement.

Windows installs the add-on program and displays a series of message boxes to keep you posted on its progress. When completed, the Web Publishing Wizard box displays.

⑪ Click OK to clear the Web Publishing Wizard dialog box.

A second Web Publishing Wizard dialog box displays to let you know that you must reboot Windows 95 before your changes will take effect (see Figure 14.6).

Figure 14.6
You must reboot before the Web Publishing Wizard can be used.

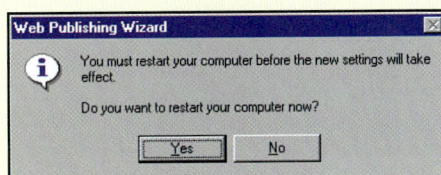

⑫ Choose Yes.

Windows 95 restarts. Both Web authoring tools are now installed on your system. Keep Windows 95 running for the next lesson, in which you create a presentation to use on the Web.

Inside Stuff

If you want to confirm that the Web Publishing Wizard is installed on your system, you can choose Start, Programs, Accessories, Internet Tools. The Web Publishing Wizard is usually listed on the Internet Tools submenu. If you use Internet Explorer, it may be listed as a submenu of the Internet Explorer program.

You can also confirm that the Save As HTML Wizard is installed. You can view the Save As HTML command on PowerPoint's File menu.

Lesson 2: Creating a Web Home Page

You don't have to jump through hoops to create a presentation for Web use. You can create any presentation as usual, then prepare it for the Web by using the Save As HTML Wizard. This means that you can convert any presentation to Web pages, no matter how you originally created it.

PowerPoint, however, includes ways to specifically create a Web presentation. You can use these methods to streamline developing a Web home page. First, you can rely on the AutoContent Wizard to help you create a Web-ready presentation. By selecting Internet as your output option in the AutoContent Wizard, you automatically add information that displays on each page of a Web presentation, such as a copyright notice, the last date updated, and your email address (see Figure 14.7).

Figure 14.7
The AutoContent Wizard automatically adds these components to each Web page.

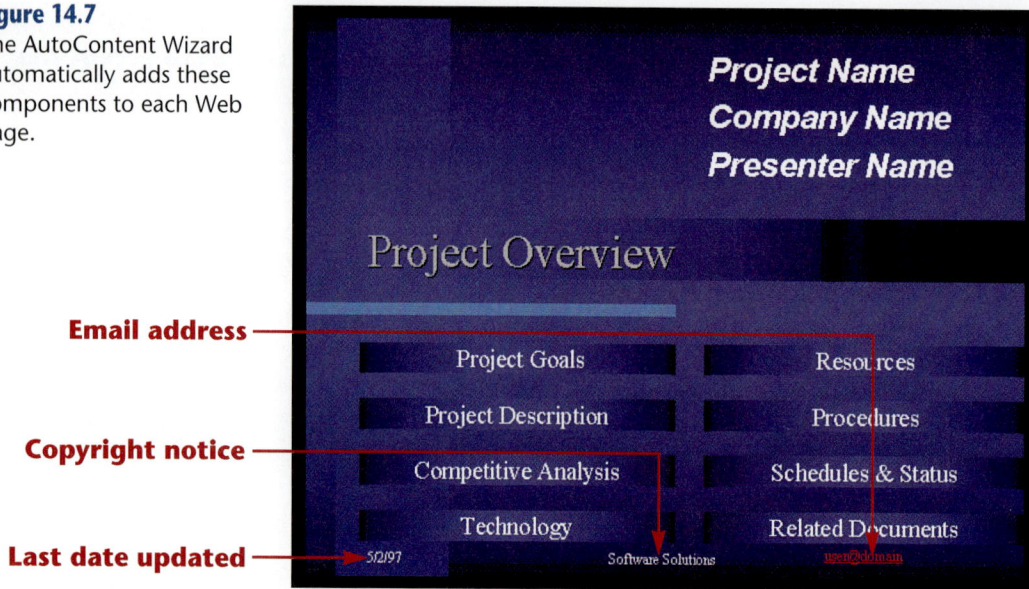

Alternately, you can create a new presentation with the templates that PowerPoint provides. Most presentations come in both Standard and Online versions. For example, PowerPoint has both Online and Standard versions of the Business Plan, Company Meeting, Corporate Financial Overview, and Flyer templates (see Figure 14.8).

The main difference between the Standard and Online versions is that the Online version adds navigation buttons to each slide so that people can use them to page through the presentation. By default, your email address, last date updated, and the copyright notice are not included, as they are when you use the AutoContent Wizard. Also, the Save As HTML Wizard can automatically add navigation buttons to any presentation whether you choose the Online template or not. Because of this, many people elect to create the presentation with their favorite template, then use the Save As HTML Wizard to add the buttons.

Figure 14.8
Many presentation templates come in both Standard and Online versions.

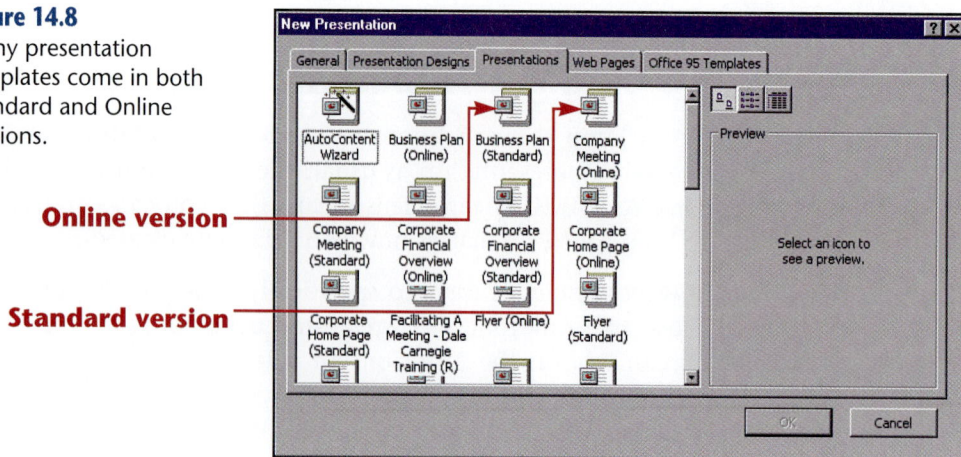

Because PowerPoint includes such strong Web support, try using the AutoContent Wizard to create a Web-ready presentation now.

Inside Stuff

When you are creating a presentation for the Web, keep a couple of things in mind. First, make sure you keep the text and graphics readable and interesting, but don't add so many graphics that your pages are sluggish to display. Many users (especially those with older and slower modems) will give up on your presentation rather than wait for slow pages to appear onscreen.

Also, keep in mind that some of PowerPoint's animation features (such as slide transitions, text builds, and so on) are not supported by most Web browsers. Unless you install the PowerPoint Animation Player (and can count on all viewers to do the same), your audience won't be able to see these enhancements.

Finally, make sure hyperlinks point to targets within your presentation (or on the network), or they won't work. For example, links to other presentation pages or Web sites generally work well, but not those to your hard drive.

To Create a Web Home Page

❶ Start PowerPoint and choose AutoContent wizard in the opening PowerPoint dialog box, then click OK.

You can also start the AutoContent Wizard by choosing File, New and then double-clicking the AutoContent Wizard icon on the Presentations page of the dialog box.

No matter which way you launch the AutoContent Wizard, the first AutoContent Wizard page displays.

❷ Click Next.

The Presentation type page appears so that you can select a type of presentation. Notice that the Wizard includes Personal Home Page and Corporate Home Page presentations. However, you don't have to choose these in order to prepare a presentation for the Web. You can choose virtually any presentation based on your sample content, then add the navigation buttons and hyperlinks later.

❸ Choose Product/Services Overview as the presentation type, then click Next.

The Output options page displays. You use this screen to designate that you want to use the presentation on the Internet.

❹ Choose the Internet, Kiosk option, then choose Next.

The Presentation options page displays (see Figure 14.9). Instead of the usual questions about if you want to print handouts, the presentation title, and so on, PowerPoint gives you the opportunity to display a copyright notice, email address, and last date updated.

continues

To Create a Web Home Page   (continued)

Figure 14.9
You can designate which elements should display on your Web page.

Check these boxes to include elements on your Web page

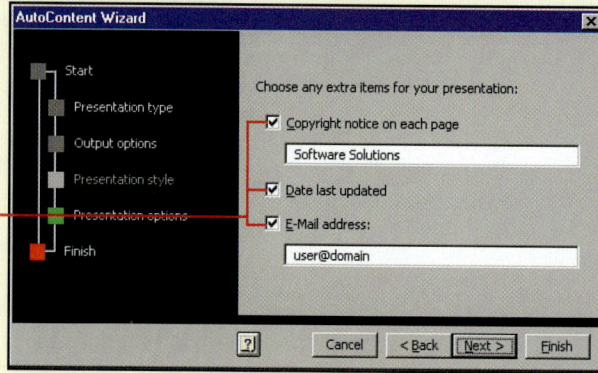

⑤ Make sure all three check boxes are selected, then enter your name and email address in the text boxes and click Next.

PowerPoint displays the final AutoContent Wizard page.

⑥ Click Finish.

The AutoContent Wizard creates your presentation and displays it in Outline view. To better view the components and navigation buttons that it automatically created as part of the presentation, try viewing the presentation in Slide view now (because Slide view emulates how the presentation appears on the Web).

⑦ Select Slide 2 and click the Slide Show button.

The slide show begins (see Figure 14.10). Notice that the AutoContent Wizard added the copyright notice, last date updated, and your email address in the footer area of the slide.

Additionally, two navigation buttons appear as part of the slide. You can use these navigation buttons to move between presentation slides. To do this, display the pointing hand icon; then click the button.

Figure 14.10
The AutoContent Wizard can automatically add several elements to your Web presentation.

Email address

Copyright notice

Last date updated

Click this navigation button to move to the next slide

Click this navigation button to move to the previous slide

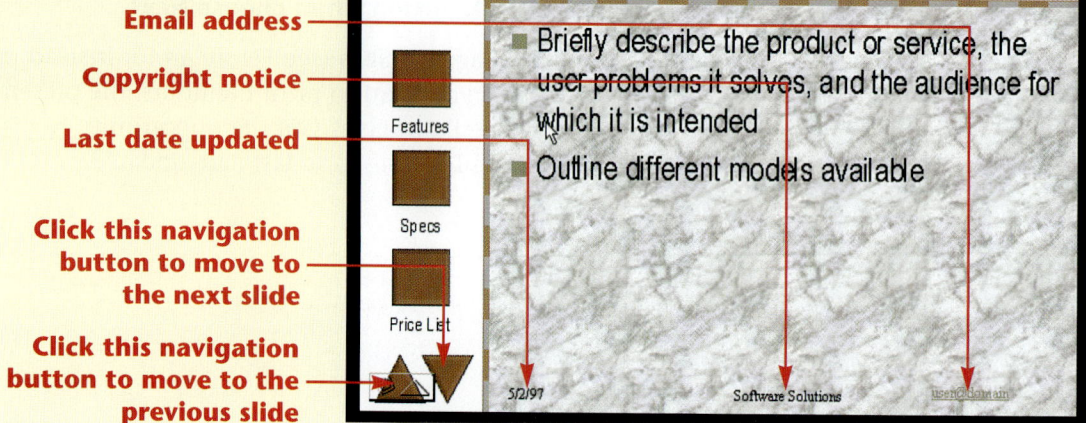

❽ Click the forward navigation button to move to the next slide.

The subsequent slide in your presentation displays.

If you have problems...

When you move your mouse pointer over the navigation buttons, PowerPoint's Control Panel icon displays in the lower-left corner of the screen in approximately the same location as the buttons. Be careful to not accidentally click PowerPoint's Control Panel icon or you will display PowerPoint's Slide Show shortcut menu. Don't worry that this will make your Web pages hard to navigate, however—when you post your presentation to the Web, PowerPoint's Control Panel icon is no longer in effect.

❾ Press Esc to end the slide show.

Keep the presentation open for the next lesson, in which you save the presentation in HTML format.

Lesson 3: Saving a Presentation as Web Pages

Most likely, during your PowerPoint career, you have saved files you create as PowerPoint presentations with the extension .ppt. However, in order for your presentation to be Web-ready, you need to save it in HTML format. You use the Save As HTML Wizard to assist you in the process. Like most Microsoft wizards, the Save As HTML Wizard displays a series of pages and gives you context-sensitive help so that you can make decisions about your presentation. When you finish making choices, the wizard automatically creates the Web pages as a series of files.

Because the Save As HTML Wizard is such a beneficial PowerPoint feature, try using it now.

To Save a Presentation as Web Pages

❶ In the open presentation, choose File, Save As HTML.

The Save as HTML Start page displays. Like all Microsoft wizards, you navigate through the dialog boxes by clicking the Next and Back buttons. You can also click Finish to jump directly to the Finish screen, or Cancel to terminate the operation. For now, you proceed step-by-step through the process.

If you have problems...

If the Office Assistant window displays, don't worry. PowerPoint is just trying to help you work through the process of saving your presentation using HTML format. Click the close button to exit the Office Assistant.

❷ Click Next to display the Layout selection page.

This page lets you specify a new group of layout settings, or use one that you've previously defined.

continues

❸ Make sure the New layout option button is selected and then click Next.

The select the page style screen displays (see Figure 14.11). The Standard option inserts your slides and navigation buttons on each Web page. In contrast, the Browser Frames option creates separate onscreen boxes for the slide, navigation buttons, and a list of presentation slides. In general, the Browser Frames option is supported by the newer browsers only, such as the latest versions of Netscape Navigator and Microsoft Internet Explorer.

Figure 14.11
You can choose the page style for your Web page.

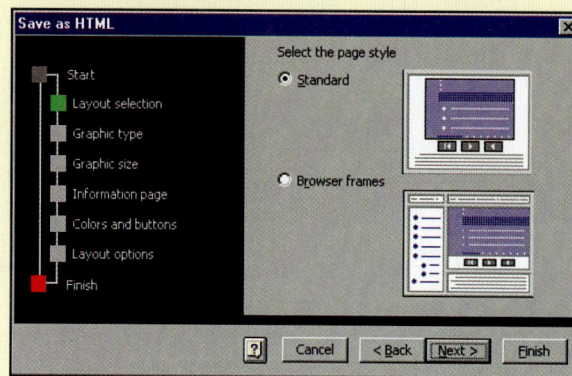

❹ Click the Standard option button, if it isn't already selected, and then click Next.

The Choose Graphic Type page displays (see Figure 14.12). You can choose GIF - Graphics Interchange Format for high-quality image reproduction. In contrast, the JPEG - Compressed file format produces smaller graphics (which draw more quickly onscreen) but with lower resolution. You can also choose PowerPoint animation so that you can use animation with your Web pages. If you choose this option, viewers are prompted to download the PowerPoint Animation Player when they access your Web site.

Figure 14.12
You can choose from three main graphic types.

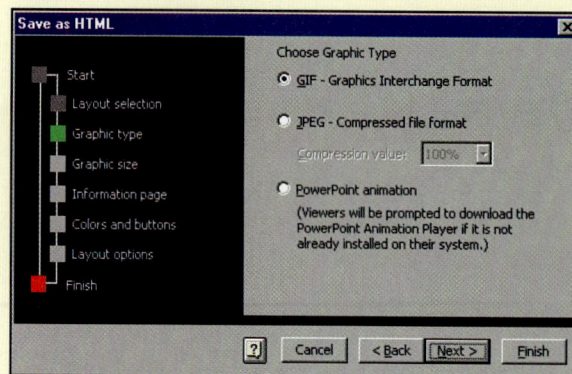

5 **Click the GIF - Graphics Interchange Format option button and click Next.**

The Graphic size page displays (see Figure 14.13). You can select the resolution and screen size for your graphics in this dialog box. In general, higher resolutions (such as 1280 × 1040) and larger graphic widths may be too large to view on some screens and will take longer to display. Because of these drawbacks, most people select a smaller width (such as 1/2 width of screen) and lower resolutions (640 × 480) for their graphics.

Figure 14.13
Consider if speed or quality is more important when choosing graphic size.

Choose the resolution here

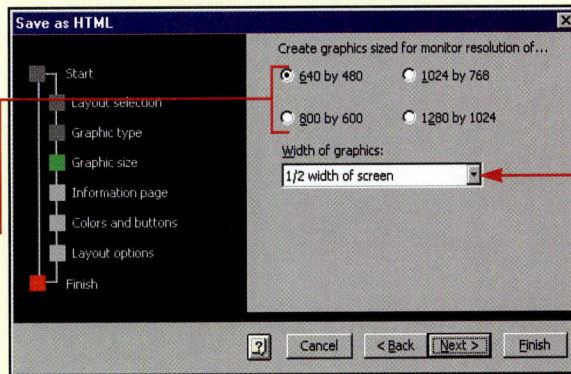

Click here to select a screen width for your graphics

6 **Select 640 × 480 and 1/2 width of screen and then choose Next.**

The Information page displays (see Figure 14.14). This page has two purposes. First, you can add information (such as your email address) that you want to display on the opening index page of your Web site. Second, you can check the boxes for Download original presentation and Internet Explorer so that the Wizard places buttons on your Web page for these features.

Figure 14.14
You can add information to the opening index page.

Check this box to allow users to download the original presentation

Check this box to allow users to download Internet Explorer

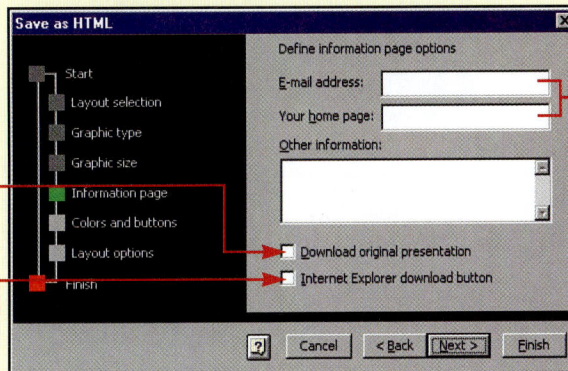

Enter your email and Web site addresses here

continues

7 Enter your email address in the <u>E</u>-mail address text box and check the boxes for <u>D</u>ownload original presentation and <u>I</u>nternet Explorer download button, then choose <u>N</u>ext. (If you don't have an email address, enter yourname@domain.com.)

The first of two Colors and Buttons pages displays (see Figure 14.15). You can accept the default browser colors or specify your own.

Figure 14.15
You can use the default colors or customize them.

Click here to choose the browser colors

Click here to customize your color combination

Samples of the default browser colors

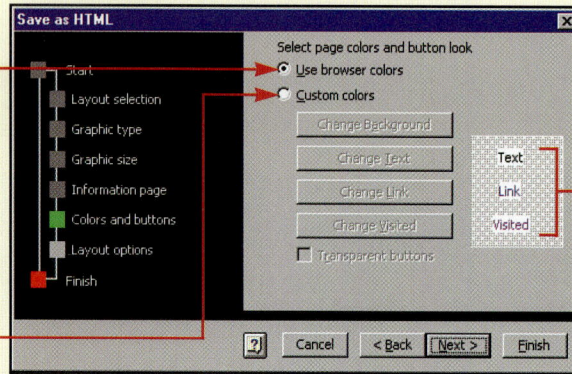

8 Make sure the <u>U</u>se browser colors option button is selected, then click <u>N</u>ext.

The second Colors and Buttons page displays (see Figure 14.16). You use this page to select a button style for your navigation buttons.

Figure 14.16
The wizard gives you a choice of button styles.

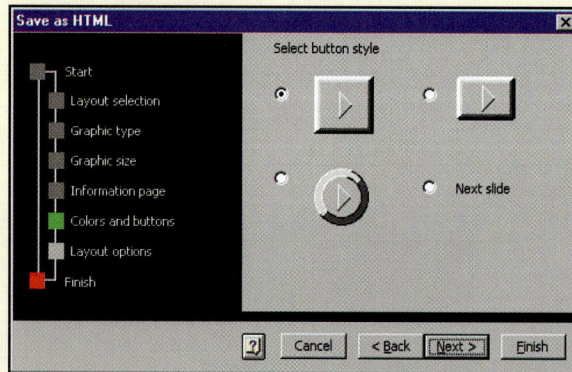

9 Select the round button style, then click <u>N</u>ext.

The first of two pages for layout options displays (see Figure 14.17). You use this page to designate the location on the Web page for your navigation buttons.

PowerPoint

Figure 14.17
You can select from four different button layouts.

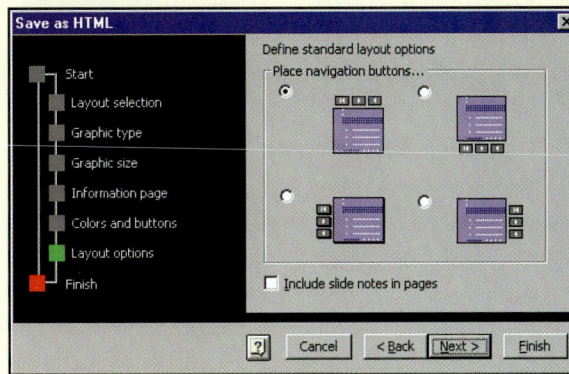

10 Choose the button layout in the upper-right corner and then click Next.

The next Layout options page displays. You use the Folder text box on this page to designate a location for the HTML files the wizard creates. Because literally tens (or even hundreds) of HTML files can be created for any presentation, you should carefully select an appropriate location. Ask your instructor where you should place the HTML files and then proceed with the next step.

11 Type C:\My Documents **(or whatever folder your instructor has indicated) in the Folder text box, then click Next.**

The final Save as HTML page displays. If you're satisfied with the settings you have designated, you can complete the process by clicking Finish.

12 Click Finish.

The Save as HTML dialog box displays. You can use this dialog box to save the HTML layout settings you just specified. If you expect to regularly create Web presentations and want to use the settings again, you can enter a name in the text box and choose Save. For now, however, you can select Don't Save because you don't need to save the settings.

13 Select Don't Save.

The Save As HTML Wizard creates the files necessary to display your presentation as a Web presentation. As the wizard creates the files, it keeps you informed of its progress with the HTML export in progress message box (see Figure 14.18).

Figure 14.18
The wizard lets you know how it's progressing as it creates the HTML files.

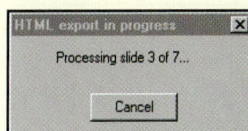

continues

When the process is completed, a message box displays telling you that the HTML export was a success.

14 Click OK to clear the message box.

After the presentation is saved as a series of HTML files, you can close it. Since saving a presentation differs from saving it as HTML files, PowerPoint will ask if you want to save the presentation before exiting it.

15 Choose File, Close to close the presentation, then choose No in the message box prompting you to save your changes.

The Wizard closes.

If you have finished your work session, exit PowerPoint and shut down Windows before turning off your computer. Otherwise, complete the "Checking Your Skills" and "Applying Your Skills" exercises at the end of this project.

Inside Stuff

If you want to see the HTML files that the wizard created, open the Presentation1 folder in My Documents (or wherever your instructor told you to save the HTML files).

After you have prepared your presentation for use on the Web, you can post it on a server so that others can access it. The process is basically copying files from your hard drive to the server. When you transfer files over the Internet, however, you must adhere to certain rules and guidelines. To help you easily transfer your Web-ready presentation to a server, you can use the Web Publishing Wizard. This wizard is most useful for copying files to the Web server of major online services (such as CompuServe or America Online) because they follow standard naming conventions for user directories.

To use the wizard, click the Windows Start button, then choose Programs, Accessories, Internet Tools and choose Web Publishing Wizard from the submenu that displays. You make decisions and work through the Web Publishing Wizard pages in the same manner as other Microsoft wizards.

Project Summary

To	Use
Install the Save As HTML Wizard	Double-click the Add/Remove Programs icon in the Windows Control Panel window.
Install the Web Publishing Wizard	Double-click the Webpost icon (located in D:\Valupack\Webpost folder), then reboot the computer.
Use PowerPoint Central	Choose Tools, PowerPoint Central.
Use the AutoContent Wizard	Start the AutoContent Wizard to create a Web home page, then choose the Internet, Kiosk option.

PowerPoint

To	Use
Use a template to create a Web home page	Choose <u>F</u>ile, <u>N</u>ew, then double-click an Online template on the Presentations page of the New Presentations dialog box.
Prepare a presentation for the Web	Choose <u>F</u>ile, Save as <u>H</u>TML.
Post your presentation to a Web server	Choose Start, <u>P</u>rograms, Accessories, Internet Tools, Web Publishing Wizard.

Checking Your Skills

True/False

For each of the following, check T or F to indicate whether the statement is true or false.

__T __F **1.** The Web is a text-only way to explore the Internet.

__T __F **2.** Utility programs that help you create presentations for the Web are called Web authoring tools.

__T __F **3.** Web browsers are software designed to help you find Web pages.

__T __F **4.** You must choose one of PowerPoint's Online templates to use a presentation on the Web.

__T __F **5.** A home page is a document on the Web dedicated to a certain topic.

__T __F **6.** The Save As HTML Wizard is installed when you use the default PowerPoint installation.

__T __F **7.** The code used by Web browsers to display Web pages is called Hyperlink Language.

__T __F **8.** You can jump from one Web page to another by clicking hyperlinks.

__T __F **9.** PowerPoint 97 includes built-in Web support.

__T __F **10.** You can publish PowerPoint presentations to the Web.

Multiple Choice

Circle the letter of the correct answer for each of the following questions.

1. HTML stands for which of the following?

    a. HyperLink Text in Many Languages

    b. HyperTransport Markup LANs

    c. Hypertext Markup Language

    d. None of the above

2. A home page _____.

    a. usually includes a number of hyperlinks to other documents

    b. makes your computer display in *home mode*

    c. is the same as a Web browser

    d. is software you use to post information to a Web server

3. Which of the following is a way to prepare a presentation for the Web?

    a. Choose an Online template.

    b. Use the AutoContent Wizard.

    c. Save a .ppt presentation as HTML.

    d. All of the above.

4. Which of the following elements can be added to a Web presentation that you create with the AutoContent Wizard?

    a. last date updated

    b. copyright notice

    c. your email address

    d. all of the above

5. Which is an example of a Web authoring tool?

    a. the Online Wizard

    b. the Internet Protocol Assistant

    c. the Internet Animation Assistant

    d. the Save As HTML Wizard

6. The Web authoring tool you can use to save your presentation as Web pages is

    a. the Online Wizard

    b. the Internet Protocol Assistant

    c. the Save As HTML Wizard

    d. the Animation Player Assistant

7. Which of the following represents PowerPoint 97's integration with the World Wide Web?

    a. PowerPoint Central

    b. Web toolbar

    c. Microsoft's home page for PowerPoint

    d. All of the above

8. HTTP is an abbreviation for

    a. Hypertext Transport Protocol

    b. Hyperlink Transfer To PowerPoint

    c. Homepage Transport Protocol

    d. None of the above

9. The main difference between the Standard and Online templates is _____.

    a. Standard templates include hyperlinks

    b. Online templates include navigation buttons

    c. Standard templates are limited to 5 slides in length

    d. There is no difference

10. Which of the following should you keep in mind as you develop a Web-ready presentation?

    a. Some Web browsers don't support animation.

    b. Including too many graphics may make your Web pages display slowly.

    c. You should test the links before publishing it to the Web.

    d. All of the above.

Completion

In the blank provided, write the correct answer for each of the following statements.

1. A Web _____ is software designed to help you find and display Web pages.

2. A worldwide system of over 100,000 networks linking every kind of information (both text and graphics) is called the _____.

3. You can click _____ on home pages to access other documents or Web pages.

4. In order for a presentation to be Web-ready, you must first save it in _____ format.

5. The graphical portion of the Internet, abbreviated as WWW is the _____.

6. A(n) _____is an interactive utility program that guides you through each step of a multi-step process by giving helpful hints and context-sensitive help.

7. A(n) _____is a utility program that transfers presentations over the Internet to a Web server.

8. A network used within a company to share information is called a(n) _____.

9. The feature used in PowerPoint to save presentations in HTML format is called the _____.

10. The main, or opening page for a Web site is called a(n) _____.

Matching

In the blank next to each of the following terms or phrases, write the letter of the corresponding term or phrase. (Note that some of the letters may be used more than once.)

a. Internet
b. intranet
c. Standard
d. wizard
e. home page
f. Web authoring tools
g. online
h. Hypertext Markup Language
i. Save As HTML Wizard
j. browser

_____ 1. Interactive utility that works you through a multi-step process

_____ 2. Programs designed to help you ready documents for the Web

_____ 3. Code used by Web browsers to display Web pages

_____ 4. International system of thousands of networks, originally used by the government to share information

_____ 5. Document first displayed at a Web site

_____ 6. Network used to share information within an organization or company

_____ 7. Feature used to save PowerPoint presentations so they can be used on the Web

_____ 8. The template type that includes navigation buttons

_____ 9. The template type you use for non-Web presentations

_____ 10. Type of software used to view Web pages

Applying Your Skills

Practice

The following exercises, found in the Project-14 folder on the CD, enable you to practice the skills you have learned in this project. Take a few minutes to work through these exercises now.

Using the Save As HTML Wizard

You have a PowerPoint presentation you want to publish to the Web. To do so, you save it using the Save As HTML Wizard

To save a presentation for the Internet, complete the following steps:

1. Make sure the Save As HTML Wizard is installed on your system, then open Proj1401 from the Project-14 folder on the CD.

2. Choose File, Save as HTML.

3. Click Next to display the Layout selection page.

4. Click Next to accept the New layout option. In the Select the page layout page, choose Standard (if necessary), then click Next.

5. In the Graphic type page, choose GIF and click Next.

6. In the Graphic size page, click Next to accept the default settings.

7. In the Information page, enter your email address and click Next.

8. Click Next in the first Color and Buttons page to accept Use browser colors.

9. Select the round button style in the second Color and Buttons page, then click Next.

10. In the first Layout options page, select the option to place the navigation buttons at the top of your Web pages and then click Next.

11. In the second Layout options page, enter the directory where you want to store the Web presentation (ask your instructor for this location or place the files in C:\My Documents). Click Next to proceed to the final page.

12. Click Finish so that the Save As HTML Wizard can save your presentation. In the Save as HTML dialog box, choose Don't Save.

13. Click OK in the Microsoft PowerPoint dialog box.

14. Close the presentation without resaving it as a .ppt file.

Creating a Web Home Page with the AutoContent Wizard

You run a small business that distributes office supplies. To create a professional impression, you decide to author a Web home page for your business. To help you quickly prepare the Web presentation, you decide to use the AutoContent Wizard.

To create a Web home page with the AutoContent Wizard, complete the following steps:

1. Choose File, New, then double-click the AutoContent Wizard on the Presentations page of the New Presentation dialog box.

2. Click Next to proceed past the opening AutoContent page.

3. Choose Product/Services Overview in the Presentation type page, then click Next.

4. In the Output options page, choose Internet, Kiosk, then click Next.

5. In the Presentation options page, enter your name and email address and check each box. Click Next when you're finished.

6. Click Finish to create the Web presentation. Keep the presentation open for the next exercise.

Entering Information in Your Web Presentation

To further develop your Web presentation, you enter information in the slides.

To enter information in your Web presentation, complete the following steps:

1. In the open presentation, switch to Slide view.

2. On Slide 1, drag over `Produce Name` in the Title placeholder, then enter `Office Storehouse`.

3. On Slide 2, erase the sample text for the bulleted points, then enter the following in the text placeholder:

   `Name-brand office products at wholesale prices!`

   `Same-day shipping!`

   `Unconditional guarantee!`

4. On Slide 3, `Features and Benefits`, erase the sample text for the bulleted points, then enter the following in the text placeholder:

   `Great selection of products!`

   `Excellent prices!`

   `Customer service oriented staff!`

   `No shipping charges on orders over $100!`

5. On Slide 6, `Pricing`, erase the sample text, then enter the following in the text placeholder:

   `Catalog with the latest prices sent upon request.`

6. Keep the presentation open for the next exercise.

Displaying Your Presentation

To preview how your presentation will look on the Web, you display it in Slide Show view.

To display your presentation, complete the following steps:

1. Display Slide 1 in the open presentation, then click the Slide Show button.

2. Click the Features button to display the Features & Benefits page.

3. Click the up-pointing triangle (navigation button) to move to the previous slide.

4. Click the Price List button to display the `Pricing` slide.

5. Press (Esc) to end the slide show.

6. Keep the presentation open for the next exercise.

Saving the Presentation for the Internet

To finish getting your presentation ready for Web use, you save it in HTML format. To do this quickly and efficiently, you use the Save As HTML Wizard.

To save a presentation as Web pages, complete the following steps:

1. In the open presentation, choose File, Save as HTML.

2. Click Next to display the Layout selection page.

3. Click Next to accept the New layout option. In the Select the page layout page, choose Standard (if necessary), then click Next.

4. In the Graphic type page, choose GIF and click Next.

5. In the Graphic size page, click Next to accept the default settings.

6. In the Information page, enter your email address and click Next.

7. Click Next in the first Color and Buttons page to accept Use browser colors.

8. Select the round button style in the second Color and Buttons page, then click Next.

9. In the first Layout options page, select the option to place the navigation buttons at the top of your Web pages and then click Next.

10. In the second Layout options page, enter the directory where you want to store the Web presentation (ask your instructor for this location or place the files in C:\My Documents). Click Next to proceed to the final page.

11. Click Finish so that the Save As HTML Wizard can save your presentation. In the Save as HTML dialog box, choose Don't Save.

12. Click OK in the Microsoft PowerPoint dialog box.

13. Close the presentation without resaving it as a .ppt file.

Challenge

The following challenges, found in the Project-14 folder on the CD, enable you to use your problem-solving skills. Take time to work through these exercises now.

Saving a Presentation for Use on the Web

You are part of an organization that recruits employees for companies. To draw in more business you save a presentation for use on the Web.

To save a presentation for use on the Web, complete the following steps:

1. Open Proj1402 from the Project-14 folder on the CD, then choose File, Save as HTML.

2. Click Next to display the Layout selection page.

3. Click Next to accept the New layout option. In the Select the page style page, choose Browser frames, then click Next.

4. In the Graphic type page, choose GIF and click Next.

5. In the Graphic size page, click Next to accept the default settings.

6. In the Information page, enter your email address and click Next.

7. Click Next in the first Color and Buttons page to accept Use browser colors.

8. Select the square button style in the second Color and Buttons page, then click Next.

9. Click Next to accept the default settings in the first Layout options page.

10. In the second Layout options page, enter the directory where you want to store the Web presentation (ask your instructor for this location or place the files in C:\My Documents). Click Next to proceed to the final page.

11. Click Finish so that the Save As HTML Wizard can save your presentation. In the Save as HTML dialog box, choose Don't Save.

12. Click OK in the Microsoft PowerPoint dialog box.

13. Close the presentation without resaving it as a .ppt file.

Creating a Web Page with a PowerPoint Presentation

You work for a company that specializes in ergonomic products. To create a Web page for your company, you save a PowerPoint presentation using the Save As HTML Wizard.

To create a Web page with a PowerPoint presentation, complete the following steps:

1. Open Proj1403 from the Project-14 folder on the CD, then choose File, Save as HTML.

2. Click Next to display the Layout selection page.

3. Click Next to accept the New layout option. In the Select the page style page, choose Browser frames, then click Next.

4. In the Graphic type page, choose GIF and click Next.

5. In the Graphic size page, click Next to accept the default settings.

6. In the Information page, click Next without entering your email address.

7. Click Next in the first Color and buttons page to accept Use browser colors.

8. Select the rectangular button style in the second Color and buttons page, then click Next.

9. Click Next to accept the default settings in the first Layout options page.

10. In the second Layout options page, enter the directory where you want to store the Web presentation (ask your instructor for this location or place the files in C:\My Documents). Click Next to proceed to the final page.

11. Click Finish so that the Save As HTML Wizard can save your presentation. In the Save as HTML dialog box, choose Don't Save.

12. Click OK in the Microsoft PowerPoint dialog box.

13. Close the presentation without resaving it as a .ppt file.

Using a Presentation on the Internet

You work for a computer training organization. To make sure you have a "Web presence," you save a presentation using the Save As HTML Wizard so you can use the presentation on the Web.

To use a presentation on the Internet, complete the following steps:

1. Open Proj1404 from the Project-14 folder on the CD, then choose File, Save as HTML.

2. Click Next to display the Layout selection page.

3. Click Next to accept the New layout option. In the Select the page style page, choose Standard, then click Next.

4. In the Graphic type page, choose PowerPoint animation and click Next.

5. In the Graphic size page, click Next to accept the default settings.

6. In the Information page, enter your email address and then click Next.

7. Click Next in the first Color and Buttons page to accept Use browser colors.

8. Select the round button style in the second Color and Buttons page, then click Next.

9. Choose the option button to place the navigation buttons on the left of the screen, then click Next.

10. In the second Layout options page, enter the directory where you want to store the Web presentation (ask your instructor for this location or place the files in C:\My Documents). Click Next to proceed to the final page.

11. Click Finish so that the Save As HTML Wizard can save your presentation. In the Save as HTML dialog box, choose Don't Save.

12. Click OK in the Microsoft PowerPoint dialog box.

13. Close the presentation without resaving it as a .ppt file.

Saving a Presentation as Web Pages

You have developed a presentation that you want to save for use on the Web. So that you can use it on the Web, you rely on the Save As HTML Wizard to save the presentation as Web pages.

To save a presentation as Web pages, complete the following steps:

1. Open Proj1405 from the Project-14 folder on the CD, then choose File, Save as HTML.

2. Click Next to display the Layout selection page.

3. Click Next to accept the New layout option. In the Select the page style page, choose Browser frames, then click Next.

4. In the Graphic type page, choose GIF and click Next.

5. In the Graphic size page, click Next to accept the default settings.

6. In the Information page, click Next without entering your email address.

7. In the first Color and buttons page, click the Custom colors button. Click each of the four command buttons (Change Background, Change Text, Change Link, and Change Visited). Click a new color of your choice in the Color dialog box for each screen element. Click Next.

8. Select the rectangular button style in the second Color and buttons page, then click Next.

9. Click Next to accept the default settings in the first Layout options page.

10. In the second Layout options page, enter the directory where you want to store the Web presentation (ask your instructor for this location or place the files in C:\My Documents). Click Next to proceed to the final page.

11. Click Finish so that the Save As HTML Wizard can save your presentation. In the Save as HTML dialog box, choose Don't Save.

12. Click OK in the Microsoft PowerPoint dialog box.

13. Close the presentation without resaving it as a .ppt file.

Utilizing a PowerPoint Presentation on the Internet

You are developing a Web site for the company for whom you work. After creating the initial presentation in PowerPoint, you decide to save it using the Save As HTML Wizard.

To utilize a PowerPoint presentation on the Internet, complete the following steps:

1. Open Proj1406 from the Project-14 folder on the CD, then choose File, Save as HTML.

2. Click Next to display the Layout selection page.

3. Click Next to accept the New layout option. In the Select the page style page, choose Standard, then click Next.

4. In the Graphic type page, choose GIF and click Next.

5. In the Graphic size page, click Next to accept the default settings.

6. In the Information page, enter your email address. Also add your company's name in the Other information section. Click Next.

7. In the first Color and buttons page click the Custom colors button. Click each of the four command buttons (Change Background, Change Text, Change Link, and Change Visited). Click a new color in the Color dialog box for each screen element. Click Next when you're finished.

8. Select the circular button style in the second Color and buttons page, then click Next.

9. Click Next to accept the default setting for button placement in the first Layout options page.

10. In the second Layout options page, enter the directory where you want to store the Web presentation (ask your instructor for this location or place the files in C:\My Documents). Click Next to proceed to the final page.

11. Click Finish so that the Save As HTML Wizard can save your presentation. In the Save as HTML dialog box, choose Don't Save.

12. Click OK in the Microsoft PowerPoint dialog box.

13. Close the presentation without resaving it as a .ppt file.

PinPoint Assessment

You have completed the project and the associated lessons, as well as the "Checking Your Skills" and "Applying Your Skills" sections. Now use the PinPoint software Evaluation mode to assess your comprehension of the specific exam tasks you have just learned. You can also use the PinPoint Trainer mode and the SHOW ME tutorials to practice these specific exam tasks.

appendix A

Working with Windows 95

Objectives

In this appendix you learn how to:

- ➤ Start Windows 95

- ➤ Use the Mouse

- ➤ Understand the Start Menu

- ➤ Identify the Elements of a Window

- ➤ Manipulate Windows

- ➤ Exit the Windows 95 Program

Graphical user interface (GUI)

A computer application that uses pictures, graphics, menus, and commands to help users communicate with their computers.

Desktop

The background of the Windows screen, on which windows, icons, and dialog boxes appear.

Icon

A picture that represents an application, a file, or a system resource.

Shortcut

Gives you quick access to frequently used objects so you don't have to look through menus each time you need to use that object.

Why Would I Do This?

Microsoft Windows 95 is a powerful operating environment that enables you to access the power of DOS without memorizing DOS commands and syntax. Windows 95 uses a *graphical user interface* (GUI) so that you can easily see onscreen the tools that you need to complete specific file- and program-management tasks.

This appendix, an overview of the Windows 95 environment, is designed to help you learn the basics of Windows 95.

Lesson 1: Starting Windows 95

The first thing you need to know about Windows is how to start the software. In this lesson, you learn how to start Windows; however, before you can start Windows, it must be installed on your computer. If you need to install Windows, refer to your Windows 95 manual or ask your instructor for assistance.

In most cases, Windows starts automatically when you turn on your computer. If your system is set up differently, you must start Windows from the DOS prompt (such as C:\>). Try starting the Windows program now.

To Start Windows 95

Taskbar

Contains the Start button, buttons for each open window, and the current time.

Start button

A click of the Start button opens the Start menu.

❶ Turn on your computer and monitor.

Most computers display technical information about the computer and the operating software installed on it.

If Windows starts, you can skip step 2. Otherwise, you will see the DOS prompt C:\>.

❷ At the DOS prompt, type win and press ↵Enter.

When you start the Windows program, a Microsoft Windows 95 banner displays for a few seconds; then the *desktop* appears (see Figure A.1).

Figure A.1
The Windows 95 desk-top appears a few seconds after a Windows 95 banner.

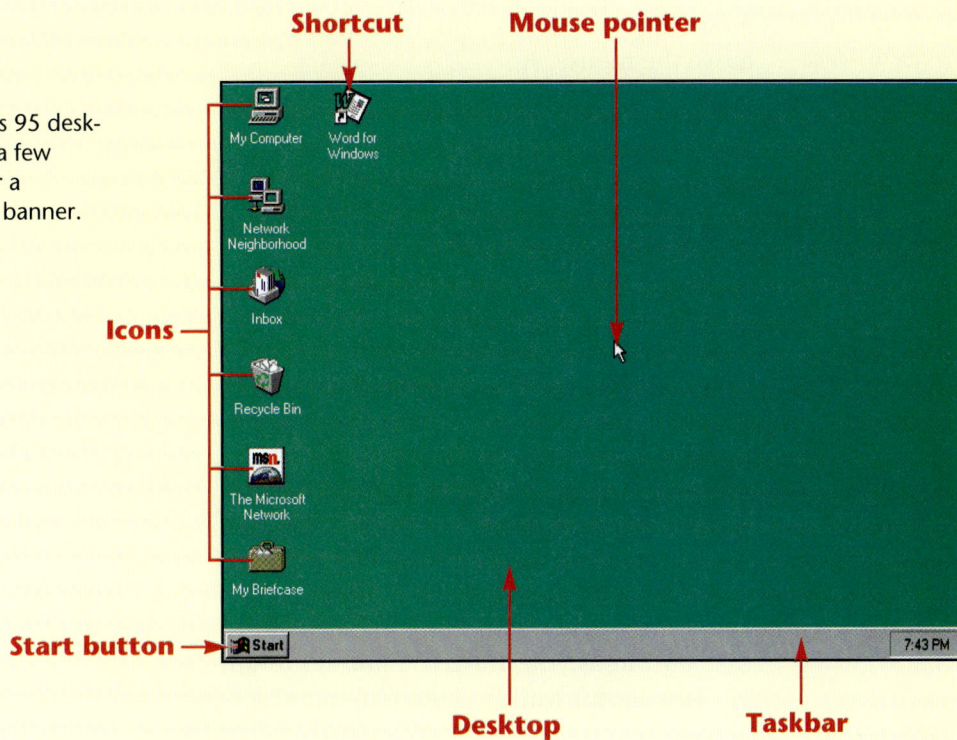

Inside Stuff

Program *icons* that were created during installation (such as My Computer, Recycle Bin, and Network Neighborhood) are displayed on the desktop. Other icons might also appear, depending on how your system is set up. *Shortcuts* to frequently used objects (such as documents, printers, and network drives) can be placed on the desktop. The *Taskbar* appears along the bottom edge of the desktop. The *Start button* appears at the left end of the Taskbar.

Mouse
A pointing device used in many programs to make choices, select data, and otherwise communicate with the computer.

Pull-down menus
Menus that cascade downward into the screen whenever you select a command from the menu bar.

Dialog box
A window that opens onscreen to provide information about the current action or to ask the user to provide additional information to complete the action.

Mouse pointer
A symbol that appears onscreen to indicate the current location of the mouse.

Lesson 2: Using the Mouse

Windows is designed to be used with a *mouse,* so it's important that you learn how to use a mouse correctly. With a little practice, using a mouse is as easy as pointing to something with your finger. You can use the mouse to select icons, to make selections from *pull-down menus* and *dialog boxes,* and to select objects that you want to move or resize.

In the Windows desktop, you can use a mouse to

- Open windows
- Close windows
- Open menus
- Choose menu commands
- Rearrange onscreen items, such as icons and windows

The position of the mouse is indicated onscreen by a *mouse pointer*. Usually, the mouse pointer is an arrow, but it sometimes changes shape depending on the current action.

Mouse pad
A pad that provides a uniform surface for the mouse to slide on.

Onscreen, the mouse pointer moves according to the movements of the mouse on your desk or on a *mouse pad*. To move the mouse pointer, simply move the mouse.

There are four basic mouse actions:

■ *Click*. To point to an item, and then press and quickly release the left mouse button. You click to select an item, such as an option on a menu. To cancel a selection, click an empty area of the desktop. Unless otherwise specified, you use the left mouse button for all mouse actions.

■ *Double-click*. To point to an item, and then press and release the left mouse button twice, as quickly as possible. You double-click to open or close windows and to start applications from icons.

■ *Right-click*. To point to an item, and then press and release the right mouse button. This opens a Context menu, which gives you a shortcut to frequently used commands. To cancel a Context menu, click the left mouse button outside the menu.

■ *Drag*. To point to an item, then press and hold down the left mouse button as you move the pointer to another location, and then release the mouse button. You drag to resize windows, move icons, and scroll.

If you have problems...

If you double-click but nothing happens, you may not be clicking fast enough. Try again.

Lesson 3: Understanding the Start Menu

Program folder
Represented by an icon of a file folder with an application window in front of it, program folders contain shortcut icons and other program folders.

The Start button on the Taskbar gives you access to your applications, settings, recently opened documents, the Find utility, the Run command, the Help system, and the Shut Down command. Clicking the Start button opens the Start menu. Choosing the Programs option at the top of the Start menu displays the Programs submenu, which lists the *program folders* on your system. Program folders are listed first, followed by shortcuts (see Figure A.2).

Programs folder

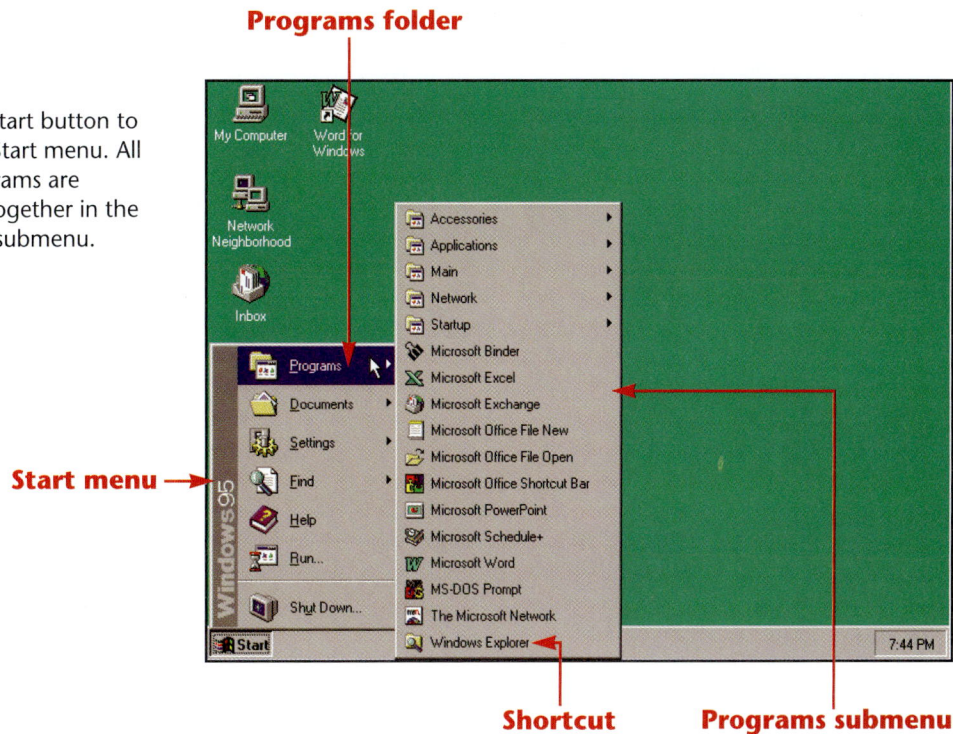

Figure A.2
Click the Start button to open the Start menu. All your programs are grouped together in the Programs submenu.

Start menu

Shortcut   **Programs submenu**

When the Start menu is open, moving the mouse pointer moves a selection bar through the menu options. When the selection bar highlights a menu command with a right-facing triangle, a submenu opens. Click the shortcut icon to start an application. If a menu command is followed by an ellipsis, clicking that command opens a dialog box.

Lesson 4: Identifying the Elements of a Window

In Windows 95, everything opens in a window. Applications, documents, and dialog boxes all open in windows. For example, double-clicking the My Computer icon opens the My Computer application into a window. Because window elements stay the same for all Windows applications, this section uses the My Computer window for illustration.

Title Bar

Across the top of each window is its title bar. A title bar contains the name of the open window, as well as three buttons to manipulate it. The Minimize button reduces the window to a button on the Taskbar. The Maximize button expands the window to fill the desktop. The Close button closes the window.

Menu Bar

The menu bar gives you access to the application's menus. Menus enable you to select options that perform functions or carry out commands (see Figure A.3). The File menu in My Computer, for example, enables you to open, save, and print files.

Word

Figure A.3
The My Computer window has window elements found in all Windows applications.

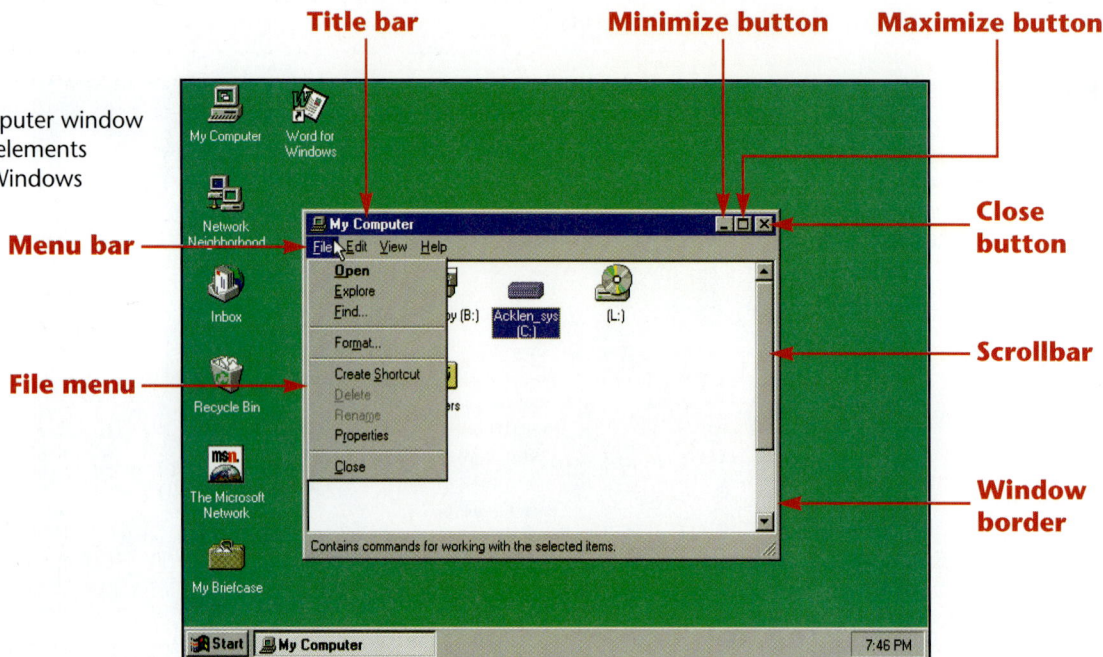

Some menu options require you to enter additional information. When you select one of these options, a dialog box opens (see Figure A.4). You type the additional information, select from a list of options, or select a button. Most dialog boxes have a Cancel button, which closes the dialog box without saving the changes; an OK button, which closes the dialog box and saves the changes; and a Help button, which opens a Help window.

Figure A.4
You can use the options in the Find dialog box to search for a file.

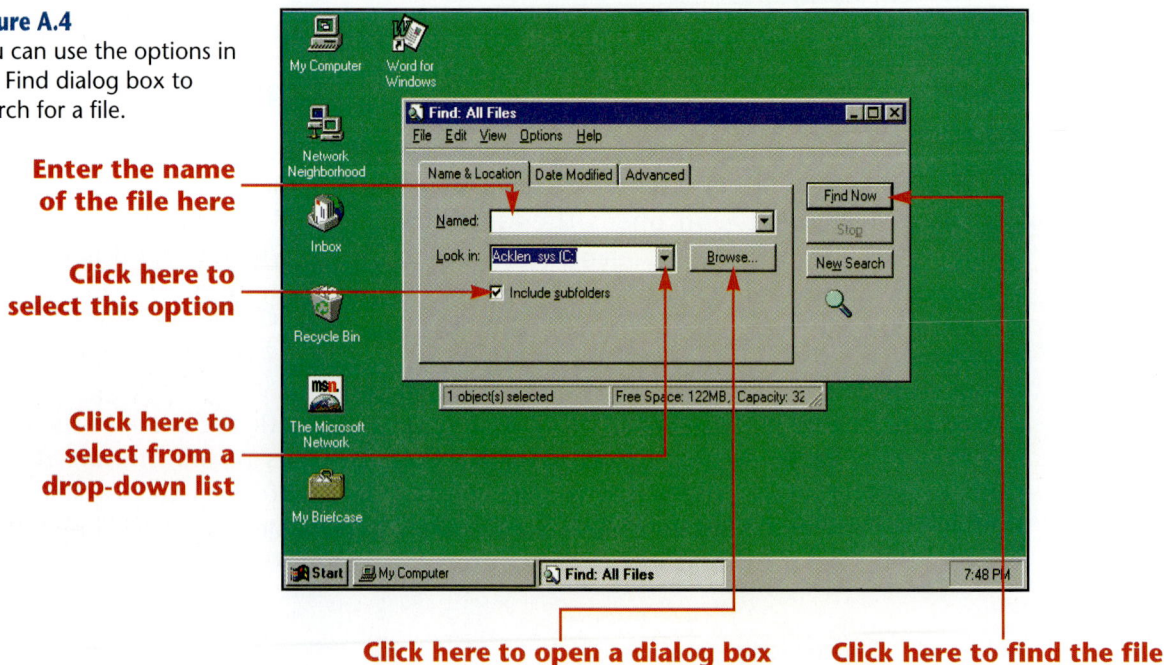

Scrollbar

Scrollbars appear when you have more information in a window than is currently displayed onscreen. A horizontal scrollbar appears along the bottom of a window, and a vertical scrollbar appears along the right side of a window.

Window Border

The window border identifies the edge of the window. In most windows, it can be used to change the size of a window. The window corner is used to resize a window on two sides at the same time.

Lesson 5: Manipulating Windows

When you work with windows, you need to know how to arrange them. You can shrink the window into an icon or enlarge the window to fill the desktop. You can stack windows together or give them each an equal slice of the desktop.

Maximizing a Window

Maximize

To increase the size of a window so that it fills the entire screen.

You can *maximize* a window so that it fills the desktop. Maximizing a window gives you more space to work in. To maximize a window, click the Maximize button on the title bar.

Minimizing a Window

Minimize

To reduce a window to an icon.

When you *minimize* a window, it shrinks the window to an icon on the Taskbar. Even though you can't see the window anymore, the application stays loaded in the computer's memory. To minimize a window, click the Minimize button on the title bar.

Restoring a Window

When a window is maximized, the Maximize button changes into a Restore button. Clicking the Restore button restores the window back to the original size and position before the window was maximized.

Closing a Window

When you are finished working in a window, you can close the window by clicking the Close button. Closing an application window exits the program, removing it from memory. When you click the Close button, the window (on the desktop) and the window button (on the Taskbar) disappear.

Arranging Windows

Changing the size and position of a window enables you to see more than one application window, which makes copying and pasting data between programs much easier. You can also move a window to any location on the desktop. By moving application windows, you can arrange your work on the Windows desktop just as you arrange papers on your desk.

Tile

To arrange open windows on the desktop so that they do not overlap.

Cascade

To arrange open windows on the desktop so that they overlap, with only the title bar of each window (behind the top window) displayed.

Use one of the following options to arrange windows:

- Right-click the Taskbar and choose Tile <u>H</u>orizontally.

- Right-click the Taskbar and choose Tile <u>V</u>ertically. See Figure A.5 for an example.

- Right-click the Taskbar and choose <u>C</u>ascade. See Figure A.6 for an example.

- Click and drag the window's title bar to move the window around on the desktop.

- Click and drag a window border (or corner) to increase or decrease the size of the window.

Figure A.5
The windows are tiled vertically across the desktop.

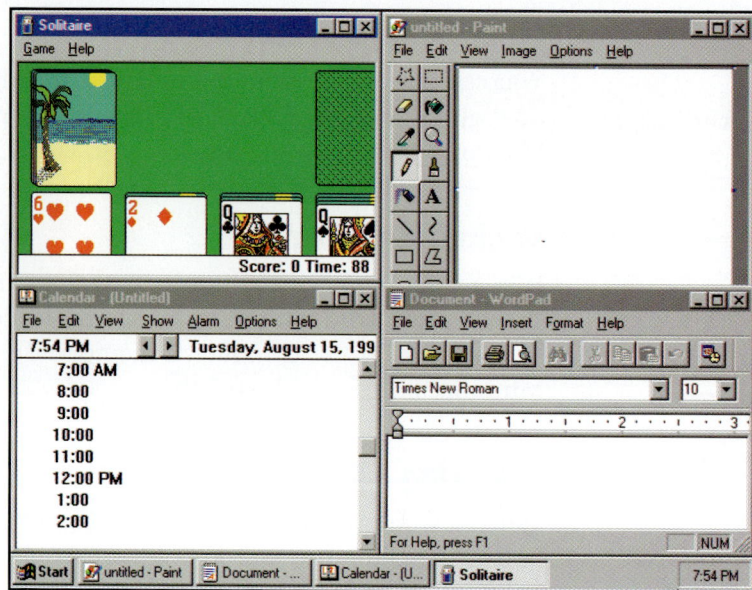

Figure A.6
The windows are cascaded on the desktop.

Lesson 6: Exiting the Windows 95 Program

In Windows 95, you use the Shut Down command to exit the Windows 95 program. You should always use this command, which closes all open applications and files, before you turn off the computer. If you haven't saved your work in an application when you choose this command, you'll be prompted to save your changes before Windows shuts down.

To Exit Windows 95

1 **Click the Start button on the Taskbar.**

2 **Choose Shut Down.**

3 **Choose Shut down the computer.**

4 **Choose Yes.**

Windows displays a message asking you to wait while the computer is shutting down. When this process is complete, a message appears telling you that you can safely turn off your computer now.

appendix B

Glossary

Active Cell   The currently selected cell in the Datasheet, marked by a heavy border.

Animation   In PowerPoint, the movement on-screen that acts as a transition from one object on the slide to the next.

AutoContent Wizard   A wizard that lets you select the type of presentation you want to create, asks for basic information about how you want to present to the audience and what you want on each slide, and then produces a presentation with sample text in it. You replace the sample text with your own information to customize the presentation for your own use.

AutoLayouts   Predefined layouts of different types of slides—title, bulleted list, graph, organization chart, and so on. The AutoLayouts have placeholders for entering text, placing graphs, or holding clip art.

Axis (plural **Axes**)   A line that serves as a major reference for plotting data in a graph. Generally, the data values are plotted along the vertical axis, called the Y or Value axis, and the categories of data are plotted along the horizontal axis, called the X or Category axis. Where the two axes intersect is the zero (0) point of the Value axis.

Bitmap Images   A bitmap image is artwork created in paint programs such as Windows Paint (*.bmp), saved in a image editing program such as Adobe PhotoShop, or captured by a scanner (*.tif). These programs color each pixel of the image and map those pixels to save them.

Browser   A program that translates the HTML codes in a Web page to a layout that is viewed by the user.

Cell   One rectangle of the Datasheet, where a row and a column intersect. You enter each piece of data in a cell.

Clip Art   A collection of previously created pictures or images that is available for use without infringement of the artist's copyright.

Clipboard *See* Windows Clipboard.

Color Scheme   Set of professionally selected complementary colors assigned to different elements in the presentation.

Control Box   The gray boxes above the row headings and to the left of the column headings. Click on a control box to highlight a row or column. Double-click the control box to exclude the data in that row or column from the chart. A control box appears black when the row or column is included in the chart and dimmed when it is not.

Copy   When you copy an object, PowerPoint places a duplicate of it in the Clipboard but leaves the original on the slide.

Cut   When you cut an object, PowerPoint removes it from the slide and stores it in the Clipboard.

Data Marker   A bar (in column and bar charts), a shape (in area and pie charts), or a dot or symbol (in line and scatter charts) that marks a single data point or value. Related markers in a graph make up a data series.

Data Point A single cell value, representing a single item in a data series. In a line chart, for example, it would be one of the points that is plotted along the line.

Data Series A row or column of data used to plot one line, one pie, or one set of bars or columns in a graph.

Datasheet The Datasheet is set up like a spreadsheet with rows and columns. Each rectangle in the Datasheet is a cell that can hold text or numbers. Microsoft Graph converts the data you enter in the Datasheet into a graph that it displays in the Graph window.

Demote To change the level of a paragraph from title down to bullet paragraph or from a bullet paragraph down to an indented bullet paragraph (or "sub-topic").

Effect An animated movement from one item to another, but it pertains to individual objects on the slide, such as a bulleted list or a movie, rather than to the appearance or disappearance of the entire slide.

Font A family of characters that share the same design or typeface, such as Courier or Arial.

Gradient Fill A gradient is where the background starts out one color on one side of the slide and gradually changes to another color. When one of the colors is white or black, the shading is called a one-color gradient. When neither color is white or black, the gradient is two-color.

Graph The entire area inside the Chart window, including all the chart elements, such as labels, axes, and markers.

Graph Text Text that describes data or items in a graph. Attached text is any label linked to a graph object such as an axis or data marker. Attached text moves with the item when it's repositioned, but cannot be moved independently of the graph object.

Gridlines Optional lines that extend from the tick marks on an axis across the plot area. Gridlines make it easier to evaluate data values.

Group A set of objects that can be moved or sized as if they were one object.

Handles Small boxes that appear around a selected object. You drag the handles to change the size of the object.

Hyperlink A graphic object or colored and underlined text that you click in order to jump to a different location in the file, to a different file, an HTML page on the World Wide Web, or to an HTML page on an intranet.

Hypertext Markup Language (HTML) HTML is a collection of instructions, or *tags*, that tell a browser program how to display a document—when the text is bold, italic, and so on.

Internet A worldwide conglomeration of computer networks that can talk to each other.

Intranet A company's computer network working with software that lets it route HTML documents. The documents can be read on the network using a browser.

Legend A key that identifies the patterns, colors, or symbols associated with the markers of a data series and shows the data series name that corresponds to each marker.

Object Any item on a slide, including text, graphics, and charts.

Orientation The orientation setting tells the printer which edge of the paper should be at the "top" of the printout. If the wide edge is at the top, the orientation is *landscape*. If the narrow edge is at the top, the orientation is *portrait*.

Paste When you paste an object, a copy of the Clipboard contents appears on your slide.

Placeholder A box on a slide where you put text, graphs, charts, tables, clip art, or objects. The position and type of the placeholders are determined by the AutoLayout.

Plot Area The area in which Microsoft Graph plots your data. It includes the axes and all markers that represent data points.

Promote Moving a indented paragraph out to a bullet paragraph or a bullet paragraph to the left to become a title.

Series Names The names that identify each row or column of data. These names appear in the legend.

Slide Background   The colors, patterns, textures, or gradients that fill the slide and appear behind all the other slide elements.

Template   A template is a set of related slide designs that comes with PowerPoint. When you select a template, PowerPoint applies the color scheme and general layout of the template to each slide in the presentation.

Text Box   A receptacle for the text on a slide. Text boxes often contain bulleted lists, notes, and labels (used to point to important parts of illustrations).

Tick Mark   A small line that intersects an axis and marks off a category, scale, or data series.

Tick Mark Label   The names that appear along the horizontal axis of an area, column, or line graph, and along the vertical axis of a bar graph. When data series are in rows, the tick mark labels are the column headings. When data series are in columns, the tick mark labels are the row headings.

Transition   A way of moving from one slide to the next. For example, with a vertical blinds transition, the slide takes on the look of window blinds that turn to reveal the next slide.

URL   The Web uses a type of address called a uniform resource locator (URL) to identify specific documents and locations.

Web   The World Wide Web (or just Web) is a component of the Internet. It's a collection of documents accessible through the Internet.

Web Page   One of the documents that make up the World Wide Web.

Windows Clipboard   A temporary memory holding area for items you have cut or copied. The items remain in the Clipboard until you cut or copy another item or until you shut down your computer. They can be pasted out again and again.

Wizard   A wizard is a feature that automates an operation and helps you perform that operation. It displays a series of dialog boxes that ask you design and content questions. You select options and type text. When you are done, the wizard creates something (in this case, a presentation) according to your instructions.

appendix C

Student Preparation Guide

The purpose of this appendix is to provide you with information you'll need about the certification tests—how to register, what is covered in the tests, how the tests work, and so on.

Studying for the Tests

Although you aren't required to take a training course to pass the Microsoft Office User Specialist exams, you certainly need to be sure you can successfully complete the tasks that are covered by the exams. Although a training class provides guidance, support, and practice, it may not be convenient or necessary for you.

This book provides the tutorial, review questions, and practice to help you complete your exams successfully. It can be used in a classroom situation, or you can work through the projects on your own. You don't have to work through the book from front to back, as each project stands on its own. The Checking and Applying Your Skills sections at the end of each project give you a chance to get familiar with the tasks. The Kelly PinPoint CBT trainer located on the accompanying CD-ROM has end-of-project computer-based training and evaluation as well as a final practice examination.

Levels of Certification

There is a single designation level for PowerPoint 97:

- **Microsoft PowerPoint 97 Expert User**: Users are expected to be able to deliver presentations in a variety of media.

Microsoft also has a special Office 97 certification, the Microsoft Office Expert. To attain this level, you must be an Expert User in each of the Microsoft Office applications (Access, Excel, Word, PowerPoint, and FrontPage) and have taken the Office Integration Exam to prove you can integrate these applications.

The specific topics covered at each level are listed in the "Required Tasks" section of this appendix. In this book, these tasks are broken down into projects. At the beginning of each project is a list of which tasks are covered in that project and which subject area they fall under in the tests.

Expert User Required Tasks

The Expert User exam involves a list of required tasks that you may be asked to perform. The list of possible tasks is categorized by skill area.

An Expert User should be able to do the following:

- Develop effective presentations
- Automate electronic slide shows
- Enhance presentations with video and graphics
- Add complex charts to presentations
- Prepare presentations for the World Wide Web

The skill areas covered in the exam and the required tasks for those skill areas are listed in Table C.1.

Table C.1 Expert User Skills	
Skill Set	Required Activity
Create a presentation	Create from a template Create from an existing presentation Delete slides
Add textual information	Enter text in Slide and Outline views Enter bulleted information Change the text alignment
Add visual elements	Add formatting Build a graph Draw an object Rotate and fill an object Scale and size an object Add a table Add shapes Animate objects Add transitions Add an organizational chart Set custom options Check styles
Bring in data from other sources	Add clip art Insert an Excel chart Import text from Word Add scanned images Add sound and movie Export an outline to Word
Modify a presentation	Change the sequence of a slide Find and replace text Modify the slide master Modify sequence in outline mode Change tabs Change fonts Change the alignment of text
Prepare for distribution	Spell check Add speaker notes Set automatic slide timing
Customize a presentation	Create a custom background Customize a color scheme Customize clip art and other objects Recolor and edit objects Apply a template from another presentation Add links to other slides within the presentation Hide slides
Deliver presentations	Start a slide show on any slide Use onscreen navigation tools Generate meeting notes Electronically incorporate meeting feedback Print slides in a variety of formats Print color presentations Export to overhead Export to 35mm slides Present with presentation conferencing Save presentation for use on another computer Save for Internet

Registering for the Exams

Microsoft Office User Specialist exams are administered by Authorized Testing Centers (ATC). To find out where the nearest ATC center is, call (800) 933-4493. Contact the ATC center to find out what their test policies and schedules are, whether they accept walk-ins or must register the candidates in advance, how the exams are conducted, and what they are charging for the tests. The estimated retail price of each exam is $50.00 in the United States, but that can vary based on the center's sales policies. Payment for the tests must be made in advance. There is no refund for missed exam appointments or failed tests.

Exams are currently available only in English, although Microsoft plans to offer the Office 97 exams in other languages as soon as the courseware in those languages becomes available.

Taking the Tests

Microsoft Office User Specialist exams are not multiple-choice or true-false tests. Instead, they are based on the types of tasks you may encounter in the everyday world. When you take the test, you sit at a computer that uses Windows® 95 or Windows NT® Workstation, work with a PowerPoint 97 presentation, and use the features of PowerPoint to perform the tasks outlined for you.

You can't use notes, manuals, laptops, tape recorders, or other aids during the tests. PowerPoint Help is available, but using it may cut down on the time you have available to complete the exam tasks.

Exams are one hour or less (some as short as 30 minutes). Your score is based on the number of tasks you successfully perform in the allotted time. This measures your productivity and efficiency, as well as your skill and knowledge.

Each test has a minimum score. If your score meets or exceeds that minimum, you pass the test. If not, you may take the test as many times as you need to until you pass. There is no refund if you don't pass the test.

You see your test results as soon as you complete the exam. Successful candidates receive a certificate a week or two after the testing. Test scores are confidential; only you and Microsoft see them.

To keep up-to-date on the Certified Microsoft Office User exams, check Microsoft's Web sites:

http://www.mous.net

http://www.microsoft.com/office/train_cert/

INDEX